# ATHENAZE

## An Introduction to Ancient Greek

Second Edition

Book II

Maurice Balme

and

Gilbert Lawall

New York   Oxford
OXFORD UNIVERSITY PRESS
2003

Oxford University Press

Oxford   New York
Auckland   Bangkok   Buenos Aires   Cape Town   Chennai
Dar es Salaam   Delhi   Hong Kong   Istanbul   Karachi   Kolkata
Kuala Lumpur   Madrid   Melbourne   Mexico City   Mumbai
Nairobi   São Paulo   Shanghai   Taipei   Tokyo   Toronto

Published by Oxford University Press, Inc.
198 Madison Avenue, New York, New York, 10016
http://www.oup-usa.org

ISBN-13 978-0-19-514957-9
ISBN 0-19-514957-2

Printing number: 9 8 7 6 5

Printed in the United States of America
on acid-free paper

# CONTENTS

# INTRODUCTION

## Part I:
## Readings in Book II

The story line continues from Book I with Dicaeopolis and Philip's arrival by boat at Epidaurus and their visit to the sacred precinct of Asclepius. In the early chapters of Book II the tail readings continue the saga of the Persian Wars. The Classical Greek readings continue with a variety of authors, including Theognis, Tyrtaeus, Solon, Hesiod, and Xenophanes; the New Testament readings in Book II are drawn from the Gospel of John. When Dicaeopolis and Philip return to Athens, the Peloponnesian War breaks out, and some of the chapter and tail readings are adapted from Thucydides' account of this war between Sparta and Athens. While in Athens, Philip attends school, and the teacher gives him the historian Herodotus to read, and the stories in the middle part of Book II are taken from some of the most memorable episodes of Herodotus's history, dealing with the Athenian Solon's visit to Croesus, King of Lydia, and the latter's ill-fated attempt to conquer the empire of Persia, ruled by Cyrus. This section ends with extracts from a beautiful poem by Bacchylides about Apollo's rescue of Croesus. The opening lines of Homer's *Iliad* and *Odyssey* are given toward the end of this section, and the last two chapters contain extracts from Thucydides on two crucial naval battles in the Peloponnesian War and extracts from Aristophanes' *Acharnians*, in which you will see Dicaeopolis making his own peace with the Spartans. The Greek Wisdom strand continues in Book II with sayings from the early Greek philosopher Heraclitus and ends in Chapter 29 with material on Socrates. You may find some links here with the sayings of the seven wise men of Archaic Greece included in Book I. A rich variety of reading awaits you in Book II.

## Part II:
## Greek Verbs

The material here will expand on the Preview of New Verb Forms in Book I, pages 154–155. It will provide additional information that will help you find your way around the charts on the following pages and give you a firm structure within which you can situate the new tenses and moods that you will study in the second half of this course.

You are not expected to learn all of the forms in the charts on pages x–xiv and xvi–xvii right away. You should begin by locating the forms that were formally presented in Book I. These include all of the forms except those of the subjunctive and optative on the first four charts (pages x–xiii). In Chapter 16 you learned that middle and passive forms are identical in the present and imperfect tenses and that they are different in the future and aorist. Thus on the second chart you will find the middle/passive forms of λύω in the present and imperfect tenses, but on the fourth chart you will find only the middle voice forms of λύω in the future and aorist. The fifth chart (page xiv) shows the passive forms of λύω in the future and aorist, and you will learn these forms in Chapter 17.

The new material on verb forms in Book II is organized as follows:

1. The aorist and future passive in Chapter 17
2. A group of verbs that end in -μι in the 1st person singular, present indicative in Chapters 18, 19, and 20 (you have already learned two such verbs, εἰμί and εἶμι)
3. The subjunctive mood (Chapter 21)
4. The optative mood (Chapter 25)
5. The perfect and pluperfect tenses (Chapters 27 and 28)

You already know from the verb charts that you filled out during your study of Greek in Book I where the subjunctive and optative forms fit into the charts, and you will find the forms of the subjunctive and optative on the charts on the following pages. The forms of the perfect and pluperfect tenses are organized on the last two charts (pages xvi–xvii). You should be pleased that you already know about half of the forms on these seven charts!

# Part III:
# Moods, Verbal Nouns, and Verbal Adjectives

Greek verbs have four moods, *indicative*, *imperative*, *subjunctive*, and *optative*, which express the manner in which the action of the verb is conceived by the speaker or writer. In the readings you have seen many verbs in the *indicative mood*, the mood used to express statements and questions about reality or fact. You have also seen many verbs in the *imperative mood*, the mood used to express commands. So far you have seen only 2nd person imperatives, e.g., "Xanthias, lift the stone!" or "Oxen, drag the plow!" Greek also has 3rd person imperative forms, not addressed directly to the person who is to do the action but to someone else, e.g., "Let Xanthias do it!" "Let the oxen drag the plow!" You will find examples of these in the reading in Chapter 30, but they are not included on the charts.

In addition to verbs in the indicative or imperative mood, you have seen *infinitives*, which are *verbal nouns* and are not limited (-*fin*- is from the Latin word *fīnis* that means "end" or "limit") by person or number and that fit into a sentence pattern such as "I am not able *to work*." You have also seen many *participles*, which are *verbal adjectives* that fit into sentence patterns such as the following: "The man *working* in the field lifted the stone."

In Book II you will learn two new moods, the *subjunctive* and the *optative*. In main clauses these do not express simple statements or questions about reality or fact but instead fit into sentence patterns such as "What are we to do?" or "I wish I had my sight restored!" They are also used in various types of subordinate clauses. Subordinate clauses that require these moods will generally use the subjunctive if the verb of the main clause is in a primary tense (present, future, or perfect) and the optative if the verb of the main clause is in a secondary tense (imperfect, aorist, or pluperfect).

Occasionally you will meet subjunctive and optative forms in the stories before they are formally introduced in the grammar. These forms are very easy to recognize. Most verbs in the subjunctive have the long vowels ω or η before the ending (find examples in the charts on the following pages). The optative has the suffix -ῑ- or -ιη-, which combines with other vowels in the verb to give forms that are immediately recognizable by the diphthongs οι, αι, or ῳ or the long-vowel digraph ει (again, find examples in the charts on the following pages). Help with translation of subjunctive and optative forms in the stories before these moods are formally introduced will be given in the glosses below the paragraphs of the stories.

# Part IV:
# Principal Parts

Once you learn the rules for the formation of the various verb forms, you will be able to recognize or make up any and all of the forms on the charts yourself if you know six basic forms of any given verb. These six forms are called the *principal parts,* and they are as follows:

| present active | future active | aorist active |
|---|---|---|
| λῡ́ω | λῡ́σω | ἔλῡσα |
| perfect active | perfect middle/passive | aorist passive |
| λέλυκα | λέλυμαι | ἐλύθην |

The other forms are constructed as follows:

The imperfect is constructed from the present stem: ἔ-λῡ-ο-ν.
The present, future, and aorist middle are constructed from the corresponding active stems: λῡ́-ο-μαι, λῡ́σ-ο-μαι, ἐ-λῡσά-μην.
The future passive is constructed from the aorist passive stem: λυθή-σ-ο-μαι.

(continued on page xv)

# VERB CHART: PRESENT AND IMPERFECT

## Active Voice

### Present

| Indicative | Subjunctive | Optative | Imperative | Infinitive | Participle |
|---|---|---|---|---|---|
| λύω | λύω | λύοιμι | | λύειν | λύων, |
| λύεις | λύῃς | λύοις | λῦε | | λύουσα, |
| λύει | λύῃ | λύοι | | | λῦον, |
| | | | | | gen., λύοντος |
| λύομεν | λύωμεν | λύοιμεν | | | |
| λύετε | λύητε | λύοιτε | λύετε | | |
| λύουσι(ν) | λύωσι(ν) | λύοιεν | | | |

### Imperfect

| Indicative |
|---|
| ἔλυον |
| ἔλυες |
| ἔλυε |
| ἐλύομεν |
| ἐλύετε |
| ἔλυον |

# VERB CHART: PRESENT AND IMPERFECT

## Middle/Passive Voice

### Present

| Indicative | Subjunctive | Optative | Imperative | Infinitive | Participle |
|---|---|---|---|---|---|
| λύομαι | λύωμαι | λυοίμην | | λύεσθαι | λυόμενος, - η, - ον |
| λύευ/η | λύῃ | λύοιο | λύου | | |
| λύεται | λύηται | λύοιτο | | | |
| λυόμεθα | λυώμεθα | λυοίμεθα | | | |
| λύεσθε | λύησθε | λύοισθε | λύεσθε | | |
| λύονται | λύωνται | λύοιντο | | | |

### Imperfect

| | | | | | |
|---|---|---|---|---|---|
| ἐλυόμην | | | | | |
| ἔλύου | | | | | |
| ἐλύετο | | | | | |
| ἐλυόμεθα | | | | | |
| ἐλύεσθε | | | | | |
| ἐλύοντο | | | | | |

# VERB CHART: FUTURE AND AORIST

## Active Voice

### Future

| Indicative | Subjunctive | Optative | Imperative | Infinitive | Participle |
|---|---|---|---|---|---|
| λύσω | | λύσοιμι | | λύσειν | λύσων, |
| λύσεις | | λύσοις | | | λύσουσα, |
| λύσει | | λύσοι | | | λῦσον, |
| | | | | | gen., λύσοντος |
| λύσομεν | | λύσοιμεν | | | |
| λύσετε | | λύσοιτε | | | |
| λύσουσι(ν) | | λύσοιεν | | | |

### Aorist

| Indicative | Subjunctive | Optative | Imperative | Infinitive | Participle |
|---|---|---|---|---|---|
| ἔλῦσα | λύσω | λύσαιμι | | λῦσαι | λύσᾱς, |
| ἔλῦσας | λύσῃς | λύσειας (-σαις) | λῦσον | | λύσᾱσα, |
| ἔλῦσε(ν) | λύσῃ | λύσειε(ν) (-σαι) | | | λῦσαν, |
| | | | | | gen., λύσαντος |
| ἐλύσαμεν | λύσωμεν | λύσαιμεν | | | |
| ἐλύσατε | λύσητε | λύσαιτε | λύσατε | | |
| ἔλῦσαν | λύσωσι(ν) | λύσειαν (-σαιεν) | | | |

# VERB CHART: FUTURE AND AORIST

## Middle Voice

| | Indicative | Subjunctive | Optative | Imperative | Infinitive | Participle |
|---|---|---|---|---|---|---|
| **Future** | | | | | | |
| | λύσομαι | | λῡσοίμην | | λύσεσθαι | λῡσόμενος, - η, - ον |
| | λύσευ/η | | λύσοιο | | | |
| | λύσεται | | λύσοιτο | | | |
| | λῡσόμεθα | | λῡσοίμεθα | | | |
| | λύσεσθε | | λύσοισθε | | | |
| | λύσονται | | λύσοιντο | | | |
| **Aorist** | | | | | | |
| | ἐλῡσάμην | λύσωμαι | λῡσαίμην | | λύσασθαι | λῡσάμενος, - η, - ον |
| | ἐλύσω | λύσῃ | λύσαιο | λῦσαι | | |
| | ἐλύσατο | λύσηται | λύσαιτο | | | |
| | ἐλῡσάμεθα | λῡσόμεθα | λῡσαίμεθα | | | |
| | ἐλύσασθε | λύσησθε | λύσαισθε | λύσασθε | | |
| | ἐλύσαντο | λύσωνται | λύσαιντο | | | |

# VERB CHART: FUTURE AND AORIST

## Passive Voice

### Future

| Indicative | Subjunctive | Optative | Imperative | Infinitive | Participle |
|---|---|---|---|---|---|
| λυθήσομαι | | λυθησοίμην | | λυθήσεσθαι | λυθησόμενος, -η, -ον |
| λυθήσει/ῃ | | λυθήσοιο | | | |
| λυθήσεται | | λυθήσοιτο | | | |
| λυθησόμεθα | | λυθησοίμεθα | | | |
| λυθήσεσθε | | λυθήσοισθε | | | |
| λυθήσονται | | λυθήσοιντο | | | |

### Aorist

| Indicative | Subjunctive | Optative | Imperative | Infinitive | Participle |
|---|---|---|---|---|---|
| ἐλύθην | λυθῶ | λυθείην | | λυθῆναι | λυθείς, |
| ἐλύθης | λυθῇς | λυθείης | λύθητι | | λυθεῖσα, |
| ἐλύθη | λυθῇ | λυθείη | | | λυθέν, |
| ἐλύθημεν | λυθῶμεν | λυθεῖμεν | | | gen., λυθέντος |
| ἐλύθητε | λυθῆτε | λυθεῖτε | λύθητε | | |
| ἐλύθησαν | λυθῶσι(ν) | λυθεῖεν | | | |

The principal parts of many verbs follow simple patterns, so that if you know the first principal part (the present active indicative) you can construct the remaining principal parts according to rules, many of which you have already learned.  Many verbs, however, follow more complex linguistic patterns, so that their principal parts cannot all be predicted on the basis of easy rules.  In some verbs the stem appears in different forms in the different tenses; for example, in the forms of the verb λύω given above you can see two slightly different stems, λῡ- and λυ-.  A knowledge of stems is useful, as you already know from Book I.  A few common verbs use etymologically unrelated stems to supply missing forms.  For example, the verb αἱρέω does not have an aorist related to the stem αἱρε- but instead uses the unrelated stem ἑλ- to supply the missing aorist.  The other principal parts of this verb are regular (except for ε instead of the expected η in the aorist passive):

$$\alpha i \rho \acute{\epsilon} \omega \qquad \alpha i \rho \acute{\eta} \sigma \omega \qquad \epsilon \hat{i} \lambda o \nu \qquad \mathring{\eta} \rho \eta \kappa \alpha \qquad \mathring{\eta} \rho \eta \mu \alpha \iota \qquad \mathring{\eta} \rho \acute{\epsilon} \theta \eta \nu$$

For convenience grammarians say that the stems of this verb are αἱρε- and ἑλ-.  Note that verbs such as this that begin with a vowel or diphthong have a temporal augment instead of reduplication in the perfect tense.  Verbs that begin with certain consonants or consonant clusters will have syllabic augment instead of reduplication, e.g., σπεύδω, perfect, ἔσπευκα.

In Book I from Chapter 10 on we gave the present, future, and aorist of most verbs in vocabulary lists, and we included the aorist participle to show the unaugmented aorist stem.  In Book II we will give in the chapter vocabulary lists full sets of principal parts for most verbs.  We will not give the principal parts of regular contract verbs that follow the patterns of the model contract verbs φιλέω, τῑμάω, and δηλόω; for the principal parts of these model verbs, see the Greek to English Vocabulary at the end of this book.  We also do not usually give the principal parts of compound verbs, for which the principal parts of the simple verb have already been given; consult the Greek to English Vocabulary as necessary.  We stop giving aorist participles, but we will occasionally include other forms, such as the imperfect, when they deserve special attention.

After the reading passages we will give full sets of principal parts of important verbs, most of which you met in Book I.  These sets are arranged according to certain linguistic principles to help you see similarities among verbs and organize them into helpful groupings in your own mind.  Seeing the similarities and shared patterns will make it easier for you to learn the principal parts.

# VERB CHART: PERFECT AND PLUPERFECT

## Active Voice

### Perfect

| Indicative | Subjunctive | Optative | Imperative** | Infinitive | Participle |
|---|---|---|---|---|---|
| λέλυκα | λελυκὼς ὦ | λελυκὼς εἴην | | λελυκέναι | λελυκώς, |
| λέλυκας | λελυκὼς ᾖς | λελυκὼς εἴης | λελυκὼς ἴσθι | | λελυκυῖα, |
| λέλυκε(ν) | λελυκὼς ᾖ | λελυκὼς εἴη | | | λελυκός, |
| | | | | | gen., λελυκότος |
| λελύκαμεν | λελυκότες ὦμεν | λελυκότες εἶμεν* | | | |
| λελύκατε | λελυκότες ἦτε | λελυκότες εἶτε* | λελυκότες ἔστε | | |
| λελύκᾱσι(ν) | λελυκότες ὦσι(ν) | λελυκότες εἶεν* | | | |

\* or εἴημεν, εἴητε, εἴησαν
\*\*very rare and not included in charts elsewhere in this book

### Pluperfect

ἐλελύκη
ἐλελύκης
ἐλελύκει

ἐλελύκεμεν
ἐλελύκετε
ἐλελύκεσαν

# VERB CHART: PERFECT AND PLUPERFECT

## Middle/Passive Voice

### Perfect

| Indicative | Subjunctive | Optative | Imperative** | Infinitive | Participle |
|---|---|---|---|---|---|
| λέλυμαι | λελυμένος ὦ | λελυμένος εἴην | | λελύσθαι | λελυμένος, -η, -ον |
| λέλυσαι | λελυμένος ᾖς | λελυμένος εἴης | λέλυσο | | |
| λέλυται | λελυμένος ᾖ | λελυμένος εἴη | | | |
| λελύμεθα | λελυμένοι ὦμεν | λελυμένοι εἶμεν* | | | |
| λέλυσθε | λελυμένοι ἦτε | λελυμένοι εἶτε* | λέλυσθε | | |
| λέλυνται | λελυμένοι ὦσι(ν) | λελυμένοι εἶεν* | | | |

\* or εἴημεν, εἴητε, εἴησαν
\*\*very rare and not included in charts elsewhere in this book

### Pluperfect

ἐλελύμην
ἐλέλυσο
ἐλέλυτο
ἐλελύμεθα
ἐλέλυσθε
ἐλέλυντο

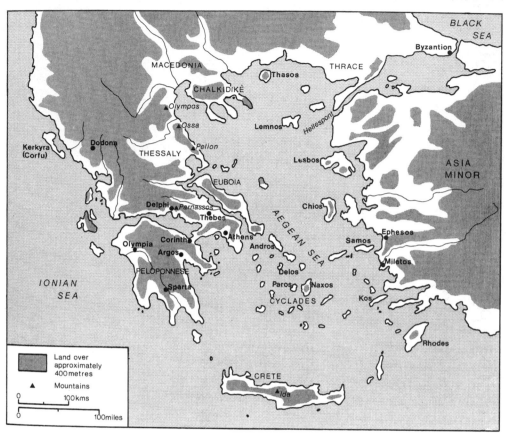

Greece and the Aegean Sea

# ATHENAZE

## An Introduction to Ancient Greek

# 17
# Η ΕΠΙΔΑΥΡΟΣ (α)

"ἐκελεύσθην ὑπὸ τοῦ ἰᾱτροῦ παρὰ τὸν Ἀσκληπιὸν ἰέναι·
ἴσως γὰρ ὠφελήσει με ὁ θεός."

## VOCABULARY

*Verbs*

αἴρω, [ἀρε-] ἀρῶ, [ἀρ-] ἦρα,
ἦρκα, ἦρμαι, ἤρθην, *I lift;*
with reflexive pronoun, *I get*
*up*

ἀπέχω [= ἀπο- + ἔχω], imperfect, ἀπεῖχον (irregular augment), ἀφέξω (irregular),
[σχ-] ἀπέσχον, *I am distant;*
+ gen., *I am distant from;*
middle + gen., *I abstain from*

ἀφικνέομαι [= ἀπο- + ἱκνέομαι],
[ἱκ-] ἀφίξομαι, ἀφῑκόμην,
ἀφῖγμαι, *I arrive;* + εἰς + acc.,
*I arrive at*

γιγνώσκω, [γνω-] γνώσομαι,
ἔγνων, ἔγνωκα, ἔγνωσμαι,
ἐγνώσθην, *I get to know,*
*learn*

δέω, δήσω, ἔδησα, δέδεκα,
δέδεμαι, ἐδέθην, *I tie, bind*

ἕπομαι, imperfect, εἱπόμην

(irregular augment), ἕψομαι,
[σπ-] ἑσπόμην + dat., *I follow*

κάθημαι [= κατα- + ἧμαι], present and imperfect only, *I sit*

οἶδα, perfect with present meaning, *I know*

πλέω, [πλευ-] πλεύσομαι,
ἔπλευσα, πέπλευκα, *I sail*

τυγχάνω, [τευχ-] τεύξομαι,
[τυχ-] ἔτυχον, [τυχε-] τετύχηκα + gen., *I hit; I hit upon;*
*I get;* + participle, *I happen to*
*be doing X*

*Pronoun*

ἔγωγε, strengthened form of
ἐγώ, *I indeed*

*Preposition*

σύν + dat., *with*

*Adverbs*

ἴσως, *perhaps*

ποῖ; *to where? whither?*

2

πρότερον, *formerly, before, ear-lier; first*

**Conjunction**

πότερον . . . ἤ, *(whether . . . ) or*

**Expression**

σὺν θεοῖς, *God willing; with luck*

οὕτως οὖν ἡ ναῦς εἰς τὸν λιμένα ἀφικομένη πρὸς τὸ χῶμα ἐδέθη ὑπὸ τῶν ναυτῶν, οἱ δὲ ἐπιβάται ἐκελεύσθησαν ἐκβῆναι. ὁ οὖν Φίλιππος ὑπὸ τοῦ πατρὸς ἀγόμενος εἰς τὴν γῆν ἐξέβη. ὁ δὲ Δικαιόπολις, "ἄγε δή, ὦ παῖ," ἔφη, "τί δεῖ ποιεῖν; ἆρα βούλει οἰνοπώλιον ζητῆσαι καὶ δεῖπνον ἑλέσθαι;" ὁ δέ, "μάλιστά γε, ὦ 5 πάτερ," ἔφη· "πεινῶ γάρ. σὺ μὲν οὖν ἡγοῦ, ἐγὼ δ' ἕψομαι." οἰνοπώλιον οὖν εὑρόντες ἐγγὺς τοῦ λιμένος ἐκάθηντο οἶνόν τε πίνοντες καὶ τοῖς παροῦσι διαλεγόμενοι.

[χῶμα, *pier*　ἐδέθη, *was tied*　ἐπιβάται, *passengers*　ἐκελεύσθησαν, *were ordered, told*　οἰνοπώλιον, *wine-shop, inn*　πεινῶ, *I am hungry*]

τῶν δὲ παρόντων γυνή τις τὸν Δικαιόπολιν ἤρετο ποῖ πορεύεται, καὶ μαθοῦσα ὅτι πρὸς τὴν Ἐπίδαυρον πορεύεται, "καὶ ἐγώ," ἔφη, 10 "πρὸς τὴν Ἐπίδαυρον πορεύομαι. νοσῶ γὰρ τὴν γαστέρα καὶ οὐδεὶς ἰᾱτρὸς δύναταί με ὠφελεῖν. ἐκελεύσθην οὖν ὑπὸ τῶν ἰᾱτρῶν παρὰ τὸν Ἀσκληπιὸν ἰέναι· ἴσως γὰρ ὑπὸ τοῦ θεοῦ ὠφεληθήσομαι. ἀλλ' εἰπέ μοι, πότε δὴ ἀποπλεύσεται ἡ ναῦς; πότερον τήμερον εἰς τὴν Ἐπίδαυρον ἀφιξόμεθα ἢ οὔ;" ὁ δὲ Δικαιόπολις, "οὐκ οἶδα ἔγωγε· 15 λέγουσι δὲ ὅτι οὐ πολὺ ἀπέχει ἡ Ἐπίδαυρος. ἴσως οὖν ἀφιξόμεθα πρὸ τῆς νυκτὸς ἢ καὶ πρότερον. ἀλλ' ἄκουε δή· δι' ὀλίγου γὰρ γνωσόμεθα· ὑπὸ γὰρ τοῦ ναυκλήρου καλούμεθα. ἆρ' οὐ ταχέως ἐπάνιμεν πρὸς τὴν ναῦν;"

[τὴν γαστέρα, *with respect to my stomach*　ὠφεληθήσομαι, *I will be helped*　τήμερον, *today*]

ἀναστάντες οὖν πρὸς τὴν ναῦν ἔσπευδον. ὁ δὲ ναύκληρος ἰδὼν 20 αὐτοὺς προσιόντας, βοήσας, "εἴσβητε ταχέως," ἔφη, "εὐθὺς γὰρ ὁρμησόμεθα· δεῖ γὰρ πρὸ τῆς νυκτὸς εἰς τὴν Ἐπίδαυρον ἀφικέσθαι." ὁ δὲ Δικαιόπολις, "πότε δή," ἔφη, "ἐκεῖσε ἀφιξόμεθα;" ὁ δὲ ναύκληρος, "οὐρίου γε ἀνέμου τυχόντες σὺν θεοῖς ταχέως

πλευσόμεθα καὶ πρὸς ἑσπέρᾱν παρεσόμεθα. ἀλλὰ σπεύδετε· εὐθὺς    25
γὰρ λυθήσεται ἡ ναῦς."

[οὐρίου, *favorable*]

οἱ μὲν οὖν ταχέως εἰσέβησαν, ἡ δὲ ναῦς δι' ὀλίγου ἐλύθη, καὶ ἐπεὶ
ἤρθη τὰ ἱστία, ἀνέμῳ οὐρίῳ διὰ τῶν κυμάτων ταχέως ἐφέρετο.

## PRINCIPAL PARTS: Stems in -υ- and -αυ-

λύω, λύσω, ἔλῡσα, [λυ-] λέλυκα, λέλυμαι, ἐλύθην, *I loosen, loose*
δακρύω, δακρύσω, ἐδάκρῡσα, δεδάκρῡκα, δεδάκρῡμαι (*I am in tears*),
    *I cry, weep*
παύω, παύσω, ἔπαυσα, πέπαυκα, πέπαυμαι, ἐπαύθην, active, transitive,
    *I stop* X; middle, intransitive + participle, *I stop* doing X; + gen., *I cease from*

## WORD STUDY

*Explain the following English words with reference to their Greek stems,
making clear the difference in meaning between 1, 2, and 4:*

1.  psychologist (ἡ ψῡχή, *soul*)          4.  psychoanalyst
2.  psychiatrist                           5.  psychic phenomena
3.  analysis

## GRAMMAR

### 1. The Passive Voice: -θη- 1st Aorist Passive and -θη- 1st Future Passive

In Chapter 16 you learned that in the present and the imperfect tenses
the middle and passive voices have identical forms. In the aorist and
future tenses the passive voice has forms different from those of the middle. In the reading passage above you met several aorist passive forms,
easily identified by the presence of the letters θη, e.g., ἐδέ**θη** ὑπὸ τῶν
ναυτῶν (1–2), **was tied** by the sailors.

To form the aorist passive, most verbs add -θη-/-θε- to the verb stem,
with the 3rd person singular ending in -θη as in the example above. The
indicative is augmented. The resulting forms are called *-θη- 1st aorist
passives* to distinguish them from a slightly different formation of aorist
passives called *-η- 2nd aorist passives* that add only -η- or -ε- to the
verb stem and will be presented in Grammar 2, page 13.

Here are the -θη- 1st aorist passive forms of λύω:

**Stem:** λυ-

| Indicative | Imperative | Infinitive | Participle |
|---|---|---|---|
| ἐ-λύ-θη-ν | | λυ-θῆ-ναι | λυ-θείς, |
| ἐ-λύ-θη-ς | λύ-θη-τι | | λυ-θεῖσα, |
| ἐ-λύ-θη | | | λυ-θέν, |
| ἐ-λύ-θη-μεν | | | gen., λυ-θέντ-ος, etc. |
| ἐ-λύ-θη-τε | λύ-θη-τε | | |
| ἐ-λύ-θη-σαν | | | |

Here is a sentence with an aorist passive participle:

ἡ ναῦς **λυθεῖσα** ὑπὸ τῶν ναυτῶν ἔπλει διὰ τὰ κύματα.
*The ship, **having been cast off (loosened)** by the sailors, was sailing through the waves.*

The 1st aorist passive participle is based on the -θε- stem as follows:

| | Masculine | Feminine | Neuter |
|---|---|---|---|
| **Nom., Voc.** | λυθέντ-ς > λυθείς | λυθεῖσα | λυθέντ > λυθέν |
| **Gen.** | λυθέντος | λυθείσης | λυθέντος |
| **Dat.** | λυθέντι | λυθείσῃ | λυθέντι |
| **Acc.** | λυθέντα | λυθεῖσαν | λυθέντ > λυθέν |
| **Nom., Voc.** | λυθέντες | λυθεῖσαι | λυθέντα |
| **Gen.** | λυθέντων | λυθεισῶν | λυθέντων |
| **Dat.** | λυθέντ-σι(ν) > λυθεῖσι(ν) | λυθείσαις | λυθέντ-σι(ν) > λυθεῖσι(ν) |
| **Acc.** | λυθέντας | λυθείσᾱς | λυθέντα |

To form the -θη- 1st future passive, add -θη- to the verb stem and then add the same letters as for the future middle. Here is an example:

εὐθὺς γὰρ **λυθήσεται** ἡ ναῦς.
*For the ship **will be cast off (loosened)** at once.*

Remember that there is no future imperative, and of course there is no augment.

| Indicative | Infinitive | Participle |
|---|---|---|
| λυ-θή-σ-ο-μαι | λυ-θή-σ-ε-σθαι | λυ-θη-σ-ό-μεν-ος, -η, -ον |
| λυ-θή-σ-ει or -ῃ | | |
| λυ-θή-σ-ε-ται | | |
| λυ-θη-σ-ό-μεθα | | |
| λυ-θή-σ-ε-σθε | | |
| λυ-θή-σ-ο-νται | | |

Stems ending in β, π, γ, and κ aspirate the last consonant in forming the -θη- 1st aorist passive and the -θη- 1st future passive, e.g.:

λαμβάνω, *I take* [ληβ-]    **Aorist:**   ἐ-λήφ-θη-ν
                            **Future:**   ληφ-θή-σ-ο-μαι

πέμπ-ω, *I send*            **Aorist:**   ἐ-πέμφ-θη-ν
                            **Future:**   πεμφ-θή-σ-ο-μαι

λέγ-ω, *I say*              **Aorist:**   ἐ-λέχ-θη-ν
                            **Future:**   λεχ-θή-σ-ο-μαι

φυλάττω, *I guard* [φυλακ-] **Aorist:**   ἐ-φυλάχ-θη-ν
                            **Future:**   φυλαχ-θή-σ-ο-μαι

Stems ending in dentals (δ, θ, and τ) and ζ change the last consonant to σ, e.g.:

ψεύδ-ω, *I deceive*         **Aorist:**   ἐ-ψεύσ-θη-ν
                            **Future:**   ψευσ-θή-σ-ο-μαι

πείθ-ω, *I persuade*        **Aorist:**   ἐ-πείσ-θη-ν
                            **Future:**   πεισ-θή-σ-ο-μαι

πάττω, *I sprinkle* [πατ-]  **Aorist:**   ἐ-πάσ-θη-ν
                            **Future:**   πασ-θή-σ-ο-μαι

κομίζ-ω, *I bring; I take*  **Aorist:**   ἐ-κομίσ-θη-ν
                            **Future:**   κομισ-θή-σ-ο-μαι

παρασκευάζ-ω, *I prepare*   **Aorist:**   παρ-ε-σκευάσ-θη-ν
                            **Future:**   παρα-σκευασ-θή-σ-ο-μαι

A number of verbs insert σ after the verb stem, e.g.:

γιγνώσκω, *I learn* [γνω-]  **Aorist:**   ἐ-γνώ-σ-θην
                            **Future:**   γνω-σ-θή-σ-ο-μαι

κελεύ-ω, *I order; I tell*  **Aorist:**   ἐ-κελεύ-σ-θη-ν
                            **Future:**   κελευ-σ-θή-σ-ο-μαι

Contract verbs lengthen the stem vowel, e.g.:

φιλέ-ω, *I love*            **Aorist:**   ἐ-φιλή-θη-ν
                            **Future:**   φιλη-θή-σ-ο-μαι

τῑμά-ω, *I honor*           **Aorist:**   ἐ-τῑμή-θη-ν
                            **Future:**   τῑμη-θή-σ-ο-μαι

δηλό-ω, *I show*            **Aorist:**   ἐ-δηλώ-θη-ν
                            **Future:**   δηλω-θή-σ-ο-μαι

Note: βάλλω [βλη-] > ἐβλήθην, ἐλαύνω [ἐλα-] > ἠλάθην, εὑρίσκω [εὑρε-] > εὑρέθην or ηὑρέθην, ὁράω [ὀπ-] > ὤφθην.

## Exercise 17α

1. *In the reading passage above, locate ten passive verbs and identify each form fully.*

2. *Make four photocopies of the Verb Chart on page 275 and fill in the future and aorist passive forms of λαμβάνω, φιλέω, τῑμάω, and δηλόω that you have learned to date; keep with your Charts for Exercise 16α.*

## Exercise 17β

*Give the corresponding passive forms of the following:*

| | | |
|---|---|---|
| 1. ἔπεμψε(ν) | 6. λέγουσι(ν) | 11. πρᾱ́ττουσι(ν) |
| 2. λῡ́σαντες | 7. φυλάξει | 12. κομίζει |
| 3. τῑμήσομεν | 8. πεῖσον | 13. ἐτῑ́μησας |
| 4. φιλήσᾱσα | 9. ἐκέλευσαν | 14. παρεσκεύασε(ν) |
| 5. δουλῶσαι | 10. παρασκευάσουσι(ν) | 15. ἔπρᾱξαν (πρᾱκ-) |

## Exercise 17γ

*Read aloud and translate:*

1. οἱ παῖδες ὑπὸ τοῦ αὐτουργοῦ ἐπείσθησαν τῷ πατρὶ συλλαβεῖν.
2. αἱ παῖδες ὑπὸ τῆς μητρὸς πρὸς τὴν κρήνην πεμφθεῖσαι τὰς ὑδρίᾱς πληροῦσιν (*fill*).
3. ὁ μὲν Δικαιόπολις τοὺς βοῦς τοῦ ἀρότρου λυθέντας οἴκαδε ἤλαυνεν, ὁ δὲ δοῦλος ἐν τῷ ἀγρῷ ἐλείφθη.
4. αὗται αἱ νῆες ὑπὸ τῶν Ἀθηναίων ἐποιήθησαν.
5. οἱ βάρβαροι ὑπὸ τῶν Ἑλλήνων νῑκηθέντες πρὸς Ἀσίᾱν ἐπανῆλθον.
6. ὁ ἄγγελος ὑπὸ τοῦ βασιλέως πεμφθεὶς τοὺς πολῑ́τᾱς ηὗρεν ἐν τῇ ἀγορᾷ μένοντας.
7. οἱ πολῖται σῑγᾶν κελευσθέντες τοῦ ἀγγέλου ἤκουον.
8. τοῦ δὲ ἀγγέλου ἀκούσαντες οἴκαδε ἔσπευδον ὡς τὰ ἀγγελθέντα ταῖς γυναιξὶ λέξοντες/ἐροῦντες.
9. "ἐκελεύσθημεν," ἔφασαν, "πολὺ ἀργύριον τῷ βασιλεῖ παρέχειν."
10. οἱ ἐν τῷ πολέμῳ ἀποθανόντες ὑπὸ πάντων τῑμηθήσονται.

## Exercise 17δ

*Translate into Greek:*

1. You were ordered to return home at once.
2. We were sent to the field to look for the ox.
3. The boy who did this (*use participle, not relative clause*) will be punished (*use* κολάζω).
4. The women left behind in the house were preparing dinner.
5. This ship was made by the sailors who had been pursued (*use aorist passive*) by pirates (*use* ὁ λῃστής, τοῦ λῃστοῦ).

# Healing Sanctuaries:
# Asclepius and Epidaurus

According to legend, Asclepius was the son of Apollo, god of healing, and a mortal girl, Coronis, who was unfaithful to him. Apollo sent his sister Artemis to punish her with death, but, as she lay on the pyre and the flames flickered around her body, Apollo snatched from her womb the unborn baby, his son. He gave him to the wise old centaur Cheiron to bring up and told him to teach the child to heal men of their sicknesses.

> And all who came to him suffering from sores caused by nature, or whose limbs were wounded by gray bronze or the far-flung stone, or whose bodies were wasting from summer's heat or winter's cold, he freed from their various pains and cured. Some he treated with soft incantations, some with soothing medicines, on the limbs of others he put healing ointments, and yet others he made straight with the surgeon's knife.
>
> (Pindar, *Pythian* 3.47–53).

In the end Asclepius attempted to restore the dead to life, and Zeus in anger struck him down with a thunderbolt.

In time the status of the mortal hero rose to reach that of a god, and shrines were dedicated to him throughout Greece as the preserver of health and healer of sickness, a god who loved mankind, their savior. Of all the sanctuaries of Asclepius, the greatest was at Epidaurus. Here, in an undulating valley, surrounded by mountains, was a site that had been holy from times immemorial, sacred first to a local hero, then to Apollo, and finally to Apollo and Asclepius. The cult of Asclepius seems to have arrived there early in the fifth century, and by the end of the century the sanctuary was visited by pilgrims from all over the Greek world.

Pilgrims arriving at the port and city of Epidaurus had a walk of five miles or eight kilometers to reach the sanctuary, through a deep ravine, cut by a stream, where wild olive and plane trees and laurel abounded. They arrived at last at a splendid entrance building resembling a temple, on the gates of which they saw this inscription:

ἁγνὸν χρὴ νᾱοῖο θυώδεος ἐντὸς ἰόντα
ἔμμεναι· ἁγνείᾱ δ' ἐστὶ φρονεῖν ὅσια.

He must be pure who enters the fragrant
shrine; purity is thinking holy thoughts.

Most of the buildings of which the remains can be seen today were built in the fourth century when the cult of Asclepius was at its height, but there would have been humbler versions of the most important buildings there when Philip visited the sanctuary. In the center stood the temple of Asclepius himself and close to it the ἄβατον, a long, narrow building in which patients seeking a cure had to sleep the night; opposite this was the θόλος, a round building that was probably the home of the sacred serpents. To the west of the main sanctuary lay the stadium, to the southeast the καταγώγιον, a large square building, where the pilgrims stayed, and beyond this on the hillside the great theater, for which Epidaurus is now most famous. Procession, choral dance, and sacrifice took place throughout the year, and every four years there was a great festival with athletic, dramatic, and musical competitions.

The procedure for consulting Asclepius was simple: patients first had to purify themselves by ritual washing and to make an offering (often a honey-cake). When night came they were conducted to the ἄβατον and waited for the god to appear while they slept. The walls of the temple were covered with tablets set up by grateful patients; the cure we ascribe to Philip is taken from one of these. Here is the record of another cure of blindness, set up by a patient who had been a sceptic:

> Ambrosia of Athens, blind in one eye. She came as a suppliant to the god, but walking around the sanctuary, she scoffed at some of the cures as incredible and impossible, that the lame and blind should be made whole, merely by seeing a vision in their sleep. But she, in her sleep, saw a vision. It seemed to her that the god stood over her and announced that he would cure her but that, in payment, he would ask her to present to the sanctuary a pig made of silver as a reminder of her ignorance. After saying this, he cut open her diseased eye and poured in some drug. When day dawned, she went out cured. (Stele 1.33–41).

Many were sceptical of the whole business, like Cicero, who said: "Few patients owe their lives to Asclepius rather than Hippocrates." The reputation of the sanctuary, however, continued to attract pilgrims for hundreds of years, and it is impossible to believe that all the cures recorded by grateful patients were mere fictions.

The inscription reads:

| ΑΣΚΛΗ | To Ascle- |
|--------|-----------|
| ΠΙΩ | pius |
| ΚΑΙ | and |
| ΥΓΕΙΑ | Health |
| ΤΥΧΗ | Tyche (dedicates this) |
| ΕΥΧΑΡΙΣ | (as a) thank |
| ΤΗΡΙΟΝ | offering |

Votive tablet dedicated for the cure of a leg

# Η ΕΠΙΔΑΥΡΟΣ (β)

## VOCABULARY

*Verbs*

Henceforth we give principal parts of contract verbs only when they show irregularities.

ἀκέομαι, ἀκοῦμαι, ἠκεσάμην (note ε instead of η), *I heal*

ἐπιτρέπω, ἐπιτρέψω, ἐπέτρεψα, [τροπ-] ἐπιτέτροφα, [τραπ-] ἐπιτέτραμμαι, ἐπετράπην, *I entrust* X (acc.) *to* Y (dat.)

θαρρέω, *I am confident*

θάρρει, *Cheer up! Don't be afraid!*

φρονέω, *I think; I am minded*

χρή, impersonal, imperfect, ἐχρῆν + infin. or acc. and infin., *it is necessary; ought, must*

χρή σε παρασκευάζεσθαι, *it is necessary that you prepare yourself, you ought to/must prepare yourself*

*Nouns*

ὁ ἱκέτης, τοῦ ἱκέτου, *suppliant*

ὁ νόμος, τοῦ νόμου, *law; custom*

τὸ τέμενος, τοῦ τεμένους, *sacred precinct*

ὁ ὑπηρέτης, τοῦ ὑπηρέτου, *servant; attendant*

ἡ ψῡχή, τῆς ψῡχῆς, *soul*

*Adjectives*

ἱερός, -ά̄, -όν, *holy, sacred*

καθαρός, -ά̄, -όν, *clean, pure*

ὅσιος, -ᾱ, -ον, *holy, pious*

*Preposition*

κατά + acc., *down;* distributive, *each, every; by; on;* according to

*Adverbs*

ὀψέ, *late; too late*

πως, enclitic, *somehow; in any way*

*Expression*

οὐ διὰ πολλοῦ, *not much later, soon*

*Proper Name*

τὸ Ἀσκληπιεῖον, τοῦ Ἀσκληπιείου, *the sanctuary of Asclepius*

πᾶσαν οὖν τὴν ἡμέρᾱν ἡ ναῦς ἀνέμῳ οὐρίῳ ἐφέρετο, ὡς δὲ ἑσπέρᾱ ἐγίγνετο, εἰς τὴν Ἐπίδαυρον ἀφίκοντο, οὐδὲν κακὸν παθόντες. ὡς δ' ἐξέβησαν εἰς τὴν γῆν, τῷ μὲν Δικαιοπόλιδι ἔδοξεν εὐθὺς πρὸς τὸ Ἀσκληπιεῖον ἰέναι· οὐ γὰρ πολὺ ἀπεῖχεν· ἡ δὲ γυνὴ ἡ τὴν γαστέρα νοσοῦσα οὕτως ἔκαμνεν ὥστε οὐκ ἤθελεν ἰέναι ἐκείνῃ τῇ ἡμέρᾳ,    5 ἀλλ' ἔμεινεν ἐν καταγωγίῳ τινὶ ἐγγὺς τοῦ λιμένος. οἱ δὲ ὥρμησαν καὶ δι' ὀλίγου ἀφικόμενοι ηὗρον τὰς πύλᾱς κεκλειμένᾱς. ὁ οὖν Δικαιόπολις, "κεκλειμέναι εἰσὶν αἱ πύλαι," ἔφη, "τί οὖν δεῖ ποιεῖν; πότερον κόψω τὰς πύλᾱς ἢ εἰς τὸν λιμένα ἐπάνιμεν; ὀψὲ γάρ ἐστιν." ὁ δὲ Φίλιππος, "ἀλλὰ κόψον, ὦ πάτερ, εἰ δοκεῖ. ἴσως γὰρ ἀκούσεται    10

τις καὶ ἡγήσεται ἡμῖν παρὰ τὸν ἱερέᾱ." ὁ μὲν οὖν Δικαιόπολις
ἔκοψεν, ἐξελθὼν δὲ ὑπηρέτης τις οὐ διὰ πολλοῦ, "τίς ὢν σύ," ἔφη,
"κόπτεις τὰς πύλᾱς τηνικαῦτα τῆς ἡμέρᾱς; πόθεν ἤλθετε καὶ τί
βουλόμενοι πάρεστε;" ὁ δὲ Δικαιόπολις, "ἐγὼ μέν εἰμι Δικαιόπολις
Ἀθηναῖος ὤν, τὸν δὲ παῖδα κομίζω, ἐᾱ́ν πως ὁ θεὸς ἐθέλῃ τοὺς    15
ὀφθαλμοὺς αὐτῷ ἀκεῖσθαι. τυφλὸς γὰρ γέγονεν. ἆρ' οὐχ ἡγήσει ἡμῖν
παρὰ τὸν σὸν δεσπότην;"

[καταγωγίῳ, inn    κεκλειμένᾱς, shut    τηνικαῦτα τῆς ἡμέρᾱς, at this time of day
ἐᾱ́ν πως . . . ἐθέλῃ, if somehow / in the hope that . . . is willing    γέγονεν, has become,
is]

ὁ δὲ ὑπηρέτης, "ὀψέ ἐστιν, ἀλλ' ὅμως μείνατε ἐνταῦθα. ἐγὼ γὰρ
εἶμι ὡς ζητήσων τὸν δεσπότην καὶ ἐρωτήσω εἰ ἐθέλει ὑμᾶς δέξασθαι."
οἱ μὲν οὖν ἔμενον ἐπὶ ταῖς πύλαις· οὐ πολλῷ δ' ὕστερον ἐπανελθὼν ὁ    20
ὑπηρέτης, "εἴσιτε," ἔφη, "ὁ γὰρ δεσπότης ὑμᾶς δέξεται." ταῦτα δ'
εἰπὼν ἡγεῖτο αὐτοῖς εἰς τὸ τέμενος.

ἀμειψάμενοι οὖν τὰς πύλᾱς εἰς αὐλὴν μεγάλην εἰσῆλθον· ἐκεῖ δὲ
ἐγγὺς τοῦ ἱεροῦ ἐκάθητο ἀνήρ τις γεραιός, ὃς ἰδὼν αὐτοὺς
προσιόντας, "χαίρετε, ὦ φίλοι," ἔφη. "τί βουλόμενοι ἥκετε;" ὁ μὲν οὖν    25
Δικαιόπολις ἐξηγήσατο τί ἔπαθεν ὁ Φίλιππος καὶ ὡς ἐκελεύσθησαν
ὑπὸ τοῦ ῑᾱτροῦ πρὸς τὴν Ἐπίδαυρον πορευθῆναι, ὁ δὲ ἱερεὺς πρὸς
τὸν παῖδα εὐμενῶς βλέψᾱς, "εἰπέ μοι, ὦ παῖ," ἔφη, "ἆρα σεαυτὸν τῷ
Ἀσκληπιῷ ἐπιτρέψεις; ἆρα τοῦτο πιστεύεις, ὅτι ὠφεληθήσει ὑπὸ τοῦ
θεοῦ;" ὁ δὲ Φίλιππος, "μάλιστά γε· πάντα γὰρ τοῖς θεοῖς δυνατά· τῷ    30
θεῷ πιστεύω καὶ ἐμαυτὸν αὐτῷ ἐπιτρέψω." ὁ δὲ γέρων, "εὖ γε, ὦ παῖ.
νῦν μὲν ἄπιτε εἰς τὸ καταγώγιον, αὔριον δὲ ὁ ὑπηρέτης ὑμῖν παρέσται
ὡς ἡγησόμενος τῷ παιδὶ παρ' ἐμέ." ἀπελθόντες οὖν ὅ τε πατὴρ καὶ ὁ
παῖς τὴν νύκτα ἔμενον ἐν τῷ καταγωγίῳ.

[ἀμειψάμενοι, having passed through    αὐλήν, courtyard    εὐμενῶς, kindly]

τῇ δὲ ὑστεραίᾳ ἐπεὶ πρῶτον ἡμέρᾱ ἐγένετο, προσελθὼν ὁ ὑπηρέτης    35
τὸν Φίλιππον ἤγαγε παρὰ τὸν ἱερέᾱ. ὁ δὲ εὐμενῶς δεξάμενος τὸν
παῖδα, "ἄγε δή, ὦ παῖ," ἔφη, "νῦν χρή σε παρασκευάζεσθαι· δεῖ γὰρ

ὅσιά τε φρονεῖν καὶ καθαρὸν εἶναι τὴν ψῡχήν. ἀλλὰ μηδὲν φοβοῦ·
φιλανθρωπότατος γάρ ἐστιν ὁ Ἀσκληπιὸς τῶν θεῶν καὶ τοῖς
καθαροῖς οὖσι τὴν ψῡχὴν ἀεὶ ἵλεώς ἐστιν. θάρρει οὖν." οὕτω δ'      40
εἰπὼν τὸν παῖδα εἰς τὸ ἱερὸν ἤγαγεν. ἐκεῖ δὲ πρῶτον μὲν ὁ Φίλιππος
ἐκαθάρθη, ἔπειτα δὲ πᾶσαν τὴν ἡμέρᾱν ἐν τῷ ἱερῷ ἔμενεν, ὅσιά τε
φρονῶν καὶ τὸν θεὸν εὐχόμενος ἐν τῷ ὕπνῳ ἐπιφανῆναι.

[ὅσια ... φρονεῖν, *to have holy thoughts*    τὴν ψῡχήν, *with respect to your soul*
φιλανθρωπότατος, *most benevolent*    ἐκαθάρθη, *was purified*    ὕπνῳ, *sleep*
ἐπιφανῆναι, -η- 2nd aorist passive infin., *to appear*]

τέλος δὲ ἐπεὶ ἑσπέρᾱ ἐγίγνετο, ἐπανελθὼν ὁ ἱερεύς, "ἄγε δή, ὦ παῖ,"
ἔφη, "πάντα γὰρ ἕτοιμά ἐστιν. ἕπου μοι." τὸν δὲ παῖδα ἐκ τοῦ ἱεροῦ    45
ἀγαγὼν πρὸς τὸν βωμόν, ἐκέλευσεν αὐτὸν σπονδὴν κατὰ νόμον
ποιεῖσθαι. ὁ δὲ τὴν φιάλην ταῖς χερσὶ λαβὼν σπονδὴν ἐποιήσατο καὶ
τὰς χεῖρας πρὸς τὸν οὐρανὸν ἄρᾱς, "Ἀσκληπιέ," ἔφη, "σῶτερ,
φιλανθρωπότατε τῶν θεῶν, ἄκουέ μου εὐχομένου, ὃς ὅσιά τε φρονῶν
καὶ καθαρὸς ὢν τὴν ψῡχὴν ἱκέτης σου πάρειμι. ἵλεως ἴσθι μοι τυφλῷ    50
γεγονότι καί, εἴ σοι δοκεῖ, τοὺς ὀφθαλμούς μοι ἀκοῦ."

[τὴν φιάλην, *the cup*    ταῖς χερσὶ, *in his hands*    ἄρᾱς (from αἴρω), *raising*    σῶτερ,
*savior*    γεγονότι, *having become / who has become*]

ἐνταῦθα δὴ ὁ ἱερεὺς τῷ παιδὶ εἰς τὸ ἄβατον ἡγησάμενος
ἐκέλευσεν αὐτὸν ἐπὶ τῇ γῇ κείμενον καθεύδειν. ὁ οὖν Φίλιππος
κατέκειτο, ἀλλὰ πολὺν δὴ χρόνον οὐκ ἐδύνατο καθεύδειν· μόνος
γὰρ καταλειφθεὶς ἐν τῷ ἀβάτῳ μάλα ἐφοβεῖτο· νὺξ γὰρ ἦν καὶ    55
πανταχοῦ σκότος καὶ σῑγή, εἰ μὴ σπανίως ἤκουε τῶν ἱερῶν ὄφεων
ἠρέμα σῡριττόντων.

[τὸ ἄβατον, *the holy place*    σκότος, *darkness*    σῑγή, *silence*    εἰ μὴ, *except*
σπανίως, *occasionally*    ὄφεων ἠρέμα σῡριττόντων, *snakes hissing gently*]

## PRINCIPAL PARTS: Stems in -ευ-

πιστεύω, πιστεύσω, ἐπίστευσα, πεπίστευκα, πεπίστευμαι, ἐπιστεύθην
  + dat., *I trust, am confident (in); I believe;* + ὡς, *I believe* (that)
κελεύω, κελεύσω, ἐκέλευσα, κεκέλευκα, κεκέλευσμαι, ἐκελεύσθην
  + acc. and infin., *I order, tell* someone to do something
πορεύομαι, πορεύσομαι, ἐπορευσάμην, aorist middle only in compounds,
  πεπόρευμαι, ἐπορεύθην (active in meaning), *I go; I walk; I march; I journey*

# WORD BUILDING

*Deduce the meanings of the words in the following sets (δυσ- = bad):*

1. τυγχάνω (τυχ-)   ἡ τύχη   εὐτυχής, -ές   δυστυχής, -ές   ἀτυχής, -ές
2. πιστεύω   ἡ πίστις   πιστός, -ή, -όν   ἄπιστος, -ον   ἀπιστέω
3. δύναμαι   ἡ δύναμις   δυνατός, -ή, -όν   ἀδύνατος, -ον
4. γιγνώσκω (γνω-)   ἡ γνώμη   γνωστός, -ή, -όν   ἄγνωστος, -ον
5. γράφω   ἡ γραφή   γραπτός, -ή, -όν   ἄγραπτος, -ον

# GRAMMAR

## 2. The Passive Voice: -η- 2nd Aorist Passive and -η- 2nd Future Passive

Some verbs add -η-/-ε- instead of -θη-/-θε- to form their aorist passives and -η- instead of -θη- to form their future passives; we call these *-η- 2nd aorist passives* and *-η- 2nd future passives*. The endings are the same as for the -θη- 1st aorist and -θη- 1st future passives. Here are some examples:

γράφω, *I write*          **Aorist:** ἐ-γράφ-η-ν
                          **Future:** γραφ-ή-σ-ο-μαι

δια-φθείρω, *I destroy* [φθαρ-]   **Aorist:** δι-ε-φθάρ-η-ν
                          **Future:** δια-φθαρ-ή-σ-ο-μαι

φαίνομαι, *I appear* [φαν-]   **Aorist:** ἐ-φάν-η-ν
                          **Future:** φαν-ή-σ-ο-μαι

Note this example from the story above:

ὁ Φίλιππος . . . ἐν τῷ ἱερῷ ἔμενεν . . . τὸν θεὸν εὐχόμενος ἐν τῷ ὕπνῳ
**ἐπιφανῆναι.** (41–43)
*Philip was waiting in the temple . . . praying the god **to appear** (= that the god appear) in (his) sleep.*

### Exercise 17ε

*Make a photocopy of the Verb Chart on page 275 and fill in the future and aorist passive forms of γράφω, except for the subjunctive and optative. Keep this chart for reference.*

## 3. Aorist of Deponent Verbs

Most deponent verbs have their aorist in the middle voice, e.g., γίγνομαι, aorist ἐγενόμην. These may be called *middle deponents*. A few deponent verbs, however, have aorists that are passive instead of middle in form, as does πορεύομαι in the list of verbs with their principal parts given above, aorist, ἐπορεύθην, *I marched, journeyed*, and as does φαίνομαι

(Grammar 2 above), aorist ἐφάνην, *I appeared.* Here are some other deponent verbs that have their aorist in the passive voice:

> βούλομαι, aorist, **ἐβουλήθην**, *I wanted; I wished*
> δύναμαι, aorist, **ἐδυνήθην**, *I was able*
> ἐπίσταμαι, aorist, **ἠπιστήθην**, *I understood; I knew*
> ὀργίζομαι, aorist, **ὠργίσθην**, *I grew angry*

These may be called *passive deponents.*

Note this example from the story above:

> . . . πρὸς τὴν Ἐπίδαυρον **πορευθῆναι.** (27)
> . . . ***to go*** to Epidaurus.

Some deponent verbs have both aorist middle and aorist passive forms, e.g.:

> διαλέγομαι, aorist middle, **διελεξάμην**, *I talked to, conversed with,*
> aorist passive, **διελέχθην**, *I talked to, conversed with*

The verb χαίρω, *I rejoice,* has its aorist in the passive, **ἐχάρην**, *I rejoiced.*

## Exercise 17ζ

*Read aloud and translate:*

1. οἱ δοῦλοι ὑπὸ τοῦ δεσπότου λυθέντες πρὸς τὸ ἄστυ ἔσπευδον.
2. οἱ πολῖται ἐκελεύσθησαν πρὸς τὸ ἄστυ πορευθῆναι.
3. οἱ νεανίαι πολὺν χρόνον τῷ γέροντι διαλεχθέντες οἴκαδε ἐπανῆλθον.
4. ὁ αὐτουργὸς τῷ λίθῳ βληθεὶς ὠργίσθη καὶ τὸν παῖδα ἐδίωκεν.
5. πᾶσαν τὴν ἡμέρᾱν πορευθέντες τέλος εἰς τὸν λιμένα ἀφίκοντο.
6. ἡ ναῦς τῷ χειμῶνι διεφθάρη καὶ πάντες οἱ ναῦται ἀπέθανον.
7. ὁ θεὸς τῷ παιδὶ καθεύδοντι ἐφάνη.
8. πρὸς τὴν Ἐπίδαυρον πορευθησόμεθα ὡς αἰτήσοντες τὸν θεὸν ἡμᾶς ὠφελεῖν.
9. αὕτη ἡ ἐπιστολὴ (*letter*) ὑπὸ τοῦ ἐμοῦ πατρὸς ἐγράφη.
10. ἡ μήτηρ μάλα ὀργισθεῖσα τοὺς παῖδας ἐκόλασεν (*punished*).

## Exercise 17η

*Translate into Greek:*

1. The ships of the barbarians, after sailing into the straits, were destroyed by the Greeks.
2. Xerxes, seeing (*use aorist participle*) the barbarians defeated, was at a loss.
3. The women, having journeyed to the city with their husbands, watched the dances.

4. The girls did not want to talk to (*use aorist of* διαλέγομαι) the old men.
5. The ship will be destroyed by the storm.

## ΟΙ ΠΕΡΣΑΙ ΤΑΣ ΑΘΗΝΑΣ ΔΕΥΤΕΡΟΝ ΑΙΡΟΥΣΙΝ

*Read the following passage (adapted from Herodotus 9.1–10) and answer the comprehension questions below:*

When Xerxes returned to Asia after Salamis, he left Mardonius with a large army to subdue Greece the following year.

ἅμα δὲ ἦρι ἀρχομένῳ ὁ Μαρδόνιος ὁρμώμενος ἐκ Θεσσαλίας ἦγε τὸν στρατὸν σπουδῇ ἐπὶ τὰς ᾿Αθήνας. προϊόντι δὲ αὐτῷ οὐδεὶς τῶν Βοιωτῶν ἀντεῖχεν, οὐδὲ ἐβοήθουν τοῖς ᾿Αθηναίοις οἱ Λακεδαιμόνιοι. ἀφικόμενος δὲ εἰς τὴν ᾿Αττικὴν οὐχ ηὗρε τοὺς ᾿Αθηναίους ἀλλὰ ἔμαθεν ὅτι ἔν τε Σαλαμῖνι οἱ πλεῖστοί εἰσι καὶ ἐν ταῖς ναυσίν· ᾑρέθη τε ἔρημον τὸ ἄστυ. ἐπεὶ δὲ ἐν ταῖς ᾿Αθήναις ἐγένετο, ἄγγελον   5
ἔπεμψεν εἰς τὴν Σαλαμῖνα, λόγους φέροντα ἐπιτηδείους· εἶπε γὰρ ὅτι ὁ βασιλεὺς τήν τε ᾿Αττικὴν τοῖς ᾿Αθηναίοις ἀποδώσει καὶ συμμαχίᾶν ποιήσεται, ἐὰν τοῦ πολέμου παύσωνται. οἱ δὲ ᾿Αθηναῖοι τοὺς λόγους οὐκ ἐδέξαντο ἀλλὰ τὸν ἄγγελον ἀπέπεμψαν.

[ἅ μ α . . . ἦ ρ ι ἀρχομένῳ, *with the beginning of spring*    ὁ Μαρδόνιος, *Mardonius*
Θεσσαλίᾶς, *Thessaly*    σπουδῇ, adv., *in haste*    προϊόντι, *going forward, advancing*
τῶν Βοιωτῶν, *of the Boeotians*    ἔρημον, *deserted*    ἐπιτηδείους, *friendly*
ἀποδώσει, *would give back*    συμμαχίᾶν, *alliance*    ἐὰν . . . παύσωνται, *if they ceased*]

1. What did Mardonius do at the coming of spring?
2. What was the response of the Boeotians and the Spartans?
3. What did Mardonius find when he reached Athens?
4. What were the terms of the proposal that Mardonius sent to the Athenians?
5. What was the response of the Athenians?

εἰς δὲ τὴν Σαλαμῖνα διέβησαν οἱ ᾿Αθηναῖοι ὧδε· ἕως μὲν ἤλπιζον στρατὸν   10
πεμφθήσεσθαι ὑπὸ τῶν Λακεδαιμονίων ὡς βοηθήσοντα, ἔμενον ἐν τῇ ᾿Αττικῇ· ἐπεὶ
δὲ οἱ μὲν Λακεδαιμόνιοι οὐκ ἐβοήθουν, ὁ δὲ Μαρδόνιος προϊὼν εἰς τὴν Βοιωτίᾶν
ἀφίκετο, ἐξεκόμισαν πάντα ἐκ τῆς ᾿Αττικῆς καὶ αὐτοὶ διέβησαν εἰς τὴν Σαλαμῖνα.
καὶ εἰς Λακεδαίμονα ἔπεμπον ἀγγέλους ὡς μεμψομένους τοῖς Λακεδαιμονίοις, διότι
οὐκ ἐβοήθουν. ὡς δὲ ἀφίκοντο εἰς τὴν Λακεδαίμονα οἱ ἄγγελοι, εἶπον τάδε,   15
"ἔπεμψαν ἡμᾶς οἱ ᾿Αθηναῖοι ὡς λέξοντας ὅτι ὁ βασιλεὺς τῶν Περσῶν ἐθέλει τήν τε
᾿Αττικὴν ἀποδοῦναι καὶ συμμαχίᾶν ποιεῖσθαι· ἡμεῖς δέ, καίπερ ἀδικούμενοι ὑφ᾿

ὑμῶν, ἐκείνους τοὺς λόγους οὐκ ἐδεξάμεθα.  νῦν δὲ κελεύομεν ὑμᾶς ὡς τάχιστα
στρατιὰν πέμψαι ὡς τοὺς βαρβάρους ἀμυνοῦσαν τῇ Ἀττικῇ."

[διέβησαν, *crossed*   ὧδε, *in this way*   ἕως, *as long as*   στρατὸν πεμφθήσεσθαι,
*that an army would be sent*   προϊών, *advancing*   τὴν Βοιωτίᾱν, *Boeotia*
ἐξεκόμισαν, *they took out, removed*   διέβησαν, *they crossed over*   Λακεδαίμονα,
*Lacedaemon, Sparta*   ὡς μεμψομένους + dat., *to blame, criticize*   διότι, *because*
ἀποδοῦναι, *to give back*   ἀδικούμενοι ὑφ' ὑμῶν, *being wronged by you*
στρατιὰν, *an army*]

6. What had the Athenians done as long as they hoped for help?
7. When did they cross to Salamis?
8. What message did they send to Sparta?

### Exercise 17θ

*Translate into Greek:*

1. The Spartans, who were holding a festival at this time, were not willing to go out against (ἐπεξιέναι ἐπί + *acc.*) the Persians but were
   still delaying (ἔμελλον).
2. And finally the messengers of the Athenians said: "On the one hand
   you, the Spartans, are betraying (προδίδοτε) your allies, and on the
   other hand the Athenians, wronged (*use* ἀδικέω, *I wrong*) by you,
   will make a peace treaty with (πρός + *acc.*) the Persians.
3. "Then having made a peace treaty and having become allies of the
   Persians (*dat.*), we will wage war with them against (ἐπί + *acc.*) the
   Peloponnesus.
4. "Then indeed you will learn by suffering (having suffered) that you
   ought not betray (προδοῦναι) your allies."
5. And finally, fearing these words, the Spartans sent their army to Attica.

## Classical Greek

### Miracle Cures

The following are inscriptions recording miracle cures from the temple
of Asclepius at Epidaurus.  They are headed: ΙΑΜΑΤΑ ΤΟΥ ΑΠΟΛΛΩΝΟΣ ΚΑΙ
ΤΟΥ ΑΣΚΛΗΠΙΟΥ.

Ἡραιεὺς Μυτιληναῖος.  οὗτος οὐκ εἶχε ἐν τῇ κεφαλῇ τρίχας, ἐν δὲ τῷ γενείῳ
παμπόλλᾱς.  αἰσχυνόμενος δὲ ὡς καταγελώμενος ὑπὸ τῶν ἄλλων ἐνεκάθευδε.
τὸν δὲ θεὸς χρῑ́σᾱς φαρμάκῳ τὴν κεφαλὴν ἐποίησε τρίχας ἔχειν.

[ἰάματα, *healings, cures*   Μυτιληναῖος, *from Mytilene*   τρίχας, *hair*   γενείῳ, *chin*
αἰσχυνόμενος, *ashamed*   ὡς καταγελώμενος, *as being laughed at*, i.e., *thinking that
he was being laughed at*   ἐνεκάθευδε, *slept (was sleeping) in* (the abaton)   χρῑ́σᾱς
φαρμάκῳ, *having anointed with an ointment*]

Ἡγέστρατος, κεφαλῆς ἄλγος. οὗτος ἀγρυπνίαις συνεχόμενος διὰ τὸν πόνον τῆς κεφαλῆς, ὡς ἐν τῷ ἀβάτῳ ἐγένετο, καθύπνωσε καὶ ἐνύπνιον εἶδε· ἐδόκει αὐτὸν ὁ θεὸς ἰασάμενος τὸ τῆς κεφαλῆς ἄλγος ὀρθὸν ἀναστήσας γυμνὸν παγκρατίου προβολὴν διδάξαι· ἡμέρας δὲ γενομένης ὑγιὴς ἐξῆλθε καὶ οὐ μετὰ πολὺν χρόνον τὰ Νέμεα ἐνίκησε παγκράτιον.

[ἄλγος, pain    ἀγρυπνίαις συνεχόμενος, suffering from insomnia    διὰ, because of κaθύπνωσε, fell asleep    ἐνύπνιον, a dream    ἰασάμενος, after curing    ἀνα-στήσας, having made him stand up    γυμνὸν, naked (athletes competed naked) παγκρατίου προβολὴν διδάξαι, to have taught him (αὐτόν) the defense in the pan-cratium (boxing and wrestling contest)    ὑγιὴς, healthy    τὰ Νέμεα (ἱερά), the Ne-mean Games (which took place in the Valley of Nemea between Argos and Corinth)]

# New Testament Greek

## John 1.1–2
### The Beginning of the Gospel

ἐν ἀρχῇ ἦν ὁ λόγος, καὶ ὁ λόγος ἦν πρὸς τὸν θεόν, καὶ θεὸς ἦν ὁ λόγος. οὗτος ἦν ἐν ἀρχῇ πρὸς τὸν θεόν.

[πρὸς, with]

## John 1.14
### The Incarnation

καὶ ὁ λόγος σὰρξ ἐγένετο καὶ ἐσκήνωσεν ἐν ἡμῖν.

[σὰρξ, flesh    ἐσκήνωσεν, tented    ἐν, among]

## John 1.29
### John the Baptist Beholds Jesus

In the following sentence the subject of the verb βλέπει is John the Baptist. The verb is transitive here.

τῇ ἐπαύριον βλέπει τὸν Ἰησοῦν ἐρχόμενον πρὸς αὐτὸν καὶ λέγει, "ἴδε ὁ ἀμνὸς τοῦ θεοῦ ὁ αἴρων τὴν ἁμαρτίᾶν τοῦ κόσμου."

[τῇ ἐπαύριον, on the next day    τὸν Ἰησοῦν, Jesus    ἐρχόμενον = ἰόντα    ἴδε, behold!    ὁ ἀμνὸς, the lamb    ὁ αἴρων, the one lifting/taking away    τὴν ἁμαρτίᾶν, the sin    τοῦ κόσμου, of the world]

See Acknowledgments, page 376.

# 18
# Ο ΑΣΚΛΗΠΙΟΣ (α)

ὁ Ἀσκληπιὸς σεμνός τ' ἦν καὶ μέγας.

## VOCABULARY

*Verbs*

γελάω, γελάσομαι (note α instead of η), ἐγέλασα, ἐγελάσθην, *I laugh*

δίδωμι [δω-/δο-], imperfect, ἐδίδουν, **δώσω, ἔδωκα,** infinitive, δοῦναι, participle, δούς, imperative, δός, **δέδωκα, δέδομαι, ἐδόθην,** *I give*
    ἀποδίδωμι, *I give back, return; I pay;* middle, *I sell*

κῑνέω, *I move*

τίθημι [θη-/θε-], imperfect, ἐτίθην, **θήσω, ἔθηκα,** infinitive, θεῖναι, participle, θείς, imperative, θές, **τέθηκα,** (τέθειμαι; κεῖμαι usually used instead), **ἐτέθην,** *I put, place*
    ἐπιτίθημι, *I put* X (acc.) *on* Y (dat.)

*Nouns*

ὁ ὕπνος, τοῦ ὕπνου, *sleep*

ἡ χάρις, τῆς χάριτος, τὴν χάριν, *thanks; gratitude*

*Adjectives*

δῆλος, -η, -ον, *clear*

εὐμενής, -ές, *kindly*

σεμνός, -ή, -όν, *holy; august*

*Prepositions*

περί + gen., *about, concerning; around;* + acc., *around*

ὑπέρ + gen., *on behalf of, for; above;* + acc., *over, above*

*Expressions*

δῆλόν ἐστι(ν), *it is clear*

χάριν ἀποδίδωμι + dat., *I give thanks to; I thank*

τέλος δὲ οὕτως ἔκαμνεν ὁ Φίλιππος ὥστε εἰς βαθὺν ὕπνον ἔπεσεν.
καθεύδοντι δ' αὐτῷ ἐπεφάνη ὁ θεός· σεμνός τ' ἦν καὶ μέγας καὶ τῇ
ἀριστερᾷ βακτηρίαν ἔφερε, περὶ ἧς εἰλίττετο ὁ ἱερὸς ὄφις.  ἔστη δὲ
παρὰ τῷ παιδί, καὶ εὐμενῶς βλέψας τάδε εἶπεν, "τί πάσχεις, ὦ παῖ; τί
καθεύδεις ἐν τῷ ἐμῷ ἀβάτῳ;" ὁ δὲ οὐδὲν φοβούμενος (εὐμενὴς γὰρ      5
ἐφαίνετο ὁ θεός), "τυφλός εἰμι, ὦ Ἀσκληπιέ," ἔφη, "ἥκω οὖν ὡς
αἰτήσων σε τοὺς ὀφθαλμούς μοι ἀκεῖσθαι."  ὁ δὲ θεός, "ἐὰν δ' ἐγὼ
ἰάσωμαί σοι τοὺς ὀφθαλμούς, τί σύ μοι δώσεις;" ὁ δὲ παῖς πολὺν δὴ
χρόνον ἠπόρει τί χρὴ λέγειν, τέλος δέ, "πολλὰ μὲν οὐκ ἔχω," ἔφη,
"δώσω δέ σοι τοὺς ἐμοὺς ἀστραγάλους."  ὁ δὲ θεὸς γελάσας      10
προσεχώρησε καὶ τὰς χεῖρας ἐπέθηκε τοῖς ὀφθαλμοῖς αὐτοῦ.  ταῦτα
δὲ ποιήσας ἀπέβη.

[βαθὺν, *deep*   ἐπεφάνη, *appeared*   βακτηρίαν, *staff*   εἰλίττετο (from ἐλίττω, *I
wind around*), *was curling itself*   ὄφις, *serpent*   ἀβάτῳ, *holy place*   ἐὰν...
ἰάσωμαί (from ἰάομαι), *if I heal*   ἀστραγάλους, *knucklebones* (used as dice in gaming)]

τῇ δ' ὑστεραίᾳ ἐπεὶ πρῶτον ἡμέρᾱ ἐγένετο, ἠγέρθη ὁ Φίλιππος καί,
ἰδού, βλέπειν ἐδύνατο· τόν τε γὰρ οὐρανὸν εἶδε καὶ τὸν ἥλιον ὑπὲρ
τοὺς λόφους ἀνίσχοντα καὶ τὰ δένδρα τῷ ἀνέμῳ κῑνούμενα· καὶ      15
ἐτέρπετο θεώμενος· πάντα γὰρ αὐτῷ κάλλιστα δὴ ἐφαίνετο.
ἔσπευδεν οὖν ὡς τὸν ἱερέᾱ ζητήσων.  ὁ δὲ ἰδὼν αὐτὸν προσιόντα,
"χαῖρε, ὦ παῖ," ἔφη, "δῆλόν ἐστιν ὅτι ὁ θεὸς εὐμενὴς προσῆλθέ σοι.
χάριν οὖν τῷ θεῷ ἀπόδος.  ἀλλ' ἴθι ὡς τὸν πατέρα ζητήσων."

[ἠγέρθη: aorist passive of ἐγείρω   λόφους, *crests of the hills*   ἀνίσχοντα (from
ἀνίσχω, a variant of ἀνέχω), *rising*   ἀπόδος: aorist imperative of ἀποδίδωμι]

## PRINCIPAL PARTS: -ε- Contract Verbs

φιλέω, φιλήσω, ἐφίλησα, πεφίληκα, πεφίλημαι, ἐφιλήθην, *I love*
δοκέω, [δοκ-] δόξω, ἔδοξα, δέδογμαι, ἐδόχθην, *I seem; I think*
καλέω, καλῶ, ἐκάλεσα, [κλη-] κέκληκα, κέκλημαι (*I am called*),
  ἐκλήθην, *I call*
πλέω, [πλευ-] πλεύσομαι or [πλευσε-] πλευσοῦμαι, [πλευ-] ἔπλευσα,
  πέπλευκα, *I sail*
σκοπέω, [σκεπ-] σκέψομαι, ἐσκεψάμην, ἔσκεμμαι, *I look at, examine; I consider*

## WORD STUDY

*Explain the meaning of the following English words with reference to their Greek stems:*

1. autobiography
2. autograph
3. automatic
4. autonomous
5. autistic

Women
playing
knucklebones

## GRAMMAR

### 1. The Verbs δίδωμι and τίθημι

These verbs have both long- and short-vowel stems:

> δίδωμι: long-vowel stem δω-; short-vowel stem δο-
> τίθημι: long-vowel stem θη-; short-vowel stem θε-

**δί-δω-μι, δώσω, ἔδωκα, δέδωκα, δέδομαι, ἐδόθην,** *I give*

**τί-θη-μι, θήσω, ἔθηκα, τέθηκα,** (τέθειμαι; κεῖμαι usually used instead), **ἐτέθην,** *I put, place*

In the present and imperfect the stems are reduplicated, i.e., the first consonant of the stem (with θ becoming τ by dissimilation, for which, see below) + ι is put before the stem. The personal endings are then added straight to the stem with no thematic vowel in between.

Note that in the present and aorist active the long-vowel stem is used in the singular forms. In the imperfect some of the forms in the singular show contractions with the short stem vowel.

The future active and future middle of these verbs are formed in the usual manner, and full sets of their forms are not included in the charts.

The aorist and future passive have their usual endings, and full sets of their forms are not included in the charts. Note, however, that for the aorist passive of τίθημι, what would be expected to be ἐ-θέ-θη-ν becomes ἐ-τέ-θη-ν by *dissimilation*, i.e., change of θ to τ to avoid two aspirated consonants in neighboring syllables.

The forms of τίθημι will be presented in the second half of this chapter.

---

## Greek Wisdom

Greek Wisdom in Book II includes the presocratic philosopher Heraclitus of Ephesus (fl. 500 B.C.), deemed "lofty-minded beyond all other men," and Socrates of Athens (Chapter 29). A saying of Heraclitus:

σωφρονεῖν ἀρετὴ μεγίστη, καὶ σοφίᾱ ἀληθῆ λέγειν καὶ ποιεῖν κατὰ φύσιν.
Fragment 112 Diels

## δίδωμι: Present, Imperfect, Future, and Aorist, Active Voice

**Stems:** δω-/δο-

### Present

| Indicative | Imperative | | Infinitive | Participle |
|---|---|---|---|---|
| δί-δω-μι | | | δι-δό-ναι | δι-δούς, |
| δί-δω-ς | δί-δο-ε > δίδου | | | δι-δοῦσα, |
| δί-δω-σι(ν) | | | | δι-δόν, |
| δί-δο-μεν | | | | gen., δι-δόντ-ος, etc. |
| δί-δο-τε | δί-δο-τε | | | |
| δι-δό-ᾱσι(ν) | | | | |

### Imperfect
### Indicative

ἐ-δί-δο-ον > ἐδίδουν

ἐ-δί-δο-ες > ἐδίδους

ἐ-δί-δο-ε > ἐδίδου

ἐ-δί-δο-μεν

ἐ-δί-δο-τε

ἐ-δί-δο-σαν

### Future:

Regular sigmatic future: δώσω, δώσεις, δώσει, etc.

### Aorist

| Indicative | Imperative | | Infinitive | Participle |
|---|---|---|---|---|
| ἔ-δωκ-α | | | δοῦ-ναι | δούς, |
| ἔ-δωκ-ας | δό-ς | | | δοῦσα, |
| ἔ-δωκ-ε(ν) | | | | δόν, |
| ἔ-δο-μεν | | | | gen., δόντ-ος, etc. |
| ἔ-δο-τε | δό-τε | | | |
| ἔ-δο-σαν | | | | |

Note the irregular stem δωκ- in the singular aorist indicative.

---

# Greek Wisdom

### Heraclitus

ἀνθρώποις πᾶσι μέτεστι γιγνώσκειν ἑαυτοὺς καὶ σωφρονεῖν. Fragment 116 Diels

## δίδωμι: Present and Imperfect, Middle/Passive Voice

**Stem:** δο-

| Present<br>Indicative | Imperative | Infinitive | Participle |
|---|---|---|---|
| δί-δο-μαι | | δί-δο-σθαι  δι-δό-μεν-ος, -η, -ον | |
| δί-δο-σαι | δί-δο-σο | | |
| δί-δο-ται | | | |
| δι-δό-μεθα | | | |
| δί-δο-σθε | δί-δο-σθε | | |
| δί-δο-νται | | | |

**Imperfect
Indicative**

ἐ-δι-δό-μην
ἐ-δί-δο-σο
ἐ-δί-δο-το
ἐ-δι-δό-μεθα
ἐ-δί-δο-σθε
ἐ-δί-δο-ντο

## δίδωμι: Future and Aorist, Middle Voice

**Stem:** δω-

**Future**

Regular sigmatic future: δώσομαι, δώσει/ῃ, δώσεται, etc.

**Stem:** δο-

| Aorist<br>Indicative | Imperative | Infinitive | Participle |
|---|---|---|---|
| ἐ-δό-μην | | δό-σθαι | δό-μεν-ος, -η, -ον |
| ἔ-δο-σο > ἔδου | δό-σο > δοῦ | | |
| ἔ-δο-το | | | |
| ἐ-δό-μεθα | | | |
| ἔ-δο-σθε | δό-σθε | | |
| ἔ-δο-ντο | | | |

## δίδωμι: Future and Aorist, Passive Voice

**Future**

Regular -θη- future passive: δοθήσομαι, δοθήσει/ῃ, δοθήσεται, etc.

**Aorist**

Regular -θη- aorist passive: ἐδόθην, ἐδόθης, ἐδόθη, etc.

## Exercise 18α

Make two photocopies of the Verb Chart on page 274 and three copies of the Verb Chart on page 275. Fill in the forms of δίδωμι, except for the subjunctive and optative, in the active voice (present, imperfect, future, and aorist), in the middle/passive voice (present and imperfect), in the middle voice (future and aorist), and in the passive voice (future and aorist). Keep these charts for reference.

## Exercise 18β

Identify and translate the following forms:

1. ἐδίδου
2. ἔδοσαν
3. δός
4. διδόᾱσι(ν)
5. διδοῦσα

6. δίδως
7. ἐδίδοτε
8. ἀποδόμενος
9. ἔδωκας
10. ἀποδοῦναι

11. δίδοσθαι (2 ways)
12. δοῦ
13. ἀπέδοσθε
14. δοῦναι
15. ἐδίδοντο (2 ways)

## Exercise 18γ

*Put into the aorist:*

1. δίδου
2. διδόᾱσι(ν)
3. διδόντα
4. διδόμενος
5. διδόναι

*Put into the present:*

6. ἐδόμεθα
7. δόμενος
8. δόσθαι
9. δούς
10. δός

*Put into the middle:*

11. δοῦναι
12. ἔδοσαν
13. ἔδωκα
14. δόντες
15. δίδομεν

## Exercise 18δ

*Read aloud and translate:*

1. ὁ γέρων οὐκ ἠθέλησε τὸ ἀργύριον τῷ ξένῳ δοῦναι.
2. οἱ παῖδες, ἐπεὶ ἡ μήτηρ σῖτον αὐτοῖς ἔδωκεν, εὐθὺς ἤσθιον.
3. ὁ δεσπότης τὸν δοῦλον ἔπεμψεν ὡς τὸ ἀργύριον ἡμῖν ἀποδώσοντα.
4. τί οὐκ ἐθέλεις τοῦτον τὸν κύνα μοι ἀποδόσθαι;
5. χάριν τῷ θεῷ ἀπόδος· ἔσωσε γὰρ ἡμᾶς.
6. τί ἀργύριον τούτῳ τῷ γέροντι ἐδίδους;
7. σὺ μὲν δός μοι τὸν οἶνον, ἐγὼ δὲ δώσω σοι τὸν σῖτον.
8. ὁ πατὴρ εὐμενῶς γελάσᾱς τῷ παιδὶ τὸν κύνα ἔδωκεν.
9. οἱ ἱκέται πρὸς τῷ βωμῷ καθήμενοι χάριν τῷ θεῷ ἀπέδοσαν.
10. ὁ αὐτουργὸς εἰς τὴν ἀγορὰν ἀφικόμενος τοὺς βοῦς ἀπέδοτο.

## Exercise 18ε

*Translate into Greek:*

1. The captain gave the money to the sailor.

2. Having thanked the god, the women went home.
3. I told you to leave the plow in the field and give food to the oxen.
4. It is clear that these women gave no money to this old man.
5. After paying the captain three drachmas, the foreigners boarded the ship.

# Sparta and Corinth

In the chaos following the breakdown of Bronze Age civilization in the Eastern Mediterranean (ca. 1200 B.C.), there were widespread migrations. New peoples entered Greece and Asia Minor from north of the civilized world and either pushed out or merged with the previous population. In Greece the newcomers were Greeks who spoke a different dialect, Doric, and this movement is traditionally called the Dorian invasion, although it probably took the form of sporadic raids over a long period of time rather than an organized invasion. When the dust settled, the whole of the Peloponnesus except the central plateau of Arcadia was occupied by Doric speakers.

Dorians calling themselves Lacedaemonians were settled in the fertile valley of the Eurotas by 1,000 B.C. and by about 850 B.C. four or five villages united to form the *polis* of Sparta. As its population increased, Sparta gradually conquered her neighbors to the north and east, reducing them to dependent status; the conquered were called περίοικοι. They had local autonomy but were obliged to serve in the Spartan army. About 735 B.C., when other states were about to solve their population problem by sending out colonies, Sparta crossed the mountain range of Taygetus and in a war lasting twenty years conquered Messenia. The inhabitants were reduced to the status of serfs, called *helots* (εἵλωτες), who worked the land for their Spartan masters.

This conquest determined the future history of Sparta. Up to this time her development had been not unlike that of other Greek states, except that she had retained a monarchy, or rather a dyarchy, since she had two hereditary kings coming from two separate royal families. Within fifty years of the conquest of Messenia she had developed into a totalitarian military state quite different from any other in Greece. The reason for this was the absolute necessity of dominating the helots, who outnumbered the Spartans by seven to one and revolted whenever the opportunity occurred.

Sometime in the seventh century there was a revolution in Sparta caused partly by economic factors (the new wealth produced by the conquest of Messenia) and partly by military reorganization (the introduction of the hoplite phalanx). Both developments gave more importance to the ordinary Spartan and challenged the authority of kings and nobles. The outcome was a revised constitution, ascribed to a lawgiver called Lycurgus. The kings were advised by a council of elders, all aged over sixty, the Gerousia. The ancient assembly of all the Spartans, the Apella, was given the final authority, i.e., the right to accept or reject proposals put by the Gerousia. In addition there were five officials called *ephors* (ἔφοροι, *overseers*), elected by the whole citizen body, whose function was to guard the rights of the people in its relation with the kings.

The other feature of the Lycurgan reforms was the ἀγωγή (*training*); this was the system by which every male Spartan was trained to devote his life to service in the army.  At birth the child was inspected by the heads of his tribe, and, if the child was weak or unhealthy, it was exposed on Mount Taygetus and left to die.  At seven the boy began his education in the state school, where the whole training was aimed at discipline, endurance, and patriotism.  At twenty he joined the army and might marry but continued to live in barracks.  At thirty he became a man and joined the ranks of the ὅμοιοι (*equals*) but continued to dine in the public mess with his fellow soldiers.

In 660 B.C. Sparta, still trying to extend her territory northward, suffered a severe defeat at the hands of her northern neighbor, Argos.  Soon after this the helots rose in revolt, no doubt supported by Argos.  There followed a long and bitter war, from which Sparta eventually emerged victorious.  By the end of the century Argive power had declined.  Sparta became the dominant power in the Peloponnesus and enrolled all the states except Argos in a loose confederacy called the Peloponnesian League.

The other Greeks either admired Sparta for her stability (εὐνομίᾱ) or hated her for her oppressive and xenophobic regime.  Nevertheless, Sparta was recognized as the most powerful state in Greece.

The *polis* of Corinth was formed from a union of seven villages perhaps about 800 B.C., and, when she emerges into the light of history, we find her ruled by a Dorian clan, the Bacchiadae.  Her position on the Isthmus, at the very center of Greece with ports on both seas, assured her future as a commercial city.  Under the Bacchiadae she founded the earliest colonies in the West (except for Ischia) at Corcyra and Syracuse (734 B.C.); she led the way in improvements in the design of ships and in the manufacture of pottery.  The distinctive Corinthian ware was exported all over the Greek world and beyond in the eighth and seventh centuries.

About 650 B.C. the Bacchiadae were overthrown and driven out by Cypselus.  He was the first of many Greek tyrants, a word which did not have its present connotations but simply meant one who seized power unconstitutionally.  The tyrants often won power as champions of the people against the oppression of the nobles and were the product of economic and military developments similar to those that occasioned the revolution at Sparta.  Under Cypselus and his son Periander, Corinth flourished and became the leading maritime and commercial state.  His regime became bloody and oppressive, as conspiracies drove him to suspect all citizens of wealth and influence.  He died in 585 B.C., and his successor was assassinated within a few years.  From then on Corinth was ruled by an oligarchy (which means rule by the few: in Corinth's case, the wealthy merchants).

Corinth remained one of the most prosperous states of Greece, achieving by the fifth century a near monopoly of western trade.  When Athens began to rival Corinth in the West, Corinth had every reason to fear her ambitions.

# Ο ΑΣΚΛΗΠΙΟΣ (β)

## VOCABULARY

*Verbs*

ἁμαρτάνω, [ἁμαρτε-] ἁμαρ-
τήσομαι, [ἁμαρτ-] ἥμαρτον,
[ἁμαρτε-] ἡμάρτηκα, ἡμάρ-
τημαι, ἡμαρτήθην + gen.,
*I miss; I make a mistake, am
mistaken*
ἀνατίθημι, *I set up; I dedicate*
ἐπιστρατεύω + dat. or ἐπί
+ acc., *I march against, attack*
κρατέω + gen., *I rule, have
power over, control; I prevail*
παραδίδωμι, *I hand over; I give*
τρέχω, [δραμε-] δραμοῦμαι,
[δραμ-] ἔδραμον, [δραμε-] δεδράμηκα, *I run*
προστρέχω, *I run toward*
τολμάω, *I dare*

*Nouns*

ἡ γνώμη, τῆς γνώμης, *opinion;
judgment; intention*
ὁ ἐχθρός, τοῦ ἐχθροῦ, *enemy*
ἡ θυσίᾱ, τῆς θυσίᾱς, *sacrifice*
τὸ κράτος, τοῦ κράτους, *power*
τὸ πρᾶγμα, τοῦ πράγματος,
*matter; trouble*
τὰ χρήματα, τῶν χρημάτων,
*things; goods; money*

*Adjectives*

ἐχθρός, -ά, -όν, *hateful; hostile*

ὑγιής, -ές, *healthy*
φιλαίτερος, -ᾱ, -ον and φιλαίτατος or φίλτατος, -η,
-ον, irregular comparative
and superlatives of φίλος, -η,
-ον, *dearer; dearest*

*Prepositions*

διά + gen., *through;* + acc. *because of*
ἐπί + dat., *at;* of price, *for;*
+ acc., *at; against; onto; upon*

*Adverbs*

ἡδέως, *sweetly; pleasantly;
gladly*
μᾶλλον, *more; rather*
μᾶλλον ἤ, *rather than*
οὔκουν, *certainly not*
πάλαι, *long ago*
πάλαι εἰσί(ν), *they have
been for a long time now*

*Conjunction*

διότι, *because*

*Particle*

μέντοι, *certainly; however*

*Expressions*

ὀρθῶς γιγνώσκω, *I am right*
πῶς ἔχει τὰ πράγματα; *How
are things?*
τίνα γνώμην ἔχεις; *What do
you think?*

τὸν δὲ Δικαιόπολιν ηὗρον πρὸ τοῦ καταγωγίου καθήμενον.  ὁ δὲ
ὡς εἶδε τὸν παῖδα βεβαίως βαδίζοντα καὶ βλέποντα, ἀνέστη καὶ
προσδραμὼν ἠσπάζετο αὐτὸν καί, "ὦ φίλτατε παῖ," ἔφη, "ἆρα
ἀληθῶς ὁρῶ σε ὑγιῆ ὄντα;  ἆρα ἀληθῶς ἠκέσατό σοι τοὺς
ὀφθαλμοὺς ὁ θεός;  δεῖ πλείστην χάριν τῷ Ἀσκληπιῷ ἀποδοῦναι."   5
καὶ πρὸς τὸν ἱερέα τρεψάμενος, "ἆρ᾽ ἔξεστι θυσίᾱν ποιεῖσθαι;  ἆρ᾽

ἔξεστι καὶ ἄγαλμα ἀναθεῖναι τῷ θεῷ;" ὁ δὲ ἱερεύς, "πῶς γὰρ οὔ;
ἔξεστί σοι. ἆρα βούλει καὶ μνημεῖον τῆς ἀκέσεως ἀναθεῖναι ἐν τῷ
ἱερῷ; σὺ μὲν γὰρ τρεῖς δραχμάς μοι παράδος, ἐγὼ δὲ θυσίαν ποιήσω
καὶ μνημεῖον ἀναθήσω ὑπὲρ σοῦ." ὁ δὲ Δικαιόπολις οἰμώξας, "τρεῖς    10
δραχμὰς λέγεις; φεῦ τῆς δαπάνης." ὁ δὲ ἱερεύς, "οὐδὲν λέγεις, ὦ
ἄνθρωπε· οὐ γὰρ μεγάλη ἡ δαπάνη. τὴν γὰρ θυσίαν ποιήσω ἐπὶ μιᾷ
δραχμῇ, τὸ δὲ μνημεῖον ἀναθήσω ἐπὶ δυοῖν. δός μοι οὖν τρεῖς
δραχμάς, εἰ βούλει με ταῦτα ποιῆσαι." ὁ δὲ Δικαιόπολις, "ἀλλὰ τρεῖς
δραχμὰς οὐκ ἔχω· ἀνὴρ γὰρ πένης εἰμί. ἆρα δύο σοι ἀρκοῦσιν;" ὁ δὲ    15
ἱερεύς, "ἔστω· δύο ἀρκοῦσιν, εἰ μὴ πλέον ἔχεις." ὁ μὲν οὖν
Δικαιόπολις δύο δραχμὰς παρέδωκεν, ὁ δὲ ἱερεὺς τὸν ὑπηρέτην
καλέσας ἐκέλευσεν ἀλεκτρυόνα ἐνεγκεῖν καὶ ἡγησάμενος αὐτοῖς
πρὸς τὸν βωμὸν τὴν θυσίαν ἐποίησεν.

[τοῦ **καταγωγίου**, _the inn_     **ἠσπάζετο**, _greeted, embraced_     **ἄγαλμα**, _gift, offering_
(often a dedicatory statuette)   **πῶς γὰρ οὔ;** _for how not? of course_   **μνημεῖον τῆς**
**ἀκέσεως**, _memorial_ (tablet) _of the cure_   **οἰμώξας** (from οἰμώζω), _groaning_   **φεῦ τῆς**
**δαπάνης**, _alas for the expense!_   **πένης**, _poor_   **ἀρκοῦσιν**, _are sufficient_   **ἔστω**, _let it_
_be! all right!_   **ἀλεκτρυόνα**, _a cock_   **ἐνεγκεῖν** (from φέρω), _to bring_]

ὁ δὲ Φίλιππος, "ἀλλὰ δεῖ καὶ ἐμέ," ἔφη, "δοῦναί τι. τῷ γὰρ θεῷ    20
εἶπον ὅτι τοὺς ἐμοὺς ἀστραγάλους δώσω. ἰδού, τούτους λαβὼν
ἀνάθες τῷ θεῷ καὶ γράψον ἐν τῷ μνημείῳ, εἴ σοι δοκεῖ, ὅτι ὁ Φίλιππος
τούτους τοὺς ἀστραγάλους τῷ Ἀσκληπιῷ ἀνέθηκε μεγίστην χάριν
ἔχων." ὁ δὲ ἱερεύς, "ἀλλὰ ἡδέως ταῦτα ποιήσω· χαιρήσει γὰρ ὁ θεὸς
τούτους δεξάμενος. ἀλλὰ νῦν γε δεῖ ὑμᾶς οἴκαδε πορεύεσθαι. ἄγε    25
δή, ἀκολουθήσω ὑμῖν πρὸς τὰς πύλας."

[**ἀκολουθήσω** + dat., _I will follow, accompany_]

ἐν ᾧ δὲ πρὸς τὰς πύλας ἐβάδιζον, ὁ ἱερεὺς τῷ Δικαιοπόλιδι, "σὺ
μέν," ἔφη, "ἐν ταῖς Ἀθήναις νεωστὶ παρῆσθα· εἰπέ μοι οὖν, πῶς ἔχει τὰ
πράγματα; πότερον πόλεμος ἔσται πρὸς τοὺς Λακεδαιμονίους ἢ
εἰρήνην δυνήσεσθε σῴζειν; δῆλον γάρ ἐστιν ὅτι οἱ Κορίνθιοι τοὺς    30
Λακεδαιμονίους εἰς πόλεμον ὀτρύνουσιν, ἐχθροὶ ὄντες τοῖς
Ἀθηναίοις. τίνα οὖν γνώμην ἔχεις; ἆρα δίκας τῶν διαφορῶν

ἐθελήσουσι διδόναι ἢ πολέμῳ τὰς διαφορὰς διαλύσονται μᾶλλον ἢ
λόγοις;"

[νεωστί, *lately*   ὀτρύνουσιν, *are urging on*   δίκᾱς τῶν διαφορῶν . . . διδόναι,
*to give (allow) arbitration of their differences*   τὰς διαφορὰς διαλύσονται, *will re-
solve their differences*]

ὁ δὲ Δικαιόπολις, "πάλαι μὲν ἐχθροί εἰσιν οἱ Κορίνθιοι καὶ ἡμῖν    35
ἐπιβουλεύουσιν, ὅμως δὲ πόλεμον οὐ ποιήσονται οἱ Λακεδαιμόνιοι·
ἀεὶ γὰρ ἡσυχάζουσιν, τὸ τῶν Ἀθηναίων κράτος φοβούμενοι." ὁ δὲ
ἱερεύς, "ἀλλ' οὐ δήπου φοβοῦνται τοὺς Ἀθηναίους οἱ
Λακεδαιμόνιοι· ἔστι γὰρ στρατὸς αὐτοῖς τε καὶ τοῖς συμμάχοις
μέγιστος δή, ᾧπερ οὐ τολμήσουσιν οἱ Ἀθηναῖοι ἀντέχειν κατὰ γῆν."    40
ὁ δὲ Δικαιόπολις ἀποκρῑνάμενος εἶπεν· "ἀλλ' ἡμεῖς τῆς γε θαλάττης
κρατοῦμεν, ὥστε πλέονα ἔχομεν τὰ τοῦ πολέμου· πλεῖστα μὲν γὰρ
χρήματά ἐστιν ἡμῖν, πλεῖσται δὲ νῆες· οὔκουν δυνήσονται ἡμᾶς
βλάπτειν οὐδὲ μακρὸν πόλεμον νῑκῆσαι, οὐδ' οὖν τολμήσουσιν ἡμῖν
ἐπιστρατεῦσαι." ὁ δὲ γέρων, "σὺ μὲν δῆλος εἶ τῇ τε σῇ πόλει μάλα    45
πιστεύων καὶ τῷ κράτει αὐτῆς. διὰ τοῦτο μέντοι, ὡς ἔμοιγε δοκεῖ,
πόλεμον ποιήσονται οἱ Λακεδαιμόνιοι, διότι τὸ τῶν Ἀθηναίων
κράτος φοβούμενοι οὐκ ἐθελήσουσι περιορᾶν αὐτὸ αὐξανόμενον.
ὅμως δὲ χαιρήσω ἐὰν σὺ μὲν ὀρθῶς γιγνώσκων φανῇς, ἐγὼ δὲ
ἁμαρτάνων."                                                          50

[ἐπιβουλεύουσιν + dat., *are plotting against*  δήπου, *surely*   τὰ τοῦ πολέμου, *resources for war*  οὐδ' οὖν, *nor indeed*   ἔμοιγε, *emphatic form*, *to me*   περιορᾶν,
*to overlook, disregard*   ἐὰν . . . φανῇς, *if you are proved*]

ἤδη δὲ εἰς τὰς πύλᾱς παρῆσαν.  χαίρειν οὖν τὸν γέροντα
κελεύσαντες ὅ τε Δικαιόπολις καὶ ὁ παῖς ἐπορεύοντο.

[ἐπορεύοντο, *began their journey*]


## PRINCIPAL PARTS:  -α- Contract Verbs; -o- Contract Verbs

τῑμάω, τῑμήσω, ἐτίμησα, τετίμηκα, τετίμημαι, ἐτῑμήθην, *I honor*
πειράω, πειράσω (note that because of the ρ the α lengthens to ᾱ rather than η),
  ἐπείρᾱσα, πεπείρᾱκα, πεπείρᾱμαι, ἐπειράθην, active or middle, *I try, attempt*

θεάομαι, θεάσομαι (note that because of the ε the α lengthens to ᾱ rather than η),
  ἐθεᾱσάμην, τεθέαμαι, *I see, watch, look at*
χράομαι (present and imperfect have η where α would be expected: χρῶμαι, χρῇ,
  χρῆται, etc.), χρήσομαι (note that here the α changes to η even after the ρ),
  ἐχρησάμην, κέχρημαι, ἐχρήσθην + dat., *I use; I enjoy; I consult* (an oracle)
γελάω, γελάσομαι (note α instead of η), ἐγέλασα, γεγέλασμαι, ἐγελάσθην,
  *I laugh*

δηλόω, δηλώσω, ἐδήλωσα, δεδήλωκα, δεδήλωμαι, ἐδηλώθην, *I show*

## WORD BUILDING

*From the meaning of the words at the left, deduce the meaning of those to the*
*right:*

1. δίδωμι (δω-/δο-)      ἡ δόσις      ἀποδίδωμι    ἐνδίδωμι    παραδίδωμι
2. προδίδωμι, *I betray*   ὁ προδότης   ἡ προδοσίᾱ
3. τίθημι                ἀνατίθημι    ἐπιτίθημι    συντίθημι

## GRAMMAR

### 2. The Verb τίθημι

τί-θη-μι, θήσω, ἔθηκα, τέθηκα, (τέθειμαι; κεῖμαι usually used instead), ἐτέθην, *I put, place*

#### τίθημι: Present, Imperfect, Future, and Aorist, Active Voice

**Stems:** θη-/θε-

| Present Indicative | Imperative | Infinitive | Participle |
|---|---|---|---|
| τί-θη-μι |  | τι-θέ-ναι | τι-θείς, |
| τί-θη-ς | τί-θε-ε > τίθει |  | τι-θεῖσα, |
| τί-θη-σι(ν) |  |  | τι-θέν, |
| τί-θε-μεν |  |  | gen., τι-θέντ-ος, etc. |
| τί-θε-τε | τί-θε-τε |  |  |
| τι-θέ-ᾱσι(ν) |  |  |  |

**Imperfect**
**Indicative**

ἐ-τί-θη-ν
ἐ-τί-θε-ες > ἐτίθεις
ἐ-τί-θε-ε > ἐτίθει
ἐ-τί-θε-μεν
ἐ-τί-θε-τε
ἐ-τί-θε-σαν

**Future**

Regular sigmatic future: θήσω, θήσεις, θήσει, etc.

**Aorist**

| Indicative | Imperative | Infinitive | Participle |
|---|---|---|---|
| ἔ-θηκ-α | | θεῖ-ναι | θείς, |
| ἔ-θηκ-ας | θέ-ς | | θεῖσα, |
| ἔ-θηκ-ε(ν) | | | θέν, |
| ἔ-θε-μεν | | | gen., θέντ-ος |
| ἔ-θε-τε | θέ-τε | | |
| ἔ-θε-σαν | | | |

Note the irregular stem θηκ- in the singular aorist indicative; cf. ἔ-δωκ-α (Grammar 1, page 21).

### τίθημι: Present and Imperfect, Middle/Passive Voice

**Stem:** θε-

**Present**

| Indicative | Imperative | Infinitive | Participle |
|---|---|---|---|
| τί-θε-μαι | | τί-θε-σθαι | τι-θέ-μεν-ος, -η, -ον |
| τί-θε-σαι | τί-θε-σο | | |
| τί-θε-ται | | | |
| τι-θέ-μεθα | | | |
| τί-θε-σθε | τί-θε-σθε | | |
| τί-θε-νται | | | |

**Imperfect**
**Indicative**

ἐ-τι-θέ-μην
ἐ-τί-θε-σο
ἐ-τί-θε-το
ἐ-τι-θέ-μεθα
ἐ-τί-θε-σθε
ἐ-τί-θε-ντο

### τίθημι: Future and Aorist, Middle Voice

**Stem:** θη-

**Future**

Regular sigmatic future: θήσομαι, θήσει/ῃ, θήσεται, etc.

**Stem:** θε-

**Aorist**

| Indicative | Imperative | | Infinitive | Participle |
|---|---|---|---|---|
| ἐ-θέ-μην | | | θέ-σθαι | θέ-μεν-ος, -η, -ον |
| ἔ-θε-σο > ἔθου | θέ-σο > θοῦ | | | |
| ἔ-θε-το | | | | |
| ἐ-θέ-μεθα | | | | |
| ἔ-θε-σθε | θέ-σθε | | | |
| ἔ-θε-ντο | | | | |

### τίθημι: Future and Aorist, Passive Voice

**Future**

-θη- future passive: τεθήσομαι, τεθήσει/ῃ, τεθήσεται, etc.

**Aorist**

-θη- aorist passive: ἐτέθην, ἐτέθης, ἐτέθη, etc.

## Exercise 18ζ

*Make two photocopies of the Verb Chart on page 274 and three copies of the Verb Chart on page 275. Fill in the forms of τίθημι, except for the subjunctive and optative, in the active voice (present, imperfect, future, and aorist), in the middle/passive voice (present and imperfect), in the middle voice (future and aorist), and in the passive voice (future and aorist). Keep these charts for reference.*

## Exercise 18η

*Identify and translate the following forms:*

| | | | | | |
|---|---|---|---|---|---|
| 1. | ἐτίθην | 6. | θήσομεν | 11. | ἐτίθεντο (2 ways) |
| 2. | τίθεται (2 ways) | 7. | ἔθεσαν | 12. | ἔθεντο |
| 3. | ἀνάθες | 8. | τιθείς | 13. | θέσθε |
| 4. | θεῖναι | 9. | ἐτέθη | 14. | τίθης |
| 5. | τιθέᾱσι(ν) | 10. | τιθεῖσα | 15. | ἔθηκε(ν) |

## Exercise 18θ

| *Put into the aorist:* | | *Put into the present:* | | *Put into the middle:* | |
|---|---|---|---|---|---|
| 1. | τιθέναι | 6. | ἔθεσαν | 11. | τίθησι(ν) |
| 2. | τίθεσο | 7. | θεῖναι | 12. | θέντες |
| 3. | τιθέμεθα | 8. | θέσθαι | 13. | θές |
| 4. | τιθέμενος | 9. | θεμένη | 14. | ἐτίθεις |
| 5. | τιθέᾱσι(ν) | 10. | ἔθεντο | 15. | ἔθηκε(ν) |

## Exercise 18ι

*Read aloud and translate:*

1. οἱ παῖδες τοὺς βοῦς λύσαντες τὸ ἄροτρον ἐπὶ τὴν γῆν ἔθεσαν.
2. αἱ παρθένοι τὰς ὑδρίᾱς ἐν τῇ οἰκίᾳ καταθεῖσαι τὴν μητέρα ἐκάλεσαν.
3. ἡ μήτηρ πέπλους εἰς τὴν κυψέλην (*chest*) ἐτίθει, τῶν δὲ παρθένων ἀκούσᾱσα ἔδραμε πρὸς αὐτάς.
4. ὁ ἱερεὺς ἱερεῖον ἐπὶ τὸν βωμὸν ἐπέθηκεν.
5. ἆρα βούλεσθε ἄγαλμα (*offering*) ἐν τῷ ἱερῷ ἀναθεῖναι;
6. οἱ ἱκέται ἄγαλμα τῷ θεῷ ἀναθέντες οἴκαδε ἔσπευδον.
7. ὁ θεός τὰς χεῖρας τοῖς τοῦ Φιλίππου ὀφθαλμοῖς ἐπιθεὶς ἀπέβη.
8. σὺ μὲν τὰς κώπᾱς εἰς τὴν ναῦν θές, ἐγὼ δὲ θήσω τὰ ἱστία.
9. τὰς ναῦς παρασκευάσαντες τοῖς βαρβάροις ἐπιθησόμεθα (ἐπιτίθεμαι + dat., *I attack*).
10. τί ἐκέλευσας τὸν σὸν κύνα τῷ ξένῳ ἐπιθέσθαι;

## Exercise 18κ

*Translate into Greek:*

1. When the god healed me, I set up an offering in the temple.
2. Having put the sails into the ship, we were waiting for the captain.
3. When the boys returned from the field, the women were putting food on the table (*use* ἡ **τράπεζα**).
4. Father told us to put the plow down on the ground.
5. When the enemy had sailed (*use aorist*) to the straits, we attacked (*use* **ἐπιτίθεμαι** + *dat.*) them.

---

## Greek Wisdom

### Heraclitus

αἱροῦνται ἓν ἀντὶ ἁπάντων οἱ ἄριστοι, κλέος ἀέναον θνητῶν.  Fragment 29 Diels

---

# Η ΕΝ ΤΑΙΣ ΠΛΑΤΑΙΑΙΣ ΝΙΚΗ

*Read the following passage (adapted from Herodotus 9.13, 19, 20, 50–51, and 63–65), describing the Plataea campaign of spring, 479 B.C., and answer the comprehension questions below:*

ὁ δὲ Μαρδόνιος μαθὼν ὅτι οἱ Λακεδαιμόνιοι ἤδη στρατεύονται, τὰς Ἀθήνᾱς ἐμπρήσᾱς καὶ πάντα τά τε οἰκήματα καὶ τὰ ἱερὰ διαφθείρᾱς, εἰς τὴν Βοιωτίᾱν ὑπεξεχώρει.  οἱ μὲν οὖν Λακεδαιμόνιοι προϊόντες εἰς τὴν Ἀττικὴν ἀφίκοντο, οἱ δὲ Ἀθηναῖοι διαβάντες ἐκ τῆς Σαλαμῖνος τοῖς Πελοποννησίοις συνεμίγησαν.

[ὁ . . . Μαρδόνιος, *Mardonius* στρατεύονται, *were* (lit., *are*) *on the march* ἐμπρήσᾱς (from ἐμπίμπρημι), *having set fire to* τὰ . . . οἰκήματα, *the dwellings* ὑπεξεχώρει, *was withdrawing* προϊόντες, *advancing* διαβάντες, *having crossed over* συνεμίγησαν (from συμμείγνῡμι), *joined with* + dat.]

1. What did Mardonius learn?
2. What three things did he then do in Athens? What did he do next?
3. What did the Lacedaemonians and Athenians do?

ἐπεὶ δὲ εἰς τὴν Βοιωτίᾱν ἀφίκοντο, ἔγνωσαν ὅτι οἱ βάρβαροι ἐπὶ τῷ Ἀσωπῷ 5
ποταμῷ στρατοπεδεύονται· ἀντετάττοντο οὖν ἐπὶ λόφῳ τινί. ὁ δὲ Μαρδόνιος, ὡς οὐ
κατέβαινον εἰς τὸ πεδίον οἱ Ἕλληνες, πᾶν τὸ ἱππικὸν ἐξέπεμψεν ἐπ᾽ αὐτούς. οἱ δὲ
Ἕλληνες τό τε ἱππικὸν ἐώσαντο καὶ αὐτὸν τὸν στρατηγὸν ἀπέκτειναν, ὥστε
ἐθάρρησαν πολλῷ μᾶλλον. μετὰ δὲ ταῦτα ἔδοξεν αὐτοῖς καταβῆναι πρὸς τὰς
Πλαταιάς. οἱ δὲ βάρβαροι, μαθόντες ὅτι οἱ Ἕλληνές εἰσιν ἐν Πλαταιαῖς, καὶ αὐτοὶ 10
ἐκεῖσε ἐπορεύοντο. ὁ δὲ Μαρδόνιος τὸν στρατὸν ἔταξεν ὡς μαχούμενος.

[τῷ Ἀσωπῷ ποταμῷ, *the Asopus River* στρατοπεδεύονται, *were* (lit., *are*) *pitching camp* ἀντετάττοντο, *they were positioning themselves opposite* (them) λόφῳ, *crest of a hill* τὸ πεδίον, *the plain* τὸ ἱππικὸν, *their cavalry* ἐώσαντο (from ὠθέω), *pushed back* τὰς Πλαταιάς, *Plataea* ἔταξεν (from τάττω), *drew up*]

4. When the Lacedaemonians and Athenians arrived in Boeotia, what did they learn? What did they do then?
5. What did Mardonius do when the Greeks did not come down onto the plain?
6. What happened to Mardonius' cavalry and its general?
7. What did the Greeks then decide to do? What did the barbarians do?

ἕνδεκα μὲν οὖν ἡμέρᾱς ἔμενον, οὐδέτεροι βουλόμενοι μάχης ἄρξαι· τῇ δὲ
δωδεκάτῃ τῷ Παυσανίᾳ ἔδοξεν αὖθις μεταστῆναι· ἅμα μὲν γὰρ σίτου ἐδέοντο καὶ
ὕδατος, ἅμα δὲ κακὰ ἔπασχον ὑπὸ τοῦ ἱππικοῦ ἀεὶ προσβάλλοντος. νύκτα οὖν
μείναντες ἐπορεύοντο. ἐπεὶ δὲ ἡμέρᾱ ἐγένετο, ὁ Μαρδόνιος εἶδεν τὸ τῶν Ἑλλήνων 15
στρατόπεδον ἔρημον ὄν· τοὺς οὖν Ἕλληνας δρόμῳ ἐδίωκεν. καὶ πρῶτον μὲν οἱ
βάρβαροι τοὺς Ἀθηναίους κατέλαβον, οἳ ἀνδρειότατα μαχόμενοι τὸ ἱππικὸν
ἐώσαντο. ἔπειτα δὲ ὁ Μαρδόνιος τοῖς Λακεδαιμονίοις ἐνέπεσεν, καὶ καρτερὰ
ἐγένετο μάχη. ἐπεὶ δὲ αὐτὸς ὁ Μαρδόνιος ἀπέθανεν, οἱ βάρβαροι τρεψάμενοι εἰς τὸ
στρατόπεδον οὐδενὶ κόσμῳ ἔφυγον. 20

[οὐδέτεροι, *neither side* ἄρξαι (from ἄρχω) + gen., *to begin* τῇ . . . δωδεκάτῃ, *on the twelfth* (day) τῷ Παυσανίᾳ, *to Pausanias* μεταστῆναι, *to change his position* ἐδέοντο + gen., *they were in need of* ὑπὸ τοῦ ἱππικοῦ, *by/at the hands of the cavalry* τὸ στρατόπεδον, *the camp* ἔρημον, *deserted* δρόμῳ, adv., *at a run, at full speed* καρτερά, *mighty*]

8. What did Pausanias finally decide to do? Why? Cite three reasons.
9. What did Mardonius discover the next day? What did he do?
10. When the barbarians and Athenians engaged in combat, who fought most bravely and with what result?
11. What happened when Mardonius attacked the Lacedaemonians?
12. What did the barbarians do when Mardonius was killed?

### Exercise 18λ

*Translate into Greek:*

1. The Spartans, pursuing the barbarians to their camp, attacked the wall but were not able to take it.
2. When the Athenians came to help (*use* βοηθέω *for the whole verbal idea here*), the barbarians did not flee but were fighting bravely.
3. And finally the Greeks climbed (went up onto) the wall, and the barbarians fled in disorder (in no order).
4. After the battle, Pausanias, being general of the Spartans, himself set up a memorial (μνημεῖον) at Delphi (ἐν Δελφοῖς):

> Ἑλλήνων ἀρχηγὸς (*leader*) ἐπεὶ στρατὸν ὤλεσε (*destroyed*) Μήδων,
> Παυσανίᾱς Φοίβῳ (*to Phoebus Apollo*) μνῆμ' ἀνέθηκε τόδε.

μνῆμα = μνημεῖον

# Classical Greek

## Miracle Cures

Εὐφάνης Ἐπιδαύριος παῖς. οὗτος λιθιῶν ἐνεκάθευδε· ἔδοξε δὴ αὐτῷ ὁ θεὸς ἐπιστὰς εἰπεῖν, "τί μοι δώσεις, εἴ σέ κε ὑγιῆ ποιήσω;" αὐτὸς δέ, "δέκα ἀστραγάλους," ἔφη. ὁ θεὸς γελάσᾱς ἔφησέ νιν παύσειν. ἡμέρᾱς δὲ γενομένης ὑγιὴς ἐξῆλθε.

[λιθιῶν, *suffering from the stone*   ἐνεκάθευδε, *slept (was sleeping) in* (the abaton) ἐπιστὰς, *standing near* (him), *appearing to* (him)   εἰ σέ κε ὑγιῆ ποιήσω, *if I make you well*   αὐτὸς δέ = ὁ δέ   ἔφησέ νιν (= αὐτὸν) παύσειν, *said that he would stop him* (from suffering)   ἡμέρᾱς . . . γενομένης, *when day came*]

Πάνδαρος Θεσσαλὸς στίγματα ἔχων ἐν τῷ μετώπῳ. οὗτος ἐγκαθεύδων ὄψιν εἶδε· ἐδόκει αὐτῷ ταινίᾳ καταδῆσαι τὰ στίγματα ὁ θεὸς καὶ κελεύειν νιν, ἐπεὶ ἂν ἔξω γένηται τοῦ ἀβάτου ἀφελόμενον τὴν ταινίᾱν ἀναθεῖναι εἰς τὸν ναόν. ἡμέρᾱς δὲ γενομένης ἐξανέστη καὶ ἀφείλετο τὴν ταινίᾱν, καὶ τὸ μὲν πρόσωπον κενὸν εἶδε τῶν στιγμάτων, τὴν δὲ ταινίᾱν ἀνέθηκε εἰς τὸν ναόν, ἔχουσαν τὰ γράμματα τὰ ἐκ τοῦ μετώπου.

[στίγματα, *marks* (these seem to have been letters, γράμματα, tattooed on his forehead, ἐν τῷ μετώπῳ, perhaps indicating that he had been a slave)   ὄψιν, *a vision*   ταινίᾳ, *with a bandage* (or *fillet*)  **καταδῆσαι** (from καταδέω), *to bind*  νιν = **αὐτόν  ἐπεὶ ἂν . . . γένηται,** *when he was*  **ἔξω** + gen., *outside of*  **ἀφελόμενον** (from ἀφαιρέω, aorist middle, ἀφειλόμην), *having taken off*  **ναόν,** *temple*  **ἐξανέστη,** *he arose and departed*  **πρόσωπον,** *face*  **κενὸν** + gen., *empty, free from*]

# New Testament Greek

### John 1.32, 33, and 49
### Pronouncements about Jesus

John the Baptist speaks in the presence of Jesus:

"τεθέαμαι τὸ πνεῦμα καταβαῖνον ὡς περιστερὰν ἐξ οὐρανοῦ καὶ ἔμεινεν ἐπ' αὐτόν."

[**τεθέαμαι** (perfect of θεάομαι), *I have seen*  **τὸ πνεῦμα,** *the spirit*  **ὡς περιστερὰν,** *as a dove*  **ἔμεινεν,** *it came to rest*  **ἐπ(ὶ),** *upon*  **αὐτόν,** i.e., Jesus]

The one who sent John to baptize in water said to him:

"ἐφ' ὃν ἂν ἴδῃς τὸ πνεῦμα καταβαῖνον καὶ μένον ἐπ' αὐτόν, οὗτός ἐστιν ὁ βαπτίζων ἐν πνεύματι ἁγίῳ."

[**ἂν ἴδῃς,** *you see*  **ὁ βαπτίζων,** *the one baptizing*  **ἁγίῳ,** *holy*]

Nathanael says to Jesus:

"ῥαββί, σὺ εἶ ὁ υἱὸς τοῦ θεοῦ, σὺ βασιλεὺς εἶ τοῦ Ἰσραήλ."

[**ῥαββί,** *rabbi, teacher, master*  **ὁ υἱὸς,** *the son*  **τοῦ Ἰσραήλ,** *of Israel*]

Epidaurus; the fourth-century theater

# 19
# Ο ΝΟΣΤΟΣ (α)

τῶν ἀνθρώπων ἐλάᾱς συλλεγόντων, παῖς τις εἰς τὸ δένδρον ἀναβαίνει.

## VOCABULARY

*Verbs*

**ἐσθίω**, [ἐδ-] **ἔδομαι**, [φαγ-]
**ἔφαγον**, [ἐδ-] **ἐδήδοκα**, *I eat*

**ἵστημι**, imperfect, **ἵστην**, [στη-]
**στήσω**, **ἔστησα**, *I make X
stand; I stop X; I am setting X
(up)*

    athematic 2nd aorist, **ἔστην**,
intransitive, *I stood*

    -κα 1st perfect, **ἕστηκα**, in-
transitive, *I stand*

    -θη- 1st aorist passive,
[στα-] **ἐστάθην**, *I was set
(up)*

**ἀνίστημι** [= ἀνα- + ἵστημι],
when transitive, *I make X
stand up; I raise X*; when
intransitive, *I stand up*

**νοστέω**, *I return home*

**συλλέγω** [= συν- + λέγω, *I pick
up, gather; I say, tell, speak*],
**συλλέξω**, **συνέλεξα**, [λογ-]
**συνείλοχα**, [λεγ-] **συνείλεγμαι**, **συνελέγην**, *I collect,
gather*

*Nouns*

**ἡ ἐλάᾱ**, **τῆς ἐλάᾱς**, *olive; olive
tree*

**ὁ νόστος**, **τοῦ νόστου**, *return
(home)*

**τὸ πεδίον**, **τοῦ πεδίου**, *plain*

ὡς δὲ εἰς τὸν λιμένα ἀφίκοντο ἔστησαν καί, ἤδη θάλποντος τοῦ
ἡλίου, ὑπὸ ἐλάᾳ καθήμενοι οἶνόν τε ἔπιον καὶ σῖτον ἔφαγον. δι᾽
ὀλίγου δὲ ὁ Δικαιόπολις εἶπεν· "τί δεῖ ποιεῖν, ὦ παῖ; οὐδενὸς γὰρ

ὄντος ἡμῖν ἀργυρίου, οὐκ ἔξεστιν ἡμῖν κατὰ θάλατταν οἴκαδε
νοστεῖν.  δεῖ οὖν πεζῇ ἰέναι." ὁ δὲ Φίλιππος, "μὴ περὶ τούτου    5
φρόντιζε, ὦ πάτερ· ἐγὼ γὰρ χαιρήσω πεζῇ ἰὼν καὶ τὰ ἔργα θεώμενος
καὶ τὰ ὄρη. ἀλλὰ πῶς εὑρήσομεν τὴν ὁδὸν τὴν πρὸς τὰς Ἀθήνας
φέρουσαν;" ὁ δὲ, "μὴ περὶ τούτου γε φρόντιζε, ὦ παῖ· ῥᾳδίως γὰρ
εὑρήσομεν αὐτήν." τὸν δὲ Φίλιππον ἀναστήσας, "ἀνάστηθι οὖν,"
ἔφη· "εἰ γὰρ δοκεῖ, καιρός ἐστιν ὁρμῆσαι."                        10

[θάλποντος, *being hot*    πεζῇ, adv., *on foot*    τὰ ἔργα, *the tilled fields* ]

ἀναστάντες οὖν ἐπορεύοντο, καὶ πρῶτον μὲν διὰ πεδίου ᾖσαν, ἐν
ᾧ πολλὰ ἦν ἔργα ἀνθρώπων· πολλοὺς δὲ ἀνθρώπους ἑώρων ἐν τοῖς
ἀγροῖς ἐργαζομένους, ὧν οἱ μὲν τοὺς βοῦς ἤλαυνον ἀροῦντες τὴν
ἄρουραν, οἱ δὲ τὰς ἐλάας συνέλεγον εἰς τὰ δένδρα ἀναβαίνοντες. ὡς
δὲ τοῖς ὄρεσι προσεχώρουν, ἀμπελῶνας ἑώρων, ἐν οἷς οἱ ἄνθρωποι    15
τοὺς βότρυας συνέλεγον· καὶ τῶν βοτρύων τοὺς μὲν οἴκαδε ἔφερον
ὄνοι ἐν μεγάλοις κανθηλίοις, τοὺς δὲ αἱ γυναῖκες ἐπὶ τῇ γῇ ἐτίθεσαν
ὥστε τῷ ἡλίῳ ξηραίνεσθαι. ὁ οὖν Φίλιππος πολὺν χρόνον ἵστατο
πάντα θεώμενος.

[ἑώρων, *imperfect of* ὁράω    ἀροῦντες, *plowing*    τὴν ἄρουραν, *the plowland*
ἀμπελῶνας, *vineyards*    τοὺς βότρυας, *bunches of grapes*    ὄνοι, *donkeys*    κανθηλίοις, *baskets*    ξηραίνεσθαι, *to become dry*]

## PRINCIPAL PARTS: Labial Stems (-β-, -π-)

βλάπ-τω, [βλαβ-] βλάψω, ἔβλαψα, βέβλαφα, βέβλαμμαι, ἐβλάφθην or
  ἐβλάβην, *I harm, hurt*
λείπω, λείψω, [λιπ-] ἔλιπον, [λοιπ-] λέλοιπα, [λειπ-] λέλειμμαι (*I am left
  behind; I am inferior*), ἐλείφθην, *I leave*
πέμπω, πέμψω, ἔπεμψα, [πομπ-] πέπομφα, [πεμπ-] πέπεμμαι, ἐπέμφθην,
  *I send*

## WORD STUDY

*Explain the meaning of the following English words with reference to their
Greek stems:*

1.  aristocracy
2.  autocracy
3.  plutocracy (ὁ πλοῦτος = wealth)
4.  theocracy
5.  bureaucracy
6.  technocracy (ἡ τέχνη, *art; skill*)

# GRAMMAR

## 1. The Genitive Absolute

Examine the following sentence:

**θάλποντος τοῦ ἡλίου**, ὑπὸ ἐλάᾳ ἐκάθηντο.
*Since the sun was hot, they were sitting under an olive tree.*

The words in boldface consist of a participle and a noun in the genitive case. This phrase has no grammatical relationship to the rest of the sentence, i.e., the participle does not modify any element such as the subject, the direct object, or the indirect object of the main clause. This use of a participle with a noun or pronoun in the genitive case is called a *genitive absolute*. The term *absolute* comes from a Latin word meaning "separated" or "independent," and genitive absolutes are grammatically separate from the rest of the sentence in which they occur. Here are other examples:

**οὐδενὸς ὄντος ἡμῖν ἀργυρίου**, οὐκ ἔξεστιν ἡμῖν κατὰ θάλατταν οἴκαδε νοστεῖν.
*There being no money for us* or *Since we have no money, it is not possible for us to return home by sea.*

**ἡμέρᾱς γενομένης**, ὁ πατὴρ τὸν παῖδα καλέσᾱς ἔπεμψε ὡς ζητήσοντα τὰ πρόβατα.
*When day came* or *When day had come* or *At daybreak, the father, calling his son, sent him to seek the sheep.*

In this sentence, the phrase ἡμέρᾱς γενομένης is absolute, i.e., not part of the structure of the rest of the sentence, whereas the participle καλέσᾱς agrees with πατήρ, the subject in the main clause, and the participle ζητήσοντα agrees with παῖδα, the direct object in the main clause.

With regard to *aspect*, present participles describe *progressive, ongoing action contemporaneous* with the action of the main verb in the sentence (see Book I, Chapter 8, Grammar 1, page 115). Thus, in the sentence above, **θάλποντος τοῦ ἡλίου**, ὑπὸ ἐλάᾳ ἐκάθηντο, a present participle is used in the genitive absolute, but it is translated into English as a past progressive, *Since the sun was hot*, indicating ongoing action contemporaneous with the imperfect tense of the main verb, ἐκάθηντο, *they were sitting*. Compare the sentence **οὐδενὸς ὄντος ἡμῖν ἀργυρίου**, οὐκ ἔξεστιν ἡμῖν κατὰ θάλατταν οἴκαδε νοστεῖν, and its English translation, *Since we have no money, it is not possible for us to return home by sea.*

With regard to aspect, the *aorist participle* in a genitive absolute expresses *simple action* (see Book I, Chapter 11, Grammar 3d, pages 179–180). Thus, the genitive absolute with its participle in the aorist in the sentence **ἡμέρᾱς γενομένης**, ὁ πατὴρ τὸν παῖδα καλέσᾱς ἔπεμψεν ὡς ζητήσοντα τὰ πρόβατα may be translated simply *When day came* or even more simply, *At daybreak*. However, aorist participles in genitive absolutes may often be translated into English so as to indicate *time before* the action of the main verb, e.g., **When day _had come_**, *the father, calling his son, sent him to seek the sheep.*

Genitive absolutes can often best be translated into English with clauses beginning with "since," "as," "when," or "although." The choice of which introductory word to use will usually be clear from the meaning of the sentence as a whole, but sometimes a word such as καίπερ, *although*, will provide a helpful clue.

### Exercise 19α

*Read aloud and translate the following sentences. Pay particular attention to aspect in the Greek and to tense in English when translating participles:*

1.  ἑσπέρας γιγνομένης, οἱ ξένοι εἰς τὸ ἄστυ ἀφίκοντο.
2.  τοῦ γέροντος ὀργιζομένου, ὁ παῖς ἐφοβεῖτο.
3.  πάντων ἑτοίμων ὄντων, ὁ ἱερεὺς τὴν θυσίᾶν ἐποιήσατο.
4.  τοῦ ἀνέμου μείζονος γενομένου, ἡ ναῦς, ὀλίγη οὖσα, ἐν κινδύνῳ ἦν.
5.  καίπερ τῆς πόλεως πολὺ ἀπεχούσης, οὐκ ἐσπεύδομεν.
6.  νυκτὸς γενομένης, ἔδοξεν ἡμῖν ἐν τῷ ἄστει μένειν.
7.  τῶν αὐτουργῶν ἐχθρῶν γενομένων, οἱ νεᾶνίαι τὸ πεδίον καταλιπόντες ἐπὶ τὸ ὄρος ἀνέβησαν.
8.  καίπερ θόρυβον ποιούντων τῶν προβάτων, ὁ αὐτουργὸς οὐκ ἔσπευδεν.
9.  τοῦ ἡλίου ἀνατέλλοντος (*rising*), ὁ παῖς ἤδη πρὸς τὸν ἀγρὸν ᾔει.
10. τοῦ ἡλίου καταδῦντος (*having set*), πᾶσαν τὴν ἡμέρᾶν ἐργασάμενος ὁ παῖς οἴκαδε ἐπανιέναι ἐβούλετο.

## 2.  The Verb ἵστημι: Formation and Meaning

This verb has both long-vowel [στη-] and short-vowel [στα-] stems.

> **ἵστημι, στήσω**, sigmatic 1st aorist, **ἔστησα**, athematic 2nd aorist, **ἔστην, ἕστηκα, ἐστάθην**, *I make to stand; I stop; I set (up);* athematic 2nd aorist, intransitive, *I stood; I stood still; I stopped;* perfect, intransitive, *I stand*

You have already studied the athematic 2nd aorist of this verb (ἔστην, *I stood*) in Chapter 15, and you have seen many examples of it in the readings.

Formation of the Active:

Present: ἵ-στη-μι                    Sigmatic 1st aorist: ἔ-στη-σα
Imperfect: ἵ-στη-ν                   Athematic 2nd aorist: ἔ-στη-ν
Future: στή-σ-ω

The present and imperfect are formed by putting ἱ- (reduplication: = σι-, cf. Latin *sistō*) before the stem and adding the personal endings, e.g., ἵ-στη-μι. In the imperfect the ἱ- augments to ῑ-. In both the present and the imperfect, the long-vowel stem (στη-) is used in the singular, and in the plural, the short (στα-). Compare δί-δω-μι and τί-θη-μι.

The future στή-σω is formed regularly, as is the sigmatic 1st aorist ἔ-στη-σα.

Meaning of the Active:

Forms in the active voice in the present, imperfect, future, and sigmatic 1st aorist are *transitive* and take direct objects. They mean *make to stand, stop,* or *set up,* e.g.:

| | |
|---|---|
| ὁ παῖς τὸν κύνα ἵστησιν. | *The boy is stopping his dog.* |
| ὁ παῖς τὸν κύνα ἵστη. | *The boy was stopping his dog.* |
| ὁ παῖς τὸν κύνα στήσει. | *The boy will stop his dog.* |
| ὁ παῖς τὸν κύνα ἔστησεν. | *The boy stopped his dog.* |
| ὁ ναύτης τὸν ἱστὸν ἔστησεν. | *The sailor set up the mast.* |

The athematic 2nd aorist, ἔστην, means *I stood, stood still, stopped,* and the perfect, ἕστηκα, means *I stand.* These forms are *intransitive* and do not take direct objects, e.g.:

ὁ κύων ἔστη. *The dog stood still / stopped.*
ἡ γυνὴ πρὸς τῇ κρήνῃ ἕστηκεν. *The woman stands near the spring.*

Formation of the Middle:

Present: ἵ-στα-μαι
Imperfect: ῑ-στά-μην
Future: στή-σ-ο-μαι
Sigmatic 1st aorist: ἐ-στη-σά-μην
Athematic 2nd aorist: none

Meaning of the Middle:

The present, imperfect, future, and sigmatic 1st aorist middle may be used *transitively*, e.g.:

| | |
|---|---|
| φύλακας ἱστάμεθα. | *We are setting up, i.e., posting, guards.* |
| φύλακας ῑστάμεθα. | *We were setting up, i.e., posting, guards.* |
| φύλακας στησόμεθα. | *We will set up, i.e., post, guards.* |
| φύλακας ἐστησάμεθα. | *We set up, i.e., posted, guards.* |

The middle voice implies that the action is performed in the interests of the subject, i.e., here, *for ourselves / for our protection.*

The present, imperfect, and future middle may also be used *intransitively*, e.g.:

| | |
|---|---|
| ἱστάμεθα. | *We are standing / standing still / stopping.* |
| ῑστάμεθα. | *We were standing / standing still / stopping.* |
| στησόμεθα. | *We will stand / stand still / stop.* |

N.B.: The sigmatic 1st aorist middle is not used intransitively; the athematic 2nd aorist active is used instead, e.g.:

ἔστημεν                              *We stood / stood still / stopped.*

Passive forms are translated exactly as you would expect, e.g., the aorist passive ἐστάθην means *I was set (up).*

The forms of ἵστημι will be presented in the second half of this chapter.

## Exercise 19β

*Translate each of the following forms, using* set up *or* stand *as meanings:*

|            | Active Transitive | Middle Transitive | Intransitive | Passive      |
|------------|-------------------|-------------------|--------------|--------------|
| Present    | ἵστημι            | ἵσταμαι           | ἵσταμαι      | ἵσταμαι      |
| Imperfect  | ἵστην             | ἱστάμην           | ἱστάμην      | ἱστάμην      |
| Future     | στήσω             | στήσομαι          | στήσομαι     | σταθήσομαι   |
| Aorist     | ἔστησα            | ἐστησάμην         | ἔστην        | ἐστάθην      |
| Perfect    |                   |                   | ἕστηκα       |              |

## Exercise 19γ

*Read aloud and translate:*

1.  οἱ παῖδες τοὺς κύνας ἔστησαν.
2.  ὁ αὐτουργὸς ἐξαίφνης (*suddenly*) ἐν τῇ ἀγορᾷ ἔστη.
3.  ὁ παῖς ἀνέστη.
4.  ὁ πατὴρ τὸν παῖδα ἀνέστησεν.
5.  οἱ ναῦται τὸν λιμένα καταλιπόντες τὸν ἱστὸν (*mast*) ἔστησαν.
6.  τοὺς Πέρσᾱς νῑκήσᾱς ὁ Παυσανίᾱς τροπαῖον (*a trophy*) ἐστήσατο.
7.  μὴ φεύγετε, ὦ φίλοι, ἀλλὰ στῆτε καὶ ἀνδρείως μάχεσθε.
8.  ἐπεὶ τὸν ξένον εἴδομεν, στάντες ἠρόμεθα ποῖ πορεύεται.
9.  ὁ νεᾱνίᾱς τὸν κύνα ἔστησε καὶ τὴν ὁδὸν ἡμῖν ἐδήλωσεν ᾗ πρὸς τὸ ἄστυ ἔφερεν.
10. τοὺς πολεμίους φοβούμενοι, φύλακας ἐστήσαντο.

---

# Greek Wisdom

### Heraclitus

ἓν τὸ σοφόν, ἐπίστασθαι γνώμην ἥτις ἐκυβέρνησε πάντα διὰ πάντων.   Fragment 41 Diels

On their return journey overland, Philip and his father visit the famous ruins of
Mycenae, which were not far off their route. The lion gate to the citadel is shown here.

# Mycenae

Mycenae stands on a hill skirted by two deep ravines. The site is a natural strong point, dominating the plain of Argos. It was first occupied about 3,000 B.C., and a new settlement was made about 2,000 B.C., which is generally believed to be the time when Greek speakers arrived in Greece. There is clear evidence for a sudden increase in the importance and prosperity of this settlement about 1,600 B.C.; two grave circles have been found, one inside the later walls and containing six shaft graves, excavated by Schliemann in the 1870s, the other rather earlier in date, outside the walls, discovered in 1950. These graves contained a mass of gold and other precious objects of great beauty, including imports from Minoan Crete and Egypt.

The power and wealth of Mycenae increased rapidly. There was soon a uniform culture in mainland Greece, stretching from Thessaly in the north to the south of the Peloponnesus, with palaces at Thebes, Athens, Mycenae, Tiryns, and Pylos and probably at other sites not yet discovered. Although the palaces were the administrative centers of separate kingdoms, it seems likely that Mycenae was the leading, if not the dominant, kingdom. From 1500 B.C. the kings of Mycenae were buried in massive stone tombs outside the walls, of which the largest, the so-called Treasury of Atreus, is a magnificent architectural achievement.

About 1450 B.C. the Achaeans, as the Greeks of the Mycenaean period were called, invaded Crete and destroyed all the Minoan palaces except Knossos, which they occupied. Succeeding to Minoan control of the seas, the Achaeans now traded widely throughout the Eastern Mediterranean and made settlements on the islands and in Asia Minor. The zenith of Mycenaean power and prosperity was in the early thirteenth century; in this period were built the walls, some of which still stand, and the lion gate. By about 1250 B.C., when the defenses were renewed and improved, there is evidence of destruction outside the walls. Trade declined; a period of upheaval and deterioration had begun. The Trojan War is thought to have occurred about this time. The traditional date for the fall of Troy is 1184 B.C., but the American archaeologist Blegen, who made the most complete recent excavations and found clear evidence of a prolonged siege, dates the destruction of Troy to about 1240 B.C. It looks as though the Trojan expedition was the last united effort of the Achaeans.

Mycenae was subjected to three successive attacks in the following years. In the first, the houses outside the walls were destroyed; in the second, the citadel was sacked; in the third, it was finally destroyed and not reoccupied. The other mainland palaces were all sacked around 1200 B.C., presumably by bands of invading Dorians.

The entrance to the Treasury of Atreus

During the Dark Ages a new settlement was made on the site of Mycenae, which developed into a miniature *polis;* this sent a small contingent to fight at Plataea, but in 468 B.C. it was attacked and destroyed by Argos. When Philip visited it in our story, the site was abandoned; the massive walls and the lion gate still stood, but the rest was overgrown and undisturbed until Schliemann arrived in 1876.

Around Mycenae centered one of the most important cycles of Greek myth. The royal house of Mycenae was doomed. Its founder had been Pelops. His father Tantalus wanted to find out whether the gods were really omniscient. He killed his own child Pelops and served him up to the gods at a feast; none of the gods would touch the meat except for Demeter, who was distracted by grief and ate part of his shoulder. The gods restored him to life and replaced his missing shoulder with one of ivory. When he had grown up, he wooed Hippodamia, daughter of Oenomaus. In order to win her hand, he had to beat her father in a chariot race. He bribed Oenomaus's charioteer to remove the linchpin of the axle. In the race, Oenomaus was thrown and killed, but as he lay dying he cursed Pelops.

Pelops carried off the dead king's daughter to Mycenae and founded a dynasty that was unremittingly haunted by the curse. His sons were Atreus and Thyestes. Thyestes seduced Atreus' wife, and Atreus banished him. Atreus then pretended to be reconciled and invited his brother to a banquet; at this feast he served up Thyestes' own children. Thyestes found a human finger in his portion and, realizing what Atreus had done, kicked over the table and fled, cursing Atreus and all his family. Thyestes had a son, Aegisthus, by his own daughter; together they murdered Atreus.

Agamemnon succeeded Atreus as king, and when he led the Greeks to Troy, he left the kingdom in the care of his wife, Clytemnestra. The Greek fleet, however, en route for Troy was held up by unceasing contrary winds. The prophet said that these winds would only cease if Agamemnon sacrificed his daughter to Artemis. Agamemnon sent for his daughter Iphigenia on the pretext that she was to wed Achilles, and with his own hand he cut her throat over the altar.

During Agamemnon's absence, Clytemnestra took Aegisthus as her lover and planned vengeance. When, after ten years, Agamemnon returned, the lovers murdered him, entrapping him in a net while he was in the bath. Orestes, the young son of Agamemnon and Clytemnestra, escaped into exile, saved by his nurse; the daughters, Chrysothemis and Electra, remained in the palace. When Orestes grew to manhood, he consulted Apollo's oracle at Delphi and was ordered to avenge his father's murder. He returned to Mycenae secretly and with Electra's help murdered both Aegisthus and his own mother. He was then pursued by the Furies and took refuge at Apollo's altar. The curse, which had haunted the family through four generations, was finally laid to rest when Athena acquitted Orestes of bloodguilt on the grounds that he had been ordered by Apollo to perform the murders.

# Classical Greek

### Theognis

Theognis laments the passing of youth and the prospect of death in the following sets of couplets (lines 1069–1070 and 1070a–1070b), which were probably composed as separate poems.  The themes were common in Greek lyric poetry.  For Theognis, see Book I, Chapter 10, page 163; Chapter 11, page 185, and Chapter 14, page 249.

ἄφρονες ἄνθρωποι καὶ νήπιοι, οἵ τε θανόντας
    κλαίουσ᾽, οὐδ᾽ ἥβης ἄνθος ἀπολλύμενον.

[**ἄφρονες**, *foolish*   **νήπιοι**, *childish*   **οἵ τε** = οἵ   **θανόντας** = ἀποθανόντας, *the dead*   **κλαίουσι**, *weep for*   **ἥβης**, *of youth*   **ἄνθος**, *the flower*   **ἀπολλύμενον**, *perishing, that perishes*]

τέρπεό μοι, φίλε θῦμέ· τάχ᾽ αὖ τινες ἄλλοι ἔσονται
    ἄνδρες, ἐγὼ δὲ θανὼν γαῖα μέλαιν᾽ ἔσομαι.

[**τέρπεο** = τέρπου, present imperative of τέρπομαι   **μοι**: not the usual dative with τέρπομαι, but a special dative used to solicit the interest of the addressee; *I beg you* or *please*   **θῦμέ**, here, *heart*   **τάχ᾽ αὖ**, *soon again*   **γαῖα**, *earth*   **μέλαιν(α)**, *black*]

Pelops and Hippodamia

# Ο ΝΟΣΤΟΣ (β)

## VOCABULARY

*Verbs*

ἀγνοέω, *I do not know*

ἀναπαύομαι, ἀναπαύσομαι, ἀνεπαυσάμην, ἀναπέπαυμαι, *I rest*

ἀφίσταμαι [= ἀπο- + ἵσταμαι], [στη-] ἀποστήσομαι, ἀπέστην, *I stand away from; I revolt from*

ἐντυγχάνω + dat., *I meet*

καθίστημι [= κατα- + ἵστημι], when transitive, *I set X up; I appoint X;* + εἰς + acc., *I put X into a certain state;* when intransitive, *I am appointed; I am established;* + εἰς + acc., *I get/fall into a certain state; I become*

εἰς ἀπορίᾱν κατέστη, *he fell into perplexity, became perplexed*

παραινέω [= παρα- + αἰνέω], παραινέσω or παραινέσομαι, παρῄνεσα, παρῄνεκα, παρῄνημαι, παρῃνέθην + dat. and infin., *I advise someone to do something*

σημαίνω, [σημανε-] σημανῶ, [σημην-] ἐσήμηνα, [σημαν-] σεσήμασμαι, ἐσημάνθην, *I signal; I sign; I show*

*Nouns*

ὁ ποιμήν, τοῦ ποιμένος, *shepherd*

ἡ ὕλη, τῆς ὕλης, *woods, forest*

ὁ φόβος, τοῦ φόβου, *fear; panic*

ὁ ὦμος, τοῦ ὤμου, *shoulder*

*Adjectives*

βαθύς, -εῖα, -ύ, *deep*

δεινός, -ή, -όν, *terrible; clever, skilled;* + infin., *clever at, skilled at*

ἔρημος, -ον, *deserted*

τρᾱχύς, -εῖα, -ύ, *rough*

*Adverbs*

ἥδιστα, superlative of ἡδέως, *most sweetly; most pleasantly; most gladly*

οὐ μέντοι διὰ πολλοῦ τὰ τῶν ἀνθρώπων ἔργα καταλιπόντες, ἀνέβησαν ἐπὶ τὰ ὄρη· καὶ σπανίως ἤδη ἐνετύγχανον ἀνθρώποις, ποιμένας δὲ ὀλίγους ἑώρων οἳ τὰ πρόβατα ἔνεμον. ἦσαν δὲ διὰ μεγάλων ὑλῶν, ἐν αἷς πολλαί τε δρύες ἦσαν καὶ πολλαὶ ἐλάται. τρᾱχείᾱς δὲ γενομένης τῆς ὁδοῦ καὶ οὐ ῥᾳδίᾱς εὑρεῖν, ὁ μὲν Δικαιόπολις εἰς ἀπορίᾱν κατέστη ἀγνοῶν τὴν ὁδόν· ὁ δὲ Φίλιππος ἄνθρωπον ἰδὼν προσιόντα, "ἰδού, ὦ πάτερ," ἔφη, "ἆρα ὁρᾷς ἐκεῖνον τὸν ἄνδρα κατιόντα πρὸς ἡμᾶς; φαίνεται κυνηγέτης εἶναι· κύων γὰρ Λάκαινα ἕπεται αὐτῷ. ἆρ' οὐ βούλει στῆσαι αὐτὸν καὶ ἐρέσθαι εἰ αὕτη ἡ ὁδὸς πρὸς Κόρινθον φέρει;" ὁ δὲ Δικαιόπολις, "μάλιστά γε," ἔφη· "στήσωμεν αὐτόν." 5

10

[σπανίως, *rarely*    ἔνεμον, *were grazing*    δρύες, *oaks*    ἐλάται, *pines*
κυνηγέτης, *hunter*    Λάκαινα, *Laconian, Spartan*    στήσωμεν, subjunctive, *let us
stop him!*]

προσχωροῦντος δὲ τοῦ νεανίου, ἡ κύων ἀγρίως ὑλακτεῖ καὶ
ὁρμᾶται ἐπ' αὐτούς· ὁ δὲ νεανίας ἔστη καὶ βοήσας, "στῆθι, Ἄργη,"
ἔφη, "καὶ σίγησον." ὁ οὖν Δικαιόπολις προσιών, "χαῖρε, ὦ νεανίᾱ,"
ἔφη, "ἆρ' οἶσθα σὺ εἰ αὕτη ἡ ἀτραπὸς πρὸς τὴν Κόρινθον φέρει;" ὁ     15
δέ, "μάλιστά γε, ἐκεῖσε φέρει· ἰδού—ἔξεστιν αὐτὴν ἰδεῖν ὑπὲρ τὸ ὄρος
φέρουσαν. ῥᾳδίως δὲ γνώσεσθε αὐτήν, τῶν γε ἑρμάτων σημαινόντων.
ἀλλὰ πολὺ ἀπέχει ἡ Κόρινθος, καὶ δι' ὀλίγου νὺξ γενήσεται· ἴσως δὲ
εἰς κίνδῡνον καταστήσεσθε μόνοι ἐν τοῖς ὄρεσι νυκτερεύοντες.
ἐρήμων γὰρ ὄντων τῶν ὀρῶν οὐδενὶ ἐντεύξεσθε ἀνθρώπων εἰ μὴ     20
ποιμένι τινί. ἀλλ' ἄγετε, πῶς ἔχετε τοῦ σίτου; ἀλλὰ μείνατε· δώσω
γὰρ ὑμῖν λαγών. ἰδού." καὶ ταῦτα εἰπὼν τὸ ῥόπαλον, ὃ ἐπὶ τοῖς ὤμοις
ἔφερε, κατέθηκεν· δύο γὰρ θηρία ἐκ τοῦ ῥοπάλου ἐκρέματο, ὧν ἓν
λύσᾱς τῷ Δικαιοπόλιδι παρέδωκεν. ὁ δὲ δεξάμενος πλείστην χάριν
ἀπέδωκεν. ὁ δὲ νεανίᾱς, "οὐδέν ἐστιν," ἔφη, "πλεῖστοι γὰρ λαγῴ     25
γίγνονται ἐν τοῖς ὄρεσιν, ἐγὼ δὲ ῥᾳδίως αἱρῶ αὐτούς· δεινότατος γὰρ
εἰμι κυνηγετεῖν. χαίρετε οὖν καὶ εὐτυχοῖτε." ταῦτα δ' εἰπὼν
ἐπορεύετο κατὰ τὴν ἀτραπόν, οἱ δὲ βραδέως ἀνῇσαν.

[ὑλακτεῖ, *barks*    ἆρ' οἶσθα, *do you know?*    ἀτραπός, *path*    τῶν . . . ἑρμάτων,
*the stone heaps, cairns*    νυκτερεύοντες, *spending the night*    πῶς ἔχετε τοῦ σίτου,
*how are you off for food?*    λαγών, *hare*    ῥόπαλον, *club, hunter's staff*    θηρία,
*beasts, animals*    ἐκρέματο (from κρέμαμαι), *were hanging*    λαγῴ: nominative
plural    κυνηγετεῖν, *to hunt* (translate, *hunting*)    εὐτυχοῖτε, optative expressing a
wish, *may you be lucky! good luck to you!*]

ἑσπέρᾱς δὲ γιγνομένης ποιμένι τινὶ ἐνέτυχον, ὃς τὰ πρόβατα κατὰ
τὴν ὁδὸν ἤλαυνεν. ὁ δὲ ἰδὼν αὐτοὺς προσιόντας εἰς φόβον καταστὰς     30
ἔστησεν αὐτοὺς καὶ βοήσας, "τίνες ἐστέ," ἔφη, "οἳ διὰ τῆς νυκτὸς
πορεύεσθε; πόθεν ἤλθετε καὶ ποῖ ἔρχεσθε;" ὁ δὲ Δικαιόπολις
προσιὼν πάντα τὰ γενόμενα ἐξηγήσατο, ὁ δὲ ποιμὴν εὐμενῶς
δεξάμενος αὐτούς, "ἀλλὰ πάντες," ἔφη, "πρὸς Διός εἰσι πτωχοί τε
ξεῖνοί τε. ἀλλὰ νυκτὸς ἤδη γιγνομένης παραινῶ ὑμῖν μόνοις οὖσι μὴ     35

νυκτερεύειν ἐν τοῖς ὄρεσιν. ἄγετε δή, ἔλθετε μετ' ἐμοῦ εἰς τὴν
καλύβην, ἐν ᾗ ἔξεστιν ὑμῖν μένειν τὴν νύκτα." οἱ δ' οὖν τοὺς τοῦ
ποιμένος λόγους ἀσμένως δεξάμενοι εἵποντο αὐτῷ εἰς ὀλίγην τινὰ
καλύβην. ὁ δὲ ποιμήν, "ἰδού· εἴσιτε. ἐγὼ μὲν τάς τ' αἶγας ἀμέλξω καὶ
τὰ πρόβατα, ὑμεῖς δὲ τὰ σκεύη καταθέντες πῦρ καύσατε καὶ      40
καθίζεσθε."

[πρὸς Διός, *under the protection of Zeus*   πτωχοί τε ξεῖνοί τε, *beggars and strangers*   τὴν καλύβην, *my hut*   ἀσμένως, *gladly*   ἀμέλξω, *I will milk*   τὰ σκεύη,
*baggage*]

ὁ μὲν οὖν Φίλιππος πῦρ ἔκαυσεν, ὁ δὲ πατὴρ καθήμενος
ἀνεπαύετο ἐκ τῆς μακρᾶς ὁδοῦ. ὁ δὲ ποιμὴν τὰ πρόβατα ἀμέλξας,
ἐπανιὼν δεῖπνον παρεσκεύαζε, σῖτόν τε καὶ τῦρὸν καὶ γάλα. ὁ δὲ
Δικαιόπολις, "ἰδού, ὦ φίλε," ἔφη, "κυνηγέτης τις, ᾧ κατὰ τὴν ὁδὸν      45
ἐνετύχομεν, τόνδε τὸν λαγὼν ἡμῖν ἔδωκεν. ἆρ' οὖν βούλει ὀπτᾶν
αὐτὸν ἐπὶ δείπνῳ;" ὁ δέ, "μάλιστά γε· οὕτω γὰρ ἥδιστα δειπνήσομεν·
μετὰ δὲ τὸ δεῖπνον ὁ παῖς μέλη ᾄσεται." τὸν οὖν λαγὼν ὀπτήσαντες
ἡδέως ἐδείπνησαν· ἔπειτα δὲ ὁ μὲν Φίλιππος μέλη ᾖδεν, ὁ δὲ ποιμὴν
μύθους ἔλεγεν, ἕως πάντες οὕτως ἔκαμνον ὥστε εἰς βαθὺν ὕπνον      50
ἔπεσον.

[τῦρὸν, *cheese*   γάλα, *milk*   ὀπτᾶν, *to roast*   μέλη ᾄσεται (from ᾄδω), *will sing
songs*   ᾖδεν, *was singing*]

## PRINCIPAL PARTS: More Labial Stems (-π-, -φ-)

κόπ-τω, κόψω, ἔκοψα, κέκοφα, κέκομμαι, ἐκόπην, *I strike; I knock on* (a
   door)
τύπ-τω, [τυπτε-] τυπτήσω, *I strike, hit*
γράφω, γράψω, ἔγραψα, γέγραφα, γέγραμμαι, ἐγράφην, *I write*

## WORD BUILDING

*From your knowledge of the prepositions at the left, deduce the meaning of the
adverbs at the right:*

1. ἀνά      ἄνω         3. ἐκ, ἐξ     ἔξω          5. κατά     κάτω
2. εἰς      εἴσω         4. ἐν         ἔνδον        6. πρός     πρόσω

# GRAMMAR

## 3. The Verb ἵστημι: Forms

ἵστημι, στήσω, ἔστησα, ἔστην, ἕστηκα, ἐστάθην, *I make* X *stand;*
*I stop* X; *I am setting* X *(up)*

### ἵστημι: Present, Imperfect, Future, and Aorist, Active Voice

**Stems:** στη-/στα-

**Present:** transitive, *I make* X *stand; I stop* X; *I am setting* X *up*

| Indicative | Imperative | Infinitive | Participle |
|---|---|---|---|
| ἵ-στη-μι | | ἱ-στά-ναι | ἱ-στάς, |
| ἵ-στη-ς | ἵ-στη | | ἱ-στᾶσα, |
| ἵ-στη-σι(ν) | | | ἱ-στάν, |
| ἵ-στα-μεν | | | gen., ἱ-στάντ-ος, etc. |
| ἵ-στα-τε | ἵ-στα-τε | | |
| ἱ-στᾶ-σι(ν) | | | |

**Imperfect:** transitive, *I was making* X *stand; I was stopping* X; *I was setting* X *(up)*

**Indicative**

ἵ-στη-ν
ἵ-στη-ς
ἵ-στη
ἵ-στα-μεν
ἵ-στα-τε
ἵ-στα-σαν

**Future**

Regular sigmatic future: στήσω, στήσεις, στήσει, etc., *I will make* X *stand;*
*I will stop* X; *I will set* X *up*

**Sigmatic 1st Aorist**

Regular sigmatic 1st aorist: ἔστησα, ἔστησας, ἔστησε(ν), etc., transitive, *I made* X *stand; I stopped* X; *I set* X *up*

**Athematic 2nd Aorist:** intransitive, *I stood*

| Indicative | Imperative | Infinitive | Participle |
|---|---|---|---|
| ἔστην | | στῆ-ναι | στάς, |
| ἔστης | στῆ-θι | | στᾶσα, |
| ἔστη | | | στάν, |
| ἔστημεν | | | gen., στάντ-ος, etc. |
| ἔστητε | στῆ-τε | | |
| ἔστησαν | | | |

### ἵστημι: Present and Imperfect, Middle/Passive Voice

**Stem:** στα-

**Present:** transitive, *I am setting* X *(up) for myself;* intransitive, *I stand*

| Indicative | Imperative | Infinitive | Participle |
|---|---|---|---|
| ἵ-στα-μαι | | ἵ-στα-σθαι | ἱ-στά-μεν-ος, -η, -ον |
| ἵ-στα-σαι | ἵ-στα-σο | | |
| ἵ-στα-ται | | | |
| ἱ-στά-μεθα | | | |
| ἵ-στα-σθε | ἵ-στα-σθε | | |
| ἵ-στα-νται | | | |

**Imperfect:** transitive, *I was setting* X *(up) for myself;* intransitive, *I was standing*

**Indicative**

ἱ-στά-μην
ἵ-στα-σο
ἵ-στα-το
ἱ-στά-μεθα
ἵ-στα-σθε
ἵ-στα-ντο

### ἵστημι: Future and Aorist, Middle Voice

**Stem:** στη-

**Future**

Regular sigmatic future: στήσομαι, στήσει/ῃ, στήσεται, etc., transitive, *I will set* X *(up) for myself;* intransitive, *I will stand*

**Aorist**

Regular sigmatic 1st aorist: ἐστησάμην, ἐστήσω, ἐστήσατο, etc., transitive, *I set* X *(up) for myself*

---

# Greek Wisdom

## Heraclitus

ἀνθρώπους μένει ἀποθανόντας ἅτινα οὐκ ἔλπονται οὐδὲ δοκοῦσιν.  Fragment 27 Diels

## ἵστημι: Future and Aorist, Passive Voice

**Stem:** στα-

### Future

Regular -θη- future passive: σταθήσομαι, σταθήσει/ῃ, σταθήσεται, etc.,  *I will be set (up)*

### Aorist

Regular -θη- aorist passive: ἐστάθην, ἐστάθης, ἐστάθη, etc., *I was set (up)*

### Exercise 19δ

*Make two photocopies of the Verb Chart on page 274 and four copies of the Verb Chart on page 275. Fill in the forms of ἵστημι, except for the subjunctive and optative, in the active voice (present, imperfect, future, sigmatic aorist, and athematic 2nd aorist), in the middle/passive voice (present and imperfect), in the middle voice (future and sigmatic 1st aorist), and in the passive voice (future and aorist). Keep these charts for reference.*

## 4.   The Verbs καθίστημι and ἀφίσταμαι

A common compound of ἵστημι is καθίστημι, transitive, *I set* X *up; I appoint* X; + εἰς + acc., *I put* X *into a certain state.* When intransitive this verb means *I am appointed; I am established;* + εἰς + acc., *I get/fall into a certain state; I become*

Study the following examples carefully and translate them:

ὁ κύων τὸν ξένον εἰς φόβον κατέστησεν. (*transitive*)

ὁ ξένος εἰς φόβον κατέστη. (*intransitive*)

ὁ δῆμος τὸν Περικλῆ στρατηγὸν κατέστησεν. (*transitive*)

ὁ Περικλῆς στρατηγὸς καθίσταται. (*middle; intransitive*)

ὁ Περικλῆς στρατηγὸς κατέστη. (*intransitive*)

οἱ Ἀθηναῖοι νόμους κατεστήσαντο. (*middle; transitive*)

Another common compound of ἵστημι is ἀφίσταμαι, ἀποστήσομαι, ἀπέστην, *I stand away from; I revolt from*, e.g.:

οἱ Ἴωνες ἀπὸ τῶν Περσῶν ἀφίστανται.

οἱ Ἴωνες ἀπὸ τῶν Περσῶν ἀποστήσονται.

οἱ Ἴωνες ἀπὸ τῶν Περσῶν ἀπέστησαν.

*The Ionians are revolting/will revolt/revolted from the Persians.*

## Exercise 19ε

*Identify and translate the following forms:*

| | | |
|---|---|---|
| 1. στῆθι | 6. ἔστησαν (2 ways) | 11. ἀφίσταται |
| 2. ἱστάναι | 7. ἵστη | 12. καθίσταντο |
| 3. στῆναι | 8. στῆσον | 13. καταστήσονται |
| 4. ἵστασθε (2 ways) | 9. στάς | 14. στήσᾱς |
| 5. στήσασθαι | 10. στησάμενος | 15. ἀφίστασο |

## Exercise 19ζ

*Read aloud and translate:*
1. οἱ Ἀθηναῖοι εἰς πόλεμον κατέστησαν.
2. οἱ πολέμιοι ὑμᾶς εἰς φυγὴν καταστήσουσιν.
3. τίς σὲ κριτὴν (*judge*) ἡμῶν κατέστησεν;
4. ὁ Θησεὺς βασιλεὺς τῶν Ἀθηναίων κατέστη.
5. οἱ Ἀθηναῖοι νόμους κατεστήσαντο.
6. οἱ Ἕλληνες τοὺς Λακεδαιμονίους ἡγεμόνας (*leaders*) κατεστήσαντο.
7. οἱ στρατηγοὶ εἰς φόβον καταστάντες ἀποφεύγειν ἐβούλοντο.
8. τοσαῦτα παθόντες οὐδέποτε (*never*) εἰς πόλεμον αὖθις καταστησόμεθα.
9. οἱ Ἴωνες ἀπὸ τῶν Περσῶν ἀποστήσονται.
10. οἱ Ἴωνες ἀπὸ τῶν Περσῶν ἀποστάντες τοῖς Ἕλλησιν ἐβοήθησαν.

## Exercise 19η

*Translate into Greek:*

1. The people appointed this (man) general again.
2. This (man), having been appointed general, advised the people not to fight.
3. He told us to cease from war and gave the city peace (= put the city into a state of peace).
4. We advise you to revolt from the Persians at once.
5. The Greeks, attacking the barbarians bravely, put them to flight.

# ΟΙ ΕΛΛΗΝΕΣ ΤΟΥΣ ΠΕΡΣΑΣ ΚΑΤΑ ΘΑΛΑΤΤΑΝ ΔΕΥΤΕΡΟΝ ΝΙΚΩΣΙΝ

*Read the following passages and answer the comprehension questions:*

The battle of Mycale took place, according to tradition, on the same day as the battle of Plataea, in spring 479 B.C. The Greek victory eliminated the Persian fleet in the Aegean and was followed by a second revolt of the Ionians from Persia. The following passages are adapted from Herodotus 9.90–104.

ἅμα ἦρι ἀρχομένῳ τὸ τῶν Ἑλλήνων ναυτικὸν εἰς τὴν Αἴγῑναν συνελέγετο, νῆες
ἀριθμὸν δέκα καὶ ἑκατόν. ἐντεῦθεν δὲ εἰς τὴν Δῆλον ἔπλευσαν, βουλόμενοι τοὺς
Ἴωνας ἐλευθερῶσαι. παρόντος δὲ τοῦ ναυτικοῦ ἐν τῇ Δήλῳ, ἦλθον ἄγγελοι ἀπὸ
τῆς Σάμου, οἳ ᾔτησαν αὐτοὺς πρὸς Σάμον πλεύσαντας τοῖς βαρβάροις ἐπιστρατεῦσαι·
"οἱ γὰρ βάρβαροι," ἔφασαν, "οὐ πολλὰς ναῦς ἔχουσιν, οἱ δὲ Ἴωνες ὑμᾶς ἰδόντες εὐθὺς   5
ἀποστήσονται ἀπὸ τῶν Περσῶν. οὕτως οὖν ἔξεστιν ὑμῖν καὶ ἄνδρας Ἕλληνας
ἐλευθερῶσαι καὶ ἀμῦναι τοὺς βαρβάρους." ὁ οὖν στρατηγὸς ὁ τῶν Ἑλλήνων
τούτους τοὺς λόγους δεξάμενος ταῖς ναυσὶ πρὸς Σάμον ἡγεῖτο.

[ἅμα ἦρι ἀρχομένῳ, *with the beginning of spring*    τὴν Αἴγῑναν, *Aegina*    ἀριθμὸν, *in number*    ἐντεῦθεν, *from there*    τὴν Δῆλον, *Delos*    τῆς Σάμου, *Samos*]

1.  Where did the Greek fleet assemble, and how many ships were there?
2.  Why did the fleet sail to Delos?
3.  What did messengers from Samos ask the Greeks at Delos to do?
4.  What two facts did the messengers cite in urging the Greeks to act?
5.  What two things do the messengers claim that the Greeks could do?
6.  What was the response of the Greek general?

ὡς δὲ εἰς Σάμον ἀφικόμενοι παρεσκευάζοντο εἰς ναυμαχίᾱν, οἱ Πέρσαι εὐθὺς
ἀπέπλευσαν πρὸς τὴν ἤπειρον· ἔδοξε γὰρ αὐτοῖς μὴ ναυμαχίᾱν ποιεῖσθαι· οὐ γὰρ   10
ἀξιόμαχοι ἦσαν αἱ νῆες αὐτῶν. ἀποπλεύσαντες οὖν πρὸς τὴν Μυκάλην τὰς ναῦς
ἀνείλκυσαν καὶ τεῖχος ἐποίησαν περὶ αὐτάς. οἱ δὲ Ἕλληνες ταῦτα γνόντες
ἐδίωκον αὐτοὺς εἰς τὴν Μυκάλην. ὡς δὲ ἐγγὺς ἐγένοντο τοῦ τῶν πολεμίων
στρατοπέδου καὶ οὐδεὶς ἐφαίνετο ἀναγόμενος ἀλλὰ ναῦς εἶδον ἀνειλκυσμένᾱς ἔσω
τοῦ τείχους, πρῶτον μὲν παραπλέοντες τοὺς Ἴωνας ἐκάλεσαν, κελεύοντες αὐτοὺς   15
ἀποστῆναι ἀπὸ τῶν Περσῶν, ἔπειτα δὲ εἰς τὴν γῆν ἐκβάντες τῷ τείχει
προσέβαλλον.

[εἰς ναυμαχίᾱν, *for a battle at sea*    τὴν ἤπειρον, *the mainland*    ἀξιόμαχοι,
*battle-worthy*    τὴν Μυκάλην, *Mycale*    ἀνείλκυσαν (from ἀνέλκω), *they beached*
τοῦ...στρατοπέδου, *the camp*    ἀναγόμενος, *putting out to sea*    ἀνειλκυσμένᾱς (perfect passive participle of ἀνέλκω, *I draw up*), *drawn up (on the shore),
beached*    ἔσω + gen., *inside*    παραπλέοντες, *sailing past* ]

7.  What did the Persians do when the Greeks arrived at Samos?  Why?
8.  How did the Persians protect their fleet?
9.  How did the Greeks respond to this maneuver of the Persians?
10. When the Greeks saw that the Persians were not putting to sea and were
    continuing to protect their beached fleet, what two things did they do?

πρῶτον μὲν οὖν ἀνδρείως ἐμάχοντο οἱ βάρβαροι, ἐπεὶ δὲ οἱ Ἕλληνες μιᾷ ὁρμῇ
προσφερόμενοι τὸ τεῖχος εἷλον, τρεψάμενοι ἔφυγον. οἱ δὲ Ἴωνες, ὡς εἶδον τοὺς

Ἕλληνας νῑκῶντας, πρὸς αὐτοὺς αὐτομολήσαντες τοῖς βαρβάροις ἐνέπεσον. οὕτως   20
οὖν τὸ δεύτερον ἀπέστησαν οἱ Ἴωνες ἀπὸ τῶν Περσῶν.

[ὁρμῇ, *rush, onset*    προσφερόμενοι, *charging*    αὐτομολήσαντες, *deserting*]

11. What action of the Greeks put the Persians to flight?
12. At what moment did the Ionians desert the Persians?
13. When the Ionians deserted the Persians, what did they do?

### Exercise 19θ

*Translate into Greek:*

1. At the Ionians' request (*use genitive absolute with* αἰτέω), the general decided to lead the fleet to Samos.
2. The messengers said, "We will not betray (προδώσομεν) you but will revolt from the Persians."
3. The barbarians, having seen the ships of the Greeks approaching, fled to the mainland.
4. The Greeks, having disembarked from their ships, attacked the wall and took (it).
5. The Ionians, having seen the Greeks winning, revolted from the Persians and came to aid the Greeks.

The death of Agamemnon

# New Testament Greek

### John 2.1–8
### The Wedding at Cana

καὶ τῇ ἡμέρᾳ τῇ τρίτῃ γάμος ἐγένετο ἐν Κανὰ τῆς Γαλιλαίας, καὶ ἦν ἡ μήτηρ
τοῦ Ἰησοῦ ἐκεῖ· ἐκλήθη δὲ καὶ ὁ Ἰησοῦς καὶ οἱ μαθηταὶ αὐτοῦ εἰς τὸν γάμον.  καὶ
ὑστερήσαντος οἴνου λέγει ἡ μήτηρ τοῦ Ἰησοῦ πρὸς αὐτόν, "οἶνον οὐκ ἔχουσιν."  λέγει
αὐτῇ ὁ Ἰησοῦς, "τί ἐμοὶ καὶ σοί, γύναι; οὔπω ἥκει ἡ ὥρα μου."

[**γάμος**, *a wedding*  **τῆς Γαλιλαίας**, *of Galilee*  **οἱ μαθηταὶ**, *the disciples*  **ὑστερήσαντος οἴνου**, *when the wine gave out*  **οὔπω**, *not yet*  **ἡ ὥρα**, *hour*]

λέγει ἡ μήτηρ αὐτοῦ τοῖς διακόνοις, "ὅ τι ἂν λέγῃ ὑμῖν ποιήσατε."  ἦσαν δὲ
ἐκεῖ λίθιναι ὑδρίαι ἓξ κατὰ τὸν καθαρισμὸν τῶν Ἰουδαίων κείμεναι, χωροῦσαι
ἀνὰ μετρητὰς δύο ἢ τρεῖς.  λέγει αὐτοῖς ὁ Ἰησοῦς, "γεμίσατε τὰς ὑδρίας ὕδατος."
καὶ ἐγέμισαν αὐτὰς ἕως ἄνω.  καὶ λέγει αὐτοῖς, "ἀντλήσατε νῦν καὶ φέρετε τῷ
ἀρχιτρικλίνῳ"· οἱ δὲ ἤνεγκαν.

[**τοῖς διακόνοις**, *to the servants*  **ὅ τι ἂν λέγῃ**, *whatever he says*  **λίθιναι**, *made
of stone*  **κατὰ τὸν καθαρισμὸν**, *for the purification*  **τῶν Ἰουδαίων**, *of the Jews*
**χωροῦσαι**, *holding*  **ἀνὰ** + *acc.*, *at the rate of, up to*  **μετρητὰς**, *measures* (one
μετρητής = about nine gallons or thirty-four liters)  **γεμίσατε**, *fill* X (acc.) *with* Y (gen.)
**ἄνω**, *up* (i.e., full)  **ἀντλήσατε**, *draw*  **τῷ ἀρχιτρικλίνῳ**, *to the master of
ceremonies*  **ἤνεγκαν**: asigmatic aorist of φέρω]

Concluded in Chapter 20

ὁ Ἰησοῦς, τοῦ Ἰησοῦ, τῷ Ἰησοῦ, τὸν Ἰησοῦν, ὦ Ἰησοῦ, *Jesus*
οἱ Ἰουδαῖοι, τῶν Ἰουδαίων, *the Jews*

Terrace of Lions on Delos; ca. 610 B.C.

# 20
# Ο ΝΟΣΤΟΣ (γ)

ἐν αὐτοῖς τοῖς δώμασι τοῦ Ἀγαμέμνονος ἵσταντο.

## VOCABULARY

*Verbs*
> ἀρέσκει, [ἀρε-] ἀρέσει, ἤρεσε,
> impersonal + dat., *it is pleas-*
> *ing*
> δείκνῡμι, imperfect, ἐδείκνῡν,
> [δεικ-] δείξω, ἔδειξα, δέδει-
> χα, δέδειγμαι, ἐδείχθην,
> *I show*
> καθοράω [= κατα- + ὁράω],
> [ὀπ-] κατόψομαι, [ἰδ-] κατ-
> εῖδον, *I look down on*

*Nouns*
> τὸ αἷμα, τοῦ αἵματος, *blood*
> ὁ λέων, τοῦ λέοντος, *lion*
> τὸ μέγεθος, τοῦ μεγέθους, *size*
> τὸ τέκνον, τοῦ τέκνου, *child*
> ὁ τόπος, τοῦ τόπου, *place*

*Adjectives*
> ἀσφαλής, -ές, *safe*
> λίθινος, -η, -ον, *of stone, made*
> *of stone*

*Adverb or Preposition*
> ἐντός, adv., *within, inside;*
> prep. + gen., *within, inside*

*Adverbs*
> ἄνω, *up; above*
> ἐξαίφνης, *suddenly*
> κάτω, *down; below*

*Particle*
> δήπου, *doubtless, surely*

*Proper Names*
> αἱ Ἐρῑνύες, τῶν Ἐρῑνυῶν,
> *the Furies* (avenging spirits)
> αἱ Μυκῆναι, τῶν Μυκηνῶν,
> *Mycenae*

ἡμέρᾱς δὲ γενομένης τὸν ποιμένα χαίρειν κελεύσαντες ἐπορεύοντο καὶ τέλος ἀφίκοντο εἰς ἄκρα τὰ ὄρη, ἀφ' ὧν κατεῖδον τό τε
πεδίον κάτω κείμενον καὶ τείχη τινὰ ἐπὶ λόφου ἑστηκότα. ὁ δὲ
Φίλιππος τὸν πατέρα στήσᾱς, "πάππα," ἔφη, "τείχη τινὰ μεγάλα ὁρῶ
ἐπ' ἐκείνου τοῦ λόφου ἑστηκότα. ἀλλ' εἰπέ μοι, τίνα ἐστίν;" ὁ δὲ     5

Δικαιόπολις πολύν τινα χρόνον πρὸς τὰ τείχη βλέπων, "ἐκεῖνά ἐστιν,
ὦ παῖ," ἔφη, "ὡς ἐμοὶ δοκεῖ, τὰ τῶν Μυκηνῶν τείχη." ὁ δὲ Φίλιππος,
"ἆρα ἀληθῆ λέγεις;" ἔφη. "ἆρα ἐκεῖ ᾤκησεν ὁ Ἀγαμέμνων; ἆρα
βούλει δεικνύναι μοι τὰ τοῦ Ἀγαμέμνονος δώματα; ἆρα ἔξεστιν ἡμῖν
ἐκεῖσε καταβῆναι καὶ τὰ δώματα θεωρεῖν;" ὁ δὲ Δικαιόπολις, "ἔξεστι    10
καταβῆναι, εἴ σοι δοκεῖ. οὐ γὰρ μάλα πολὺ ἀπέχει τὰ τείχη τῆς
ὁδοῦ, καί—ὀψὲ γάρ ἐστιν—τὴν νύκτα ἐντὸς τῶν τειχῶν ἀσφαλεῖς
μενοῦμεν."

[λόφου, *crest of a hill*    ἑστηκότα, perfect participle, *standing*    τὰ ... δώματα, *the
palace*]

οὕτως εἰπών, τῷ παιδὶ κατὰ τὸ ὄρος ἡγήσατο. δι' ὀλίγου οὖν τοῖς
τείχεσι ἐπλησίαζον καὶ ἐπὶ τὸν λόφον ἀναβάντες εἰς τὰς πύλας    15
ἀφίκοντο. ὁ δὲ Φίλιππος τὰ τείχη θεώμενος τὸ μέγεθος ἐθαύμαζε καί,
"ὦ πάτερ," ἔφη, "γίγαντες δήπου ταῦτα τὰ τείχη ᾠκοδόμησαν·
ἄνθρωποι γὰρ τοσούτους λίθους αἴρειν οὐκ ἐδύναντο." ὁ δὲ
Δικαιόπολις, "ἀληθῆ λέγεις, ὦ τέκνον," ἔφη· "οἱ γὰρ Κύκλωπες, ὥς
φασιν, ταῦτα ἐποίησαν. ἀλλ' ἰδού, ἔργον θαυμάσιόν σοι δείξω·    20
βλέπε ἄνω." ὁ δὲ Φίλιππος ἀναβλέπων δύο λέοντας λιθίνους εἶδε τὰς
πύλας φυλάττοντας. τούτους δὲ θεασάμενοι προὐχώρουν καὶ εἰς
ἄκρον τὸν λόφον ἀφικόμενοι ἐν αὐτοῖς τοῖς δώμασι τοῦ
Ἀγαμέμνονος ἵσταντο, τό τε πεδίον καθορῶντες καὶ τὴν θάλατταν τῷ
ἡλίῳ λαμπομένην.    25

[ἐπλησίαζον + dat., *they were approaching*    γίγαντες, *giants*    ᾠκοδόμησαν, *built*
θαυμάσιόν, *wonderful, marvelous*    λαμπομένην, *shining*]

ἐξαίφνης δὲ ἔφρῑξεν ὁ Φίλιππος καὶ εἰς φόβον κρυερὸν κατέστη.
"ὦ πάτερ," ἔφη, "οὐκ ἀρέσκει μοι οὗτος ὁ τόπος. αἵματος γὰρ ὄζει."
ὁ δὲ Δικαιόπολις, "μηδὲν φοβοῦ, ὦ τέκνον," ἔφη· "ἴσως αἱ Ἐρῑνύες
Ἀγαμέμνονός τε καὶ τῆς παγκάκου γυναικὸς ἔτι καὶ νῦν
περιφοιτῶσιν. ἀλλ' οὐ βλάψουσί σε, τέκνον. ἐλθέ. δός μοι τὴν    30
χεῖρα. ἐγώ σοι ἡγήσομαι." καὶ οὕτως εἰπών, τῷ παιδὶ ὡς τάχιστα
κάτω ἡγήσατο.

[ἔφρῑξεν (from φρίττω), *shuddered*   κρυερὸν, *icy*   ὄζει + gen., *it smells of*   παγκά-κου, *completely evil*   περιφοιτῶσιν, *wander about*]

## PRINCIPAL PARTS: Velar Stems (-γ-, -κ-)

ἄγ-ω, ἄξω, [ἀγαγ-] ἤγαγον, [ἀγ-] ἦχα, ἦγμαι, ἤχθην, *I lead; I take*
φεύγ-ω, φεύξομαι, [φυγ-] ἔφυγον, [φευγ-] πέφευγα, *I flee; I escape*
πράττω, [πρᾱκ-] πρᾱ́ξω, ἔπρᾱξα, πέπρᾱγα, πέπρᾱγμαι, ἐπρᾱ́χθην, intransitive,
    *I fare;* transitive, *I do*

## WORD STUDY

*Deduce the meaning of the Greek word from which the first part of each of the following words is derived. Then give a definition of the English word:*

1. photograph (τὸ φῶς, τοῦ φωτός = ?)   4. paleography (παλαιός, -ά, -όν = ?)
2. seismograph (ὁ σεισμός = ?)            5. cryptography (κρύπτω = ?)
3. telegraph (τῆλε = ?)

*Give two other English words beginning with* tele- *and explain their meanings and Greek stems.*

## GRAMMAR

### 1. The Verb δείκνῡμι

**Stem:** δεικ-, *show*

δείκ-νῡ-μι, δείξω, ἔδειξα, δέδειχα, δέδειγμαι, ἐδείχθην, *I show*

In the present and imperfect tenses of this verb, endings are added directly to the extended present stem δεικ-νῡ-/-νυ-. Note the nasal suffix -νῡ-/-νυ-. The other principal parts are formed regularly from the stem δεικ-. The following verbs are conjugated like δείκνῡμι in the present and imperfect:

ζεύγ-νῡ-μι, ζεύξω, ἔζευξα, ἔζευγμαι, ἐζεύχθην or ἐζύγην, *I yoke*
ἀνοίγ-νῡ-μι [= ἀνα- + οἴγ-νῡ-μι], imperfect, ἀνέῳγον (double augment),
    ἀνοίξω, ἀνέῳξα, ἀνέῳχα, ἀνέῳγμαι (*I stand open*), ἀνεῴχθην,
    *I open*
ῥήγ-νῡ-μι, ῥήξω, ἔρρηξα, ἔρρωγα (intransitive, *I have broken out*),
    ἐρράγην, aorist passive participle, ῥαγείς, *I break*
σβέν-νῡμι, [σβε-] σβέσω, ἔσβεσα, ἔσβηκα (intransitive, *I have gone out*),
    ἐσβέσθην, *I put out, extinguish*

---

## Greek Wisdom

### Heraclitus

ὕβριν χρὴ σβεννύναι μᾶλλον ἢ πυρκαϊάν. Fragment 43 Diels

## δείκνῡμι: Active Voice

**Stems:** δεικνῡ-/δεικνυ-

### Present
| Indicative | Imperative | | Infinitive | Participle |
|---|---|---|---|---|
| δείκνῡμι | | | δεικνύναι | δεικνύς, |
| δείκνῡς | δείκνῡ | | | δεικνῦσα, |
| δείκνῡσι(ν) | | | | δεικνύν, |
| δείκνυμεν | | | | gen., δεικνύντος, etc. |
| δείκνυτε | δείκνυτε | | | |
| δεικνύᾱσι(ν) | | | | |

### Imperfect
### Indicative

ἐδείκνῡν
ἐδείκνῡς
ἐδείκνῡ
ἐδείκνυμεν
ἐδείκνυτε
ἐδείκνυσαν


## δείκνῡμι: Middle /PassiveVoice

**Stem:** δεικνυ-

### Present
| Indicative | Imperative | | Infinitive | Participle |
|---|---|---|---|---|
| δείκνυμαι | | | δείκνυσθαι | δεικνύμενος, -η, -ον |
| δείκνυσαι | δείκνυσο | | | |
| δείκνυται | | | | |
| δεικνύμεθα | | | | |
| δείκνυσθε | δείκνυσθε | | | |
| δείκνυνται | | | | |

### Imperfect
### Indicative

ἐδεικνύμην
ἐδείκνυσο
ἐδείκνυτο
ἐδεικνύμεθα
ἐδείκνυσθε
ἐδείκνυντο

### Exercise 20 α

*Make two photocopies of the Verb Charts on pages 274 and 275 and a third copy of the chart on page 275. Fill in the forms of ζεύγνῡμι, except for the subjunctive and optative, in the active voice on the first set, in the middle voice on the second, and in the future and aorist passive on the third copy of the chart on page 275. Keep these charts for reference.*

### Exercise 20 β

*Identify and translate the following forms of* δείκνῡμι, ἀνοίγνῡμι, ζεύγνῡμι, *and* ῥήγνῡμι:

1. δεικνύᾱσι(ν)
2. δείκνυσθαι (2 ways)
3. ἐδείκνῡ
4. δεικνῦσα
5. ἐδείκνυσο (2 ways)

6. δεῖξαι (2 ways)
7. ἀνοίγνυτε (2 ways)
8. ἔρρηξαν
9. ζεύξᾱς
10. ἀνέῳξε(ν)

11. ῥήξουσι(ν)
12. δείκνυσο (2 ways)
13. ἀνοίξαντες
14. ῥηγνύναι
15. ζεύγνυμεν

### Exercise 20 γ

*Read aloud and translate:*

1. ὁ στρατηγὸς τὸν ἄγγελον ἐκέλευσε τὰς πύλᾱς ἀνοῖξαι καὶ τοὺς πρέσβεις (*ambassadors*) δέχεσθαι.
2. ὁ ἄγγελος τοὺς φύλακας (*the guards*) ἤρετο τί οὐκ ἀνοιγνύᾱσι τὰς πύλᾱς.
3. ὁ αὐτουργὸς τοὺς βοῦς ζεύξᾱς ἀροῦν (*to plow*) ἤρξατο (*began*).
4. τὸν δοῦλον καλέσᾱς λίθον μέγιστον ἔδειξεν αὐτῷ καὶ ἐκέλευσεν ἐκφέρειν ἐκ τοῦ ἀγροῦ.
5. λίθος τοσοῦτος τὸ ἄροτρον ῥήξει· δεῖ οὖν τὸν λίθον αἴρειν καὶ ἐκφέρειν.

# War Clouds

The alliance formed between Sparta and Athens during Xerxes' invasion did not last. When the allies rejected the general whom the Spartans sent to command the fleet in 478 B.C. and formed the Delian League under Athenian leadership, Sparta did not demur. However, she watched the successes of the League and the growth of Athenian power with increasing anxiety. In 464 B.C. there was an earthquake at Sparta, and in the ensuing chaos the helots revolted. The Spartans asked their allies, including Athens, to send help, and the Assembly was persuaded by Cimon to send a force under his command. When this force failed to take the helot stronghold, the Spartans dismissed them.

This rebuff resulted in a volte-face in Athenian policy. As soon as Cimon returned (461 B.C.), an ostracism was held, and Cimon was sent into exile for ten years. Pericles emerged as the dominant statesman, a position he held until his death in 429 B.C. Under his leadership, Athens broke with Sparta, made an alliance with Argos, and soon became involved in a sporadic war with Sparta and her allies, which lasted intermittently for fifteen years.

On the whole, Athens was successful, and at one time her empire extended to include Boeotia and Megara, but she was overextended. In 446 B.C. when Euboea and Megara revolted and a Lacedaemonian army advanced to the borders of Attica, she was glad to make peace. The Thirty Years' Peace stipulated that each side should respect the other's sphere of influence and not admit into her alliance an ally of the other.

There followed a period of peace and retrenchment, during which Pericles eschewed imperialistic adventures, observed the terms of the peace, and built up Athenian resources. Sparta and her allies, however, especially Corinth, continued to distrust Athens and to fear her ambitions. The Aegean and Black Sea were already Athenian preserves; when she began to extend her influence in the west, Corinthian fears increased.

In 433/432 B.C. the Corinthian colony of Corcyra (Corfu) was embroiled in a quarrel with her mother city and asked Athens for help. Athens agreed to make a defensive alliance, and when Corinth attacked Corcyra an Athenian squadron, which had been sent to "observe," joined in the battle and routed the Corinthian fleet. Shortly after this, Potidaea, which was both a colony of Corinth and a member of the Athenian Empire, revolted from Athens and asked Corinth for help. The Corinthians sent "volunteers," and Athens laid siege to the city.

In late summer 432 B.C., representatives of the Peloponnesian League voted that Athens had broken the terms of the peace and that war should be declared. Both sides tried to make the other appear the aggressor. Finally, the Spartans sent an ultimatum: "The Lacedaemonians desire peace, and there will be peace, if you let the Greeks be independent." Pericles advised the Athenians to reject this ultimatum and to call on the Spartans to submit their differences to arbitration under the terms of the peace. By now the Peloponnesian army was mustered, and in early summer 431 B.C. it invaded Attica.

Corinth: the site of the ancient city, dominated by the remains of the temple of Apollo

# Ο ΝΟΣΤΟΣ (δ)

## VOCABULARY

*Verbs*

δειπνέω, *I eat (dinner)*

ἵημι, imperative, ἵει, infinitive,
ἱέναι, participle, ἱείς, imperfect, ἵην, [ἡ-] ἥσω, ἧκα, imperative, [ἑ-] ἕς, infinitive,
εἷναι, participle, εἵς, εἷκα,
εἷμαι, εἵθην, *I let go, release;
I send; I throw;* middle, ἵεμαι,
imperfect, ἱέμην, *I hasten*

ἀφίημι [= ἀπο- + ἵημι], *I let
go, release; I send; I throw*

ἐφίημι [= ἐπι- + ἵημι], *I
throw;* + ἐπί + acc., *I throw
at*

συνίημι + gen. of person,
acc. of thing, *I understand*

κρύπτω, [κρυφ-] κρύψω, ἔκρυψα, κέκρυμμαι, ἐκρύφθην,
*I hide*

λανθάνω, [ληθ-] λήσω, [λαθ-]
ἔλαθον, [ληθ-] λέληθα + acc.
and/or participle, *I escape
someone's* notice *doing something = I do something without*

someone's noticing; *I escape
the notice of* someone

οἰκτίρω, [οἰκτιρε-] οἰκτιρῶ,
[οἰκτῑρ-] ᾤκτῑρα, *I pity*

παρέρχομαι, *I go past; I pass in,
enter; I come forward (to
speak)*

προέρχομαι, *I go forward, advance*

*Noun*

ἡ ὀργή, τῆς ὀργῆς, *anger*

*Adjective*

ἔνιοι, -αι, -α, *some*

*Adverb or Preposition*

ἔξω, adv., *outside;* prep. + gen.,
*outside*

*Preposition*

ἐπί + gen., *toward, in the direction of;* + dat., *at;* of price, *for;*
+ acc., *at; against; onto; upon*

*Adverbs*

μή, with infin., *not*

πολύ, *far, by far*

τήμερον, *today*

ἔδοξεν οὖν αὐτοῖς μὴ ἐγγὺς τῶν Μυκηνῶν νυκτερεύειν, ἀλλὰ τὰ
τείχη καταλιπόντες ἵεντο ἐπὶ τῆς Κορίνθου. δι' ὀλίγου, ἤδη
καταδύντος τοῦ ἡλίου, εἰς κώμην τινὰ ἀφίκοντο. ἐκεῖ δὲ αὐτουργός
τις αὐτοῖς πρὸς τῇ ὁδῷ ἀναπαυομένοις ἐντυχὼν ᾤκτῑρε καὶ οἴκαδε
ἤγαγεν. ἡ μὲν οὖν γυνὴ αὐτοῦ σῖτον παρέσχε, ὁ δὲ αὐτουργὸς      5
ἐκέλευσεν αὐτοὺς ἐγγὺς τοῦ πυρὸς καθίσαι. ἐπεὶ δὲ ἐδείπνησαν, ὁ
αὐτουργὸς ἤρετο αὐτοὺς ποῖ πορεύονται, καὶ ἀκούσᾱς ὅτι πρὸς τὴν
Κόρινθον πορεύονται, "ἡ Κόρινθος," ἔφη, "πολὺ ἀπέχει. οὔκουν
δύνασθε ἐκεῖσε ἀφικέσθαι τήμερον. ἀλλ' εἰ δοκεῖ, ἔξεστιν ὑμῖν
ἐνθάδε νυκτερεύειν." οἱ δὲ χάριν μεγίστην αὐτῷ ἀπέδοσαν καὶ ἐγγὺς  10
τοῦ πυρὸς κατέκειντο. τῇ δὲ ὑστεραίᾳ, ἀνατέλλοντος τοῦ ἡλίου, τὸν

αὐτουργὸν χαίρειν κελεύσαντες ἐπὶ τῆς Κορίνθου ἵεντο.  ἀλλὰ
μακρὰ ἦν ἡ ὁδός, καὶ ἑσπέρας ἤδη γιγνομένης εἰς τὴν πόλιν ἀφίκοντο
καὶ καταγώγιον ἐζήτουν.

[νυκτερεύειν, *to spend the night*    καταδύντος, *setting, having set*    κώμην, *village*
ἀνατέλλοντος, *rising*    καταγώγιον, *inn*]

προσιόντες οὖν πρὸς ἄνδρα τινὰ ὃς διὰ τῆς ὁδοῦ παρῄει, ἤροντο    15
ποῦ ἐστι καταγώγιόν τι.  ὁ δὲ δεινὸν βλέψας καὶ εἰς ὀργὴν καταστάς,
"πρὸς τῶν σιῶν," ἔφη, "Ἀθηναῖοι φαίνεσθε ἐόντες.  τί βούλεσθε; τί δὰ
πράττετε ἐν τᾷ Κορίνθῳ;" τοῖς δὲ παροῦσι βοήσας, "δεῦρο ἕρπετε,"
ἔφη, "φίλοι.  Ἀθηναῖοί τινες πάρεντιν· κατάσκοποι δᾶπου ἐντίν, οἳ
ἦνθον τὰ νεώρια κατασκεψόμενοι." ὁ δὲ Δικαιόπολις, "τί λέγεις, ὦ    20
ἄνθρωπε;  οὐκ ἐσμὲν κατάσκοποι ἀλλ' αὐτουργοί, οἵπερ ἀπὸ τῆς
Ἐπιδαύρου Ἀθήναζε ἱέμεθα." ἀλλ' ἤδη συνῆλθεν ὅμιλος Κορινθίων
οἳ ἀγρίως ἐβόων· ἔνιοι δὲ καὶ λίθους ἐλάμβανον καὶ ἐπ' αὐτοὺς
ἐφίεσαν.

[πρὸς τῶν σιῶν = Doric Greek for the Attic πρὸς τῶν θεῶν, *by the gods!*    ἐόντες =
Doric for ὄντες    δὰ = Doric for δή    τᾷ = Doric for τῇ    ἕρπετε = Doric for ἔλθετε
πάρεντιν = Doric for πάρεισιν    κατάσκοποι *spies*    δᾶπου = Doric for δήπου
ἐντίν = Doric for εἰσίν    ἦνθον = Doric for ἦλθον    τὰ νεώρια, *the docks*    κατασκεψόμενοι, *about to spy on, to spy on*]

ὁ οὖν Δικαιόπολις εἰς φόβον καταστάς, "φύγε, Φίλιππε," ἔφη, "ὡς    25
τάχιστα." οἱ μὲν οὖν ἔφυγον πρὸς τὰς πύλας, οἱ δὲ Κορίνθιοι
διώκοντες λίθους ἐφίεσαν.  τρέχοντες δὲ ὅ τε Φίλιππος καὶ ὁ πατὴρ
τοὺς διώκοντας ἔφυγον καὶ ἔλαθον ἐν τάφρῳ τινὶ κρυψάμενοι, ἐν ᾗ
ἅπασαν τὴν νύκτα ἔμενον.  ἡμέρας δὲ γενομένης εὐθὺς ἐπορεύοντο
καὶ πάντας ἀνθρώπους ἔλαθον ταχέως ἱέμενοι.  ὡς δὲ τοῖς Μεγάροις    30
προσεχώρουν, οὐκ εἰσῆλθον εἰς τὴν πόλιν ἀλλὰ παρῆλθον ἔξω τῶν
τειχῶν.  οὕτως οὖν τέλος ἔλαθον εἰς τὴν Ἀττικὴν εἰσελθόντες καὶ ἐπεὶ
πρῶτον ἀφίκοντο εἰς τὴν Ἐλευσῖνα, κείμενοι πρὸς τῇ ὁδῷ
ἀνεπαύοντο· πολλὰ γὰρ καὶ δεινὰ παθόντες μάλα ἔκαμνον, ὥστε
οὐκ ἐδύναντο προϊέναι.                                              35

[τάφρῳ, *ditch*    τοῖς Μεγάροις, *Megara*]

## PRINCIPAL PARTS: More Velar Stems (-κ-, -χ-)

διώκω, διώξω or διώξομαι, ἐδίωξα, δεδίωχα, ἐδιώχθην, *I pursue, chase*
φυλάττω, [φυλακ-] φυλάξω, ἐφύλαξα, πεφύλαχα, πεφύλαγμαι (*I am on my guard*), ἐφυλάχθην, *I guard*
δοκέω, [δοκ-] δόξω, ἔδοξα, δέδογμαι, ἐδόχθην, *I seem; I think*
εὔχομαι, εὔξομαι, ηὐξάμην, ηὖγμαι, *I pray;* + dat., *I pray to*

## WORD BUILDING

*The following table illustrates some ways in which nouns and verbs can be formed from a single stem.  Define each word:*

**Stem**

| | | | | | |
|---|---|---|---|---|---|
| 1. | τῑμα- | ἡ τῑμή | τῑμάω | | |
| 2. | ἀναγκα- | ἡ ἀνάγκη | ἀναγκάζω | | |
| 3. | ὀργα- | ἡ ὀργή | ὀργίζομαι | | |
| 4. | οἰκο/ε- | ὁ οἶκος | οἰκέω | ἡ οἴκησις | ὁ οἰκητής | τὸ οἴκημα |
| 5. | δουλο- | ὁ δοῦλος | δουλόω | ἡ δούλωσις | | |
| 6. | κηρῡκ- | ὁ κῆρυξ | κηρύττω | | | τὸ κήρῡγμα |

## GRAMMAR

### 2. The Verb ἵημι

**Stems:** long-vowel stem ἡ-; short-vowel stem ἑ-, *send*

ἵημι, ἥσω, ἧκα, εἷκα, εἷμαι, εἵθην, *I let go, release; I send; I throw;*
middle, *I hasten* (present and imperfect only)

This verb is particularly common in compounds. In the present and imperfect the stem is reduplicated, but its reduplication is linguistically more complex than that seen in δίδωμι, τίθημι, and ἵστημι.

#### ἵημι: Active Voice

| **Present** Indicative | Imperative | | Infinitive | Participle |
|---|---|---|---|---|
| ἵημι | | | ἱέναι | ἱείς, |
| ἵης | ἵει | | | ἱεῖσα, |
| ἵησι(ν) | | | | ἱέν, |
| ἵεμεν | | | | gen., ἱέντος, etc. |
| ἵετε | ἵετε | | | |
| ἱᾶσι(ν) | | | | |

**Imperfect**
**Indicative**

ἵην
ἵεις
ἵει
ἵεμεν
ἵετε
ἵεσαν

**Future:** ἥσω, ἥσεις, ἥσει, etc.

**Aorist**

| Indicative | Imperative | Infinitive | Participle |
|------------|------------|------------|------------|
| ἧκα | | εἶναι | εἵς, |
| ἧκας | ἕς | | εἶσα, |
| ἧκε(ν) | | | ἕν, |
| εἷμεν | | | gen., ἕντος, etc. |
| εἷτε | ἕτε | | |
| εἷσαν | | | |

## ἵημι: Middle /PassiveVoice

**Present**

| Indicative | Imperative | Infinitive | Participle |
|------------|------------|------------|------------|
| ἵεμαι | | ἵεσθαι | ἱέμενος, -η, -ον |
| ἵεσαι | ἵεσο | | |
| ἵεται | | | |
| ἱέμεθα | | | |
| ἵεσθε | ἵεσθε | | |
| ἵενται | | | |

**Imperfect**
**Indicative**

ἱέμην
ἵεσο
ἵετο
ἱέμεθα
ἵεσθε
ἵεντο

## ἵημι: Middle Voice

**Future:** ἥσομαι, ἥσει/ῃ, ἥσεται, etc.

### Aorist

| Indicative | Imperative | | Infinitive | Participle |
|---|---|---|---|---|
| εἵμην | | | ἕσθαι | ἕμενος, -η, -ον |
| εἷσο | οὗ | | | |
| εἷτο | | | | |
| εἵμεθα | | | | |
| εἷσθε | ἕσθε | | | |
| εἷντο | | | | |

## ἵημι: Passive Voice

**Aorist Passive:** εἵθην, εἵθης, εἵθη, etc.

**Future Passive:** εἱθήσομαι, εἱθήσει/ῃ, εἱθήσεται, etc.

For compounds of ἵημι, see page 62.

### Exercise 20 δ

*Make two photocopies of the Verb Chart on page 274 and three copies of the Verb Chart on page 275. Fill in the forms of ἵημι, except for the subjunctive and optative, in the active voice (present, imperfect, future, and aorist), in the middle/passive voice (present and imperfect), in the middle voice (future and aorist), and in the passive voice (future and aorist). Keep these charts for reference.*

### Exercise 20 ε

*Identify and translate the following forms of ἵημι, ἀφίημι, ἐφίημι, συνίημι, εἰμί, and εἶμι:*

1. ἵεσθαι (2 ways)
2. συνιᾶσι(ν)
3. ἱέμενος (2 ways)
4. ἀφῆκε(ν)
5. ἀφείς
6. ἀφεῖσαν (2 ways)
7. ἄφες
8. ἀφεῖσθε
9. ἵεντο (2 ways)
10. συνῆκας
11. ἀφοῦ
12. ἱέναι
13. ἐφῑέναι
14. εἶναι
15. εἶναι

### Exercise 20 ζ

*Read aloud and translate into English:*

1. οἱ ἔμποροι πρὸς τὸν λιμένα ἱέμενοι ναῦν ἐζήτουν μέλλουσαν πρὸς τὰς Ἀθήνᾱς πλεύσεσθαι.
2. οὗτος ὁ δοῦλος δεῦρο ἱέμενος ἦλθεν καὶ ἡμᾶς ἐκ κινδύνου ἔσωσε.
3. οἴκαδε οὖν ἱέμενοι τὸν πατέρα ᾐτήσαμεν αὐτὸν ἐλεύθερον ἀφεῖναι.

4.   ἡ μὲν γυνή, "μὴ ἄφες τὸν δοῦλον, ὦ ἄνερ," ἔφη.

5.   ὁ δὲ ἀνὴρ τὸν δοῦλον ἀφεὶς Ἀθήναζε ἵετο καὶ ἄλλον δοῦλον ἐπρίατο
     (aorist of ὠνέομαι, I buy).

6.   ἆρα συνίης πάντα ἃ εἶπεν ὁ γέρων;

7.   οὐ πάντα συνῆκα ἐγώ. ἆρα σὺ πάντα συνιέναι ἐδύνασο;

8.   ἐγώ, πάντα συνείς, τῷ γέροντι χάριν ἀπέδωκα.

9.   ὁ κυνηγέτης λαγὼν ἰδὼν τὸν κύνα ἀφῆκεν.

10.  τοὺς κύνας ἀφέντες τὸν λαγὼν ἐδιώκομεν.

## 3.   Verbs That Take Supplementary Participles: λανθάνω, τυγχάνω, φθάνω, and φαίνομαι

The verb λανθάνω, λήσω, ἔλαθον, λέληθα, meaning *I escape notice, escape the notice of*, is used idiomatically with a supplementary participle. The participle contains the main idea of the sentence and is usually translated with a finite verb, while the form of λανθάνω becomes an adverbial phrase. Note these examples from the last paragraph of the reading passage above:

<u>ἔλαθον</u> ἐν τάφρῳ τινὶ **κρυψάμενοι**.

**They *hid themselves*** in a ditch <u>without anyone's noticing</u> (that they were doing so).

πάντας ἀνθρώπους <u>ἔλαθον</u> ταχέως **ἱέμενοι**.

**They** quickly **hurried**, <u>unobserved</u> by everyone.

Note that in the second example ἔλαθον takes a direct object, πάντας ἀνθρώπους, lit., *they escaped notice of all men*.

Here are two more examples:

ἔλαθον εἰσελθόντες.

*They entered without being seen.*

ἔλαθεν ἑαυτὸν τοῦτο ποιήσας.

*He did this unawares.*

Some other Greek verbs may also be used with supplementary participles:

a.   τυγχάνω, τεύξομαι, ἔτυχον, τετύχηκα, *I happen to* (of a coincidence)

     <u>ἔτυχον</u> **παρόντες** οἱ πρέσβεις.

     *The ambassadors **were present** <u>by chance</u>.*

b.   φθάνω, φθήσομαι, ἔφθασα or ἔφθην, *I anticipate; I do* something *before* someone else

     <u>ἐφθάσαμεν</u> ὑμᾶς **ἀφικόμενοι**.

     **We arrived** <u>before</u> you.

c. φαίνομαι, φανήσομαι or φανοῦμαι, πέφηνα, ἐφάνην, *I appear; I seem*

You have seen this verb meaning *I appear; I seem*, and used with an infinitive, e.g.:

ἡ γυνὴ <u>φαίνεται</u> σώφρων **εἶναι**.

*The woman <u>appears</u> **to be** sensible.*

With a participle instead of an infinitive, it means *I am shown to be; I am proved to be; I am clearly*, e.g.:

ἡ γυνὴ σώφρων **οὖσα** <u>φαίνεται</u>.

*The woman <u>is shown</u> **being/to be** sensible = is clearly sensible.*

## Exercise 20 η

*Read aloud and translate:*

1. οἱ Κορίνθιοι ἐχθροὶ γίγνεσθαι ἐφαίνοντο.
2. οἱ Κορίνθιοι ἐχθροὶ ὄντες φαίνονται.
3. ἄγε, Φίλιππε, τοὺς διώκοντας λάθε ἐν ταύτῃ τῇ τάφρῳ κρυψάμενος.
4. ὁ Φίλιππος τὸν πατέρα ἔφθασε τὸ ὄρος καταβάς.
5. προσιόντος τοῦ ἀνδρὸς ἡ γυνὴ ἔτυχε καθιζομένη ἐν τῇ αὐλῇ (*courtyard*).
6. "φαίνει ἀργὸς οὖσα, ὦ γύναι," ἔφη· "τί οὐκ ἐργάζει;"
7. οἱ Πέρσαι τοὺς Ἕλληνας ἔφθασαν ἀποπλεύσαντες πρὸς τὴν ἤπειρον (*mainland*).
8. οἱ Πέρσαι ἐφαίνοντο οὐ βουλόμενοι ναυμαχεῖν.
9. ὁ δεσπότης τυγχάνει καθεύδων.
10. ἔφθασαν τὸν χειμῶνα εἰς τὸν λιμένα εἰσπλέοντες.

# ΟΙ ΑΘΗΝΑΙΟΙ
# ΤΟΥΣ ΛΑΚΕΔΑΙΜΟΝΙΟΥΣ
# ΑΝΑΜΙΜΝΗΙΣΚΟΥΣΙΝ

*Read the following passages (adapted from Thucydides 1.73–75) and answer the comprehension questions below:*

Nearly fifty years after the battle of Salamis, the Corinthians were urging the Spartans to make war on Athens. Athenian ambassadors, who happened to be in Sparta on other business, took the opportunity to remind the Spartans of what they owed to Athens.

λέγομεν ὅτι ἔν τε τῷ Μαραθῶνι μόνοι ἐκινδῡνεύσαμεν τοῖς βαρβάροις μαχόμενοι, καὶ ἐπεὶ τὸ δεύτερον ἦλθον, οὐ δυνάμενοι κατὰ γῆν ἀμύνεσθαι, εἰσβάντες εἰς τὰς ναῦς πανδημεὶ ἐν Σαλαμῖνι ἐναυμαχήσαμεν, ὥστε οὐκ ἐδύναντο

οἱ βάρβαροι κατὰ πόλιν ἐπιπλέοντες τὴν Πελοπόννησον διαφθείρειν. τεκμήριον δὲ
μέγιστον τούτων αὐτοὶ οἱ βάρβαροι ἐποίησαν· ἐπεὶ γὰρ ταῖς ναυσὶν ἐνῑκήσαμεν, 5
ἐκεῖνοι ὡς τάχιστα τῷ πλέονι τοῦ στρατοῦ ἀνεχώρησαν.

[τῷ Μαραθῶνι, *Marathon* ἐκινδῡνεύσαμεν, *we ran/took the risk* πανδημεί, *all
of us together* κατὰ πόλιν, *city by city* τεκμήριον, *proof* τῷ πλέονι τοῦ
στρατοῦ, *with the greater part of their army*]

1. Who were the only ones to risk fighting the barbarians at Marathon?
2. When the barbarians came a second time how did the Athenians prevent
   them from destroying the Peloponnesus?
3. What proof did the barbarians give of the point that the Athenians are
   making here?

οἱ δὲ Ἀθηναῖοι ἐν τούτοις τρία τὰ ὠφελιμώτατα παρέσχομεν, ἀριθμόν τε νεῶν
πλεῖστον, καὶ ἄνδρα στρατηγὸν σοφώτατον, καὶ προθῡμίᾱν ἀοκνοτάτην. νεῶν μὲν
γὰρ τὰ δύο μέρη τῶν πᾱσῶν παρέσχομεν, Θεμιστοκλέᾱ δὲ στρατηγόν, ὃς ἔπεισε τοὺς
ἄλλους στρατηγοὺς ἐν τοῖς στενοῖς ναυμαχῆσαι, προθῡμίᾱν δὲ τοσαύτην 10
ἐδηλώσαμεν ὥστε ἐπεὶ ἡμῖν κατὰ γῆν οὐδεὶς ἐβοήθει, ἐκλιπόντες τὴν πόλιν καὶ
τὰ οἰκεῖα διαφθείραντες, εἰσβάντες εἰς τὰς ναῦς ἐκινδῡνεύσαμεν. ὑμεῖς μὲν γὰρ
ἐπεὶ ἐφοβεῖσθε ὑπὲρ ὑμῶν καὶ οὐχ ἡμῶν, ἐβοηθήσατε (ὅτε γὰρ ἦμεν ἔτι σῶοι, οὐ
παρεγένεσθε)· ἡμεῖς δὲ κινδῡνεύοντες ἐσώσαμεν ὑμᾶς τε καὶ ἡμᾶς αὐτούς.

[τὰ ὠφελιμώτατα, *the most useful things* ἀριθμόν, *number* προθῡμίᾱν, *eagerness, spirit* ἀοκνοτάτην, *most unhesitating, resolute* τὰ δύο μέρη, *two-thirds*
ἐκλιπόντες, *having left behind* τὰ οἰκεῖα, *our property, belongings* ἔτι, *still*
σῶοι, *safe*]

4. What three most useful things did the Athenians offer in the struggle
   against the barbarians?
5. What percentage of the ships did they supply?
6. What was Themistocles responsible for?
7. By what four actions did the Athenians show their προθῡμίᾱ?
8. What was it that finally prompted the Spartans to send aid?
9. Whom do the Athenians claim to have saved?

τοσαύτην τε προθῡμίᾱν τότε δηλώσαντες καὶ τοσαύτην γνώμην, ἆρ' ἄξιοί 15
ἐσμεν, ὦ Λακεδαιμόνιοι, τοσαύτης ἔχθρᾱς τῶν Ἑλλήνων διὰ τὴν ἀρχὴν ἣν ἔχομεν;
καὶ γὰρ αὐτὴν τήνδε ἀρχὴν ἐλάβομεν οὐ βιασάμενοι, ἀλλὰ ὑμῶν οὐκ ἐθελησάντων
παραμεῖναι πρὸς τὰ ὑπόλοιπα τῶν βαρβάρων, ἡμῖν δὲ προσελθόντων τῶν
συμμάχων καὶ αὐτῶν αἰτησάντων ἡμᾶς ἡγεμόνας καταστῆναι.

[ἔχθρᾱς, *hatred* τὴν ἀρχήν, *the empire* βιασάμενοι, *using force* παραμεῖναι,
*to stand fast, stand your ground* τὰ ὑπόλοιπα, *the remnants, those remaining*
ἡγεμόνας, *leaders*]

10. What do the Athenians ask the Spartans?
11. How do the Athenians claim to have secured their empire?
12. Why did the allies of the Athenians choose the Athenians to be their leaders rather than the Spartans?

### Exercise 20 θ

*Translate into Greek:*

1. The Spartans, having heard both the accusations (τὰ ἐγκλήματα) of (their) allies and the words of the Athenians, were debating (*use* βουλεύομαι περί) the matter alone.
2. Many were saying that the Athenians were acting wrongly (*use present tense of* ἀδικέω) and (that) it was necessary (*use present tense*) to wage war immediately.
3. But Archidamus, being king, advised them not to get into war.
4. "For," he said, "they have (*use dative of the possessor*) very much money and very many ships. We are not able to defeat them by sea. And so we will suffer terribly (*use* κακά *and* πάσχω) ourselves more than we will harm them."
5. But he was not able to persuade the Spartans, who decided to wage war.

# New Testament Greek

### John 2.9–11
### The Wedding at Cana (concluded)

ὡς δὲ ἐγεύσατο ὁ ἀρχιτρίκλῑνος τὸ ὕδωρ οἶνον γεγενημένον καὶ οὐκ ᾔδει πόθεν ἐστίν, οἱ δὲ διάκονοι ᾔδεισαν οἱ ἠντληκότες τὸ ὕδωρ, φωνεῖ τὸν νυμφίον ὁ ἀρχιτρίκλῑνος καὶ λέγει αὐτῷ, "πᾶς ἄνθρωπος πρῶτον τὸν καλὸν οἶνον τίθησιν καὶ ὅταν μεθυσθῶσιν τὸν ἐλάσσω· σὺ τετήρηκας τὸν καλὸν οἶνον ἕως ἄρτι." ταύτην ἐποίησεν ἀρχὴν τῶν σημείων ὁ Ἰησοῦς ἐν Κανὰ τῆς Γαλιλαίᾱς καὶ ἐφανέρωσεν τὴν δόξαν αὐτοῦ, καὶ ἐπίστευσαν εἰς αὐτὸν οἱ μαθηταὶ αὐτοῦ.

[ἐγεύσατο, *tasted* ὁ ἀρχιτρίκλῑνος, *the master of ceremonies* γεγενημένον, *that had become* ᾔδει, *he was aware* (lit., *was knowing*) ᾔδεισαν, *were aware* οἱ ἠντληκότες, *the ones who had drawn* φωνεῖ, *calls* τὸν νυμφίον, *the bridegroom* τίθησιν, *serves* (lit., *puts, places*) ὅταν μεθυσθῶσιν, *when they are drunk* τὸν ἐλάσσω, *the inferior* (wine) τετήρηκας (from τηρέω), *you have saved* ἄρτι, *now* τῶν σημείων, *of his signs/miracles* ἐφανέρωσεν, *he showed* τὴν δόξαν, *the glory* ἐπίστευσαν, ingressive aorist, *came to believe* εἰς, *in* οἱ μαθηταὶ, *the disciples*]

# Classical Greek

## Tyrtaeus

Tyrtaeus of Sparta (fl. 600 B.C.) composed poems to encourage his fellow Spartans to fight bravely in the war against the rebelling Messenians (see essay in Chapter 18). In this poem (12, of which we give lines 23–24, 27–28, and 31–32) he says that the only virtue that matters is courage in war.

αὐτὸς δ' ἐν προμάχοισι πεσὼν φίλον ὤλεσε θῡμόν,

　　ἄστυ τε καὶ λαοὺς καὶ πατέρ' εὐκλεΐσᾱς. . . .

τὸν δ' ὀλυφύρονται μὲν ὁμῶς νέοι ἠδὲ γέροντες,

　　ἀργαλέῳ τε πόθῳ πᾶσα κέκηδε πόλις . . .

οὐδέ ποτε κλέος ἐσθλὸν ἀπόλλυται οὐδ' ὄνομ' αὐτοῦ,

　　ἀλλ' ὑπὸ γῆς περ ἐὼν γΐνεται ἀθάνατος.

[**αὐτὸς δ'**, *and he* (Tyrtaeus has been describing the ideal warrior, and he continues his description here)　**ἐν προμάχοισι**, *in the front line*　**φίλον**, here not *dear*, but *his own* (a Homeric usage)　**ὤλεσε** (from ὄλλῡμι, Attic, ἀπόλλῡμι), gnomic aorist; translate as present, *loses*　**θῡμόν**, *spirit; life*　**λαοὺς**, *the people*　**εὐκλεΐσᾱς**, *bringing glory to* + acc.　**τὸν δ'**, *and him*　**ὀλυφύρονται**, *lament*　**ὁμῶς**, *alike*　**νέοι**, *young men*　**ἠδὲ**, *and*　**ἀργαλέῳ . . . πόθῳ**, *with grievous longing*　**κέκηδε** (from κήδω), perfect with present sense, *mourns*　**κλέος ἐσθλὸν**, *his good fame*　**ἀπόλλυται**, *perishes*　**περ**, *although*　**ἐὼν** = ὢν　**γΐνεται** = γίγνεται]

# New Testament Greek

## John 3.1–3
## Nicodemus Visits Jesus

ἦν δὲ ἄνθρωπος ἐκ τῶν Φαρισαίων, Νικόδημος ὄνομα αὐτῷ, ἄρχων τῶν Ἰουδαίων· οὗτος ἦλθεν πρὸς αὐτὸν νυκτὸς καὶ εἶπεν αὐτῷ, "ῥαββί, οἴδαμεν ὅτι ἀπὸ θεοῦ ἐλήλυθας διδάσκαλος· οὐδεὶς γὰρ δύναται ταῦτα τὰ σημεῖα ποιεῖν ἃ σὺ ποιεῖς, ἐὰν μὴ ᾖ ὁ θεὸς μετ' αὐτοῦ." ἀπεκρίθη Ἰησοῦς καὶ εἶπεν αὐτῷ, "ἀμὴν ἀμὴν λέγω σοι, ἐὰν μή τις γεννηθῇ ἄνωθεν, οὐ δύναται ἰδεῖν τὴν βασιλείᾱν τοῦ θεοῦ."

[**τῶν Φαρισαίων**, *the Pharisees*　**ἄρχων**, *a leader*　**αὐτὸν**: i.e., Jesus　**ῥαββί**, *rabbi, teacher, master*　**ἐλήλυθας**, *you have come*　**διδάσκαλος**, *teacher*　**σημεῖα**, *signs, miracles*　**ἐὰν μὴ**, *unless*　**ᾖ**, subjunctive, *is*　**ἀμὴν**, *verily*　**γεννηθῇ**, *is born*　**ἄνωθεν**, *from above; anew*　**τὴν βασιλείᾱν**, *the kingdom*]

Concluded at the end of Chapter 21

# 21
# Η ΕΚΚΛΗΣΙΑ (α)

πρὸς τὴν Πύκνα σπεύδουσιν ἵνα εἰς τὴν ἐκκλησίᾱν ἐν καιρῷ παρῶσιν.

## VOCABULARY

*Verbs*
  **ἀγορεύω,** *I speak in the Assembly;* more generally,
  *I speak; I say*
  **ἀναγιγνώσκω,** [γνω-] **ἀναγνώσομαι, ἀνέγνων,** *I read*
  **βουλεύω, βουλεύσω, ἐβούλευσα, βεβούλευκα, βεβούλευμαι, ἐβουλεύθην,** active
  or middle, *I deliberate; I plan*
  **θύω, θύσω, ἔθῡσα,** [θυ-] **τέθυκα, τέθυμαι, ἐτύθην,** *I sacrifice*
  **πολεμέω,** *I make war; I go to war*
  **πρόκειμαι, προκείσομαι** + dat.,
  *I lie before*
  **ψηφίζομαι,** [ψηφιε-] **ψηφιοῦμαι,** [ψηφι-] **ἐψηφισάμην, ἐψήφισμαι,** *I vote*
*Nouns*
  **ἡ ἀρχή, τῆς ἀρχῆς,** *beginning; rule; empire*
  **ἡ ἐκκλησίᾱ, τῆς ἐκκλησίᾱς,** *assembly*

  **ὁ πρέσβυς, τοῦ πρέσβεως,** *old man; ambassador;* usually
  pl., **οἱ πρέσβεις, τῶν πρέσβεων,** *ambassadors*
  **ὁ ῥήτωρ, τοῦ ῥήτορος,** *speaker; politician*
*Adjectives*
  **μύριοι, -αι, -α,** *10,000*
  **μῡρίοι -αι, -α,** *numberless, countless*
  **νέος, -ᾱ, -ον,** *young; new*
*Prepositions*
  **ἕνεκα** + preceding gen., *for the sake of; because of*
*Conjunctions*
  **ἐάν** + subjunctive, *if*
  **ἵνα** + subjunctive, *so that, in order to* (expressing purpose)
*Proper Names*
  **οἱ Πελοποννήσιοι, τῶν Πελοποννησίων,** *Peloponnesians*
  **ἡ Πνύξ, τῆς Πυκνός,** *the Pnyx* (the hill in Athens on which the Assemblies were held)

72

οὐ πολλῷ δ' ὕστερον ἀναστὰς ὁ Δικαιόπολις τῷ Φιλίππῳ,
"ἀνάστηθι, ὦ παῖ," ἔφη· "καιρὸς γάρ ἐστι πορεύεσθαι. εὐθὺς οὖν
σπεύδωμεν πρὸς τὴν πόλιν." ὁρμήσαντες οὖν δι' ὀλίγου πολλοῖς
ἐνετύγχανον αὐτουργοῖς Ἀθήνᾱζε πορευομένοις. ὁ οὖν Δικαιόπολις
γέροντί τινι προσχωρήσᾱς, ὃς ἐγγὺς αὐτοῦ ἐβάδιζεν, ἤρετο τίνος      5
ἕνεκα τοσοῦτοι Ἀθήνᾱζε σπεύδουσιν. ὁ δέ, "τί λέγεις, ὦ ἄνθρωπε;"
ἔφη· "ἆρα τοῦτο ἀγνοεῖς, ὅτι τήμερον ἐκκλησίᾱ γενήσεται; πάντες
οὖν πρὸς τὸ ἄστυ σπεύδομεν τούτου ἕνεκα, ἵνα ἐν τῇ ἐκκλησίᾳ τῶν
ῥητόρων ἀκούωμεν. πράγματα γὰρ μέγιστα τῷ δήμῳ πρόκειται περὶ
ὧν χρὴ βουλεύεσθαι." ὁ δὲ Δικαιόπολις, "ἀλλὰ τίνα δὴ πρόκειται τῷ      10
δήμῳ, ὦ γέρον;" ὁ δέ, "ἀλλὰ τίς τοῦτο ἀγνοεῖ, ὅτι χρὴ βουλεύεσθαι
πότερον πόλεμον ποιησώμεθα πρὸς τοὺς Πελοποννησίους ἢ τὴν
εἰρήνην σώσωμεν;"

[σπεύδωμεν, *let us hurry*    ἀκούωμεν, *we may hear*    ποιησώμεθα, *we should
make*]

ὁ δὲ Δικαιόπολις, "ἀλλὰ τί νέον ἐγένετο; πάλαι γὰρ ἐχθροί εἰσιν
οἱ Πελοποννήσιοι ἀλλ' οὐκ εἰς πόλεμον κατέστημεν ἀλλὰ μένουσιν      15
αἱ σπονδαί. τί οὖν νῦν γε δεῖ περὶ τοῦ πολέμου διακρίνειν;" ὁ δὲ
γέρων, "ἀλλὰ καὶ τοῦτο ἀγνοεῖς, ὅτι πρέσβεις νεωστὶ ἔπεμψαν οἱ
Λακεδαιμόνιοι οἳ ταῦτα εἶπον· 'Λακεδαιμόνιοι βούλονται τὴν
εἰρήνην εἶναι· εἰρήνη δ' ἔσται, ἐὰν τοὺς Ἕλληνας αὐτονόμους
ἀφῆτε'; κελεύουσιν οὖν ἡμᾶς τὴν ἀρχὴν ἀφιέναι. τοῦτο οὖν      20
βουλεύεσθαι δεῖ, πότερον τὴν ἀρχὴν ἀφῶμεν ἢ πόλεμον πρὸς τοὺς
Πελοποννησίους ποιησώμεθα." ὁ δὲ Δικαιόπολις, "ὦ Ζεῦ," ἔφη·
"τοῦτ' ἔστιν ἐκεῖνο. νῦν γὰρ ἐπίσταμαι τί οἱ Κορίνθιοι εἰς ὀργὴν
καταστάντες λίθους ἐφ' ἡμᾶς ἐφίεσαν, γνόντες ὅτι Ἀθηναῖοί ἐσμεν.
ἀλλὰ σπεύδωμεν, ὦ παῖ, ἵνα ἐν καιρῷ παρῶμεν."      25

[διακρίνειν, *to decide*   νεωστὶ, *recently*   αὐτονόμους, *independent, free*   ἀφῆτε
(from ἀφίημι), *you let . . . go*   ἀφῶμεν (from ἀφίημι), *we should let go, give up*
παρῶμεν (from πάρειμι), *we may be present*]

εὐθὺς οὖν ὥρμησαν καὶ εἰς τὰς πύλᾱς ἀφικόμενοι πρὸς τὴν
Πύκνα ἔτρεχον. ἐκεῖ δὲ ἤδη συνηγείρετο ὁ δῆμος καὶ μῡρίοι

παρῆσαν, τοὺς πρυτάνεις μένοντες. δι' ὀλίγου δ' εἰσελθόντες οἵ τε
πρυτάνεις καὶ ὁ ἐπιστάτης καὶ οἱ ἄλλοι βουλευταὶ ἐκάθιζον. ἔπειτα
δὲ ἐσίγησαν μὲν οἱ παρόντες, ὁ δὲ ἱερεὺς πρὸς τὸν βωμὸν προσελθὼν    30
τό τε ἱερεῖον ἔθῡσε καὶ τοῖς θεοῖς ηὔξατο, ἵνα τῷ δήμῳ εὐμενεῖς ὦσιν.
ἐνταῦθα δὴ ὁ μὲν ἐπιστάτης τὸν κήρῡκα ἐκέλευσε τὸ προβούλευμα
ἀναγνῶναι. ὁ δὲ κῆρυξ τὸ προβούλευμα ἀναγνοὺς τὸν δῆμον ἤρετο
πότερον δοκεῖ εὐθὺς ψηφίζεσθαι ἢ χρὴ πρότερον βουλεύεσθαι περὶ
τοῦ πρᾱ́γματος. ὁ δὲ δῆμος ἐχειροτόνησε, δηλῶν ὅτι πάντες βού-     35
λονται περὶ τοῦ πρᾱ́γματος βουλεύεσθαι τοσούτου ὄντος. ἐνταῦθα
δὴ ὁ κῆρυξ εἶπεν· "τίς ἀγορεύειν βούλεται;" τῶν οὖν ῥητόρων πολλοὶ
πρὸς τὸ βῆμα παριόντες ἠγόρευον, ἄλλοι μὲν λέγοντες ὅτι χρὴ
πολεμεῖν, ἄλλοι δὲ ὅτι οὐδὲν χρὴ ἐμπόδιον εἶναι τῆς εἰρήνης.

[τοὺς **πρυτάνεις**, *the presidents of the tribes of citizens*   ὁ **ἐπιστάτης**, *the chairman*
**βουλευταὶ**, *councilors*   **ὦσιν** (from εἰμί), *they might be*   τὸ **προβούλευμα**, *the motion for deliberation*   **ἐχειροτόνησε**, *voted* (by show of hands)   τὸ **βῆμα**, *the
speakers' platform*   **ἄλλοι**...**ἄλλοι**, *some ... others*   **ἐμπόδιον** + gen., *in the way
of* ]

### PRINCIPAL PARTS: Dental Stems (-δ-, -θ-)

σπεύδω, σπεύσω, ἔσπευσα, ἔσπευκα, ἔσπευσμαι, *I hurry*
πείθω, πείσω, ἔπεισα, πέπεικα (*I have persuaded*) or [ποιθ-] πέποιθα (+ dat.,
   *I trust*), [πειθ-] πέπεισμαι, ἐπείσθην, *I persuade;* middle, present, imperfect,
   and future + dat., *I obey*

### WORD STUDY

*Explain the meaning of the following English words with reference to their
Greek stems:*

1. anthropology
2. philanthropy
3. anthropomorphous (ἡ μορφή = ?)
4. anthropophagous (φαγ- = ?)
5. misanthrope (μῑσέω = ?)
6. pithecanthropus (ὁ πίθηκος = ?)

---

### Greek Wisdom

#### Heraclitus

ἀνθρώπων ὁ σοφώτατος πρὸς θεὸν πίθηκος φανεῖται καὶ σοφίᾳ καὶ κάλλει καὶ τοῖς
ἄλλοις πᾶσιν. Fragment 83 Diels

# GRAMMAR

## 1.  The Subjunctive Mood

Verbs in the subjunctive mood are used in certain types of main and subordinate clauses (see Grammar 3).  Subjunctives are usually very easy to recognize from the long vowels ω or η, which occur in all forms, except when obscured in some forms of the contract verbs.  Here are some sentences with subjunctives taken from the reading passage above:

a.  εὐθὺς οὖν **σπεύδωμεν** πρὸς τὴν πόλιν.
    ***Let us hurry*** *immediately to the city.*

b.  σπεύδομεν τούτου ἕνεκα, ἵνα ἐν τῇ ἐκκλησίᾳ τῶν ῥητόρων **ἀκούωμεν.**
    *We are hurrying for this reason, so that **we may hear** the speakers in the Assembly.*

c.  πότερον πόλεμον **ποιησώμεθα** πρὸς τοὺς Πελοποννησίους ἢ εἰρήνην **σώσωμεν**;
    ***Should we make*** *war against the Peloponnesians or **should we keep** peace?*

## 2.  Forms of the Subjunctive

There are no imperfect or future subjunctives.

The subjunctive of εἰμί, *I am*, is as follows: ὦ, ᾖ-ς, ᾖ, ὦ-μεν, ἦ-τε, ὦ-σι(ν). These same letters are used to form other active subjunctives, as seen in the charts below.

### Present Active

| Indicative | Subjunctive | |
|---|---|---|
| λύω | λύ-ω | |
| λύεις | λύ-η-ς | |
| λύει | λύ-η | |
| λύομεν | λύ-ω-μεν | |
| λύετε | λύ-η-τε | |
| λύουσι(ν) | λύ-ω-σι(ν) | |
| | | |
| φιλῶ | φιλέ-ω  > | φιλῶ |
| φιλεῖς | φιλέ-η-ς  > | φιλῇς |
| φιλεῖ | φιλέ-η  > | φιλῇ |
| φιλοῦμεν | φιλέ-ω-μεν  > | φιλῶμεν |
| φιλεῖτε | φιλέ-η-τε  > | φιλῆτε |
| φιλοῦσι(ν) | φιλέ-ω-σι(ν)  > | φιλῶσι(ν) |

| | | |
|---|---|---|
| τῑμῶ | τῑμά-ω > | τῑμῶ |
| τῑμᾷς | τῑμά-ῃ-ς > | τῑμᾷς |
| τῑμᾷ | τῑμά-ῃ > | τῑμᾷ |
| τῑμῶμεν | τῑμά-ω-μεν > | τῑμῶμεν |
| τῑμᾶτε | τῑμά-η-τε > | τῑμᾶτε |
| τῑμῶσι(ν) | τῑμά-ω-σι(ν) > | τῑμῶσι(ν) |

| | | |
|---|---|---|
| δηλῶ | δηλό-ω > | δηλῶ |
| δηλοῖς | δηλό-ῃ-ς > | δηλοῖς |
| δηλοῖ | δηλό-ῃ > | δηλοῖ |
| δηλοῦμεν | δηλό-ω-μεν > | δηλῶμεν |
| δηλοῦτε | δηλό-η-τε > | δηλῶτε |
| δηλοῦσι(ν) | δηλό-ω-σι(ν) > | δηλῶσι(ν) |

Note that the usual contractions take place. Note that -α- contract verbs have identical forms in the indicative and subjunctive, singular and plural, and that -o- contract verbs have identical forms in the singular indicative and subjunctive.

## Present Middle
### (Contracted Forms Only)

| Indicative | Subjunctive | Indicative | Subjunctive |
|---|---|---|---|
| λΰομαι | λΰωμαι | φιλοῦμαι | φιλῶμαι |
| λΰει or λΰῃ | λΰῃ | φιλεῖ or φιλῇ | φιλῇ |
| λΰεται | λΰηται | φιλεῖται | φιλῆται |
| λῡόμεθα | λῡώμεθα | φιλούμεθα | φιλώμεθα |
| λΰεσθε | λΰησθε | φιλεῖσθε | φιλῆσθε |
| λΰονται | λΰωνται | φιλοῦνται | φιλῶνται |
| τῑμῶμαι | τῑμῶμαι | δηλοῦμαι | δηλῶμαι |
| τῑμᾷ | τῑμᾷ | δηλοῖ | δηλοῖ |
| τῑμᾶται | τῑμᾶται | δηλοῦται | δηλῶται |
| τῑμώμεθα | τῑμώμεθα | δηλούμεθα | δηλώμεθα |
| τῑμᾶσθε | τῑμᾶσθε | δηλοῦσθε | δηλῶσθε |
| τῑμῶνται | τῑμῶνται | δηλοῦνται | δηλῶνται |

## Aorist Active and Middle Subjunctives

Note that there is no augment in the subjunctive mood and that the middle voice uses primary endings.

Sigmatic 1st Aorist (e.g., of λΰω):

Sigmatic 1st Aorist **Active Indicative**: ἔλῡσα, etc.

Sigmatic 1st Aorist **Active Subjunctive**:
λΰσω, λΰσῃς, λΰσῃ, λΰσωμεν, λΰσητε, λΰσωσι(ν)

Sigmatic 1st Aorist **Middle Indicative**: ἐλῡσάμην, etc.
Sigmatic 1st Aorist **Middle Subjunctive**:
λύσωμαι, λύσῃ, λύσηται, λῡσώμεθα, λύσησθε, λύσωνται

Asigmatic 1st Aorist of Liquid Verbs (e.g., of αἴρω):

Asigmatic 1st Aorist **Active Indicative**: ἦρα, etc.
Asigmatic 1st Aorist **Active Subjunctive**:
ἄρω, ἄρῃς, ἄρῃ, ἄρωμεν, ἄρητε, ἄρωσι(ν)

Asigmatic 1st Aorist **Middle Indicative**: ἠράμην, etc.
Asigmatic 1st Aorist **Middle Subjunctive**:
ἄρωμαι, ἄρῃ, ἄρηται, ἀρώμεθα, ἄρησθε, ἄρωνται

Thematic 2nd Aorist (e.g., of λείπω):

Thematic 2nd Aorist **Active Indicative**: ἔλιπον, etc.
Thematic 2nd Aorist **Active Subjunctive**:
λίπω, λίπῃς, λίπῃ, λίπωμεν, λίπητε, λίπωσι(ν)

Thematic 2nd Aorist **Middle Indicative**: ἐλιπόμην, etc.
Thematic 2nd Aorist **Middle Subjunctive**:
λίπωμαι, λίπῃ, λίπηται, λιπώμεθα, λίπησθε, λίπωνται

Athematic 2nd Aorist (e.g., of βαίνω):

Athematic 2nd Aorist **Active Indicative**: ἔβην, etc.
Athematic 2nd Aorist **Active Subjunctive**:
βῶ, βῇς, βῇ, βῶμεν, βῆτε, βῶσι(ν)

### Aorist Passive Subjunctives

Verbs with -θη- 1st aorist passives (e.g., λύω):

-θη- 1st Aorist **Passive Indicative**: ἐλύθην, etc.
-θη- 1st Aorist **Passive Subjunctive** (note the -θε- stem and
the accent; λυ-θέ-ω > λυθῶ):
λυθῶ, λυθῇς, λυθῇ, λυθῶμεν, λυθῆτε, λυθῶσι(ν)

Verbs with -η- 2nd aorist passives (e.g., γράφω):

-η- 2nd Aorist **Passive Indicative**: ἐγράφην, etc.
-η- 2nd Aorist **Passive Subjunctive** (note the -θε- stem and
the accent; γραφ-έ-ω > γραφῶ):
γραφῶ, γραφῇς, γραφῇ, γραφῶμεν, γραφῆτε, γραφῶσι(ν)

---

## Greek Wisdom

### Heraclitus

μάχεσθαι χρὴ τὸν δῆμον ὑπὲρ τοῦ νόμου ὥσπερ τείχους.  Fragment 44 Diels

### Exercise 21α

*Fill in the subjunctive forms on all Verb Charts completed for Book I except for the charts for Exercise 11θ. Keep the charts for reference.*

## 3. Uses of the Subjunctive Mood

a. The subjunctive (usually 1st person plural) is used in exhortations, as in example a in Grammar 1 above (page 75). This is called the *hortatory subjunctive*, and its negative is μή, e.g.:

ἀνδρείως **μαχώμεθα**. ***Let us fight*** bravely.

μὴ εὐθὺς **ἴωμεν**. ***Let us*** not ***go*** immediately.

μὴ τοιοῦτο **ποιήσωμεν**. ***Let us*** not ***do*** such a thing.

Note that the difference between the present and aorist subjunctive is in aspect, not in time; i.e., the present subjunctive is used when the action is viewed as a process, and the aorist is used when the action is viewed as an event. This applies to the other uses below as well.

b. The present or aorist subjunctive (usually 1st person) may be used in *deliberative questions*, as in example c in Grammar 1 above (page 75) and in the following:

τί **ποιῶμεν**; πότερον **μένωμεν** ἢ οἴκαδε **ἐπανίωμεν**;
*What **are we to do**? **Are we to stay** or **return** home?*

Remember that the double question is introduced by πότερον, *whether*, which is not translated.

c. The *aorist* subjunctive (2nd person singular or plural) is used with μή in *prohibitions* or *negative commands*, e.g.:

μὴ τοῦτο **ποιήσῃς**. ***Do*** not ***do*** this.

d. The subjunctive is used in subordinate clauses introduced by ἵνα, ὅπως, or ὡς to express *purpose*, as in example b in Grammar 1 above (page 75). A negative purpose clause is introduced by ἵνα μή, ὅπως μή, ὡς μή, or simply μή. The following are further examples:

ἀνδρείως μαχόμεθα **ἵνα** τὴν πατρίδα **σώσωμεν**.
*We are fighting bravely **so that we may save** our fatherland (= **to save** our fatherland).*

σπεύδουσιν **ὅπως μὴ** ὀψὲ **ἀφίκωνται**.
*They are hurrying **so that they may not arrive** late (= **lest they arrive** late = **so as not to arrive** late).*

Note that several different translations are possible in English. Note also, however, that Attic Greek prose does not use a simple infinitive to express purpose as we most commonly do in English.

e.  The subjunctive is used in some types of *conditional clauses*, e.g.:

εἰρήνη δ' ἔσται, **ἐὰν** τοὺς Ἕλληνας αὐτονόμους **ἀφῆτε**.
*There will be peace, **if you let** the Greeks **go** free.*

Note the use of ἐάν (= εἰ + ἄν).

## Exercise 21β

*Change the following to the subjunctive:*

| | | | | | |
|---|---|---|---|---|---|
| 1. | λύομεν | 8. | εἵλοντο | 15. | ηὔξατο |
| 2. | ἔλῡσε(ν) | 9. | ἐγένετο | 16. | ἐλύθησαν |
| 3. | τῑμᾷ | 10. | ἐφίλησας | 17. | ἐγράφη |
| 4. | δηλοῦμεν | 11. | μαχόμεθα | 18. | ἐβάλομεν |
| 5. | λύονται | 12. | ἀπέθανε(ν) | 19. | ἐτῑμήθης |
| 6. | ἐλῡσάμην | 13. | εἴδετε | 20. | ἀφῑκόμεθα |
| 7. | ἔλαβον (2 ways) | 14. | ἐβουλεύσατο | 21. | ἐφάνησαν |

## Exercise 21γ

*Read aloud and translate into English; identify each use of the subjunctive:*

1.  στῆτε, ὦ φίλοι· σκοπῶμεν τί ποιήσωμεν.
2.  πότερον οἴκαδε ἐπανέλθωμεν ἢ ἐν τοῖς ὄρεσιν μένωμεν;
3.  ἑσπέρᾱς γιγνομένης, μὴ μένωμεν ἐν τοῖς ὄρεσιν ἀλλὰ οἴκαδε σπεύδωμεν.
4.  πῶς οἴκαδε ἀφικώμεθα; τὴν γὰρ ὁδὸν ἀγνοοῦμεν.
5.  ἰδού, ἔξεστιν ἐκεῖνον τὸν ποιμένα ἐρέσθαι τίνα ὁδὸν ἑλώμεθα.
6.  μὴ ἀποφύγῃς, ὦ γέρον, ἀλλ' εἰπὲ ἡμῖν τίς ὁδὸς πρὸς τὸ ἄστυ φέρει.
7.  μὴ ἐκεῖσε νῦν γε ὁρμήσητε· οὐ γὰρ ἀφίξεσθε πρὸ νυκτός.
8.  τί ποιῶμεν, ὦ φίλοι; ὁ γὰρ ποιμὴν λέγει ὅτι οὐ δυνάμεθα ἀφικέσθαι πρὸ νυκτός.
9.  εἰς τὸ πεδίον καταβάντες οἰκίᾱν τινὰ ζητῶμεν ἵνα ἀναπαυώμεθα.
10.  ἡμέρᾱς δὲ γενομένης, εὐθὺς ὁρμήσωμεν.

## Exercise 21δ

*Translate into Greek:*

1.  The Athenians are deliberating whether they are to make war against the Peloponnesians.
2.  Let us hurry to the city and listen to the speakers.
3.  Are we to yield to the enemy or save the city? (*Use aorist subjunctives in this and the next sentences.*)
4.  Don't listen to the ambassadors; they are not telling the truth.
5.  Let us send them away immediately.

# The Athenian Democracy

The radical democracy of Pericles' time had evolved over many years. Solon, in his reforms of 594/593 B.C. (see essay, Book I, Chapter 8, page 118), had broken the old aristocratic (*eupatrid*) monopoly of power by making wealth, not birth, the criterion for political privilege. He also gave the Assembly a more important role in decision making; it elected the nine magistrates (archons) from the top two property classes and was supported by a new Council of 400, which prepared business for debate in the Assembly and which also formed a counterweight to the old Council of the Areopagus, which before Solon's reforms had been the governing body of Athens. The most democratic feature of Solon's constitution was the Heliaea; this was the Assembly sitting as a court of appeals from the decisions of magistrates.

Solon's constitution continued to function throughout the following period of strife between factions of the nobility and throughout the ensuing tyranny of Pisistratus and his son Hippias. When Hippias was driven out in 510 B.C., the noble families began to compete for power once more. Herodotus (5.66) says, "Two men were preeminent, Cleisthenes the Alcmeonid and Isagoras. These were involved in a struggle for power, and Cleisthenes, being worsted, took the people into partnership." In 508 Isagoras was driven into exile, and Cleisthenes put through a program of reforms, which established a moderate democracy.

First, he probably extended the citizenship, so that every free man, landless or not, had the right to vote. Secondly, to prevent the recurrence of dynastic rivalry, he instituted an elaborate system that destroyed the territorial basis of the nobles' power. He divided Attica into 139 demes (see essay, Book I, Chapter 3, pages 28–29), each with its own assembly and *demarch*; he abolished the four old Athenian tribes (φῦλαί), based on kinship, and replaced them with ten new tribes, which were artificial political units, so constituted that the political influence of clan and locality was ended.

This photograph shows the Acropolis from the west with the Areopagus (the hill of Ares, god of war) in the foreground; here the ancient Council of the Areopagus met.

The ten new tribes formed the basic administrative and military units of the state. Each tribe (φῦλή) provided fifty members (*councilors*, βουλευταί) to the Council (βουλή) of 500, which now replaced Solon's Council of 400; every deme elected a fixed number of councilors in proportion to its size. The new Council had a key role; it prepared business for the Assembly in its probouleutic function and was also responsible as an executive committee of the Assembly for seeing that decisions of the people were carried out. In the military sphere, each tribe provided one brigade, which was commanded by one of the ten generals elected by the Assembly.

The Assembly of all adult male citizens was sovereign. It elected the nine archons, whose functions were largely judicial, and the ten generals; it met regularly to debate issues brought before the people by the Council, and it continued to function as a court of appeals as the Heliaea. The ancient Council of the Areopagus still had important but vague powers, especially in judicial matters and as guardian of the constitution.

To Cleisthenes, probably, should also be ascribed the institution of ostracism. Once a year the Assembly was asked whether it wished to send one of the citizens into exile. If the people voted in favor of an ostracism, a meeting was held at which every citizen scratched on a fragment of pottery (ὄστρακον) the name of the politician he would like to see banished. The man against whom most ostraca were cast was sent off into honorable exile for ten years.

In 487 B.C. a change was introduced by which the nine archons were selected by lot (from the top two property classes) instead of by election. It followed that the importance of the archons declined while that of the generals, who were still elected, increased. In 462 B.C. a statesman named Ephialtes, supported by the young Pericles, put through measures that stripped the Areopagus of its powers and transferred them to the Assembly, Council, or popular courts, which now became courts of first instance instead of courts of appeal.

Ephialtes was assassinated soon after his reforms, and his place as leader of the people was taken by Pericles, who dominated the Assembly until his death in 429 B.C., thirty-two years later. The key principles of democracy that had long been recognized were the rule of law and the equality of all citizens before the law (ἰσονομία). To these Pericles added two further principles, which the Greeks considered characteristic of radical democracy, namely, selection for office by lot and payment of all officials. Lot had been used for selecting the archons since 487 B.C., but now it was extended to the selection of councilors. At the same time the archonship was opened to the third property class, the ζευγῖται, those able to keep only a team of oxen (ζεῦγος). Now that any citizen, rich or poor, might be selected for office, it became essential that officials should be paid. Soon pay was instituted not only for the archons and councilors but also for the 10,000 members of the jury panel, who received a small wage for each day they sat in one of the courts into which the Heliaea was now divided.

# Η ΕΚΚΛΗΣΙΑ (β)

## VOCABULARY

*Verbs*

ἄρχω, ἄρξω, ἦρξα, ἦργμαι,
ἤρχθην + gen., active or middle, *I begin;* + gen., active,
*I rule*

ἐπιβουλεύω + dat., *I plot
against*

νομίζω, [νομιε-] νομιῶ, [νομι-]
ἐνόμισα, νενόμικα, νενό-
μισμαι, ἐνομίσθην, *I think*

πληρόω, *I fill*

προάγω, *I lead forward*

*Nouns*

ἡ ἀνάγκη, τῆς ἀνάγκης, *necessity*

ἡ δίκη, τῆς δίκης, *custom; justice; right; lawsuit; penalty*

ἡ δύναμις, τῆς δυνάμεως,
*power; strength; forces
(military)*

ὁ ἰδιώτης, τοῦ ἰδιώτου, *private
person*

ἡ στρατιᾱ, τῆς στρατιᾶς,
*army*

ἡ τῑμή, τῆς τῑμῆς, *honor*

ὁ τρόπος, τοῦ τρόπου, *manner;
way*

ἡ χώρᾱ, τῆς χώρᾱς, *land*

*Adjectives*

ἀδύνατος, -ον, *impossible; incapable*

δυνατός, -ή, -όν, *possible; capable*

ἑκάτερος, -ᾱ, -ον, *each* (of two)

ὅμοιος, -ᾱ, -ον + dat., *like*

τελευταῖος, -ᾱ, -ον, *last*

τοιόσδε, τοιάδε (note the accent), τοιόνδε, *such* (as the following)

τοιοῦτος, τοιαύτη, τοιοῦτο,
*such*

χρόνιος, -ᾱ, -ον, *lengthy*

*Preposition*

κατά + acc., *down;* distributive, *each; by; on; according
to;* of time, <u>*at*</u>

*Adverbs*

ἰδίᾳ, *privately*

πεζῇ, *on foot*

*Expression*

ἀνάγκη ἐστί(ν), *it is necessary*

## Spelling

The following passage and the passage at the end of this chapter are
adapted from the historian Thucydides. He used the Ionic spelling -σσ- in
words that in Attic have -ττ-, e.g., πράσσειν for πράττειν; he used the Homeric
and early Attic spelling ξύν (ξυν-) for σύν (συν-); and he used ἐς (ἐσ-) instead
of εἰς (εἰσ-) and αἰεί instead of ἀεί. We have preserved these spellings in the
passages from Thucydides. In Chapter 22 when the narrative returns to Dicaeopolis and his family, we use the Attic forms. Chapter 23, based on Thucydides, again uses his spellings. Chapter 24 on the education of Philip, which
includes a passage adapted from Plato, uses the Attic forms. In chapters 25
and 26 the readings are based on Herodotus, and some features of his Ionic
Greek are preserved, e.g., ἐς for εἰς and πρᾱ́σσω for πρᾱ́ττω. More features of
his Ionic Greek are preseved in the readings in chapters 27 and 28.

τέλος δὲ παρελθὼν Περικλῆς ὁ Ξανθίππου, ἀνὴρ κατ᾽ ἐκεῖνον
τὸν χρόνον πρῶτος Ἀθηναίων, λέγειν τε καὶ πράσσειν δυνατώτατος,
παρῄνει τοιάδε· "τῆς μὲν γνώμης, ὦ Ἀθηναῖοι, αἰεὶ τῆς αὐτῆς ἔχομαι,
μὴ εἴκειν Πελοποννησίοις. δῆλον γάρ ἐστιν ὅτι οἱ Λακεδαιμόνιοι καὶ
πρότερον καὶ νῦν ἡμῖν ἐπιβουλεύουσιν. ἐν μὲν γὰρ ταῖς ξυνθήκαις    5
εἴρητο ὅτι χρὴ δίκας μὲν τῶν διαφορῶν ἀλλήλοις διδόναι καὶ
δέχεσθαι, ἔχειν δὲ ἑκατέρους ἃ ἔχομεν· νῦν δὲ οὔτε δίκας αὐτοὶ
ᾔτησαν οὔτε ἡμῶν διδόντων δέχονται, ἀλλὰ βούλονται πολέμῳ
μᾶλλον ἢ λόγοις τὰ ἐγκλήματα διαλύεσθαι. πολλά τε γὰρ ἄλλα ἡμῖν
ἐπιτάσσουσιν, καὶ οἱ τελευταῖοι οἵδε ἥκοντες ἡμᾶς κελεύουσι τοὺς    10
Ἕλληνας αὐτονόμους ἀφιέναι. ἐγὼ οὖν ὑμῖν παραινῶ μηδὲν εἴκειν
ἀλλὰ τὴν ἀρχὴν σῴζειν καὶ πολεμεῖν παρασκευάζεσθαι.

[ἔχομαι + gen., *I cling to*     ταῖς ξυνθήκαις, *the treaty*     εἴρητο (from εἴρω; see page
195) *it was stated* (lit., pluperfect, *it had been stated*)     δίκας ... τῶν διαφορῶν ...
διδόναι καὶ δέχεσθαι, *to give one another and to accept arbitration of (our) differences*     τὰ ἐγκλήματα διαλύεσθαι, *to settle their complaints*     ἐπιτάσσουσιν, *they
impose, dictate*]

"ἐὰν δὲ ἐς πόλεμον καταστῶμεν, τὰ τοῦ πολέμου οὐκ
ἀσθενέστερα ἕξομεν· γνῶτε γὰρ ἀκούοντες· αὐτουργοὶ γάρ εἰσιν οἱ
Πελοποννήσιοι καὶ οὔτε ἰδίᾳ οὔτ᾽ ἐν κοινῷ χρήματά ἐστιν αὐτοῖς.    15
καὶ οἱ τοιοῦτοι οὔτε ναῦς πληροῦν οὔτε πεζὰς στρατιὰς πολλάκις
ἐκπέμπειν δύνανται· οὐ γὰρ ἐθέλουσιν ἀπὸ τῶν κλήρων πολὺν
χρόνον ἀπεῖναι, καὶ τὰ χρήματα δεῖ ἀπὸ τῶν ἑαυτῶν ἐσφέρειν. μάχῃ
οὖν μιᾷ πρὸς ἅπαντας Ἕλληνας δυνατοί εἰσιν οἱ Πελοποννήσιοι καὶ
οἱ ξύμμαχοι ἀντέχειν, πόλεμον δὲ χρόνιον ποιεῖσθαι πρὸς ἡμᾶς    20
ἀδύνατοι.

[ἀσθενέστερα, *weaker*     ἐν κοινῷ, *in the treasury*     τῶν κλήρων, *their farms*
ἀπὸ τῶν ἑαυτῶν, *from their own (private property)*]

"ἡμεῖς γὰρ τῆς θαλάσσης κρατοῦμεν. καὶ ἐὰν ἐπὶ τὴν χώρᾱν
ἡμῶν πεζῇ ἴωσιν, ἡμεῖς ἐπὶ τὴν ἐκείνων πλευσόμεθα. μέγα γάρ ἐστι τὸ
τῆς θαλάσσης κράτος. πόλιν γὰρ οἰκοῦμεν νήσῳ ὁμοίᾱν ἣν οὐδεὶς
πολέμιος δύναται λαβεῖν. χρὴ οὖν τὴν μὲν γῆν καὶ τὰς οἰκίᾱς    25
ἀφεῖναι, τὴν δὲ θάλασσαν καὶ τὴν πόλιν φυλάσσειν.

"νῦν δὲ τούτοις ἀποκρῑνάμενοι ἀποπέμπωμεν ὅτι τὰς πόλεις αὐτονόμους ἀφήσομεν ἐᾱν καὶ ἐκεῖνοι ἀφῶσι τὰς πόλεις ἃς ὑπηκόους ἔχουσιν, δίκᾱς τε ὅτι ἐθέλομεν δοῦναι κατὰ τὰς ξυνθήκᾱς, πολέμου δὲ οὐκ ἄρξομεν, εἰ δὲ ἄρξουσιν ἐκεῖνοι, ἀμυνούμεθα.　　　30

[ὑπηκόους, subjected, obedient　δίκᾱς ... δοῦναι, to submit to arbitration　τὰς ξυνθήκᾱς, the treaty]

"ταῦτα δὲ ἐπίστασθαι χρή, ὅτι ἀνάγκη ἐστὶ πολεμεῖν, καὶ ὅτι ἐκ τῶν μεγίστων κινδῡνων καὶ πόλει καὶ ἰδιώτῃ μέγισται τῑμαὶ περιγίγνονται. οἱ μὲν πατέρες ῡμῶν τούς τε βαρβάρους ἀπεώσαντο καὶ ἐς τὴν νῦν δύναμιν προήγαγον τὴν πόλιν, ῡμᾶς δὲ οὐ χρὴ αὐτῶν κακῑ́ονας γίγνεσθαι, ἀλλὰ τούς τε ἐχθροὺς παντὶ τρόπῳ ἀμῡ́νεσθαι　35 καὶ τοῖς ἐπιγιγνομένοις τὴν πόλιν μὴ ἐλάσσονα παραδοῦναι."

[περιγίγνονται, result　ἀπεώσαντο (from ἀπωθέω), they pushed back, drove off τοῖς ἐπιγιγνομένοις, those coming after, your descendants]

ὁ μὲν οὖν Περικλῆς τοιαῦτα εἶπεν, οἱ δὲ Ἀθηναῖοι νομίσαντες αὐτὸν ἄριστα παραινεῖν, ἐψηφίσαντο ἃ ἐκέλευε, καὶ τοῖς Λακεδαιμονίοις ἀπεκρῑ́ναντο κατὰ πάντα ὡς ἔφρασεν. οἱ δὲ πρέσβεις ἀπεχώρησαν ἐπ' οἴκου καὶ οὐκέτι ὕστερον ἐπρεσβεύοντο.　　40

[κατὰ πάντα, point by point　ἐπρεσβεύοντο, were not coming as ambassadors]

—adapted from Thucydides 1.140–146

## PRINCIPAL PARTS: Stems in -ζ- and -ιζ-

θαυμάζω, θαυμάσομαι, ἐθαύμασα, τεθαύμακα, τεθαύμασμαι, ἐθαυμάσθην, intransitive, I am amazed; transitive, I wonder at; I admire
φράζω, φράσω, ἔφρασα, πέφρακα, πέφρασμαι, ἐφράσθην, I show; I tell (of); I explain; middle and aorist passive in middle sense, I think about; I consider
κομίζω, [κομιε-] κομιῶ, [κομι-] ἐκόμισα, κεκόμικα, κεκόμισμαι, ἐκομίσθην, I bring; I take
ὀργίζομαι, [ὀργιε-] ὀργιοῦμαι or [ὀργισ-] ὀργισθήσομαι, ὤργισμαι, ὠργίσθην, I grow angry; I am angry; + dat., I grow angry at; I am angry at

## WORD BUILDING

*Deduce or find the meanings of the words in the following sets:*

1. ἡ δίκη; δίκαιος, -ᾱ, -ον; ἡ δικαιοσύνη; ἄδικος, -ον; ἀδικέω; τὸ ἀδίκημα
2. ἡ βουλή; βουλεύω; ὁ βουλευτής; τὸ βούλευμα; προβουλεύω; τὸ προβούλευμα

# GRAMMAR

## 4. The Subjunctive of -μι Verbs

εἰμί, *I am*
Present Active:

    ὦ, ᾖς, ᾖ, ὦμεν, ἦτε, ὦσι(ν)

εἶμι, *I will go*
Present Active:

    ἴω, ἴῃς, ἴῃ, ἴωμεν, ἴητε, ἴωσι(ν)

### δίδωμι

Present Active:

    διδῶ, διδῷς, διδῷ, διδῶμεν, διδῶτε, διδῶσι(ν)

Present Middle/Passive:

    διδῶμαι, διδῷ, διδῶται, διδώμεθα, διδῶσθε, διδῶνται

Aorist Active:

    δῶ, δῷς, δῷ, δῶμεν, δῶτε, δῶσι(ν)

Aorist Middle:

    δῶμαι, δῷ, δῶται, δώμεθα, δῶσθε, δῶνται

Aorist Passive:

    δοθῶ, δοθῇς, δοθῇ, δοθῶμεν, δοθῆτε, δοθῶσι(ν)

### τίθημι

Present Active:

    τιθῶ, τιθῇς, τιθῇ, τιθῶμεν, τιθῆτε, τιθῶσι(ν)

Present Middle/Passive:

    τιθῶμαι, τιθῇ, τιθῆται, τιθώμεθα, τιθῆσθε, τιθῶνται

Aorist Active:

    θῶ, θῇς, θῇ, θῶμεν, θῆτε, θῶσι(ν)

Aorist Middle:

    θῶμαι, θῇ, θῆται, θώμεθα, θῆσθε, θῶνται

Aorist Passive:

    τεθῶ, τεθῇς, τεθῇ, τεθῶμεν, τεθῆτε, τεθῶσι(ν)

### ἵστημι

Present Active:

    ἱστῶ, ἱστῇς, ἱστῇ, ἱστῶμεν, ἱστῆτε, ἱστῶσι(ν)

Present Middle/Passive:

    ἱστῶμαι, ἱστῇ, ἱστῆται, ἱστώμεθα, ἱστῆσθε, ἱστῶνται

Aorist Active:

στῶ, στῇς, στῇ, στῶμεν, στῆτε, στῶσι(ν)

Aorist Middle:

στῶμαι, στῇ, στῆται, στώμεθα, στῆσθε, στῶνται

Aorist Passive:

σταθῶ, σταθῇς, σταθῇ, σταθῶμεν, σταθῆτε, σταθῶσι(ν)

### δείκνῡμι

Present Active:

δεικνύω, δεικνύῃς, δεικνύῃ, δεικνύωμεν δεικνύητε, δεικνύωσι(ν)

Present Middle/Passive:

δεικνύωμαι, δεικνύῃ, δεικνύηται, δεικνυώμεθα, δεικνύησθε, δεικνύωνται

Aorist Active:

δείξω, δείξῃς, δείξῃ, δείξωμεν, δείξητε, δείξωσι(ν)

Aorist Middle:

δείξωμαι, δείξῃ, δείξηται, δειξώμεθα, δείξησθε, δείξωνται

Aorist Passive:

δειχθῶ, δειχθῇς, δειχθῇ, δειχθῶμεν, δειχθῆτε, δειχθῶσι(ν)

### ἵημι

Present Active:

ἱῶ, ἱῇς, ἱῇ, ἱῶμεν, ἱῆτε, ἱῶσι(ν)

Present Middle/Passive:

ἱῶμαι, ἱῇ, ἱῆται, ἱώμεθα, ἱῆσθε, ἱῶνται

Aorist Active:

ὧ, ᾗς, ᾗ, ὧμεν, ἧτε, ὧσι(ν)

Aorist Middle:

ὧμαι, ᾗ, ἧται, ὥμεθα, ἧσθε, ὧνται

Aorist Passive:

ἑθῶ, ἑθῇς, ἑθῇ, ἑθῶμεν, ἑθῆτε, ἑθῶσι(ν)

N.B. Many verbs that are compounded with prepositional prefixes are sometimes found with recessive accent in the subjunctive and sometimes with the accent of the uncompounded form retained, e.g., πάρωμεν or παρῶμεν. We follow the latter accentuation in this book.

### Exercise 21ε

*Fill in the subjunctive forms on all Verb Charts completed to date for Book II and on the charts for Exercise 11θ. Keep the charts for reference.*

## Exercise 21ζ

*Identify the tense, voice, person, and number of these subjunctive forms:*

1. δοθῶμεν
2. διδῶτε
3. δῷς
4. τιθῇ (3 ways)
5. θώμεθα

6. τιθῆσθε (2 ways)
7. ἱστῶσι(ν)
8. σταθῇς
9. στῶ
10. δείξῃς

11. δειξώμεθα
12. δεικνύῃ (3 ways)
13. ᾖ (2 ways)
14. ἱῶσι(ν)
15. ἐθῇ

## Exercise 21η

*Read aloud and translate into English; identify each use of the subjunctive:*

1. μὴ οἴκοι μένωμεν ἀλλὰ πρὸς τὸ ἄστυ ἰώμεθα ὅπως τῇ ἐκκλησίᾳ παρῶμεν.
2. εἰς τὴν Πύκνα ἴωμεν ἵνα τῶν ῥητόρων ἀκούωμεν βουλευομένων τί ποιήσωμεν.
3. οἱ γὰρ Πελοποννήσιοι πρέσβεις πεπόμφασι (*have sent*) λέξοντας ὅτι πόλεμος ἔσται ἐὰν μὴ τὴν ἀρχὴν ἀφῶμεν.
4. ὁ Περικλῆς, "μὴ ἀφῆτε τὴν ἀρχήν," φησίν.
5. τί οὖν ποιήσωμεν; πότερον τὴν ἀρχὴν ἀφῶμεν ἢ ἐς πόλεμον καταστῶμεν;
6. τὰς ὑδρίᾱς καταθῶμεν καὶ πρὸς τὸν ἀγρὸν σπεύδωμεν ἵνα τὸν κύνα ζητῶμεν.
7. καλὸν δῶρον (*gift*) τῇ παιδὶ δῶμεν τῇ τὸν κύνα εὑρούσῃ.
8. μὴ δείξῃς τὴν ὁδὸν τῷ ξένῳ· ψευδῆ γὰρ λέγει.
9. ἄκουσον, ὦ παῖ, ἵνα συνῑῇς τί λέγει ὁ διδάσκαλος.
10. μὴ ἀνοίξητε τὰς πύλᾱς, ὦ φύλακες· οἱ γὰρ πολέμιοι προσχωροῦσιν.

## Exercise 21θ

*Translate into Greek:*

1. If (ἐάν + subjunctive) you give us money, friends, we will help you.
2. Let us stop and look at the temple.
3. Let us go to the temple (in order) to put up an offering (*use* τὸ ἄγαλμα) to the god.
4. Are we to show (to) the priest the offering that we intend to give?
5. Let us revolt from the Persians and sail at once (in order) to come to aid the Greeks.

# ΟΙ ΑΥΤΟΥΡΓΟΙ ΑΝΙΣΤΑΝΤΑΙ

*Read the following passage (adapted from Thucydides 2.14 and 16–17) and answer the comprehension questions:*

οἱ δὲ Ἀθηναῖοι ἐπείθοντό τε τῷ Περικλεῖ καὶ ἐσεκομίζοντο ἐκ τῶν ἀγρῶν παῖδας καὶ γυναῖκας καὶ τὴν ἄλλην κατασκευὴν ᾗ κατ' οἶκον ἐχρῶντο· πρόβατα δὲ καὶ ὑποζύγια ἐς τὴν Εὔβοιαν ἔπεμψαν καὶ τὰς νήσους τὰς ἐπικειμένᾱς. χαλεπὴ δὲ αὐτοῖς ἐγίγνετο ἡ ἀνάστασις, διότι αἰεὶ εἰώθεσαν οἱ πολλοὶ ἐν τοῖς ἀγροῖς οἰκεῖν. ἐβαρύνοντό τε οἰκίᾱς τε καταλείποντες καὶ ἱερά, δίαιτάν τε μέλλοντες μετα- 5
βάλλειν. ἐπειδὴ δὲ ἀφίκοντο ἐς τὸ ἄστυ, ὀλίγοις μέν τισιν ὑπῆρχον οἰκήσεις· οἱ δὲ πολλοὶ τά τε ἐρῆμα τῆς πόλεως ᾤκησαν καὶ τὰ ἱερά. καὶ κατεσκευάσαντο καὶ ἐν τοῖς πύργοις τῶν τειχῶν πολλοὶ καὶ ὡς ἕκαστός που ἐδύνατο. οὐ γὰρ ἐχώρησε ξυνελθόντας αὐτοὺς ἡ πόλις, ἀλλ' ὕστερον δὴ τά τε μακρὰ τείχη ᾤκησαν καὶ τοῦ Πειραιῶς τὰ πολλά. 10

[ἐσεκομίζοντο, *they brought in* κατασκευὴν, *equipment, household furniture* ὑποζύγια, *beasts of burden* (yoked) ἐπικειμένᾱς, *lying nearby* ἡ ἀνάστασις, *the removal* εἰώθεσαν (from ἔθω), pluperfect with imperfect sense, *were accustomed* οἱ πολλοί, *the majority* ἐβαρύνοντό, *they were distressed* δίαιτάν, *way of life* μεταβάλλειν, *to change* ἐπειδή, *when* ὑπῆρχον, *were (ready)* οἰκήσεις, *dwellings* κατεσκευάσαντο, *they set up house* καί, *even* τοῖς πύργοις, *the towers* ἕκαστος, *each* που, *anywhere* ἐχώρησε, *accommodated, was large enough for* τὰ πολλά, *the greater part*]

1. What did the Athenians bring with them from the country?
2. Why was the removal from the countryside difficult and distressing?
3. What problem confronted them when they arrived at the city?
4. Where did most of them settle?
5. In what other places did some of them set up their households?

---

### Exercise 21ι

*Translate into Greek*

1. As the enemy was advancing into Attica (*use genitive absolute*), obeying Pericles we all went to the city.
2. We were very distressed (*use* βαρύνομαι) (at) leaving (our) homes behind.
3. When (ἐπεί) we arrived at the city, no house was ready (*use* ὑπάρχω) for us.
4. And so at first we lived in a tower (*use* πύργος), but later we set up house (*use* κατασκευάζομαι) near the long walls.
5. But when (ἐπεί) the enemy withdrew, we returned to (our) homes.

## Classical Greek

### Solon

Solon, besides being a statesman who saved the Athenian state from revolution by his reforms (see page 80), was a poet, who used his poetry as propaganda to warn and inform his fellow citizens.   In the following lines (fragment 9),  he warns them of the danger of tyranny.  His warning was prescient; thirty years later Pisistratus became tyrant of Athens.

ἐκ νεφέλης πέλεται χιόνος μένος ἠδὲ χαλάζης,

  βροντὴ δ᾽ ἐκ λαμπρῆς γίγνεται ἀστεροπῆς·

ἀνδρῶν δ᾽ ἐκ μεγάλων πόλις ὄλλυται, ἐς δὲ μονάρχου

  δῆμος ἀϊδρίῃ δουλοσύνην ἔπεσεν.

λίην δ᾽ ἐξάραντ᾽ οὐ ῥᾴδιόν ἐστι κατασχεῖν

  ὕστερον, ἀλλ᾽ ἤδη χρή τινα πάντα νοεῖν.

[**νεφέλης,** *cloud*   **πέλεται,** *comes*   **χιόνος μένος ἠδὲ χαλάζης,** *the might of snow and hail*   **βροντή,** *thunder*   **ἀστεροπῆς,** *lightning*   **ὄλλυται,** *perishes*   **ἐς . . . μονάρχου . . . δουλοσύνην,** *under the slavery of a monarch*   **ἀϊδρίῃ,** *through its folly*   **ἔπεσεν:** gnomic aorist; translate as present   **λίην . . . ἐξάραντ(α),** *if you raise (having raised)* (a man) *too high*   **κατασχεῖν,** *to restrain* (him)   **τινα,** *someone, one*   **νοεῖν,** *to think about*]

## New Testament Greek

### John 3.4–7
### Nicodemus visits Jesus (concluded)

λέγει πρὸς αὐτὸν Νικόδημος, "πῶς δύναται ἄνθρωπος γεννηθῆναι γέρων ὤν; μὴ δύναται εἰς τὴν κοιλίαν τῆς μητρὸς αὐτοῦ δεύτερον εἰσελθεῖν καὶ γεννηθῆναι;" ἀπεκρίθη Ἰησοῦς, "ἀμὴν ἀμὴν λέγω σοι, ἐὰν μή τις γεννηθῇ ἐξ ὕδατος καὶ πνεύματος, οὐ δύναται εἰσελθεῖν εἰς τὴν βασιλείαν τοῦ θεοῦ. τὸ γεγεννημένον ἐκ τῆς σαρκὸς σάρξ ἐστιν, καὶ τὸ γεγεννημένον ἐκ τοῦ πνεύματος πνεῦμά ἐστιν. μὴ θαυμάσῃς ὅτι εἶπόν σοι, ʽδεῖ ὑμᾶς γεννηθῆναι ἄνωθεν.ʼ"

[**γεννηθῆναι** (from **γεννάω,** *I give birth to;* passive, *I am born*), *to be born*   **μὴ:** here introducing a question expecting the answer "no"   **τὴν κοιλίαν,** *the womb*   **ἀμὴν,** *verily*   **ἐὰν μὴ,** *unless*   **πνεύματος,** *spirit*   **τὴν βασιλείαν,** *the kingdom*   **τὸ γεγεννημένον,** *that which has been born*   **τῆς σαρκὸς,** *the flesh*   **ἄνωθεν,** *from above; anew*]

# 22
# Η ΑΝΑΣΤΑΣΙΣ (α)

φοβοῦμαι μὴ δι᾽ ὀλίγου εἰς πόλεμον καταστῶμεν·
ὁ γὰρ νεᾱνίᾱς τόν τε πατέρα καὶ τὴν γυναῖκα χαίρειν κελεύει.

## VOCABULARY

*Verbs*

**ἀνθίσταμαι** [= ἀντι- + ἵσταμαι],
[στη-] **ἀντιστήσομαι, ἀντέστην, ἀνθέστηκα** + dat.,
*I stand up against, withstand*

**ἀνίσταμαι** [= ἀνα- + ἵσταμαι],
[στη-] **ἀναστήσομαι, ἀν-
έστην, ἀνέστηκα,** *I stand up;
I am forced to move; I move;
I evacuate*

**εἰσβάλλω** + εἰς + acc., *I invade*

**λούω,** λούεις, λούει, λοῦμεν, λοῦτε,
λοῦσι(ν), imperfect, ἔλουν,
**λούσομαι, ἔλουσα, λέλου-
μαι,** *I wash;* middle, *I wash
myself, bathe*

**ὑπάρχω** [= ὑπο- + ἄρχω], *I am;
I exist; I am ready*

*Nouns*

**ἡ ἀνάστασις, τῆς ἀναστά-
σεως,** *forced move; move;
evacuation*

**ἡ οἴκησις, τῆς οἰκήσεως,**
*dwelling*

**ἡ φυλακή, τῆς φυλακῆς,**
*guard; garrison*

*Relative Pronoun*

**ὅστις, ἥτις** (note the accent), **ὅ
τι,** often in indefinite or general clauses with ἄν and subjunctive, *anyone who, whoever; anything that, whatever;*
pl., *all that; whoever; whatever*

*Relative and Interrogative Adjec-
tive*

**ὅσος, -η, -ον,** *as great as; as
much as;* pl., *as many as*
**πάντες ὅσοι,** *all that, whoever;* **πάντα ὅσα,** *all that,
whatever*

*Conjunctions*

**ἐπειδή,** *when; since*

**ἐπειδάν** [= ἐπειδή + ἄν], *in indefinite or general clauses
with subjunctive, when
(ever)*

**πρίν** + indicative or + ἄν and
subjunctive, *until;* + infin.,
*before*

τελευτησάσης δὲ τῆς ἐκκλησίᾱς καὶ τῶν πολῑτῶν ἀπιόντων, ὁ
Δικαιόπολις, "ἄγε δή, ὦ παῖ," ἔφη· "οἴκαδε σπεύδωμεν ἵνα τῇ μητρὶ
ἅπαντα τὰ γενόμενα ἐξηγώμεθα." τάχιστα οὖν ἐπορεύοντο καὶ ἤδη
νυκτὸς γενομένης εἰς τὴν οἰκίᾱν ἀφίκοντο.  τοῦ δὲ Δικαιοπόλιδος
κόψαντος τὴν θύρᾱν, ἐξῆλθεν ἡ Μυρρίνη καὶ τὸν Φίλιππον ἰδοῦσα      5
ὑγιῆ τ' ὄντα καὶ βλέποντα ἠσπάζετο καὶ χαίρουσα ἐδάκρῡσεν.  ὡς δ'
εἰσελθόντες ἐλούσαντό τε καὶ ἐδείπνησαν, ὁ μὲν Φίλιππος πάντα
ἐξηγεῖτο ὅσα ἐγένετο ἐν τῇ ὁδῷ καὶ ἐν τῷ Ἀσκληπιείῳ· ἡ δὲ ἐτέρπετο
ἀκούουσα.

[ἠσπάζετο, *embraced*]

ὁ δὲ Δικαιόπολις ἅπαντα ἐξηγεῖτο ὅσα ἤκουσαν τῶν ῥητόρων ἐν      10
τῇ ἐκκλησίᾳ ἀγορευόντων.  "οὕτως οὖν," ἔφη, "φοβοῦμαι μὴ δι'
ὀλίγου εἰς πόλεμον καταστῶμεν.  χρὴ δὲ ἡμᾶς τῷ Περικλεῖ
πειθομένους ἅπαντα παρασκευάζεσθαι ὡς εἰς τὸ ἄστυ ἀνα-
στησομένους· ἐπειδὰν γὰρ οἱ Πελοποννήσιοι εἰς τὴν Ἀττικὴν
εἰσβάλωσιν, ἀνάγκη ἔσται τὴν οἰκίᾱν καταλιπόντας Ἀθήναζε      15
ἀναστῆναι." ἡ δὲ Μυρρίνη, "οἴμοι," ἔφη· "τί λέγεις, ὦ ἄνερ; πῶς γὰρ
δυνησόμεθα τήν τε οἰκίᾱν καταλιπεῖν καὶ τὰ πρόβατα καὶ τοὺς βοῦς;
καὶ εἰς τὰς Ἀθήνᾱς ἀναστάντες ποῦ δὴ οἰκήσομεν; οὐδεμία γὰρ ἡμῖν
ὑπάρχει οἴκησις ἐν τῷ ἄστει.  ἀλλ' οὐ δυνατόν ἐστι ταῦτα πρᾶξαι."

ὁ δὲ Δικαιόπολις, "ἀλλ' ἀνάγκη ἔσται, ὦ γύναι, ταῦτα πρᾶξαι      20
τούτων ἕνεκα· ἐπειδὰν γὰρ οἱ Πελοποννήσιοι εἰς τὴν γῆν εἰσβάλωσιν,
ἡμεῖς οὐ δυνησόμεθα αὐτοῖς μάχῃ ἀντιστῆναι τοσούτοις οὖσιν· ὥστε
ὅστις ἂν ἔξω τῶν τειχῶν μένῃ, ἀποθανεῖται ὑπὸ τῶν πολεμίων·
συνελθόντες δὲ εἰς τὴν πόλιν, πάντες ἀσφαλεῖς ἐσόμεθα καὶ οὐδεὶς
κίνδῡνος ἔσται μὴ οἱ πολέμιοι ἡμᾶς βλάπτωσιν, τὴν μὲν γῆν ἀφέντας      25
καὶ τὰς οἰκίᾱς, τῆς δὲ θαλάττης καὶ πόλεως φυλακὴν ἔχοντας."

[ἀποθανεῖται, *will die*, i.e., *will be killed* (ἀποθνήσκω = passive of ἀποκτείνω)]

## PRINCIPAL PARTS: Liquid and Nasal Stems (-λ-, -ν-)

ἀγγέλλ-ω, [ἀγγελε-] ἀγγελῶ, [ἀγγειλ-] ἤγγειλα, [ἀγγελ-] ἤγγελκα,
    ἤγγελμαι, ἠγγέλθην, *I announce; I tell*

βάλλ-ω, [βαλε-] βαλῶ, [βαλ-] ἔβαλον, [βλη-] βέβληκα, βέβλημαι,
    ἐβλήθην, *I throw; I put; I pelt; I hit, strike*

φαίν-ω, [φανε-] φανῶ or φανοῦμαι, [φην-] ἔφηνα, [φαν-] πέφασμαι, *I show*

φαίν-ομαι, [φαν-] φανήσομαι (2nd future passive) or [φανε-] φανοῦμαι,
    [φην-] πέφηνα, [φαν-] ἐφάνην + infin., *I appear; I seem;* + participle, *I am*
    *shown to be; I am proved to be; I am clearly*

## WORD STUDY

*Give the Greek words from which the following English words for subjects of*
*academic study are derived:*

1. mathematics
2. arithmetic
3. geometry
4. physics
5. biology
6. zoology

## GRAMMAR

### 1. Clauses of Fearing

Examine these sentences from the reading passage above:

φοβοῦμαι **μὴ δι' ὀλίγου εἰς πόλεμον καταστῶμεν.**
*I am afraid **that we will (may) soon get into war.***

οὐδεὶς κίνδῡνος ἔσται **μὴ οἱ πολέμιοι ἡμᾶς βλάπτωσιν.**
*There will be no danger **that the enemy will (may) harm us.***

Subordinate clauses introduced by μή state what is feared; such clauses of
fearing may be introduced by verbs such as φοβοῦμαι or expressions such
as κίνδῡνός ἐστιν, and the verb of the clause of fearing is in the subjunctive
(present or aorist, differing in aspect only).

When the clause of fearing is negative, the introductory μή is accompanied somewhere in the clause by οὐ, e.g.:

ἐφοβούμην **μὴ ἐν καιρῷ οὐκ ἀφίκωμαι.**
*I was afraid **that I would (might) not arrive in time.***

Where English uses the infinitive, so does Greek, e.g.:

φοβοῦμαι τοῦτο **ποιῆσαι.**
*I am afraid **to do** this.*

Note that if the introductory verb or clause is in the present tense, we
translate the subjunctive with *will* or *may*, but if the introductory verb or
clause is in a past tense, we translate the subjunctive with *would* or *might*.

## Exercise 22 α

*Read aloud and translate into English:*

1. ἆρ' οὐ φοβεῖσθε μὴ κακόν τι πάθωμεν;
2. κίνδυνός ἐστι μὴ χειμὼν δι' ὀλίγου γένηται.
3. καίπερ φοβουμένη μὴ χαλεπὴ γένηται ἡ ἀνάστασις, ἡ γυνὴ τῷ ἀνδρὶ πείθεται.
4. ὁ γέρων ἐλῡπεῖτο, φοβούμενος μὴ οὐδέποτε (*never*) ἐπανίῃ.
5. φοβοῦμαι μὴ οἱ φύλακες (*guards*) οὐκ ἐθέλωσιν ἀνοῖξαι (*to open*) τὰς πύλᾱς.
6. οἱ δοῦλοι ἐφοβοῦντο μὴ ὁ δεσπότης σφίσιν (*at them*) ὀργίζηται.
7. οὐ φοβούμεθα ἔξω τῶν τειχῶν μένειν.
8. οἱ παῖδες ἐφοβοῦντο τὰ ἀληθῆ λέγειν.
9. φοβούμενοι νυκτὸς ἐπανιέναι οἱ αὐτουργοὶ ἐν τῷ ἄστει ἔμενον.
10. ὁ ναύκληρος ἐφοβεῖτο μὴ ὁ χειμὼν τὴν ναῦν διαφθείρῃ.

## Exercise 22 β

*Translate into Greek:*

1. I fear we will (may) not arrive at the city in time.
2. There is a danger that the enemy will (may) soon come into the land.
3. We set out toward the city immediately, being afraid to stay in the country.
4. The farmers were afraid that the enemy would (might) destroy their homes.
5. Are you not more afraid (Don't you fear rather) to sail home than to go by land?

## 2. Indefinite or General Clauses

In relative, temporal, and conditional clauses, the indicative mood is used if the clauses are *definite*, i.e., specific in reference or in time. If the reference or time is *indefinite* or *general*, ἄν + the subjunctive (present or aorist) is used; ἄν is placed after the relative pronoun or combined with some temporal conjunctions and with the conditional conjunction εἰ.

Relative: Definite:

πάντες ἐκείνους τῑμῶσιν **οἳ ἐν Σαλαμῖνι ἐμαχέσαντο.**
*All honor the men **who fought at Salamis.***

Relative: Indefinite or General:

**ὅστις ἂν ἔξω τῶν τειχῶν μένῃ,** ἀποθανεῖται ὑπὸ τῶν πολεμίων.
***Whoever remains outside the walls** will be killed by the enemy.*

(Present subjunctive = ongoing process)

ὅστις ἂν τοῦτο ποιήσῃ, τῑμῆς ἄξιός ἐστιν.
**Whoever does this** *is worthy of honor.*
(Aorist subjunctive = simple action)

Temporal: Definite:
ἐπεὶ εἰς τὸ ἄστυ ἀφῑκόμεθα, πρὸς τὴν ἀγορὰν ἐσπεύσαμεν.
**When we arrived at the city,** *we hurried to the agora.*

Temporal: Indefinite or General:
**ἐπειδὰν** (= ἐπειδή + ἄν) **εἰς τὸ ἄστυ ἴωμεν,** πρὸς τὴν ἀγορὰν σπεύδομεν.
**Whenever we go to the city,** *we hurry to the agora.*

Temporal: Definite:
οἱ Σπαρτιᾶται ἐμάχοντο **ἕως ἅπαντες ἔπεσον.**
*The Spartans were fighting* **until all fell.**

After a negative main clause, πρίν is usually used:
αἱ γυναῖκες <u>οὐκ ἀπῆλθον</u> **πρὶν ἀφίκετο ὁ ἱερεύς.**
*The women <u>did not go away</u>* **until the priest arrived.**

Temporal: Indefinite or General:
μείνατε **ἕως ἂν ἐπανέλθῃ ὁ πατήρ.**
*Wait* **until father returns.**

Again, after a negative main clause, πρίν is usually used:
αἱ γυναῖκες <u>οὐκ ἀπίᾱσι</u> **πρὶν ἂν ἀφίκηται ὁ ἱερεύς.**
*The women <u>will not go away</u>* **until the priest arrives.**

Conditional: Definite:
εἰ τῷ Περικλεῖ πιστεύεις, μῶρος εἶ.
**If you believe Pericles (now),** *you are foolish.*

Conditional: Indefnite or General:
**ἐὰν** (= εἰ + ἄν) **τῷ Περικλεῖ πιστεύωμεν,** μῶροί ἐσμεν.
**If we ever believe Pericles,** *we are (always) foolish.*

The last example above is also called a *present general condition.*

Indefinite Relative Clauses:

Note that ὅστις, ἥτις, ὅ τι, *anyone who, whoever; anything that, whatever; pl., all that; whoever; whatever*, is commonly used with ἄν in indefinite relative clauses with the subjunctive, as in the second example in the list above. Both halves of the word decline, as follows (but note the alternative forms):

|         | **Masculine**          | **Feminine**     | **Neuter**            |
|---------|------------------------|------------------|-----------------------|
| Nom.    | ὅστις                  | ἥτις             | ὅ τι                  |
| Gen.    | οὗτινος or ὅτου        | ἧστινος          | οὗτινος or ὅτου       |
| Dat.    | ᾧτινι or ὅτῳ           | ᾗτινι            | ᾧτινι or ὅτῳ          |
| Acc.    | ὅντινα                 | ἥντινα           | ὅ τι                  |
| Nom.    | οἵτινες                | αἵτινες          | ἅτινα or ἅττα         |
| Gen.    | ὧντινων                | ὧντινων          | ὧντινων               |
| Dat.    | οἷστισι(ν)             | αἷστισι(ν)       | οἷστισι(ν)            |
| Acc.    | οὕστινας               | ἅστινας          | ἅτινα or ἅττα         |

The word ὅσοι, ὅσαι, ὅσα, *as many as*, often reinforced by πάντες, πᾶσαι, πάντα, *all*, is also used with ἄν and the subjunctive to mean *all that; whoever; whatever*, e.g.:

ὁ πατὴρ τῷ παιδὶ δίδωσιν **πάντα ὅσ' ἂν αἰτῇ**.
*The father gives the child **whatever he asks for**.*
[πάντα ὅσα = lit., *all the things as many as* = *whatever*]

Indefinite Temporal Clauses:

Note the following words that may introduce indefinite temporal clauses.  They all mean *whenever* and are used with verbs in the subjunctive:

ἐπειδάν = ἐπειδή + ἄν
ὅταν = ὅτε + ἄν
ὁπόταν = ὁπότε + ἄν

Aspect:

The difference between the present and aorist subjunctive in indefinite clauses is in aspect, not in time, i.e., the present subjunctive is used when the action is viewed as *continuous*, and the aorist subjunctive is used when the action is viewed as *a simple event* (you will find this contrast illustrated in the two examples of indefinite or general relative clauses above and in the first two sentences below).

Future Time:

Note that relative, temporal, and conditional clauses referring to *future* time are usually treated as indefinite in Greek, although sometimes we do not translate with the indefinite *ever* in English, e.g.:

**ὅστις ἂν ἔξω τῶν τειχῶν μένῃ**, ἀποθανεῖται ὑπὸ τῶν πολεμίων.
***Whoever remains outside the walls*** *will be killed by the enemy.*

**ἐπειδὰν ἐπανέλθῃ ὁ πατήρ**, πάντα μαθησόμεθα.
***When father returns****, we will learn everything.*

μείνατε ἕως ἂν ἐπανέλθῃ ὁ πατήρ.
*Wait **until father returns**.*

αἱ γυναῖκες οὐκ ἀπίασι **πρὶν ἂν ἀφίκηται ὁ ἱερεύς.**
*The women will not go away **until the priest arrives**.*
(Remember that πρίν instead of ἕως is usually used after a negative
main clause.)

**ἐ ἂν οἴκαδε ἐπανέλθωμεν,** πάντα μαθησόμεθα.
***If we return home,*** *we will learn everything.*

The last example above is also called a *future more vivid condition,*
and it is in the form that future conditions usually take, with ἄν and the
subjunctive in the if-clause. Greek may, however, use εἰ + the future indicative in conditional clauses referring to future time, but this is less
common and is usually reserved for threats and warnings, e.g.:

εἰ τοῦτο **ποιήσεις, ἀποθανεῖ.**
***If you do** this, **you will die**.*

Note that in this kind of condition we translate the future tense in the if-
clause (here, ποιήσεις) as present in English.

## Exercise 22γ

*Translate the following pairs of sentences.   In the Greek sentences,
identify subordinate clauses as relative, temporal, or conditional and as
definite or indefinite:*

1. ὅστις ἂν ἔξω τῶν τειχῶν μένῃ, ἐν κινδύνῳ ἔσται.
   Whoever arrives first will receive the money.
2. ἐπειδὰν γένηται ἡ ἐκκλησία, οἱ πολῖται εἰς τὴν Πύκνα σπεύδουσιν.
   Whenever the enemy invades the land, we all come together into the
   city.
3. μενοῦμεν ἐν τῇ ἀγορᾷ ἕως ἂν ἐπανέλθῃ ὁ ἄγγελος.
   We will not return home until day breaks (*use* γίγνομαι).
4. μὴ εἰσβῆτε εἰς τὴν ναῦν πρὶν ἂν κελεύσῃ ὁ ναύκληρος.
   Don't climb that mountain until spring (τὸ ἔαρ) begins (*use* γίγνομαι).
5. ἐὰν οἱ Πελοποννήσιοι ἐπὶ τὴν γῆν ἡμῶν πεζῇ ἴωσιν, ἡμεῖς ἐπὶ τὴν
   ἐκείνων ναυσὶ πλευσόμεθα.
   If the farmers hurry into the city, they will all be safe.
6. ὅσ’ ἂν ἔχωσιν οἱ παῖδες, πάντα ἡμῖν διδόναι ἐθέλουσιν.
   We must do whatever the king orders.
7. ἐπειδὴ ὁ αὐτουργὸς τοὺς βοῦς εἰς τὸν ἀγρὸν εἰσήλασεν, δι’ ὀλίγου ἀροῦν
   (*to plow*) ἤρξατο.
   When the boy (had) gone into the field, he immediately called (his)
   father.

8.  οἱ ποιμένες τὰ πρόβατα ἐν τοῖς ὄρεσιν οὐ νεμοῦσιν (*will pasture*) πρὶν ἂν γένηται τὸ ἔαρ (*spring*).

    We will not set out for home until the shepherd shows us the way.

9.  ὅταν ἀπῇ ὁ δεσπότης, οἱ δοῦλοι παύονται ἐργαζόμενοι.

    Whenever the master approaches, the slaves, getting up (*use aorist*), work.

10. εἰς κίνδῡνον καταστήσεσθε, ὦ παῖδες, εἰ μὴ ποιήσετε ὅσ' ἂν παραινέσωμεν.

    Unless you listen to me, you will suffer terribly (terrible things).

11. οὗτοι οἱ παῖδες, οἳ τοῖς πατράσι συνελάμβανον, εἰργάζοντο ἕως ἐγένετο νύξ.

12. ἐάν τις τούτου πίῃ, ἀποθνῄσκει.

13. οὐκ ἄπιμεν πρὶν ἂν ἐπανέλθῃ ὁ πατήρ.

14. οἱ αὐτουργοὶ εἰς τοὺς ἀγροὺς οὐκ ἐπανῆλθον πρὶν οἱ πολέμιοι ἀπὸ τῆς Ἀττικῆς ἀνεχώρησαν.

15. μὴ ἀπὸ τῆς ἀγορᾶς ἀπέλθητε πρὶν ἂν τοῦ ἀγγέλου ἀκούσητε.

## Athenian Democracy in Action

The Assembly (ἡ ἐκκλησία) was sovereign. Consisting of all adult male citizens, it had forty regular meetings each year, four in each *prytany* (a period of time equal to one-tenth of a year). It met on the Pnyx (ἡ Πνύξ), the slope of a hill opposite the Acropolis. All eligible citizens were expected and required to attend, but in fact an attendance of 6,000 (the legal quorum for an ostracism) out of a citizen body of about 50,000 was probably a respectable number for a routine meeting. It must be remembered that the majority of the people lived in the country and could not possibly have come into the city for every meeting. The Assembly decided all issues by direct vote, by a show of hands.

The Council of 500 (ἡ βουλή) formed the steering committee of the Assembly. No matter could come before the Assembly that had not first been discussed in the Council. It presented motions to the Assembly in the form of "preliminary decrees" (προβουλεύματα), which were debated in the Assembly and passed, rejected, or amended by the people. If passed, the motion became a "decree" (ψήφισμα), which was recorded, usually on stone, and set up in public for all to read. Hundreds of fragments of such decrees survive, some fairly complete, which show the democracy in action. All begin ἔδοξε τῇ βουλῇ καὶ τῷ δήμῳ and then give the name of the prytany and chairman.

When the Assembly met, proceedings were opened by prayer and libation. Then the herald read out the preliminary decree (τὸ προβούλευμα) and asked whether it should be accepted without debate or debated. If the people voted for a debate, the herald then asked "τίς ἀγορεύειν βούλεται;" and any citizen could come forward to the platform (τὸ βῆμα) and address the people. The Assembly did not tolerate the foolish or ill-informed, and in practice the

speakers were usually drawn from a limited number of politicians (οἱ
ῥήτορες). The regular meetings of the Assembly had a fairly standard
agenda. At the first meeting of each prytany (i.e., of each one-tenth of a year)
a vote was taken on whether to continue the magistrates in office or to depose
any of them. Then the grain supply and security (especially the state of the
navy) were discussed. At the second meeting of the prytany any citizen could
bring up any topic of public or private interest (provided he had first introduced his proposal to the Council). At the third and fourth meetings current
problems were dealt with under the headings of sacred affairs, foreign policy,
and secular affairs. Besides the regular meetings, extraordinary meetings
could be called by the Council in any emergency.

The 500 councilors (βουλευταί) were selected by lot in the demes from citizens over thirty years old. They served for one year only and might not serve
more than twice in a lifetime. It follows statistically that most citizens would
sooner or later have to serve their turn on the Council. Each of the ten tribes
(φῦλαί) provided fifty councilors, and each group of fifty served in rotation for
one-tenth of the year (i.e., for each prytany) as "presidents" (*prytaneis*,
πρυτάνεις). Every day a "chairman" (ὁ ἐπιστάτης) was selected by lot from
those serving as prytaneis for that one-tenth of the year, and for twenty-four
hours he held the seal of state and the keys to the temples where the public
moneys and archives were stored. The chairman and one-third of the prytaneis were on twenty-four hour duty and slept and ate in the Tholos (Θόλος),
the round building next to the Council House (Βουλευτήριον). The Council had
a "secretary" (ὁ γραμματεύς), who was responsible for recording all business.
The Council met daily, and the public could attend as observers. Any citizen
could ask for leave to introduce business, and, possibly, the generals could
attend *ex officio*.

The Council was divided into committees, usually of ten, each responsible for a different sphere of business. One was in charge of shipbuilding,
another was responsible for the dockyards, a third for the upkeep of public
buildings, and so forth. The audit committee checked the accounts of all
magistrates who handled public moneys. All magistrates on entering office
were scrutinized by the Council to see that they were fit and proper persons,
and on resigning office they had to submit to a public examination of their
record by the Council. The Council was in fact the linchpin that held the
whole constitution together, and it is worth reflecting on the fact that at any
given time there may have been 15,000 citizens in the Assembly who had
served on the Council with all the political and administrative experience
that this entailed. This gives substance to Pericles' claim that "we are all
concerned alike with our personal affairs and the affairs of the city, and, despite our various occupations, we are adequately informed on politics."

It is remarkable that the Athenian democracy worked so well, considering that all offices, except for military commands and offices entailing tech-
nical expertise, were filled by lot and that all important decisions were taken
by direct vote in a large and emotional assembly. Its success in the Periclean
period may be ascribed to the dominance of one outstanding statesman, who

could control and guide the Assembly by his eloquence and his known integrity: "it was (in Pericles' time) in theory a democracy but in practice rule by the leading man" (Thucydides 2.65). Thucydides, however, overstates his case. Pericles could have been dropped at any time (he was in fact deposed for a short time in 430 B.C.), and credit must be paid to the average Athenians, who had the political acumen to follow a great leader. Thucydides says that Pericles' successors as leaders of the people, because they did not have his influence and powers of persuasion and were motivated by personal ambition and the pursuit of private gain, gave the people what they wanted and made a series of political blunders that led to the downfall of Athens. Failures in the war certainly did result in the growth of an antidemocratic party (οἱ ὀλίγοι) and eventually to revolution and counterrevolution. After the war, however, the restored democracy continued to function throughout the fourth century without any outstanding leaders and with good success on the whole.

# New Testament Greek

### John 5.1–9
### The Healing at the Pool Called Bethzatha

μετὰ ταῦτα ἦν ἑορτὴ τῶν Ἰουδαίων καὶ ἀνέβη Ἰησοῦς εἰς Ἱεροσόλυμα. ἔστιν δὲ ἐν τοῖς Ἱεροσολύμοις ἐπὶ τῇ προβατικῇ κολυμβήθρᾱ ἡ ἐπιλεγομένη Ἑβραϊστὶ Βηθζαθὰ πέντε στοὰς ἔχουσα. ἐν ταύταις κατέκειτο πλῆθος τῶν ἀσθενούντων, τυφλῶν, χωλῶν, ξηρῶν. ἦν δέ τις ἄνθρωπος ἐκεῖ τριάκοντα ὀκτὼ ἔτη ἔχων ἐν τῇ ἀσθενείᾳ αὐτοῦ.

[Ἱεροσόλυμα, *Jerusalem*  τῇ προβατικῇ (πύλη), *the sheep gate*  κολυμβήθρᾱ, *pool*  ἡ ἐπιλεγομένη, *the one called*  Ἑβραϊστὶ, *in Hebrew*  Βηθζαθὰ, *Bethzatha*  στοὰς, *porticoes*  τῶν ἀσθενούντων, *of the weak/sick*  χωλῶν, ξηρῶν, *of the lame, of the withered/paralyzed*  τριάκοντα, *thirty*  ἔχων, intransitive here, *being* (with accusative of duration of time)  τῇ ἀσθενείᾳ, *weakness/sickness*]

τοῦτον ἰδὼν ὁ Ἰησοῦς κατακείμενον καὶ γνοὺς ὅτι πολὺν ἤδη χρόνον ἔχει, λέγει αὐτῷ, "θέλεις ὑγιὴς γενέσθαι;" ἀπεκρίθη αὐτῷ ὁ ἀσθενῶν, "κύριε, ἄνθρωπον οὐκ ἔχω ἵνα ὅταν ταραχθῇ τὸ ὕδωρ βάλῃ με εἰς τὴν κολυμβήθρᾱν· ἐν ᾧ δὲ ἔρχομαι ἐγώ, ἄλλος πρὸ ἐμοῦ καταβαίνει." λέγει αὐτῷ ὁ Ἰησοῦς, "ἔγειρε ἆρον τὸν κράβαττόν σου καὶ περιπάτει." καὶ εὐθέως ἐγένετο ὑγιὴς ὁ ἄνθρωπος καὶ ἦρεν τὸν κράβαττον αὐτοῦ καὶ περιεπάτει.

[ἔχει: supply ἐν τῇ ἀσθενείᾳ αὐτοῦ from the previous sentence; translate, *he has been in his sickness*  θέλεις = ἐθέλεις  κύριε, *lord; sir*  ταραχθῇ (from ταράττω), *is disturbed, is stirred up*  ἔγειρε, here, *get up!*  κράβαττόν, *bed, cot*  περιπάτει (from περιπατέω), *walk!*  εὐθέως, *immediately*]

# Η ΑΝΑΣΤΑΣΙΣ (β)

## VOCABULARY

*Verbs*
  **ἐνδίδωμι**, *I give in, yield*
  **ζεύγνῡμι, ζεύξω, ἔζευξα,**
  **ἔζευγμαι, ἐζεύχθην** or
  **ἐζύγην**, *I yoke*
  **ὀδΰρομαι**, rare in tenses other
  than present, *I grieve*
  **προσδέχομαι**, *I receive, admit;*
  *I await, expect*
*Nouns*
  **ἡ ἅμαξα, τῆς ἁμάξης**, *wagon*
  **ἡ βουλή, τῆς βουλῆς**, *plan; ad-*
  *vice; Council*
  **τὸ ἔαρ, τοῦ ἦρος**, *spring*
  **οἱ οἰκεῖοι, τῶν οἰκείων**, *the*
  *members of the household;*
  *family; relations*
  **ὁ πύργος, τοῦ πύργου**, *tower*

**τὸ στρατόπεδον, τοῦ στρατο-**
**πέδου**, *camp; army*
*Adjectives*
  **τοσόσδε, τοσήδε** (note the accent), **τοσόνδε**, *so great;* pl., *so*
  *many*
    = τοσοῦτος, τοσαύτη, τοσοῦτο, *so*
    *great;* pl., *so many*
    cf. τοιοῦτος, τοιαύτη, τοιοῦτο,
    *such; of this kind*
*Preposition*
  **ἐκτός** + gen., *outside*
*Adverb*
  **οὐδέποτε**, *never*
*Conjunction*
  **ὅπως** + subjunctive, *so that, in*
  *order to*

ταῦτα οὖν ἀκούσᾶσα ἡ Μυρρίνη σῑγήσᾶσα τῷ ἀνδρὶ ἐπείθετο,
καίπερ φοβουμένη μὴ χαλεπὴ γένηται ἡ ἀνάστασις.  πάντα οὖν τὸν
χειμῶνα παρεσκευάζοντο ὡς Ἀθήνᾱζε ἀναστησόμενοι ἐπειδὰν
εἰσβάλωσιν οἱ Πελοποννήσιοι.  ἅμα δ' ἦρι ἀρχομένῳ ἄγγελος ἀπὸ
τῶν Ἀθηνῶν ἀφίκετο λέγων ὅτι ἤδη συλλέγονται οἵ τε Λακεδαιμόνιοι    5
καὶ οἱ σύμμαχοι εἰς τὸν Ἰσθμόν· ὁ οὖν Δικαιόπολις τὸν Φίλιππον καὶ
τὸν Ξανθίᾱν ἔπεμψεν ὡς τὰ ποίμνια εἰς τὴν Εὔβοιαν κομιοῦντας.
ἔπειτα δὲ αὐτός τε καὶ ἡ Μυρρίνη τὴν ἅμαξαν ἐξαγαγόντες πάνθ'
ὅσα φέρειν ἐδύναντο εἰσέθεσαν.  πάντων δ' ἑτοίμων ὄντων ὁ
Δικαιόπολις τοὺς βοῦς ζεύξᾱς τὸν πάππον πολλὰ ὀδῡρόμενον          10
ἀνεβίβασεν.  τέλος δὲ ἥ τε Μυρρίνη καὶ ἡ Μέλιττα αὐταὶ ἀνέβησαν.
οὕτως οὖν ἐπορεύοντο δακρΰοντες καὶ ὀδῡρόμενοι, φοβούμενοι μὴ
οὐδέποτε ἐπανίωσιν.

[τὰ ποίμνια, *the flocks*    ἀνεβίβασεν (from ἀναβιβάζω), *put* (him) *onto* (the wagon)]

μακρὰ δ' ἦν ἡ ὁδὸς καὶ χαλεπή. ἔδει γὰρ κατὰ τὴν ἀμαξιτὸν
ἰέναι, πολλοῖς δ' ἐνετύγχανον αὐτουργοῖς οἵπερ πρὸς τὴν πόλιν     15
σπεύδοντες ἀλλήλοις ἐνεπόδιζον. τέλος δὲ ἑσπέρας ἤδη γιγνομένης ἐς
τὰς πύλας ἀφίκοντο, καὶ μόλις εἰσελθόντες τὴν νύκτα ἐν ἡρῴῳ τινὶ
ἔμειναν. τῇ δ' ὑστεραίᾳ ὁ Δικαιόπολις παρὰ τὸν ἀδελφὸν ἦλθεν ἵνα
αἰτῇ αὐτὸν εἴ πως βοηθεῖν δύναται. ὁ δ' ἀδελφὸς οὐκ ἐδύνατο
αὐτοὺς εἰς τὴν οἰκίαν δέχεσθαι τοσούτους ὄντας ἀλλὰ πύργον τινὰ     20
αὐτῷ ἔδειξεν ὃς πάντας χωρήσει. ὁ οὖν Δικαιόπολις πρὸς τοὺς
οἰκείους ἐπανελθὼν ἡγήσατο αὐτοῖς πρὸς τὸν πύργον, ἐν ᾧ ἔμελλον
διὰ παντὸς οἰκήσειν, ἕως οἱ μὲν Πελοποννήσιοι ἀπίοιεν, αὐτοὶ δὲ
πρὸς τοὺς ἀγροὺς ἐπανίοιεν.

[τὴν **ἀμαξιτὸν**, *the wagon road*   **ἀλλήλοις ἐνεπόδιζον**, *were getting in one another's way*   **ἡρῴῳ**, *shrine of a hero*   **χωρήσει**, *would* (lit., *will*) *hold*   **ἕως . . .**
**ἀπίοιεν . . . ἐπανίοιεν**: the optative without ἄν is used in indefinite or general
clauses when the verb in the governing clause is in the imperfect tense.]

—The following is adapted from Thucydides 2.12:

ἐν δὲ τούτῳ κῆρυξ ἀφίκετο ἐς τὰς Ἀθήνας, πέμψαντος τοῦ     25
Ἀρχιδάμου τῶν Λακεδαιμονίων βασιλέως· οἱ δὲ Ἀθηναῖοι οὐ
προσεδέξαντο αὐτὸν ἐς τὴν πόλιν οὐδ' ἐπὶ τὴν βουλήν· ἦν γὰρ
Περικλέους γνώμη κήρυκα καὶ πρεσβείᾱν μὴ δέχεσθαι Λακεδαιμονίων ἤδη στρατευομένων· ἀποπέμπουσιν οὖν αὐτὸν πρὶν
ἀκοῦσαι καὶ ἐκέλευον ἐκτὸς ὁρίων εἶναι αὐθημερόν, ξυμπέμπουσί τε     30
αὐτῷ ἀγωγούς, ὅπως μηδενὶ ξυγγένηται. ὁ δ' ἐπειδὴ ἐπὶ τοῖς ὁρίοις
ἐγένετο καὶ ἔμελλε διαλύσεσθαι, τοσόνδε εἰπὼν ἐπορεύετο ὅτι, "ἥδε ἡ
ἡμέρᾱ τοῖς Ἕλλησι μεγάλων κακῶν ἄρξει." ὡς δὲ ἀφίκετο ἐς τὸ
στρατόπεδον καὶ ἔγνω ὁ Ἀρχίδᾱμος ὅτι οἱ Ἀθηναῖοι οὐδέν πω
ἐνδώσουσιν, οὕτω δὴ ἄρᾱς τῷ στρατῷ προὐχώρει ἐς τὴν γῆν αὐτῶν.     35

[**πρεσβείᾱν**, *embassy*   **πρὶν ἀκοῦσαι** (πρίν + infin.), *before to hear (him) = before*
*hearing (him)*   **ὁρίων**, *boundaries*   **αὐθημερόν**, *that very day*   **ξυμπέμπουσί**, *they*
*send* X (acc.) *with* Y (dat.)   **ἀγωγούς**, *escorts*   **ξυγγένηται** + dat., *he would meet*
**διαλύσεσθαι**, *to part* (from the escort)   **πω**, *at all*   **ἄρᾱς** (from αἴρω, ἀρῶ, ἦρα),
here intransitive, *setting out / having set out*   **τῷ στρατῷ**, *with his army*]

## PRINCIPAL PARTS: More Nasal Stems (-ν-)

ἀποκτείν-ω, [κτενε-] ἀποκτενῶ, [κτειν-] ἀπέκτεινα, [κτον-] ἀπέκτονα, *I kill*
  The passive of ἀποκτείνω is supplied by ἀποθνῄσκω, *I die; I am killed.*

κρίν-ω, [κρινε-] κρινῶ, [κρῑν-] ἔκρῑνα, [κρι-] κέκρικα, κέκριμαι, ἐκρίθην,
    *I judge*
      ἀποκρίν-ομαι, [κρινε-] ἀποκρινοῦμαι, [κρῑν-] ἀπεκρῑνάμην, [κριν-]
        ἀποκέκριμαι, [κρι-] ἀπεκρίθην (New Testament), *I answer*

μέν-ω, [μενε-] μενῶ, [μειν-] ἔμεινα, [μενε-] μεμένηκα, intransitive, *I stay* (in
  one place); *I wait;* transitive, *I wait for*

## WORD BUILDING

Verbs with present stems ending in -ττ- are formed from stems ending in κ
and χ, e.g., πρᾱκ- > πρᾱττω, *I fare; I do;* τακ- > τάττω, *I marshal; I draw up;*
ταραχ- > ταράττω, *I confuse,* and φυλακ- > φυλάττω, *I guard.*

*Give the meanings of the words in the following sets:*

1. πρᾱττω    ἡ πρᾶξις    τὸ πρᾶγμα    πρᾱκτικός, -ή, -όν
2. τάττω     ἡ τάξις     τὸ τάγμα     τακτός, -ή, -όν    ἄτακτος, -ον
3. ταράττω   ἡ ταραχή    ἡ ἀταραξίᾱ   ἀτάρακτος, -ον
4. φυλάττω   ὁ φύλαξ     ἡ φυλακή

## GRAMMAR

### 3. Indirect Statements and Questions

Indirect statements and indirect questions have been used in the sentences of the stories from nearly the beginning of this course. Indirect
statements may be introduced by ὅτι or ὡς, *that,* and have their verbs in the
indicative.

You may have noticed that in indirect statements and indirect questions, Greek, unlike English, retains the tense of the original statement
or question, even when the main verb is in a past tense. Study the following examples:

Direct Statement:
    "ἡ ἐμὴ μήτηρ πρὸς τὴν κρήνην ἔρχεται."
    *"My mother is going to the spring."*

Indirect Statement:
    ἡ παρθένος εἶπεν **ὅτι ἡ μήτηρ πρὸς τὴν κρήνην ἔρχεται.**
    *The girl said **that her mother was going to the spring.***
    (The present tense is retained in the indirect statement in Greek
    but is changed to the past in English.)

Indirect questions may be introduced by the same words that introduce direct questions, e.g., τίς, *who?* Usually, however, certain indefinite

forms are used instead, as in the third row of the following chart:

| whence? | whither? | how much? | when? | where? | who? |
|---------|----------|-----------|-------|--------|------|
| πόθεν; | ποι; | πόσος; | πότε; | που; | τίς; |
| ὁπόθεν | ὅποι | ὁπόσυς | ὁπότε | ὅπου | ὅστις |

Direct Questions:

"πότε ἐπάνεισιν;"
*"When will she return?"*

"πόσον χρόνον ἀπέσται;"
*"How long will she be away?"*

Indirect Questions:

ὁ πατὴρ ἤρετο **ὁπότε/πότε ἐπάνεισιν.**
*The father asked **when she would return.***
(The future indicative is retained in the indirect question in Greek but is changed to *would return* in English.)

"οὐκ εἶπεν ἡ μήτηρ **ὁπόσον/πόσον χρόνον ἀπέσται.**"
*"Mother did not say **how long she would be away.**"*

Indirect Statement with Indirect Question:

ἡ παρθένος ἀπεκρίνατο <u>**ὡς οὐκ εἶπεν ἡ μήτηρ ὁπόσον/πόσον χρόνον ἀπέσται.**</u>
*The girl answered <u>**that mother had not said how long she would be away.**</u>*

## Exercise 22 δ

*Read aloud and translate.   Identify indirect statements and indirect questions.   Give in English the original direct statement or question:*

1.   ὁ πατὴρ τὴν παρθένον ἤρετο ὁπόθεν/πόθεν ἦλθεν.
2.   ἡ δὲ ἀποκρῑναμένη εἶπεν ὅτι ἦλθεν ἀπὸ τῆς οἰκίας καὶ δι' ὀλίγου ἐκεῖσε ἐπάνεισιν.
3.   ὁ ἄγγελος εἶπεν ὅτι οἱ πρέσβεις ἤδη προσχωροῦσι καὶ δι' ὀλίγου παρέσονται.
4.   ὁ δοῦλος εἶπεν ὅτι οὐ δυνατόν ἐστι λίθον τοσοῦτον αἴρειν.
5.   ὁ δὲ δοῦλος εἶπεν ὅτι ἐὰν μὴ συλλαμβάνῃ ὁ δεσπότης, οὐ δυνήσεται αἴρειν τὸν λίθον.
6.   οὐδεὶς ἠγνόει ὅτι οἱ πολέμιοι δι' ὀλίγου εἰς τὴν γῆν εἰσβαλοῦσιν.
7.   ὁ Δικαιόπολις τῇ γυναικὶ εἶπεν ὡς δεῖ εἰς τὸ ἄστυ ἀναστῆναι.
8.   ἡ γυνὴ ἤρετο ὅπου/ποῦ εἰς τὸ ἄστυ ἀναστάντες οἰκήσουσιν.
9.   ἀπεκρίνατο ὁ Δικαιόπολις ὅτι ἐπειδὰν εἰσβάλωσιν οἱ πολέμιοι, ἐν τῷ ἄστει ἀσφαλεῖς ἔσονται.
10.   ἡ οὖν γυνὴ εἶπεν ὅτι πάντα ποιήσει ὅσ' ἂν κελεύῃ ὁ ἀνήρ.

# Η ΝΟΣΟΣ

*Read the following passages (adapted from Thucydides 2.47–48) and answer the comprehension questions:*

In early summer of 430 B.C., when the Peloponnesians invaded Attica for the second time, plague struck Athens. The city was crowded with refugees from the country, and living conditions were not healthy.

τοῦ δὲ θέρους εὐθὺς ἀρχομένου Πελοποννήσιοι καὶ οἱ ξύμμαχοι ἐσέβαλον ἐς τὴν Ἀττικήν· καὶ ὄντων αὐτῶν ἐν τῇ Ἀττικῇ οὐ πολλὰς ἡμέρας, ἡ νόσος πρῶτον ἤρξατο γενέσθαι τοῖς Ἀθηναίοις· λέγουσιν ὅτι πρότερον πολλαχόσε ἐγκατέσκηψεν, οὐ μέντοι τοσοῦτός γε λοιμὸς ἐγένετο οὐδὲ τοσοῦτοι ἄνθρωποι ἀπέθανον.

[τοῦ ... θέρους, *the summer*   ἡ νόσος, *the disease, plague*   πολλαχόσε, *onto many places*   ἐγκατέσκηψεν* (from ἐγκατασκήπτω), *it had fallen* (lit., *fell*) *upon*   οὐ μέντοι ... γε, *but (that)* . . . *not*   λοιμὸς, *plague*]

1  What did the Peloponnesians do at the beginning of summer?
2.  When did the plague begin in Athens?
3.  How were the plague and its effects different in Athens from elsewhere?

οὔτε γὰρ ἰατροὶ ὠφέλουν τὸ πρῶτον, ἀγνοοῦντες τὴν νόσον, ἀλλ' αὐτοὶ μάλιστα   5
ἔθνησκον ὅσῳ καὶ μάλιστα προσῇσαν τοῖς νοσοῦσιν, οὔτε ἄλλη ἀνθρωπείᾱ τέχνη ὠφέλει οὐδεμία. ἤρξατο δὲ ἡ νόσος τὸ μὲν πρῶτον, ὡς λέγουσιν, ἐξ Αἰθιοπίᾱς τῆς ὑπὲρ Αἰγύπτου, ἔπειτα δὲ καὶ ἐς Αἴγυπτον κατέβη καὶ ἐς τὴν βασιλέως γῆν τὴν πολλήν.

[ἔθνησκον, *they were dying*   ὅσῳ, *in as much as*   προσῇσαν, *were going near, were consorting with*   ἀνθρωπείᾱ, *human*   τέχνη, *skill, art*   Αἰθιοπίᾱς, *Ethiopia*   ὑπὲρ + gen., *above*, here, *south of*   βασιλέως, *the king of Persia*   γῆν τὴν πολλήν, *the greater part of the land*]

4.  Why were doctors of no help? Why did they, especially, perish?
5.  To what avail were other human efforts?
6.  Where is the plague said to have originated?
7.  What countries had it already ravaged?

ἐς δὲ τὴν Ἀθηναίων πόλιν ἐξαίφνης ἐσέπεσε, καὶ τὸ πρῶτον ἐν τῷ Πειραιεῖ   10
ἥψατο τῶν ἀνθρώπων· ὕστερον δὲ καὶ ἐς τὴν ἄνω πόλιν ἀφίκετο, καὶ ἔθνησκον πολλῷ πλέονες ἤδη ἄνθρωποι. ἐγὼ δὲ οἷον ἐγίγνετο λέξω, αὐτός τε νοσήσᾱς καὶ αὐτὸς ἰδὼν ἄλλους πάσχοντας.

[ἥψατο (from ἅπτω, *I fasten*) + gen., *it took hold of*   οἷον ἐγίγνετο, *what it was like*]

9.  Where did the plague begin to ravage the Athenians?
10.  What happened when the plague reached the upper city of Athens?

11. What two reasons does Thucydides give for why he is a reliable source of information about the plague?

### Exercise 22 ε

*Translate into Greek:*

1. The doctors are afraid to approach the sick (*use participle*).
2. For whoever touches (*use* ἅπτομαι + *gen.*) a sick man (*use participle of* νοσέω), himself catches (falls into–*use aorist participle of* ἐμπίπτω + εἰς + acc.) the plague and dies.
3. The doctors said that they could not help, not knowing the disease.
4. Although we are afraid that we may become sick (fall into the sickness), we must stay in the city until the enemy goes away.
5. If they go away soon, we will hurry to the country to escape the plague.

# Classical Greek

## Solon

In the following lines Solon proudly defends the reforms he has put through (fragment 5):

δήμῳ μὲν γὰρ ἔδωκα τόσον γέρας ὅσσον ἀπαρκεῖν

    τῑμῆς οὔτ᾽ ἀφελὼν οὔτ᾽ ἐπορεξάμενος·

οἳ δ᾽ εἶχον δύναμιν καὶ χρήμασιν ἦσαν ἀγητοί,

    καὶ τοῖς ἐφρασάμην μηδὲν ἀεικὲς ἔχειν·

ἔστην δ᾽ ἀμφιβαλὼν κρατερὸν σάκος ἀμφοτέροισι,

    νῑκᾶν δ᾽ οὐκ εἴᾱσ᾽ οὐδετέρους ἀδίκως.

[τόσον γέρας, *as much privilege*   ὅσσον (= ὅσον) ἀπαρκεῖν, *as to be enough*   ἐπορεξάμενος (from ἐπορέγω), *giving too much*   οἱ δ(ὲ), *and (for those) who*   ἀγητοί, *admired*   καὶ τοῖς ἐφρασάμην, *I contrived for them too*   μηδὲν ἀεικὲς, *nothing improper*   ἀμφιβαλὼν, *having put around/over*   κρατερὸν σάκος, *my mighty shield*   ἀμφοτέροισι = ἀμφοτέροις, *both*   εἴασ(α) (from ἐάω), *I allowed*   οὐδετέρους, *neither* (side)   ἀδίκως, *unjustly*]

Solon's reforms replaced the aristocracy (rule of the nobles) by a timocracy, in which political privilege was related to property; he divided the people into four property classes, each of which had appropriate political status.

# 23

# Η ΕΣΒΟΛΗ (α)

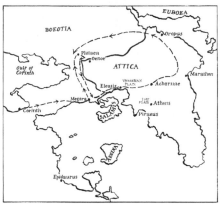

ἡ Ἀττικὴ γῆ τέμνεται ὑπὸ τῶν πολεμίων.

## VOCABULARY

*Verbs*

ἐπεξέρχομαι [= ἐπι- + ἐκ- + ἔρχομαι] + dat., *I march out against, attack*

καθέζομαι [= κατα- + ἕζομαι], [ἑδε-] καθεδοῦμαι, *I sit down; I encamp*

περιοράω, *I overlook, disregard*

τάττω (τάσσω), [τακ-] τάξω, ἔταξα, τέταχα, τέταγμαι, ἐτάχθην, *I marshal, draw up in battle array; I station, post*

τέμνω, [τεμε-] τεμῶ, [τεμ-] ἔτεμον, [τμε-] τέτμηκα, τέτμημαι, ἐτμήθην, *I cut; I ravage*

*Nouns*

ἡ αἰτίᾱ, τῆς αἰτίᾱς, *blame; responsibility; cause*

ὁ δῆμος, τοῦ δήμου, *the people; township; deme*

ἡ εἰσβολή (ἐσ-), τῆς εἰσβολῆς, *invasion*

ἡ πεῖρα, τῆς πείρᾱς, *trial; attempt; test*

ἡ προσβολή, τῆς προσβολῆς, *attack*

τὸ φρούριον, τοῦ φρουρίου, *garrison*

τὸ χωρίον, τοῦ χωρίου, *place; district*

ὁ χῶρος, τοῦ χώρου, *place*

*Adjective*

ἐπιτήδειος, -ᾱ, -ον, *friendly;* + infin., *suitable for*

*Adverb*

ᾗπερ, *where*

*Conjunctions*

ὁπότε, *when*

ὁπόταν [= ὁπότε + ἄν] + subjunctive, *when(ever)*

*Proper Names and Adjectives*

αἱ Ἀχαρναί, τῶν Ἀχαρνῶν, *Acharnae*

οἱ Ἀχαρνῆς, τῶν Ἀχαρνέων, *inhabitants of Acharnae, the Acharnians*

ὁ δὲ στρατὸς τῶν Πελοποννησίων προϊὼν ἀφίκετο τῆς Ἀττικῆς ἐς
Οἰνόην πρῶτον, ᾗπερ ἔμελλον ἐσβαλεῖν.  καὶ ὡς ἐκαθέζοντο,
προσβολὰς παρεσκευάζοντο τῷ τείχει ποιησόμενοι μηχαναῖς τε καὶ
ἄλλῳ τρόπῳ· ἡ γὰρ Οἰνόη οὖσα ἐν μεθορίοις τῆς Ἀττικῆς καὶ
Βοιωτίᾱς ἐτετείχιστο, καὶ αὐτῷ φρουρίῳ οἱ Ἀθηναῖοι ἐχρῶντο ὁπότε      5
πόλεμος γένοιτο.  τάς τε οὖν προσβολὰς παρεσκευάζοντο καὶ ἄλλως
ἐνδιέτρῑψαν χρόνον περὶ αὐτήν.  αἰτίᾱν τε οὐκ ὀλίγην Ἀρχίδᾱμος
ἔλαβεν ἀπ᾽ αὐτοῦ· οἱ γὰρ Ἀθηναῖοι πάντα ἐσεκομίζοντο ἐν τῷ
χρόνῳ τούτῳ.

[τῆς Ἀττικῆς, gen. of place, *in Attica*    προσβολὰς . . . τῷ τείχει ποιησόμενοι, future participle expressing purpose, *to make attacks on the wall*    μηχαναῖς, *siege engines*    ἄλλῳ τρόπῳ, *otherwise*    μεθορίοις, *borders*    ἐτετείχιστο (pluperfect, from τειχίζω), *had been fortified with a wall*    αὐτῷ, *it*    φρουρίῳ, *as a garrison*    ὁπότε πόλεμος γένοιτο (optative), *whenever war occurred*    ἄλλως, *in other ways*    ἐνδιέτρῑψαν (from ἐνδιατρίβω), *they spent, wasted*    αὐτήν, i.e., Oenoe    αὐτοῦ, i.e., *from wasting time there*]

ἐπειδὴ μέντοι προσβαλόντες τῇ Οἰνόῃ καὶ πᾶσαν ἰδέᾱν      10
πειρᾱ́σαντες οὐκ ἐδύναντο ἑλεῖν, οἵ τε Ἀθηναῖοι οὐδὲν ἐπεκηρῡκεύοντο, οὕτω δὴ ὁρμήσαντες ἀπ᾽ αὐτῆς ἐσέβαλον ἐς τὴν Ἀττικήν·
ἡγεῖτο δὲ Ἀρχίδᾱμος Λακεδαιμονίων βασιλεύς.

[ἰδέᾱν, *sort; form; way*    ἐπεκηρῡκεύοντο, *were sending ambassadors to make peace proposals*]

καὶ καθεζόμενοι ἔτεμνον πρῶτον μὲν Ἐλευσῖνα καὶ τὸ Θρῑάσιον
πεδίον.  ἔπειτα δὲ προὐχώρουν ἕως ἀφίκοντο ἐς Ἀχαρνάς, χωρίον      15
μέγιστον τῆς Ἀττικῆς τῶν δήμων καλουμένων, καὶ καθεζόμενοι ἐς
αὐτὸ στρατόπεδόν τε ἐποιήσαντο χρόνον τε πολὺν ἐμμείναντες
ἔτεμνον.  λέγεται δὲ ὅτι γνώμῃ τοιᾷδε ὁ Ἀρχίδᾱμος περί τε τὰς
Ἀχαρνὰς ὡς ἐς μάχην ταξάμενος ἔμεινε καὶ ἐς τὸ πεδίον ἐκείνη τῇ
ἐσβολῇ οὐ κατέβη· ἤλπιζε γὰρ τοὺς Ἀθηναίους ἐπεξιέναι καὶ τὴν γῆν      20
μὴ περιόψεσθαι τεμνομένην.

[καλουμένων, *so-called*    ἐς αὐτὸ, *in it*, i.e., *there*    ἐμμείναντες, *remaining there*
ὡς ἐς μάχην, *as for battle*    τοὺς Ἀθηναίους ἐπεξιέναι, *that the Athenians would
march out against* (him)    τὴν γῆν . . . τεμνομένην, *(the fact) that their land was
being ravaged*]

ἐπειδὴ οὖν αὐτῷ ἐς Ἐλευσῖνα καὶ τὸ Θρῑάσιον πεδίον οὐκ
ἀπήντησαν, πεῖραν ἐποιεῖτο περὶ Ἀχαρνὰς καθήμενος εἰ ἐπεξίᾱσιν·
ἅμα μὲν γὰρ αὐτῷ ὁ χῶρος ἐπιτήδειος ἐφαίνετο ἐνστρατοπεδεῦσαι,
ἅμα δὲ ἐνόμιζε τοὺς Ἀχαρνέᾱς μέγα μέρος ὄντας τῆς πόλεως
(τρισχίλιοι γὰρ ὁπλῖται ἐγένοντο) οὐ περιόψεσθαι τὰ σφέτερα
διαφθειρόμενα ἀλλὰ ὁρμήσειν καὶ τοὺς πάντας ἐς μάχην.

[ἀπήντησαν (from ἀπαντάω) + dat., *they went to meet*    καθήμενος, *sitting, i.e., en-camped*   ἅμα μὲν ... ἅμα δέ, *at the same time*   ἐνστρατοπεδεῦσαι, *to encamp in*   τρισχίλιοι, *three thousand*   τὰ σφέτερα διαφθειρόμενα, *(the fact) that their own property* (lit., *things) was being destroyed*   ὁρμήσειν, *would urge on, rouse* τοὺς πάντας, *everyone*]

—adapted from Thucydides 2.18–20

## PRINCIPAL PARTS: More Liquid Stems (-ρ-)

αἴρω, [ἀρε-] ἀρῶ, [ἀρ-] ἦρα, ἦρκα, ἦρμαι, ἤρθην, *I lift, raise up;* with reflexive pronoun, *I get up;* intransitive, *I get under way, set out*

διαφθείρω, [φθερε-] διαφθερῶ, [φθειρ-] διέφθειρα, [φθαρ-] διέφθαρκα or [φθορ-] διέφθορα, [φθαρ-] διέφθαρμαι, διεφθάρην, *I destroy*

ἐγείρω, [ἐγερε-] ἐγερῶ, [ἐγειρ-] ἤγειρα, [thematic 2nd aorist middle; ἐγρ-] ἠγρόμην (*I awoke*), [ἐγορ-] ἐγρήγορα (*I am awake*), [ἐγερ-] ἐγήγερμαι, ἠγέρθην, active, transitive, *I wake X up;* middle and passive, intransitive, *I wake up*

## WORD STUDY

*Give the Greek words from which the following English political terms are derived:*

1. politics
2. demagogue
3. rhetoric
4. democracy
5. monarchy
6. tyranny
7. ochlocracy (ὁ ὄχλος, *mob*)
8. autonomy

## GRAMMAR

### 1. Indirect Statements with Infinitives

Indirect statements may be expressed with the infinitive instead of with ὅτι or ὡς and the indicative (see Chapter 22, Grammar 3, pages 102–103).

a. When the subject of the infinitive is different from that of the leading verb it is in the accusative, e.g.:

ὁ πατήρ μοι ἔφη <u>τὸν νεανίαν</u> τῷ γέροντι <u>συλλήψεσθαι</u>.
*The father said to me **that <u>the young man</u> <u>would help</u> the old man**.*

The tense of the infinitive in the indirect statement in Greek is the same as the tense of the verb in the original or direct statement. In the example above the direct statement would have been ὁ νεανίας τῷ γέροντι συλλήψεται, *The young man will help the old man*, with a future indicative, which becomes a future infinitive in the indirect statement. The nominative subject of the verb in the direct statement, i.e., ὁ νεανίας, becomes the accusative subject of the infinitive in the indirect statement, <u>τὸν νεανίαν</u> τῷ γέροντι <u>συλλήψεσθαι</u>, *that the young man will help the old man*, or, after a leading verb in a past tense, *that the young man would help the old man*.

b. When the subject of the infinitive is the same as that of the leading verb it may be unexpressed in Greek but it must be supplied in English, e.g.:

<u>ὁ νεανίας</u> μοι ἔφη τῷ γέροντι συλλήψεσθαι.
*The <u>young man</u> said to me **that <u>he</u> would help the old man**.*

If the subject of the infinitive is the same as that of the leading verb and is expressed or modified by an adjective or participle, it will be in the nominative case, e.g.:

<u>ὁ νεανίας</u> μοι ἔφη <u>αὐτὸς</u> τῷ γέροντι συλλήψεσθαι.
*<u>The young man</u> said to me **that he <u>himself</u> would help the old man**.*

<u>ὁ νεανίας</u> μοι ἔφη οἴκαδε <u>ἐπανελθὼν</u> τῷ γέροντι συλλήψεσθαι.
*<u>The young man</u> said to me **that <u>having returned home</u> he would help the old man**.*

c. Indirect statements with the infinitive may be introduced by other verbs as well as φημί, especially verbs of *thinking*, *believing*, and *hoping*, e.g.:

<u>ἐνόμιζε</u> τοὺς Ἀχαρνέας οὐ περιόψεσθαι τὰ σφέτερα διαφθειρόμενα.
*<u>He was thinking</u> that the Acharnians would not disregard (the fact) that their own property was being destroyed.*

<u>ἐπίστευεν</u> τοὺς Ἀχαρνέας ὁρμήσειν τοὺς πάντας ἐς μάχην.
*<u>He was believing</u> that the Acharnians would rouse everyone to battle.*

<u>ἤλπιζε</u> τοὺς Ἀχαρνέας ὁρμήσειν τοὺς πάντας ἐς μάχην.
*<u>He was hoping</u> that the Acharnians would rouse everyone to battle.*

d. The negative is usually the same in the indirect statement as it was in the direct statement, e.g.:

Direct:
τῷ γέροντι **οὐ** βοηθήσω.
*I will **not** come to the old man's aid.*

Indirect:

οὐκ ἔφη τῷ γέροντι βοηθήσειν.

*He said that he would **not** come to the old man's aid.*

*He denied that he would come to the old man's aid.*

Note that in the indirect statement the negative is placed before ἔφη.

Verbs of *hoping, threatening,* and *promising* and equivalent phrases are often followed by the negative μή in indirect statements, e.g.:

ἤλπιζε τοὺς Ἀθηναίους τὴν γῆν **μὴ** περιόψεσθαι τεμνομένην.

*He was hoping that the Athenians would **not** disregard (the fact) that their land was being ravaged.*

ἐλπίδα εἶχε τοὺς Ἀθηναίους τὴν γῆν **μὴ** περιόψεσθαι τεμνομένην.

*He was holding hope that the Athenians would **not** disregard (the fact) that their land was being ravaged.*

N.B. In indirect statements the present infinitive refers to the same time as that of the leading verb, the future infinitive refers to time subsequent to that of the leading verb, and the aorist infinitive refers to time prior to that of the leading verb. The infinitive of εἶμι and its compounds may, in indirect statements, refer to time subsequent to that of the leading verb, replacing a future indicative of a direct statement. Observe these temporal relationships carefully in your translations of the following sentences.

## Exercise 23 α

*Read aloud and translate:*

1.  ὁ παῖς τῷ νεᾱνίᾳ ἔφη πρὸς τὸν ἀγρὸν ἰέναι ὡς τὸν πατέρα ζητήσων.
2.  ὁ δὲ νεᾱνίᾱς οὐκ ἔφη τὸν πατέρα αὐτοῦ ἐν τῷ ἀγρῷ ἰδεῖν.
3.  ὁ παῖς ἔφη τὸν πατέρα ἐν τῷ ἄστει ζητήσειν.
4.  ἤλπιζε γὰρ ἐκεῖ εὑρήσειν αὐτὸν τὰ πρόβατα ἀποδιδόμενον.
5.  ὁ νεᾱνίᾱς ἐπίστευε τὸν πατέρα αὐτοῦ ἤδη οἴκαδε ἐπανελθεῖν.
6.  ὁ παῖς ἔφη αὐτὸς δι' ὀλίγου οἴκαδε ἐπανιέναι.
7.  ὁ Περικλῆς ἔφη ἀεὶ τῆς αὐτῆς γνώμης ἔχεσθαι.
8.  ἐνόμιζε γὰρ τοὺς Ἀθηναίους εἰς πόλεμον καταστάντας τοὺς Πελοποννησίους νῑκήσειν.
9.  οὐκ ἔφη τοὺς Πελοποννησίους πόλεμον χρόνιον ποιεῖσθαι δύνασθαι.
10. ἔφη τοὺς πατέρας αὐτῶν ἀνδρείως μαχομένους τοὺς Πέρσᾱς νῑκῆσαι.
11. ἤλπιζεν αὐτοὺς μὴ κακίονας τῶν πατέρων γενήσεσθαι.
12. οἱ Ἀθηναῖοι ἐνόμιζον τὸν Περικλῆ ἄριστα παραινέσαι.
13. ὁ Δικαιόπολις ἔφη ἀνάγκην εἶναι εἰς τὸ ἄστυ ἀναστῆναι.
14. ἡ δὲ Μυρρίνη οὐκ ἔφη δυνατὸν εἶναι τοῦτο ποιεῖν.
15. τέλος δὲ ἔφη πάντα πράξειν ὅσα παραινεῖ ὁ Δικαιόπολις.

## 2. Indirect Statements with Participles

After verbs of *knowing*, *learning*, and *perceiving* indirect statements may be expressed with a participle, e.g.:

ὄψονται τὴν γῆν <u>τεμνομένην</u>.
*They will see **that their land is being ravaged**.*

ὄψονται τὰ σφέτερα <u>διαφθειρόμενα</u>.
*They will see **that their own property is being destroyed**.*

In the following examples note that, as with the infinitive construction, the subject of the indirect statement is not expressed if it is the same as that of the leading verb. Note also that in this case the participle is in the nominative case. Also, αὐτός, αὐτή, αὐτό may be used in the nominative case to emphasize the subject of the indirect statement. Note the following:

ἐπίστανται εἰς μέγιστον κίνδῡνον <u>καταστάντες</u>.
*They know **that they have gotten** into the greatest danger.*

οἶδα <u>αὐτὸς</u> μὲν <u>ὀρθῶς γιγνώσκων</u>, ἐκείνους δὲ ἁμαρτάνοντας.
*I know **that I myself am right**, and that they are wrong.*

The rules for tenses and negatives are the same for the participle construction as for the infinitive construction.

### Exercise 23 β

1. ὁ αὐτουργὸς εἶδε τὸν δοῦλον ὑπὸ τῷ δένδρῳ καθεύδοντα.
2. ὁ δοῦλος ἔγνω τὸν δεσπότην μάλα ὀργιζόμενον.
3. αἱ γυναῖκες εἶδον λύκον μέγαν πρὸς τὴν κρήνην προσιόντα.
4. ἡ μήτηρ ἔγνω τὴν θυγατέρα τὸν λύκον μάλα φοβουμένην.
5. ἡ μήτηρ ἠπίστατο αὐτὴ μὲν ἀσφαλὴς οὖσα, τὴν δὲ θυγατέρα εἰς κίνδῡνον ἐμπῑπτουσαν.
6. δι᾽ ὀλίγου εἶδε τὸν λύκον τρεψάμενον πρὸς τὰ ὄρη ἀποφεύγοντα.
7. τὴν οὖν θυγατέρα καλέσᾱσα, "ἐπάνελθε," ἔφη· "ἆρ᾽ οὐκ οἶσθα τὸν λύκον ἤδη ἀπιόντα;"
8. οἶδα τοὺς πολεμίους εἰς τὴν γῆν δι᾽ ὀλίγου εἰσιόντας.
9. οἱ αὐτουργοὶ ἠπίσταντο εἰς μέγιστον κίνδῡνον καταστάντες.
10. ὁ ἰᾱτρὸς ἔγνω αὐτὸς τῇ νόσῳ ἀποθανούμενος.

## Greek Wisdom

### Heraclitus

ἐκ τῶν διαφερόντων καλλίστην ἁρμονίᾱν γίγνεσθαι ὁ Ἡράκλειτός φησιν. **Fragment 8 Diels**

# The Peloponnesian War:
# First Phase (431–421 B.C.)

The events that led up to the war are briefly outlined in Chapter 20, pages 60–61. Pericles was convinced that war was inevitable and, while observing the terms of the Thirty Years' Peace to the letter, he was not prepared to make any concessions to the Peloponnesians. He believed firmly that Athenian naval and financial superiority would bring victory in a war of attrition and that the war had better be fought now than later.

He had a clearly conceived strategy, which he outlined to the people in the speech from which you read extracts in Chapter 21β. The Athenian army could not risk battle in the field against the Peloponnesians, whose army outnumbered theirs by two to one and included the best hoplites in Greece. But the Athenians with a fleet of 300 triremes controlled the seas and the empire, so that Athens was invulnerable, provided that she was prepared to abandon Attica: "You must make up your minds to abandon your land and houses and keep guard over the sea and the city." At the same time, he intended to use the navy to make landings on enemy territory in the Peloponnesus and would attempt to regain control of Megara and its ports and to win over northwest Greece, so that a blockade of the Corinthian Gulf would bring Corinth to her knees.

Whether this Periclean strategy of a war of attrition, undermining the determination of the enemy, would have been successful, we cannot tell; for Pericles' calculations were upset by unforeseen factors, in particular by the plague that swept the city in 430–429 B.C. and by the cost of the war, which proved far higher than Pericles had calculated, so that by 422 B.C. the huge financial reserves on which he had relied were exhausted.

The war lasted from 431 to 404 B.C. with an intermission from 421 to 416. In this essay we will outline the events of the first half only, the Archidamian War, as it is called. In early summer 431 B.C. the Peloponnesian army under the Spartan king Archidamus invaded Attica, staying for about a month, while the Athenians withdrew behind the walls of Athens and saw their land ravaged. As soon as the Peloponnesian army withdrew, Pericles led the Athenian army out and devastated Megara. At the same time a fleet of 100 triremes together with allied contingents sailed around the Peloponnesus, landing at various points and causing havoc. In the autumn this force joined up with the Athenian army for a second attack on Megara.

The operations of the next few years followed a similar pattern with the northwest of Greece seeing more activity. Both sides had allies in this area and sent expeditions to help them win control of the approaches to the Corinthian Gulf. The outcome was inconclusive except in the Gulf itself, where the brilliant victories of the Athenian admiral Phormio over a much larger Peloponnesian fleet finally established Athenian naval supremacy beyond all doubt (see Chapter 29).

In 425 B.C. a minor operation nearly brought the war to an end. An Athenian fleet sailing around the Peloponnesus was forced by bad weather to land

at Pylos, on the west coast of the Peloponnesus.  When the fleet continued on
its way, it left behind a small force that fortified the promontory of Pylos and
held it against Spartan attacks until reinforcements arrived.  In the course of
this operation, 420 Spartans were cut off on the island of Sphacteria.  Eventually, the surviving 292 Spartans surrendered and were taken to Athens.  The
Spartan authorities in their eagerness to recover the prisoners sent an embassy to Athens to negotiate peace; the generous terms offered were rejected by
the Assembly on the advice of Cleon, who had succeeded Pericles, who had
died in 429 B.C., as the most influential speaker in the Assembly.

The following year the war took a new turn when a Spartan officer named
Brasidas led a small force overland through northern Greece to Thrace.
There he fomented revolt among the cities of Chalcidice, which belonged to
the Athenian Empire, and succeeded in taking Amphipolis, a city of great
strategic importance on the river Strymon.  The historian Thucydides was
one of the generals commanding in this area.  He arrived with a fleet just too
late to save the city, and for this failure he was brought to trial and exiled.

The Spartans were still eager for peace, and the Athenians were weary of
the war.  There was now a strong peace party, led by Nicias.  In 423 B.C. a
one-year truce was agreed upon, during which time negotiations for a permanent settlement were to go forward.  When the truce ended, however, Cleon
persuaded the Assembly to send him in command of an expedition to recover
Amphipolis.  He scored some initial successes, but then Brasidas attacked
him outside the walls of Amphipolis.  In the ensuing battle both he and Brasidas were killed.

With their deaths, the chief obstacles to peace were removed, and in 421
B.C. a treaty was negotiated between Athens and Sparta, which is known as
the Peace of Nicias.  Each side agreed to abandon nearly all the gains they
had made in the war and to observe the peace for fifty years.  The outcome of
these ten years of costly and bitter struggle was thus a return to the position
that had existed before the war.  It proved to be a stalemate, nor were the
prospects for long-term peace good.  Nothing had been resolved.  The basic
reason for the war, the Peloponnesian fears of Athenian power, was still
valid, nor, as events showed, was Athenian ambition quenched.  Five years
later the war was to start again, this time with consequences disastrous for
Athens.

---

## Greek Wisdom

### Heraclitus

ἦθος ἀνθρώπῳ δαίμων.  Fragment 119 Diels

# Η ΕΣΒΟΛΗ (β)

## VOCABULARY

*Verbs*

**διαλύω**, *I disband* (an army);
*I disperse* (a fleet)

**ἐάω**, imperfect, εἴων (irregular augment), **ἐάσω** (note ᾱ instead of η after the ε), **εἴᾱσα** (irregular augment), **εἴᾱκα**, **εἴᾱμαι, εἰάθην**, *I allow, let be*

**ἐμμένω** [= ἐν- + μένω], *I remain in*

**ἐξαμαρτάνω** [= ἐκ- + ἁμαρτάνω], *I miss; I fail; I make a mistake*

**οἴομαι** or **οἶμαι**, imperfect, ᾠόμην or ᾤμην, [οἰε-] **οἰήσομαι, ᾠήθην**, *I think*

*Nouns*

**ἡ ἐλπίς, τῆς ἐλπίδος**, *hope; expectation*

**ἡ ἔξοδος, τῆς ἐξόδου**, *going out; marching forth; military expedition*

**τὸ στάδιον, τοῦ σταδίου**, pl., **τὰ στάδια** or **οἱ στάδιοι**, *stade* (1 stade = 607 feet or 185 meters; 8.7 stades = 1 mile; 5.4 stades = 1 kilometer)

*Adjective*

**ἕκαστος, -η, -ον**, *each*

*Proper Name*

**οἱ Βοιωτοί, τῶν Βοιωτῶν**, *Boeotians*

Ἀθηναῖοι δέ, μέχρι μὲν οὗ περὶ Ἐλευσῖνα καὶ τὸ Θριάσιον πεδίον ὁ στρατὸς ἦν, ἐλπίδα τινὰ εἶχον αὐτοὺς ἐς τὸ ἐγγυτέρω μὴ προϊέναι· ἐπειδὴ δὲ περὶ τὰς Ἀχαρνὰς εἶδον τὸν στρατὸν ἑξήκοντα σταδίους τῆς πόλεως ἀπέχοντα, οὐκέτι ἀνασχετὸν ἐποιοῦντο, ἀλλά, τῆς γῆς τεμνομένης ἐν τῷ ἐμφανεῖ, δεινὸν αὐτοῖς ἐφαίνετο καὶ ἐδόκει τοῖς τε    5 ἄλλοις καὶ μάλιστα τοῖς νεᾱνίαις ἐπεξιέναι καὶ μὴ περιορᾶν. κατὰ ξυστάσεις τε γιγνόμενοι ἐν πολλῇ ἔριδι ἦσαν, οἱ μὲν κελεύοντες ἐπεξιέναι, οἱ δέ τινες οὐκ ἐῶντες. οἵ τε Ἀχαρνῆς οἰόμενοι αὐτοὶ μέγιστον μέρος εἶναι τῶν Ἀθηναίων, ὡς αὐτῶν ἡ γῆ ἐτέμνετο, ἐνῆγον τὴν ἔξοδον μάλιστα.    10

[**μέχρι ... οὗ**, *as long as*    **ἐς τὸ ἐγγυτέρω**, *closer*    **ἀνασχετὸν**, *tolerable* **ἐποιοῦντο**, *they were considering*    **ἐν τῷ ἐμφανεῖ**, *visibly, within eyesight*    **κατὰ ξυστάσεις ... γιγνόμενοι**, *assembling into groups*    **ἔριδι**, *contention, strife* **ἐνῆγον** (from ἐν- + ἄγω), *were urging*]

παντί τε τρόπῳ ἀνηρέθιστο ἡ πόλις καὶ τὸν Περικλέᾱ ἐν ὀργῇ εἶχον, καὶ ἐκείνων ὧν παρῄνεσε πρότερον ἐμέμνηντο οὐδέν, ἀλλ' ἐκάκιζον αὐτὸν ὅτι στρατηγὸς ὢν οὐκ ἐπεξάγει, αἴτιόν τε ἐνόμιζον

αὐτὸν εἶναι πάντων ὧν ἔπασχον.  Περικλῆς δὲ ὁρῶν μὲν αὐτοὺς πρὸς
τὸ παρὸν ὀργιζομένους καὶ οὐ τὰ ἄριστα φρονοῦντας, πιστεύων δὲ   15
ὀρθῶς γιγνώσκειν περὶ τοῦ μὴ ἐπεξιέναι, ἐκκλησίᾱν οὐκ ἐποίει οὐδὲ
ξύλλογον οὐδένα, ἵνα μὴ ὀργῇ μᾶλλον ἢ γνώμῃ ξυνελθόντες
ἐξαμάρτωσί τι, ἀλλὰ τήν τε πόλιν ἐφύλασσε καὶ δι' ἡσυχίᾱς μάλιστα
ὅσον ἐδύνατο εἶχεν.

[ἀνηρέθιστο (pluperfect passive of ἀνερεθίζω), *had been stirred up, was excited*
ἐμέμνηντο + gen., *they remembered*  ἐκάκιζον, *they were abusing*  ὅτι, *because*
ἐπεξάγει, *he was (not) leading (them) out against (the enemy)*  πρὸς τὸ παρὸν, *at
the present state of affairs*  περὶ τοῦ μὴ ἐπεξιέναι, *about not going out to attack*
ξύλλογον, *gathering, meeting*  δι' ἡσυχίᾱς . . . εἶχεν, *he was keeping (it) quiet*]

οἱ δὲ Πελοποννήσιοι, ἐπειδὴ οὐκ ἐπεξῇσαν αὐτοῖς οἱ Ἀθηναῖοι ἐς   20
μάχην, ἄραντες ἐκ τῶν Ἀχαρνῶν ἐδῄουν τῶν δήμων τινὰς ἄλλους
καὶ ἐμμείναντες ἐν τῇ Ἀττικῇ πολύν τινα χρόνον, ἀνεχώρησαν διὰ
Βοιωτῶν, οὐχ ᾗπερ ἐσέβαλον.  ἀφικόμενοι δὲ ἐς Πελοπόννησον
διέλῡσαν τὸν στρατὸν καὶ ἕκαστοι ἐς τὴν ἑαυτῶν πόλιν ἐπανῆλθον.

[αὐτοῖς: dat. with ἐπεξῇσαν  ἐδῄουν (from δηιόω), *were laying waste, ravaging*]

—adapted from Thucydides 2.21–23

## PRINCIPAL PARTS: Verbs with Present Stem Suffix -αν-

αὐξ-άν-ω, [αὐξε-] αὐξήσω, ηὔξησα, ηὔξηκα, ηὔξημαι, ηὐξήθην, *I increase*

λαμβ-άν-ω, [ληβ-] λήψομαι, [λαβ-] ἔλαβον, [ληβ-] εἴληφα, εἴλημμαι,
ἐλήφθην, *I take*; middle + gen., *I seize, take hold of*

μανθ-άν-ω, [μαθε-] μαθήσομαι, [μαθ-] ἔμαθον, [μαθε-] μεμάθηκα, *I learn*;
*I understand*

Note that λαμβάνω and μανθάνω have nasal infixes as well as the nasal suffix -αν-.

## WORD BUILDING

*Verbs and nouns are formed by adding suffixes to a stem.  Give the meaning
of the verbs and nouns in the following sets:*

|    | Stem   | Verb      | Noun       |
|----|--------|-----------|------------|
| 1. | λεγ-   | λέγ-ω     | ὁ λόγο-ς   |
|    | τρεπ-  | τρέπ-ω    | ὁ τρόπο-ς  |
|    | γραφ-  | γράφ-ω    | ἡ γραφ-ή   |
|    | μαχ-   | μάχ-ομαι  | ἡ μάχ-η    |

2.  The following noun suffixes denote *agent*:

| | | | |
|---|---|---|---|
| -τη (nominative -της) | ποιε-/ποιη- | ποιέ-ω | ὁ ποιη-τής |
| | κρῑ-/κρι- | κρῑ-νω | ὁ κρι-τής |
| -ευ (nominative -ευς) | γραφ- | γράφ-ω | ὁ γραφ-εύς |
| | γν-/γεν-/γον- | γί-γν-ομαι | ὁ γον-εύς |
| -τηρ (nominative -τηρ) | σω- | σώ-ζω | ὁ σω-τήρ |
| | δω-/δο- | δί-δω-μι | ὁ δο-τήρ |
| -τρο (nominative -τρος) | ῑᾱ- | ῑᾱ-ομαι | ὁ ῑᾱ-τρός |

3.  The following noun suffixes denote *action*:

| | | | |
|---|---|---|---|
| -σι (nominative -σις) | λῡ-/λυ- | λῡ́ω | ἡ λύσις |
| | ποιε-/ποιη- | ποιέ-ω | ἡ ποίη-σις |
| | κρῑ-/κρι- | κρῑ-νω | ἡ κρί-σις |
| -μη (nominative -μη) | φη-/φα- | φη-μί | ἡ φή-μη |
| | γνω-/γνο- | γι-γνώ-σκω | ἡ γνώ-μη |

4. The following noun suffix denotes *result of action*:

| | | | |
|---|---|---|---|
| -ματ (nominative -μα) | ποιε-/ποιη- | ποιέ-ω | τὸ ποίη-μα |
| | πρᾱκ- | πρᾱ́ττω | τὸ πρᾶγ-μα |
| | γραφ- | γράφ-ω | τὸ γράμ-μα |

The suffixes illustrated above are the most common ones, but there are many others.


# GRAMMAR

## 3.  Indirect Statements with ὅτι/ὡς, Infinitive, or Participle?

| After | Expect usually |
|---|---|
| a.  Verbs of saying: | |
|    i.   φημί or ἔφην | infinitive |
|    ii.  λέγω | infinitive or ὅτι/ὡς |
|    iii. εἶπον | ὅτι/ὡς |
| b.  verbs of thinking and believing δοκῶ, νομίζω, οἴομαι, πιστεύω | infinitive or sometimes ὅτι/ὡς |
| c.  ἐλπίζω | infinitive (negative usually μή) |
| d.  verbs of knowing and learning γιγνώσκω, ἐπίσταμαι, μανθάνω, οἶδα | participle or ὅτι/ὡς |
| e.  verbs of perceiving ἀκούω, ὁρῶ | participle or, of intellectual perception, ὅτι/ὡς |

## 4. The Verb φημί

This verb shows a long-vowel stem φη- and a short-vowel stem φα-, which lengthens in the 3rd person plural of the present tense, e.g., 3rd person singular, *he/she says* = φησί(ν); 3rd person plural, *they say* = φᾱσί(ν). Imperfect: *he/she was saying/said*, ἔφη; *they were saying/said*, ἔφασαν. Study the chart of this verb in the Forms section, page 307. The future and aorist are regular: φήσω, ἔφησα (rare).

### Exercise 23 γ

*Translate the following pairs of sentences. State which pattern in Grammar 3 above each sentence exemplifies.*

1. ὁ ἄγγελος ἔφη τοὺς πρέσβεις ἤδη ἀφικέσθαι ἐς τὰς πύλας.
   The old man said that the boy had already returned home.

2. οἱ νεᾱνίαι νομίζουσιν αὐτοὶ τοὺς πολεμίους ῥᾳδίως νῑκήσειν.
   We think that we ourselves will easily take the city.

3. οἱ παῖδες εἶπον ὅτι/ὡς τὸν πατέρα ἐν τῇ ἀγορᾷ εἶδον.
   The foreigners said that they had found the money.

4. ὁρῶ ὑμᾶς πολλὰ καὶ κακὰ πάσχοντας.
   We see that they are mistaken.

5. χειμῶνος γιγνομένου οἱ ναῦται ἔγνωσαν ὅτι/ὡς μόλις εἰς τὸν λιμένα ἀφίξονται.
   The women perceived that they would get into great danger.

6. ἡ παρθένος ᾤετο τὴν μητέρα πρὸς τῇ κρήνῃ ὄψεσθαι.
   The shepherd was thinking that he would find (his) dog by the river.

7. οἱ δοῦλοι ἤλπιζον τὸν δεσπότην σφίσι (*with them*) μὴ ὀργιεῖσθαι.
   We hope that the dog will not harm the sheep.

8. αἱ γυναῖκες ἠπιστήθησαν οὐδένα σῖτον ἐν τῷ οἴκῳ σφίσιν (*for them*) ὑπάρχοντα.
   The farmers knew that there was no dwelling ready (*use* ὑπάρχω) for them in the city.

9. οἱ Ἀθηναῖοι ᾤοντο τοὺς ἐχθροὺς σφίσιν (*against them*) ἐπιβουλεύειν.
   We were thinking that the foreigner was leading us to the temple.

10. ἡ γυνὴ ἐπίστευεν αὐτὴ μὲν ὀρθῶς γιγνώσκειν, τὸν δὲ ἄνδρα ἁμαρτάνειν.
    Each (man) was thinking that he was safe and the others in danger.

## 5. The Articular Infinitive

The infinitive can be used as a verbal noun in any case, simply by introducing it with the neuter of the definite article (the negative is μή), e.g.:

τοῦτό ἐστι **τὸ ἀδικεῖν, τὸ** πλέον τῶν ἄλλων **ζητεῖν** ἔχειν.
*This is **wrongdoing, seeking** to have more than others.* (Plato, *Gorgias* 483e)
(Here τὸ ἀδικεῖν is nominative, subject of ἐστί, and τὸ . . . ζητεῖν is another nominative, in apposition to τοῦτο.)

ὁ Περικλῆς πιστεύει ὀρθῶς γιγνώσκειν περὶ **τοῦ μὴ ἐπεξιέναι.**
*Pericles believes that he is right about **not going out to attack**.*

**τῷ ταχέως ἱππεύειν** ἐν καιρῷ ἀφίκοντο.
***By riding fast** they arrived on time.*

δεῖ τοὺς νεᾱνίᾱς ἀγαθοὺς γίγνεσθαι εἰς **τὸ λέγειν** τε καὶ **πρᾱττειν.**
*The young men must become good for both **speech** and **action** / **speaking** and **acting**.*

The infinitive may have its own subject in the accusative (see sentence no. 5 in Exercise 23δ below) and its own complement (such as a direct object), e.g.:

**τῷ ταχέως διώκειν** <u>**τὸ θηρίον**</u>, δι' ὀλίγου καταληψόμεθα.
***By quickly pursuing** <u>**the wild beast**</u>, we will soon catch (it).*

### Exercise 23 δ

*Read aloud and translate:*

1. ὁ Θεμιστοκλῆς μάλιστα αἴτιος ἦν τοῦ ἐν τοῖς στενοῖς ναυμαχῆσαι.
2. τί ἐστι τὸ δίκαιον; τὸ δίκαιόν ἐστι τὸ τοὺς μὲν φίλους ὠφελεῖν, τοὺς δὲ ἐχθροὺς βλάπτειν.
3. πρὸς τὴν πόλιν προσβαλόντες ἐς ἐλπίδα ἦλθον τοῦ ἑλεῖν.
4. τῷ ζῆν ἐστί τι ἐναντίον (*opposite*), ὥσπερ τῷ ἐγρηγορέναι (*to be awake*) τὸ καθεύδειν;
5. Περικλῆς δὲ στρατηγὸς ὢν περὶ τοῦ μὴ ἐπεξιέναι τοὺς Ἀθηναίους τὴν ὀρθὴν γνώμην εἶχεν.

---

# Greek Wisdom

### Heraclitus

οὐ δεῖ ὥσπερ καθεύδοντας ποιεῖν καὶ λέγειν. Fragment 73 Diels

συντομωτάτην ὁδὸν ἔλεγεν εἰς εὐδοξίᾱν τὸ γενέσθαι ἀγαθόν. Fragment 135 Diels

# 6. Relative Pronouns and Their Antecedents: Some Special Cases

### a. Attraction of Relative Pronoun to the Case of Its Antecedent

Examine the following from pages 114–115, lines 11–14:

τὸν Περικλέα ἐν ὀργῇ εἶχον, καὶ ἐκείνων **ὧν** παρῄνεσε πρότερον ἐμέμνηντο οὐδέν . . . αἴτιόν τε ἐνόμιζον αὐτὸν εἶναι πάντων **ὧν** ἔπασχον.

*They were angry with Pericles and remembered nothing of those things **that** he had formerly advised . . . and they thought that he was responsible for all **that** they were suffering.*

In this sentence the relative pronouns, which would normally be accusative, have been attracted into the case of their antecedents ἐκείνων and πάντων respectively.

Such attraction to the case of the antecedent often occurs when the relative pronoun would normally be in the accusative case and its antecedent is in the genitive or dative case. The attraction is optional.

### b. Antecedent Incorporated into the Relative Clause

Sometimes the antecedent does not precede the relative pronoun but is incorporated into the relative clause, e.g.:

ὁ στρατηγὸς ἐπορεύετο σὺν **ᾗ εἶχε δυνάμει** (= σὺν <u>δυνάμει</u> ἣν/ᾗ εἶχε).
*The general was marching with the (military) forces that he had.*

### c. Omission of Antecedent

Where the antecedent is a demonstrative pronoun, it is frequently omitted and attraction takes place. For example, instead of

ἐπαινῶ σε ἐπὶ <u>τούτοις</u> **ἃ/οἷς λέγεις**.
*I praise you for <u>these things</u> **that you say**.*

the antecedent would usually be omitted, as follows:

ἐπαινῶ σε ἐφ' **οἷς λέγεις**.
*I praise you for **what you say**.*

## Exercise 23 ε

*Read aloud and translate. For each relative pronoun, give the form in which it would have been if attraction had not taken place, and give (where applicable) the omitted demonstrative pronoun antecedent.*

1. μὴ πιστεύωμεν τοῖς πρέσβεσιν οἷς ἔπεμψαν οἱ Λακεδαιμόνιοι.
2. ἄξιοι ἔστε, ὦ ἄνδρες, τῆς ἐλευθερίας ἧς κέκτησθε (*you have won*).
3. δεῖ ὑμᾶς ἀφ' ὧν ἴστε (*you know*) αὐτοὶ τὰ πράγματα κρῖναι (*to judge*).
4. ὁ στρατηγὸς ἀφίκετο ἄγων ἀπὸ τῶν πόλεων ὧν ἔπεισε στρατιάν.
5. ἀμαθέστατοί (*most ignorant*) ἔστε ὧν ἐγὼ οἶδα Ἑλλήνων.

## 7.   Prepositional Prefixes and Euphony

Certain changes in spelling take place when prefixes are attached to verbs (see Book I, Chapter 5, Grammar 4, pages 58–59).  Note what happens with prefixes that end in ν:

Before β, π, φ, and ψ, ν becomes μ, e.g., ἐν- + πίπτω > ἐμπίπτω (cf. ἐνέπεσον, ἐμπεσών).

Before γ, κ, ξ, and χ, ν becomes γ, e.g., συν- + γράφω > συγγράφω and ἐν- + καλέω > ἐγκαλέω.

Before λ or μ, ν is fully assimilated, e.g., συν- + λέγω > συλλέγω and ἐν + μένω > ἐμμένω.

# Ο ΠΕΡΙΚΛΗΣ

*Read the following passages (adapted from Thucydides 2.65) and answer the comprehension questions:*

The plague undermined Athenian morale.  The people blamed Pericles for their sufferings and sent envoys to Sparta to discuss peace terms.  Pericles made a speech to try to raise their spirits.  Thucydides here summarizes the achievements of Pericles.

τοιαῦτα ὁ Περικλῆς λέγων ἐπειρᾶτο τοὺς Ἀθηναίους τῆς ἐς αὐτὸν ὀργῆς παραλύειν.  οἱ δὲ δημοσίᾳ μὲν τοῖς λόγοις ἐπείθοντο καὶ οὔτε πρὸς τοὺς Λακεδαιμονίους πρέσβεις ἔτι ἔπεμπον ἔς τε τὸν πόλεμον μᾶλλον ὥρμηντο, ἰδίᾳ δὲ τοῖς παθήμασιν ἐλυποῦντο.  οὐ μέντοι πρότερόν γε ἐπαύσαντο ἐν ὀργῇ ἔχοντες αὐτὸν πρὶν ἐζημίωσαν χρήμασιν.  ὕστερον δὲ οὐ πολλῷ αὖθις στρατηγὸν αὐτὸν εἵλοντο   5
καὶ πάντα τὰ πράγματα ἐπέτρεψαν.

[ἐς + acc., *against*   παραλύειν, *to rid* X (acc.) *of* Y (gen.)   δημοσίᾳ, *publicly*   οὔτε = οὐ   ὥρμηντο (pluperfect passive of ὁρμάω), *they had been aroused, were in a state of eagerness*   τοῖς παθήμασιν, *sufferings*   πρὶν, *until*   ἐζημίωσαν, *they penalized, fined*   χρήμασιν, dat. of χρήματα, *money*, with ἐζημίωσαν   εἵλοντο, *they chose*]

1.  What was Pericles attempting to do?
2.  What three things did the Athenians publicly do in response?
3.  What did they do in private?
4.  What did the Athenians have to do before they could stop being angry at Pericles?
5.  What did they do shortly thereafter?

ὅσον τε γὰρ χρόνον προύστη τῆς πόλεως ἐν τῇ εἰρήνῃ, μετρίως ἡγεῖτο καὶ ἀσφαλῶς ἐφύλαξεν αὐτήν, καὶ ἐγένετο ἐπ᾽ ἐκείνου μεγίστη· ἐπειδή τε πόλεμος κατέστη, φαίνεται ὁ Περικλῆς καὶ ἐν τούτῳ προγνοὺς τὴν δύναμιν αὐτῆς.  ἐπεβίω

δὲ δύο ἔτη καὶ ἓξ μῆνας· καὶ ἐπειδὴ ἀπέθανεν, ἐπὶ πλέον ἐγνώσθη ἡ πρόνοια    10
αὐτοῦ ἡ ἐς τὸν πόλεμον.

[ὅσον ... χρόνον, *as long as*    προύστη (from προΐστημι) + gen., *he was at the head of, in charge of*    μετρίως, *moderately*    ἐπ᾽ ἐκείνου, *in his time*    κατέστη, *began*    προγνούς (from προγιγνώσκω), *having foreknown*    ἐπεβίω (from ἐπιβιόω), *he lived on, survived*    μῆνας, *months*    ἐπὶ πλέον, *more, further*    ἐγνώσθη ἡ πρόνοια αὐτοῦ, *his foresight was recognized*    ἐς τὸν πόλεμον, *with regard to the war*]

6. How did the city fare with Pericles in charge of it during peacetime?
7. When war came did Pericles appear to be right or wrong in his thinking about the city?
8. What was recognized even more after Pericles' death?

ὁ μὲν γὰρ ἔφη ἡσυχάζοντάς τε καὶ τὸ ναυτικὸν φυλάσσοντας καὶ ἀρχὴν μὴ ἐπικτωμένους ἐν τῷ πολέμῳ μηδὲ τῇ πόλει κινδῡνεύοντας αὐτοὺς νῑκήσειν. οἱ δὲ ταῦτα πάντα ἐς τὸ ἐναντίον ἔπρᾱξαν καὶ κατὰ τὰς ἰδίᾱς φιλοτῑμίᾱς καὶ ἴδια κέρδη κακῶς ἐπολίτευσαν. αἴτιον δὲ ἦν ὅτι ἐκεῖνος δυνατὸς ὢν οὐκ ἤγετο ὑπὸ τοῦ    15
δήμου μᾶλλον ἢ αὐτὸς ἦγε. ἐγίγνετό τε λόγῳ μὲν δημοκρατίᾱ, ἔργῳ δὲ ὑπὸ τοῦ πρώτου ἀνδρὸς ἀρχή.

[ἐπικτωμένους, *increasing, adding to*    τῇ πόλει κινδῡνεύοντας, *putting the city at risk*    οἱ δὲ, *but they* (i.e., his successors)    ἐς τὸ ἐναντίον, *in the opposite way*    τὰς ἰδίᾱς φιλοτῑμίᾱς, *their private ambitions*    κέρδη, *profits*    κακῶς ἐπολίτευσαν, *pursued bad policies*    αἴτιον, *the reason*]

9. What four things had Pericles said the citizens should do if they were to be victorious?
10. Did the Athenians do as Pericles said they should?
11. What two things motivated the Athenians?
12. How did they conduct themselves as citizens?
13. What reasons does Thucydides give for Pericles' success as a leader?
14. How does Thucydides describe the system of government under Pericles?

### Exercise 23 ζ

*Translate into Greek:*

1. When Pericles died, his successors (οἱ ὕστερον) were not leading the citizens but were being led by them.
2. For each wishing to be first said, "I will give the citizens all that (whatever) they want."
3. But they made many mistakes (*use* πολλά + ἁμαρτάνω) and sent away the expedition to Sicily (*use* ἡ Σικελίᾱ), hoping that they would thus oblige (*use* χαρίζομαι + *dat.*) the people.
4. But when they heard that the generals were being defeated by the enemy, they did not send aid (*use* ἡ βοήθεια).

5. Competing (*use* ἀγωνίζομαι) against each other about the leadership (*use* ἡ προστασίᾱ) of the people, they were being persuaded to neglect (*use* ἀμελέω + *gen.*) the war.

# Classical Greek

### Solon

Solon's poems were not confined to political themes. The following lines come from a long poem in which he reflects on men's desire to win wealth; ill-gotten gains earn punishment from Zeus. He here lists some ways in which men try to make a living (fragment 13.43–44, 47–50, 53–54):

σπεύδει δ' ἄλλοθεν ἄλλος· ὁ μὲν κατὰ πόντον ἀλᾶται

ἐν νηυσὶν χρῄζων οἴκαδε κέρδος ἄγειν. . . .

ἄλλος γῆν τέμνων πολυδένδρεον εἰς ἐνιαυτὸν

λατρεύει, τοῖσιν καμπύλ' ἄροτρα μέλει·

ἄλλος Ἀθηναίης τε καὶ Ἡφαίστου πολυτέχνεω

ἔργα δαεὶς χειροῖν ξυλλέγεται βίοτον. . . .

ἄλλον μάντιν ἔθηκεν ἄναξ ἑκάεργος Ἀπόλλων,

ἔγνω δ' ἀνδρὶ κακὸν τηλόθεν ἐρχόμενον.

[ἄλλοθεν ἄλλος, *one man one way, one another*   κατὰ πόντον, *over the sea* ἀλᾶται, *wanders*   νηυσὶν = ναυσὶν   χρῄζων, *longing*   κέρδος (τό), *gain, wealth*   τέμνων, *cutting*   πολυδένδρεον, *with many a tree, tree-clad*   εἰς ἐνιαυτόν, *year in, year out*   λατρεύει, *slaves*   τοῖσιν, *for whom*   καμπύλ(α), *bent*   μέλει, *are a concern*   Ἀθηναίης = Ἀθηνᾶς   πολυτέχνεω (gen. of πολυτέχνης), *of many crafts* (Hephaestus was the god of fire and crafts)   δαεὶς, *knowing, skilled in*   χειροῖν, *with his (two) hands*   βίοτον, *his livelihood*   μάντιν, *a prophet*   ἔθηκεν, *made*   ἄναξ ἑκάεργος, *the Lord, the far-shooter* (lit., *far-worker*)   ἔγνω, gnomic aorist, *he* (the prophet) *knows*   τηλόθεν, *from afar*]

# New Testament Greek

### John 6.47–51
### Jesus the Bread of Life

Jesus speaks to the Jews.

"ἀμὴν ἀμὴν λέγω ὑμῖν, ὁ πιστεύων ἔχει ζωὴν αἰώνιον. ἐγώ εἰμι ὁ ἄρτος τῆς ζωῆς. οἱ πατέρες ὑμῶν ἔφαγον ἐν τῇ ἐρήμῳ τὸ μάννα καὶ ἀπέθανον· οὗτός ἐστιν ὁ ἄρτος ὁ ἐκ τοῦ οὐρανοῦ καταβαίνων, ἵνα τις ἐξ αὐτοῦ φάγῃ καὶ μὴ ἀποθάνῃ. ἐγώ εἰμι ὁ ἄρτος ὁ ζῶν ὁ ἐκ τοῦ οὐρανοῦ καταβάς· ἐάν τις φάγῃ ἐκ τούτου τοῦ ἄρτου ζήσει εἰς τὸν αἰῶνα, καὶ ὁ ἄρτος δὲ ὃν ἐγὼ δώσω ἡ σάρξ μού ἐστιν ὑπὲρ τῆς τοῦ κόσμου ζωῆς."

[ἀμὴν, *verily*   ζωὴν, *life*  αἰώνιον, *eternal*   ὁ ἄρτος, *the bread*   ἔφαγον, *ate*   τῇ ἐρήμῳ, *the desert*   τὸ μάννα, *the manna*   αἰῶνα, *eternity*   καὶ ... δὲ, *moreover also*   ἡ σάρξ, *the flesh*   τοῦ κόσμου, *the world*]

Departure of a warrior

# 24
# ΕΝ ΔΙΔΑΣΚΑΛΩΝ (α)

ἐν διδασκάλων· ἐπ' ἀριστερᾷ μὲν ὁ παῖς κιθαρίζειν διδάσκεται ὑπὸ κιθαριστοῦ· ἐπὶ δὲ δεξιᾷ κάθηται ὁ παιδαγωγός· μεταξὺ δὲ ὁ γραμματιστὴς τὰ γράμματα διδάσκει.

## VOCABULARY

*Verbs*
**διδάσκω,** [διδαχ-] **διδάξω, ἐδίδαξα, δεδίδαχα, δεδί-δαγμαι, ἐδιδάχθην,** *I teach* someone (acc.) something (acc.); passive, *I am taught* something (acc.)

*****ζάω** (unattested, hypothetical form) (**ζῶ, ζῇς, ζῇ,** etc.), infinitive, **ζῆν,** imperfect, **ἔζων, ἔζης, ἔζη,** etc., **ζήσω** or **ζή-σομαι,** *I live*

**μελετάω,** *I study; I practice*

**παιδεύω, παιδεύσω, ἐπαί-δευσα, πεπαίδευκα, πε-παίδευμαι, ἐπαιδεύθην,** *I educate*

**φοιτάω,** *I go; I visit*

*Nouns*
**τὸ γράμμα, τοῦ γράμματος,** *letter* (of the alphabet); pl., *writing*

**ὁ γραμματιστής, τοῦ γραμ-ματιστοῦ,** *schoolmaster*

**ἡ γυμναστική, τῆς γυμνα-στικῆς,** *gymnastics*

**ὁ διδάσκαλος, τοῦ διδασκά-λου,** *teacher*

**ὁ κιθαριστής, τοῦ κιθαριστοῦ,** *lyre player*

**ἡ μουσική, τῆς μουσικῆς,** *music*

**ἡ παίδευσις, τῆς παιδεύσεως,** *education*

**ὁ σοφιστής, τοῦ σοφιστοῦ,** *wise man; sophist*

**ὁ τεκών, τοῦ τεκόντος,** *parent*

**ὁ υἱός, τοῦ υἱοῦ,** *son*

*Adjectives*
**ἄδικος, -ον,** *unjust*

**αἰσχρός, -ά, -όν,** *shameful*

**ἄσμενος, -η, -ον,** *glad(ly)*

**δίκαιος, -ά, -ον,** *just*

**σμῑκρός, -ά, -όν,** *small*

| | |
|---|---|
| *Conjunction* | **περὶ πολλοῦ ποιοῦμαι,** *I con-* |
| **ὅπως** + subjunctive, *so that, in* | *sider of great importance* |
| *order to;* + future indicative, | **περὶ πλείστου ποιοῦμαι,** *I* |
| *(to see to it) that* | *consider of greatest impor-* |
| *Expressions* | *tance* |
| **καθ' ἡμέρᾱν,** *every day* | |

μέχρι μὲν οὗ οἵ τε Πελοποννήσιοι ἐν τῇ Ἀττικῇ ἔμενον καὶ οἱ
Ἀθηναῖοι ἐπολιορκοῦντο, ὁ Φίλιππος καθ' ἡμέρᾱν ἤγετο ὑπὸ τῶν
ἀνεψιῶν εἰς διδασκάλων. τά τ' οὖν γράμματα ἐδιδάσκετο ὑπὸ τοῦ
γραμματιστοῦ καὶ ὑπὸ τοῦ κιθαριστοῦ τὴν μουσικήν· ἐφοίτᾱ δὲ καὶ
εἰς τοῦ παιδοτρίβου ὅπως τὴν γυμναστικὴν μελετᾷ. ἐπεὶ δ' ἠγγέλθη　5
ὅτι οἱ Πελοποννήσιοι ἀπῆλθον, ἅπαντες οἱ αὐτουργοὶ φόβου
λελυμένοι εἰς τοὺς ἀγροὺς ἐπανῇσαν. ὁ μὲν οὖν Δικαιόπολις τήν τε
γυναῖκα καὶ τοὺς παῖδας ἔμελλεν οἴκαδε κομιεῖν, ὁ δὲ ἀδελφὸς ἤρετο
αὐτὸν εἰ ἐθέλει τὸν Φίλιππον παρ' ἑαυτῷ λείπειν ἵνα μὴ παύηται
παιδευόμενος. ὁ μὲν οὖν Δικαιόπολις ταῦτα ἅσμενος δεξάμενος καὶ　10
τὸν υἱὸν τῷ ἀδελφῷ ἐπιτρέψᾱς ἐπορεύετο, ὁ δὲ Φίλιππος καταλειφθεὶς
ἔτι πλέονα ἐπαιδεύετο.

[**μέχρι ... οὗ,** *as long as*　**τῶν ἀνεψιῶν,** *his cousins*　**τοῦ παιδοτρίβου,** *trainer*
**λελυμένοι,** perfect passive participle + gen., *freed from*　**παρ' ἑαυτῷ,** *at his house*]

ὁποῖᾱ δ' ἦν αὕτη ἡ παίδευσις δύναταί τις γιγνώσκειν διάλογόν
τινα τοῦ Πλάτωνος σκοπῶν, ἐν ᾧ σοφιστής τις, Πρωταγόρᾱς ὀνόματι,
ἐνδείκνυσθαι πειρᾶται ὅτι διδακτόν ἐστιν ἡ ἀρετή. ὁ γὰρ　15
Πρωταγόρᾱς λέγει ὅτι ἅπαντες οἱ τεκόντες τοῦτο περὶ πλείστου
ποιοῦνται, ὅπως ἀγαθοὶ γενήσονται οἱ παῖδες.

[**ὁποῖᾱ,** *of what sort*　**διάλογόν,** *dialogue*　**ἐνδείκνυσθαι,** *to show, prove*　**διδακτόν,** *a teachable thing*]

"ἐκ παίδων σμῑκρῶν," φησίν, "ἀρξάμενοι, μέχρι οὗπερ ἂν ζῶσιν,
καὶ διδάσκουσι καὶ νουθετοῦσιν. ἐπειδὰν πρῶτον συνῑῇ τις τὰ
λεγόμενα, καὶ τροφὸς καὶ μήτηρ καὶ παιδαγωγὸς καὶ αὐτὸς ὁ πατὴρ　20
περὶ τούτου διαμάχονται, ὅπως ὡς βέλτιστος ἔσται ὁ παῖς, παρ'
ἕκαστον ἔργον καὶ λόγον διδάσκοντες καὶ ἐνδεικνύμενοι ὅτι τὸ μὲν
δίκαιον, τὸ δὲ ἄδικον, καὶ τόδε μὲν καλόν, τόδε δὲ αἰσχρόν, καὶ τόδε

μὲν ὅσιον, τόδε δὲ ἀνόσιον, καὶ τὰ μὲν ποίει, τὰ δὲ μὴ ποίει. καὶ ἐὰν

μὲν πείθηται—, εἰ δὲ μή, ὥσπερ ξύλον διαστρεφόμενον καὶ   25

καμπτόμενον εὐθύνουσιν ἀπειλαῖς καὶ πληγαῖς."

[νουθετοῦσιν, *warn, advise*   τὰ λεγόμενα, *things being said, speech*   τροφός,
*nurse*   παιδαγωγός, *tutor*   διαμάχονται, *strive hard*   ὡς βέλτιστος, *as good as
possible*   παρ' + acc., *in respect of*   ἐνδεικνύμενοι, *pointing out, showing*   τὸ μὲν
... τὸ δὲ..., *this is* ... *but that is*   ἀνόσιον, *unholy*   ὥσπερ ξύλον διαστρεφόμενον καὶ καμπτόμενον, *like a piece of bent and warped wood*   εὐθύνουσιν,
*they straighten* (him) *out*   ἀπειλαῖς, *with threats*   πληγαῖς, *with blows*]

—The last paragraph above is adapted from Plato, *Protagoras* 325c5–d7.

## PRINCIPAL PARTS: More Verbs with Nasal Present Stem Suffixes: -ν-, -νε-, and -νῡ-/-νυ-

κάμ-ν-ω, [καμε-] καμοῦμαι, [καμ-] ἔκαμον, [κμη-] κέκμηκα, *I am sick; I am
tired*

ἀφικ-νέ-ομαι, [ἰκ-] ἀφίξομαι, ἀφῑκόμην, ἀφῖγμαι, *I arrive;* + εἰς + acc., *I arrive at*

δείκ-νῡ-μι, [δεικ-] δείξω, ἔδειξα, δέδειχα, δέδειγμαι, ἐδείχθην, *I show*

## WORD STUDY

See page 134.

## GRAMMAR

### 1. Comparison of Adjectives

Review: Book I, Chapter 14, Grammar 1:

    Adjectives have three *degrees*, e.g., "beautiful" (*positive*), "more
beautiful" (*comparative*), and "most beautiful" (*superlative*) or "brave"
(*positive*), "braver" (*comparative*), and "bravest" (*superlative*).

    In Greek the comparative and superlative of adjectives are regularly
formed by adding -τερος, -τέρᾱ, -τερον and -τατος, -τάτη, -τατον to the
stem of the positive:

| Positive | Comparative | Superlative |
|---|---|---|
| ἀνδρεῖος, -ᾱ, -ον, *brave* | | |
| **Stem:** ἀνδρειο- | ἀνδρειό-τερος, -ᾱ, -ον<br>*braver* | ἀνδρειό-τατος, -η, -ον<br>*bravest* |
| χαλεπός, -ή, -όν, *difficult* | | |
| **Stem:** χαλεπο- | χαλεπώ-τερος, -ᾱ, -ον<br>*more difficult* | χαλεπώ-τατος, -η, -ον<br>*most difficult* |

Note that in 1st and 2nd declension adjectives as in the examples above, the o at the end of the stem of the positive is lengthened to ω if the syllable preceding it is regarded as short (e.g., contains a short vowel).

3rd Declension:

ἀληθής, ἀληθές, *true*
**Stem:** ἀληθεσ-    ἀληθέσ-τερος, -ᾱ, -ον        ἀληθέσ-τατος, -η, -ον
                    *truer*                      *truest*

Note what happens when the stem ends in -ον-:

σώφρων, σῶφρον, *of sound mind; prudent; self-controlled*
**Stem:** σωφρον-    σωφρον-έσ-τερος, -ᾱ, -ον    σωφρον-έσ-τατος, -η, -ον
                    *more prudent*              *most prudent*

The endings -έσ-τερος, -ᾱ, -ον and -έσ-τατος, -η, -ον are constructed by analogy with ἀληθέσ-τερος, -ᾱ, -ον and ἀληθέσ-τατος, -η, -ον.

Remember that comparatives can mean *rather/somewhat* X and superlatives, *very* X, e.g.

οἱ βάρβαροι **ἀνδρειότεροί** εἰσιν.
*The barbarians are **rather/somewhat** brave.*

οἱ ἀθάνατοι **ἀνδρειότατοί** εἰσιν.
*The Immortals are **very** brave.*

## 2.  Irregular Comparison of Adjectives

Review Book I, Chapter 14, Grammar 2, and then study the following:

| Positive | Comparative | Superlative |
|---|---|---|
| ἀγαθός, -ή, -όν<br>*good* | ἀμείνων, ἄμεινον<br>*better*<br>(stronger, braver, preferable, superior) | ἄριστος, -η, -ον<br>*best* |
|  | βελτίων, βέλτῑον<br>*better*<br>(more fitting, morally superior) | βέλτιστος, -η, -ον<br>*best* |
|  | κρείττων, κρεῖττον<br>*better, stronger* | κράτιστος, -η, -ον<br>*best; strongest* |
| κακός, -ή, -όν<br>*bad* | κακῑων, κάκῑον<br>*worse*<br>(morally inferior, more cowardly) | κάκιστος, -η, -ον<br>*worst* |
|  | χείρων, χεῖρον<br>*worse*<br>(inferior in strength, rank, or quality) | χείριστος, -η, -ον<br>*worst* |
|  | ἥττων, ἧττον<br>*inferior; weaker; less* |  |

## Exercise 24 α

*Read aloud and translate into English:*

1. οἱ βάρβαροι, καίπερ πολλῷ πλέονες ὄντες, ἥττονες ἦσαν τῶν Ἑλλήνων.
2. οἱ γὰρ Ἕλληνες εἰς τὰ στενὰ ἀνδρειότατα προχωροῦντες καὶ ἄριστα μαχόμενοι τοὺς βαρβάρους εἰς φυγὴν κατέστησαν.
3. οὕτως οὖν οἱ Ἕλληνες τοὺς βαρβάρους νῑκήσαντες παντὶ τρόπῳ κρείττονες ὄντες ἐφάνησαν.
4. ὁ Περικλῆς ἀνὴρ ἄριστος ὢν ἐφάνη· τῇ γὰρ πόλει σωφρονέστατα ἡγεῖτο.
5. τῶν ἄλλων ῥητόρων πολλῷ βελτίων ἦν· ἐκεῖνοι γὰρ χείρονες ὄντες πλεῖστα ἡμάρτανον.
6. αὗται αἱ γυναῖκες σωφρονέστεραι οὖσαι τῶν ἀνδρῶν ἀμείνονα παρήνουν.
7. οὗτος μὲν κακίων ἐστίν, ἐκεῖνος δὲ κάκιστος.
8. πάντων τῶν διδασκάλων οὗτος βέλτιστός ἐστιν· τοὺς γὰρ παῖδας ἄριστα παιδεύει.
9. ἐκεῖνος δὲ διδάσκαλος χείριστός ἐστιν· τοὺς γὰρ παῖδας οὐδὲν διδάσκει.
10. οἱ διδάσκαλοι οἱ ἄριστοι τοὺς παῖδας καθ' ἡμέρᾱν βελτίονας ποιοῦσιν.

## 3. ὅπως + Future Indicative in Object Clauses after Verbs Expressing Care or Effort

Note the use of ὅπως + future indicative in the following sentences:

διαμάχονται, **ὅπως ὡς βέλτιστος ἔσται ὁ παῖς**.
*They strive hard (to see to it)* **that the child will be as good as possible**.

The negative is ὅπως μή, e.g.:

οἱ διδάσκαλοι πάντα πράττουσιν, **ὅπως μηδὲν κακὸν ποιήσουσιν οἱ παῖδες**.
*The teachers do everything (to see to it)* **that the children will do nothing bad**.

## Exercise 24 β

*Read aloud and translate into English:*

1. περὶ πλείστου ποιοῦ ὅπως ἀεὶ τοὺς θεοὺς τῑμήσεις.
2. περὶ πολλοῦ ποιούμεθα ὅπως μὴ κακίονες τῶν πατέρων γενησόμεθα.
3. οἱ διδάσκαλοι διαμάχονται (*strive hard*), ὅπως μὴ ἁμαρτήσονται οἱ παῖδες.
4. πάντα πράττωμεν, ὦ φίλοι, ὅπως μὴ ὑπὸ τῶν πολεμίων ληφθησόμεθα.
5. ὁ πατὴρ πάντα ἔπραττεν ὅπως εὖ παιδευθήσεται ὁ υἱός.

At the trainer's: boys practice boxing, throwing
javelins and the discus, and running

## Exercise 24 γ

*Translate into Greek:*

1.  Do everything (to see to it) that you become better, boys.
2.  Let us consider it of great importance (to see to it) that we not get/fall into danger.
3.  The shepherds were striving hard (*use* διαμάχομαι) (to see to it) that they would guard the sheep well.
4.  They were considering it of greatest importance (to see to it) that the sheep would not flee into the hills.
5.  They were doing everything (to see to it) that they would kill the wolf that was attacking the sheep.

# Greek Education

The Greeks divided education into "music" and "gymnastics." Music meant everything concerned with the Muses, including literacy, literature, and music in our sense. Gymnastics meant physical training. It was commonly said that "music" educated the soul and "gymnastics" trained the body.

Girls did not, as far as we know, attend schools. Their education was at home and centered on the domestic arts but must have also included music and dancing. Boys went to school from about the age of seven and usually had three different teachers. The writing master (ὁ γραμματιστής) taught basic literacy, numbers, and literature, the latter consisting of the traditional poets, especially Homer. The music teacher (ὁ κιθαριστής) taught the lyre and sometimes also the double pipe, singing, and dancing. The trainer (ὁ παιδοτρίβης) taught exercises such as running, jumping, throwing the javelin and discus, and wrestling.

There were no state schools, though the state did pay for the education of some children, in particular the sons of those who had died fighting for the city. Other parents had to pay the teachers a small fee. A boy was usually accompanied by a slave called a παιδαγωγός, who was responsible for his safety on the way to and from school and for his good behavior.

It is impossible to say confidently how large a proportion of the citizens received this education or how widespread literacy was. It seems likely that the vast majority received schooling. The Athenian democracy functioned on the assumption that all male citizens were literate. Officers of state were selected by lot, and an illiterate could hardly have carried out the duties of a councilor, let alone act as chairman of the Assembly. Moreover, laws and decrees were displayed in public places for all to read, and at an ostracism it was assumed that every citizen could at least write on an ostracon the name of the politician he wished to see exiled.

The education we have described was elementary. There was no higher education until the sophists arrived on the scene (see below), and, as Protagoras says in the passages quoted in this chapter, the moral element in education was considered quite as important as the intellectual. In fact, the purpose of the educational system was not to train the intellect at all, but to impart basic skills that would be essential in adult life and, above all, to hand down the traditional values of piety, morality, and patriotism, which were enshrined in poetry, especially in Homer. Plato says of Homer: "This poet has educated Greece." Boys learned extensive passages of the *Iliad* by heart and in so doing imbibed Homeric values.

With the development of democracy there arose a demand for a new sort of education. Birth was no longer the passport to political power. The aspiring politician needed the ability to persuade others, especially in the law courts and the Assembly. It was this ability that had given Pericles, for instance, his pre-eminence. This demand was met by the sophists, who were itinerant teachers who began to appear on the scene in the second half of the fifth century. They offered to the sons of the rich a form of higher education in return for large fees. Different sophists included different topics in their courses, but common to all was rhetoric, that is, the art of speaking persuasively, especially in public.

One of the earliest and greatest of the sophists was Protagoras, born in Abdera on the coast of Thrace about 485 B.C. He was extremely successful and had such a reputation that wherever he went rich and clever young men flocked to hear him. In Plato's *Protagoras*, Socrates takes the young Hippocrates to meet Protagoras. When they arrive at the house where he is staying, they find Protagoras walking around in a portico accompanied by some of the richest and noblest young men of Athens, including two sons of Pericles. They see other famous sophists who have come to meet Protagoras, including one who is teaching astronomy. They then approach the great man, and Socrates explains the purpose of their visit: "Hippocrates here wishes to make a mark in the city and thinks he would be most likely to achieve this if he became your pupil; and so he would like to know what he will gain if he comes to you." "Young man," replies Protagoras, "this is what you will gain, if you come to me; on the very day you join me you will go home a better man, and on the next day the same will happen, and every day you will continually progress toward the better." Socrates answers that this may well be so, but in what particular sphere will he become better? Protagoras replies that anyone who comes to him will not learn irrelevant subjects such as arithmetic, astronomy, or geometry, but will learn precisely the subject for which he has come, namely good judgment in managing both his personal affairs and the affairs of the city, so that he may be most capable in political action and speech. Socrates asks: "Do I follow what you are saying? I think you mean the art of politics (ἡ πολῑτικὴ τέχνη) and profess to make men good citizens." "That," replies Protagoras, "is exactly what I do profess."

Protagoras accuses other sophists of teaching "irrelevant subjects," such as mathematics. Those who did teach such subjects would have said that they provided an intellectual training that was an essential preparation for further studies. The idea of training the intellect had come to stay.

The next century saw the foundation of institutes of higher education. Socrates' pupil Plato founded the Academy in 387 B.C. to train statesmen by teaching them philosophy; for only the philosopher knew what was really "good," and only one trained in philosophy could know what was good for the city. He believed in a rigorous intellectual training, based on the study of mathematics. Soon other schools were founded, such as Aristotle's Lyceum, which was a center for research in the sciences as well as a school of philosophy, and schools of rhetoric, such as that of Isocrates.

At school: (from left to right) a boy being taught to play the double pipe, a teacher examining a pupil's exercise, and a seated παιδαγωγός

# ΕΝ ΔΙΔΑΣΚΑΛΩΝ (β)

## VOCABULARY

*Verbs*
ἐπιμελέομαι, ἐπιμελήσομαι,
  ἐπιμεμέλημαι, ἐπεμελήθην
  + gen., *I take care for;* + ὅπως
  + future indicative, *I take care*
  (*to see to it that*)
ἥδομαι, ἡσθήσομαι, ἥσθην,
  *I am glad, delighted;* + participle or dat., *I enjoy*
κιθαρίζω, [κιθαριε-] κιθαριῶ,
  [κιθαρι-] ἐκιθάρισα, *I play the*
  *lyre*
*Nouns*
ἡ ἁρμονίᾱ, τῆς ἁρμονίᾱς,
  *harmony*
τὸ βιβλίον, τοῦ βιβλίου, *book*
ἡ διάνοια, τῆς διανοίᾱς, *in-*
  *tention; intellect*
ὁ ἔπαινος, τοῦ ἐπαίνου, *praise*
ὁ μαθητής, τοῦ μαθητοῦ, *pupil*
ἡ πονηρίᾱ, τῆς πονηρίᾱς, *fault;*
  *wickedness*
ἡ πρᾶξις, τῆς πρᾱ́ξεως, *deed*

ὁ ῥυθμός, τοῦ ῥυθμοῦ, *rhythm*
τὸ σῶμα, τοῦ σώματος, *body*
ἡ σωφροσύνη, τῆς σωφροσύνης,
  *soundness of mind, prudence;*
  *moderation, self-control*
ἡ φωνή, τῆς φωνῆς, *voice;*
  *speech*
*Adjectives*
ὄλβιος, -ᾱ, -ον, *happy; blest;*
  *prosperous*
παλαιός, -ᾱ́, -όν, *old; of old*
χρήσιμος, -η, -ον, *useful*
χρηστός, -ή, -όν, *useful; good*
*Prepositions*
ἐπί + gen., *toward, in the direc-*
  *tion of; on;* + dat., *at; of price,*
  *for;* + acc., *at; against; onto,*
  *upon*
πρός + dat., *at; near; by; in*
  *addition to;* + acc., *to, toward;*
  *upon; against*
*Adverb*
αὖ, *again*

"μετὰ δὲ ταῦτα εἰς διδασκάλων πέμποντες πολὺ μᾶλλον τοὺς διδασκάλους κελεύουσιν ἐπιμελεῖσθαι εὐκοσμίᾱς τῶν παίδων ἢ γραμμάτων τε καὶ κιθαρίσεως· οἱ δὲ διδάσκαλοι τούτων τε ἐπιμελοῦνται, καὶ ἐπειδὰν αὖ γράμματα μάθωσι καὶ μέλλωσι συνήσειν τὰ γεγραμμένα ὥσπερ τότε τὴν φωνήν, παρατιθέᾱσιν αὐτοῖς    5 ἐπὶ τῶν βάθρων ἀναγιγνώσκειν ποιητῶν ἀγαθῶν ποιήματα καὶ ἐκμανθάνειν ἀναγκάζουσιν, ἐν οἷς πολλαὶ μὲν νουθετήσεις ἔνεισιν, πολλοὶ δὲ ἔπαινοι παλαιῶν ἀνδρῶν ἀγαθῶν, ἵνα ὁ παῖς μῑμῆται καὶ βούληται τοιοῦτος γενέσθαι.

[εὐκοσμίᾱς, *good behavior*    κιθαρίσεως, *lyre-playing*    τὰ γεγραμμένα, *things written, writing*    παρατιθέᾱσιν, *they* (i.e., the teachers) *set* X (acc., ποιήματα) *in front of* Y (dat., αὐτοῖς)    τῶν βάθρων, *the benches*    ποιήματα, *poems*    ἐκμανθάνειν, *to learn thoroughly*    νουθετήσεις, *warnings, advice*    μῑμῆται, *may imitate*]

"οἵ τ' αὖ κιθαρισταὶ σωφροσύνης τε ἐπιμελοῦνται καὶ ὅπως μηδὲν    10
κακουργήσουσιν οἱ νέοι.  πρὸς δὲ τούτοις, ἐπειδὰν κιθαρίζειν
μάθωσιν, ἄλλων αὖ ποιητῶν ἀγαθῶν ποιήματα διδάσκουσι
μελοποιῶν, εἰς τὰ κιθαρίσματα ἐντείνοντες, καὶ τοὺς ῥυθμούς τε καὶ
τὰς ἁρμονίας ἀναγκάζουσιν οἰκειοῦσθαι ταῖς ψυχαῖς τῶν παίδων, ἵνα
ἡμερώτεροί τ' ὦσιν, καὶ εὐρυθμότεροι καὶ εὐαρμοστότεροι γιγνό-    15
μενοι χρήσιμοι ὦσιν εἰς τὸ λέγειν τε καὶ πράττειν.

[κακουργήσουσιν, (will) do wrong    μελοποιῶν, of song writers (the word here
stands in apposition to ἄλλων . . . ποιητῶν ἀγαθῶν)    εἰς τὰ κιθαρίσματα ἐντείνοντες (from τείνω, I stretch), setting them to the music of the lyre    οἰκειοῦσθαι +
dat., to be made familiar to    ἡμερώτεροι, gentler    εὐρυθμότεροι, more rhythmical,
orderly, graceful    εὐαρμοστότεροι, better joined, more harmonious    εἰς τὸ λέγειν
τε καὶ πράττειν, for both speech and action]

"ἔτι δὲ πρὸς τούτοις εἰς παιδοτρίβου πέμπουσιν, ἵνα τὰ σώματα
βελτίονα ἔχοντες ὑπηρετῶσι τῇ διανοίᾳ χρηστῇ οὔσῃ, καὶ μὴ
ἀναγκάζωνται ἀποδειλιᾶν διὰ τὴν πονηρίαν τῶν σωμάτων καὶ ἐν τοῖς
πολέμοις καὶ ἐν ταῖς ἄλλαις πράξεσιν."    20

[εἰς παιδοτρίβου, to the trainer's    βελτίονα, better    ὑπηρετῶσι + dat., they may
serve    ἀποδειλιᾶν, to play the coward]

—adapted from Plato, Protagoras 325d8–326c3

τοιαῦτα οὖν ἐπαιδεύετο ὁ Φίλιππος, καὶ ταύτῃ τῇ παιδεύσει
ἡδόμενος οὕτως ἀγαθὸς μαθητὴς ἐφαίνετο ὥστε ὁ διδάσκαλος βιβλία
τινὰ αὐτῷ ἔδωκεν ἵνα αὐτὸς πρὸς ἑαυτὸν ἀναγιγνώσκῃ.  τούτων δὲ
τῶν βιβλίων ἑνί τινι μάλιστα ἥσθη, τῇ τοῦ Ἡροδότου συγγραφῇ, ἐν ᾗ
ὁ Ἡρόδοτος τὰ Μηδικὰ ἐξηγεῖται· ὁ γὰρ Ἡρόδοτος οὐ μόνον τόν τε    25
πρὸς τοὺς Μήδους πόλεμον συγγράφει καὶ πάσας τὰς μάχας, ἀλλὰ
καὶ τὰς αἰτίας τοῦ πολέμου ἀποδεικνῦσιν, δηλῶν τίνι τρόπῳ οἱ Μῆδοι
τὴν δύναμιν ηὔξησαν καὶ τίνα ἔθνη ἐφεξῆς ἐνίκησαν· ἐν οἷς πολλά τε
ἄλλα λέγεται καὶ ὁ περὶ Κροίσου λόγος· ὁ γὰρ Κροῖσος βασιλεὺς ἦν
τῶν Λυδῶν, ἀνὴρ ὀλβιώτατος γενόμενος καὶ δυνατώτατος, ὃς τοὺς    30
μὲν Ἕλληνας τοὺς ἐν Ἀσίᾳ κατεστρέψατο, αὐτὸς δὲ ὑπὸ τοῦ Κύρου,
βασιλέως ὄντος τῶν Μήδων, τέλος ἐνικήθη.

[συγγραφῇ, history, book    τὰ Μηδικὰ, Median affairs, i.e., the Persian Wars    συγγράφει, *writes about*    ἀποδείκνῦσιν, *reveals*    ἔθνη, *nations, peoples*    ἐφεξῆς, *in succession*    δυνατώτατος, *very powerful*    κατεστρέψατο, *overthrew*]

## PRINCIPAL PARTS: Verbs in -(ί)σκω

ἀποθνῄ-σκω, [θανε-] ἀποθανοῦμαι, [θαν-] ἀπέθανον, [θνη-] τέθνηκα,
     *I die;* perfect, *I am dead*

γιγνώ-σκω, [γνω-] γνώσομαι, ἔγνων, ἔγνωκα, ἔγνωσμαι, ἐγνώσθην,
     *I come to know; I perceive; I learn*

εὑρ-ίσκω, [εὑρε-] εὑρήσω, [εὑρ-] ηὗρον or εὗρον, [εὑρε-] ηὕρηκα or
     εὕρηκα, ηὕρημαι or εὕρημαι, ηὑρέθην or εὑρέθην, *I find*

## WORD STUDY

*Give the Greek words from which the following English musical terms are derived:*

1. music
2. harmony
3. rhythm
4. orchestra
5. chorus
6. symphony
7. melody
8. chord
9. diapason

## WORD BUILDING

Many verbs are formed from the stems of nouns. They are called denominative verbs.

*Note the following six different types of formation and give the meaning of each noun and verb:*

1. ἡ τῑμή > τῑμάω
2. ὁ οἶκος > οἰκέω
3. ὁ δοῦλος > δουλόω
4. ὁ βασιλεύς > βασιλεύω
5. ἡ ἀνάγκη > ἀναγκάζω
6. ἡ ὀργή > ὀργίζομαι

## GRAMMAR

### 4. More Irregular Comparative and Superlative Adjectives

Four of the following were given in Chapter 14, and six are new:

| Positive | Comparative | Superlative |
|---|---|---|
| αἰσχρός, -ά, -όν<br>*shameful* | αἰσχίων, αἴσχῑον<br>*more shameful* | αἴσχιστος, -η, -ον<br>*most shameful* |
| ἐχθρός -ά, -όν<br>*hateful; hostile* | ἐχθίων, ἔχθῑον<br>*more hateful, more hostile* | ἔχθιστος, -η, -ον<br>*most hateful,<br>most hostile* |

| ἡδύς, ἡδεῖα, ἡδύ | ἡδίων, ἥδῑον | ἥδιστος, -η, -ον |
|---|---|---|
| *sweet; pleasant* | *sweeter; more pleasant* | *sweetest;* |
| | | *most pleasant* |

| καλός, -ή, -όν | καλλίων, κάλλῑον | κάλλιστος, -η, -ον |
|---|---|---|
| *beautiful* | *more beautiful* | *most beautiful* |

| μέγας, μεγάλη, μέγα | μείζων, μεῖζον | μέγιστος, -η, -ον |
|---|---|---|
| *big* | *bigger* | *biggest* |

| ὀλίγος, -η, -ον | ἐλάττων, ἔλαττον | ὀλίγιστος, -η, -ον |
|---|---|---|
| *small; pl., few* | *smaller, pl., fewer* | *smallest; least* |
| | | ἐλάχιστος, -η, -ον |
| | | *smallest; least;* |
| | | *pl., fewest* |

| πολύς, πολλή, πολύ | πλείων/πλέων, | πλεῖστος, -η, -ον |
|---|---|---|
| *much; pl., many* | πλεῖον/πλέον | *most, very much;* |
| | *more, rather much* | *pl., most, very many* |

| ῥᾴδιος, -ᾱ, -ον | ῥᾴων, ῥᾷον | ῥᾷστος, -η, -ον |
|---|---|---|
| *easy* | *easier* | *easiest* |

| ταχύς, ταχεῖα, ταχύ | θάττων, θᾶττον | τάχιστος, -η, -ον |
|---|---|---|
| *quick, swift* | *quicker, swifter* | *quickest, swiftest* |

| φίλος, -η, -ον | φιλαίτερος, -ᾱ, -ον | φιλαίτατος, -η, -ον |
|---|---|---|
| *dear* | *dearer* | or φίλτατος -η, -ον |
| | | *dearest* |

## 5. Declension of Comparative Adjectives

Note that comparatives have some alternative, contracted forms, shown in parentheses in the following chart:

|  | Singular | | Plural | |
|---|---|---|---|---|
|  | **M. & F.** | **N.** | **M. & F.** | **N.** |
| **Nom.** | βελτῑων | βέλτῑον | βελτῑονες | βελτῑονα |
|  |  |  | (βελτῑους) | (βελτῑω) |
| **Gen.** | βελτῑονος | βελτῑονος | βελτῑόνων | βελτῑόνων |
| **Dat.** | βελτῑονι | βελτῑονι | βελτῑοσι(ν) | βελτῑοσι(ν) |
| **Acc.** | βελτῑονα | βέλτῑον | βελτῑονας | βελτῑονα |
|  | (βελτῑω) |  | (βελτῑους) | (βελτῑω) |
| **Voc.** | βέλτῑον | βέλτιον | βελτῑονες | βελτῑονα |

## Exercise 24 δ

*Read aloud and translate into English:*

1. ἐπιμελοῦ, ὦ φίλε, ὅπως βέλτῑον κιθαριεῖς ἢ ὁ ἀδελφός.
2. οἱ χρηστοὶ οὐκ ἀεὶ ὀλβιώτεροι γίγνονται τῶν πονηρῶν (*the wicked*) οὐδὲ ῥᾷον ζῶσιν.
3. φοβοῦμαι μὴ αἱ τῶν πολεμίων νῆες θάττονες ὦσι τῶν ἡμετέρων.
4. ἐὰν τοῦτο ποιήσῃς, ἔχθιστός μοι γενήσῃ.
5. ὅστις ἂν τὰ τῶν ἀγαθῶν ποιητῶν ποιήματα ἀναγιγνώσκῃ, βελτῑων γενήσεται.
6. οἱ Πέρσαι ναῦς μείζονας ἔχουσιν ἢ ἡμεῖς καὶ πλέονας.
7. ἡμεῖς, καίπερ ἐλάττονας ἔχοντες ναῦς, αὐτοὺς ῥᾷστα νῑκήσομεν.
8. αἱ γὰρ ἡμέτεραι νῆες θάττονές εἰσιν.
9. τίς φιλαιτέρᾱ μοί ἐστιν ἢ ἡ μήτηρ;
10. οὐδείς σου ἥδιον κιθαρίζει.

# Ο ΗΡΟΔΟΤΟΣ ΤΗΝ ΙΣΤΟΡΙΑΝ ΑΠΟΔΕΙΚΝΥΣΙΝ

*Read the following passages (adapted from Herodotus's introduction to his history–1.1–6) and answer the comprehension questions:*

Ἡροδότου Ἁλικαρνᾱσσέως ἱστορίᾱς ἀπόδειξίς ἐστιν ἥδε, ὅπως μήτε τὰ γενόμενα ἐξ ἀνθρώπων τῷ χρόνῳ ἐξίτηλα γένηται, μήτε ἔργα μεγάλα τε καὶ θαυμαστά, τὰ μὲν ὑπὸ τῶν Ἑλλήνων, τὰ δὲ ὑπὸ τῶν βαρβάρων ἐργασθέντα, ἀκλεᾶ γένηται, τά τε ἄλλα καὶ δι' ἣν αἰτίᾱν ἐπολέμησαν ἀλλήλοις.

[Ἁλικαρνᾱσσέως, *of Halicarnassus*   ἱστορίᾱς, *of the inquiry*   ἀπόδειξίς, *display*   μήτε ... μήτε, *neither ... nor*   ἐξίτηλα, *faded*   θαυμαστά, *wondrous*   ἀκλεᾶ, *without fame*   δι' ἣν αἰτίᾱν, *for what reason*]

1. What four words in the sentence above would best serve as a title for Herodotus's book?
2. For what two purposes is Herodotus publishing the results of his investigations?
3. What are at least four of the subjects that Herodotus indicates that he will treat in his work?

Herodotus first gives a semi-mythical account of the origin of the feud between Europe (the Greeks) and Asia (the barbarians, including the Persians). Persian chroniclers, according to Herodotus, said that first some Phoenician traders carried off a Greek princess (Io) to Egypt; in retaliation the Greeks stole a Phoenician princess (Europa); then Greeks, led by Jason, carried off Medea from Colchis. Finally, the Trojan prince Paris stole

Helen from Sparta and took her back to Troy; Agamemnon led the Greeks to Troy to recover her.

οὕτω μὲν οἱ Πέρσαι λέγουσι, καὶ διὰ τὴν Ἰλίου ἅλωσιν εὑρίσκουσι σφίσι οὖσαν   5
τὴν ἀρχὴν τῆς ἔχθρᾱς τῆς ἐς τοὺς Ἕλληνας. ἐγὼ δὲ περὶ μὲν τούτων οὐκ ἔρχομαι
ἐρέων ὅτι οὕτως ἢ ἄλλως πως ταῦτα ἐγένετο, ὃν δὲ οἶδα αὐτὸς ἄρξαντα ἀδίκων
ἔργων ἐς τοὺς Ἕλληνας, περὶ τούτου ἐξηγησάμενος προβήσομαι ἐς τὸ πρόσω τοῦ
λόγου.

[τὴν . . . ἅλωσιν, *the sack*      Ἰλίου, *of Ilium, Troy*      σφίσι, lit., *for themselves;*
translate with τῆς ἔχθρᾱς, *of their hatred*      ἐς + acc., *toward*      ἔρχομαι ἐρέων, *I am
going to say*      ἄλλως πως, *in some other way*      προβήσομαι, *I will go forward*      τὸ
πρόσω, *the further (part)* + partitive gen.]

4.  What do the Persians say was the origin of their hatred of the Greeks?
5.  Does Herodotus commit himself as to the truth of the Persian account?
6.  How will Herodotus begin his own account?

Κροῖσος ἦν Λῡδὸς μὲν γένος, παῖς δὲ Ἀλυάττεω, τύραννος δὲ ἐθνῶν τῶν ἐντὸς   10
Ἅλυος ποταμοῦ. οὗτος ὁ Κροῖσος πρῶτος ἐκείνων οὓς ἡμεῖς ἴσμεν τοὺς μὲν Ἑλλήνων
κατεστρέψατο, τοὺς δὲ φίλους ἐποιήσατο. κατεστρέψατο μὲν Ἴωνας τοὺς ἐν Ἀσίᾳ,
φίλους δὲ ἐποιήσατο Λακεδαιμονίους. πρὸ δὲ τῆς Κροίσου ἀρχῆς πάντες Ἕλληνες
ἦσαν ἐλεύθεροι.

[Λῡδός, *Lydian*      γένος, *by race*      Ἀλυάττεω, *of Alyattes*      τύραννος, *ruler*
ἐθνῶν, *of the peoples*      Ἅλυος (gen. of Ἅλυς), *Halys*      ἴσμεν, *we know*      κατεστρέψατο, *subdued*      ἀρχῆς, *reign*      ἐλεύθεροι, *free*]

7.  What four things do we learn about Croesus in the first sentence?
8.  What was Croesus the first to do?
9.  Whom did Croesus subdue and whom did he make his friends?
10. In what condition were the Greeks before the time of Croesus?

### Exercise 24 ε

*Translate into Greek (these sentences are based on Herodotus 1.27):*

1.  When his father died (*genitive absolute*), Croesus became king, who, waging war against (*use* στρατεύομαι + ἐπί + acc. *throughout this exercise*) the Greeks in Asia, subdued (*use* καταστρέφομαι) (them).
2.  When all the Greeks in Asia had been defeated (*use genitive absolute with aorist passive participle*), having built (made for himself) very many ships, he prepared to wage war against (ὡς + *future participle*) the islanders (*use* ὁ νησιώτης, τοῦ νησιώτου).
3.  But a certain Greek (man) having arrived at Sardis (τὰς Σάρδῑς) and having heard what Croesus was having in mind, said, "King, the is-

landers are gathering very many cavalry (ἱππέᾱς), to wage war (*use* ὡς + *future participle or purpose clause*) against you."

4. And Croesus, thinking that the Greek was speaking the truth, said, "I hope that the islanders will wage war against me; for they will clearly (σαφῶς) be defeated."

5. But the Greek answered these things, "Don't you think that the islanders hope that you will wage war against them (σφᾱς) by sea, believing that they will defeat you?"

6. So thus Croesus was persuaded not (μή) to wage war against the islanders but to make (them) friends.

# Classical Greek

## Hesiod

Hesiod (fl. 700 B.C.?) was a farmer in Boeotia who composed a long poem in which he intermingled practical advice on farming with moral homilies and myth. In the following lines (*Works and Days* 109–110, 112–118, ed., M. L. West) he gives an account of the Golden Age, which was followed by the Silver, Bronze, and Iron Ages, each worse than its predecessor:

χρύσεον μὲν πρώτιστα γένος μερόπων ἀνθρώπων

ἀθάνατοι ποίησαν Ὀλύμπια δώματ' ἔχοντες.

ὥστε θεοὶ δ' ἔζωον, ἀκηδέα θῦμὸν ἔχοντες,

νόσφιν ἄτερ τε πόνου καὶ ὀϊζύος· οὐδέ τι δειλόν

γῆρας ἐπῆν, αἰεὶ δὲ πόδας καὶ χεῖρας ὁμοῖοι

τέρποντ' ἐν θαλίῃσι κακῶν ἔκτοσθεν ἁπάντων·

θνῆσκον δ' ὥσθ' ὕπνῳ δεδμημένοι· ἐσθλὰ δὲ πάντα

τοῖσιν ἔην· καρπὸν δ' ἔφερε ζείδωρος ἄρουρα

αὐτομάτη πολλόν τε καὶ ἄφθονον. . . .

[χρύσεον, *golden*   γένος, *race*   μερόπων, *of mortal speech*   ποίησαν = ἐποίησαν  Ὀλύμπια δώματ(α), *homes on Mount Olympus*   ὥστε, *like, as though*   ἔζωον = ἔζων   ἀκηδέα, *free from sorrow*   θῦμὸν, *heart*   νόσφιν ἄτερ τε, *away from and without*   ὀϊζύος (gen. of ὀϊζύς), *woe, misery*   δειλόν / γῆρας, *sad old age*   ἐπῆν, *was present*   πόδας καὶ χεῖρας ὁμοῖοι, *the same in feet and hands*   τέρποντ' = ἐτέρποντο   θαλίῃσι = θαλίαις, *festivities*   ἔκτοσθεν + gen., *outside of; far from*   θνῆσκον = ἀπόθνησκον   δεδμημένοι (from δαμάζω), *subdued, overcome*   ἐσθλὰ, *good things*   τοῖσιν = τοῖς = ἐκείνοις   ἔην = ἦν   καρπὸν, *fruit*   ζείδωρος ἄρουρα, *the bountiful earth*   αὐτομάτη, *of its own accord*  (as in the Garden of Eden, earth produced food spontaneously)   πολλόν = πολύν   ἄφθονον, *plentiful*]

Concluded at the end of Chapter 26

# New Testament Greek

John 8.12
Jesus the Light of the World

Jesus speaks to the Pharisees.

πάλιν οὖν αὐτοῖς ἐλάλησεν ὁ Ἰησοῦς λέγων, "ἐγώ εἰμι τὸ φῶς τοῦ κόσμου· ὁ ἀκολουθῶν ἐμοὶ οὐ μὴ περιπατήσῃ ἐν τῇ σκοτίᾳ, ἀλλ᾽ ἕξει τὸ φῶς τῆς ζωῆς."

[**πάλιν**, *again*   **ἐλάλησεν**, *spoke*   **τὸ φῶς**, *the light*   **ὁ ἀκολουθῶν** + dat., *the one following*   **οὐ μὴ περιπατήσῃ**, *will never walk*   **τῇ σκοτίᾳ**, *the darkness*]

John 8.31–32
The Truth Will Make You Free

Jesus speaks to Jewish believers.

ἔλεγεν οὖν ὁ Ἰησοῦς πρὸς τοὺς πεπιστευκότας αὐτῷ Ἰουδαίους, "ἐὰν ὑμεῖς μείνητε ἐν τῷ λόγῳ τῷ ἐμῷ, ἀληθῶς μαθηταί μού ἐστε καὶ γνώσεσθε τὴν ἀλήθειαν, καὶ ἡ ἀλήθεια ἐλευθερώσει ὑμᾶς."

[**πεπιστευκότας** + dat., *who had come to believe in*   **τὴν ἀλήθειαν**, *the truth*]

John 9.1–7
Jesus Heals a Man Born Blind

καὶ παράγων εἶδεν ἄνθρωπον τυφλὸν ἐκ γενετῆς.  καὶ ἠρώτησαν αὐτὸν οἱ μαθηταὶ αὐτοῦ λέγοντες, "ῥαββί, τίς ἥμαρτεν, οὗτος ἢ οἱ γονεῖς αὐτοῦ, ἵνα τυφλὸς γεννηθῇ;" ἀπεκρίθη Ἰησοῦς, "οὔτε οὗτος ἥμαρτεν οὔτε οἱ γονεῖς αὐτοῦ, ἀλλ᾽ ἵνα φανερωθῇ τὰ ἔργα τοῦ θεοῦ ἐν αὐτῷ.  ἡμᾶς δεῖ ἐργάζεσθαι τὰ ἔργα τοῦ πέμψαντός με ἕως ἡμέρα ἐστίν· ἔρχεται νὺξ ὅτε οὐδεὶς δύναται ἐργάζεσθαι.  ὅταν ἐν τῷ κόσμῳ ὦ, φῶς εἰμι τοῦ κόσμου."

[**παράγων**: the subject is Jesus, *passing along*   **γενετῆς**, *birth*   **οἱ μαθηταί**, *the disciples*   **ῥαββί**, *rabbi, teacher, master*   **οἱ γονεῖς**, *the parents*   **γεννηθῇ**, *he was born*   **ἀλλ᾽ ἵνα φανερωθῇ** (from φανερόω) *but* (he was born blind) *so that X might be shown*   **ἕως**, *while*]

ταῦτα εἰπὼν ἔπτυσεν χαμαὶ καὶ ἐποίησεν πηλὸν ἐκ τοῦ πτύσματος καὶ ἐπέχρισεν αὐτοῦ τὸν πηλὸν ἐπὶ τοὺς ὀφθαλμοὺς καὶ εἶπεν αὐτῷ, "ὕπαγε νίψαι εἰς τὴν κολυμβήθραν τοῦ Σιλωάμ (ὃ ἑρμηνεύεται Ἀπεσταλμένος)." ἀπῆλθεν οὖν καὶ ἐνίψατο καὶ ἦλθεν βλέπων.

[**ἔπτυσεν**, *he spat*   **χαμαί**, *on the ground*   **πηλόν**, *mud*   **ἐπέχρισεν** (from ἐπιχρίω), *he smeared*   **αὐτοῦ**: take with τοὺς ὀφθαλμοὺς   **ὕπαγε**, *go*   **νίψαι** (from νίπτω, aorist middle imperative), *wash yourself*   **τὴν κολυμβήθραν**, *pool*   **ἑρμηνεύεται**, *is translated*   **Ἀπεσταλμένος**, *Having Been Sent*   **ἐνίψατο**, *he washed himself*]

# 25
# Ο ΚΡΟΙΣΟΣ
# ΤΟΝ ΣΟΛΩΝΑ ΞΕΝΙΖΕΙ (α)

ὁ Σόλων ἀφικόμενος ἐς τὰς Σάρδῑς ἵνα πάντα θεωροίη ἐξενίζετο ὑπὸ τοῦ Κροίσου.

## VOCABULARY

*Verbs*
   ἀποδημέω, *I am abroad; I go abroad*
   θάπτω, [θαφ-] θάψω, ἔθαψα, τέθαμμαι, [ταφ-] ἐτάφην, *I bury*
   καταστρέφω, καταστρέψω, κατέστρεψα, [στραφ-] κατέστραμμαι, κατεστράφην, *I overturn; middle, I subdue*
   κρίνω, [κρινε-] κρινῶ, [κρῑν-] ἔκρῑνα, [κρι-] κέκρικα, κέκριμαι, ἐκρίθην, *I judge*
   ξενίζω, [ξενιε-] ξενιῶ, [ξενι-] ἐξένισα, ἐξενίσθην, *I entertain*
   περιάγω, *I lead around*
*Nouns*
   ἡ βασιλείᾱ, τῆς βασιλείᾱς, *kingdom*
   τὰ βασίλεια, τῶν βασιλείων, *palace*

   ὁ θεράπων, τοῦ θεράποντος, *attendant; servant*
   ἡ θεωρίᾱ, τῆς θεωρίᾱς, *viewing; sight-seeing*
   ὁ θησαυρός, τοῦ θησαυροῦ, *treasure; treasury*
   ἡ σοφίᾱ, τῆς σοφίᾱς, *wisdom*
   ἡ τελευτή, τῆς τελευτῆς, *end*
*Preposition*
   κατά + acc., *down;* distributive, *each, every; by; on; according to;* of time, *at; through*
*Adverb*
   μετά, *afterward; later*
*Expressions*
   οἷός τ' εἰμί, *I am able*
*Proper Names*
   ὁ Ἀλυάττης, τοῦ Ἀλυάττεω (Ionic genitive), *Alyattes*
   αἱ Σάρδεις, τῶν Σάρδεων; Ionic, αἱ Σάρδιες, τῶν Σαρδίων, τὰς Σάρδῑς, *Sardis*

τελευτήσαντος δὲ Ἀλυάττεω, ἐδέξατο τὴν βασιλείᾱν Κροῖσος ὁ
Ἀλυάττεω, ἔτη γενόμενος πέντε καὶ τριάκοντα, ὃς δὴ τοῖς ἐν Ἀσίᾳ
Ἕλλησι ἐπιστρατεύων ἐν μέρει κατεστρέψατο. ὡς δὲ τοὺς ἐν Ἀσίᾳ
Ἕλληνας κατεστρέψατο, ἀφικνοῦνται ἐς τᾱς Σάρδῑς ἄλλοι τε ἐκ τῆς
Ἑλλάδος σοφισταὶ καὶ δὴ καὶ ὁ Σόλων, ἀνὴρ Ἀθηναῖος, ὃς      5
Ἀθηναίοις νόμους ποιήσᾱς ἀπεδήμησε ἔτη δέκα, λόγῳ μὲν θεωρίᾱς
ἕνεκα ἐκπλεύσᾱς, ἔργῳ δὲ ἵνα μή τινα τῶν νόμων ἀναγκασθείη λῦσαι
ὧν ἔθετο. αὐτοὶ γὰρ οὐχ οἷοί τ’ ἦσαν τοῦτο ποιῆσαι Ἀθηναῖοι·
κατείχοντο γὰρ δέκα ἔτη χρήσεσθαι νόμοις οὕστινας σφίσι Σόλων
θεῖτο. ἀποδημήσᾱς οὖν ἐς Αἴγυπτον ἀφίκετο παρὰ Ἄμασιν καὶ δὴ      10
καὶ ἐς Σάρδῑς παρὰ Κροῖσον. ἀφικόμενος δὲ ἐξενίζετο ἐν τοῖς
βασιλείοις ὑπὸ τοῦ Κροίσου. μετὰ δέ, ἡμέρᾳ τρίτῃ ἢ τετάρτῃ,
κελεύσαντος Κροίσου, τὸν Σόλωνα θεράποντες περιῆγον κατὰ τοὺς
θησαυροὺς ἵνα δείξειαν πάντα ὄντα μεγάλα καὶ ὄλβια.

[ἐν μέρει, *in turn*    λῦσαι, *to repeal*    ἔθετο (from τίθημι), *he enacted*    κατείχοντο, *they were being constrained*    σφίσι, *for them*]

θεᾱσάμενον δὲ αὐτὸν τὰ πάντα καὶ σκεψάμενον ἤρετο ὁ Κροῖσος      15
τάδε· "ξένε Ἀθηναῖε, παρὰ ἡμᾶς περὶ σοῦ λόγος ἥκει πολὺς καὶ
σοφίᾱς ἕνεκα σῆς καὶ πλάνης, ὡς θεωρίᾱς ἕνεκα γῆν πολλὴν
ἐπελήλυθας. νῦν οὖν βούλομαι ἐρέσθαι σε τίς ἐστιν ὀλβιώτατος
πάντων ὧν εἶδες." ὁ μὲν ἐλπίζων αὐτὸς εἶναι ὀλβιώτατος ταῦτα
ἠρώτᾱ, Σόλων δὲ οὐδὲν ὑποθωπεύσᾱς ἀλλὰ τῷ ἀληθεῖ χρησάμενος      20
λέγει· "ὦ βασιλεῦ, Τέλλος Ἀθηναῖος." θαυμάσᾱς δὲ Κροῖσος τὸ
λεχθέν, ἤρετο, "πῶς δὴ κρῑνεις Τέλλον εἶναι ὀλβιώτατον;" ὁ δὲ εἶπε·
"Τέλλῳ καὶ παῖδες ἦσαν καλοί τε κἀγαθοὶ καὶ τοῖς παισὶ εἶδε τέκνα
ἐκγενόμενα καὶ πάντα παραμείναντα, καὶ τελευτὴ τοῦ βίου
λαμπροτάτη ἐγένετο· γενομένης γὰρ Ἀθηναίοις μάχης πρὸς γείτονας      25
ἐν Ἐλευσῖνι, βοηθήσᾱς καὶ τροπὴν ποιήσᾱς τῶν πολεμίων ἀπέθανε
κάλλιστα, καὶ αὐτὸν Ἀθηναῖοι δημοσίᾳ τε ἔθαψαν ὅπου ἔπεσε καὶ
ἐτίμησαν μεγάλως."

[σκεψάμενον (from σκοπέω), *having examined*    πλάνης, *wandering*    ἐπελήλυθας, *you have passed through*   ὑποθωπεύσᾱς, *flattering*   τὸ λεχθέν, *what was said*   κἀγαθοὶ = καὶ ἀγαθοὶ   ἐκγενόμενα, *being born (having been born) from / to + dat.*   παραμείναντα, *surviving, remaining alive*   γείτονας, *neighbors*   τροπὴν, *rout*   δημοσίᾳ, *publicly*]

—adapted from Herodotus 1.26 and 29–30

## PRINCIPAL PARTS: Three Deponent Verbs

δύνα-μαι, δυνήσομαι, δεδύνημαι, ἐδυνήθην, *I am able; I can*

ἐπίστα-μαι, ἐπιστήσομαι, ἠπιστήθην, *I understand; I know*

κεῖ-μαι, κείσομαι, *I lie;* also used in the present and imperfect instead of the perfect and pluperfect passive of τίθημι, with the meanings *I am laid; I am placed*

## WORD STUDY

*Give the Greek words from which the following English terms used in the study of history are derived:*

1. history
2. chronicle
3. chronology

4. genealogy
5. paleography
6. archaeology *or* archeology

## GRAMMAR

### 1. The Optative Mood Used to Express Wishes

The last mood of the Greek verb for you to learn is the *optative*, so called from its use in wishes and named from the Latin word for "to wish," *optāre*. The suffixes for the optative mood are -ῑ- or -ιη-, which combine with other vowels in the verb to give forms that are immediately recognizable by the diphthongs οι, αι, or ῳ or the long-vowel digraph ει, e.g., λύοιμι, λύσαιμι, τῑμῴην and λυθείην.

One use of the optative in main clauses is to express wishes for the future (the negative is μή), e.g.:

ὠφελοίη σε ὁ θεός, ὦ παῖ.
***May* the god *help* you, son.**

μὴ εἰς κακὰ **πέσοιτε**, ὦ φίλοι.
***May you not fall* into trouble, friends. *I hope you don't.* . . .**

Both the present optative (ὠφελοίη) and the aorist optative (πέσοιτε) refer to the future; they differ in aspect, not time.

The word εἴθε or the words εἰ γάρ, *if only, oh that,* are often used to introduce wishes with the optative, e.g.:

εἴθε/εἰ γὰρ μὴ **ὀργίζοιτο** ἡμῖν ὁ δεσπότης.
***If only* the master *would* not *be angry* with us!**

## Exercise 25 α

*Read aloud and translate:*

1. εἴθε ταχέως παραγένοιτο ἡ μήτηρ.
2. τοὺς πολεμίους νῑκήσαιμεν καὶ τὴν πατρίδα σῴζοιμεν.
3. εἰ γὰρ μὴ ἴδοιμι τοὺς κακοὺς εὖ πράττοντας.
4. εἴθε μὴ διαφθαρείη ἡ ναῦς τῷ χειμῶνι.
5. κακῶς ἀποθάνοιεν πάντες οἱ τοιαῦτα πράττοντες.

## 2.  The Potential Optative

The optative (present or aorist) with the particle ἄν in main clauses expresses a possibility or likelihood, sometimes dependent on a condition, stated or implied.  This is called the *potential optative*; compare English statements with "would," "should," and "may," e.g.:

**I *would like*** to see the doctor (*if I may*).

**βουλοίμην ἄν** τὸν ῑ̓ᾱτρὸν ἰδεῖν.

There is no one way of translating such clauses; the following examples illustrate some of the uses of the potential optative (the negative is οὐ):

οὐκ ἂν βοηθοίην σοι. *I wouldn't come to your aid.*

ἴσως ἂν ἡμῖν βοηθοίης. *Perhaps you would come to our aid.*

οὐκ ἂν δυναίμεθά σοι βοηθεῖν. *We couldn't come to your aid.*

χωροῖς ἂν εἴσω; *Would you go in? = Please go in.*

## Exercise 25 β

*Read aloud and translate:*

1. οὐκ ἂν βουλοίμην τὸ παιδίον βλάπτειν.
2. οὐκ ἂν δυναίμην τοῦτο ποιῆσαι.
3. ἡδέως ἂν ἀκούσαιμι τί βούλεται ὁ νεᾱνίᾱς.
4. ἴσως ἂν ἀργύριόν τι ἡμῖν δοίη ὁ βασιλεύς.
5. μόλις ἂν πειθοίμεθα τῷ στρατηγῷ τοιαῦτα κελεύοντι.
6. εἴποιτε ἄν μοι τί ἐγένετο;
7. τίς ἂν τούτῳ πιστεύοι, ὅσπερ ἡμῖν πολλάκις ἐψεύσατο;
8. οὐκ ἂν λάθοις τοὺς θεοὺς τοιοῦτο ποιῶν.
9. ἐχθροὶ ὄντες οὐκ ἂν βούλοιντο ἡμῖν συλλαμβάνειν.
10. δὶς εἰς τὸν αὐτὸν ποταμὸν οὐκ ἂν ἐμβαίης (from ἐμβαίνω, *I step into*).
    (Heraclitus, as quoted by Plato, *Cratylus* 402a10)

## 3.  The Optative Mood in Subordinate Clauses

a.  In some subordinate clauses, the optative may be used as an alternative to the subjunctive.  This option is available only if the verb of the main clause is in the imperfect, aorist, or pluperfect tense.  The subordinate clause is then said to be in *secondary* sequence.  (If the main

verb of the sentence is in the present, future, or perfect tense or in the
present or aorist imperative, the subordinate clause is said to be in
*primary* sequence.)

In the following examples of sentences with subordinate clauses
in secondary sequence, the optional optative verb forms are given after the slash. Note that the translation into English is the same re-
gardless of whether the optative or the subjunctive mood is used in
Greek; Greek authors seem to have used the subjunctive or optative
indifferently in secondary sequence, with no difference in meaning.

Primary Sequence (Purpose Clause):

ὁ Σόλων <u>ἀποδημεῖ</u> **ἵνα** μή τινα τῶν νόμων **ἀναγκασθῇ** λῦσαι ὧν
ἔθετο.
*Solon <u>goes abroad</u>* **in order that he might** *not* **be compelled** *to repeal
any of the laws that he enacted.*

Secondary Sequence:

ὁ Σόλων <u>ἀπεδήμησε</u> **ἵνα** μή τινα τῶν νόμων **ἀναγκασθῇ/ἀναγ-
κασθείη** λῦσαι ὧν ἔθετο.
*Solon <u>went abroad</u>* **in order that he might** *not* **be compelled** *to repeal
any of the laws that he  had enacted.*

Primary Sequence (Clause of Fearing):

οἱ πολῖται <u>φοβοῦνται</u> **μὴ** οἱ πολέμιοι εἰς τὴν γῆν **εἰσβάλωσιν**.
*The citizens <u>are afraid</u> the enemy* **may invade** *the land.*

Secondary Sequence:

οἱ πολῖται <u>ἐφοβοῦντο</u> **μὴ** οἱ πολέμιοι εἰς τὴν γῆν **εἰσβάλωσιν/εἰσ-
βάλοιεν**.
*The citizens <u>were afraid</u> the enemy* **would invade** *the land.*

b.  In secondary sequence, indefinite or general clauses regularly have
their verbs in the optative without ἄν, e.g.:

Primary Sequence (Indefinite or General Temporal Clause):

οἱ Ἀθηναῖοι αὐτῷ φρουρίῳ <u>χρῶνται</u>, **ὁπόταν** πόλεμος **γένηται**.
*The Athenians <u>use</u> it as a garrison,* **whenever** *war* **occurs**.

Secondary Sequence:

οἱ Ἀθηναῖοι αὐτῷ φρουρίῳ <u>ἐχρῶντο,</u> **ὁπότε** πόλεμος **γένοιτο**.
*The Athenians <u>used to use</u> it as a garrison,* **whenever** *war* **occurred**.

Primary Sequence (Indefinite or General Relative Clause):

οἱ Ἀθηναῖοι <u>κατέχονται</u> χρῆσθαι νόμοις **οὕστινας ἂν** σφίσι Σόλων **θῆται.**

*The Athenians <u>are constrained</u> to use **whatever** laws Solon **lays down** for them.*

Secondary Sequence:

οἱ Ἀθηναῖοι <u>κατείχοντο</u> χρῆσθαι νόμοις **οὕστινας** σφίσι Σόλων **θεῖτο.**

*The Athenians <u>were being constrained</u> to use **whatever** laws Solon **laid down** for them.*

## 4.  The Forms of the Optative

The optative, associated with secondary sequence, uses secondary endings, -μην, -σο, -το, -μεθα, -σθε, -ντο, in the present middle and passive and in the aorist middle; the σ of the 2nd person singular is lost between vowels.  The optative suffixes -ῑ- or -ιη- produce forms that are recognizable from the diphthongs οι, αι, or ῳ or the long-vowel digraph ει; be sure you can recognize person, tense, and voice markers.

| Pres. Act. | Pres. M./P. | Aor. Act. | Aor. Mid. | Aor. Pass. |
|---|---|---|---|---|
| λῡοιμι | λῡοίμην | λῡσαιμι | λῡσαίμην | λυθείην |
| λῡοις | λῡοιω | λῡσειας (-σαις) | λῡσαιο | λυθείης |
| λῡοι | λῡοιτο | λῡσειε(ν) (-σαι) | λῡσαιτο | λυθείη |
| λῡοιμεν | λῡοίμεθα | λῡσαιμεν | λῡσαίμεθα | λυθεῖμεν |
| λῡοιτε | λῡοισθε | λῡσαιτε | λῡσαισθε | λυθεῖτε |
| λῡοιεν | λῡοιντο | λῡσειαν (-σαιεν) | λῡσαιντο | λυθεῖεν |
|  |  |  |  | γραφείην etc. |

Liquid Stems:

| | | | | |
|---|---|---|---|---|
| αἴροιμι | αἱροίμην | ἄραιμι | ἀραίμην | ἀρθείην |
| αἴροις | αἴροιο | ἄρειας (-αις) | ἄραιο | ἀρθείης |
| αἴροι | αἴροιτο | ἄρειε(ν) (-αι) | ἄραιτο | ἀρθείη |
| αἴροιμεν | αἱροίμεθα | ἄραιμεν | ἀραίμεθα | ἀρθεῖμεν |
| αἴροιτε | αἴροισθε | ἄραιτε | ἄραισθε | ἀρθεῖτε |
| αἴροιεν | αἴροιντο | ἄρειαν (-αιεν) | ἄραιντο | ἀρθεῖεν |

Contract Verbs:

| | | | | |
|---|---|---|---|---|
| φιλοίην | φιλοίμην | φιλήσαιμι | φιλησαίμην | φιληθείην |
| φιλοίης | φιλοῖο | φιλήσειας (-σαις) | φιλήσαιο | φιληθείης |
| φιλοίη | φιλοῖτο | φιλήσειε(ν) (-σαι) | φιλήσαιτο | φιληθείη |
| φιλοῖμεν | φιλοίμεθα | φιλήσαιμεν | φιλησαίμεθα | φιληθεῖμεν |
| φιλοῖτε | φιλοῖσθε | φιλήσαιτε | φιλήσαισθε | φιληθεῖτε |
| φιλοῖεν | φιλοῖντο | φιλήσειαν (-σαιεν) | φιλήσαιντο | φιληθεῖεν |

| | | | | |
|---|---|---|---|---|
| τῑμῴην | τῑμῴμην | τῑμήσαιμι | τῑμησαίμην | τῑμηθείην |
| τῑμῴης | τῑμῷο | τῑμήσειας (-σαις) | τῑμήσαιο | τῑμηθείης |
| τῑμῴη | τῑμῷτο | τῑμήσειε(ν) (-σαι) | τῑμήσαιτο | τῑμηθείη |
| τῑμῷμεν | τῑμῴμεθα | τῑμήσαιμεν | τῑμησαίμεθα | τῑμηθεῖμεν |
| τῑμῷτε | τῑμῷσθε | τῑμήσαιτε | τῑμήσαισθε | τῑμηθεῖτε |
| τῑμῷεν | τῑμῷντο | τῑμήσειαν (-σαιεν) | τῑμήσαιντο | τῑμηθεῖεν |

| | | | | |
|---|---|---|---|---|
| δηλοίην | δηλοίμην | δηλώσαιμι | δηλωσαίμην | δηλωθείην |
| δηλοίης | δηλοῖο | δηλώσειας (-σαις) | δηλώσαιο | δηλωθείης |
| δηλοίη | δηλοῖτο | δηλώσειε(ν) (-σαι) | δηλώσαιτο | δηλωθείη |
| δηλοῖμεν | δηλοίμεθα | δηλώσαιμεν | δηλωσαίμεθα | δηλωθεῖμεν |
| δηλοῖτε | δηλοῖσθε | δηλώσαιτε | δηλώσαισθε | δηλωθεῖτε |
| δηλοῖεν | δηλοῖντο | δηλώσειαν (-σαιεν) | δηλώσαιντο | δηλωθεῖεν |

Thematic 2nd Aorists:

| **Active** | **Middle** |
|---|---|
| λίποιμι | λιποίμην |
| λίποις | λίποιο |
| λίποι | λίποιτο |
| λίποιμεν | λιποίμεθα |
| λίποιτε | λίποισθε |
| λίποιεν | λίποιντο |

Athematic 2nd Aorists:  βαίην, βαίης, βαίη, βαῖμεν, βαῖτε, βαῖεν
σταίην, σταίης, σταίη, σταῖμεν, σταῖτε, σταῖεν
γνοίην, γνοίης, γνοίη, γνοῖμεν, γνοῖτε, γνοῖεν

Future Active and Middle Optatives:

The future active and middle optatives are formed from the future indicative stem, and their endings are the same as those for the present optative of λύω, except for liquid stem verbs, which have the same endings in the future as -ε- contract verbs have in the present, e.g.:

λύσοιμι / λῡσοίμην           τῑμήσοιμι / τῑμησοίμην           ἀροίην / ἀροίμην
φιλήσοιμι / φιλησοίμην      δηλώσοιμι / δηλωσοίμην

Future Passive Optatives:

λυθησοίμην     φιληθησοίμην     τῑμηθησοίμην     δηλωθησοίμην     ἀρθησοίμην
γραφησοίμην

## Exercise 25 γ

*Fill in the optative forms on all Verb Charts completed for Book I, except for the charts for Exercise 11θ.  Keep the charts for reference.*

## Exercise 25 δ

*Change the following indicative forms first to the subjunctive and then to the optative:*

| | | |
|---|---|---|
| 1. λῡ́ουσιν | 6. νῑκῶμεν | 11. λῡόμεθα |
| 2. λῡ́εται | 7. φιλεῖ | 12. ἔλαβον (2 ways) |
| 3. ἐλῡ́σαμεν | 8. ἐποιήσαντο | 13. ἐγένετο |
| 4. ἐλύθη | 9. εἴδετε | 14. ἐφιλήσαμεν |
| 5. βούλομαι | 10. τῑμᾷ | 15. ἀφίκοντο |

## Exercise 25 ε

*Rewrite the following sentences, changing the main verbs to the designated past tenses and the subjunctives to optatives; then translate the new sentences:*

1. οἱ νέοι παιδεύονται (*imperfect*) ἵνα ἀγαθοὶ γένωνται.
2. ὁ Σόλων ἀποδημεῖ (*aorist*) ἵνα μὴ ἀναγκασθῇ τοὺς νόμους λῦσαι.
3. οἱ παῖδες φοβοῦνται (*imperfect*) μὴ ὁ πατὴρ ὀργίζηται.
4. οἱ ὁπλῖται φοβοῦνται (*imperfect*) μὴ οὐκ ἀμῡ́νωσι τοὺς πολεμίους.
5. ὁ Δικαιόπολις πρὸς τὸ ἄστυ πορεύεται (*aorist*) ὅπως τοὺς χοροὺς θεᾶται.
6. φοβούμενος τὸν κίνδῡνον, τοὺς φίλους καλῶ (*aorist*) ὅπως ῡ̔μῖν βοηθῶσιν.
7. ἐν τῷ ἄστει μενοῦμεν (*aorist*) ἵνα τὰς τραγῳδίᾱς θεώμεθα.
8. οἱ αὐτουργοὶ εἰς τὸ ἄστυ σπεύδουσιν (*aorist*) ἵνα μὴ ὑπὸ τῶν πολεμίων ληφθῶσιν.
9. φοβούμεθα (*imperfect*) μὴ οὐκ ἐν καιρῷ οἴκαδε ἐπανέλθωμεν.
10. ὁπόταν ἔαρ γένηται, οἱ ποιμένες τὰ πρόβατα πρὸς τὰ ὄρη ἐλαύνουσιν (*imperfect*).

## Exercise 25 ζ

*Translate into Greek:*

1. The Greeks used to send their children to school to learn writing.
2. The children were always afraid that the teacher might be angry.
3. Whenever winter came, the shepherds were driving their flocks to the plain.
4. The slaves were always doing whatever (their) master ordered.
5. We hurried home to find our mother.

Bust of Herodotus

# Herodotus

Herodotus was born at Halicarnassus, on the southern fringe of Ionia, some years before Xerxes' invasion of Greece. As a boy, he must have seen the queen of Halicarnassus, Artemisia, lead her fleet to join the invasion force. As a young man he joined the unsuccessful uprising against the tyrant Lygdamis, Artemisia's grandson, and after its failure went into exile in Samos. From there he embarked on his travels, which eventually took him around most of the known world. He visited Lydia, including Sardis, and Syria, from where he reached the Euphrates and sailed down the river to Babylon. From Babylon he went on to the Persian capital, Susa. In the North he sailed right around the Black Sea (Pontus Euxinus), stayed some time at Olbia at the mouth of the Dnieper (Borysthenes) and traveled up the river into the wild interior of Scythia. In the South, he visited Egypt twice, staying for several months, and sailed up the Nile as far as Elephantine. In the West he knew Sicily and south Italy. Whether he traveled as a merchant or, as Solon, simply for sightseeing (θεωρίας ἕνεκα), he continually amassed information, seeing and listening, gathering oral tradition, and studying records and monuments, all of which he was to use in his history.

During this period he settled in Athens for some time. He became a friend of the tragedian Sophocles, who wrote an ode to him when he left Athens to join the panhellenic colony of Thurii in south Italy (443 B.C.). Thurii became his home thereafter, though he continued to travel and returned to Athens to give recitations of his history in the 430s. He lived through the first years of the Peloponnesian War (he refers to events of 431–430 B.C.), and his history must have been published before 425 B.C., when Aristophanes parodies its introduction in the *Acharnians*.

He has rightly been called the "father of history." He had no predecessor except Hecataeus of Miletus (fl. 500 B.C.), who wrote a description of the earth in two books, one on Asia, the other on Europe. Herodotus knew this work and refers to it twice, when he disagrees with Hecataeus's statements. It is hard for us, with books and libraries at hand, to imagine the difficulties that confronted a man who set out to write a history of events that took place a generation or more earlier. The only written sources he could consult were local records, e.g., temple lists and oracles, and in some cases official documents, e.g., he must have had access to some Persian records, such as the Persian army list. Otherwise he had to rely entirely on what he saw on his travels and what he heard from the people he met. He was a man of infinite curiosity with an unflagging interest in the beliefs and customs of foreign peoples. Free from all racial prejudice, he listened to what strangers had to tell him with an open mind, and he could never resist passing on a good story. Not that he believed all that he was told. He had a healthy scepticism: "I am obliged to report what people say, but I feel no obligation to believe it always; this principle applies to my whole history" (7.152).

He was a deeply religious man, and his interpretation of history is theological. He believed firmly that the gods did intervene in human affairs and that no man could escape his fate. In particular, he believed that human pride (ὕβρις) resulted in divine vengeance (νέμεσις). This is clearly seen in the story of Croesus and on a larger scale in the whole treatment of the pride, defeat, and downfall of Xerxes. Dreams, signs, and oracles play an important part in his narrative. These are the means by which man might know his fate, which could not be changed but which might be postponed. Myth permeates his work. He moves in a world where mythical explanations of phenomena are commonplace; he is not a thoroughgoing sceptic, nor does he swallow the mythical tradition whole.

Before telling the story of Croesus, he goes back to give an account of the kings of Lydia, from whom Croesus was descended, and the whole section ends with the words Λυδοὶ μὲν δὴ ὑπὸ Πέρσῃσι ἐδεδούλωντο, "the Lydians had been enslaved by the Persians." One of the major themes of the history is freedom and slavery.

There follows a description of the rise of Persia, including the subjugation of the Greeks in Asia Minor and the defeat and capture of Babylon, ending with the death of Cyrus. Book 2 opens with the accession of Cyrus's son Cambyses, who invaded and conquered Egypt. The remainder of Book 2 is then taken up with a description and history of Egypt, the longest of Herodotus's digressions from his main theme. Book 3 starts with the conquest of Egypt and Cambyses' subsequent madness and death. After a digression on Polycrates of Samos, we have an account of the accession of Darius and the organization and resources of the Persian Empire. Book 4 is devoted to Darius's invasions of Scythia and Cyrene; Book 5, to the reduction of Thrace and the Ionian revolt. The Persian menace is seen to be looming larger and larger over Greece. Book 6 centers on Darius's expedition to punish the Athenians for helping the Ionians in their revolt, an expedition that culminates in the Marathon campaign. Book 7 opens with the accession of Xerxes and his decision to invade Greece. It ends with the Thermopylae campaign. Books 8 and 9 continue the story of the invasion and end with the battle of Mycale and the revolt of Ionia.

Within this broad framework, Herodotus continually makes digressions wherever a topic that interests him crops up. He is particularly fascinated by the strange customs and beliefs of the remoter peoples he met, but he also tells us a great deal about the earlier history of Greece, as occasion arises. The whole story moves in a leisurely and expansive way, not unlike Homer's *Iliad* in this respect, and like Homer he also continually uses speeches to heighten the drama of events and to illuminate the characters of the leading actors. Despite the poetic qualities of his work, he is usually found to be correct on matters of historical fact where we can check them from any other source.

# Ο ΚΡΟΙΣΟΣ
# ΤΟΝ ΣΟΛΩΝΑ ΞΕΝΙΖΕΙ (β)

## VOCABULARY

*Verbs*
  ἕλκω, imperfect, εἷλκον (irreg-
    ular augment), ἕλξω, [ἑλκυ-]
    εἵλκυσα, εἵλκυκα, εἵλκυ-
    σμαι, εἱλκύσθην, *I drag*
  καταφρονέω + gen., *I despise*
*Nouns*
  ἡ εὐδαιμονίᾱ, τῆς εὐδαιμο-
    νίᾱς, *happiness; prosperity;
    good luck*

ἡ εὐχή, τῆς εὐχῆς, *prayer*
ὁ πλοῦτος, τοῦ πλούτου, *wealth*
ἡ ῥώμη, τῆς ῥώμης, *strength*
*Adjectives*
  ἀμφότερος, -ᾱ, -ον, *both*
  ἱκανός, -ή, -όν, *sufficient; ca-
    pable*
*Proper Name*
  οἱ Δελφοί, τῶν Δελφῶν, *Delphi*


ὡς δὲ ταῦτα περὶ τοῦ Τέλλου ὁ Σόλων εἶπε, ὁ Κροῖσος ἤρετο τίνα
δεύτερον μετ᾽ ἐκεῖνον ὀλβιώτατον ἴδοι, νομίζων πάγχυ δευτερεῖα
οἴσεσθαι. ὁ δέ, "Κλέοβίν τε καὶ Βίτωνα. τούτοις γὰρ οὖσι γένος
Ἀργείοις πλοῦτός τε ἦν ἱκανὸς καὶ πρὸς τούτῳ ῥώμη σώματος
τοιᾶδε· ἀεθλοφόροι τε ἀμφότεροι ἦσαν, καὶ δὴ καὶ λέγεται ὅδε ὁ      5
λόγος· οὔσης ἑορτῆς τῇ Ἥρᾳ τοῖς Ἀργείοις, ἔδει πάντως τὴν μητέρα
αὐτῶν ζεύγει κομισθῆναι ἐς τὸ ἱερόν, οἱ δὲ βόες ἐκ τοῦ ἀγροῦ οὐ
παρεγίγνοντο ἐν καιρῷ. οἱ δὲ νεᾱνίαι, ἵνα παραγένοιτο ἡ μήτηρ ἐν
καιρῷ, αὐτοὶ εἷλκον τὴν ἅμαξαν, ἐπὶ δὲ τῆς ἁμάξης ἐφέρετο ἡ μήτηρ,
σταδίους δὲ πέντε καὶ τεσσαράκοντα κομίσαντες ἀφίκοντο ἐς τὸ       10
ἱερόν.

[πάγχυ, *certainly*  δευτερεῖα (neut. pl.), *second prize*  οἴσεσθαι (future middle
infinitive of φέρω), *he would carry (off)*  γένος, *by race*  ἀεθλοφόροι, *prize winners*
(in athletic contests)  πάντως, *absolutely*  ζεύγει, *by means of a yoke of oxen*
σταδίους . . . πέντε καὶ τεσσαράκοντα, *forty-five stades* = about five miles or
eight kilometers]

ταῦτα δὲ αὐτοῖς ποιήσᾱσι καὶ ὀφθεῖσι ὑπὸ τῶν παρόντων τελευτὴ
τοῦ βίου ἀρίστη ἐγένετο, ἔδειξέ τε ἐν τούτοις ὁ θεὸς ὅτι ἄμεινον εἴη
ἀνθρώπῳ τεθνάναι μᾶλλον ἢ ζῆν. οἱ μὲν γὰρ Ἀργεῖοι περιστάντες
ἐμακάριζον τῶν νεᾱνιῶν τὴν ῥώμην, αἱ δὲ Ἀργεῖαι τὴν μητέρα αὐτῶν   15

ἐμακάριζον, διότι τοιούτων τέκνων ἐκύρησε. ἡ δὲ μήτηρ στᾶσα ἀντίον τοῦ ἀγάλματος τῆς θεοῦ ηὔχετο Κλεόβει τε καὶ Βίτωνι τοῖς ἑαυτῆς τέκνοις, οἳ αὐτὴν ἐτίμησαν μεγάλως, τὴν θεὸν δοῦναι ὅ τι ἀνθρώπῳ τυχεῖν ἄριστον εἴη. μετὰ δὲ ταύτην τὴν εὐχήν, ὡς ἔθυσάν τε καὶ εὐωχήθησαν, κατακοιμηθέντες ἐν αὐτῷ τῷ ἱερῷ οἱ νεανίαι 20 οὐκέτι ἀνέστησαν ἀλλ' οὕτως ἐτελεύτησαν. Ἀργεῖοι δὲ αὐτῶν εἰκόνας ποιησάμενοι ἀνέθεσαν ἐν Δελφοῖς, ὡς ἀνδρῶν ἀρίστων γενομένων."

[ὀφθεῖσι: aorist passive participle of ὁράω    τεθνάναι, *to have died = to be dead*  περιστάντες, *standing around*    ἐμακάριζον, *called blessed, praised*    ἐκύρησεν + gen., *obtained, had*    ἀντίον τοῦ ἀγάλματος, *in front of the statue*    εὐωχήθησαν (from εὐωχέω), *had feasted*    κατακοιμηθέντες (from κατακοιμάω), *having gone to sleep*    εἰκόνας, *statues*]

Σόλων μὲν οὖν εὐδαιμονίᾱς δευτερεῖα ἔνειμε τούτοις, Κροῖσος δὲ ὀργισθεὶς εἶπε· "ὦ ξέν' Ἀθηναῖε, τῆς δὲ ἡμετέρᾱς εὐδαιμονίᾱς οὕτω 25 καταφρονεῖς ὥστε οὐδὲ ἰδιωτῶν ἀνδρῶν ἀξίους ἡμᾶς ἐποίησας;"

[ἔνειμε (aorist of νέμω), *gave*    ἰδιωτῶν (adjective here), *private*]

—adapted from Herodotus 1.31–32

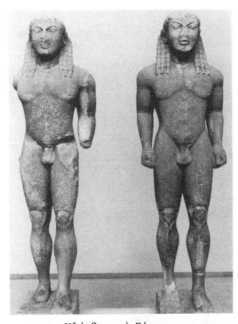

Κλέοβις καὶ Βίτων

# PRINCIPAL PARTS: Verbs that Augment to εἰ- in One or More Tenses

ἐάω, imperfect, εἴων, ἐάσω (note ᾱ instead of η after the ε), εἴᾱσα, εἴᾱκα, εἴᾱμαι, εἰάθην, *I allow, let be*

ἕλκω, imperfect, εἷλκον, ἕλξω, [ἑλκυ-] εἵλκυσα, εἵλκυκα, εἵλκυσμαι, εἱλκύσθην, *I drag*

ἐργάζομαι, imperfect, ἠργαζόμην or εἰργαζόμην, ἐργάσομαι, ἠργασάμην or εἰργασάμην, εἴργασμαι, εἰργάσθην, *I work; I accomplish*

ἕπομαι, imperfect, εἱπόμην, ἕψομαι, [σπ-] ἑσπόμην + dat., *I follow*

ἔχω, imperfect, εἶχον, ἕξω (irregular) (*I will have*) or [σχε-] σχήσω (*I will get*), [σχ-] ἔσχον, [σχε-] ἔσχηκα, ἔσχημαι, *I have; I hold;* middle + gen., *I hold onto*

# WORD BUILDING

Nouns formed from the stem of another noun or of an adjective are called denominative nouns.

*Give the meanings of the nouns in the following sets:*

1.  Suffixes -της and -εύς (nominative) denote the person concerned or occupied with anything, e.g.:

    ὁ πολῑ-της (ἡ πόλι-ς), ὁ ναύ-της (ἡ ναῦ-ς)

    ὁ ἱππ-εύς (ὁ ἵππ-ος), ὁ ἱερ-εύς (ἱερ-ός, -ά, -όν)

2.  Abstract nouns denoting qualities are formed by adding suffixes to adjectives, e.g.,

    | -ίᾱ/-ια (nominative) | φίλος, -η, -ον | ἡ φιλίᾱ |
    |---|---|---|
    | | ἀληθής, -ές | ἡ ἀλήθε-ια |
    | -σύνη (nominative) | δίκαιος, -ᾱ, -ον | ἡ δικαιο-σύνη |
    | | σώφρων, σώφρον-ος | ἡ σωφρο(ν)-σύνη |
    | -της (nominative) | ἴσος, -η, -ον | ἡ ἰσό-της, τῆς ἰσότητος |
    | | νέος, -ᾱ, -ον | ἡ νεό-της, τῆς νεότητος |

3.  Patronymics, i.e., nouns meaning "son of . . . ," "descended from . . . ," are most commonly formed with the suffix -ίδης (nominative), e.g., ὁ Ἀλκμεων-ίδης.

4.  Various suffixes are added to nouns to express smallness; the resulting words are called diminutives. The most common are:

    | -ιον (nominative) | τὸ παιδίον (ὁ παῖς, τοῦ παιδ-ός) |
    |---|---|
    | -ίδιον | τὸ οἰκ-ίδιον (ἡ οἰκί-ᾱ) |
    | -ίσκος | ὁ παιδ-ίσκος (ὁ παῖς, τοῦ παιδ-ός) |
    | | ὁ νεᾱν-ίσκος (ὁ νεᾱνί-ᾱς) |

Diminutives can express affection, e.g., πατρίδιον, *daddy dear*, or contempt, e.g., ἀνθρώπιον, *wretched little man*.

# GRAMMAR

## 5.  The Optative of -μι Verbs

εἰμί, *I am*

Present:

εἴην, εἴης, εἴη, εἶμεν/εἴημεν, εἶτε/εἴητε, εἶεν/εἴησαν

εἶμι, *I will go*

Present or Future:

ἴοιμι/ἰοίην, ἴοις, ἴοι, ἴοιμεν, ἴοιτε, ἴοιεν

### δίδωμι

Present Active:

διδοίην, διδοίης, διδοίη, διδοῖμεν, διδοῖτε, διδοῖεν

Present Middle/Passive:

διδοίμην, διδοῖο, διδοῖτο, διδοίμεθα, διδοῖσθε, διδοῖντο

Aorist Active:

δοίην, δοίης, δοίη, δοῖμεν, δοῖτε, δοῖεν

Aorist Middle:

δοίμην, δοῖο, δοῖτο, δοίμεθα, δοῖσθε, δοῖντο

Aorist Passive:

δοθείην, δοθείης, δοθείη, δοθεῖμεν, δοθεῖτε, δοθεῖεν

### τίθημι

Present Active:

τιθείην, τιθείης, τιθείη, τιθεῖμεν, τιθεῖτε, τιθεῖεν

Present Middle/Passive:

τιθείμην, τιθεῖο, τιθεῖτο, τιθείμεθα, τιθεῖσθε, τιθεῖντο

Aorist Active:

θείην, θείης, θείη, θεῖμεν, θεῖτε, θεῖεν

Aorist Middle:

θείμην, θεῖο, θεῖτο, θείμεθα, θεῖσθε, θεῖντο

Aorist Passive:

τεθείην, τεθείης, τεθείη, τεθεῖμεν, τεθεῖτε, τεθεῖεν

### ἵστημι

Present Active:

ἱσταίην, ἱσταίης, ἱσταίη, ἱσταῖμεν, ἱσταῖτε, ἱσταῖεν

Present Middle/Passive:

ἱσταίμην, ἱσταῖο, ἱσταῖτο, ἱσταίμεθα, ἱσταῖσθε, ἱσταῖντο

Aorist Active:
σταίην, σταίης, σταίη, σταῖμεν, σταῖτε, σταῖεν

Aorist Middle:
σταίμην, σταῖο, σταῖτο, σταίμεθα, σταῖσθε, σταῖντο

Aorist Passive:
σταθείην, σταθείης, σταθείη, σταθεῖμεν, σταθεῖτε, σταθεῖεν

## δείκνῡμι

Present Active:
δεικνύοιμι, δεικνύοις, δεικνύοι, δεικνύοιμεν δεικνύοιτε, δεικνύοιεν

Present Middle/Passive:
δεικνυοίμην, δεικνύοιο, δεικνύοιτο, δεικνυοίμεθα, δεικνύοισθε, δεικνύοιντο

Aorist Active:
δείξαιμι, δείξειας/δείξαις, δείξειε/δείξαι, δείξαιμεν, δείξαιτε, δείξειαν/δείξαιεν

Aorist Middle:
δειξαίμην, δείξαιο, δείξαιτο, δειξαίμεθα, δείξαισθε, δείξαιντο

Aorist Passive:
δειχθείην, δειχθείης, δειχθείη, δειχθεῖμεν, δειχθεῖτε, δειχθεῖεν

## ἵημι

Present Active:
ἱείην, ἱείης, ἱείη, ἱεῖμεν, ἱεῖτε, ἱεῖεν

Present Middle/Passive:
ἱείμην, ἱεῖο, ἱεῖτο, ἱείμεθα, ἱεῖσθε, ἱεῖντο

Aorist Active:
εἵην, εἵης, εἵη, εἷμεν, εἷτε, εἷεν

Aorist Middle:
εἵμην, εἷο, εἷτο, εἵμεθα, εἷσθε, εἷντο

Aorist Passive:
None

|           | Future Active: | Future Middle: | Future Passive: |
|-----------|----------------|----------------|-----------------|
| εἰμί      |                | ἐσοίμην (deponent) |             |
| δίδωμι    | δώσοιμι        | δωσοίμην       | δοθησοίμην      |
| τίθημι    | θήσοιμι        | θησοίμην       | τεθησοίμην      |
| ἵστημι    | στήσοιμι       | στησοίμην      | σταθησοίμην     |
| δείκνῡμι  | δείξοιμι       | δειξοίμην      | δειχθησοίμην    |
| ἵημι      | ἥσοιμι         | ἡσοίμην        | no future passive |

**Exercise 25 η**

*Fill in the optative forms on all Verb Charts completed to date for exercises in Book II and on the charts for Exercise 11θ. Keep the charts for reference.*

**Exercise 25 θ**

*Identify the person, number, tense, and voice of these optative forms:*

1. εἴη
2. ἴοιτε
3. δοίμεθα
4. διδοίην
5. διδοῖο (2 ways)
6. τιθεῖτο (2 ways)
7. τιθεῖεν
8. τεθεῖεν
9. ἱσταῖτο (2 ways)
10. ἱσταίην
11. σταίης
12. δείξαιμεν
13. δεικνύοιεν
14. εἶεν
15. ἱείη

## 6. The Optative Mood in Indirect Statements and Indirect Questions

In indirect statements and indirect questions the optative may be used as an alternative to the indicative in *secondary sequence*, or the indicative may be preserved. If the optative is used, its tense is the same as the tense of the verb in the direct statement or direct question. In the following examples, the optional optative is given after the slash (in the examples from Herodotus we do not use the movable ν).

Direct Statement:

ἄμεινόν ἐστι ἀνθρώπῳ τεθνάναι μᾶλλον ἢ ζῆν.
*It is better for a man to be dead than to be alive.*

Indirect Statement, Primary Sequence:

<u>δείκνῡσι</u> ὁ θεὸς ὅτι ἄμεινόν **ἐστι** ἀνθρώπῳ τεθνάναι μᾶλλον ἢ ζῆν.
*The god <u>shows</u> that **it is** better for a man to be dead than to be alive.*

Indirect Statement, Secondary Sequence:

<u>ἔδειξε</u> ὁ θεὸς ὅτι ἄμεινόν **ἐστι/εἴη** ἀνθρώπῳ τεθνάναι μᾶλλον ἢ ζῆν.
*The god <u>showed</u> that **it was** better for a man to be dead than to be alive.*

Direct Question:

τίνα δεύτερον μετ' ἐκεῖνον ὀλβιώτατον εἶδες;
*Whom did you see second most happy after him?*

Indirect Question, Primary Sequence:

ὁ Κροῖσος <u>ἐρωτᾷ</u> τίνα δεύτερον μετ' ἐκεῖνον ὀλβιώτατον **εἶδε**.
*Croesus <u>asks</u> whom **he saw** second most happy after him.*

Indirect Question, Secondary Sequence:

ὁ Κροῖσος <u>ἤρετο</u> τίνα δεύτερον μετ' ἐκεῖνον ὀλβιώτατον **εἶδε/ἴδοι**.

*Croesus <u>asked</u> whom **he had seen** second most happy after him.*

Remember that it is only in secondary sequence that indicatives may be changed to optatives.

The only use of the future optative in Greek is as an alternative to the future indicative in indirect statements or indirect questions in secondary sequence, e.g.:

ὁ πατὴρ <u>εἶπεν</u> ὅτι τοῖς παισὶν πρὸς τὸ ἄστυ **ἡγήσεται/ἡγήσοιτο**.

*The father <u>said</u> that **he would lead** his sons to the city.*

οἱ παῖδες <u>ἤροντο</u> πότε οἴκαδε **ἐπανίᾱσιν/ἐπανίοιεν**.

*The sons <u>asked</u> when **they would return** home.*

Note that ἐπανίοιεν is here regarded as future, substituting for the future ἐπανίᾱσιν of the direct question.

### Exercise 25 ι

*Rewrite the following sentences, making the leading verb aorist and changing the verbs in indirect statements from indicative to optative. Then translate the new sentences:*

1. ἡ γυνὴ ἡμᾶς ἐρωτᾷ εἰ τῷ παιδὶ αὐτῆς ἐν τῇ ὁδῷ ἐνετύχομεν.
2. ἀποκρῑνόμεθα ὅτι οὐδένα ἀνθρώπων εἴδομεν ἀλλ' εὐθὺς ἐπάνιμεν ὡς αὐτὸν ζητήσοντες.
3. τῷ παιδὶ ἐντυχόντες λέγομεν ὅτι ἡ μήτηρ αὐτὸν ζητεῖ.
4. ὁ ἄγγελος λέγει ὅτι τῶν πολεμίων ἀπελθόντων τοῖς αὐτουργοῖς ἔξεστιν οἴκαδε ἐπανιέναι.
5. ὁ Πρωταγόρᾱς λέγει ὅτι τοῦτο περὶ πλείστου ποιοῦνται οἱ πατέρες, ὅπως ἀγαθοὶ γενήσονται οἱ παῖδες.
6. ὁ Ἡρόδοτος ἐξηγεῖται ὅπως εἰς πόλεμον κατέστησαν οἵ τε βάρβαροι καὶ οἱ Ἕλληνες.
7. ὁ Σόλων ἐπίσταται ὅτι οἱ Ἀθηναῖοι οὐ λύσουσι τοὺς νόμους.
8. ὁ Κροῖσος τὸν Σόλωνα ἐρωτᾷ τίνα ὀλβιώτατον εἶδεν.
9. ὁ Σόλων λέγει ὅτι οἱ νεᾱνίαι, τὴν μητέρα εἰς τὸ ἱερὸν κομίσαντες, ἀπέθανον.
10. οὕτω δείκνῡσιν ὁ θεὸς ὅτι ἄμεινόν ἐστι ἀνθρώπῳ τεθνάναι μᾶλλον ἢ ζῆν.

## Greek Wisdom

### Heraclitus

(οἱ Ἕλληνες) δαιμόνων ἀγάλμασιν εὔχονται οὐκ ἀκούουσιν, ὥσπερ ἀκούοιεν.
Fragment 128 Diels

# Ο ΣΟΛΩΝ ΤΟΝ ΚΡΟΙΣΟΝ ΟΡΓΙΖΕΙ

*Read the following passages (adapted from Herodotus 1.32–33) and answer the comprehension questions:*

Solon explains to Croesus why he does not count him happy:

ὁ δὲ Σόλων εἶπεν· "ὦ Κροῖσε, ἐρωτᾷς με περὶ ἀνθρωπίνων πρᾱγμάτων, ἐγὼ δὲ ἐπίσταμαι πᾶν τὸ θεῖον φθονερὸν ὂν καὶ ταραχῶδες. ἐν μὲν γὰρ τῷ μακρῷ χρόνῳ πολλὰ μέν ἐστιν ἰδεῖν ἃ μή τις ἐθέλει, πολλὰ δὲ καὶ παθεῖν. ἐς γὰρ ἑβδομήκοντα ἔτη ὅρον τῆς ζωῆς ἀνθρώπῳ τίθημι. ταῦτα δὲ ἔτη ἑβδομήκοντα ὄντα παρέχεται ἡμέρᾱς διᾱκοσίᾱς καὶ ἑξακισχῑλίᾱς καὶ δισμῡρίᾱς. ἡ δὲ ἑτέρᾱ αὐτῶν τῇ ἑτέρᾳ οὐδὲν ὅμοιον προσάγει πρᾶγμα. 5

[ἀνθρωπίνων, *human*   τὸ θεῖον, *divinity*   φθονερὸν, *jealous*   ταραχῶδες (cf. ταράττω), *troublemaking*   ὅρον, *boundary, limit*   τῆς ζωῆς, *of the life*   παρέχεται, *offer*   διᾱκοσίᾱς, *200*   ἑξακισχῑλίᾱς, *6,000*   δισμῡρίᾱς, *20,000*   ἡ ... ἑτέρᾱ ... τῇ ἑτέρᾳ, *the one . . . to the other*   προσάγει, *brings*]

1.   What two realms does Solon distinguish?
2.   How does he characterize divinity?
3.   What do men see and experience in the length of their lives?
4.   At how many years does Solon set the limit of a man's life?  At how many days?
5.   What does each day bring?

"ἐμοὶ δὲ σὺ καὶ πλουτεῖν μέγα φαίνῃ καὶ βασιλεὺς εἶναι πολλῶν ἀνθρώπων· ἐκεῖνο δὲ ὃ ἐρωτᾷς με οὔπω σε λέγω, πρὶν ἄν σε τελευτήσαντα καλῶς βίον μάθω. οὐ γὰρ ὁ μέγα πλούσιος ὀλβιώτερός ἐστι τοῦ ἐφ᾽ ἡμέρᾱν βίον ἔχοντος, εἰ μὴ αὐτῷ ἡ τύχη παραμείνειε ὥστε εὖ τελευτῆσαι τὸν βίον. πολλοὶ γὰρ πλούσιοι ἀνθρώπων ἄνολβοί εἰσι, πολλοὶ δὲ μέτριον ἔχοντες βίον εὐτυχεῖς. σκοπεῖν δὲ χρὴ παντὸς χρήματος τὴν τελευτήν, πῶς ἀποβήσεται. πολλοῖς γὰρ δὴ ὑποδείξᾱς ὄλβον ὁ θεὸς προρρίζους ἀνέτρεψε." 10

[πλουτεῖν, *to be rich*   μέγα, *very*   οὔπω, *not yet*   πρὶν ἄν . . . μάθω, *until I learn*   πλούσιος, *rich*   τοῦ ἐφ᾽ ἡμέρᾱν βίον ἔχοντος, *gen. of comparison, than the one having livelihood for a day*   εἰ μὴ . . . παραμείνειε + dat., *unless . . . should stay with*   ἄνολβοί, *unhappy*   μέτριον . . . βίον, *a moderate livelihood*   εὐτυχεῖς, *lucky, happy*   παντὸς χρήματος, *of every event*   ἀποβήσεται, *it will turn out*   ὑποδείξᾱς, *having shown, having given a glimpse of*   ὄλβον, *happiness*   προρρίζους, *by the roots, root and branch*   ἀνέτρεψεν, *overturned*]

6.   How does Croesus appear to Solon?
7.   What does Solon need to know before he can answer Croesus's question with certainty?

8.  What, according to Solon, does the rich man need in order to be called truly happy?
9.  With what Greek words does Solon describe the men whom he contrasts with the πλούσιοι?
10. What Greek word does Solon use as the opposite of ἄνολβοι?
11. When assessing men's lives, what, according to Solon, must be examined in each case?
12. What two things does Solon say that god often does to men?

ὁ Σόλων ταῦτα λέγων τῷ Κροίσῳ οὐκέτι ἐχαρίζετο, ἀλλὰ ὁ Κροῖσος ἀποπέμπει αὐτόν, δόξᾱς αὐτὸν ἀμαθῆ εἶναι, ὃς τὰ παρόντα ἀγαθὰ μεθεὶς τὴν τελευτὴν   15 παντὸς χρήματος ὁρᾶν ἐκέλευε.

[ἐχαρίζετο + dat., *was finding favor with*   δόξᾱς, *thinking*   ἀμαθῆ, *stupid*   μεθεὶς (aorist participle of μεθίημι), *letting go, ignoring*]

13. What two things resulted from the "lecture" that Solon gave to Croesus?
14. What opinion of Solon did Croesus have?
15. What did Croesus think should be considered when judging a man's happiness?

## Exercise 25 κ

*Translate into Greek:*

1.  Croesus was thinking that he was the happiest of men, but Solon said that he had seen others happier.
2.  Croesus asked Solon why he judged that the others were (*use infinitive*) happier.
3.  Solon answered that he called no one happy until he learned that he had ended his life well.
4.  Croesus having grown angry at Solon, sent him away, thinking that he was stupid.
5.  After this Croesus, having suffered terrible things, learned that Solon was right.

---

# Greek Wisdom

## Heraclitus

ὁ ἄναξ, οὗ τὸ μαντεῖόν ἐστι τὸ ἐν Δελφοῖς, οὔτε λέγει οὔτε κρύπτει ἀλλὰ σημαίνει.
Fragment 93 Diels

# New Testament Greek

John 10.2–4, 9, and 11–16
The Parable of the Sheepfold

Jesus addresses the Pharisees.

"ὁ δὲ εἰσερχόμενος διὰ τῆς θύρας ποιμήν ἐστιν τῶν προβάτων. τούτῳ ὁ θυρωρὸς ἀνοίγει, καὶ τὰ πρόβατα τῆς φωνῆς αὐτοῦ ἀκούει καὶ τὰ ἴδια πρόβατα φωνεῖ κατ' ὄνομα καὶ ἐξάγει αὐτά. ὅταν τὰ ἴδια πάντα ἐκβάλῃ, ἔμπροσθεν αὐτῶν πορεύεται, καὶ τὰ πρόβατα αὐτῷ ἀκολουθεῖ, ὅτι οἴδασιν τὴν φωνὴν αὐτοῦ. . . . ἐγώ εἰμι ἡ θύρα· δι' ἐμοῦ ἐάν τις εἰσέλθῃ σωθήσεται καὶ εἰσελεύσεται καὶ ἐξελεύσεται καὶ νομὴν εὑρήσει. . . . ἐγώ εἰμι ὁ ποιμὴν ὁ καλός. ὁ ποιμὴν ὁ καλὸς τὴν ψυχὴν αὐτοῦ τίθησιν ὑπὲρ τῶν προβάτων· ὁ μισθωτὸς καὶ οὐκ ὢν ποιμήν, οὗ οὐκ ἔστιν τὰ πρόβατα ἴδια, θεωρεῖ τὸν λύκον ἐρχόμενον καὶ ἀφίησιν τὰ πρόβατα καὶ φεύγει— καὶ ὁ λύκος ἁρπάζει αὐτὰ καὶ σκορπίζει—ὅτι μισθωτός ἐστιν καὶ οὐ μέλει αὐτῷ περὶ τῶν προβάτων. ἐγώ εἰμι ὁ ποιμὴν ὁ καλὸς καὶ γῑνώσκω τὰ ἐμὰ καὶ γῑνώσκουσί με τὰ ἐμά, καθὼς γῑνώσκει με ὁ πατὴρ κᾱγὼ γῑνώσκω τὸν πατέρα, καὶ τὴν ψυχήν μου τίθημι ὑπὲρ τῶν προβάτων. καὶ ἄλλα πρόβατα ἔχω ἃ οὐκ ἔστιν ἐκ τῆς αὐλῆς ταύτης· κᾱκεῖνα δεῖ με ἀγαγεῖν καὶ τῆς φωνῆς μου ἀκούσουσιν, καὶ γενήσονται μία ποίμνη, εἷς ποιμήν."

[ὁ εἰσερχόμενος = ὁ εἰσιών   ποιμήν, *shepherd*   ὁ θυρωρὸς, *the gatekeeper*   ἀνοίγει, *opens*   τὰ ἴδια, *his own*   φωνεῖ, *he calls*   ἐκβάλῃ, *he puts/leads out*   ἔμπροσθεν + gen., *in front of*   ἀκολουθεῖ, *follow*   ὅτι, *because*   οἴδασιν, *they know*   εἰσελεύσεται = εἴσεισι   νομὴν, *pasture*   ψυχὴν, *soul; life*   τίθησιν, *puts/lays (down)*   μισθωτὸς, *hired laborer*   ἐρχόμενον = ἰόντα   ἁρπάζει, *seizes (perhaps attacks)*   σκορπίζει, *scatters*   οὐ μέλει αὐτῷ, *there is no care to him, he has no care*   γῑνώσκω = γιγνώσκω   καθὼς, *just as*   κᾱγὼ = καὶ ἐγώ   αὐλῆς, *sheepfold*   κᾱκεῖνα = καὶ ἐκεῖνα, *and them*   ἀκούσουσιν = ἀκούσονται   ποίμνη, *flock*]

New Testament Greek uses ἐλεύσομαι as the future of ἔρχομαι, for which Attic Greek uses εἶμι. New Testament Greek also uses ἐρχόμενος as the present participle of ἔρχομαι, for which Attic Greek uses ἰών.

# 26

# Ο ΚΡΟΙΣΟΣ
# ΤΟΝ ΠΑΙΔΑ ΑΠΟΛΛΥΣΙΝ (α)

ὁ Κροῖσος ἄγεται τῷ παιδὶ γυναῖκα· ἰδού, ὁ Ἄτῡς τὴν νύμφην οἴκαδε φέρει ἐν ἀμάξῃ.

## VOCABULARY

*Verbs*

ἀπόλλῡμι [= ἀπο- + ὄλλῡμι],
[ὀλε-] ἀπολῶ, ἀπώλεσα,
*I destroy; I ruin; I lose*
  Middle:
  ἀπόλλυμαι, [ὀλε-] ἀπολοῦ-
  μαι, [ὀλ-] ἀπωλόμην,
  *I perish*
  Perfect:
  [ὀλε-] ἀπολώλεκα, *I have
  ruined*, [ὀλ-] ἀπόλωλα,
  *I am ruined*

δέομαι, [δεε-] δεήσομαι, ἐδεήθην, *I ask for* X (acc.) *from* Y
(gen.); + infin., *I beg*; + gen.,
*I want*

ἐφίσταμαι [= ἐπι- + ἵσταμαι],
[στη-] ἐπέστην + dat., *I stand
near*; of dreams, *I appear to*

καθαίρω, [καθαρε-] καθαρῶ,
[καθηρ-] ἐκάθηρα, [καθαρ-]
κεκάθαρμαι, ἐκαθάρθην,
*I purify*

ὀνομάζω, ὀνομάσω, ὠνόμασα,
ὠνόμακα, ὠνόμασμαι, ὠνο-
μάσθην, *I name; I call*

πυνθάνομαι, [πευθ-] πεύσομαι,
[πυθ-] ἐπυθόμην, πέπυσμαι,
*I inquire; I learn by inquiry;
I hear; I find out about* X (acc.)
*from* Y (gen.)

φαίνω, [φανε-] φανῶ or φανοῦμαι, [φην-] ἔφηνα, [φαν-]
πέφασμαι, *I show*

φονεύω, φονεύσω, ἐφόνευσα,
πεφόνευκα, πεφόνευμαι,
ἐφονεύθην, *I slay*

*Nouns*

ἡ ἀλήθεια, τῆς ἀληθείᾱς, *truth*

ὁ γάμος, τοῦ γάμου, *marriage*

τὸ δόρυ, τοῦ δόρατος, *spear*

ἡ νέμεσις, τῆς νεμέσεως, *retribution*

τὸ οἰκίον, τοῦ οἰκίου, *house;
palace* (often in plural for a
single house or palace)

ὁ ὄνειρος, τοῦ ὀνείρου, *dream*

*Adjectives*

ἄκων, ἄκουσα, ἆκον, *unwill-
ing(ly); involuntary(-ily)*

160

ἕτερος, -ᾱ, -ον, *one or the other*
  *(of two)*
    ὁ μὲν ἕτερος . . . ὁ δὲ
    ἕτερος, *the one . . . the*
    *other*
Prepositions
  ἐπί + gen., *toward, in the direc-*
    *tion of; on;* + dat., *at; of price,*
    *for;* + acc., *at; against; onto;*

*upon; of direction or purpose,*
  *to, for*
κατά + acc., *down;* distributive, *each, every; by; on; ac-*
  *cording to; of time, at;*
  *through;* with regard to
Adverb
  ὁπόθεν, indirect interrogative,
    *whence, from where*

ὡς δὲ ἀπῆλθε ὁ Σόλων, ἔλαβε ἐκ τοῦ θεοῦ νέμεσις μεγάλη
Κροῖσον, διότι ἐνόμισε ἑαυτὸν εἶναι ἀνθρώπων ἁπάντων ὀλβιώτατον.
καθεύδοντι γὰρ αὐτῷ ἐπέστη ὄνειρος, ὃς αὐτῷ τὴν ἀλήθειαν ἔφαινε
τῶν μελλόντων γενέσθαι κακῶν κατὰ τὸν παῖδα.  ἦσαν δὲ Κροίσῳ
δύο παῖδες, ὧν ὁ μὲν ἕτερος κωφὸς ἦν, ὁ δὲ ἕτερος τῶν ἡλίκων πολὺ   5
πρῶτος· ὄνομα δὲ αὐτῷ ἦν Ἄτῡς.  τοῦτον οὖν τὸν Ἄτῡν σημαίνει τῷ
Κροίσῳ ὁ ὄνειρος ἀποθανεῖσθαι αἰχμῇ σιδηρέᾳ βληθέντα.  ὁ δὲ ἐπεὶ
ἐξηγέρθη, φοβούμενος τὸν ὄνειρον, ἄγεται μὲν τῷ παιδὶ γυναῖκα, ἐπὶ
πόλεμον δὲ οὐκέτι ἐξέπεμψεν αὐτόν, ἀκόντια δὲ καὶ δόρατα καὶ
πάντα οἷς χρῶνται ἐς πόλεμον ἄνθρωποι ἐκ τῶν ἀνδρεώνων   10
ἐκκομίσᾱς ἐς τοὺς θαλάμους συνένησε, μή τι τῷ παιδὶ ἐμπέσοι.

[κωφὸς, *dumb, mute*  τῶν ἡλίκων, *of those the same age*  αἰχμῇ σιδηρέᾳ, *an iron*
*spear point*  ἀκόντια, *javelins*  τῶν ἀνδρεώνων, *the men's chambers*  τοὺς
θαλάμους, *the storerooms*  συνένησε (from συννέω), *he piled up*]

ἔχοντος δὲ ἐν χερσὶ τοῦ παιδὸς τὸν γάμον, ἀφικνεῖται ἐς τὰς
Σάρδῑς ἀνὴρ οὐ καθαρὸς ὢν τὰς χεῖρας.  παρελθὼν δὲ οὗτος ἐς τὰ
Κροίσου οἰκία καθαρσίου ἐδέετο ἐπικυρῆσαι· ὁ δὲ Κροῖσος αὐτὸν
ἐκάθηρεν.  ἐπεὶ δὲ τὰ νομιζόμενα ἐποίησεν ὁ Κροῖσος, ἐπυνθάνετο   15
ὁπόθεν τε ἥκοι καὶ τίς εἴη, λέγων τάδε· "ὦ ἄνθρωπε, τίς τ' ὢν καὶ
πόθεν ἥκων ἐς τὰ ἐμὰ οἰκία παρεγένου;" ὁ δὲ ἀπεκρίνατο· "ὦ
βασιλεῦ, Γορδίου μέν εἰμι παῖς, ὀνομάζομαι δὲ Ἄδρηστος, φονεύσᾱς
δὲ τὸν ἐμαυτοῦ ἀδελφὸν ἄκων πάρειμι, ἐξεληλαμένος ὑπὸ τοῦ
πατρός." ὁ δὲ Κροῖσος ἀπεκρίνατο· "ἀνδρῶν τε φίλων ἔκγονος εἶ καὶ   20
ἥκεις ἐς φίλους, ὅπου ἀμηχανήσεις οὐδενὸς μένων ἐν τοῖς ἡμετέροις
οἰκίοις.  συμφορὰν δὲ ταύτην παραινῶ σοι ὡς κουφότατα φέρειν."

[τὰς χεῖρας, *with respect to his hands*   καθαρσίου, *purification*   ἐδέετο = ἐδεῖτο, from δέομαι   ἐπικυρῆσαι + gen., *to obtain*   τὰ νομιζόμενα, *the customary rituals* ἐξεληλαμένος (perfect passive participle of ἐξελαύνω), *having been driven out* ἔκγονος, *offspring*   ἀμηχανήσεις + gen., *you will lack*   ὡς κουφότατα, *as lightly as possible*]

—adapted from Herodotus 1.34–35

## PRINCIPAL PARTS: Verbs with Present Reduplication

γί-γνομαι, [γενε-] γενήσομαι, [γεν-] ἐγενόμην, [γον-] γέγονα, [γενε-] γεγένημαι, *I become; I happen*

γι-γνώ-σκω, [γνω-] γνώσομαι, ἔγνων, ἔγνωκα, ἔγνωσμαι, ἐγνώσθην, *I come to know; I perceive; I learn*

δι-δά-σκω, [διδαχ-] διδάξω, ἐδίδαξα, δεδίδαχα, δεδίδαγμαι, ἐδιδάχθην, *I teach* someone (acc.) something (acc.); passive, *I am taught* something (acc.)

πί-πτω, πεσοῦμαι (irregular), ἔπεσον (irregular), [πτω-] πέπτωκα, *I fall*

## WORD STUDY

*Give the Greek words from which the following English literary terms are derived:*

1. epic
2. lyric
3. drama
4. tragedy
5. comedy
6. biography

*What genre of modern literature is missing from this list?*

## GRAMMAR

### 1. Conditional Sentences

Conditional sentences, in both English and Greek, may be organized under two broad headings:

a. *Simple conditions*, in which nothing is implied as to whether the condition was, is, or will be fulfilled

These may be of two kinds:

i. *Particular conditions*
ii. *General conditions*, in which the conditional clause is a type of *indefinite clause* (see Chapter 22, Grammar 2, pages 93–96).

b. *Contrary to fact* and *remote conditions*, in which it is implied that the condition was not fulfilled, is not being fulfilled, or is not likely to be fulfilled in the future

### a.  Simple Conditions:

*Past Particular:*

> *If Philip said this, he was lying.*
>
> εἰ ὁ Φίλιππος τοῦτο **εἶπεν, ἐψεύδετο.**
> (a past tense, i.e., imperfect, aorist, or pluperfect, of the indicative in both clauses)

*Past General:*

> *If Philip (ever) said this, he was (always) lying.*
>
> εἰ ὁ Φίλιππος τοῦτο **λέγοι, ἐψεύδετο.**
> (εἰ + optative, aorist or present; imperfect indicative)

*Present Particular:*

> *If you believe Philip, you are foolish.*
>
> εἰ τῷ Φιλίππῳ **πιστεύεις,** μῶρος **εἶ.**
> (present or perfect indicative in both clauses)

*Present General:*

> *If you (ever) believe Philip, you are (always) foolish.*
>
> **ἐὰν** τῷ Φιλίππῳ **πιστεύῃς,** μῶρος **εἶ.**
> (ἐὰν + subjunctive, aorist or present; present indicative)

*Future Minatory:*

> *If you do this, you will die.*
>
> εἰ τοῦτο **ποιήσεις, ἀποθανεῖ.**
> (εἰ + future indicative; future indicative)
> (Conditions with the future indicative in both clauses usually express threats and warnings, hence the term *minatory*.)

*Future More Vivid (Particular or General):*

> Particular:
> *If the doctor does this, he will receive his pay.*
> General:
> *If the doctor (ever) does this, he will (always) receive his pay.*
>
> **ἐὰν** ὁ ἰατρὸς τοῦτο **ποιήσῃ,** τὸν μισθὸν **δέξεται.**
> (ἐάν + subjunctive, aorist or present; future indicative)

> The imperative may be used in the main clause, e.g.:
>
> *If you see father, tell him what happened.*
>
> **ἐὰν** τὸν πατέρα **ἴδῃς, εἰπὲ** αὐτῷ τί ἐγένετο.

### b. *Contrary to Fact and Remote Conditions:*

*Past Contrary to Fact:*

> If the doctor had done this, he would have received his pay.
> (It is implied that he did not do this and did not receive his pay.)

εἰ ὁ ἰᾱτρὸς τοῦτο **ἐποίησεν, ἐδέξατο ἂν** τὸν μισθόν.
> (aorist indicative; aorist indicative with ἄν)

*Present Contrary to Fact:*

> If our father were living, he would be coming to our aid.
> (It is implied that he is not living and is not coming to X's aid.)

εἰ **ἔζη** ὁ πατήρ, ἡμῖν **ἂν ἐβοήθει.**
> (imperfect indicative; imperfect indicative with ἄν)

*Future Remote or Future Less Vivid:*

> If the doctor should do this, he would not receive his pay.
> (If the doctor were to do this, . . . )
> (If the doctor did this, . . . )
> (It is implied that the doctor is not likely to do this.)

εἰ ὁ ἰᾱτρὸς τοῦτο **ποιήσειεν,** οὐκ **ἂν δέξαιτο** τὸν μισθόν.
> (εἰ + optative, aorist or present; optative, aorist or present, with ἄν)

In contrary to fact and remote or future less vivid conditions, the potential particle ἄν always appears near the beginning of the main clause, although not as the first word; it is often next to the verb. Note that in these clauses the aorist indicative refers to past time, the imperfect indicative to present time, and the optative to future time.

Note that the difference between aorist and present subjunctives and optatives in conditional clauses is in aspect, not time. The aorist subjunctive or optative is used when the action of the verb is looked on as a simple event, the present, when it is looked on as a process.

✳ In all conditional sentences, the negative is μή in the conditional clause and οὐ in the main clause.

## Exercise 26 α

*Translate the following sentences and identify the type of condition each represents:*

1. ἐὰν μὴ περὶ εἰρήνης λέγητε, οὐκ ἀκούσομαι ὑμῶν.
2. εἰ τοὺς βαρβάρους ἐνῑκήσαμεν, πάντες ἂν ἐτίμησαν ἡμᾶς.
3. εἰ οἴκαδε σπεύδοιμεν, ἴσως ἂν ἀφικοίμεθα ἐν καιρῷ.
4. εἰ τῷ βασιλεῖ πάντα εἶπες, μῶρος ἦσθα.
5. εἰ οἴκοι ἐμείνατε, οὐκ ἂν κατέστητε εἰς τοσοῦτον κίνδῡνον.

6. εἰ παρῆσαν οἱ σύμμαχοι, ἡμῖν ἂν ἐβοήθουν.
7. ἐὰν τοὺς συμμάχους παρακαλῶμεν, ἡμῖν βοηθήσουσιν.
8. εἰ τοῦτο ποιήσεις, ἐγώ σε ἀποκτενῶ.
9. εἰ εὐθὺς ὡρμησάμεθα, ἤδη ἀφῑκόμεθα ἂν εἰς τὸ ἄστυ.
10. εἰ τὰ ἀληθῆ λέγοις, πιστεύοιμι ἄν σοι.
11. ἐὰν τῷ πατρὶ συλλάβῃς, ἐπαινῶ σε.
12. εἰ οὗτος ὁ κύων λύκον ἴδοι, ἀπέφευγεν.


## Exercise 26 β

*Translate the following pairs of sentences:*

1. εἰ εὐθὺς πρὸς τὸ ἄστυ σπεύδοιμεν, ἴσως ἂν ἀφικοίμεθα πρὶν γενέσθαι ἑσπέρᾱν.
   If you should lead me, I would gladly follow.
2. εἰ μὴ τῷ ποιμένι ἐνετύχομεν, ἡμάρτομεν ἂν τῆς ὁδοῦ.
   If we had not hurried, we would have arrived home late.
3. ἐὰν μου ἀκούητε, πάντα δι' ὀλίγου γνώσεσθε.
   If you (*pl.*) follow me quickly, we will arrive before (*use* **πρίν** + *infin.*) night falls.
4. εἰ οἱ παῖδες τῷ πατρὶ ἐπείσθησαν, οὐκ ἂν κατέστησαν ἐς τοσοῦτον κίνδῡνον.
   If we had stayed at home, we would not have seen (*use* **θεάομαι**) the contests.
5. εἰ μή σοι ἐπίστευον, οὐκ ἂν ταῦτά σοι ἔλεγον.
   If father were here, he would be helping us.
6. εἰ μὴ ἐβοήθησεν ὁ ποιμήν, ἀπέθανεν ἂν πάνα τὰ πρόβατα.
   If the shepherd had not hurried to the sheepfold (**τὸ αὔλιον**), he would not have saved the sheep.
7. ἐὰν τὴν μητέρα ἐν τῇ ἀγορᾷ ἴδῃς, αἴτησον αὐτὴν οἴκαδε σπεύδειν.
   If mother does not come home soon, I will go myself to look for (*use* **ὡς** + *future participle*) her.
8. εἰ μὴ ὁ ἀδελφὸς κακὰ ἔπασχεν, οὐκ ἂν οὕτω ἐλῡπούμην.
   If mother were here, she would know what we must (*use* **δεῖ**) do.
9. ἐὰν οἱ πολέμιοι ἐς τὴν γῆν ἐσβάλωσιν, οἱ αὐτουργοὶ ἐς τὸ ἄστυ ἀνίστανται.
   If the farmers (ever) remove to the city, they are (always) safe within the walls.
10. εἰ προσβάλοιεν οἱ Ἀθηναῖοι, οἱ πολέμιοι ἀνεχώρουν.
    If the Athenians (ever) withdrew, the enemy (always) attacked them.

# Shame and Guilt

When Solon explained to Croesus why he would not call him the happiest man he had seen, he said: ἐπίσταμαι πᾶν τὸ θεῖον φθονερὸν ὂν καὶ ταραχῶδες. When Solon had left Sardis, ἔλαβεν ἐκ τοῦ θεοῦ νέμεσις μεγάλη Κροῖσον. Shortly after Solon's departure, Adrastus arrived οὐ καθαρὸς ὢν τὰς χεῖρας and καθαρσίου ἐδέετο ἐπικυρῆσαι. The concepts in these passages from Herodotus are quite alien to our modes of thought but are central to the Greek view of man's relation to the gods and his place in the universe.

In the *Iliad*, there is a division between morality (man's relations with his fellow men) and religion (man's relations with the gods). The gods are not usually interested in how men behave toward each other but are very interested in how men behave toward themselves, the gods. They demand from men a proper honor (τῑμή), just as a king demands honor from his nobles. The gods must receive prayer and sacrifice from mortals, accompanied by the appropriate rituals. Provided you fulfill these obligations, you may expect the gods to be well disposed toward you, although, of course, you cannot constrain them by any amount of prayer and sacrifice. The gods are often arbitrary in their behavior, and they, like men, are bound by the dictates of fate (μοῖρα), which even they cannot change. Nevertheless, in the *Iliad* men, though recognizing the power of the gods, do not generally go in fear of them, and religion shows little of the darker side that is prominent in Herodotus and the poets of his time.

Homeric heroes in their relations with their fellow men are motivated not by religious considerations but by what their peers think of them. The mainspring of their action is honor, which is literally dearer than life. Conversely, they avoid certain actions through fear of what others may say or think of them. They are restrained by αἰδώς (*sense of shame, self-respect*). So the whole plot of the *Iliad* turns on Achilles' refusal to fight when Agamemnon has insulted his honor. Life was a competition in which honor was the prize. Achilles' father told him: αἰὲν ἀριστεύειν καὶ ὑπείροχον ἔμμεναι ἄλλων, "always to be the best and to excel over others" (*Iliad* 11.784).

The *honor ethic* (a *shame culture*, as the anthropologists call it) persisted throughout Greek history, but in the time of Herodotus there was alongside it a very different ethic, which was based on a different view of the gods and the whole human predicament. According to this view, to court the preeminence that Achilles' father recommended to his son was positively dangerous and wrong. In Herodotus and the poets of his time, Zeus is the agent of justice (δίκη). Man is helpless before the power of the gods and the dictates of μοῖρα (*one's allotted portion, fate*), and all who offend must suffer. The surest way of offending the gods and bringing down νέμεσις (*divine vengeance*) on yourself is to become too prosperous or too great. Such excess leads to pride (ὕβρις), a condition in which you may think yourself more than mortal and so incur the jealousy (φθόνος) of the gods: φιλέει γὰρ ὁ θεὸς τὰ ὑπερέχοντα πάντα κολούειν "for God is accustomed to cut down everything that excels (overtops others)" (Herodotus 7.10).

What of those who have not offended but still suffer? One answer was inherited or corporate guilt. If a righteous man suffers, he must be paying for the offense of one of his kin (so the family curse is a prominent theme in Greek tragedy, e.g., Aeschylus's *Oresteia* or Sophocles' *Antigone*). Such corporate guilt can infect not just one family but whole societies: "Often a whole city reaps the reward of an evil man who sins and plots wicked deeds" (Hesiod, *Works and Days* 240–241). So man is helpless (ἀμήχανος) in a frightening and unpredictable world, governed by gods who are jealous and troublemaking.

What could man do to avoid disaster (συμφορά)? The only way was to refrain from offending the gods and if offense occurred, to seek purification, a cleansing of guilt. Purification (κάθαρσις) was a ritual washing away of pollution, as Christian baptism is a symbolic washing away of sin, and was regularly performed on all occasions that brought man into contact with the gods, e.g., before sacrifice or feasting (which was a meal shared with the gods). Rituals, of which we know little, were prescribed for various occasions, e.g., after childbirth.

The greatest pollution (μίασμα) was blood-guilt. Adrastus arrived at Croesus's court οὐ καθαρὸς ὢν τὰς χεῖρας. He had involuntarily killed his own brother. Whether the act was voluntary or involuntary was beside the point as far as his family was concerned. He had to go into exile, since otherwise he would have infected the whole family with his μίασμα. He comes to Croesus as a suppliant (ἱκέτης), and Croesus, a god-fearing man, is bound to accept him. Such were the rules of supplication, which had its own ritual. Suppliants were under the protection of Zeus. Croesus, although he does not know Adrastus, at once understands the situation and purifies him, using the customary rites. We do not know precisely what these rites were, but they involved the sacrifice of a suckling pig, in the blood of which the guilty man was cleansed. Pollution could infect a whole people. In the opening scene of Sophocles' *Oedipus the King*, the whole land of Thebes is devastated by plague. Oedipus sends Creon to Delphi to ask Apollo what he should do. Apollo's answer is that they must drive out the pollution of the land (μίασμα χώρᾱς); "By what sort of purification (ποίῳ καθάρμῳ)?" asks Oedipus. The answer is "By driving out (the guilty man), or by exacting blood for blood."

The society that accepted such ideas must have been suffering from a deep sense of guilt, all the more terrifying because one could not always know the cause of one's pollution, nor, in the last resort, was there any way of escaping it. When Croesus had been saved by Apollo, he sent messengers to Delphi to ask why Apollo had deceived him. The answer came back: "It is impossible even for a god to escape his destined lot. Croesus has paid for the sin of his ancestor five generations back, who murdered his master and took the honor (i.e., the throne) which was not rightly his" (Herodotus 1.91). Zeus might be just, but it was a harsh justice.

# Ο ΚΡΟΙΣΟΣ
# ΤΟΝ ΠΑΙΔΑ ΑΠΟΛΛΥΣΙΝ (β)

## VOCABULARY

*Verbs*

**ἀποφαίνω**, *I show; I reveal; I prove*

**μεθῑ́ημι** [= μετα- + ῑ́ημι], *I set loose; I let go*

**μέλει**, [μελε-] **μελήσει, ἐμέλησε, μεμέληκε**, impersonal + dat., X *is a care to; there is a care to* X (dat.) *for* Y (gen.)

**μεταπέμπομαι**, *I send for*

**χαρίζομαι**, [χαριε-] **χαριοῦμαι**, [χαρι-] **ἐχαρισάμην, κεχάρισμαι** + dat., *I show favor to; I oblige*

*Nouns*

**ἡ ἄγρᾱ, τῆς ἄγρᾱς**, *hunt; hunting*

**ἡ ἀθῡμίᾱ, τῆς ἀθῡμίᾱς**, *lack of spirit; despair*

**ἡ δειλίᾱ, τῆς δειλίᾱς**, *cowardice*

**τὸ θηρίον, τοῦ θηρίου**, *beast, wild beast*

**ὁ κύκλος, τοῦ κύκλου**, *circle*

**ἡ φήμη, τῆς φήμης**, *saying; report; voice; message*

**ὁ φόνος, τοῦ φόνου**, *murder*

**ὁ φύλαξ, τοῦ φύλακος**, *guard*

*Adjective*

**ποῖος; ποίᾱ; ποῖον;** *what kind of?*

*Preposition*

**πρός** + gen., <u>*from*</u> (i.e., <u>*at the hand of*</u>); + dat., *at; near; by; in addition to*; + acc., *to, toward; upon; against*

*Conjunction*

**ἐπεί**, *when; since*

*Proper Names*

**οἱ Μῡσοί, τῶν Μῡσῶν**, *Mysians*

**ὁ Ὄλυμπος, τοῦ Ὀλύμπου**, *Mount Olympus* (here, a mountain in Mysia)

ὁ μὲν οὖν Ἄδρηστος δίαιταν εἶχε ἐν Κροίσου, ἐν δὲ τῷ αὐτῷ χρόνῳ ἐν τῷ Ὀλύμπῳ τῷ ὄρει ὗς μέγας γίγνεται· ὁρμώμενος δὲ οὗτος ἐκ τοῦ ὄρους τούτου τὰ τῶν Μῡσῶν ἔργα διέφθειρε, πολλάκις δὲ οἱ Μῡσοὶ ἐπ' αὐτὸν ἐξελθόντες ἐποίουν μὲν κακὸν οὐδέν, ἔπασχον δὲ κακὰ πρὸς αὐτοῦ. τέλος δὲ ἀφικόμενοι παρὰ τὸν Κροῖσον τῶν    5
Μῡσῶν ἄγγελοι ἔλεγον τάδε· "ὦ βασιλεῦ, ὗς μέγιστος ἀνεφάνη ἡμῖν ἐν τῇ χώρᾳ, ὃς τὰ ἔργα διαφθείρει. τοῦτον προθῡμούμενοι ἑλεῖν οὐ δυνάμεθα. νῦν οὖν δεόμεθά σου τὸν παῖδα καὶ λογάδας νεᾱνίᾱς καὶ κύνας πέμψαι ἡμῖν, ἵνα αὐτὸν ἐξέλωμεν ἐκ τῆς χώρᾱς."

[**δίαιταν εἶχε**, *he was having a mode of life, he was living*    **ἐν Κροίσου**, *in Croesus's* (palace)    **ὗς**, *a wild boar*    **τὰ . . . ἔργα**, *the tilled fields*    **ἀνεφάνη** (from ἀναφαίνω), *appeared*   **προθῡμούμενοι**, *being very eager*   **λογάδας**, *picked, selected*]

Κροῖσος δὲ μεμνημένος τοῦ ὀνείρου τὰ ἔπη ἔλεγε τάδε· "τὸν παῖδα   10
οὐκ ἐθέλω πέμψαι· νεόγαμος γάρ ἐστι καὶ ταῦτα αὐτῷ νῦν μέλει.
Λῡδῶν μέντοι λογάδας καὶ κύνας πέμψω καὶ κελεύσω τοὺς ἰόντας
ἐξελεῖν τὸ θηρίον ἐκ τῆς χώρᾱς."

[**μεμνημένος**, *remembering*   **τὰ ἔπη**, *the words*   **νεόγαμος**, *newly married*]

οἱ Μῡσοὶ ἐπὶ τὸν ὗν ἐξελθόντες ἐποίουν μὲν κακὸν οὐδέν,
ἔπασχον δὲ κακὰ πρὸς αὐτοῦ.

ὁ δὲ παῖς ἀκούσᾱς ἃ εἶπεν Κροῖσος τοῖς Μῡσοῖς, πρὸς αὐτὸν
προσῆλθε καί, "ὦ πάτερ," φησίν, "τί οὐκ ἐθέλεις με πέμψαι ἐς τὴν   15
ἄγρᾱν; ἆρα δειλίᾱν τινὰ ἐν ἐμοὶ εἶδες ἢ ἀθῡμίᾱν;" ὁ δὲ Κροῖσος
ἀποκρίνεται τοῖσδε· "ὦ παῖ, οὔτε δειλίᾱν οὔτε ἄλλο οὐδὲν ἄχαρι ἰδὼν
ποιῶ ταῦτα, ἀλλά μοι ὄψις ὀνείρου ἐν τῷ ὕπνῳ ἐπιστᾶσα ἔφη σε
ὀλιγοχρόνιον ἔσεσθαι· ὑπὸ γὰρ αἰχμῆς σιδηρέᾱς ἀπολεῖσθαι."
ἀποκρίνεται δὲ ὁ νεᾱνίᾱς τοῖσδε· "συγγνώμη μέν ἐστί σοι, ὦ πάτερ,   20
ἰδόντι ὄψιν τοιαύτην περὶ ἐμὲ φυλακὴν ἔχειν. λέγεις δὲ ὅτι ὁ ὄνειρος
ἔφη ὑπὸ αἰχμῆς σιδηρέᾱς ἐμὲ τελευτήσειν· ὑὸς δὲ ποῖαι μέν εἰσι χεῖρες,
ποίᾱ δὲ αἰχμὴ σιδηρέᾱ; ἐπεὶ οὖν οὐ πρὸς ἄνδρας ἡμῖν γίγνεται ἡ
μάχη, μέθες με." ἀμείβεται Κροῖσος· "ὦ παῖ, νῑκᾷς με γνώμην
ἀποφαίνων περὶ τοῦ ὀνείρου. μεταγιγνώσκω οὖν καὶ μεθῑημί σε ἰέναι   25
ἐπὶ τὴν ἄγρᾱν."

[**ἄχαρι**, *unpleasant, objectionable*   **ὄψις**, *sight, vision, apparition*   **ὀλιγοχρόνιον**,
*short-lived*   **αἰχμῆς σιδηρέᾱς**, *an iron spear-point*   **συγγνώμη ... ἐστί σοι**, *you
have an excuse, you may be pardoned*   **ὑὸς** (gen. of **ὗς**), *of a wild boar*   **ἀμείβεται**,
*answers*   **μεταγιγνώσκω**, *I change my mind*]

εἰπὼν δὲ ταῦτα ὁ Κροῖσος τὸν Ἄδρηστον μεταπέμπεται καὶ αὐτῷ
λέγει τάδε· "Ἄδρηστε, ἐγώ σε ἐκάθηρα καὶ ἐν τοῖς οἰκίοις ἐδεξάμην·
νῦν οὖν φύλακα τοῦ παιδὸς ἐμοῦ σε χρῄζω γενέσθαι ἐς ἄγρᾱν
ὁρμωμένου." ὁ δὲ Ἄδρηστος ἀπεκρίνατο· "ἐπεὶ σὺ σπεύδεις καὶ δεῖ    30
μέ σοι χαρίζεσθαι, ἕτοιμός εἰμι ποιεῖν ταῦτα, τόν τε παῖδα σὸν, ὃν
κελεύεις φυλάσσειν, ἀσφαλῆ τοῦ φυλάσσοντος ἕνεκα προσδόκᾱ σοι
νοστήσειν."

[χρῄζω, *I want, need*  σπεύδεις, *you are (so) earnest*  τοῦ φυλάσσοντος ἕνεκα,
*as far as his guardian is concerned*  προσδόκᾱ (imperative of προσδοκάω), *expect*]

ἦσαν μετὰ ταῦτα ἐξηρτῦμένοι λογάσι τε νεᾱνίαις καὶ κυσίν.
ἀφικόμενοι δὲ ἐς τὸν Ὄλυμπον τὸ ὄρος ἐζήτουν τὸ θηρίον, εὑρόντες    35
δὲ καὶ περιστάντες αὐτὸ κύκλῳ ἐσηκόντιζον. ἐνταῦθα δὴ ὁ ξένος, ὁ
καθαρθεὶς τὸν φόνον, ἀκοντίζων τὸν ὗν, τοῦ μὲν ἁμαρτάνει,
τυγχάνει δὲ τοῦ Κροίσου παιδός.  ὁ μὲν οὖν βληθεὶς τῇ αἰχμῇ
ἐξέπλησε τοῦ ὀνείρου τὴν φήμην, ἔτρεχε δέ τις ὡς ἀγγελῶν τῷ Κροίσῳ
τὸ γενόμενον. ἀφικόμενος δὲ ἐς τᾱς Σάρδῑς τήν τε μάχην καὶ τὸν τοῦ    40
παιδὸς μόρον εἶπεν αὐτῷ.

[ἐξηρτῦμένοι (perfect passive participle of ἐξαρτύω), *equipped*  ἐσηκόντιζον, *they
were throwing their javelins at (it)*  ὁ καθαρθεὶς τὸν φόνον, *the man who had been
purified with respect to murder*  ἀκοντίζων, *throwing/aiming his javelin at*
ἐξέπλησε (from ἐκπίμπλημι), *fulfilled*  τὸν ... μόρον, *the fate, death*]

—adapted from Herodotus 1.36–43

## PRINCIPAL PARTS: Verbs with Three or Four Variations within Their Stems

[γν-] γί-γν-ο-μαι, [γενε-] γενήσομαι, [γεν-] ἐγενόμην, [γον-] γέγονα,
[γενε-] γεγένημαι, *I become; I happen*

διαφθείρω, [φθερε-] διαφθερῶ, [φθειρ-] διέφθειρα, [φθαρ-] διέφθαρκα or
[φθορ-] διέφθορα, [φθαρ-] διέφθαρμαι, διεφθάρην, *I destroy*

ἐγείρω, [ἐγερε-] ἐγερῶ, [ἐγειρ-] ἤγειρα, [thematic aorist middle; ἐγρ-] ἠγρόμην
(*I awoke*), [ἐγορ-] ἐγρήγορα (*I am awake*), [ἐγερ-] ἐγήγερμαι, ἠγέρθην,
active, transitive, *I wake X up;* middle and passive, intransitive, *I wake up*

λείπω, λείψω, [λιπ-] ἔλιπον, [λοιπ-] λέλοιπα, [λειπ-] λέλειμμαι (*I am left
behind; I am inferior*), ἐλείφθην, *I leave*

## WORD BUILDING

*Adjectives are formed by adding suffixes to verb or noun stems. Study the ways in which the following are formed and give their meanings:*

1. λείπ-ω              λοιπ-ός, -ή, -όν          9. ὁ λίθ-ος      λίθ-ινος, -η, -ον
2. ἥδ-ομαι            ἡδ-ύς, -εῖα, -ύ         10. ἡ μάχ-η      μάχ-ιμος, -η, -ον
3. ψεύδ-ομαι        ψευδ-ής, -ές           11. χρά-ομαι    χρή-σιμος, -η, -ον
4. ὁ πόλεμ-ος      πολέμ-ιος, -ᾱ, -ον     12. λάμπ-ω      λαμπ-ρός, -ά, -όν
5. ἡ δίκ-η            δίκα-ιος, -ᾱ, -ον      13. φοβέ-ομαι   φοβε-ρός, -ά, -όν
6. ὁ οἶκ-ος          οἰκε-ῖος, -ᾱ, -ον      14. ποιέ-ω        ποιη-τός, -ή, -όν
7. ὁ πόλεμ-ος      πολεμ-ικός, -ή, -όν    15. γράφ-ω       γραπ-τός, -ή, -όν
8. πράττω (πρᾱκ-)  πρᾱκ-τικός, -ή, -όν    16. χρά-ομαι     χρη-στός, -ή, -όν

## GRAMMAR

### 2. Adverbial Accusatives and the Accusative of Respect

The neuter accusative of adjectives is often used *adverbially*, e.g., the comparative adverb is the neuter accusative singular of the comparative adjective; thus, θᾶσσον = *more quickly*. The superlative adverb is the neuter accusative plural of the superlative adjective; thus, τάχιστα = *most quickly, very quickly*. The words μέγα, πολύ, ὀλίγον, οὐδέν, and τί are commonly used adverbially, e.g.:

μέγα βοᾷ. *He/she shouts **loudly**.*

οὐδέν σε φοβεῖται. *He/she does **not** fear you **at all**.*

τί τοῦτο ποιεῖς; ***Why** are you doing this?*

Another kind of adverbial accusative is the *accusative of duration of time* or *extent of space*, e.g.:

ἐμείναμεν **πέντε ἡμέρᾱς**.
*We stayed **five days**.*

τὸ ἄστυ **πολλοὺς σταδίους** ἀπέχει.
*The city is **many stades** distant.*

A new adverbial use of the accusative case is the *accusative of respect*, e.g.:

Κροῖσος ἦν Λῡδὸς μὲν **γένος**. . . .
*Croesus was Lydian **with respect to his race**, i.e., **by birth**. . . .*

ἀνήρ τις ἀφίκετο οὐ καθαρὸς **τὰς χεῖρας**.
*A man arrived impure **with respect to his hands**.*

The accusative of respect is very similar to the dative of respect (see Book I, Chapter 6, Grammar 6c, page 88).

## 3.  The Accusative Absolute

Another adverbial use of the accusative case is the *accusative absolute*, used with participles of impersonal verbs instead of the genitive absolute, e.g.:

**δόξαν** τὸν παῖδα ἐς τὴν ἄγρᾱν πέμψαι, ὁ Κροῖσος μάλιστα ἐφοβεῖτο.
***When he had decided** to send his son to the hunt, Croesus was very afraid.*
(The word δόξαν is the accusative neuter of the aorist participle of δοκεῖ = *it having seemed best* = *it having been decided*.)

**ἐξὸν** ἐς τὴν ἄγρᾱν ἰέναι, ὁ Ἄτῡς εὐθὺς ὁρμᾶται.
***Being allowed** to go to the hunt, Atys sets out at once.*
(The word ἐξόν is the accusative neuter of the participle of ἔξεστι(ν) = *it being possible, it being allowed*.)

**δέον** τὸ θηρίον αἱρεῖν, ἐς τὸ ὄρος ἔσπευδον.
***Since it was necessary** to take the beast, they hurried to the mountain.*
(The word δέον is the accusative neuter of the participle of δεῖ = *it being necessary*.)

## Exercise 26 γ

*Translate each sentence and explain the uses of the accusative case in the underlined words and phrases:*

1.  ἀνήρ τις, Φρύγιος <u>τὸ γένος</u>, ἐς τὰς Σάρδῑς ἀφικόμενος, τὸν Κροῖσον κάθαρσιν ᾔτησεν.

2.  <u>δόξαν</u> καθῆραι αὐτόν, ὁ Κροῖσος ἐπυνθάνετο πόθεν ἥκει καὶ τίνος πατρὸς ἐγένετο.

3.  <u>δέον</u> τὸ ἀληθὲς εἰπεῖν, ὁ ξένος ἀπεκρίνατο· "Γορδίου μὲν ἐγενόμην, ὄνομα δέ μοί ἐστιν Ἄδρηστος, φονεύσᾱς δὲ τὸν ἐμαυτοῦ ἀδελφὸν ἄκων πάρειμι."

4.  ὁ δὲ Κροῖσος δεξάμενος αὐτόν, "ἥκεις ἐς φίλους," ἔφη. "μένε οὖν ἐν τοῖς ἡμετέροις οἰκίοις <u>ὅσον</u> ἂν <u>χρόνον</u> βούλῃ."

5.  ἄγγελοί τινες, Μῡσοὶ <u>τὸ γένος,</u> ἐς Σάρδῑς ἀφικόμενοι, "πέμψον ἡμῖν, ὦ βασιλεῦ," ἔφασαν, "τὸν σὸν παῖδα ἵνα μέγα θηρίον τῆς χώρᾱς ἐξέλωμεν."

6.  ὁ δὲ παῖς, <u>οὐδὲν</u> φοβούμενος τὴν ἄγρᾱν, τὸν πατέρα ἔπεισε ἑαυτὸν πέμψαι· "οὐ γάρ," φησί, "πρὸς ἄνδρας ἡμῖν γίγνεται ἡ μάχη."

7.  <u>ἐξὸν</u> οὖν ἐς τὴν ἄγρᾱν ἰέναι, ὁ Ἄτῡς εὐθὺς ὡρμήσατο.

8.  <u>μακρὰν</u> οὖν <u>ὁδὸν</u> πορευθέντες καὶ τὸ θηρίον εὑρόντες, τῶν νεᾱνιῶν οἱ μὲν αὐτὸ ἐδίωκον, οἱ δὲ περιστάντες κύκλῳ ἐσηκόντιζον.

## 4. The Verbal Adjective in -τέος

The suffix -τέος, added usually to the verbal stem of the aorist passive, may give a passive adjective, e.g., λυ-τέος, -ᾱ, -ον = *to be loosed*, which expresses obligation or necessity and is often used with the verb εἰμί, e.g.:

λυτέοι εἰσὶν οἱ βόες.
*The oxen **are to be loosed**.*
*The oxen **must be loosed**.*

The person by whom the action must be performed is in the dative, e.g.:

ὠφελητέᾱ <u>σοι</u> ἡ πόλις ἐστίν.   (Xenophon, *Memorabilia* 3.6)
*The city **must be helped** by <u>you</u>. <u>You</u> **must help** the city.*

The person is often omitted in the Greek, although we prefer to express it in English, e.g.:

ἄλλαι νῆες ἐκ τῶν ξυμμάχων **μεταπεμπτέαι εἰσίν**.
*Other ships **must be summoned** from the allies (<u>by us</u>).*
<u>We</u> **must summon** other ships from the allies.*

The verb εἰμί is often omitted, e.g.:

λυτέοι οἱ βόες.
*The oxen **must be loosed**.*

The neuter verbal adjective of intransitive verbs is used impersonally with an active sense, e.g.:

ἰτέον <u>ἡμῖν</u>.
*It is necessary <u>for us</u> to go.*
<u>We</u> **must go**.*

The neuter plural is often used in this way instead of the singular, e.g.:

<u>ἐμοὶ</u> **βαδιστέα ἐστὶν** πρὸς τὴν ἀγορᾱν.
*It is necessary <u>for me</u> to walk to the agora.*
<u>I</u> **must walk** to the agora.*

The neuter verbal adjective of transitive verbs is also used impersonally with an active sense and an object, e.g.:

ἀλήθειάν γε **περὶ πολλοῦ ποιητέον**.   (Plato, *Republic* 389b2)
***It is necessary to consider** the truth **of great importance**.*
*We **must consider** the truth **of great importance**.*

## Exercise 26 δ

*The following examples are all taken with minor omissions of words from Plato, Republic, Books 2–5, in which Plato is discussing (a) the education of the guardians of his ideal state (1–3), (b) the selection of the rulers from the guardian class (4), and (c) the education of women (5). Translate the sentences and see how far you can reconstruct Plato's views on the education of his "guardians":*

1. ἆρ' οὖν οὐ μουσικῇ πρότερον ἀρξόμεθα παιδεύοντες ἢ γυμναστικῇ; λόγων (of stories) δὲ διττὸν εἶδος (two sorts), τὸ μὲν ἀληθές, ψεῦδος (falsehood) δ' ἕτερον; παιδευτέον δ' ἐν ἀμφοτέροις; (376e6–377a1)

2. οὗτοι οἱ λόγοι οὐ λεκτέοι ἐν τῇ ἡμετέρᾳ πόλει. (378a7–378b2)

3. μετὰ δὴ μουσικὴν γυμναστικῇ θρεπτέοι (from τρέφω, I rear, train) οἱ νεᾱνίαι. (403c9)

4. ἐκλεκτέον (from ἐκλέγω, I select) ἐκ τῶν ἄλλων φυλάκων τοιούτους ἄνδρας, οἳ ἂν μάλιστα φαίνωνται, ὃ ἂν τῇ πόλει ἡγήσωνται συμφέρειν (to benefit + dat.), πάσῃ προθῡμίᾳ (eagerness) ποιεῖν. (412d9–412e2)

5. εἰ ταῖς γυναιξὶν ἐπὶ ταὐτὰ (for the same purpose, i.e., for acting as guardians) χρησόμεθα καὶ (as) τοῖς ἀνδράσι, ταὐτὰ (= τὰ αὐτὰ) καὶ διδακτέον αὐτάς. (451e)

# Ο ΑΔΡΗΣΤΟΣ ΕΑΥΤΟΝ ΣΦΑΖΕΙ

*Read the following passages (adapted from Herodotus 1.44–45) and answer the comprehension questions:*

The story of Croesus and Adrastus concluded:

ὁ δὲ Κροῖσος τῷ μὲν θανάτῳ τοῦ παιδὸς συνεταράχθη, ἔτι δὲ μᾶλλον ὠδύρετο διότι τὸν παῖδα ἀπέκτεινε ἐκεῖνος ὃν αὐτὸς φόνου ἐκάθηρε. λῡπούμενος δὲ τῇ συμφορᾷ δεινῶς, ἐκάλει μὲν Δία καθάρσιον, μαρτυρόμενος ἃ ὑπὸ τοῦ ξένου ἔπαθεν, ἐκάλει δὲ Δία ἐφέστιον, διότι ἐν τοῖς οἰκίοις δεξάμενος τὸν ξένον ἐλάνθανε βόσκων τὸν φονέᾱ τοῦ παιδός, ἐκάλει δὲ καὶ Δία ἑταιρεῖον, διότι φύλακα συμπέμψᾱς αὐτὸν    5 ηὗρε πολεμιώτατον.

[**συνεταράχθη** (from συνταράττω), *was thrown into confusion, confounded* **καθάρσιον**, *of purification* (a title of Zeus)    **μαρτυρόμενος**, *calling (him) to witness* **ἐφέστιον**, *who presides over the hearth* (ἑστίᾱ) *and hospitality* (a title of Zeus) **βόσκων**, *feeding, sheltering*    **τὸν φονέᾱ**, *the murderer*    **ἑταιρεῖον**, *presiding over companionship* (a title of Zeus)]

1. By what was Croesus confounded?
2. Why did he grieve even more?
3. With what three titles did Croesus call upon Zeus?
4. To what irony does Croesus call attention when invoking Zeus as καθάρσιος?
5. To what irony does he call attention when invoking Zeus as ἐφέστιος?
6. To what irony does he call attention when invoking Zeus as ἑταιρεῖος?

παρῆσαν δὲ μετὰ τοῦτο οἱ Λῡδοὶ φέροντες τὸν νεκρόν, ὄπισθε δὲ εἵπετο αὐτῷ ὁ φονεύς. στὰς δὲ οὗτος πρὸ τοῦ νεκροῦ παρεδίδου ἑαυτὸν Κροίσῳ προτείνων τὰς χεῖρας, ἐπικατασφάξαι ἑαυτὸν κελεύων τῷ νεκρῷ, λέγων ὅτι οὐκέτι χρὴ βιοῦν.

[ὄπισθε, *behind*    παρεδίδου, *tried to surrender*    προτείνων, *stretching forth*
ἐπικατασφάξαι, *to slaughter* X (acc.) *over* Y (dat.)    βιοῦν, *to live*]

7.   Who follows the corpse of Croesus's son?
8.   With what gesture does Adrastus attempt to surrender to Croesus?
9.   What does Adrastus order Croesus to do?
10.  What reason does Adrastus give for ordering Croesus to do this?

Κροῖσος δὲ ταῦτα ἀκούσας τόν τε Ἄδρηστον οἰκτίρει, καίπερ ὢν ἐν κακῷ    10
οἰκείῳ τοσούτῳ, καὶ λέγει πρὸς αὐτόν· "ἔχω, ὦ ξένε, παρὰ σοῦ πᾶσαν δίκην,
ἐπειδὴ σεαυτοῦ καταδικάζεις θάνατον. οὐ σύ μοι τοῦδε τοῦ κακοῦ αἴτιος εἶ, ἀλλὰ
θεῶν τις, ὅς μοι πάλαι προεσήμαινε τὰ μέλλοντα ἔσεσθαι." Κροῖσος μὲν οὖν ἔθαψε
τὸν ἑαυτοῦ παῖδα, Ἄδρηστος δέ, οὗτος δὴ ὁ φονεὺς μὲν τοῦ ἑαυτοῦ ἀδελφοῦ, φονεὺς
δὲ τοῦ καθήραντος, ἐπεὶ οὐδεὶς ἀνθρώπων ἐγένετο περὶ τὸ σῆμα, βαρυσυμφορώτατος    15
ὤν, ἐπικατασφάζει τῷ τύμβῳ ἑαυτόν.

[κακῷ, *trouble*    οἰκείῳ, *of his own*    παρὰ* + gen., *from*    καταδικάζεις, *you con-
demn someone* (gen.) *to some punishment* (acc.)    προεσήμαινε, *foretold*    τὸ σῆμα,
*the tomb*    βαρυσυμφορώτατος, *very weighed down by his bad luck*    ἐπικατασφάζει, *he slaughters* X (acc.) *over* Y (dat.)    τῷ τύμβῳ, *the tomb*]

11.  Why is it surprising that Croesus pities Adrastus?
12.  How does Croesus explain that he has received full justice from Adras-
     tus?
13.  Who, in Croesus's view, is responsible for what has happened?
14.  What does Adrastus do at the end of the story?
15.  What hints does Herodotus give in the last sentence as to why Adrastus
     did what he did?
16.  Does Adrastus seem to have been able to accept Croesus's explanation of
     who was responsible for what happened?
17.  Is there any indication in the story of Herodotus's own views as to who
     was responsible for what happened?  Can Croesus himself be held re-
     sponsible in any way?  Look back at the beginning of the story at the be-
     ginning of this chapter.

### Exercise 26 ε

*Translate into Greek:*

1.   A foreigner, Phrygian by race, arriving at Sardis with impure hands,
     asked Croesus to purify him.
2.   When the Mysians asked Croesus for help (*use* βοήθεια; *use two
     accusatives*), at first Croesus was not willing to send his son.
3.   But his son said, "Our (*use dative of the possessor*) battle is not against
     men; and so fear nothing but send me."

4. So Croesus was persuaded by these words, but, having sent for the foreigner, he told him to guard his son.

5. Being allowed to go, Atys, having set out immediately, arrived at the mountain on the third day.

6. When they found the boar, the foreigner threw his spear (*use* ἀκοντίζω) and missed the boar but hit Croesus's son.

## Classical Greek

### Hesiod (concluded from Chapter 24)

Hesiod wishes that he had not been born in the Iron Age (*Works and Days*, 174–181). When the fifth, iron, age is destroyed, the world cycle will begin again with a new Golden Age; hence Hesiod's wish to have been born later.

μηκέτ' ἔπειτ' ὤφελλον ἐγὼ πέμπτοισι μετεῖναι

ἀνδράσιν, ἀλλ' ἢ πρόσθε θανεῖν ἢ ἔπειτα γενέσθαι.

νῦν γὰρ δὴ γένος ἐστὶ σιδήρεον· οὐδέ ποτ' ἦμαρ

παύσονται καμάτου καὶ ὀϊζύος οὐδέ τι νύκτωρ

τειρόμενοι· χαλεπὰς δὲ θεοὶ δώσουσι μερίμνας.

ἀλλ' ἔμπης καὶ τοῖσι μεμείξεται ἐσθλὰ κακοῖσιν.

Ζεὺς δ' ὀλέσει καὶ τοῦτο γένος μερόπων ἀνθρώπων,

εὖτ' ἂν γεινόμενοι πολιοκρόταφοι τελέθωσιν.

[μηκέτ(ι) . . . ὤφελλον . . . μετεῖναι + dat., *I wish I were not among . . . any longer* πέμπτοισι = πέμπτοις πρόσθε, *before* θανεῖν = ἀποθανεῖν γένος, *race* σιδήρεον, *of iron* ἦμαρ, *in the day* καμάτου, *from weariness* ὀϊζύος (gen. of ὀϊζύς), *woe, misery* νύκτωρ, *in the night* τειρόμενοι, *being distressed* (supply παύσονται) μερίμνας, *anxieties* ἔμπης, *all the same* τοῖσι = τοῖς, *for them* μεμείξεται, rare future perfect passive, *will have been mixed* ἐσθλὰ, *good things* κακοῖσιν = κακοῖς ὀλέσει = ἀπολεῖ μερόπων, *of mortal speech* εὖτ(ε) ἂν = ἐπειδὰν γεινόμενοι, *being born, at birth* πολιοκρόταφοι, *gray-haired* τελέθωσιν, *they are*]

## Greek Wisdom

### Heraclitus

πολυμαθίᾱ νοῦν ἔχειν οὐ διδάσκει· Ἡσίοδον γὰρ ἂν ἐδίδαξε καὶ Πῡθαγόρᾱν αὖθις τε Ξενοφάνη τε καὶ Ἑκαταῖον. Fragment 40 Diels

# New Testament Greek

### John 11.1, 3–5, 17, 19–27, and 38–44
### The Death and Resurrection of Lazarus

ἦν δέ τις ἀσθενῶν, Λάζαρος ἀπὸ Βηθανίας, ἐκ τῆς κώμης Μαρίας καὶ Μάρθας τῆς ἀδελφῆς αὐτῆς. . . . ἀπέστειλαν οὖν αἱ ἀδελφαὶ πρὸς αὐτὸν λέγουσαι, "κύριε, ἴδε ὃν φιλεῖς ἀσθενεῖ." ἀκούσας δὲ ὁ Ἰησοῦς εἶπεν, "αὕτη ἡ ἀσθένεια οὐκ ἔστιν πρὸς θάνατον ἀλλ᾽ ὑπὲρ τῆς δόξης τοῦ θεοῦ, ἵνα δοξασθῇ ὁ υἱὸς τοῦ θεοῦ δι᾽ αὐτῆς. ἠγάπα δὲ ὁ Ἰησοῦς τὴν Μάρθαν καὶ τὴν ἀδελφὴν αὐτῆς καὶ τὸν Λάζαρον. . . . ἐλθὼν οὖν ὁ Ἰησοῦς εὗρεν αὐτὸν τέσσαρας ἤδη ἡμέρας ἔχοντα ἐν τῷ μνημείῳ. . . . πολλοὶ δὲ ἐκ τῶν Ἰουδαίων ἐληλύθεισαν πρὸς τὴν Μάρθαν καὶ Μαριὰμ ἵνα παραμυθήσωνται αὐτὰς περὶ τοῦ ἀδελφοῦ.

[ἀσθενῶν, *being sick*    τῆς κώμης, *the village*    ἀπέστειλαν (from ἀποστέλλω), *they sent*    αὐτὸν, *i.e., Jesus*    ὃν, *(the one) whom*    δοξασθῇ (from δοξάζω), *may be glorified*    ἠγάπα (from ἀγαπάω), *was loving, loved*    ἔχοντα, *here, being* (with accusative of duration of time)    τῷ μνημείῳ, *the tomb*    ἐληλύθεισαν (= Attic ἐληλύθεσαν, pluperfect of ἔρχομαι), *had come*    ἵνα παραμυθήσωνται, *to console*]

ἡ οὖν Μάρθα ὡς ἤκουσεν ὅτι Ἰησοῦς ἔρχεται ὑπήντησεν αὐτῷ· Μαριὰμ δὲ ἐν τῷ οἴκῳ ἐκαθέζετο. εἶπεν οὖν ἡ Μάρθα πρὸς τὸν Ἰησοῦν, "κύριε, εἰ ἦς ὧδε οὐκ ἂν ἀπέθανεν ὁ ἀδελφός μου· καὶ νῦν οἶδα ὅτι ὅσα ἂν αἰτήσῃ τὸν θεὸν δώσει σοι ὁ θεός." λέγει αὐτῇ ὁ Ἰησοῦς, "ἀναστήσεται ὁ ἀδελφός σου." λέγει αὐτῷ ἡ Μάρθα, "οἶδα ὅτι ἀναστήσεται ἐν τῇ ἀναστάσει ἐν τῇ ἐσχάτῃ ἡμέρᾳ." εἶπεν αὐτῇ ὁ Ἰησοῦς, "ἐγώ εἰμι ἡ ἀνάστασις καὶ ἡ ζωή· ὁ πιστεύων εἰς ἐμὲ κἂν ἀποθάνῃ ζήσεται, καὶ πᾶς ὁ ζῶν καὶ πιστεύων εἰς ἐμὲ οὐ μὴ ἀποθάνῃ εἰς τὸν αἰῶνα. πιστεύεις τοῦτο;" λέγει αὐτῷ, "ναὶ κύριε, ἐγὼ πεπίστευκα ὅτι σὺ εἶ ὁ Χρῑστὸς ὁ υἱὸς τοῦ θεοῦ ὁ εἰς τὸν κόσμον ἐρχόμενος."

[ὑπήντησεν (from ὑπαντάω) + dat., *met*    Μαριὰμ: nominative here    εἰ ἦς ὧδε (ἦς = Attic ἦσθα, here used in a past contrary to fact condition), *if you had been here*    ἂν ἀπέθανεν, *would have died*    ὅσα ἂν αἰτήσῃ, *as many things as you ask*    ἀναστήσεται, *will stand up*    ἀναστήσεται, *he will be resurrected*    τῇ ἀναστάσει, *the resurrection*    ἐσχάτῃ, *last*    κἂν ἀποθάνῃ (κἂν = καὶ ἐάν), *even if he dies*    ζήσεται (from *ζάω), *he will live*    οὐ μὴ ἀποθάνῃ, *will never die*    εἰς τὸν αἰῶνα, *into eternity, forever*    ναί, *yes*    πεπίστευκα, *I have come to believe*    ὁ Χρῑστὸς, *the Christ* (i.e., the anointed one)]

And having said this, she went away and called Mary her sister secretly, saying, "The Master is here, and he calls you." And when she heard this, she got up quickly and began to go to him. And Jesus had not yet come into the village, but was in the place where Martha had met him. . . . Then when Mary had come where Jesus was, having seen him, she fell at his feet, saying to him, "Lord, if you had been here, my brother would not have died." Then when Jesus saw her weeping, . . . he was deeply moved (ἐνεβρῑμήσατο) in his spirit and was troubled, and said, "Where have you laid him?" They say to him, "Lord, come and see." Jesus burst into tears. . . .

Ἰησοῦς οὖν πάλιν ἐμβρῑμώμενος ἐν ἑαυτῷ ἔρχεται εἰς τὸ μνημεῖον· ἦν δὲ σπήλαιον καὶ λίθος ἐπέκειτο ἐπ' αὐτῷ. λέγει ὁ Ἰησοῦς, "ἄρατε τὸν λίθον." λέγει αὐτῷ ἡ ἀδελφὴ τοῦ τετελευτηκότος Μάρθᾱ, "κύριε, ἤδη ὄζει, τεταρταῖος γάρ ἐστιν." λέγει αὐτῇ ὁ Ἰησοῦς, "οὐκ εἶπόν σοι ὅτι ἐὰν πιστεύσῃς ὄψῃ τὴν δόξαν τοῦ θεοῦ;" ἦραν οὖν τὸν λίθον. ὁ δὲ Ἰησοῦς ἦρεν τοὺς ὀφθαλμοὺς ἄνω καὶ εἶπεν, "πάτερ, εὐχαριστῶ σοι ὅτι ἤκουσάς μου. ἐγὼ δὲ ᾔδειν ὅτι πάντοτέ μου ἀκούεις, ἀλλὰ διὰ τὸν ὄχλον τὸν περιεστῶτα εἶπον, ἵνα πιστεύσωσιν ὅτι σύ με ἀπέστειλας." καὶ ταῦτα εἰπὼν φωνῇ μεγάλῃ ἐκραύγασεν, "Λάζαρε, δεῦρο ἔξω." ἐξῆλθεν ὁ τεθνηκὼς δεδεμένος τοὺς πόδας καὶ τὰς χεῖρας κειρίαις καὶ ἡ ὄψις αὐτοῦ σουδαρίῳ περιεδέδετο. λέγει αὐτοῖς ὁ Ἰησοῦς, "λύσατε αὐτὸν καὶ ἄφετε αὐτὸν ὑπάγειν."

[**πάλιν**, *again*   **ἐμβρῑμώμενος** (from ἐμβρῑμάομαι), *being deeply moved*   **σπή-λαιον**, *a cave*   **τοῦ τετελευτηκότος**, *of the one who had died*   **ὄζει**, *he stinks*   **τεταρταῖος**, *(dead) for four days*   **εὐχαριστῶ**, *I give thanks*   **ὅτι**, *because*   **ᾔδειν**, *I knew*   **πάντοτε**, *always*   **τὸν ὄχλον**, *the crowd*   **τὸν περιεστῶτα**, *the one standing around*   **ἀπέστειλας**, *you sent*   **ἐκραύγασεν**, *he shouted*   **ὁ τεθνηκὼς**, *the one who had died, the dead man*   **κειρίαις**, *strips of cloth*   **ἡ ὄψις**, *his face*   **σουδαρίῳ**, *handkerchief, cloth used to wrap the face of a dead person*   **περιεδέδετο**, *had been bound around*   **ἄφετε** (from ἀφίημι), *allow*   **ὑπάγειν**, *to go, depart*]

Aerial photograph of Delphi, showing the stadium, the theater, the temple of Apollo, and the Sacred Way lined with treasuries

# 27
# Ο ΚΡΟΙΣΟΣ ΕΠΙ ΤΟΝ ΚΥΡΟΝ ΣΤΡΑΤΕΥΕΤΑΙ (α)

οἱ τοῦ Κροίσου ἄγγελοι ἐς τοὺς Δελφοὺς ἀφῑγμένοι τῷ θεῷ ἐχρήσαντο.

## Herodotus's Ionic Dialect

Herodotus wrote in a literary version of the Ionic dialect; in the preceding chapters we changed most of his Ionic forms to their Attic equivalents, preserving only ἐς (ἐσ-), -σσ-, and a few others, but from now on in the readings we leave more Ionic forms as Herodotus actually wrote them. Note the following:

1. Ionic has η where Attic has ᾱ after ε, ι, and ρ, e.g., Ionic ἡμέρη = Attic ἡμέρᾱ; Ionic πρῆξις = Attic πρᾶξις.
2. Contraction does not take place in Herodotus's Ionic with verbs and nouns, the stems of which end in -ε-, e.g., Herodotus has φιλέω, φιλέεις, φιλέει, etc., instead of the Attic φιλῶ, φιλεῖς, φιλεῖ, etc. As examples of nouns, note that Herodotus has the uncontracted forms γένεος (= Attic γένους), γένεα (= Attic γένη), and Περσέων (= Attic Περσῶν). The noun νόος does not contract in Herodotus.
3. Herodotus has ἐών, ἐοῦσα, ἐόν for the present participle of the verb εἰμί.
4. Dative plurals of the 1st and 2nd declensions end in -ῃσι and -οισι, e.g., κρήνῃσι and ἀγροῖσι.
5. Occasionally Ionic has ει where Attic has ε and ου where Attic has ο, e.g., Ionic ξεῖνος (= Attic ξένος) and Ionic μοῦνος (= Attic μόνος).
6. Ionic has some pronouns not common in Attic prose, e.g., οἱ (dative, enclitic) *to him/her/it*, and μιν (accusative, enclitic) *him/her*.
7. Herodotus usually does not use the movable ν (see 27 α:14, 26, and 29).

179

## VOCABULARY

*Verbs*

ἀγείρω, [ἀγερε-] ἀγερῶ,
[ἀγειρ-] ἤγειρα, *I gather*
ἀγωνίζομαι, [ἀγωνιε-] ἀγωνιοῦμαι, [ἀγωνι-] ἠγωνισάμην, ἠγώνισμαι, *I contend*
ἀντιόομαι, ἀντιώσομαι, ἠντιώθην + dat., *I oppose*
διαβαίνω, *I cross*
ἐπέρχομαι [= ἐπι- + ἔρχομαι],
*I approach;* + dat., *I attack*
καταλύω , *I dissolve; I break
up; I destroy*
μέμφομαι, μέμψομαι, ἐμεμψάμην or ἐμέμφθην + dat. or
acc., *I blame, find fault with*
παρακαλέω, *I summon*
φωνέω, *I speak*

*Nouns*

τὸ ἀνάθημα, τοῦ ἀναθήματος,
*temple offering*
ὁ ἀριθμός, τοῦ ἀριθμοῦ, *number*
τὸ δῶρον, τοῦ δώρου, *gift*
τὸ μαντεῖον, τοῦ μαντείου, *oracle*
τὸ μέτρον, τοῦ μέτρου, *measure*
τὸ ὅρκιον, τοῦ ὁρκίου, *oath;* pl.,
*treaty*
τὸ στράτευμα, τοῦ στρατεύματος, *army*
ἡ συμμαχίᾱ, τῆς συμμαχίᾱς,
*alliance*
ὁ χρησμός, τοῦ χρησμοῦ, *oracular response*

τὸ χρηστήριον, τοῦ χρηστηρίου
(often pl. with sing. meaning), *oracle* (either the seat of
the oracle or the oracular response)

*Adjectives*

καρτερός, -ά, -όν, *strong;
fierce*
οὐδέτερος, -ᾱ, -ον, *neither*

*Prepositions*

ἐπί + gen., *toward, in the direction of; on;* + dat., *upon, on; at;*
of price, *for;* + acc., *at;
against; onto, upon;* of direction or purpose, *to; for;* of time,
*for*
πρός + gen., *from* (i.e., *at the
hand of*); + dat., *at, near, by;
in addition to;* + acc., *to, toward; upon, onto; against;
with* (i.e., *in relation to*)

*Adverbs*

ἄλλοσε, *to another place; to
other places*
αὐτίκα, *straightway, at once*
πάνυ, *altogether; very; exceedingly*

*Expressions*

ἄλλοι ἄλλοσε, *some to some
places . . . others to other
places*

*Proper Name*

ἡ Πῡθίᾱ, τῆς Πῡθίᾱς, *Pythia*
(the Delphic priestess of
Apollo)

Κροῖσος δὲ ἐπὶ δύο ἔτεα ἐν πένθει μεγάλῳ ἐκάθητο τοῦ παιδὸς
ἐστερημένος· μετὰ δὲ ταῦτα, ἐπεὶ ὁ Κῦρος βασιλεὺς γενόμενος τῶν
Περσέων τούς τε Μήδους ἐνίκησε καὶ τὰ τῶν Περσέων πρήγματα
ηὔξανε, ἤθελε ὁ Κροῖσος, εἴ πως δύναιτο, τὴν δύναμιν αὐτῶν παῦσαι
πρὶν μεγάλους γενέσθαι. ἔδοξε οὖν αὐτῷ χρῆσθαι τῷ μαντείῳ τῷ        5
ἀρίστῳ, ἵνα μάθοι εἰ δέοι ἐπὶ τοὺς Πέρσᾱς στρατεύεσθαι· πρῶτον

μέντοι ἔδει γιγνώσκειν τί μαντεῖόν ἐστι ἄριστον. πάντων οὖν τῶν
μαντείων ἀπεπειρᾶτο, ἀγγέλους πέμψας, τοὺς μὲν ἐς Δωδώνην, τοὺς
δὲ ἐς Δελφούς, ἄλλους δὲ ἄλλοσε. τοὺς δὲ ἀγγέλους ἐκέλευε τῇ
ἑκατοστῇ ἡμέρῃ ἀφ' ἧς ἂν ὁρμηθῶσι ἐκ Σαρδίων, χρῆσθαι τοῖς 10
χρηστηρίοις, ἐρωτῶντας ὅ τι ποιῶν τυγχάνοι ὁ Λυδῶν βασιλεὺς
Κροῖσος, καὶ ὅσ' ἂν λέγῃ τὰ χρηστήρια γράψαντας ἀναφέρειν παρ'
ἐαυτόν.

[πένθει, sorrow  ἐστερημένος (perfect passive participle of στερέω) + gen., *having
been bereft of*  ἀπεπειρᾶτο + gen., *made trial of*  τοὺς δὲ ἀγγέλους ἐκέλευε: the
infinitives with the construction are χρῆσθαι (10) and ἀναφέρειν (12)  ἑκατοστῇ,
*hundredth*  χρῆσθαι + dat., *to consult (an oracle)*  ἀναφέρειν, *to bring back, report*]

ὅ τι μὲν τὰ ἄλλα χρηστήρια ἐθέσπισε οὐ λέγεται ὑπ' οὐδενός, ἐν
δὲ Δελφοῖσι ἐπεὶ τάχιστα εἰσῆλθον οἱ Λυδοὶ χρησόμενοι τῷ θεῷ, ἡ 15
Πυθίη λέγει τάδε·

οἶδα δ' ἐγὼ ψάμμου τ' ἀριθμὸν καὶ μέτρα θαλάσσης,
καὶ κωφοῦ συνίημι, καὶ οὐ φωνεῦντος ἀκούω.
ὀδμή μ' ἐς φρένας ἦλθε κραταιρίνοιο χελώνης
ἑψομένης ἐν χαλκῷ ἅμ' ἀρνείοισι κρέεσσιν.          20

[ἐθέσπισε, *prophesied*  ἐπεὶ τάχιστα, *as soon as*  ψάμμου, *of the sand(s)*  κωφοῦ
(gen. with συνίημι), *dumb, mute*  συνίημι = συνίημι, with short ι, as is usual in dactylic
verse  φωνεῦντος = Ionic for φωνοῦντος  ὀδμή, *smell*  μ' = μοι  φρένας, *mind*
κραταιρίνοιο χελώνης ἑψομένης ἐν χαλκῷ ἅμ' ἀρνείοισι κρέεσσιν, *of a hard-
shelled tortoise being boiled in a bronze (kettle) along with the flesh of a lamb*]

ταῦτα θεσπισάσης τῆς Πυθίης, οἱ Λυδοὶ γράψαντες ἀπῆλθον ἐς τὰς
Σάρδῑς. ὡς δὲ καὶ οἱ ἄλλοι οἱ περιπεμφθέντες παρῆσαν φέροντες τοὺς
χρησμούς, ὁ Κροῖσος πάντα τὰ γεγραμμένα ἀνεγίγνωσκε. τῶν μὲν
οὖν ἄλλων οὐδὲν ἤρεσκέ οἱ, ὡς δὲ τὸ ἐκ Δελφῶν ἤκουσε, αὐτίκα
ηὔχετο καὶ ἐδέξατο, νομίσᾱς μοῦνον εἶναι μαντεῖον τὸ ἐν Δελφοῖσι, 25
διότι ἐξηῦρε ἃ αὐτὸς ἐποίησε.

[τὰ γεγραμμένα, perfect passive participle, *the things that had been written*]

μετὰ δὲ ταῦτα ὁ Κροῖσος τὸν ἐν Δελφοῖσι θεὸν ἐτίμᾱ, Λυδούς τε
πάντας ἐκέλευε θύειν ὅ τι ἔχοι ἕκαστος. καὶ πλεῖστα καὶ κάλλιστα
δῶρα ἔπεμψε ἐς Δελφοὺς καὶ τοὺς ἄγειν μέλλοντας ἐκέλευε ἐρωτᾶν

τὰ χρηστήρια εἰ δέοι Κροῖσον στρατεύεσθαι ἐπὶ Πέρσας. ὡς δὲ    30
ἀφικόμενοι οἱ Λῡδοὶ ἀνέθεσαν τὰ ἀναθήματα, ἐχρήσαντο τοῖς
χρηστηρίοις. ἡ δὲ Πῡθίη τάδε ἀπεκρίνατο, ὅτι ἐὰν στρατεύηται
Κροῖσος ἐπὶ Πέρσας, μεγάλην ἀρχὴν καταλύσει. ἐπεὶ δὲ τὸν χρησμὸν
ἐπύθετο ὁ Κροῖσος, ἥσθη, πάνυ ἐλπίσᾱς καταλύσειν τὴν Κύρου
ἀρχήν. οὕτως οὖν ἐλπίσᾱς ἐστρατεύετο ἐς τὴν Περσέων ἀρχήν. καὶ    35
ὡς ἀφίκετο ἐς τὸν Ἅλυν ποταμὸν διαβὰς σὺν τῷ στρατῷ τῶν Πτερίων
εἷλε τὴν πόλιν.

     Κῦρος δὲ ἀγείρᾱς τὸν ἑαυτοῦ στρατὸν ἠντιοῦτο Κροίσῳ. μάχης
δὲ καρτερῆς γενομένης καὶ πεσόντων ἀμφοτέρων πολλῶν, τέλος
οὐδέτεροι νῑκήσαντες διέστησαν νυκτὸς ἐπελθούσης. καὶ τὰ μὲν    40
στρατόπεδα ἀμφότερα οὕτως ἠγωνίσατο. Κροῖσος δὲ μεμφθεὶς κατὰ
τὸ πλῆθος τὸ ἑαυτοῦ στράτευμα (ἦν γὰρ οἱ στρατὸς πολλῷ ἐλάσσων
ἢ ὁ Κύρου), τοῦτο μεμφθείς, ὡς τῇ ὑστεραίῃ οὐκ ἐπειρᾶτο ἐπιὼν ὁ
Κῦρος, ἀπήλαυνε ἐς τὰς Σάρδῑς, ἐν νόῳ ἔχων τούς τε Αἰγυπτίους
παρακαλεῖν κατὰ τὸ ὅρκιον (ἐποιήσατο γὰρ πρὸς Ἄμᾱσιν    45
βασιλεύοντα Αἰγύπτου συμμαχίην) καὶ μεταπέμψασθαι τοὺς
Βαβυλωνίους (καὶ γὰρ πρὸς τούτους αὐτῷ ἐπεποίητο συμμαχίη),
καλέσᾱς τε δὴ τούτους καὶ τὴν ἑαυτοῦ συλλέξᾱς στρατιήν, ἐν νόῳ
εἶχε ἅμα τῷ ἦρι στρατεύειν ἐπὶ τοὺς Πέρσας.

[διέστησαν, *they parted*    τὰ...στρατόπεδα, here, *the armies*    κατὰ τὸ
πλῆθος, *with regard to its size*    οἱ, *to/for him, his*    ἀπήλαυνε, intransitive, *he was
marching away*    αὐτῷ, *by him*    ἐπεποίητο, pluperfect, *had been made*]

                 —adapted from Herodotus 1.46–50, 53–54, and 76–77

---

# Greek Wisdom

## Heraclitus

ἀνθρώποις γίγνεσθαι ὁπόσα θέλουσιν οὐκ ἄμεινον. Fragment 110 Diels

# PRINCIPAL PARTS: Verbs from Unrelated Stems

αἱρέω, αἱρήσω, [ἑλ-] εἷλον (irregular augment), [αἱρε-] ᾕρηκα, ᾕρημαι,
ᾑρέθην, *I take;* middle, *I choose*

ἔρχομαι (present indicative only in Attic), *I come; I go*

Stems grouped for convenience with ἔρχομαι:

[ἰ-]: present subjunctive, ἴω; present or future optative, ἴοιμι or ἰοίην; present imperative, ἴθι; present or future infinitive, ἰέναι; present or future participle, ἰών

[εἰ-]: imperfect, ᾖα

[εἰ-/ἰ-]: future indicative, εἶμι

[ἐλθ-]: aorist, ἦλθον

[ἐλυθ-]: perfect, ἐλήλυθα (for the Attic reduplication, see page 235)

Note: Ionic and New Testament Greek use ἐλεύσομαι for the future.

τρέχω, [δραμε-] δραμοῦμαι, [δραμ-] ἔδραμον, [δραμε-] δεδράμηκα, δεδράμημαι, *I run; I sail*

# WORD STUDY

*From what Greek words are the following English philosophical terms derived:*

1. philosophy
2. logic
3. ethics
4. epistemology
5. metaphysics
6. political theory

*Explain the meaning of the terms with reference to their Greek stems.*

# GRAMMAR

## 1. The Perfect Tense: Middle/Passive Participles

The perfect tense has the same forms for middle and passive voices, just as do the present and the imperfect. Deponent verbs are, of course, in the middle voice; the context will tell whether other verbs are being used as middle or passive.

You have met a number of perfect passive participles in the stories. In the Greek sentences quoted below, all perfect passive participles are in boldface; they all have one of the following:

a. Reduplication: repetition of the first consonant of the stem + ε, e.g., κλει-, *shut*, reduplicates to κεκλει-.

b. Temporal augment: e.g., ἑλκυ-, *drag; draw*, augments to εἱλκυ-.

c. Syllabic augment: e.g., στερε-, *deprive; bereave*, augments to ἐστερε-.

Note the perfect *passive* participles in the following sentences:

ηὗρον τὰς πύλας **κεκλειμένᾱς**.  (17β:7)
*They found the gates **having been closed** = closed.*
*They found that the gates **had been closed**.*

οἱ Ἕλληνες . . . ναῦς εἶδον **ἀνειλκυσμένᾱς** ἔσω τοῦ τείχους.  (19 tail:12–15)
*The Greeks saw the ships **having been drawn up (on the shore)** = **beached** inside the wall.*
*The Greeks saw that the ships **had been beached** inside the wall.*

Κροῖσος . . . ἐν πένθει μεγάλῳ ἐκάθητο τοῦ παιδὸς **ἐστερημένος**.  (27α:1–2)
*Croesus was sitting in great grief, **(having been) bereft** of his son.*
*Croesus was sitting in great grief, **since he had been bereft** of his son.*

The actions described by these participles in the perfect tense were necessarily completed *prior* to the action of the main verb.  When the main verb is in a past tense, the perfect participles can often best be translated with the word "had" in English, as in the second translations of the examples above.

Here are sentences with a pefect *middle* participle of the deponent verb ἀφικνέομαι (with temporal augment: ικ- augments to ῑκ-, which becomes ῑγ- in ἀφῑγμένᾱς):

ὁρῶσι τὰς ναῦς ἤδη εἰς τὸν λιμένα **ἀφῑγμένᾱς**.
*They see that the ships **have** already **arrived** at the harbor.*

εἶδον τὰς ναῦς ἤδη εἰς τὸν λιμένα **ἀφῑγμένᾱς**.
*They saw that the ships **had** already **arrived** at the harbor.*

## 2.  Perfective Aspect

Perfect participles describe enduring states or conditions resulting from completed actions.  Let us say that the gates *were closed* by the gatekeeper at one moment in time; Greek would use the *aorist tense* here for simple action in past time.  When Dicaeopolis and Philip arrived at Epidaurus, they found the gates *closed* (κεκλειμένᾱς, the enduring condition produced by the action of the person who shut them); Greek uses the *perfect tense* to describe this enduring result of a completed action.

Greek thus distinguishes clearly between progressive, aorist, and perfective aspects:

While *closing* the gates, the gatekeeper slipped and fell.
(*Closing* would be translated with a present, progressive participle in Greek.)

*Having closed/After closing/Closing* the gates, the gatekeeper went home.
(*Having shut/After shutting/Shutting* would be translated with an aorist participle in Greek, expressing a simple action, here one that took place just prior to the gatekeeper's departure for home.)

Dicaeopolis and Philip found the gates *having been closed/closed*.
(*Having been closed/closed* would be translated with a perfect passive participle in Greek, expressing the enduring result of the action completed by the gatekeeper.)

The term *perfect* comes from a Latin verb meaning "to complete." The reduplication or augment in the perfect tense indicates that the verb expresses the enduring result of an action *completed* in the past.

Here is an example that you are familiar with of a perfect *active* verb:

οὐδὲν ὁρᾷ ὁ Φίλιππος· τυφλὸς γὰρ **γέγονεν.** (10β:34)
*Philip sees nothing; for **he has become** = **he is** blind.*

## 3. The Perfect Tense: Middle/Passive: Indicative, Subjunctive, Optative, Imperative, and Infinitive

### a. *Perfect Indicative Middle (Deponent):*

ἡ ναῦς εἰς τὸν λιμένα ἤδη **ἀφῖκται.**
*The ship **has** already **arrived** at the harbor.*

### b. *Perfect Indicative Passive:*

πάντα τῷ Κροίσῳ ἤδη **βεβούλευται.**
*Everything **has** already **been planned** by Croesus.*

### c. *Perfect Subjunctive Middle (Deponent):*

φοβούμεθα μὴ ἡ ναῦς εἰς τὸν λιμένα οὐκ ἤδη **ἀφῖγμένη ᾖ.**
*We are afraid that the ship **has** not already **arrived** at the harbor.*

### d. *Perfect Subjunctive Passive:*

φοβούμεθα μὴ πάντα τῷ Κροίσῳ καλῶς οὐ **βεβουλευμένα ᾖ.**
*We are afraid that everything **has** not **been** well **planned** by Croesus.*

### e. *Perfect Optative Middle (Deponent):*

ἤρετο εἰ ἡ ναῦς εἰς τὸν λιμένα ἤδη **ἀφῖγμένη εἴη.**
*He asked whether the ship **had** already **arrived** at the harbor.*

### f. *Perfect Optative Passive:*

ἤρετο εἰ πάντα τῷ Κροίσῳ ἤδη **βεβουλευμένα εἴη.**
*He asked whether everything **had** already **been planned** by Croesus.*

**g. Perfect Imperative:**

Very rare in either middle or passive.

μέμνησο. *Remember!*  μὴ **πεφόβησθε**. *Don't be afraid!*

The perfect imperative is so rare that forms are not given in the chart below.

**h. Perfect Infinitive Middle (Deponent):**

λέγει τὴν ναῦν εἰς τὸν λιμένα ἤδη **ἀφῖχθαι**.

*He says that the ship **has** already **arrived** at the harbor.*

**i. Perfect Infinitive Passive:**

ἔφη πάντα τῷ Κροίσῳ ἤδη **βεβουλεῦσθαι**.

*He said that everything **had** already **been planned** by Croesus.*

## 4. The Perfect Tense: Middle/Passive Forms

To form the perfect middle/passive of λύω, reduplicate the stem (i.e., put the first consonant + ε before the stem, which appears here with short υ), and add the primary middle/passive endings with no thematic vowel (ο or ε) between the stem and the ending.

| **Indicative** | **Infinitive** | **Participle** |
|---|---|---|
| λέ-λυ-μαι | λε-λύ-σθαι | λε-λυ-μένος, -η, -ον |
| λέ-λυ-σαι | | |
| λέ-λυ-ται | | |
| λε-λύ-μεθα | | |
| λέ-λυ-σθε | | |
| λέ-λυ-νται | | |

| **Subjunctive** | **Optative** |
|---|---|
| λελυμένος ὦ | λελυμένος εἴην |
| λελυμένος ᾖς | λελυμένος εἴης |
| λελυμένος ᾖ | λελυμένος εἴη |
| λελυμένοι ὦμεν | λελυμένοι εἶμεν/εἴημεν |
| λελυμένοι ἦτε | λελυμένοι εἶτε/εἴητε |
| λελυμένοι ὦσι(ν) | λελυμένοι εἶεν/εἴησαν |

The above forms may be either middle or passive in sense, according to the context, e.g., λέλυμαι may mean either *I have ransomed* (middle sense) or *I have been loosed* (passive sense).

Note:

1. There is no thematic vowel (ο/ε) between the stem and the ending.
2. The reduplication is retained in all forms.
3. The accents of the infinitive and participle are always on the next to the last syllable.
4. The perfect middle/passive subjunctive and optative are per-

iphrastic, that is, they are formed from the perfect middle/passive participle plus the subjunctive and optative of the verb εἰμί.

Note that contract verbs lengthen the stem vowel, e.g.:

φιλέ-ω > πεφίλη-μαι     (For φιλε- reduplicating to πεφιλε-, see
τῑμά-ω > τετίμη-μαι     Grammar 8, page 196.)
δηλό-ω > δεδήλω-μαι

## 5. The Pluperfect Tense: Indicative Only

Look at these examples from the stories:

ἐν μὲν γὰρ ταῖς ξυνθήκαις **εἴρητο** ὅτι χρὴ δίκᾱς μὲν διαφορῶν ἀλλήλοις διδόναι καὶ δέχεσθαι, ἔχειν δὲ ἑκατέρους ἃ ἔχομεν. (21β:5–7, with pluperfect of εἴρω, *I say;* for principal parts, see page 195)
*For in the treaty **it had been stated** that (we) must give and accept arbitration of our differences, and that each side should keep what we hold.*

ἡ γὰρ Οἰνόη οὖσα ἐν μεθορίοις τῆς Ἀττικῆς καὶ Βοιωτίᾱς, **ἐτετείχιστο**. (23α:4–5)
*For Ocnoe, being on the borders of Attica and Boeotia, **had been fortified**.*

καὶ γὰρ πρὸς τούτους αὐτῷ **ἐπεποίητο** συμμαχίη. (27α:47)
*For an alliance **had been made** by him with them, too.*

The pluperfect records a state that existed in the past as the result of an action completed at some time more remote: ἐλελύμην = *I was free* (at some time in the past) *as a consequence of having been freed* (at some earlier time) = *I had been freed = I was free.* Only indicative forms appear in the pluperfect tense; there are no pluperfect subjunctives, optatives, imperatives, infinitives, or participles.

## 6. The Pluperfect Tense: Middle/Passive Forms

To form the pluperfect middle/passive indicative of λύω, augment the reduplicated stem and add the secondary middle/passive endings with no thematic vowels. Again, the same forms serve as middle or passive.

### Indicative

ἐ-λε-λύ-μην
ἐ-λέ-λυ-σο
ἐ-λέ-λυ-το
ἐ-λε-λύ-μεθα
ἐ-λέ-λυ-σθε
ἐ-λέ-λυ-ντο

Contract verbs:

φιλέω > ἐπεφιλήμην

τῑμάω > ἐτετῑμήμην

δηλόω > ἐδεδηλώμην

The augment here indicates past time. The perfect tense describes an action as completed as of the present: *I have come;* the pluperfect describes an action as completed as of some time in the past: *I had come.*

Verbs that augment in the perfect do not add an additional augment for the pluperfect, thus, στερέω, *I deprive; I bereave;* perfect middle/passive, ἐστέρημαι, pluperfect middle/passive, ἐστερήμην.

## 7.  The Dative of Agent with Perfect and Pluperfect Passives

Note that with perfect and pluperfect passive verbs the dative case without a preposition is usually used to designate the person or agent by whom the action is carried out, instead of the preposition ὑπό with the genitive case, as is usual with passive verbs in other tenses, e.g.:

ἔργα μεγάλα τὰ μὲν **τοῖς Ἕλλησι**, τὰ δὲ **τοῖς βαρβάροις** εἴργασται.

*Great deeds <u>have been done</u>, some **by the Greeks**, others **by the barbarians**.*

Compare 24 tail:2–3, where the aorist passive and ὑπό + gen. is used.

### Exercise 27 α

*Make four photocopies of the Verb Chart for the perfect and pluperfect tenses on page 276 and fill in the forms of πορεύομαι (middle voice) and of φιλέω, τῑμάω, and δηλόω (middle/passive).  Keep these sheets for reference.*

### Exercise 27 β

*Change the following present forms to the corresponding perfect forms:*

| | | | |
|---|---|---|---|
| 1. λῡ́ονται | 3. ποιεῖται | 5. παιδευόμεθα | 7. αἱρούμενος |
| 2. λῡόμενος | 4. νῑκᾶσθαι | 6. οἰκεῖσθαι | 8. δίδοται [δο-] |

### Exercise 27 γ

*Change the following present forms to the corresponding pluperfect forms:*

| | | |
|---|---|---|
| 1. λῡ́εται | 3. νῑκᾶται | 5. βουλεύεται |
| 2. ποιοῦνται | 4. αἱρεῖται | 6. ἀγγέλλεται |

### Exercise 27 δ

*Read aloud and translate into English (remember that the pluperfect is a secondary tense and that dependent subjunctives may be changed to optatives; see Chapter 25, Grammar 3a, page 144):*

1. ὁ αὐτουργὸς εἰς τὸν ἀγρὸν ἀφῑγμένος τοὺς βοῦς ἔζευξεν.
2. τῶν βοῶν ἐζευγμένων τὸν ἀγρὸν ἤροσεν (*plowed*).
3. τοῦ ἔργου πεπαυμένος οἴκαδε ἐπανιέναι ἔμελλεν.
4. οἱ βόες τῷ δούλῳ λελυμένοι ἐκ τοῦ ἀγροῦ ἠλαύνοντο.
5. ὁ αὐτουργὸς αὐτὸς ὕπνῳ νενῑκημένος πρὸς τῇ ὁδῷ ἐκάθευδεν.
6. τῷ Κροίσῳ ἐβεβούλευτο γιγνώσκειν τί μαντεῖον εἴη ἄριστον.
7. οἱ ἄγγελοι τῇ Πῡθίᾳ κεχρημένοι εἰς Σάρδῑς ἀπῆλθον.
8. ὁ θεὸς ὁ ἐν Δελφοῖς τῷ Κροίσῳ τετίμηται.
9. συμμαχίᾱ τοῖς Λῡδοῖς ἐπεποίητο πρὸς τὸν Ἄμασιν.
10. ὁ Κροῖσος τῷ μαντείῳ ἐπηρμένος (from ἐπαίρω, *I raise; I induce*) ἐπὶ τὸν Κῦρον στρατεύεσθαι ἔμελλεν.

### Exercise 27 ε

*Translate into Greek (note that the perfect is a primary tense and that dependent subjunctives do not change to optatives; see Chapter 25, Grammar 3a, page 144):*

1. Freed (*use* λύω) by (their) master, the slaves were all delighted.
2. We have journeyed to the city to see the dances.
3. Have you used the plow that I gave you?
4. Many ships had been built (made) by the Athenians.
5. The general told us what had been planned (= the having been planned things; *use neuter plural definite article + perfect passive participle*).

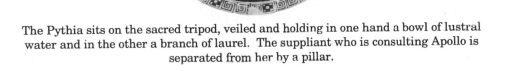

The Pythia sits on the sacred tripod, veiled and holding in one hand a bowl of lustral water and in the other a branch of laurel. The suppliant who is consulting Apollo is separated from her by a pillar.

The Charioteer of Delphi

# Signs, Dreams, and Oracles

In a world that was dangerous and controlled by gods who were arbitrary, the Greeks needed means of ascertaining the will of the gods. There were several ways of trying to do this. First, the gods were thought to send signs to men, particularly in the behavior of birds and in dreams. Interpretation of these signs was open to anyone, but throughout Greek history there were always prophets who were especially gifted in this sphere. In the second book of the *Odyssey* Telemachus, Odysseus's son, addressed an assembly of the people of Ithaca, complaining of the behavior of Penelope's suitors:

Zeus sent two eagles from the top of the mountain, which flew down close to each other on the breath of the wind. And when they reached the middle of the meeting place, they wheeled around and flapped their wings. They went for the heads of all who were there, and they foreboded death, tearing with their talons at their cheeks and necks; then they flew off on the right over the houses and city. The people were amazed at the birds when they saw them and wondered in their hearts what was destined to happen. The old hero Halitherses spoke to them, for he excelled all his generation in understanding birds and expounding omens: "Listen to me, men of Ithaca, I speak particularly to the suitors. Great trouble is rolling toward you, for Odysseus will not be long away. . . ." (*Odyssey* 2.146–164)

Such prophets were not always believed; on this occasion the leader of the suitors, Eurymachus, replied:

> "Old man, go home and prophesy to your children, in case they get into trouble. I can make a much better prophecy on this than you; lots of birds fly under the rays of the sun and not all bring omens: Odysseus died far away, and you should have died with him." (*Odyssey* 2.178–184)

Dreams were also thought to be sent by the gods. In the first book of the *Iliad*, when the Greeks are struck by plague, Achilles called a meeting and said: "Let us consult a prophet (μάντις) or a priest (ἱερεύς) or an interpreter of dreams (for dreams also come from Zeus), who may tell us why Apollo is so angry with us" (*Iliad* 1.62–64). In the story of Adrastus, Croesus was warned by a dream, which revealed the truth of the disaster that was going to strike his son.

If either states or individuals were in some serious dilemma and needed to know what to do, they had recourse to oracles. There were many oracles in Greece, but by far the most prestigious and wealthy at this time was Apollo's oracle at Delphi. It was consulted by inquirers from all over the Greek world and beyond. Apollo, god of light, music, poetry, healing, and prophecy, was a comparative latecomer to the Greek pantheon. He seems to have arrived at Delphi early in the eighth century, and his oracle rapidly acquired a high reputation. Grateful states and individuals showered gifts upon it, and by the sixth century the sanctuary was an elaborate complex. The Sacred Way wound up the hill toward the great temple. On either side of the way stood treasuries (little temples in which states stored their offerings) and dedications of statues and tripods. Above the temple was the theater, and high above this again was the stadium. Every four years games second in importance only to those of Olympia were held in honor of Apollo. The wealth and beauty of the sanctuary in its remote and awe-inspiring site on the slopes of the foothills of Mount Parnassus must have made a deep impression on all visitors.

There were full-time priests or prophets (προφῆται) at Delphi. The priestess (ἡ Πῡθία) was chosen from an ordinary family, a woman past middle age and of blameless life. She received no special training, since, when she prophesied, she was simply the mouthpiece of Apollo. The procedure for consulting the oracle was elaborate. Consultations were held only nine times a year. There were consequently always many state embassies and individuals waiting for their turn. At dawn the Pythia purified herself in the water of the Castalian spring. The priest then prepared to sacrifice a goat and tested the omens by sprinkling it with water. If the omens were satisfactory, the day was declared auspicious, and the Pythia was admitted to the inner sanctuary of the temple. There she drank sacred water and may have chewed laurel leaves (the laurel was sacred to Apollo) before ascending the sacred tripod.

Inquirers purified themselves in the water of Castalia and offered a sacred cake on the altar outside the temple. On entering the temple they sacrificed a goat on the inner hearth where the eternal fire burned. They were then conducted to the inner sanctuary. They were told "to think holy thoughts and speak well-omened words." The priest put the inquirer's question to the Pythia and brought back the answer, usually in verse form. The Greeks believed that when the Pythia sat on the sacred tripod, after completing the rituals, she was possessed by Apollo and "filled with god" (ἔνθεος). Descriptions certainly suggest that she fell into some kind of trance, in which her voice changed, like modern spiritualist mediums.

It is probably true to say that the vast majority of Herodotus's contemporaries believed firmly in the Delphic oracle and that in a serious crisis they would choose to consult it, if they were rich enough to afford the procedure. Individuals went for advice on religious questions, cult and pollution, and on practical questions, "Should I marry?" "Should I go abroad?" These individuals must have far outnumbered the deputations from the cities, but it is of the latter that we hear most in our sources. One of the most famous was the deputation sent by the Athenians when Xerxes' invasion was threatening. The moment the deputies had taken their seat in the inner sanctuary, before their question had been put, the Pythia exclaimed: "Unhappy men, why do you sit here? Leave your homes and flee to the ends of the earth. . . . For fire and war strike you down. . . . Be gone from my shrine, and steep your hearts in woe." The deputies were aghast, but, on the advice of a prominent Delphian, they went for a second consultation as suppliants and said: "Lord, give us a better answer about our country, respecting our suppliant branches." The second reply was ambiguous:

> "Pallas Athena cannot propitiate Olympian Zeus, though she prays to him with many words and all her skill. All else will be taken, . . . but far-seeing Zeus grants to Athena that only the wooden wall will be unsacked. Do not wait for the host of cavalry and infantry that come from the mainland but turn your backs and flee; yet some day you will face them. O divine Salamis, you will destroy the sons of women, when the grain is scattered or gathered in." (Herodotus 7.140–141)

The answer was brought back to Athens, and a debate followed in which its meaning was discussed. Some of the older men said that the wooden wall meant the wall with which the Acropolis had once been fortified. Others said it meant their ships, and this view prevailed when Themistocles argued that the last two lines foretold the death not of Athenians but of their enemies, for Salamis is called "divine Salamis." If the oracle foretold their own destruction, it would have said "unhappy Salamis." This story illustrates the difficulty of interpreting some of Apollo's oracles correctly and the seriousness with which the oracles were treated. It is impossible for us to distinguish which oracles quoted by Herodotus are genuine and which forged later to suit past events (the first oracle given the Athenians in the case above certainly rings true). In any case the prestige of Delphi survived, and states and individuals consulted Apollo throughout Greek history until the oracle was closed in A.D. 390 by a Roman emperor in the name of Christianity.

# New Testament Greek

### John 20.11–18
### Jesus, Risen from the Dead, Appears to Mary Magdalene

Μαρία δὲ εἱστήκει πρὸς τῷ μνημείῳ ἔξω κλαίουσα. ὡς οὖν ἔκλαιεν παρέκυψεν εἰς τὸ μνημεῖον καὶ θεωρεῖ δύο ἀγγέλους ἐν λευκοῖς καθεζομένους, ἕνα πρὸς τῇ κεφαλῇ καὶ ἕνα πρὸς τοῖς ποσίν, ὅπου ἔκειτο τὸ σῶμα τοῦ Ἰησοῦ. καὶ λέγουσιν αὐτῇ ἐκεῖνοι, "γύναι, τί κλαίεις;" λέγει αὐτοῖς ὅτι "ἦραν τὸν κύριόν μου, καὶ οὐκ οἶδα ποῦ ἔθηκαν αὐτόν." ταῦτα εἰποῦσα ἐστράφη εἰς τὰ ὀπίσω καὶ θεωρεῖ τὸν Ἰησοῦν ἑστῶτα καὶ οὐκ ᾔδει ὅτι Ἰησοῦς ἐστιν. λέγει αὐτῇ Ἰησοῦς, "γύναι, τί κλαίεις; τίνα ζητεῖς;" ἐκείνη δοκοῦσα ὅτι ὁ κηπουρός ἐστιν λέγει αὐτῷ, "κύριε, εἰ σὺ ἐβάστασας αὐτόν, εἰπέ μοι ποῦ ἔθηκας αὐτόν, κἀγὼ αὐτὸν ἀρῶ." λέγει αὐτῇ Ἰησοῦς, "Μαριάμ." στραφεῖσα ἐκείνη λέγει αὐτῷ Ἑβραϊστί, "'Ραββουνι" (ὃ λέγεται Διδάσκαλε). λέγει αὐτῇ Ἰησοῦς, "μή μου ἅπτου, οὔπω γὰρ ἀναβέβηκα πρὸς τὸν πατέρα· πορεύου δὲ πρὸς τοὺς ἀδελφούς μου καὶ εἰπὲ αὐτοῖς, "ἀναβαίνω πρὸς τὸν πατέρα μου καὶ πατέρα ὑμῶν καὶ θεόν μου καὶ θεὸν ὑμῶν." ἔρχεται Μαριὰμ ἡ Μαγδαληνὴ ἀγγέλλουσα τοῖς μαθηταῖς ὅτι "ἑώρακα τὸν κύριον," καὶ ταῦτα εἶπεν αὐτῇ.

[εἱστήκει, pluperfect, *was standing*  μνημείῳ, *tomb*  κλαίουσα, *weeping* παρέκυψεν, *she stooped to look*  ἀγγέλους, *angels*  λευκοῖς, *white (garments)* τοῖς ποσίν (from πούς, ποδός), *the feet*  ἐστράφη, *she turned*  εἰς τὰ ὀπίσω, *around* (lit., *to the things in back*)  ἑστῶτα, perfect participle, *standing*  οὐκ ᾔδει (see οἶδα), *she was not aware* (*was not knowing*)  ὁ κηπουρός, *the gardener*  ἐβά- στασας (from βαστάζω), *you took away*  κἀγὼ = καὶ ἐγώ  Ἑβραϊστί, *in Hebrew* 'Ραββουνι = ῥαββί, *rabbi, teacher, master*  λέγεται, *is said, means*  ἅπτου (from ἅπτομαι) + gen., *touch*  οὔπω, *not yet*  ἀναβέβηκα, *I have gone up*  ἑώρακα (perfect of ὁράω), *I have seen*]

The stadium at Delphi

# Ο ΚΡΟΙΣΟΣ ΕΠΙ ΤΟΝ ΚΥΡΟΝ ΣΤΡΑΤΕΥΕΤΑΙ (β)

## VOCABULARY

*Verbs*

**ἀναστρέφω**, *I turn around*

**ἀνέχομαι** [= ἀνα- + ἔχομαι], imperfect, ἠνειχόμην (double augment), **ἀνέξομαι**, [σχ-] **ἠνεσχόμην**, *I endure; I am patient*

**ἱππεύω, ἱππεύσω, ἵππευσα**, active or middle, *I am a horseman; I ride a horse*

**κτείνω**, usually compounded with ἀπο- in Attic prose, [κτενε-] **κτενῶ**, [κτειν-] **ἔκτεινα**, [κτον-] **ἔκτονα**, *I kill*

**προστάττω**, *I command*

**φείδομαι, φείσομαι, ἐφεισάμην** + gen., *I spare*

*Nouns*

**τὸ ἔθνος, τοῦ ἔθνους**, *tribe; people*

**τὸ ἱππικόν, τοῦ ἱππικοῦ**, *cavalry*

**ὁ ἵππος, τοῦ ἵππου**, *horse*

**ἡ ἵππος, τῆς ἵππου**, *cavalry*

**ἡ κάμηλος, τῆς καμήλου**, *camel*

**ὁ πεζός, τοῦ πεζοῦ**, *infantry*

*Adjectives*

**ἄχρηστος, -ον**, *useless*

**δειλός, -ή, -όν**, *cowardly*

*Preposition and Adverb*

**ὄπισθε(ν)**, adv. or prep. + gen., *behind*

**ὀπίσω**, *backward*

*Expression*

**κατὰ τάχος**, *quickly*

Κῦρος δὲ αὐτίκα ἀπελαύνοντος Κροίσου μετὰ τὴν μάχην τὴν γενομένην ἐν τῇ Πτερίῃ, ἐπιστάμενος ὡς ἀπελάσᾱς μέλλοι Κροῖσος διασκεδᾶν τὸν στρατόν, ἐβουλεύσατο ἐλαύνειν ὡς τάχιστα δύναιτο ἐπὶ τᾱς Σάρδῑς. ὡς δέ οἱ ταῦτα ἔδοξε, καὶ ἐποίεε κατὰ τάχος· ἐλάσᾱς γὰρ τὸν στρατὸν ἐς τὴν Λῡδίην αὐτὸς ἄγγελος ἦλθε Κροίσῳ. 5 ἐνταῦθα Κροῖσος ἐς ἀπορίην πολλὴν ἀφῑγμένος, ὅμως τοὺς Λῡδοὺς ἐξῆγε ἐς μάχην. ἦν δὲ τοῦτον τὸν χρόνον ἔθνος οὐδὲν ἐν τῇ Ἀσίῃ οὔτε ἀνδρειότερον οὔτε ἀλκιμώτερον τοῦ Λῡδίου. ἡ δὲ μάχη αὐτῶν ἦν ἀφ' ἵππων καὶ αὐτοὶ ἦσαν ἱππεύεσθαι ἀγαθοί.

[**ἀπελαύνοντος**, *marching away*   **διασκεδᾶν** (from διασκεδάννῡμι), *to disperse*   **ἐλαύνειν**, *to march*   **καὶ ἐποίεε**, *he also began to do* (it)   **ἀλκιμώτερον**, *more stalwart*]

ἐς δὲ τὸ πεδίον συνελθόντων αὐτῶν τὸ πρὸ τοῦ ἄστεως, ὁ Κῦρος 10 ὡς εἶδε τοὺς Λῡδοὺς ἐς μάχην τασσομένους, φοβούμενος τὴν ἵππον,

ἐποίησε τοιόνδε· πάσας τὰς καμήλους, αἳ τόν τε σῖτον ἔφερον καὶ τὰ
σκεύεα, προσέταξε πρὸ τῆς ἄλλης στρατιῆς προϊέναι πρὸς τὴν
Κροίσου ἵππον, ταῖς δὲ καμήλοις ἕπεσθαι τὸν πεζὸν ἐκέλευε. ὄπισθε
δὲ τοῦ πεζοῦ ἔταξε τὴν πᾶσαν ἵππον. ὡς δὲ πάντες τεταγμένοι ἦσαν,    15
παρήνεσε αὐτοῖς τῶν μὲν ἄλλων Λυδῶν μὴ φειδομένοις κτείνειν
πάντας, Κροῖσον δὲ αὐτὸν μὴ κτείνειν. τὰς δὲ καμήλους ἔταξε
ἀντίον τῆς ἵππου τῶνδε εἵνεκα· κάμηλον γὰρ ἵππος φοβεῖται καὶ οὐκ
ἀνέχεται οὔτε τὴν ἰδέην αὐτῆς ὁρῶν οὔτε τὴν ὀσμὴν ὀσφραινόμενος.
ταῦτα οὖν ἐσεσόφιστο ἵνα τῷ Κροίσῳ ἄχρηστον ᾖ τὸ ἱππικόν. ὡς δὲ    20
καὶ συνῆσαν ἐς τὴν μάχην, ἐνταῦθα ὡς τάχιστα ὤσφροντο τῶν
καμήλων οἱ ἵπποι καὶ εἶδον αὐτάς, ὀπίσω ἀνέστρεφον, διέφθαρτό τε
τῷ Κροίσῳ ἡ ἐλπίς.

[τὴν ἵππον, i.e., of Croesus   σκεύεα, *baggage*   τῆς ἄλλης στρατιῆς, *the rest of
his army*   ἀντίον + gen., *opposite*   τὴν ἰδέην, *the form, appearance*   τὴν ὀσμὴν
ὀσφραινόμενος, *smelling its smell*   ἐσεσόφιστο (pluperfect of σοφίζομαι), *he had
devised*   ὡς τάχιστα, *as soon as*   ὤσφροντο (from ὀσφραίνομαι) + gen., *they caught
the scent of, smelled*]

οὐ μέντοι οἵ γε Λυδοὶ δειλοὶ ἦσαν. ἀλλ᾽ ὡς ἔμαθον τὸ γιγνόμενον,
ἀποθορόντες ἀπὸ τῶν ἵππων πεζοὶ τοῖς Πέρσῃσι συνέβαλλον. χρόνῳ    25
δὲ πεσόντων ἀμφοτέρων πολλῶν, ἐτράποντο οἱ Λυδοὶ καὶ
κατειληθέντες ἐς τὸ τεῖχος ἐπολιορκέοντο ὑπὸ τῶν Περσέων.

[ἀποθορόντες (from ἀποθρῴσκω), *having leaped off*   ἐτράποντο (thematic aorist
middle of τρέπω), *turned tail*   κατειληθέντες (from κατειλέω), *cooped up*]

—adapted from Herodotus 1.79–80

## PRINCIPAL PARTS: Three Verbs of Saying

*I say; I tell; I speak:*

| | | | | | |
|---|---|---|---|---|---|
| λέγω | λέξω | ἔλεξα | | λέλεγμαι | ἐλέχθην |
| ἔπω* | | εἶπον | | | |
| εἴρω** | [ἐρε-] ἐρῶ | | [ῥη-] εἴρηκα | εἴρημαι | ἐρρήθην |

N.B. The boldface forms are used in Attic.

*very rare; not Attic
**Homeric

## WORD BUILDING

*If you know the meaning of each part of a compound word, you can usually deduce the meaning of the word as a whole. Give the meaning of each part of the following compound words and then the meaning of the whole:*

Compound words formed by prefixing an adverb or ἀ-privative:

1. εὐγενής, -ές        3. εὐτυχής, -ές        5. ἀμαθής, -ές
2. δυσγενής, -ές       4. ἀτυχής, -ές         6. ἀείμνηστος, -ον

Note that compound adjectives have the same form for masculine and feminine.

Compound words formed by combining the stem of an adjective with another word:

1. φιλάνθρωπος, -ον    3. φιλότῑμος, -ον      5. μεγαλόψῡχος, -ον
2. φιλόσοφος, -ον      4. ὀλιγοχρόνιος, -ον   6. ὁ ψευδόμαντις

Compound words formed by combining the stem of a noun with another word:

1. ἡ ναυμαχίᾱ          3. ἡ δημοκρατίᾱ       5. ὁ παιδαγωγός
2. ὁ ναυβάτης          4. θαλαττοκρατέω

## GRAMMAR

### 8. Perfect Reduplication and Augment

Most verbs form their perfect and pluperfect by reduplication or augment as described in Grammar 1 above, but note the following:

a. If the verb starts with one of the aspirated stops, φ (labial), θ (dental), or χ (velar), the reduplication uses the unaspirated equivalents of these consonants, namely, π, τ, and κ, e.g.:

   φιλέω > πεφίλημαι
   θάπτω > τέθαμμαι
   χράομαι > κέχρημαι

b. If the verb starts with a vowel or double consonant (ζ, ξ, or ψ), it does not reduplicate but augments, e.g.:

   ἀγγέλλω > ἤγγελμαι
   ἀφικνέομαι [ἱκ-] > ἀφῖγμαι
   οἰκέω > ᾤκημαι
   ζητέω > ἐζήτημαι
   ξενίζω > ἐξένισμαι
   ψεύδομαι > ἔψευσμαι

The augment, just as the reduplication, is retained in all forms, e.g.: ἠγγελμένος, ᾠκῆσθαι, ἐψευσμένος.

c. If the verb starts with two consonants, in most cases the first is reduplicated, e.g.:

γράφω > γέγραμμαι

βλάπτω > βέβλαμμαι

In some combinations, there is augment instead of reduplication, e.g.:

σκ-  σκοπέω [σκεπ-] > ἔσκεμμαι

γν-  γιγνώσκω [γνω-] > ἔγνωσμαι

σπ-  σπεύδω > ἔσπευσμαι

στ-  στερέω > ἐστέρημαι

Κροῖσος . . . ἐν πένθει μεγάλῳ ἐκάθητο τοῦ παιδὸς **ἐστερημένος**. (27α:1–2)

*Croesus was sitting in great grief, **bereft** of his son.*

d. For Attic reduplication, see the list of principal parts on page 235.

## 9. Perfect and Pluperfect Middle/Passive of Verbs with Stems Ending in Consonants

When the stem of the verb ends in a consonant, sound and spelling changes take place. The 3rd person plural of the indicative and all the subjunctives and optatives are periphrastic and consist of a perfect middle/passive participle and a form of the verb "to be." The extremely rare perfect imperative is not given in the charts below. Be sure you are able to identify the markers for voice, mood, person, and number of these forms when you see them.

| Labial Stems<br>(-β, -π, -φ) | Dental Stems<br>(-δ, -θ, -τ and ζ) | Velar Stems<br>(-γ, -κ, -χ) |
|---|---|---|
| λείπω<br>**Stem:** λειπ- | πείθω<br>**Stem:** πειθ- | δέχομαι<br>**Stem:** δεκ- |

**Perfect**

Indicative

| | | |
|---|---|---|
| λέλειμμαι | πέπεισμαι | δέδεγμαι |
| λέλειψαι | πέπεισαι | δέδεξαι |
| λέλειπται | πέπεισται | δέδεκται |
| λελείμμεθα | πεπείσμεθα | δεδέγμεθα |
| λέλειφθε | πέπεισθε | δέδεχθε |
| λελειμμένοι εἰσί(ν) | πεπεισμένοι εἰσί(ν) | δεδεγμένοι εἰσί(ν) |

Subjunctive

| | | |
|---|---|---|
| λελειμμένος ὦ<br>etc. | πεπεισμένος ὦ<br>etc. | δεδεγμένος ὦ<br>etc. |

### Optative

| | | |
|---|---|---|
| λελειμμένος εἴην | πεπεισμένος εἴην | δεδεγμένος εἴην |
| etc. | etc. | etc. |

### Infinitive

| | | |
|---|---|---|
| λελεῖφθαι | πεπεῖσθαι | δεδέχθαι |

### Participle

| | | |
|---|---|---|
| λελειμμένος, -η, -ον | πεπεισμένος, -η, -ον | δεδεγμένος, -η, -ον |

## Pluperfect

### Indicative

| | | |
|---|---|---|
| ἐλελείμμην | ἐπεπείσμην | ἐδεδέγμην |
| ἐλέλειψο | ἐπέπεισο | ἐδέδεξο |
| ἐλέλειπτο | ἐπέπειστο | ἐδέδεκτο |
| ἐλελείμμεθα | ἐπεπείσμεθα | ἐδεδέγμεθα |
| ἐλέλειφθε | ἐπέπεισθε | ἐδέδεχθε |
| λελειμμένοι ἦσαν | πεπεισμένοι ἦσαν | δεδεγμένοι ἦσαν |

| **Liquid Stems** | **Nasal Stems** | |
|---|---|---|
| (-λ, -ρ) | (-μ, -ν) | |
| ἀγγέλλω | φαίνω | κρίνω |
| **Stem:** ἄγγελ- | **Stem:** φαν- (ν retained) | **Stem:** κρι- (ν dropped) |

## Perfect

### Indicative

| | | |
|---|---|---|
| ἤγγελμαι | πέφασμαι | κέκριμαι |
| ἤγγελσαι | πεφασμένος εἶ* | κέκρισαι |
| ἤγγελται | πέφανται | κέκριται |
| ἠγγέλμεθα | πεφάσμεθα | κεκρίμεθα |
| ἤγγελθε | πέφανθε | κέκρισθε |
| ἠγγελμένοι εἰσί(ν) | πεφασμένοι εἰσί(ν) | κεκριμένοι εἰσί(ν) |

### Subjunctive

| | | |
|---|---|---|
| ἠγγελμένος ὦ | πεφασμένος ὦ | κεκριμένος ὦ |
| etc. | etc. | etc. |

### Optative

| | | |
|---|---|---|
| ἠγγελμένος εἴην | πεφασμένος εἴην | κεκριμένος εἴην |
| etc. | etc. | etc. |
| | *hypothetical form | |

Infinitive

| | | |
|---|---|---|
| ἠγγέλθαι | πεφάνθαι | κεκρίθαι |

Participle

| | | |
|---|---|---|
| ἠγγελμένος, -η, -ον | πεφασμένος -η, -ον | κεκριμένος -η, -ον |

**Pluperfect**

Indicative

| | | |
|---|---|---|
| ἠγγέλμην | ἐπεφάσμην | ἐκεκρίμην |
| ἤγγελσο | πεφασμένος ἦσθα* | ἐκέκρισο |
| ἤγγελτο | ἐπέφαντο | ἐκέκριτο |
| ἠγγέλμεθα | ἐπεφάσμεθα | ἐκεκρίμεθα |
| ἤγγελθε | ἐπέφανθε | ἐκέκρισθε |
| ἠγγελμένοι ἦσαν | πεφασμένοι ἦσαν | κεκριμένοι ἦσαν |

*hypothetical form

## Exercise 27 ζ

*Locate four perfect or pluperfect verb forms in the reading above, translate the sentences in which they occur, identify each element of each verb form, and explain why each form is used in its context.*

## Exercise 27 η

*Make two photocopies of the Verb Chart for the perfect and pluperfect tenses on page 276 and fill in the forms of λαμβάνω in the middle/passive (εἴλημμαι, perfect stem, ληβ-) on one chart and the forms of πράττω in the middle/passive (πέπρᾱγμαι, perfect stem, πρᾱκ-) on the other. Keep these charts for reference.*

## Exercise 27 θ

*Change the following present forms to the corresponding perfect forms:*

| | | |
|---|---|---|
| 1. δέχονται | 5. γράφεται | 9. νομίζεται |
| 2. ἀγγελλόμενα | 6. λείπεσθε | 10. ψεύδεσθε |
| 3. ἀφικνεῖσθαι | 7. πράττονται | 11. πείθομαι |
| 4. διωκόμενοι | 8. ἀγγέλλεται | 12. πέμπονται |

## Exercise 27 ι

*Change the following present forms to the corresponding pluperfect forms:*

| | | |
|---|---|---|
| 1. πέμπεσθε | 3. πείθῃ | 5. ἀφικνεῖται |
| 2. δέχονται | 4. ἄγομαι | 6. παρασκευάζομαι |

## Exercise 27 κ

*Read aloud and translate into English:*

1. συμμαχίᾳ πρὸς τοὺς Βαβυλωνίους ἐπεποίητο τῷ Κροίσῳ.
2. οἱ ὁπλῖται ἐν τῷ πεδίῳ τεταγμένοι τοὺς πολεμίους ἔμενον.
3. πάντα τῷ στρατηγῷ ἤδη ἐβεβούλευτο.
4. ὁ Κροῖσος τῷ χρησμῷ ἐπέπειστο ἐς τὴν τοῦ Κύρου ἀρχὴν εἰσβαλεῖν.
5. οἱ Λῡδοὶ εἰς μάχην ἐξηγμένοι ἦσαν ἵνα τοὺς πολεμίους ἀμύνοιεν.
6. αἱ πύλαι ἀνεῳγμέναι εἰσίν· ἐσέλθωμεν οὖν ταχέως.
7. ἆρα πέπεισαι τῷ ἰᾱτρῷ τὸν παῖδα ἐς Ἐπίδαυρον κομίζειν;
8. ἆρα συνῑῆς τὰ γεγραμμένα; ἐγὼ γὰρ δύναμαι αὐτὰ συνῑέναι.
9. ὁ ἔμπορος οὐκ ἔφη τὸ ἀργύριον δεδέχθαι.
10. οἱ παῖδες οἱ ἐν τῷ ἄστει τοῖς πατράσι λελειμμένοι ἐς διδασκάλων καθ᾽ ἡμέρᾱν ἐφοίτων.

## Exercise 27 λ

*Translate into Greek:*

1. The children, left at home, were distressed.
2. The ambassadors had already arrived at the gates.
3. The messenger said that the king had been persuaded to spare (**φείδεσθαι** + *gen.*) the old man.
4. We have been sent to tell (*use* **ὡς** + *future participle*) you that the ship has already arrived at the harbor.
5. Have you received the money that I sent you?

# Η ΛΑΒΔΑ ΣΩΙΖΕΙ ΤΟ ΠΑΙΔΙΟΝ

*Read the following passages (adapted from Herodotus 5.92) and answer the comprehension questions:*

The following story from Herodotus is concerned with events a hundred years before the time of Croesus. In the seventh century a family called the Bacchiadae ruled Corinth. They received an oracle that the child born to Labda, wife of Eetion, would overthrow them. They decided to kill the child as soon as it was born. The child survived and became tyrant of Corinth about 650 B.C.

ὡς δὲ ἔτεκε ἡ Λάβδα, οἱ Βακχιάδαι πέμπουσι δέκα ἄνδρας ἐς τὸν δῆμον ἐν ᾧ ᾤκεε ὁ Ἠετίων, ὡς ἀποκτενέοντας τὸ παιδίον. ἀφικόμενοι δὲ οὗτοι καὶ παρελθόντες ἐς τὴν αὐλήν, τὴν Λάβδαν ᾔτεον τὸ παιδίον. ἡ δὲ οὐκ ἐπισταμένη τί ἦλθον καὶ δοκέουσα αὐτοὺς φίλους εἶναι τοῦ ἀνδρός, φέρουσα τὸ παιδίον ἔδωκε αὐτῶν ἑνί. τοῖσι δὲ ἐβεβούλευτο ἐν τῇ ὁδῷ τὸν πρῶτον αὐτῶν λαβόντα τὸ παιδίον 5 ἀποκτεῖναι. ἐπεὶ οὖν Λάβδα φέρουσα ἔδωκε, τὸ παιδίον θείῃ τύχῃ προσεγέλασε τὸν λαβόντα τῶν ἀνδρῶν· ὁ δὲ οἰκτίρας οὐκ ἐδύνατο αὐτὸ ἀποκτεῖναι, ἀλλὰ τῷ δευτέρῳ παρέδωκεν, ὁ δὲ τῷ τρίτῳ· οὕτω τε διεξῆλθε διὰ πάντων παραδιδόμενον, οὐδενὸς βουλομένου τὸ ἔργον ἐργάσασθαι.

[ἔτεκε (from τίκτω), *gave birth*    ἡ Λάβδα, *Labda*    οἱ Βακχιάδαι, *the Bacchiadae*  ὁ Ἠετίων, *Eetion*    τὸ παιδίον, *the baby*    τὴν αὐλήν, *the courtyard*    τοῖσι, *dative plural pronoun in Herodotus, by them*    ἐβεβούλευτο (from βουλεύομαι), *it had been planned that* + acc. and infin.    θείῃ, *divine*    προσεγέλασε (from προσγελάω), *smiled at*    διεξῆλθε, *passed through*]

1. What do the Bacchiadae send men to do?
2. What do the men do when they enter the courtyard of Labda's house?
3. What does Labda know of the men's purpose?
4. What had the men agreed upon among themselves?
5. What did the baby do when one of the men took it?
6. To what does Herodotus attribute the baby's action?
7. Why was the man not able to kill the baby?
8. What did he do with it?

ἀποδόντες οὖν τῇ μητρὶ τὸ παιδίον καὶ ἐξελθόντες, ἑστῶτες ἐπὶ τῇ θύρῃ  10
ἀλλήλους ᾐτιῶντο, καὶ μάλιστα τὸν πρῶτον λαβόντα, ὅτι οὐκ ἐποίησε κατὰ τὰ δεδογμένα, ἕως μετὰ πολύν τινα χρόνον ἔδοξεν αὐτοῖς αὖθις ἐσελθοῦσι πᾶσι μετέχειν τοῦ φόνου. ἡ δὲ Λάβδα πάντα ταῦτα ἤκουε, ἑστῶσα πρὸς αὐτῇ τῇ θύρῃ· φοβουμένη δὲ μὴ τὸ δεύτερον λαβόντες τὸ παιδίον ἀποκτείνωσι, φέρουσα ἀποκρύπτει ἐς κυψέλην, ἐπισταμένη ὡς εἰ ἐπανίοιεν, πάντα ἐρευνήσειν μέλλοιεν· ὃ δὴ καὶ  15
ἐγένετο. ἐσελθοῦσι δὲ καὶ ἐρευνήσασι, ὡς οὐκ ἐφαίνετο τὸ παιδίον, ἔδοξεν ἀπιέναι καὶ λέγειν πρὸς τοὺς πέμψαντας ὡς πάντα ἐποίησαν ἃ ἐκεῖνοι ἐκέλευσαν. οἱ μὲν δὴ ἀπελθόντες ταῦτα ἔλεγον. μετὰ δὲ ταῦτα ὁ παῖς ηὐξάνετο, καὶ τοῦτον τὸν κίνδῡνον διαφυγών, Κύψελος ὠνομάσθη ἀπὸ τῆς κυψέλης ἐν ᾗ ἐκρύφθη.

[ἑστῶτες, *standing*    ᾐτιῶντο (from αἰτιάομαι), *they were accusing*    ὅτι, *because*  τὰ δεδογμένα, *what had been decided*    μετέχειν, *to share in* + gen.    ἑστῶσα, *standing*    ἀποκρύπτει, *hides*    κυψέλην, *chest*    ἐρευνήσειν (from ἐρευνάω), *to search*    διαφυγών, *having escaped*    Κύψελος, *Cypselus*]

9. When they left the house, where did the men stop to talk?
10. Whom did they especially accuse?
11. What did the men decide to do now?
12. What did Labda hear and why was she able to hear it?
13. What did she do with the baby? Why did she do it?
14. What did the men do when they returned into the house?
15. What did they decide to tell those who had sent them?
16. Why was the child named Cypselus?

## Exercise 27 μ

*Translate into Greek:*

1. Cyrus has already arrived at Sardis. We must prepare to fight (*use* ὡς + *future participle*).
2. The army of the enemy, having been drawn up by Cyrus, is waiting on the plain before the city.
3. The camels have been drawn up before the rest of the army. Why has this been done by the Persians?
4. The horses, overcome (*use perfect passive participle of* νῑκάω) by fear, are fleeing; we must fight on foot (*use* πεζός).
5. We have fought bravely, but we have been defeated by Cyrus's trick (*use* τὸ σόφισμα).

# Classical Greek

### Xenophanes of Kolophon

Xenophanes of Kolophon in Ionia (fl. 550 B.C.) was a philosopher who wrote in verse. He attacked the anthropomorphism of contemporary religion in pronouncements such as the following (fragment 23 Diels):

εἷς θεός, ἔν τε θεοῖσι καὶ ἀνθρώποισι μέγιστος,
οὔτι δέμας θνητοῖσιν ὁμοίιος οὐδὲ νόημα.

[δέμας, *with respect to his body*    θνητοῖσιν, *mortals*    ὁμοίιος = ὅμοιος    νόημα, *with respect to his thought / mind*]

He makes his point again in the following hypothetical conditional statement (fragment 15 Diels):

ἀλλ᾽ εἰ χεῖρας ἔχον βόες ἵπποι τ᾽ ἠὲ λέοντες
ἢ γράψαι χείρεσσι καὶ ἔργα τελεῖν ἅπερ ἄνδρες,
ἵπποι μὲν θ᾽ ἵπποισι βόες δέ τε βουσὶν ὁμοίᾱς
καὶ κε θεῶν ἰδέᾱς ἔγραφον καὶ σώματ᾽ ἐποίουν
τοιαῦθ᾽ οἷόν περ καὐτοὶ δέμας εἶχον ἕκαστοι.

[εἰ . . . ἔχον (= εἶχον), introducing a present contrary to fact condition, *if they had*    ἠὲ = ἤ, *or*    γράψαι, here, *to draw;* with this and the next infinitive (τελεῖν), repeat εἰ ἔχον from line 1, here in the sense *if they were able*    χείρεσσι = χερσί    τελεῖν, *to accomplish*    ἵπποι . . . κε (= ἄν) . . . ἔγραφον, *horses would draw*    ἰδέᾱς, *the shapes*    τοιαῦθ᾽ (= τοιαῦτα) οἷον περ, *such as*    καὐτοὶ = καὶ αὐτοὶ    δέμας, *the body*]

# Homeric Greek

## Homer, *Iliad* 1.1–7

μῆνιν ἄειδε, θεά, Πηληϊάδεω Ἀχιλῆος
οὐλομένην, ἣ μυρί' Ἀχαιοῖς ἄλγε' ἔθηκε,
πολλὰς δ' ἰφθίμους ψυχὰς Ἄϊδι προΐαψεν
ἡρώων, αὐτοὺς δὲ ἑλώρια τεῦχε κύνεσσιν
οἰωνοῖσί τε πᾶσι, Διὸς δ' ἐτελείετο βουλή,
ἐξ οὗ δὴ τὰ πρῶτα διαστήτην ἐρίσαντε
Ἀτρείδης τε ἄναξ ἀνδρῶν καὶ δῖος Ἀχιλλεύς.

[**μῆνιν**, *wrath* **ἄειδε**, uncontracted = Attic ᾆδε, *sing* **Πηληϊάδεω**, Homeric gen. of Πηληϊάδης, *son of Peleus* **Ἀχιλῆος**, Homeric gen. of Ἀχιλ(λ)εύς, *Achilles* **οὐλομένην** = ὀλομένην, *destructive* **ἄλγε(α)**, *woes* **ἰφθίμους**, *mighty* **Ἄϊδι**, *to Hades* **προΐαψεν** (from προιάπτω), *sent forth* **ἡρώων** (from ἥρως), *of heroes* **ἑλώρια**, neuter pl.; translate as sing., *prey* **τεῦχε** = ἔτευχε (Homer often omits the augment), *was making, causing X to be* **κύνεσσιν** = κυσίν **οἰωνοῖσι** = οἰωνοῖς, *for birds* **ἐτελείετο** (uncontracted imperfect passive of τελέω), *was being accomplished* **ἐξ οὗ δὴ**, *from which very time* **τὰ πρῶτα**, adverbial, *first* **διαστήτην** = δι-εστήτην, dual number, *the two of them stood apart* **ἐρίσαντε** (aorist nominative dual participle of ἐρίζω), *the two of them having quarreled/quarreling* **Ἀτρείδης**, *the son of Atreus* (i.e., Agamemnon) **ἄναξ**, *king; lord* **δῖος**, *bright, shining; noble, illustrious*]

A rhapsode recites Homer.

# 28

# Ο ΑΠΟΛΛΩΝ
# ΤΟΝ ΚΡΟΙΣΟΝ ΣΩΙΖΕΙ (α)

## VOCABULARY

*Verbs*

ἀλίσκομαι, [ἀλο-] ἀλώσομαι,
ἐάλων or ἥλων, ἐάλωκα or
ἥλωκα, *I am caught; I am
taken*

ἀναιρέομαι [= ἀνα- + αἱρέομαι],
*I take up; I pick up*

διαφέρει, impersonal + dat., (it)
*makes a difference to*

ἐπιβαίνω + gen., *I get up on,
mount;* + dat., *I board*

κατακαίω or κατακάω, [καυ-]
κατακαύσω, κατέκαυσα,
κατακέκαυκα, κατα-
κέκαυμαι, κατεκαύθην,
*I burn completely*

καταπαύω, *I put an end to*

πορθέω, *I sack*

προλέγω, *I proclaim*

*Nouns*

ἡ ἀκρόπολις, τῆς ἀκροπόλεως,
*citadel*

ὁ δαίμων, τοῦ δαίμονος, *spirit;
god; the power controlling
one's destiny, fate, lot*

τὸ δέος, τοῦ δέους, *fear*

ἡ ζωή, τῆς ζωῆς, *life*

ὁ ἱππεύς, τοῦ ἱππέως, *horseman; cavalryman*

ἡ πυρά, τῆς πυρᾶς, *funeral
pyre*

*Preposition*

κατά + acc., *down;* distributive, *each, every; by; on; according to;* of time, *at;
through; with regard to; after*

*Conjunction*

εἴτε . . . εἴτε, note the accent,
*either . . . or*

Σάρδιες δὲ ἑάλωσαν ὧδε· ἐπειδὴ τεσσερεσκαιδεκάτη ἐγένετο
ἡμέρη πολιορκεομένῳ Κροίσῳ, Κῦρος τῇ στρατιῇ τῇ ἑαυτοῦ
διαπέμψας ἱππέας προεῖπε τῷ πρώτῳ ἐπιβάντι τοῦ τείχεος δῶρα
δώσειν. μετὰ δὲ τοῦτο πειρησαμένης τῆς στρατιῆς, ὡς οὐ προεχώρεε,
ἐνταῦθα τῶν ἄλλων πεπαυμένων ἀνήρ τις, Ὑροιάδης ὀνόματι, 5
ἐπειρᾶτο προσβαίνων κατὰ τοῦτο τῆς ἀκροπόλεως ὅπου οὐδεὶς
ἐτέτακτο φύλαξ· ἀπότομός τε γὰρ ἔστι ταύτῃ ἡ ἀκρόπολις καὶ
ἄμαχος. ὁ δὲ Ὑροιάδης οὗτος, ἰδὼν τῇ προτεραίῃ τινὰ τῶν Λυδῶν
κατὰ τοῦτο τῆς ἀκροπόλεως καταβάντα ἐπὶ κυνέην ἄνωθεν
κατακυλισθεῖσαν καὶ ἀνελόμενον, ἐφράσθη καὶ ἐς θυμὸν ἐβάλετο. 10
τότε δὲ δὴ αὐτός τε ἀνεβεβήκει καὶ κατ' αὐτὸν ἄλλοι Περσέων

ἀνέβαινον.  προσβάντων δὲ πολλῶν οὕτω δὴ Σάρδιές τε ἑάλωσαν καὶ
πᾶν τὸ ἄστυ ἐπορθέετο.

[ἑάλωσαν: this aorist is conjugated like ἔγνων    τεσσερεσκαιδεκάτη, *fourteenth*
διαπέμψας, *sending* X (acc.) *through* Y (dat.)    ὡς οὐ προεχώρεε, *as it was not succeeding*  ἀπότομος, *steep, sheer*  ἄμαχος, *impregnable*  κυνέην, *helmet*  ἄνωθεν, *from above*  κατακυλισθεῖσαν (from κατακυλίνδω), *which had been rolled
down*  ἐς θυμὸν ἐβάλετο, *he laid it to heart*  ἀνεβεβήκει: pluperfect, translate, *he
had already climbed up*]

κατ᾽ αὐτὸν δὲ Κροῖσον τάδε ἐγένετο.  ἦν οἱ παῖς τὰ μὲν ἄλλα
ἐπιεικής, ἄφωνος δέ.  ἁλισκομένου δὴ τοῦ τείχεος ἤιε τῶν τις Περσέων    15
ὡς Κροῖσον ἀποκτενέων· καὶ ὁ μὲν Κροῖσος ὁρέων αὐτὸν ἐπιόντα
ὑπὸ τῆς παρεούσης συμφορῆς παρημελήκει οὐδέ τί οἱ διέφερε
ἀποθανεῖν.  ὁ δὲ παῖς οὗτος ὁ ἄφωνος, ὡς εἶδε ἐπιόντα τὸν Πέρσην,
ὑπὸ δέους ἔρρηξε φωνήν, εἶπε δέ· "ὦ ἄνθρωπε, μὴ κτεῖνε Κροῖσον."
οὗτος μὲν δὴ τοῦτο πρῶτον ἐφθέγξατο, μετὰ δὲ τοῦτο ἤδη ἐφώνεε τὸν    20
πάντα χρόνον τῆς ζωῆς.

[οἱ = αὐτῷ    τὰ ... ἄλλα, *in other respects*  ἐπιεικής, *able, capable*  ἄφωνος,
*dumb, mute*  ἤιε = Ionic for ᾔει, *was going* (imperfect of εἶμι)  ὁρέων = Ionic for
ὁρῶν  ὑπό + gen., *because of*  παρημελήκει (pluperfect of παραμελέω), translate as
a simple past, *took no heed*  ἔρρηξε (from ῥήγνυμι), we say "broke his silence" or
"broke into speech" rather than "broke his voice"  ἐφθέγξατο (from φθέγγομαι),
*spoke*]

οἱ δὲ Πέρσαι τάς τε Σάρδῖς ἔσχον καὶ αὐτὸν Κροῖσον ἐζώγρησαν,
ἄρξαντα ἔτεα τεσσερεσκαίδεκα καὶ τεσσερεσκαίδεκα ἡμέρας
πολιορκηθέντα, κατὰ τὸ χρηστήριόν τε καταπαύσαντα τὴν ἑαυτοῦ
μεγάλην ἀρχήν.  λαβόντες δὲ αὐτὸν οἱ Πέρσαι ἤγαγον παρὰ Κῦρον.    25
ὁ δὲ ποιήσας μεγάλην πυρὴν ἀνεβίβασε ἐπ᾽ αὐτὴν τὸν Κροῖσόν τε ἐν
πέδῃσι δεδεμένον καὶ δὶς ἑπτὰ Λυδῶν παρ᾽ αὐτὸν παῖδας, εἴτε ἐν νόῳ
ἔχων αὐτοὺς θεῶν τινι θύσειν, εἴτε πυθόμενος τὸν Κροῖσον εἶναι
θεοσεβέα τοῦδε εἵνεκα ἀνεβίβασε ἐπὶ τὴν πυρήν, βουλόμενος
γιγνώσκειν εἴ τις αὐτὸν δαιμόνων σώσει ὥστε μὴ ζῶντα    30
κατακαυθῆναι.

[ἐζώγρησαν (from ζωγρέω), *took alive, captured*    τεσσερεσκαίδεκα, *fourteen*
ἀνεβίβασε (from ἀναβιβάζω), *put him up on*  πέδῃσι, *shackles*  δὶς ἑπτά, *twice
seven*  παρ᾽ αὐτόν, *beside him*  θεοσεβέα, *god-fearing, religious*]

—adapted from Herodotus 1.84–86.2

## PRINCIPAL PARTS: Another Verb from Unrelated Stems

φέρω, [οἰ-] οἴσω, [ἐνεγκ-] ἤνεγκα or ἤνεγκον, [ἐνεκ-] ἐν-ήνοχ-α (see pages 211 and 235), ἐν-ήνεγ-μαι, ἠνέχθην, *I carry;* of roads, *lead*

## WORD STUDY

*In what branches of medicine do the following specialize?*

1. gynecologist
2. pharmacologist
3. physiotherapist
4. pediatrician
5. gerontologist
6. anesthetist

*Give the Greek stems from which these words are formed.*

## GRAMMAR

### 1. The Perfect Active

#### a. *Indicative:*

οἱ δοῦλοι τοὺς βοῦς ἤδη **λελύκᾱσιν**.
*The slaves **have** already **loosed** the oxen.*

#### b. *Subjunctive:*

φοβούμεθα μὴ οἱ δοῦλοι τοὺς βοῦς οὐκ ἤδη **λελυκότες ὦσιν**.
*We are afraid that the slaves **have** not already **loosed** the oxen.*

#### c. *Optative:*

ἤρετο εἰ οἱ δοῦλοι τοὺς βοῦς ἤδη **λελυκότες εἶεν**.
*He asked whether the slaves **had** already **loosed** the oxen.*

#### d. *Imperative:*

Very rare; Achilles, addressing the body of Hector, whom he has just slain, uses the perfect imperative, **τέθναθι**, *be dead!* (*Iliad* 22.365). The forms of the perfect imperative are not given in the chart below.

#### e. *Infinitive:*

λέγει τοὺς δούλους τοὺς βοῦς ἤδη **λελυκέναι**.
*He says that the slaves **have** already **loosed** the oxen.*

#### f. *Participle:*

εἶδε τοὺς δούλους τοὺς βοῦς ἤδη **λελυκότας**.
*He saw that the slaves **had** already **loosed** the oxen.*

All these perfect verb forms describe states or conditions existing as a result of completed actions. The state or condition described is ongoing or permanent: οἱ δοῦλοι τοὺς βοῦς ἤδη λελύκᾱσιν; this sentence states that the slaves have already loosed the oxen and that the oxen are still loose now, in present time.

In indirect questions and indirect statements when the leading verb is in a past tense, the perfect tense forms will be translated with "had" in English to show completion of the action prior to the time of the leading verb (see the third and last examples above).

## 2. The -κα 1st Perfect Active: Forms

Some verbs have -κα in the perfect active, and some have only -α (see below, Grammar 7, pages 210–211). We call the former -κα *1st perfect active* and the latter -α *2nd perfect active*. Both types reduplicate or augment the stem, as does the perfect middle/passive (see Chapter 27, Grammar 1, pages 183–184, and Grammar 8, pages 196–197). Perfects in -κα then have endings as shown below. Remember that the perfect stem of λύω has a short υ, and note the accent of the infinitive. The perfect imperative is rare and is not shown in the chart below.

| Indicative | Infinitive | Participle |
|---|---|---|
| λέ-λυ-κα | λε-λυ-κέναι | λε-λυ-κώς, |
| λέ-λυ-κας | | λε-λυ-κυῖα, |
| λέ-λυ-κε(ν) | | λε-λυ-κός, |
| λε-λύ-καμεν | | gen., λε-λυ-κότ-ος, etc. |
| λε-λύ-κατε | | |
| λε-λύ-κᾱσι(ν) | | |

| Subjunctive | or very rarely | Subjunctive |
|---|---|---|
| λελυκὼς ὦ | | λελύκω |
| λελυκὼς ᾖς | | λελύκῃς |
| λελυκὼς ᾖ | | λελύκῃ |
| λελυκότες ὦμεν | | λελύκωμεν |
| λελυκότες ἦτε | | λελύκητε |
| λελυκότες ὦσι(ν) | | λελύκωσι(ν) |

| Optative | or occasionally | Optative |
|---|---|---|
| λελυκὼς εἴην | | λελύκοιμι |
| λελυκὼς εἴης | | λελύκοις |
| λελυκὼς εἴη | | λελύκοι |
| λελυκότες εἶμεν or εἴημεν | | λελύκοιμεν |
| λελυκότες εἶτε or εἴητε | | λελύκοιτε |
| λελυκότες εἶεν or εἴησαν | | λελύκοιεν |

Note: εὑρίσκω may either retain εὑ- or augment to ηὑ-, thus giving either εὕρηκα or ηὕρηκα for the perfect active.

The declension of the -κα 1st perfect active participle is as follows:

|              | Masculine    | Feminine     | Neuter       |
|--------------|--------------|--------------|--------------|
| Nom., Voc.   | λελυκώς      | λελυκυῖα     | λελυκός      |
| Gen.         | λελυκότος    | λελυκυίᾱς    | λελυκότος    |
| Dat.         | λελυκότι     | λελυκυίᾳ     | λελυκότι     |
| Acc.         | λελυκότα     | λελυκυῖαν    | λελυκός      |
| Nom., Voc.   | λελυκότες    | λελυκυῖαι    | λελυκότα     |
| Gen.         | λελυκότων    | λελυκυιῶν    | λελυκότων    |
| Dat.         | λελυκόσι(ν)  | λελυκυίαις   | λελυκόσι(ν)  |
| Acc.         | λελυκότας    | λελυκυίᾱς    | λελυκότα     |

## 3. The Perfect Tense: Stems

Contract verbs lengthen the stem vowel, e.g.:

τῑμά-ω > τετῑμη-κα
φιλέ-ω > πεφίλη-κα
δηλό-ω > δεδήλω-κα

Consonant stems:

a. Verbs with stems ending in dentals (δ, θ) and ζ drop the final consonant, e.g.:

δείδ-ω > δέ-δοι-κα
πείθ-ω > πέ-πει-κα
νομίζ-ω > νε-νόμι-κα

b. Some verbs with stems ending in liquids (λ, ρ) and nasals (μ, ν) drop the final consonant of the stem, e.g.:

κρῑν-ω > κέ-κρι-κα

Others extend the stem with an ε, which is lengthened to η in the perfect, e.g.:

εὑρίσκω: [εὑρ- > εὑρε-] ηὕρη-κα
μέν-ω: [μεν- > μενε-] με-μένη-κα
τρέχω: [δραμ- > δραμε-] δε-δράμη-κα

So also μανθάνω: [μαθ- > μαθε-] με-μάθη-κα

c. Note the following:

ἀπο-θνῄσκω: [θνη-] τέ-θνη-κα
βάλλω: [βλη-] βέ-βλη-κα
καλέω: [κλη-] κέ-κλη-κα

## 4. Aspect

The perfect tense denotes or records a state that is the result of an action *completed* in the past (see Chapter 27, Grammar 2, page 184) and thus describes *a present state*. Many verbs in the perfect tense can therefore best be translated with the present tense in English, e.g.:

ἀπο-θνῄσκω: perfect [θνη-] τέθνηκα (no prefix in the perfect tense) = *I have died* and therefore *I am dead*    οἱ τεθνηκότες = *the dead*
ἵστημι: perfect [στη-] ἕστηκα = *I have stood up* and therefore *I stand*
βαίνω: perfect [βη-] βέβηκα = *I have taken a step, made a stand*, and therefore *I stand; I stand firm; I am set*

## 5. The Pluperfect Tense: Indicative Only

οἱ δοῦλοι τοὺς βοῦς **ἐλελύκεσαν** πρὶν καταδῦναι τὸν ἥλιον.
*The slaves **had loosed** the oxen before the sun set.*

The pluperfect records a state that existed in the past as the result of an action completed at some time more remote. It will normally be translated with "had" in English.

Note the following sentences with verbs in the pluperfect from the reading passage at the beginning of this chapter:

τότε δὲ δὴ αὐτός τε **ἀνεβεβήκει** καὶ κατ᾽ αὐτὸν ἄλλοι Περσέων ἀν-έβαινον. (11–12)
*And then indeed he himself **had climbed up**, and others of the Persians were climbing up after him.*
(The action of Hyroeades was completed before the others ascended, and hence the pluperfect ἀνεβεβήκει is appropriate, but sometimes, as here, the pluperfect is used to describe a past action that occurs so suddenly as to be almost simultaneous with another or other past actions. Thus, the others climbed up almost at the same moment at which Hyroeades had made his ascent.)

καὶ ὁ μὲν Κροῖσος ὀρέων αὐτὸν ἐπιόντα ὑπὸ τῆς παρεούσης συμφορῆς **παρημελήκει** οὐδέ τί οἱ διέφερε ἀποθανεῖν. (16–18)
*And Croesus, seeing him coming against (him), because of his present misfortune **had gotten into a state of heedlessness** = **was paying no heed**, nor was it making any difference to him at all whether he died.*

(The pluperfect παρημελήκει implies that Croesus had gotten into a state of heedlessness by the time he was attacked; therefore at that moment in time he was not caring whether he died or not.)

## 6. The -κη 1st Pluperfect Active: Forms

Verbs that reduplicate the stem in the perfect are augmented with ε to form the pluperfect:

**Indicative**                                    **Contract Verbs**

ἐ-λε-λύ-κη                                         ἐπεφιλήκη, etc.
ἐ-λε-λύ-κης                                        ἐτετῑμήκη, etc.
ἐ-λε-λύ-κει(ν)                                     ἐδεδηλώκη, etc.
ἐ-λε-λύ-κεμεν
ἐ-λε-λύ-κετε
ἐ-λε-λύ-κεσαν

### Exercise 28 α

*Make four photocopies of the Verb Chart for the perfect and pluperfect tenses on page 276 and fill in the forms of βάλλω, φιλέω, τῑμάω, and δηλόω in the active voice. Keep these charts for reference.*

## 7. The - α 2nd Perfect Active and the - η 2nd Pluperfect Active

Some verbs in the perfect and pluperfect active do not have the κ that appears in all the forms given above; we call these *-α 2nd perfects* and *-η 2nd pluperfects*. Here are examples:

ὁ Φίλιππος τυφλὸς **γέγονεν.**
*Philip **has become** = is blind.*

ἵλεως ἴσθι μοι τυφλῷ **γεγονότι.** (17β:50–51)
*Be propitious to me **having become** blind.*
*Be propitious to me who **have become** blind.*
*Be propitious to me who **am** blind.*

-α 2nd perfect active and -η 2nd pluperfect active:

Present: γράφ-ω
-α 2nd perfect active: γέ-γραφ-α
-η 2nd pluperfect active: ἐ-γε-γράφ-η

Present: ἔρχομαι
-α 2nd perfect active: ἐλήλυθ-α
-η 2nd pluperfect active: ἐληλύθ-η (rare)

The endings for the -α 2nd perfect and the -η 2nd pluperfect are the same as for the -κα 1st perfect and the -κη 1st pluperfect given in Grammar 2 and Grammar 6 above. The periphrastic forms of the subjunctive and optative are, with few exceptions, the only ones used.

Most verbs with stems in labials (β, π, φ) and velars (γ, κ, χ) form -α 2nd perfects and -η 2nd pluperfects and usually aspirate the final consonant of the stem if it is not already aspirated, e.g.:

κρύπ-τ-ω: [κρυφ-]  κέ-κρυφ-α
ἄγ-ω: [ἀγ-]  ἦχ-α
τάττω: [ταγ-]  τέ-ταχ-α
δείκνῡμι: [δεικ-]  δέ-δειχ-α

Note the change of vowel from ε to ο or from ει to οι or ο in verbs with -α perfects and -η pluperfects, e.g.:

πέμπ-ω > πέπομφ-α
τρέπ-ω > τέτροφ-α
λείπ-ω > λέλοιπ-α
κτείν-ω > ἔκτον-α

Note: for φέρ-ω, the perfect stem ἐνεκ- gives perfect ἐνήνοχ-α (for the Attic reduplication, see page 235).

## Exercise 28 β

1. *Make one photocopy of the Verb Chart for the perfect and pluperfect tenses on page 276 and fill in the forms of γίγνομαι, perfect, γέγονα. Keep this chart for reference*
2. *Make ten photocopies of the Verb Chart for the perfect and pluperfect on page 276, choose five verbs from previous charts for which you have not filled in perfect and pluperfect forms and fill in active and middle/passive perfect and pluperfect forms of those five verbs.*

## Exercise 28 γ

*Change the following present forms to the corresponding perfect forms:*

| | | |
|---|---|---|
| 1. λῡ́ουσι(ν) | 5. ἀποθνῄσκει | 9. δεικνύᾱσι(ν) |
| 2. λῡ́οντες | 6. ἄγετε | 10. λείπειν |
| 3. μανθάνειν | 7. δηλοῦμεν | 11. γράφουσα |
| 4. πέμπεις | 8. νῑκῶντες | 12. πείθομεν |

---

### Greek Wisdom

#### Heraclitus

ἀοιδοῖς πείθονται καὶ διδασκάλῳ χρῶνται ὁμίλῳ οὐκ εἰδότες ὅτι "οἱ πολλοὶ κακοί, ὀλίγοι δὲ ἀγαθοί." Fragment 104 Diels

## Exercise 28 δ

*Change the following present forms to the corresponding pluperfect forms:*

1. λύομεν
2. τῑμᾷ
3. ἄγουσι(ν)
4. πείθεις
5. πέμπουσι(ν)
6. δηλῶ

## Exercise 28 ε

*Read aloud and translate:*

1. ἆρα πεποίηκας πάνθ' ὅσα κεκέλευκεν ὁ πατήρ;
2. ἆρα πέπεικέ σε ἡ μήτηρ οἴκοι μένειν;
3. οἱ Ἀθηναῖοι ἐς μέγιστον κίνδῡνον καθεστήκᾱσιν.
4. οἵ τε ὁπλῖται ὑπὸ τῶν πολεμίων νενίκηνται καὶ αὐτὸς ὁ στρατηγὸς τέθνηκεν.
5. οἱ ἐν τῇ μάχῃ τεθνηκότες ὑπὸ τοῦ δήμου τετίμηνται.
6. οἱ δοῦλοι τοὺς βοῦς λελυκότες οἴκαδε ἤλαυνον.
7. τί τὸ ἄροτρον ἐν τῷ ἀγρῷ λελοίπατε;
8. ἐγὼ νεᾱνίᾱς τότε ὢν οὔπω ἐμεμαθήκη τὴν γεωμετρίᾱν.
9. νῦν δὲ σοφιστής τις πάντα τὰ μαθηματικά με δεδίδαχεν.
10. ὁ Ἀρχιμήδης ἐν τῷ λουτρῷ (*bath*) καθήμενος, ἐξαίφνης βοήσᾱς, "εὕρηκα," ἔφη.

## Exercise 28 ζ

*Translate into Greek:*

1. The slaves have loosed the oxen and have led (*use* ἄγω) them home.
2. We have sent the women and children to the islands.
3. The woman is standing by the door, waiting for her husband.
4. Why have you done this? The teacher has shown you what you ought to do.
5. It is better to be dead than to live shamefully.

# Rationalism and Mysticism

In the essay on Greek science and medicine (Chapter 11), we saw that the Ionian cosmologists attempted to explain the world in terms of natural causation. This intellectual revolution involved rejection of the old mythical explanations of phenomena and led inevitably to criticism of the traditional religion, to agnosticism, and to atheism. The criticism was not all destructive. For instance, the poet and philosopher Xenophanes, born ca. 570 B.C., attacked the immorality of the gods as they are portrayed in myth: "Homer and Hesiod attributed to the gods all that is a shame and a rebuke to men, theft, adultery, and deceit" (Kirk and Raven, *The Presocratic Philosophers*, Cambridge,

1964, page 169). He criticizes anthropomorphism: "The Ethiopians say that their gods are snub-nosed and black, the Thracians that theirs are blue-eyed and red-haired. . . . There is one god, like mortals neither in body nor in thought" (*ibid.*, pages 171 and 173). (See the Classical Greek readings on page 202.)

An example of the agnostic is provided by Protagoras, the first and greatest of the sophists (see essay, Chapter 24), who begins his work *On the Gods* as follows: "Concerning the gods, I am unable to discover whether they exist or not, or what they are like in form" (Protagoras, fragment 4).

The clearest surviving statement of the atheist's position is a fragment from a play by Critias (born ca. 460 B.C.):

> There was a time when the life of men was disorderly and beast-like. . . . Then, as I believe, man laid down laws to chastise, and who-ever sinned was punished. Then when the laws prevented men from open deeds of violence but they continued to commit them in secret, I be-lieve that a man of shrewd and subtle mind invented for men the fear of the gods, so that there might be something to frighten the wicked even if they acted, spoke, or thought in secret. From this motive he introduced the conception of divinity. (Translated by Guthrie, *The Sophists*, Cambridge, 1971, pages 82 and 243)

The sixth century saw the development of religious ideas that were to have profound influence on Western thought, including Christian theology. The central tenet of this new mysticism was the duality of body and soul. The soul was conceived as a spiritual entity that existed before its confinement in the body and that survives the body's dissolution. This teaching was attributed to a poet-prophet named Orpheus, who was said to have lived in Thrace; his followers were called Orphics. Little is known about their beliefs. We are on firmer ground with Pythagoras, who seems to have incorporated Orphic beliefs into his teaching. Born ca. 550 B.C. in Samos, he settled in southern Italy, where he founded a religious community of men and women. He is best remembered today as a mathematician, but he also taught a way of life that was based on the belief that our present life is but a preparation for a further life or lives. The soul is divine and immortal; in successive reincarnations it is imprisoned in the body, and in its lives it must try to rid itself of bodily impurity by living as well as possible. Eventually it may be freed from the cycle of life and death and return to its divine origins.

The beliefs we have outlined were those of a limited circle of intellectuals, but the ordinary Greeks, who adhered to the traditional religion, could also find comfort in mysteries. There were various mystery cults in different parts of Greece, of which the most important were the Eleusinian mysteries. Starting as an ancient agrarian cult in honor of Demeter, goddess of grain, these mysteries by the middle of the seventh century offered initiates a blessed afterlife, from which the uninitiated were excluded: "Blessed is the man among mortals on earth who has seen these things. But he who has not taken part in the rites and has no share in them, he never knows these good things when he is dead beneath the grim darkness" (Homeric *Hymn to Demeter*, ca. 625 B.C.).

The mysteries were open to all, men and women, Athenians and foreigners, slave and free. On the first day of the festival, the sacred herald made a proclamation, inviting all who wished to be initiated to assemble; they were warned that they must be of pure hands and "have a soul conscious of no evil and have lived well and justly." After three days of sacrifice and preparation, the initiates (μύσται), numbering over 10,000, made their pilgrimage of fourteen miles or twenty-two and a half kilometers from Athens to Eleusis, led by the officials of the Eleusinian cult. The last day was spent in fasting and sacrifice. In the evening the rites were performed in the Hall of the Mysteries. The rites were secret, and all who participated took a vow of silence, so that we know very little of what happened. At the climax of the ceremony, in the darkness of the night, the ἱεροφάντης (*revealer of holy things*) appeared in a brilliant light and revealed the holy objects. We are told that these included a sheaf of grain, which may have had symbolical significance, offering the hope of resurrection.

The cult of Eleusis, with its emphasis on moral as well as ritual purity and with the hope it offered the initiates of a blessed life hereafter, answered a deep spiritual need. The mysteries were celebrated with unbroken continuity from the archaic age until the site at Eleusis was finally devastated by Alaric the Goth in A.D. 395. "In a civilization where official religion did little to support the soul, Eleusis provided some comfort to those who faced the anxieties of this world and the next" (Parke, *Festivals of the Athenians*, London, Thames & Hudson, 1977, page 71).

Triptolemus, a hero of Eleusis, sowing Demeter's grain

# Homeric Greek

### Homer, *Odyssey* 1.1–10

ἄνδρα μοι ἔννεπε, Μοῦσα, πολύτροπον, ὃς μάλα πολλὰ

πλάγχθη, ἐπεὶ Τροίης ἱερὸν πτολίεθρον ἔπερσεν·

πολλῶν δ' ἀνθρώπων ἴδεν ἄστεα καὶ νόον ἔγνω,

πολλὰ δ' ὅ γ' ἐν πόντῳ πάθεν ἄλγεα ὃν κατὰ θῦμόν,

ἀρνύμενος ἥν τε ψῦχὴν καὶ νόστον ἑταίρων.

ἀλλ' οὐδ' ὣς ἑτάρους ἐρρύσατο, ἱέμενός περ·

αὐτῶν γὰρ σφετέρῃσιν ἀτασθαλίῃσιν ὄλοντο,

νήπιοι, οἳ κατὰ βοῦς Ὑπερίονος Ἠελίοιο

ἤσθιον· αὐτὰρ ὁ τοῖσιν ἀφείλετο νόστιμον ἦμαρ.

τῶν ἀμόθεν γε, θεά, θύγατερ Διός, εἰπὲ καὶ ἡμῖν.

[μοι: a polite use of the dative case, not *to me*, but *please tell about, tell the tale* of **Μοῦσα**, *Muse*  **πολύτροπον**, *much-traveled* or *of many devices, resourceful* **πολλὰ**, adverbial, *greatly; far and wide*  **πλάγχθη** = ἐπλάγχθη (aorist passive of πλάζω, *I turn X aside;* passive, *I wander*), *wandered*  **Τροίης** = Τροίας  **πτολίεθρον** = πόλιν  **ἔπερσεν:** aorist of πέρθω, *I sack, ravage*  **ἴδεν** = εἶδεν  **ἄστεα** = ἄστη  **νόον** = νοῦν  **ὅ**, *he*  **πάθεν** = ἔπαθεν  **ἄλγεα**, *woes*  **ὃν**, *his* (with θῦμόν)  **ἀρνύμενος**, conative present participle, *trying to win*  **ἥν**, *his*  **ψῦχὴν**, *soul; life*  **ὣς**, *so*  **ἑτάρους** = ἑταίρους  **ἐρρύσατο** (aorist middle of ἐρύω), *saved, rescued*  **ἱέμενος** (present middle participle of Homeric ἵημι, distinct in origin from ἵημι and usually with initial short ι, but with long ι in the participle), *desiring, being eager*  **περ**, with participle, *although*  **αὐτῶν** = ἑαυτῶν (enhancing the sense of σφετέρῃσιν)  **σφετέρῃσιν**, *their own*  **ἀτασθαλίῃσιν** = ἀτασθαλίαις, *recklessness*  **ὄλοντο** = ἀπώλοντο, *they perished*  **νήπιοι**, *childish; foolish*  **κατὰ:** prepositional prefix to be taken with ἤσθιον in the next line (= κατήσθιον)  **Ὑπερίονος**, *of Hyperion* (the one on high)  **Ἠελίοιο** = Ἠλίου  **αὐτὰρ**, *but*  **ὁ**, *he*  **τοῖσιν** = τοῖς, dative of separation, pronoun here, *them*  **νόστιμον ἦμαρ**, *the day of their return*  **τῶν**, pronoun, take with εἰπὲ, *tell of these things*  **ἀμόθεν**, *from some point*]

The Sirens sing to Odysseus as he sails by.

# Ο ΑΠΟΛΛΩΝ
# ΤΟΝ ΚΡΟΙΣΟΝ ΣΩΙΖΕΙ (β)

## VOCABULARY

*Verbs*
αἱρέομαι, *I choose*
ἀναμιμνῄσκω, [μνη-] ἀνα-
μνήσω, ἀνέμνησα, *I remind*
someone (acc.) of something
(acc. or gen.)
  μέμνημαι (perfect middle =
  present), *I have reminded
  myself = I remember*
  μνησθήσομαι (future passive in middle sense),
  *I will remember*
  ἐμνήσθην (aorist passive in
  middle sense), *I remembered*
ἀναστενάζω, *I groan aloud*
ἐνθῡμέομαι, ἐνθῡμήσομαι,
ἐντεθῡμημαι, ἐνεθῡμήθην,
*I take to heart; I ponder*
ἐπικαλέω, *I call upon*; middle,
*I call upon X to help*

μεταγιγνώσκω, *I change my
mind; I repent*
παρίσταμαι [= παρα- + ἵστα-
μαι], παρέστην, παρέστηκα
+ dat., *I stand near, stand by;
I help*
*Nouns*
ἡ ἡσυχίᾱ, τῆς ἡσυχίᾱς, *quietness*
ἡ νεφέλη, τῆς νεφέλης, *cloud*
ὁ ὄλβος, τοῦ ὄλβου, *happiness,
bliss; prosperity*
ἡ σῑγή, τῆς σῑγῆς, *silence*
*Adjectives*
ἀνόητος, -ον, *foolish*
ἔσχατος, -η, -ον, *furthest; extreme*
*Preposition*
ἀντί + gen., <u>*instead of*</u>; *against*
*Expression*
περὶ οὐδενὸς ποιοῦμαι, *I consider of no importance*

ὁ μὲν Κῦρος ἐποίεε ταῦτα, ὁ δὲ Κροῖσος ἑστηκὼς ἐπὶ τῆς πυρῆς,
καίπερ ἐν κακῷ ἐὼν τοσούτῳ, ἐμνήσθη τὸν τοῦ Σόλωνος λόγον, ὅτι
οὐδεὶς τῶν ζώντων εἴη ὄλβιος.  ὡς δὲ τοῦτο ἐμνήσθη ἀναστενάξᾱς ἐκ
πολλῆς ἡσυχίης τρὶς ὠνόμασε, "Σόλων."  καὶ Κῦρος ἀκούσᾱς
ἐκέλευσε τοὺς ἑρμηνέᾱς ἐρέσθαι τὸν Κροῖσον τίνα τοῦτον          5
ἐπικαλέοιτο.  Κροῖσος δὲ πρῶτον μὲν σῑγὴν εἶχεν ἐρωτώμενος, τέλος
δὲ ὡς ἠναγκάζετο, εἶπε ὅτι ἦλθε παρ' ἑαυτὸν ὁ Σόλων ἐὼν Ἀθηναῖος,
καὶ θεησάμενος πάντα τὸν ἑαυτοῦ ὄλβον περὶ οὐδενὸς ἐποιήσατο,
καὶ αὐτῷ πάντα ἀποβεβήκοι ᾗπερ ἐκεῖνος εἶπε.

[ἑστηκὼς, *standing*    τρὶς, *three times*    τοὺς ἑρμηνέᾱς, *interpreters*    ἀποβεβήκοι
(perfect optative of ἀποβαίνω), *had turned out*]

ὁ μὲν Κροῖσος ταῦτα ἐξηγήσατο, τῆς δὲ πυρῆς ἤδη ἀμμένης    10
ἐκαίετο τὰ ἔσχατα. καὶ ὁ Κῦρος ἀκούσᾱς τῶν ἑρμηνέων ἃ Κροῖσος
εἶπε, μεταγνούς τε καὶ ἐνθῡμεόμενος ὅτι καὶ αὐτὸς ἄνθρωπος ἐὼν
ἄλλον ἄνθρωπον, γενόμενον ἑαυτοῦ εὐδαιμονίῃ οὐκ ἐλάσσονα,
ζῶντα πυρῇ διδοίη, καὶ ἐπιστάμενος ὅτι οὐδὲν εἴη τῶν ἐν ἀνθρώποις
ἀσφαλές, ἐκέλευσε σβεννύναι ὡς τάχιστα τὸ καιόμενον πῦρ καὶ    15
καταβιβάζειν Κροῖσόν τε καὶ τοὺς μετὰ Κροίσου. καὶ οἱ πειρώμενοι
οὐκ ἐδύναντο ἔτι τοῦ πυρὸς ἐπικρατῆσαι.

[ἀμμένης (perfect passive participle of ἅπτω, I fasten; I set on fire), kindled, lit    σβεννύναι (from σβέννῡμι), (his men) to put out    καταβιβάζειν, to bring down    ἐπικρατῆσαι + gen., to master, get control of]

ἐνταῦθα λέγεται ὑπὸ τῶν Λῡδῶν τὸν Κροῖσον, μαθόντα τὴν
Κύρου μετάγνωσιν, βοῆσαι τὸν Ἀπόλλωνα, καλέοντα παραστῆναι
καὶ σῶσαί μιν ἐκ τοῦ παρεόντος κακοῦ· τὸν μὲν δακρύοντα    20
ἐπικαλέεσθαι τὸν θεόν, ἐκ δὲ αἰθρίης καὶ νηνεμίης συνδραμεῖν
ἐξαίφνης νεφέλᾱς, καὶ χειμῶνά τε γενέσθαι καὶ πολὺ ὕδωρ,
σβεσθῆναί τε τὴν πυρήν. οὕτω δὴ μαθόντα τὸν Κῦρον ὡς εἴη ὁ
Κροῖσος καὶ θεοφιλὴς καὶ ἀνὴρ ἀγαθός, ἐρέσθαι τάδε· "Κροῖσε, τίς
σε ἀνθρώπων ἔπεισε ἐπὶ γῆν τὴν ἐμὴν στρατευσάμενον πολέμιον ἀντὶ    25
φίλου ἐμοὶ καταστῆναι;" ὁ δὲ εἶπε· "ὦ βασιλεῦ, ἐγὼ ταῦτα ἔπρηξα τῇ
σῇ μὲν εὐδαιμονίῃ, τῇ δὲ ἐμαυτοῦ κακοδαιμονίῃ· αἴτιος δὲ τούτων
ἐγένετο ὁ Ἑλλήνων θεὸς ἐπάρᾱς ἐμὲ στρατεύεσθαι. οὐδεὶς γὰρ οὕτω
ἀνόητός ἐστι ὅστις πόλεμον πρὸ εἰρήνης αἱρέεται· ἐν μὲν γὰρ τῇ
εἰρήνῃ οἱ παῖδες τοὺς πατέρας θάπτουσι, ἐν δὲ τῷ πολέμῳ οἱ πατέρες    30
τοὺς παῖδας. ἀλλὰ ταῦτα δαίμονί που φίλον ἦν οὕτω γενέσθαι." ὁ
μὲν ταῦτα ἔλεγε, Κῦρος δὲ αὐτὸν λύσᾱς καθεῖσέ τε ἐγγὺς ἑαυτοῦ καὶ
μεγάλως ἐτίμᾱ.

[μετάγνωσιν, change of mind    μιν, him    αἰθρίης . . . νηνεμίης, clear sky . . .
windless calm    σβεσθῆναι (from σβέννῡμι; aorist passive infinitive in indirect
statement), was put out    θεοφιλὴς, dear to the gods    οὕτω δὴ . . . τὸν
Κῦρον . . . ἐρέσθαι, still indirect statement, reporting what was said    καταστῆναι,
to become    τῇ . . . εὐδαιμονίῃ, τῇ . . . κακοδαιμονίῃ: datives of accompanying
circumstances or manner, with good luck for you . . .    κακοδαιμονίῃ, bad luck
ἐπάρᾱς (from ἐπαίρω), having raised; having induced    ὅστις = ὥστε    πρὸ, in prefer-

ence to   **που**, *perhaps, I suppose*   **καθεῖσέ** (= ἐκάθισε, aorist of καθίζω), *made X sit*
down]

—adapted from Herodotus 1.86.3–88.1

## PRINCIPAL PARTS: Verbs Adding ε to Stem

**βούλομαι**, [βουλε-] **βουλήσομαι, βεβούλημαι, ἐβουλήθην** + infin., *I want;*
  *I wish*

**ἐθέλω** or **θέλω**, imperfect, **ἤθελον**, [ἐθελε-] **ἐθελήσω, ἠθέλησα, ἠθέληκα**
  + infin., *I am willing; I wish*

**μάχομαι**, [μαχε-] **μαχοῦμαι, ἐμαχεσάμην, μεμάχημαι,** *I fight;* + dat., *I fight*
  *against*

**χαίρω**, [χαιρε-] **χαιρήσω**, [χαρε-] **κεχάρηκα**, [χαρ-] **ἐχάρην** (*I rejoiced*),
  *I rejoice;* + participle, *I am glad to*

## WORD BUILDING

*The following verbs have present reduplication, i.e., in the present and
imperfect only, the first consonant of the stem + ι are prefixed to the verb stem:*

| | | | |
|---|---|---|---|
| δί-δω-μι | (δω-/δο-) | γί-γν-ομαι | (γν-/γεν-/γον-) |
| τί-θη-μι | (θη-/θε-) | γι-γνώ-σκω | (γνω-/γνο-) |
| ἵ-στη-μι (see page 40) | (στη-/στα-) | ἀνα-μι-μνή-σκω | (μνη-/μνα-) |

*Give the meaning of the following sets formed from these verbs. Note that
nouns and adjectives formed from such verbs are formed from the verb stem
proper, not the reduplicated form:*

1. δω-/δο-    ἡ δόσις    τὸ δῶρον    προ-δο- >    ὁ προδότης    ἡ προδοσίᾱ
2. θη-/θε-    ἡ θέσις    ὁ νομο-θέτης    ἡ ὑπό-θεσις
3. στη-/στα-    ἡ στάσις    προ-στα- >    ὁ προστάτης    ἡ προστασίᾱ
4. γεν-/γον-    τὸ γένος    ἡ γένεσις    ὁ πρόγονος
5. γνω-/γνο-    ἡ γνώμη    ἡ γνῶσις    γνωστός, -ή, -όν
6. μνη-/μνα-    ἡ μνήμη    τὸ μνῆμα    τὸ μνημεῖον    ἀεί-μνηστος, -ον

---

## Greek Wisdom

### Heraclitus

τῷ μὲν θεῷ καλὰ πάντα καὶ ἀγαθὰ καὶ δίκαια, ἄνθρωποι δὲ ἃ μὲν ἄδικα
ὑπειλήφασιν ἃ δὲ δίκαια. Fragment 102 Diels

# GRAMMAR

## 8.   Verbs Found Most Commonly in the Perfect and Pluperfect Tenses

The following verbs are found most commonly in the perfect tense with present meanings. The pluperfect of these verbs is translated as imperfect in English. The present forms given below in parentheses do not occur in Attic Greek:

| Present | Aorist | Perfect |
|---------|--------|---------|
| (δείδω, *I fear*) | ἔδεισα, *I feared* | δέδοικα, *I am afraid* |
| (ἔθω, *I am accustomed*) | | εἴωθα, *I am accustomed to* + infin. |
| (εἴκω, *I am like*; *I seem likely*) | | ἔοικα, *I am like*; *I am likely to* ὡς ἔοικε(ν), *as it seems* |
| (ἰδ-, *see*) | | οἶδα, *I know* |
| φύω or φύω, *I produce* | ἔφυσα, *I produced* | πέφυκα, *I am by nature* |

Keep in mind also that the perfect tense forms μέμνημαι and ἕστηκα have present meanings, *I remember* and *I stand*.

### Exercise 28 η

*Read aloud and translate into English:*

1.   αὕτη ἡ γυνή, ὡς ἔοικε, σωφρονεστάτη πέφυκεν.
2.   οὐκ οἶδα γυναῖκα σωφρονεστέρᾱν· βούλομαι οὖν γαμεῖν (*to marry*) αὐτήν.
3.   δέδοικα δὲ μὴ ὁ πατὴρ οὐκ ἐθέλῃ αὐτήν μοι ἐκδοῦναι.
4.   οἱ νεᾱνίαι ἀνδρειότατοι πεφῡκότες οὐκ ἐδεδοίκεσαν.
5.   οἱ παῖδες εἰώθᾱσιν εἰς διδασκάλων καθ᾽ ἡμέρᾱν φοιτᾶν.
6.   ἀλλ᾽ οὐκ ἀεὶ μέμνηνται ὅσα λέγει ὁ διδάσκαλος.
7.   ὁ Κροῖσος ἐμνήσθη πάνθ᾽ ὅσα εἶπεν ὁ Σόλων.
8.   τῶν Ἀθηναίων οἱ πολλοὶ (*the majority*) ἐν τοῖς ἀγροῖς οἰκεῖν εἰώθεσαν.

## 9.   The Verb οἶδα

The verb οἶδα is an irregular -α 2nd perfect (see above, Grammar 8) formed from the stem ἰδ- (originally ϝιδ-, pronounced *wid*, cf. Latin *videō*, "I see"), which appears also in εἶδον, *I saw*. The verb οἶδα means *I have found out = I know*, and is present in meaning. The corresponding pluperfect ᾔδη or ᾔδειν means *I had found out = I was aware, was knowing; I knew*, and is imperfect in meaning. As seen in the chart below, the subjunctive, infinitive, and participle are formed regularly from the stem εἰδ-; the indicative and imperative are irregular and must be carefully learned.

| Indic. | Subj. | Opt. | Imper. | Infin. | Part. |
|--------|-------|------|--------|--------|-------|

-α 2nd Perfect (present in meaning), *I know*

| Indic. | Subj. | Opt. | Imper. | Infin. | Part. |
|--------|-------|------|--------|--------|-------|
| οἶδα | εἰδῶ | εἰδείην | | εἰδέναι | εἰδώς, |
| οἶσθα | εἰδῇς | εἰδείης | ἴσθι | | εἰδυῖα, |
| οἶδε(ν) | εἰδῇ | εἰδείη | | | εἰδός |
| ἴσμεν | εἰδῶμεν | εἰδεῖμεν | | | gen., εἰδότος, etc. |
| ἴστε | εἰδῆτε | εἰδεῖτε | ἴστε | | |
| ἴσᾱσι(ν) | εἰδῶσι(ν) | εἰδεῖεν | | | |

-η 2nd Pluperfect (imperfect in meaning), *I was aware, was knowing; I knew*

| | | |
|--------|-----|--------|
| ᾔδη | or | ᾔδειν |
| ᾔδησθα | or | ᾔδεις |
| ᾔδει(ν) | | |
| ᾖσμεν | or | ᾔδεμεν |
| ᾖστε | or | ᾔδετε |
| ᾖσαν | or | ᾔδεσαν |

The future, εἴσομαι, *I will know*, is regular (like λύσομαι).

## Exercise 28 θ

*Read aloud and translate into English:*

1. ἆρ᾽ οἶσθα ὁπόθεν ἐληλύθᾱσιν οἱ ξένοι;
2. οὐδεὶς ᾔδει ὅποι ἔπλευσαν οἱ ἔμποροι.
3. οὐδέποτε ἑώρᾱκα τοσοῦτον θόρυβον. ἆρ᾽ ἴστε τί γέγονεν;
4. ὁ αὐτουργός, οὐκ εἰδὼς τί βούλεται ὁ ξένος, ἠπόρει τί δεῖ ποιῆσαι.
5. οὗτοι οὔτ᾽ ἴσᾱσι πότε γενήσεται ἡ ἐκκλησίᾱ οὔτε βούλονται εἰδέναι.
6. ὦ κάκιστε, εὖ ἴσθι κακὰ πεισόμενος, οὕτω κακὰ πρᾱ́ξᾱς.
7. οἱ πολῖται οὐκ ᾔδεσαν τὸν ῥήτορα ψευδῆ εἰπόντα.
8. οἱ ἄγγελοι ἀπῆλθον πρὶν εἰδέναι πότερον ἡμεῖς τοὺς λόγους δεξόμεθα ἢ οὔ.
9. μείνατε ἕως ἂν εἰδῆτε τί βουλόμεθα.
10. αἱ γυναῖκες, εἰδυῖαι τοὺς ἄνδρας ἐς κίνδῡνον καταστάντας, μάλα ἐφοβοῦντο.

## Exercise 28 ι

*Translate into Greek:*

1. Be assured (= Know well) that the king is becoming angry.
2. Do you know where the children have gone?
3. I wish to know why you did this.

4. Knowing well what had happened, the woman told her husband (*dative*) the truth.

5. Not knowing when the ship would arrive, they were waiting all day at (ἐν) the harbor.

# Ο ΚΡΟΙΣΟΣ ΓΙΓΝΩΣΚΕΙ
# ΤΗΝ ΕΑΥΤΟΥ ΑΜΑΡΤΙΑΝ

*Read the following passages (adapted from Herodotus 1.90–91) and answer the comprehension questions:*

ὁ δὲ Κῦρος τὸν Κροῖσον θαυμάζων τῆς σοφίης εἵνεκα ἐκέλευε αὐτὸν αἰτεῖν ἥντινα ἂν δόσιν βούληται. ὁ δὲ Κροῖσος εἶπε· "ὦ δέσποτα, χαριεῖ μοι μάλιστα, ἐάν με ἐᾶς τὸν θεὸν τῶν Ἑλλήνων, ὃν ἐγὼ ἐτίμησα μάλιστα, ἐρέσθαι εἰ ἐξαπατᾶν τοὺς εὖ ποιέοντας νόμος ἐστί οἱ." Κῦρος δὲ ἤρετο τί τοῦτο αἰτέει. Κροῖσος δὲ πάντα οἱ ἐξηγέετο, τάς τε ἀποκρίσεις τῶν χρηστηρίων διεξιὼν καὶ τὰ ἀναθήματα ἃ ἐς   5
Δελφοὺς ἔπεμψε καὶ ὅπως ἐπαρθεὶς τῷ μαντείῳ ἐστρατεύσατο ἐπὶ τοὺς Πέρσας. Κῦρος δὲ γελάσας εἶπε· "καὶ τούτου τεύξεαι παρ' ἐμοῦ καὶ ἄλλου παντὸς οὗ ἂν δέῃ."

[δόσιν, *gift*   ἐξαπατᾶν, *to deceive*   οἱ, dative of possession, *for him, his*   οἱ, indirect object, *to him*   τάς . . . ἀποκρίσεις, *the answers*   διεξιών (from διεξέρχομαι), *going through in detail, relating*   ἐπαρθεὶς (from ἐπαίρω), *having been raised; having been induced*   τεύξεαι* = τεύξει (future of τυγχάνω) + gen., *you will get*]

1. Why does Cyrus admire Croesus?
2. What does Cyrus order Croesus to do?
3. What does Croesus want to ask the Greek god in Delphi?
4. What three things does Croesus recount to Cyrus?
5. What is Cyrus's reaction and response?

ὡς δὲ ταῦτα ἤκουσε ὁ Κροῖσος πέμπων ἀγγέλους ἐς Δελφοὺς ἐκέλευε αὐτοὺς τιθέντας τὰς πέδας ἐν τῷ ἱερῷ τὸν θεὸν ἐρωτᾶν εἰ οὔ τι ἐπαισχύνεται τοῖσι   10
μαντείοισι ἐπάρας Κροῖσον στρατεύεσθαι ἐπὶ Πέρσας.

[τὰς πέδας, *the shackles* (that Croesus wore when he was bound on the pyre)   ἐπαισχύνεται, *he is ashamed*]

6. What did Croesus order the messengers to do first when they arrived in Delphi?
7. What were the messengers to ask the god?

ἀφικομένοισι δὲ τοῖσι Λυδοῖσι καὶ λέγουσι τὰ ἐντεταλμένα ἡ Πῡθίη εἶπε τάδε· "τὴν πεπρωμένην μοῖραν ἀδύνατόν ἐστι ἀποφυγεῖν καὶ θεῷ. κατὰ δὲ τὸ μαντεῖον τὸ γενόμενον, οὐκ ὀρθῶς Κροῖσος μέμφεται· προηγόρευε γὰρ ὁ Ἀπόλλων, ἐὰν

στρατεύηται ἐπὶ Πέρσᾱς, μεγάλην ἀρχὴν αὐτὸν καταλύσειν. τὸν δὲ εὖ μέλλοντα    15
βουλεύεσθαι ἐχρῆν ἐπερέσθαι πότερον τὴν ἑαυτοῦ ἢ τὴν Κῡ́ρου λέγοι ἀρχήν."
ταῦτα μὲν ἡ Πῡθίη ἀπεκρῑ́νατο τοῖσι Λῡδοῖσι, οἱ δὲ ἐπανῆλθον ἐς Σάρδῑς καὶ ταῦτα
ἀπήγγειλαν Κροίσῳ. ὁ δὲ ἀκούσᾱς συνέγνω ἑαυτοῦ εἶναι τὴν ἁμαρτίᾱν καὶ οὐ τοῦ
θεοῦ.

[τὰ ἐντεταλμένα (from ἐντέλλω), *the things that had been commanded* = Croesus's
commands   πεπρωμένην (from πόρω, *I furnish, offer, give*), *fated*   μοῖραν, *fate* (=
*portion, allotment, lot*)   καὶ, *even*   προηγόρευε, *foretold*   τὸν δὲ εὖ μέλλοντα
βουλεύεσθαι, *and he, if he was going to plan well*   ἐπερέσθαι, *to ask in addition*
λέγοι, *meant*   ἀπήγγειλαν, *announced*   συνέγνω (from συγγιγνώσκω), *he acknowl-
edged, admitted*   τὴν ἁμαρτίᾱν, *the mistake*]

8.  What does the Pythia say is impossible?
9.  Does the Pythia agree with Croesus's criticism of the oracle?
10. What, exactly, had the oracle said?
11. What should Croesus have asked in addition?
12. What words suggest that the Pythia thinks that Croesus was not suffi-
    ciently cautious?
13. Whom does Croesus finally blame?

## Exercise 28 κ

*Translate into Greek:*

1.  Croesus has sent messengers to Delphi to ask the god why he has be-
    trayed (*use* προδίδωμι) him (ἑαυτόν).
2.  The messengers have arrived at Delphi, and, standing in the temple,
    have consulted the oracle.
3.  The Pythia has interpreted (*use* ἐξηγέομαι) the oracle of Apollo; the
    god blames Croesus for (= as, *use* ὡς) not being prudent.
4.  Croesus, having heard (*use* ἀκούω, *perfect* ἀκήκοα) the oracle, comes
    to know that he himself was wrong.
5.  "Alas, alas," he says, "how foolish (*use* ἀνόητος, -ον) I was! I my-
    self, as it seems, have destroyed my own empire."

Apollo enthroned in his temple

The nine Muses

# ΑΛΛΟΣ ΛΟΓΟΣ ΠΕΡΙ ΤΟΥ ΚΡΟΙΣΟΥ

The lyric poet Bacchylides was born on the island of Ceos ca. 524 B.C. None of his poetry was known to us until 1896, when a papyrus was found in Egypt containing the remains of fourteen odes in honor of victors in the great games and four odes in honor of Dionysus. All Bacchylides' poems belong to the genre called "choral lyric," that is to say, poems written for public performance, usually on religious occasions, by a chorus that sang the poem to the accompaniment of flute and lyre and expressed the drama of the poem through dance. Such performances had been a central part of Greek festivals since the Bronze Age and took place everywhere in Greece.

The lines below are part of a poem commissioned to celebrate the victory of Hieron, tyrant of Syracuse, in the chariot race at the Olympic Games of 468 B.C. This was the most prestigious of all victories in the games and would have been celebrated on Hieron's return to Syracuse at a religious festival.

The dialect of choral lyric by tradition had a Doric coloring, most clearly seen in the predominance of long α, e.g., ἀρχᾱγέτᾱν = ἀρχηγέτην (as an aid in reading, Attic equivalents are given for words glossed in the notes with Doric spellings). Other features of the genre are swift changes of direction in thought or scene, the abbreviated form in which mythical examples are given (it is assumed that the story is known to the audience, and the poet concentrates on the dramatic moments), and the free use of colorful compound adjectives, often coined for the particular context.

In choral odes the central feature is often a myth, which is more or less closely connected with the main subject of the poem. Croesus was an historical figure, but his story is here told as a myth. In Bacchylides' version Croesus builds the pyre himself and ascends it with his family in order to commit suicide and so avoid slavery. Apollo rescues him and takes him and his family to live with the Hyperboreans, a legendary people who live in the far North. The connection with Hieron is that both were exceptionally generous to Delphi and both were rewarded for their generosity.

## VOCABULARY

1    ἐπεί, *for*    καί, *even*    δαμασίππου, *horse-taming*
2    ἀρχᾱγέτᾱν (= ἀρχηγέτην), *ruler*
3    εὖτε, *when*
     τὰν πεπρωμένᾱν (= τὴν πεπρωμένην) ... κρίσιν (4), *the fated judgment*
4    Ζηνὸς τελέσσαντος = Διὸς τελέσαντος, *Zeus having brought to pass*
5    Περσᾶν = Περσῶν    ἁλίσκοντο = ἡλίσκοντο
6    ὁ χρῡσάορος ... Ἀπόλλων (7), *Apollo of the golden sword*
7    φύλαξ' = ἐφύλαξε    ἄελπτον ἇμαρ (= ἦμαρ), *the unexpected day*
8    μολών, *having come*
     πολυδάκρυον ... δουλοσύνᾱν (9), *tearful slavery*
9    μίμνειν (= μένειν), *to wait for*
10    χαλκοτειχέος ... αὐλᾶς, *the bronze-walled courtyard*
     προπάροιθεν + gen., *before, in front of*

ὁ Κροῖσος τῆς πυρῆς ἐπιβεβηκὼς σπονδὴν ποιεῖται.

 

ἐπεί ποτε καὶ δαμασίππου
  Λῡδίᾱς ἀρχᾱγέτᾱν,
εὖτε τὰν πεπρωμένᾱν
  Ζηνὸς τελέσσαντος κρίσιν
5  Σάρδιες Περσᾶν ἁλίσκοντο στρατῷ,
  Κροῖσον ὁ χρῡσάορος

φύλαξ᾽ Ἀπόλλων. ὁ δ᾽ ἐς ἄελπτον ἆμαρ
μολὼν πολυδάκρυον οὐκ ἔμελλε
μίμνειν ἔτι δουλοσύνᾱν· πυρὰν δὲ
10  χαλκοτειχέος προπάροιθεν αὐλᾶς

11  νᾱήσατ' (= ἐνᾱήσατο; from νηέω), *he heaped up*     ἔνθα, *where*
    ἀλόχῳ ... κεδνᾷ, *his dear wife*
12  εὐπλοκάμοις (with θυγατράσι, 13), *fair-haired*
    ἄλαστον, *inconsolably*
13  δῡρομέναις = ὀδῡρομέναις      χέρας = χεῖρας
14  αἰπὺν αἰθέρα, *the high air*
    σφετέρᾱς, *his*      ἀείρᾱς = ἄρᾱς
15  γέγωνεν (perfect with present sense) *he calls aloud*
    ὑπέρβιε, *mighty*
17  Λᾱτοΐδᾱς (= Λητοΐδης) ἄναξ, *lord son of Leto* (i.e., Apollo, whose mother was
       Leto)
18  ἔρρουσιν, *are gone, have vanished*
    Ἀλυάττᾱ δόμοι = Ἀλυάττου δόμος, *the house of Alyattes*
19  ἀμοιβᾱ́ (= ἀμοιβή) + gen., *return for*
20  Πῡθωνόθεν, *from Delphi* (Pytho was the old name for Delphi)
21  πέρθουσι = πορθοῦσι
    δοριάλωτον, *taken by the spear*
22  ἐρεύθεται, *is reddened, runs red*
    χρῡσοδῑνᾱς (= χρῡσοδῑνης) Πακτωλός, *the Pactolus eddying with gold* (the river
       Pactolus, which ran through Sardis, contained gold)
23  ἀεικελίως, *shamefully*
24  ἐΰκτίτων μεγάρων, *their well-built houses*
25  τὰ πρόσθεν ἐχθρὰ φίλα, *what was hateful before* (is now) *dear*
    γλύκιστον, (is) *sweetest* (the subject is θανεῖν)
26  τόσ(α), *so much; this*
    ἀβροβάτᾱν (= ἀβροβάτην), *delicately-stepping* (servant)
    κέλευσεν = ἐκέλευσεν
27  ἅπτειν ξύλινον δόμον, *to light the wooden pyre* (lit., *structure, house*)
    ἔκλαγον, *were shrieking*
28  ἀνὰ ... ἔβαλλον (29) = ἀνέβαλλον      φίλᾱς, *their own*      μᾱτρί = μητρί
29  προφανής, *clear beforehand, foreseen*
    θνᾱτοῖσιν (= θνητοῖς), *for mortals*
30  ἔχθιστος, *most hateful*      φόνων, *of deaths*
32  λαμπρὸν ... μένος, *the bright strength*
    διάϊσσεν (= διῆσσεν), *was rushing through* (the pyre)
33  ἐπιστᾱ́σᾱς (= ἐπιστήσᾱς), *having set above*
    μελαγκευθὲς νέφος, *a black-covering cloud*
34  σβέννῡεν (= ἐσβέννῡ), *was quenching*
    ξανθᾱ̀ν φλόγα, *the yellow flame*
35  ἄπιστον, (is) *incredible*
    μέριμνα, *the care, providence*
36  τεύχει, *brings to pass*
    Δᾱλογενής (= Δηλογενής), *born in Delos*
37  Ὑπερβορέους, *the Hyperboreans* (a mythical people living in the far North)
    γέροντα, i.e., Croesus
38  τανισφύροις ... κούραις, *the maidens of the slender ankles*
    κατένασσε (aorist of καταναίω), *settled*
39  εὐσέβειαν, *his piety*      ὅτι, *because*
    θνᾱτῶν (= θνητῶν), *of* (all) *mortals*
40  ἀγαθέᾱν ... Πῡθώ, *holy Pytho* (Delphi)

νᾱήσατ', ἔνθα σὺν ἀλόχῳ τε κεδνᾷ
σὺν εὐπλοκάμοις τ' ἐπέβαιν' ἄλαστον
θῡγατράσι δῡρομέναις· χέρας δ' ἐς
      αἰπὺν αἰθέρα σφετέρᾱς ἀείρᾱς

15  γέγωνεν· "ὑπέρβιε δαῖμον,
      ποῦ θεῶν ἐστιν χάρις;
ποῦ δὲ Λᾱτοίδᾱς ἄναξ;
      ἔρρουσιν Ἀλυάττᾱ δόμοι,
τίς δὲ νῦν δώρων ἀμοιβᾷ μῡρίων
20      φαίνεται Πῡθωνόθεν;

      πέρθουσι Μῆδοι δοριάλωτον ἄστυ,
      ἐρεύθεται αἵματι χρῡσοδῑνᾱς
Πακτωλός, ἀεικελίως γυναῖκες
      ἐξ ἐϋκτίτων μεγάρων ἄγονται·

25  τὰ πρόσθεν ἐχθρὰ φίλα· θανεῖν γλύκιστον."
      τόσ' εἶπε, καὶ ἁβροβάτᾱν κέλευσεν
ἅπτειν ξύλινον δόμον.  ἔκλαγον δὲ
      παρθένοι, φίλᾱς τ' ἀνὰ μᾱτρὶ χεῖρας

      ἔβαλλον· ὁ γὰρ προφανὴς θνᾱ-
30      τοῖσιν ἔχθιστος φόνων·
ἀλλ' ἐπεὶ δεινοῦ πυρὸς
      λαμπρὸν διάϊσσεν μένος,
Ζεὺς ἐπιστᾱ́σᾱς μελαγκευθὲς νέφος
      σβέννῡεν ξανθὰν φλόγα.

35  ἄπιστον οὐδέν, ὅ τι θεῶν μέριμνα
      τεύχει· τότε Δᾱλογενὴς Ἀπόλλων
φέρων ἐς Ὑπερβορέους γέροντα
      σὺν τανισφύροις κατένασσε κούραις

      δι' εὐσέβειαν, ὅτι μέγιστα θνᾱτῶν
40  ἐς ἀγαθέᾱν ἀνέπεμψε Πῡθώ.

                                    Bacchylides 3.23–62

Greece

# 29
# ΜΕΓΑ ΤΟ ΤΗΣ
# ΘΑΛΑΣΣΗΣ ΚΡΑΤΟΣ (α)

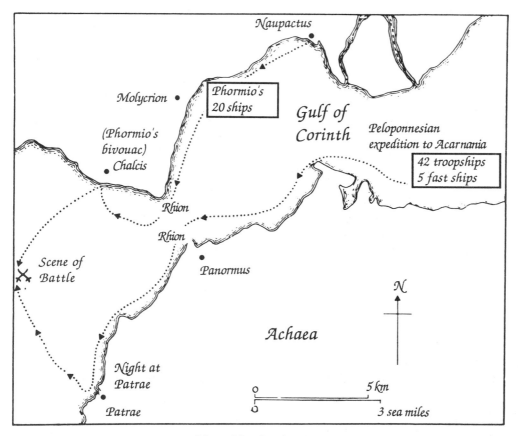

Map of the first battle

In this chapter we return to excerpts from Thucydides' account of the Peloponnesian War. That war has been described as a struggle between an elephant and a whale; the Athenians could not face the Peloponnesian army in the field, and the Peloponnesians could not risk a naval battle against the Athenian fleet. In this chapter we give Thucydides' accounts of two naval victories achieved by the Athenian admiral Phormio against heavy odds in the summer of 429 B.C. These victories were decisive; the Peloponnesians were forced to acknowledge the naval supremacy of the Athenians not only in the Aegean but also here in the Gulf of Corinth (Κρῖσαῖος κόλπος), and they made no attempt to challenge the Athenians by sea throughout the rest of the Archidamian War, i.e., until the truce of 421 B.C.

229

## VOCABULARY

*Verbs*
ἐκπνέω, [πνευσε-] ἐκπνευ-
σοῦμαι and [πνευ-] ἐκπνεύ-
σομαι, ἐξέπνευσα, ἐκπέ-
πνευκα, *I blow out; I blow
from*
ἐπιγίγνομαι, *I come after*
ἐπιτίθεμαι, [θη-] ἐπιθήσομαι,
[θε-] ἐπεθέμην + dat., *I attack*
ἐπιχειρέω + dat., *I attempt;
I attack*
παραπλέω, *I sail by; I sail
past; I sail along*
στέλλω, [στελε-] στελῶ,
[στειλ-] ἔστειλα, [σταλ-]
ἔσταλκα, ἔσταλμαι, ἐστά-
λην, *I send; I equip; I take
down* (sails)
συνάγω (ξυνάγω), *I bring together; I compress*
φρουρέω, transitive, *I guard;*
intransitive, *I am on guard*

*Nouns*
ἡ ἕως, τῆς ἕω, *dawn*
ἡ ἤπειρος, τῆς ἠπείρου, *land;
mainland*
ὁ κόλπος, τοῦ κόλπου, *lap; gulf*
ἡ ναυμαχίᾱ, τῆς ναυμαχίᾱς,
*naval battle*
τὸ πλοῖον, τοῦ πλοίου, *boat*
τὸ πνεῦμα, τοῦ πνεύματος,
*breeze*
ἡ πρύμνη, τῆς πρύμνης, *stern*
(of a ship)
ἡ πρῷρα, τῆς πρῴρᾱς, *bow* (of a
ship)
ἡ τάξις, τῆς τάξεως, *rank; position*
ἡ ταραχή, τῆς ταραχῆς, *confusion*

*Adverb*
εἴσω (ἔσω), *inward*

*Conjunction*
μήτε, *and not*
μήτε . . . μήτε, *neither . . .
nor*

*Expressions*
ἐπὶ τὴν ἕω, *at dawn*
κατὰ μέσον . . . , *in the middle
of . . .*

τοῦ δὲ ἐπιγιγνομένου χειμῶνος Ἀθηναῖοι ναῦς ἔστειλαν εἴκοσι μὲν
περὶ Πελοπόννησον καὶ Φορμίωνα στρατηγόν, ὃς ὁρμώμενος ἐκ
Ναυπάκτου φυλακὴν εἶχεν ὥστε μήτ᾽ ἐκπλεῖν ἐκ Κορίνθου καὶ τοῦ
Κρῑσαίου κόλπου μηδένα μήτ᾽ ἐσπλεῖν.

[ὁρμώμενος, *starting from, based on*     τοῦ Κρῑσαίου κόλπου: Κρῖσα was a city near
Delphi that gave its name to what we call the Gulf of Corinth]

In the summer of 429 B.C. a Corinthian fleet of forty-seven ships tried to
slip through Phormio's blockade and take reinforcements to their allies
fighting in Acarnania in northwest Greece (see map, page 228).

οἱ δὲ Κορίνθιοι καὶ οἱ ἄλλοι ξύμμαχοι ἠναγκάσθησαν περὶ τὰς    5
αὐτὰς ἡμέρᾱς ναυμαχῆσαι πρὸς Φορμίωνα καὶ τὰς εἴκοσι ναῦς τῶν
Ἀθηναίων αἳ ἐφρούρουν ἐν Ναυπάκτῳ. ὁ γὰρ Φορμίων παραπλέοντας αὐτοὺς ἔξω τοῦ κόλπου ἐτήρει, βουλόμενος ἐν τῇ
εὐρυχωρίᾳ ἐπιθέσθαι.

[ἔξω + gen., here, *out of*    ἐτήρει (from τηρέω), *was watching*    τῇ εὐρυχωρίᾳ, *the broad waters*]

οἱ δὲ Κορίνθιοι καὶ οἱ ξύμμαχοι ἔπλεον μὲν οὐχ ὡς ἐπὶ ναυμαχίᾳ    10
ἀλλὰ στρατιωτικώτερον παρεσκευασμένοι ἐς τὴν Ἀκαρνανίαν, καὶ
οὐκ οἰόμενοι τοὺς Ἀθηναίους ἂν τολμῆσαι ναυμαχίαν ποιήσασθαι·
παρὰ γῆν σφῶν μέντοι κομιζόμενοι τοὺς Ἀθηναίους ἀντιπαραπλέοντας ἑώρων καί, ἐπεὶ ἐκ Πατρῶν τῆς Ἀχαΐας πρὸς τὴν ἀντιπέρας
ἤπειρον διέβαλλον, εἶδον τοὺς Ἀθηναίους ἀπὸ Χαλκίδος    15
προσπλέοντας σφίσιν· οὕτω δὴ ἀναγκάζονται ναυμαχεῖν κατὰ μέσον
τὸν πορθμόν.

[ἐπὶ + dat., *for* (of purpose)    στρατιωτικώτερον, *more for carrying troops*    τὴν Ἀκαρνανίᾶν, *Acarnania* (see map, page 228)    ἂν τολμῆσαι, ἄν + infin., representing a potential optative in indirect statement, *would dare*    παρὰ γῆν σφῶν, *past their own land*    κομιζόμενοι, *being conveyed, sailing along*    ἀντιπαραπλέοντας, *sailing along opposite*    ἑώρων = imperfect of ὁράω    ἀντιπέρᾱς, adv., *opposite* διέβαλλον, *were crossing*    σφίσιν, dative plural pronoun, *(toward) them*    Χαλκί-δος, *Chalcis*    τὸν πορθμόν, *straits*]

καὶ οἱ μὲν Πελοποννήσιοι ἐτάξαντο κύκλον τῶν νεῶν ὡς μέγιστον
οἷοί τ' ἦσαν, τὰς πρῴρᾱς μὲν ἔξω, ἔσω δὲ τὰς πρύμνᾱς, καὶ τὰ λεπτὰ
πλοῖα ἃ ξυνέπλει ἐντὸς ποιοῦνται. οἱ δὲ Ἀθηναῖοι κατὰ μίαν ναῦν    20
τεταγμένοι περιέπλεον αὐτοὺς κύκλῳ καὶ ξυνῆγον ἐς ὀλίγον, ἐν χρῷ
αἰεὶ παραπλέοντες· προείρητο δ' αὐτοῖς ὑπὸ Φορμίωνος μὴ ἐπιχειρεῖν
πρὶν ἂν αὐτὸς σημήνῃ. ἤλπιζε γὰρ αὐτῶν οὐ μενεῖν τὴν τάξιν ἀλλὰ
τὰς ναῦς ξυμπεσεῖσθαι πρὸς ἀλλήλᾱς καὶ τὰ πλοῖα ταραχὴν
παρέξειν· εἴ τ' ἐκπνεύσειεν ἐκ τοῦ κόλπου τὸ πνεῦμα, ὅπερ εἰώθει    25
γίγνεσθαι ἐπὶ τὴν ἕω, οὐδένα χρόνον ἡσυχάσειν αὐτούς.

[ἔξω, here, *outward*    λεπτὰ, *light*    κατὰ μίαν ναῦν, *in single file*    ἐς ὀλίγον, *into a small* (space)    ἐν χρῷ, lit., *on the skin* = within a hair's breadth    προείρητο (pluperfect passive of προερέω, *I order beforehand*), *an order had been given*    μενεῖν, *remain, hold* (the subject of the infin. is αὐτῶν . . . τὴν τάξιν)    ξυμπεσεῖσθαι (future infin. of συμπῑπτω), *would fall together, clash*)]

—adapted from Thucydides 2.69 and 2.83.2–84.2

## PRINCIPAL PARTS: ὁράω and οἶδα, Seeing and Knowing

ὁράω, imperfect, ἑώρων (note the double augment in this and some of the following forms), [ὀπ-] ὄψομαι, [ἰδ-] εἶδον (irregular augment), [ὁρᾱ-] ἑόρᾱκα or ἑώρᾱκα, ἑώρᾱμαι or [ὀπ-] ὦμμαι, ὤφθην, I see

The stem ἰδ- (seen in εἶδον above) and its variants οἰδ- and εἰδ- also give οἶδα (perfect with present meaning), I know, ᾔδη or ᾔδειν (pluperfect with imperfect meaning), I was aware, was knowing; I knew, and εἴσομαι, I will know. See Chapter 28, Grammar 9, pages 219–220.

## WORD STUDY

*From what Greek words are the following theological terms derived:*

1. theology
2. Bible
3. dogma
4. orthodoxy
5. heresy
6. ecclesiastical

# Thucydides

Thucydides was born about 455 B.C. of a noble Athenian family, probably related to that of the aristocratic Cimon. Little is known about his life. He suffered from the plague (2.48). He was general in 424 B.C. and was exiled for failing to prevent Brasidas from taking the strategic city of Amphipolis (4.105–106 and see page 113 above). He returned to Athens in 404 B.C. after the end of the war and died there about 400 B.C. In the introduction to his history (1.1), he says that he began writing it as soon as war broke out, feeling certain that it would be the most important war in history up to his time. He died before completing it, breaking off abruptly in his account of 411 B.C.

Unlike Herodotus, Thucydides was writing the history of events through which he had lived and at many of which he had himself been present. Even so, he is well aware of the difficulty of getting the facts right. In his introduction (1.22) he discusses this problem:

> With regard to the factual reporting of the events in the war, I did not think it right to give the account of the first man I happened to meet, nor to give my personal impressions, but I have examined each question with a view to the greatest possible accuracy both in events at which I was present myself and in those of which I heard from others. But it was a laborious business to find the truth, because eyewitnesses at each event did not give the same report about it, but their reports differed according to their partiality to either side or their powers of memory.

It should be remembered that his sources were not only Athenian. His long exile gave him the chance of making inquiries on the other side. He says (1.22) that the absence of the storytelling element (τὸ μῦθῶδες) may make his history less attractive to his audience:

I shall be satisfied if those who want to examine an accurate account of events that happened in the past and that are likely to be repeated some time in the future in similar form, human nature being what it is, find my history useful.  It is composed to be a possession forever (κτῆμα ἐς αἰεί), not a performance to please an immediate public.

So there are lessons to be learned from his history, especially by statesmen.  Although Thucydides restricts his history to military and political events, it is human nature, as revealed in both individual and social psychology, that most interests him.  When, for instance, he has given a clinical account of the physical symptoms and effects of the plague (2.49–51), he goes on to discuss its psychological effects on the Athenian people (2.52–53).

Such passages of explicit analysis are rare.  More often Thucydides uses speeches to show motives, underlying causes of events, and principles at stake.  These speeches are placed at key points throughout most of the history.  For example, when the Spartans send their final ultimatum, the Athenians debate their reply (see Chapter 21).  Of this debate, Thucydides quotes one speech only, that of Pericles (1.140–44).  In his speech, which extends to five printed pages, Pericles not only gives reasons for rejecting the Spartan ultimatum but also outlines the military and economic resources of each side and the strategy on which they should conduct the war, which he considered inevitable.  The following narrative shows this strategy put into practice.  The speech enables the reader to understand why the Athenians acted as they did.

Although fewer than thirty years separate the publication of Herodotus's history from that of Thucydides, there is a great gulf between them, which is not to be explained simply by the personalities of the authors.  Herodotus was a child of the old order, accepting traditional values and beliefs.  Thucydides is a product of the sophistic movement.  He always searches for rational explanations of events, is sceptical in matters of religion, discounts oracles, and is austerely scientific in intent.  Despite the austerity of his narrative, which appears impartial and impersonal even when he is writing of himself, his deep feelings are apparent from the way he tells the story, notably, for instance, in his description of the defeat of the Athenian fleet in the Great Harbor of Syracuse, which sealed the fate of the expedition to Sicily and ultimately led to the downfall of Athens.

---

### Greek Wisdom

#### Socrates

The Pythian priestess at Delphi is said to have made the following pronouncement about Socrates (Scholiast, Aristophanes, *Clouds* 144, and see Diogenes Laertius 2.37 and Plato, *Apology* 21a):

σοφὸς Σοφοκλῆς, σοφώτερος δ' Εὐριπίδης,
ἀνδρῶν ἁπάντων Σωκράτης σοφώτατος.

# ΜΕΓΑ ΤΟ ΤΗΣ ΘΑΛΑΣΣΗΣ ΚΡΑΤΟΣ (β)

## VOCABULARY

*Verbs*

ἀποστέλλω, *I send off*

ἐξαρτύω [= ἐκ + ἀρτύω ], ἐξαρτύσω, ἐξήρτῡσα, ἐξήρτῡκα, ἐξήρτῡμαι, ἐξηρτύθην, *I equip*

καταδύω, καταδύσω, κατέδῡσα, [δυ-] καταδέδυκα, καταδέδυμαι, κατεδύθην, transitive, *I sink;* athematic aorist, κατέδῡν, intransitive, *I sank;* of the sun, *set*

προσπῑ́πτω + dat., *I fall against; I fall on*

ταράττω (ταράσσω), [ταραχ-] ταράξω, ἐτάραξα, τετάραγμαι, ἐταράχθην, *I confuse*

χωρέω, *I go; I come*

*Nouns*

ἡ παρασκευή, τῆς παρασκευῆς, *preparation*

τὸ τρόπαιον, τοῦ τροπαίου, *trophy*

ὡς δὲ τό τε πνεῦμα κατῄει καὶ αἱ νῆες, ἐν ὀλίγῳ ἤδη οὖσαι, ὑπὸ τοῦ τ' ἀνέμου καὶ τῶν πλοίων ἅμα ἐταράσσοντο, καὶ ναῦς τε νηὶ προσέπῑπτε, οἱ δὲ ναῦται βοῇ τε χρώμενοι καὶ λοιδορίᾳ οὐδὲν ἤκουον τῶν παραγγελλομένων, τότε δὴ σημαίνει ὁ Φορμίων· καὶ οἱ Ἀθηναῖοι προσπεσόντες πρῶτον μὲν καταδύουσι τῶν στρατηγίδων 5 νεῶν μίαν, ἔπειτα δὲ καὶ τὰς ἄλλᾱς ᾗ χωρήσειαν διέφθειρον, καὶ κατέστησαν αὐτοὺς ἐς φόβον, ὥστε φεύγουσιν ἐς Πάτρᾱς καὶ Δύμην τῆς Ἀχαΐᾱς. οἱ δὲ Ἀθηναῖοι διώξαντες καὶ ναῦς δώδεκα λαβόντες τούς τε ἄνδρας ἐξ αὐτῶν τοὺς πλείστους ἀνελόμενοι, ἐς Μολύκρειον ἀπέπλεον, καὶ τροπαῖον στήσαντες ἐπὶ τῷ Ῥίῳ ἀνεχώρησαν ἐς 10 Ναύπᾱκτον.

[ἐν ὀλίγῳ, *in a little* (space) λοιδορίᾳ, *abuse* τῶν παραγγελλομένων, *of the orders that were being passed along* τῶν στρατηγίδων νεῶν, *of the ships of the generals* (the flagships) ᾗ, *where, wherever* Δύμην, *Dyme, three miles or a little more than four and three-quarters kilometers southwest of Patrae* τῷ Ῥίῳ, *the Headland* (Rhion on the north shore of the Gulf of Corinth)]

παρέπλευσαν δὲ καὶ οἱ Πελοποννήσιοι εὐθὺς ταῖς περιλοίποις τῶν νεῶν ἐκ τῆς Δύμης καὶ Πατρῶν ἐς Κυλλήνην. καὶ ἀπὸ Λευκάδος Κνῆμός τε καὶ αἱ ἐκείνων νῆες ἀφικνοῦνται ἐς τὴν Κυλλήνην.

πέμπουσι δὲ καὶ οἱ Λακεδαιμόνιοι τῷ Κνήμῳ ξυμβούλους ἐπὶ τὰς    15
ναῦς, κελεύοντες ἄλλην ναυμαχίαν βελτίω παρασκευάζεσθαι καὶ
μὴ ὑπ' ὀλίγων νεῶν εἴργεσθαι τῆς θαλάσσης. οὐ γὰρ ᾤοντο σφῶν τὸ
ναυτικὸν λείπεσθαι ἀλλὰ γεγενῆσθαί τινα μαλακίαν· ὀργῇ οὖν
ἀπέστελλον τοὺς ξυμβούλους. οἱ δὲ μετὰ τοῦ Κνήμου ἀφικόμενοι
ἄλλας τε ναῦς μετεπέμψαντο τοὺς ξυμμάχους παρακαλοῦντες    20
βοηθεῖν καὶ τὰς προϋπαρχούσας ναῦς ἐξηρτύοντο ὡς ἐπὶ μάχην.

[εὐθὺς, here, *straight* (with ἐκ τῆς Δύμης . . . ἐς Κυλλήνην)  **ταῖς περιλοίποις**, *with
the rest*  **Κυλλήνην**, *Cyllene*, about fifty-six miles or ninety kilometers southwest of
Patrae (see map, page 228)  **Λευκάδος**, *Leucas*, an island off the coast of Acarnania
(see map, page 228)  **Κνῆμος**: Cnemus was the Peloponnesian commander-in-chief,
based in Leucas  **ἐκείνων**, i.e., of the Leucadians  **ξυμβούλους**, *advisers*
**εἴργεσθαι** (from εἴργω) + gen., *to be shut out from*  **ᾤοντο** (from οἴομαι), *they were
thinking*  **σφῶν**, *of themselves, their*  **λείπεσθαι**, *to be deficient*  **μαλακίαν**, *soft-
ness, cowardice*  **ὀργῇ**, adv., *in anger*  **τὰς προϋπαρχούσας**, *the (ships) already
there*]

πέμπει δὲ καὶ ὁ Φορμίων ἐς τὰς Ἀθήνας ἀγγέλους τήν τε
παρασκευὴν αὐτῶν ἀγγελοῦντας καὶ περὶ τῆς ναυμαχίας ἣν
ἐνίκησαν φράσοντας, καὶ κελεύων αὐτοὺς ἑαυτῷ ναῦς ὡς πλείστας
ταχέως ἀποστεῖλαι, ὡς καθ' ἡμέραν ἐλπίδος οὔσης ναυμαχήσειν. οἱ    25
δὲ Ἀθηναῖοι πέμπουσιν εἴκοσι ναῦς αὐτῷ, τῷ δὲ κομίζοντι αὐτὰς
προσεπέστειλαν ἐς Κρήτην πρῶτον ἀφικέσθαι, ἵνα ξυμμάχοις τισὶν
ἐκεῖ βοηθοίη.

[**προσεπέστειλαν** (from προσεπιστέλλω) + dat., *they instructed in addition*]

—adapted from Thucydides 2.84.3–85.5

## PRINCIPAL PARTS: Verbs with Attic Reduplication

**ἀκούω, ἀκούσομαι, ἤκουσα,** [ἀκο-] **ἀκ-ήκο-α,** [ἀκου-] **ἠκούσθην,** intransitive, *I listen;* transitive + gen. of person, acc. of thing, *I listen to; I hear*
**ἐλαύνω,** [ἐλα-] **ἐλῶ, ἐλᾷς, ἐλᾷ,** etc., **ἤλασα, ἐλ-ήλα-κα, ἐλ-ήλα-μαι,**
**ἠλάθην,** transitive, *I drive; I march* (an army);  intransitive, *I march*
**ἐσθίω,** [ἐδ-] **ἔδομαι,** [φαγ-] **ἔφαγον,** [ἐδ-] **ἐδ-ήδο-κα,** *I eat*
In verbs that have Attic reduplication, the initial vowel and consonant of the
stem on which the perfect is based are repeated, and what was originally the initial
vowel is lengthened, thus ἀκο- > ἀκ-ήκο-α.

## WORD BUILDING

*Give the meanings of the following words:*

1.  ἡ δίκη
2.  δίκαιος, -ᾱ, -ον
3.  δικάζω
4.  ὁ δικαστής
5.  δικαστικός, -ή, -όν
6.  ἄδικος, -ον

# ΜΕΓΑ ΤΟ ΤΗΣ ΘΑΛΑΣΣΗΣ ΚΡΑΤΟΣ (γ)

## VOCABULARY

*Verbs*
  **κατέχω**, *I hold back*
  **ὁρμίζω**, *I bring* (a ship) *into harbor;* middle, *I come to anchor*
  **παρακελεύομαι**, *I encourage, exhort*
*Nouns*
  **ἡ εὐρυχωρίᾱ, τῆς εὐρυχωρίᾱς,** *broad waters*

  **ἡ ἧττα (ἧσσα), τῆς ἥττης,** *defeat*
  **τὸ πάθος, τοῦ πάθους,** *experience; misfortune*
*Adjective*
  **πρόθῡμος, -ον,** *eager*
*Adverb*
  **οὗπερ,** *where*

οἱ δὲ ἐν Κυλλήνῃ Πελοποννήσιοι, ἐν ᾧ οἱ Ἀθηναῖοι περὶ τὴν Κρήτην κατείχοντο, παρεσκευασμένοι ὡς ἐπὶ ναυμαχίᾱν παρέπλευσαν ἐς Πάνορμον τὸν Ἀχαϊκόν, οὗπερ αὐτοῖς ὁ κατὰ γῆν στρατὸς τῶν Πελοποννησίων προσεβεβοηθήκει. παρέπλευσε δὲ καὶ ὁ Φορμίων ἐπὶ τὸ Ῥίον τὸ Μολυκρικόν, καὶ ὡρμίσατο ἔξω αὐτοῦ ναυσὶν εἴκοσι, αἷσπερ καὶ ἐναυμάχησεν. ἐπὶ οὖν τῷ Ῥίῳ τῷ Ἀχαϊκῷ οἱ Πελοποννήσιοι, ἀπέχοντι οὐ πολὺ τοῦ Πανόρμου, ὡρμίσαντο καὶ αὐτοὶ ναυσὶν ἑπτὰ καὶ ἑβδομήκοντα, ἐπειδὴ καὶ τοὺς Ἀθηναίους εἶδον. 5

[**Πάνορμον**, *Panormus* **Ἀχαϊκόν**, *Achaean* **προσεβεβοηθήκει** (from προσβοηθέω), *had come to their aid* **Μολυκρικόν**, *Molycrian*]

καὶ ἐπὶ μὲν ἓξ ἢ ἑπτὰ ἡμέρᾱς ἀνθώρμουν ἀλλήλοις, μελετῶντές τε καὶ παρασκευαζόμενοι τὴν ναυμαχίᾱν, γνώμην ἔχοντες οἱ μὲν Πελοποννήσιοι μὴ ἐκπλεῖν ἔξω τῶν Ῥίων ἐς τὴν εὐρυχωρίᾱν, φοβούμενοι τὸ πρότερον πάθος, οἱ δὲ Ἀθηναῖοι μὴ ἐσπλεῖν ἐς τὰ 10

στενά, νομίζοντες πρὸς ἐκείνων εἶναι τὴν ἐν ὀλίγῳ ναυμαχίᾶν. ἔπειτα
ὁ Κνῆμος καὶ οἱ ἄλλοι τῶν Πελοποννησίων στρατηγοί, βουλόμενοι    15
ταχέως τὴν ναυμαχίᾶν ποιῆσαι, πρίν τι καὶ ἀπὸ τῶν ᾿Αθηναίων
ἐπιβοηθῆσαι, ξυνεκάλεσαν τοὺς στρατιώτᾱς, καὶ ὁρῶντες αὐτῶν
τοὺς πολλοὺς διὰ τὴν προτέρᾱν ἧσσαν φοβουμένους καὶ οὐ
προθύμους ὄντας παρεκελεύσαντο.

[ἀνθώρμουν (from ἀνθορμέω) + dat., *they were lying at anchor opposite*    π ρ ὸ ς
ἐκείνων, *in their* (i.e., the Peloponnesians') *favor*    τι . . . ἐπιβοηθῆσαι, *any aid
came*]

—Adapted from Thucydides 2.86

The reconstructed trireme *Olympias* at sea

# ΜΕΓΑ ΤΟ ΤΗΣ
# ΘΑΛΑΣΣΗΣ ΚΡΑΤΟΣ (δ)

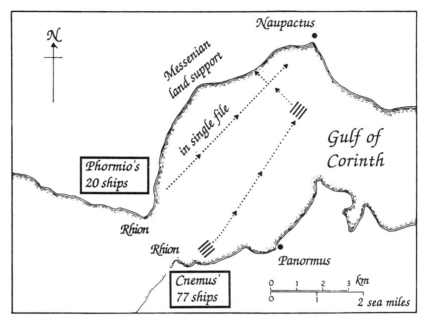

Map of the second battle

## VOCABULARY

*Verbs*

**ἀνάγομαι** [= ἀνα- + ἄγομαι],
   *I put out to sea*

**ἀπολαμβάνω**, *I cut off, intercept*

**ἀφαιρέομαι** [= ἀπο- + αἰρέομαι],
   *I take away for myself; I save*

**διαφεύγω**, *I escape*

**ἐπεισβαίνω (ἐπεσβαίνω)**
   [= ἐπι- + εἰσ/ἐσ- + βαίνω], *I go
   into*

**ἐπιβοηθέω** + dat., *I come to aid*

**ἐπιστρέφω**, 2nd aorist passive,
   active and intransitive in
   meaning, **ἐπεστράφην**, *I turn
   around*

**ὁρμέω**, *I lie at anchor*

**παραβοηθέω** + dat., *I come to
   (X's) aid*

**ὑπεκφεύγω** [= ὑπο- + ἐκ- +
   φεύγω], *I escape*

*Nouns*

**τὸ κέρας, τοῦ κέρως**, *wing* (of
   a fleet or army)

**τὰ ὅπλα, τῶν ὅπλων**, *weapons*

**τὸ σημεῖον, τοῦ σημείου**, *sign*

*Adjective*

**κενός, -ή, -όν**, *empty*

*Prepositions*

**παρά** + dat., *at the house of;*
   + acc., of persons only, *to;*
   <u>*along*</u>, <u>*past*</u>; *in respect of*

**περί** + gen., *about, concerning;
   around;* + dat., <u>*concerning*</u>;
   + acc., *around*

*Expression*

**ἅμα ἕῳ**, *at dawn*

οἱ δὲ Πελοποννήσιοι, ἐπειδὴ αὐτοῖς οἱ Ἀθηναῖοι οὐκ ἐπέπλεον ἐς
τὸν κόλπον, βουλόμενοι ἄκοντας ἔσω προαγαγεῖν αὐτούς,
ἀναγαγόμενοι ἅμα ἕῳ ἔπλεον ἐπὶ τοῦ κόλπου, ἐπὶ τεσσάρων
ταξάμενοι τὰς ναῦς, δεξιῷ κέρᾳ ἡγουμένῳ, ὥσπερ καὶ ὥρμουν· ἐπὶ δὲ
τούτῳ τῷ κέρᾳ εἴκοσι ἔταξαν τὰς ναῦς τὰς ἄριστα πλεούσας, ἵνα, εἰ ὁ   5
Φορμίων, νομίσας ἐπὶ τὴν Ναύπακτον αὐτοὺς πλεῖν, ἐπιβοηθῶν
ἐκεῖσε παραπλέοι, μὴ διαφύγοιεν τὸν ἐπίπλουν σφῶν οἱ Ἀθηναῖοι,
ἀλλὰ αὗται αἱ νῆες περικλήσειαν.

[ἐπὶ τεσσάρων, *four deep* (they were drawn up at anchor four deep; when they
weighed anchor, they turned right and sailed in column four abreast, with their twenty
fastest ships leading)   τὸν ἐπίπλουν, *the attack*   σφῶν, *of them, their*   περικλήσειαν (from περικλήω), *would shut* (them) *in, trap* (them)]

ὁ δὲ Φορμίων, ὅπερ ἐκεῖνοι προσεδέχοντο, φοβηθεὶς περὶ τῷ
χωρίῳ ἐρήμῳ ὄντι, ὡς ἑώρα ἀναγομένους αὐτούς, ἄκων καὶ κατὰ   10
σπουδὴν ἐμβιβάσας, ἔπλει παρὰ τὴν γῆν· καὶ ὁ πεζὸς στρατὸς ἅμα
τῶν Μεσσηνίων παρεβοήθει. ἰδόντες δὲ οἱ Πελοποννήσιοι αὐτοὺς
κατὰ μίαν παραπλέοντας καὶ ἤδη ὄντας ἐντὸς τοῦ κόλπου τε καὶ
πρὸς τῇ γῇ, ὅπερ ἐβούλοντο μάλιστα, ἀπὸ σημείου ἑνὸς εὐθὺς
ἐπιστρέψαντες τὰς ναῦς μετωπηδὸν ἔπλεον ὡς τάχιστα ἐπὶ τοὺς   15
Ἀθηναίους, καὶ ἤλπιζον πάσας τὰς ναῦς ἀπολήψεσθαι.

[κατὰ σπουδὴν, *hastily*   ἐμβιβάσας (from ἐμβιβάζω), *having embarked*   ἅμα: adverbial here   τῶν Μεσσηνίων: genitive with ὁ πεζὸς στρατὸς (Messenian refugees
from the Peloponnesus had been settled at Naupactus by the Athenians in 459 B.C.)
κατὰ μίαν, *in single file*   πρὸς τῇ γῇ, *near the land*   μετωπηδὸν, *with their fronts
forward, in close line* (i.e., they turned left and advanced four deep toward the north)]

τῶν δὲ Ἀθηναίων νεῶν ἕνδεκα μὲν αἵπερ ἡγοῦντο ὑπεκφεύγουσι
τὸ κέρας τῶν Πελοποννησίων· τὰς δὲ ἄλλας καταλαβόντες οἱ
Πελοποννήσιοι ἐξέωσάν τε πρὸς τὴν γῆν ὑπεκφευγούσας καὶ
διέφθειραν· ἄνδρας τε τῶν Ἀθηναίων ἀπέκτειναν ὅσοι μὴ ἐξένευσαν   20
αὐτῶν. καὶ τῶν νεῶν τινας ἀναδούμενοι εἷλκον κενάς (μίαν δὲ
αὐτοῖς ἀνδράσιν εἷλον ἤδη), τὰς δέ τινας οἱ Μεσσήνιοι,
παραβοηθήσαντες καὶ ἐπεσβαίνοντες ξὺν τοῖς ὅπλοις ἐς τὴν
θάλασσαν καὶ ἐπιβάντες, ἀπὸ τῶν καταστρωμάτων μαχόμενοι
ἀφείλοντο ἑλκομένας ἤδη.   25

[ἐξέωσαν (from ἐξωθέω), *pushed out* ὑπεκφευγούσᾱς, *as they (tried to) escape*
διέφθειραν, not *destroyed*, but *disabled* ἐξένευσαν (from ἐκνέω), *swam out, swam*
*to shore* ἀναδούμενοι (from ἀναδέομαι), *fastening with a rope, taking in tow*
αὐτοῖς ἀνδράσιν, *with the men themselves* τῶν καταστρωμάτων, *the decks*]

—adapted from Thucydides 2.90

## PRINCIPAL PARTS: ἀναμιμνῄσκω and μέμνημαι

ἀναμιμνῄσκω, [μνη-] ἀναμνήσω, ἀνέμνησα, *I remind* someone (acc.) *of*
something (acc. or gen.)
   μέμνημαι (perfect middle = present), *I have reminded myself = I remem-*
   *ber*
   μνησθήσομαι (future passive in middle sense), *I will remember*
   ἐμνήσθην (aorist passive in middle sense), *I remembered*

## WORD STUDY

*The following passage contains twenty words derived from Greek; list them*
*and explain their derivation and meaning. Then try to rewrite the passage*
*without using these Greek derivatives.*

The philosopher in his study can analyze political situations logically; he
can propose hypotheses and produce ideal solutions to problems. The
politician, however, agonizes in the sphere of the practical; he is beset by a
recurring cycle of crises, for which the therapy is empirical. Whatever
his ideology, in the event, he is guided not by dogma or theoretical analysis but by pragmatic considerations.

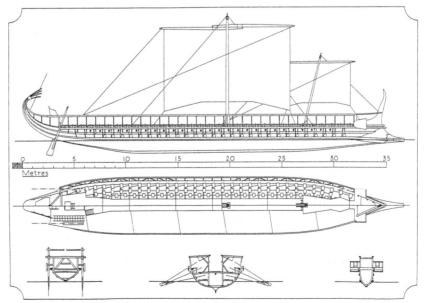

Plan of the reconstructed trireme *Olympias*

# The Downfall of Athens

The essay in Chapter 23 carried the story of the Peloponnesian War as far as the Peace of Nicias, concluded by Sparta and Athens in 421 B.C., when both sides were physically and economically exhausted by the ten years' war. There was little hope of the peace holding. It was not accepted by Corinth and Boeotia, and at Athens a rival to the peace-loving Nicias appeared in the person of Alcibiades, a cousin and ward of Pericles, rich, handsome, unscrupulous, and ambitious. Opposing Nicias, who did all he could to preserve peaceful relations with Sparta, Alcibiades initiated a policy of backing Argos, Sparta's old rival in the Peloponnesus, and forming a coalition of states that were dissatisfied with Spartan leadership. In 419 B.C. a sporadic war broke out, in which Athens was halfheartedly involved as the ally of Argos, but in 418 B.C. Sparta inflicted a crushing defeat on Argos and re-established her hegemony in the Peloponnesus, while the Athenians became interested in other imperial ventures.

In the winter of 416/415 B.C. the Athenians made the fateful decision to add Sicily to their empire. They were given a pretext for intervention by the arrival of ambassadors from a small Sicilian city, which asked for help against a neighboring city, which was backed by the greatest city in the West, Syracuse. When the matter was debated in the Assembly, Nicias advised caution, but Alcibiades argued strongly in favor of the venture. His view prevailed. In a burst of enthusiasm, the people voted for an expedition and for all the resources that the generals in command (Nicias, Alcibiades, and Lamachus) required.

The expedition departed in midsummer 415 B.C.: "It was," says Thucydides, "the most costly and splendid force that ever sailed from one Greek city." It was dogged by disaster. No sooner had it arrived in Sicily than Alcibiades was recalled to stand trial on a charge trumped up by his political enemies, but he jumped ship and fled to Sparta, where he advised the authorities to send help to Syracuse, which the Athenians were by now besieging. Just as the Athenians were about to complete an encircling wall around Syracuse, a Spartan relief force arrived and saved the city (winter 414 B.C.). Nicias decided to lift the siege and retire by sea, but the Syracusans blocked the entrance to the Great Harbor, and in the battle that followed the Athenian fleet suffered a crushing defeat. Nicias decided to destroy what was left of the fleet and retreat over land; his army was split up into two halves. Both were ambushed and annihilated:

This was the greatest action which took place in this war, . . . the most brilliant for the victors and the most disastrous for the conquered; for they were utterly defeated at all points and after undergoing the extremities of suffering were completely annihilated, infantry, ships, and all. Few of the many returned home.

(Thucydides 7.87)

Despite this terrible loss, the Athenians immediately began to build a new fleet and fought on for another nine years. This last phase of the war was quite different from what had gone on before. It was a war of movement, fought all over the Aegean. The Spartans, who bartered away the freedom of the Ionian Greeks for Persian gold, built a fleet and roused most of the Athenian Empire to revolt. In 411 B.C. Athens, reduced to desperate straits, underwent an oligarchic revolution. This was fostered by Alcibiades, who had now fled from Sparta to the Persians and undertook to win Persian support for Athens if the Athenians would modify their extreme democracy and recall him. The people agreed that the franchise should be limited to the 5,000 richest citizens and that for the moment there should be a provisional government formed by a council of 400. No sooner were the 400 in power than they tried to make their position permanent and began to negotiate peace terms with Sparta. A counterrevolution followed. The Assembly deposed the 400 and instituted the moderate democracy originally proposed, government by the 5,000. Alcibiades was elected general in his absence and won a brilliant victory at Cyzicus, annihilating the Spartan fleet. This was followed by the restoration of the radical democracy at Athens and a series of operations in which Athens recovered most of her empire in the north Aegean. In 407 B.C. Alcibiades returned to Athens and received a hero's welcome.

A new Spartan commander, Lysander, was soon to change the situation. With Persian support, he rebuilt the Spartan fleet and defeated a squadron of Alcibiades' fleet. Alcibiades, although he was not present at the battle, fearing the volatility of the *demos*, fled to a castle, which he had prepared as a refuge in the Hellespont. The following year (405 B.C.) the Athenians won another major victory at Arginusae, destroying over half the Spartan fleet. In 405 B.C., however, Lysander, again in command, made a surprise attack on the Athenian fleet when it was beached at Aegospotami and annihilated it.

This was the end for Athens. When the news reached the Piraeus, "A wail of lamentation spread from the Piraeus through the Long Walls to the city; and on that night not a man slept" (Xenophon, *Hellenica* 2.2.3). The Spartans now controlled the seas. They did not attack Athens but proceeded to starve her into submission. At last, when the people were desperate, they sent envoys to Sparta to discuss terms of surrender. The Peloponnesian League was summoned to discuss the issue. The majority voted for the utter destruction of Athens and the enslavement of the whole population, but Sparta resisted these savage terms. Eventually it was settled that Athens should surrender her whole empire; the entire fleet except for twelve triremes was to be handed over; all exiles were to return, and Athens should become an ally of Sparta.

---

## Greek Wisdom

### Socrates

ἔλεγε δὲ καὶ ἓν μόνον ἀγαθὸν εἶναι, τὴν ἐπιστήμην, καὶ ἓν μόνον κακόν, τὴν ἀμαθίᾱν· πλοῦτον δὲ καὶ εὐγένειαν οὐδὲν σεμνὸν ἔχειν· πᾶν δὲ τοὐναντίον κακόν. Diogenes Laertius 2.31

Hera and Athena shake hands.

Hera was the patron goddess of Samos.  After the Athenian defeat at Aegospotami, all the subject states of the Athenian Empire except Samos revolted.  In gratitude for this loyalty, the Athenians passed a decree praising the Samians and making them Athenian citizens. In 403 B.C. this marble stele was set up on the Acropolis with the decree inscribed below the figures of Hera and Athena.

---

## Greek Wisdom

### Socrates

οὐκ ἔστιν ἀνδρὶ ἀγαθῷ κακὸν οὐδὲν οὔτε ζῶντι οὔτε τελευτήσαντι.   Plato, *Apology* 41d

# ΜΕΓΑ ΤΟ ΤΗΣ
# ΘΑΛΑΣΣΗΣ ΚΡΑΤΟΣ (ε)

## VOCABULARY

*Verbs*
ἐπιδιώκω, *I pursue*
καταφεύγω, *I flee for refuge*
περιμένω, *I wait for*
σφάζω and σφάττω, [σφαγ-]
  σφάξω, ἔσφαξα, ἔσφαγμαι,
  ἐσφάγην, *I slay*
ὑπομένω, *I await* (an attack);
  *I stand firm*
φθάνω, [φθη-] φθήσομαι, [φθα-]
  ἔφθασα or [φθη-] ἔφθην +
  acc. and/or participle, *I antic-*
  *ipate; I do* something *before*
  someone else
*Nouns*
ἡ ἀταξίᾱ, τῆς ἀταξίᾱς, *disor-*
  *der*
ἡ βοήθεια, τῆς βοηθείᾱς, *help;*
  *aid*
ἡ κώπη, τῆς κώπης, *oar*
τὸ ναυᾱγιον, τοῦ ναυᾱγίου,
  *wrecked ship*

ἡ ὁλκάς, τῆς ὁλκάδος, *mer-*
  *chant ship*
ἡ τροπή, τῆς τροπῆς, *turn; turn-*
  *ing; rout* (of the enemy)
*Adjective*
ἄτακτος, -ον, *disordered*
ἐναντίος, -ᾱ, -ον, *opposed; op-*
  *posite; hostile;* as noun, *the*
  *enemy*
*Prepositions*
πλήν + gen., *except, except for*
ὑπό + gen., *under;* of agent, *by;*
  *because of;* + dat., *under;*
  + acc., of motion, *under;* of
  time, <u>*at*</u>
*Adverbs*
ἀτάκτως, *in disorder*
ὅθεν, *from where, whence*
ὅθενπερ: -περ added for emphasis

ταύτῃ μὲν οὖν οἱ Πελοποννήσιοι ἐκράτουν τε καὶ διέφθειραν τὰς
Ἀττικὰς ναῦς· αἱ δὲ εἴκοσι νῆες αὐτῶν αἱ ἀπὸ τοῦ δεξιοῦ κέρως
ἐδίωκον τὰς ἕνδεκα ναῦς τῶν Ἀθηναίων αἵπερ ὑπεξέφυγον τὴν
ἐπιστροφήν.  καὶ φθάνουσιν αὐτοὺς πλὴν μιᾶς νεὼς καταφυγοῦσαι ἐς
τὴν Ναύπᾱκτον, καὶ σχοῦσαι ἀντίπρωροι παρεσκευάζοντο          5
ἀμῡνούμενοι, ἐὰν ἐς τὴν γῆν ἐπὶ σφᾶς πλέωσιν οἱ Πελοποννήσιοι.  οἱ
δὲ παραγενόμενοι ἐπαιάνιζον ὡς νενῑκηκότες· καὶ τὴν μίαν ναῦν τῶν
Ἀθηναίων τὴν ὑπόλοιπον ἐδίωκε Λευκαδίᾱ ναῦς μία πολὺ πρὸ τῶν
ἄλλων.  ἔτυχε δὲ ὁλκὰς ὁρμοῦσα μετέωρος, περὶ ἣν ἡ Ἀττικὴ ναῦς
περιπλεύσᾱσα τῇ Λευκαδίᾳ διωκούσῃ ἐμβάλλει μέσῃ καὶ καταδῡει.   10

[τὴν ἐπιστροφήν, *their turning movement*     φθάνουσιν . . . καταφυγοῦσαι, *they*
(i.e., the eleven Athenian ships) *anticipate* (them) *fleeing for refuge* (i.e., they flee for

refuge before they could be caught)  **σχοῦσαι** (aorist participle of ἔχω, here intransitive), *facing*  **ἀντίπρῳροι**, *with prows toward the enemy*  **σφᾶς**, *t h e m*  **ἐπαιάνιζον**, *raised the victory song* (παιάν, *paean*)  **ὑπόλοιπον**, *r e m a i n i n g*  **μετέωρος**, *raised off the ground, at sea*  **ἐμβάλλει** + dat., *strikes with its ram* (ἔμβολος)]

τοῖς μὲν οὖν Πελοποννησίοις γενομένου τούτου ἀπροσδοκήτου φόβος ἐμπίπτει, καὶ ἀτάκτως διώκοντες αἱ μέν τινες τῶν νεῶν καθεῖσαι τὰς κώπᾱς ἐπέστησαν τοῦ πλοῦ, βουλόμενοι τοὺς ἄλλους περιμεῖναι, αἱ δὲ ἐς βράχεα ὤκειλαν. οἱ δὲ Ἀθηναῖοι ἰδόντες ταῦτα γιγνόμενα ἐθάρσουν τε καὶ βοήσαντες ἐπ' αὐτοὺς ὥρμησαν. οἱ δὲ διὰ τὴν  15
παροῦσαν ἀταξίᾱν ὀλίγον μὲν χρόνον ὑπέμειναν, ἔπειτα δὲ ἐτράποντο ἐς τὸν Πάνορμον ὅθενπερ ἀνηγάγοντο.

[**ἀπροσδοκήτου**, *unexpected*  **καθεῖσαι** (aorist participle of καθίημι), *dropping*  **ἐπέστησαν τοῦ πλοῦ**, *they stopped sailing*  **ἐς βραχέα** (from βραχύς, βραχεῖα, βραχύ, *short*), *onto the shallows*  **ὤκειλαν** (from ὀκέλλω), *ran aground*  **ἐθάρσουν** = ἐθάρρουν  **ἐτράποντο** (thematic aorist middle of τρέπω), *they turned, fled*]

ἐπιδιώκοντες δὲ οἱ Ἀθηναῖοι τάς τε ἐγγὺς οὔσᾱς ναῦς ἔλαβον ἓξ καὶ τὰς ἑαυτῶν ἀφείλοντο, ἃς ἐκεῖνοι πρὸς τῇ γῇ διαφθείραντες ἀνεδήσαντο· ἄνδρας τε τοὺς μὲν ἀπέκτειναν, τινὰς δὲ ἐζώγρησαν. ἐπὶ  20
δὲ τῆς Λευκαδίᾱς νεώς, ἣ περὶ τὴν ὁλκάδα κατέδῡ, Τῑμοκράτης ὁ Λακεδαιμόνιος πλέων, ὡς ἡ ναῦς διεφθείρετο, ἔσφαξεν ἑαυτόν, καὶ ἐξέπεσεν ἐς τὸν Ναυπᾱκτίων λιμένα.

[**ἐγγύς**, adv., *nearby*  **ἀνεδήσαντο** (from ἀναδέομαι), *they fastened with ropes, took in tow*  **ἐζώγρησαν** (from ζωγρέω), *they took alive, took captive*  **ἐξέπεσεν**, *fell out* (of the sea), *was cast ashore*]

ἀναχωρήσαντες δὲ οἱ Ἀθηναῖοι τροπαῖον ἔστησαν καὶ τοὺς νεκροὺς καὶ τὰ ναυάγια, ὅσα πρὸς τῇ ἑαυτῶν γῇ ἦν, ἀνείλοντο, καὶ  25
τοῖς ἐναντίοις τὰ ἐκείνων ὑπόσπονδα ἀπέδοσαν. ἔστησαν δὲ καὶ οἱ Πελοποννήσιοι τροπαῖον ὡς νενῑκηκότες τῆς τροπῆς τῶν νεῶν ἃς πρὸς τῇ γῇ διέφθειραν. μετὰ δὲ ταῦτα φοβούμενοι τὴν ἀπὸ τῶν Ἀθηναίων βοήθειαν ὑπὸ νύκτα ἐσέπλευσαν ἐς τὸν κόλπον τὸν Κρῑσαῖον καὶ Κόρινθον ἅπαντες πλὴν Λευκαδίων.  30

[**ὑπόσπονδα**, *under truce*]

—adapted from Thucydides 2.91–92

## PRINCIPAL PARTS: Verbs with -αν-/-ν- That Take Supplementary Participles

λα-ν-θ-άν-ω, [ληθ-] λήσω, [λαθ-] ἔλαθον, [ληθ-] λέληθα + acc. and/or participle, *I escape* someone's *notice* doing something = I do something without someone's noticing; *I escape the notice of* someone

τυ-γ-χ-άν-ω, [τευχ-] τεύξομαι, [τυχ-] ἔτυχον, [τυχε-] τετύχηκα + gen., *I hit; I hit upon; I get;* + participle, *I happen* to be doing X

φθά-ν-ω, [φθη-] φθήσομαι, [φθα-] ἔφθασα or [φθη-] ἔφθην + acc. and/or participle, *I anticipate; I do* something *before* someone else

## WORD BUILDING

*Explain how the words in the following sets are formed and give their meanings:*

stem: παιδ-
1. ὁ or ἡ παῖς
2. τὸ παιδίον
3. παιδικός, -ή, -όν
4. παίζω
5. εὔπαις
6. ἄπαις
7. παιδεύω
8. ἡ παίδευσις
9. ὁ παιδαγωγός
10. παιδαγωγικός, -ή, -όν

stem: λεγ-/λογ-
1. λέγω
2. ἡ λέξις
3. λεκτικός, -ή, -όν
4. ὁ λόγος
5. λογικός, -ή, -όν
6. λογίζομαι
7. ὁ λογιστής
8. ἄλογος, -ον
9. ἡ εὐλογίᾱ
10. ὁ λογογράφος

N.B. ὁ λόγος = *word; story; speech; account; calculation; reasoning*

## Greek Wisdom

### Socrates Addresses the Jurors at His Trial

τυγχάνει μέγιστον ἀγαθὸν ὂν ἀνθρώπῳ τοῦτο, ἑκάστης ἡμέρᾱς περὶ ἀρετῆς τοὺς λόγους ποιεῖσθαι καὶ τῶν ἄλλων, περὶ ὧν ὑμεῖς ἐμοῦ ἀκούετε διαλεγομένου καὶ ἐμαυτὸν καὶ ἄλλους ἐξετάζοντος, ὁ δὲ ἀνεξέταστος βίος οὐ βιωτὸς ἀνθρώπῳ.
Plato, *Apology* 38a

# GRAMMAR

## 1. Complex Sentences in Indirect Statement: Primary Sequence

When complex sentences (i.e., sentences containing a main clause and a subordinate clause) are stated indirectly after a leading verb in the present, future, or perfect tense (primary sequence), no changes in the tenses or moods of the verbs in the original sentence are made except to substitute an infinitive or participle for the finite verb in the main clause of the original sentence, as required by the introductory verb, e.g.:

a. Direct statement:

εἰ ὁ Φίλιππος τοῦτο εἶπεν, ἐψεύδετο.          (past particular condition)
*If Philip said this, he was lying.*

Indirect Statement with λέγει + ὅτι or ὡς
λέγει ὅτι/ὡς εἰ ὁ Φίλιππος τοῦτο εἶπεν, ἐψεύδετο.
*He/She says that if Philip said this, he was lying.*

Indirect statement with φησί(ν) + infinitive:
τὸν Φίλιππόν φησι ψεύδεσθαι, εἰ τοῦτο εἶπεν.
*He/She says that Philip was lying, if he said this.*

Indirect statement with οἶδε and participle:
οἶδε τὸν Φίλιππον ψευδόμενον, εἰ τοῦτο εἶπεν.
He/She knows *that Philip was lying, if he said this*
(Note that the imperfect indicative ἐψεύδετο of the original statement remains unchanged after ὅτι and is replaced by a present infinitive and a present participle after φησί and οἶδε respectively. The present infinitive and participle represent progressive, continuous, ongoing action and so can substitute here for the imperfect indicative of the direct statement.)

b. The particle ἄν must be retained with the infinitive and participle constructions as well as with the indicative construction in indirect speech, e.g.:

Direct statement:
εἰ ὁ Φίλιππος τοῦτο ἔλεγεν, ἐψεύδετο ἄν. (present contrary to fact condition)
*If Philip said this, he would be lying.*

Indirect Statement with λέγει + ὅτι or ὡς:
λέγει ὅτι/ὡς εἰ ὁ Φίλιππος τοῦτο ἔλεγεν, ἐψεύδετο ἄν.
*He/She says that if Philip said this, he would be lying.*

Indirect statement with φησί(ν) + infinitive:
τὸν Φίλιππόν φησι ψεύδεσθαι ἄν, εἰ τοῦτο ἔλεγεν.
*He/She says that Philip would be lying, if he said this.*

Indirect statement with οἶδε and participle:

οἶδε τὸν Φίλιππον ψευδόμενον ἄν, εἰ τοῦτο ἔλεγεν.

*He/She knows that Philip would be lying, if he said this.*

## Exercise 29 α

*Translate the following sentences and then put them into indirect statement:*

1. οἱ παῖδες οὐκ ἂν κατέστησαν εἰς κίνδῡνον, εἰ εὐθὺς οἴκαδε ἐπανῆλθον.
   α. ὁ πατὴρ λέγει ὅτι. . . .
   β. ὁ πατήρ φησι. . . .
   γ. ὁ πατὴρ οἶδε. . . .

2. ὁ ἄγγελος, ἐπεὶ εἰς τὸ ἄστυ ἀφίκετο, εἰς τὴν ἀγορὰν ἔσπευσεν.
   α. οἱ ἄνδρες λέγουσιν ὅτι. . . .
   β. οἱ ἄνδρες φᾶσὶ. . . .
   γ. οἱ ἄνδρες ἴσᾱσι. . . .

3. ἡ γυνὴ οἴκοι μενεῖ, ἕως ἂν ἐπανέλθῃ ὁ ἀνήρ.
   α. ὁ παῖς λέγει ὅτι. . . .
   β. ὁ παῖς φησι. . . .
   γ. ὁ παῖς οἶδε. . . .

4. εἰ οἱ σύμμαχοι ἡμῖν βοηθοῖεν, οὐκ ἂν φοβοίμεθα τοὺς πολεμίους.
   α. πάντες λέγουσιν ὅτι. . . .
   β. πάντες φᾶσὶν. . . .
   γ. πάντες ἴσᾱσιν. . . .

5. εἰ ὁ πατὴρ ἔζη, συνελάμβανεν ἂν τοῖς παισίν.
   α. ἡ γυνὴ λέγει ὅτι. . . .
   β. ἡ γυνή φησι. . . .
   γ. ἡ γυνὴ οἶδε. . . .

Nike erecting a trophy

# 30
# ΑΧΑΡΝΗΣ (α)

## Aristophanes and Old Comedy

In 486 B.C. a prize was first offered for a comedy in the dramatic competition at the Greater Dionysia, which until then had been for tragedies only. At the time of Aristophanes' first play (427 B.C.), three comedies were put on every year at the Lenaea, a festival of Dionysus held in January, and three at the Greater Dionysia, held in March.

The theater of Dionysus, in which both tragedies and comedies were performed, consisted of a circular dancing place (ὀρχήστρᾱ) about sixty-six feet or twenty meters in diameter (see illustration, page 258). Behind it was the auditorium, rising in concentric rows up the south slope of the Acropolis. In front of it was the stage (σκηνή), a permanent set representing a building with two doors. The stage was raised slightly above the level of the orchestra. In both tragedy and comedy the chorus played a leading role. In comedy they numbered twenty-four. Whereas the actors spoke their dialogue, the chorus sang their lyrics to the accompaniment of the lyre and flute.

Aristophanes' first play, the *Banqueters*, was produced in 427 B.C., his last extant play, *Wealth*, in 388 B.C. Eleven of his comedies survive, the earliest being the *Acharnians*, which won first prize at the Lenaea in 425 B.C. When this play was produced, Athens had been at war for more than five years. The people had suffered terribly from the plague, and the war seemed a stalemate. The farmers suffered the most, abandoning their farms every year when the Peloponnesians invaded in late spring, living in the city under appalling conditions during the invasions, and returning home to find their crops destroyed and their vines cut down. The heroes of several of Aristophanes' plays, including Dicaeopolis in the *Acharnians*, are war-weary farmers.

We last saw the family of Dicaeopolis when Philip was left behind in Athens to continue his schooling (Chapter 24). The rest of the family returned to the country when the Peloponnesians withdrew from Attica, only to return to the city every year when the Peloponnesians invaded in late spring. In reading the words of Dicaeopolis in the *Acharnians* you will hear the voice that Aristophanes gave him. He dreams of peace, and after being rebuffed in the normal course of political activity in the Assembly, he makes his own separate peace with Sparta. At the end of the selections from the play that you will read in this chapter, he joyfully assembles his family and celebrates his private peace with a sacred procession and a song in honor of Dionysus.

## VOCABULARY

*Verbs*

**δάκνω, δήξομαι, ἔδακον,**
**δέδηγμαι, ἐδήχθην,** *I bite;*
*I sting*

**ἐράω,** imperfect, **ἤρων** + gen.,
*I love*

**λαλέω,** *I talk; I chatter*

**λοιδορέω,** *I abuse*

**ὀδυνάω,** future and aorist passive, **ὀδυνηθήσομαι, ὠδυνή-**
**θην,** *I cause pain;* passive,
*I suffer pain*

**ποθέω,** *I long for*

**στυγέω,** *I hate*

*Nouns*

**ἡ καρδίᾱ, τῆς καρδίᾱς,** *heart*

**οἱ πρυτάνεις, τῶν πρυτά-**
**νεων,** *prytaneis = presidents*
(see essay in Chapter 22)

*Adjective*

**κύριος, -ᾱ, -ον,** *having author-*
*ity; legitimate; regular*

*Adverbs*

**ἀτεχνῶς,** *simply; really*

**εἶτα,** *then, next*

**οὐδεπώποτε,** *never yet*

1  **ὅσα δὴ δέδηγμαι,** *how much I've been stung,* lit., *as to how many things;* ὅσα,
βαιά. . . βαιά, τέτταρα (2), and ἃ (3) are adverbial accusatives.

2  **βαιά,** *few things* (accusative with ἥσθην = *I have had few pleasures*)

3  **ψαμμακοσιογάργαρα,** *sand-hundred-heaps,* a typical Aristophanic coinage

6  **οὔσης . . . ἑωθινῆς** (7): translate the genitive absolute as concessive,
*although . . .*

7  **ἑωθινῆς,** *at dawn,* the usual time for an Assembly to begin
**αὑτηΐ,** *this here,* the suffix -ῑ adds demonstrative force and often suggests that
the actor points with his finger.

8  **οἱ δ',** *but they,* i.e., the people     **κἄνω** = καὶ ἄνω (a vowel or diphthong at the
end of a word sometimes coalesces with a vowel or diphthong at the beginning
of the next word; this is called *crasis;* note that crasis is marked by a breathing)

9  **τὸ σχοινίον . . . τὸ μεμιλτωμένον,** *the red rope,* i.e., a rope covered with red
ocherous iron ore used to round up and drive loiterers from the agora to the
Pnyx for assemblies; those marked with the red would be fined.

10  **ἀωρίᾱν,** adv., *too late*

11  **ὠστιοῦνται . . . ἀλλήλοισι** (12), *will jostle each other*
**πῶς δοκεῖς,** lit., *how do you think? = you can't think how, astonishingly, like
mad*

12  **ξύλου,** *wood = bench, seat*

13  **ἀθρόοι,** *all together*     **καταρρέοντες,** *flowing down, streaming in*
**εἰρήνη δ' ὅπως . . . οὐδέν** (14): = οὐδὲν προτῑμῶσι (= *they don't care a bit*)
ὅπως εἰρήνη ἔσται

16  **νοστῶν,** *coming*
**κᾆτ'** = καὶ εἶτα, crasis, see line 8

17  **κέχηνα, σκορδινῶμαι, πέρδομαι,** *I yawn, stretch, fart*

18  **παρατίλλομαι,** *I pluck out my hairs*
**λογίζομαι,** *I count; I make calculations*

21  **ἀτεχνῶς:** take with παρεσκευασμένος

22  **ὑποκρούειν,** *to interrupt*

## Speaking Characters

ΔΙΚΑΙΟΠΟΛΙΣ (ΔΙΚ.) Dicaeopolis  
ΚΗΡΥΞ (ΚΗΡ.) Herald  
ΑΜΦΙΘΕΟΣ (ΑΜΦ.) Amphitheus  
ΠΡΕΣΒΥΣ (ΠΡΕ.) Ambassador  

ΨΕΥΔΑΡΤΑΒΑΣ (ΨΕΥ.) Pseudartabas  
ΧΟΡΟΣ Chorus of Acharnian men  
ΘΥΓΑΤΗΡ Daughter of Dicaeopolis  

*The opening scene is set on the Pnyx where there is to be a meeting of the Assembly. Dicaeopolis sits alone, waiting for the people to assemble and the prytaneis to arrive. While waiting, he complains that it has been a terrible year, in which almost nothing has occurred that gave him any pleasure.*

### ΔΙΚΑΙΟΠΟΛΙΣ *(soliloquizing)*

1    ὅσα δὴ δέδηγμαι τὴν ἐμαυτοῦ καρδίαν,

2    ἥσθην δὲ βαιά, πάνυ δὲ βαιά, τέτταρα·

3    ἃ δ' ὠδυνήθην, ψαμμακοσιογάργαρα. . . .

4    ἀλλ' οὐδεπώποτ' . . .

5    οὕτως ἐδήχθην . . .

6    ὡς νῦν, ὁπότ' οὔσης κῡρίας ἐκκλησίας

7    ἑωθινῆς ἔρημος ἡ πνὺξ αὑτηΐ,

8    οἱ δ' ἐν ἀγορᾷ λαλοῦσι κἄνω καὶ κάτω

9    τὸ σχοινίον φεύγουσι τὸ μεμιλτωμένον.

10   οὐδ' οἱ πρυτάνεις ἥκουσιν, ἀλλ' ἀωρίᾱν

11   ἥκοντες, εἶτα δ' ὠστιοῦνται πῶς δοκεῖς

12   ἐλθόντες ἀλλήλοισι περὶ πρώτου ξύλου,

13   ἀθρόοι καταρρέοντες· εἰρήνη δ' ὅπως

14   ἔσται προτῑμῶσ' οὐδέν· ὦ πόλις, πόλις.

15   ἐγὼ δ' ἀεὶ πρώτιστος εἰς ἐκκλησίᾱν

16   νοστῶν κάθημαι· κᾆτ' ἐπειδὰν ὦ μόνος,

17   στένω, κέχηνα, σκορδινῶμαι, πέρδομαι,

18   ἀπορῶ, γράφω, παρατίλλομαι, λογίζομαι,

19   ἀποβλέπων εἰς τὸν ἀγρόν, εἰρήνης ἐρῶν,

20   στυγῶν μὲν ἄστυ, τὸν δ' ἐμὸν δῆμον ποθῶν. . . .

21   νῦν οὖν ἀτεχνῶς ἥκω παρεσκευασμένος

22   βοᾶν, ὑποκρούειν, λοιδορεῖν τοὺς ῥήτορας,

24  ἀλλ' οἱ πρυτάνεις γὰρ οὑτοιί, *But (look!) for the prytaneis (are) here*
    μεσημβρινοί, *at midday*
25  οὐκ ἠγόρευον; *Didn't I tell you?*
    τοῦτ' ἐκεῖν' οὑγὼ 'λεγον: = τοῦτό (ἐστιν) ἐκεῖνο ὃ ἐγὼ ἔλεγον: οὑγὼ: crasis,
      see line 8; οὑγὼ 'λεγον: an ε at the beginning of a word following a word
      ending in a long vowel or diphthong is sometimes elided; this is called *prodeli-
      sion*
26  τὴν προεδρίᾱν, *the front seat*
    ὠστίζεται, *pushes and shoves, jostles*

# ΑΧΑΡΝΗΣ (β)

## VOCABULARY

*Verbs*

ἀδικέω, intransitive, *I do
  wrong;* transitive, *I wrong;
  I injure*
αἰσθάνομαι, αἰσθήσομαι,
  ἠσθόμην, ᾔσθημαι + gen. or
  acc., *I perceive; I learn; I apprehend*
ἄχθομαι, ἀχθέσομαι, ἠχθέ-
  σθην + dat., *I am vexed* (at);
  *I am grieved* (by)
ἡγέομαι + dat., *I lead; I think,
  consider*
οἴχομαι, present in perfect
  sense, *I have gone, have departed;* imperfect in pluperfect
  sense, *I had gone, had departed*
προσδοκάω, *I expect*

*Nouns*

ὁ or ἡ ἀλαζών, τοῦ or τῆς
  ἀλαζόνος, *imposter, charlatan, quack*
ἡ ἀσπίς, τῆς ἀσπίδος, *shield*
ἡ βίᾱ, τῆς βίᾱς, *force; violence*
ὁ μήν, τοῦ μηνός, *month*

ὁ or ἡ ὄρνῑς, τοῦ or τῆς ὄρνῑθος,
  *bird*
τὸ χρῡσίον, τοῦ χρῡσίου, *gold
  coin; money; jewelry*

*Adjectives*

ἀθάνατος, -ον, *immortal*
κακοδαίμων, κακοδαίμονος,
  *having an evil spirit, having
  bad luck*
ὅλος, -η, -ον, *whole, entire*
χρῡσοῦς, -ῆ, -οῦν, *golden*

*Preposition*

παρά + gen., *from;* + dat., *at the
  house of;* + acc., *of persons
  only, to; along, past; in respect
  of*

*Adverbs*

πρόσθε(ν), *before* (of time or
  place)
πώποτε, *ever*
σαφῶς, *clearly*

*Expressions*

εἰς τὸ πρόσθεν, *forward*
ναὶ μὰ Δία, *yes, by Zeus!*
οἴμοι κακοδαίμων, *poor devil!
  oh misery!*

28  ὡς ἄν = ἵνα
    καθάρματος, *the purified area.* Before the Assembly began, a suckling pig was
      sacrificed and carried around the boundaries of the meeting place to purify it.
    ΑΜΦΙΘΕΟΣ: the name means something like *divine on both sides of his family.*
29  τίς ἀγορεύειν βούλεται; = the formula for throwing open a motion to debate
      (see essay in Chapter 22)

23    ἐάν τις ἄλλο πλὴν περὶ εἰρήνης λέγῃ.

24    (*seeing the prytaneis arrive*) ἀλλ' οἱ πρυτάνεις γὰρ
         οὑτοιῒ μεσημβρινοί.

25    οὐκ ἠγόρευον; τοῦτ' ἐκεῖν' οὑγὼ 'λεγον·

26    εἰς τὴν προεδρίαν πᾶς ἀνὴρ ὠστίζεται.

ἔρημος ἡ πνύξ

27    **ΚΗΡΥΞ** (*addressing the people who are milling around the edge of
         the area of assembly*) πάριτ' ἐς τὸ πρόσθεν,

28    πάριθ', ὡς ἂν ἐντὸς ἦτε τοῦ καθάρματος.

29    **ΑΜΦΙΘΕΟΣ** (*running in breathless*) ἤδη τις εἶπε; **ΚΗΡ.**
         (*ignoring Amphitheus and opening the Assembly with a
         formal question*) τίς ἀγορεύειν βούλεται;

34    **ἀθάνατος ὤν**: translate the participle as concessive, *although being* . . .
       **ἐφόδι(α)**, *journey money*, i.e., an allowance paid by the Council for journeys
          made for public purposes

35    **οἱ τοξόται**, *archers.*     Scythian archers (see illustration below) were used as po-
         lice. It was considered improper to use a citizen in this capacity.

36    **ὦνδρες** = ὦ ἄνδρες, crasis, see line 8

38    **κρεμάσαι τὰς ἀσπίδας**, *to hang up our shields;* shields were usually hung on
         the wall when they were out of use.

39    **σῖγα**, *be quiet*, lit., *quietly*; σῖγα is an adverb (the imperative of σῑγάω is σῖγᾱ, as
         in line 44).
       **'γὼ** = ἐγὼ, prodelision, see line 25

40    **ἢν** = ἐὰν
       **ἢν μὴ**, *unless*
       **πρυτανεύσητέ μοι**, *prytanize for me = introduce a motion for debate for me.*
         All motions for debate had to be first discussed by the Council, that was
         presided over by the prytaneis (see essay in Chapter 22). The prytaneis intro-
         duced the motion to the Assembly as a προβούλευμα.

42    **ποίου βασιλέως;** Dicaeopolis's indignant question is occasioned by the finery
         of the Persian ambassadors. They are peacocks (τοῖς ταῶσι, 43), who are
         likely to prove imposters (τοῖς ἀλαζονεύμασιν, 43, *impostures*, abstract
         noun for concrete).
       **'γὼ** = ἐγὼ, prodelision, see line 25

43    **ταῶσι**: the Athenians pronounced the word with aspiration before its second syl-
         lable.

45    **ἐπέμψαθ'** = ἐπέμψατε, *you* (the people) *sent us*
       **ὡς** + acc., *to*

ὁ τοξότης

30  **ΑΜΦ.** ἐγώ. **ΚΗΡ.** τίς ὤν; **ΑΜΦ.** Ἀμφίθεος. **ΚΗΡ.** οὐκ
       ἄνθρωπος; **ΑΜΦ.** οὔ,
31      ἀλλ’ ἀθάνατος. . . .
32           . . . ἐμοὶ δ’ ἐπέτρεψαν οἱ θεοὶ
33      σπονδὰς ποιεῖσθαι πρὸς Λακεδαιμονίους μόνῳ.
34      ἀλλ’ ἀθάνατος ὤν, ἄνδρες, ἐφόδι’ οὐκ ἔχω·
35      οὐ γὰρ διδόασιν οἱ πρυτάνεις. **ΚΗΡ.** (*calling for the
       archers to eject Amphitheus for interrupting the
       proceedings*) οἱ τοξόται. . . .

    **ΔΙΚ.** (*standing up and shouting an appeal to the prytaneis on
36      Amphitheus’ behalf*) ὦνδρες πρυτάνεις, ἀδικεῖτε
       τὴν ἐκκλησίᾱν
37      τὸν ἄνδρ’ ἀπάγοντες, ὅστις ἡμῖν ἤθελεν
38      σπονδὰς ποιῆσαι καὶ κρεμάσαι τὰς ἀσπίδας.
39  **ΚΗΡ.** κάθησο, σῖγα. **ΔΙΚ.** μὰ τὸν Ἀπόλλω, ’γὼ μὲν οὔ,
40      ἢν μὴ περὶ εἰρήνης γε πρυτανεύσητέ μοι. (*Dicaeopolis
       reluctantly sits down, but far from remaining silent he will
       keep up a running commentary on the proceedings.*)

The first item on the agenda of the Assembly is a report from ambassadors who were sent to Persia to ask the King to help in the war against the Peloponnesians. These ambassadors were dispatched from Athens in 437/436 when Euthymenes was archon, eleven years before this play was staged! They bring with them envoys from Persia, dressed in Oriental splendor (i.e., as peacocks).

41  **ΚΗΡ.** (*formally announcing the arrival of the
       ambassadors*) οἱ πρέσβεις οἱ παρὰ βασιλέως.
42  **ΔΙΚ.** ποίου βασιλέως; ἄχθομαι ’γὼ πρέσβεσιν
43      καὶ τοῖς ταῶσι τοῖς τ’ ἀλαζονεύμασιν.
44  **ΚΗΡ.** σῖγᾱ. . . .
45  **ΠΡΕΣΒΥΣ** (*addressing the Assembly*) ἐπέμψαθ’ ἡμᾶς ὡς
       βασιλέᾱ τὸν μέγαν

47 ἐπ' Εὐθυμένους ἄρχοντος, *in the time of Euthymenes being archon.* Year
dates are given by the name of the eponymous archon. The archon list shows
that this was the year 437/6.

οἴμοι τῶν δραχμῶν: genitive of exclamation, *oh my, (those) drachmas!*

48 πρὸς βίαν, *forcibly, perforce;* the ambassadors *had to, were forced to drink*

49 ὑαλίνων ἐκπωμάτων, *crystal goblets*

χρῡσίδων, *golden vessels*

50 ἄκρᾱτον, *unmixed,* i.e., undiluted with water. Wine was normally mixed with
water, unless the drinker intended to get drunk.

ὦ Κραναὰ πόλις, *O Cranian city.* Κρανααί was the most ancient name for
Athens, and the word suggests the adjective κραναός, *rocky, rugged,* and the
proper noun Κραναός, the name of a mythical king of Athens. Dicaeopolis al-
ludes to the good old days, now replaced by the effeminate luxury of the ambassadors.

51 τὸν κατάγελων, *the mockery,* i.e., how the ambassadors mock you

53 καταφαγεῖν (thematic aorist infinitive of κατεσθίω), *to eat*

55 ἀπόπατον, *latrine*

56 κἄχεζεν = καὶ ἔχεζεν, crasis, see line 8, *and he was shitting*

57 πόσου . . . χρόνου, *within what time*     τὸν πρωκτὸν, *his ass*

ξυνήγαγεν; *did he close?*

58 τῇ πανσελήνῳ, *at the full moon* (σελήνη)

κᾆτ' = καὶ εἶτα, crasis, see line 8

60 κρῑβάνου, *a ceramic oven* (for baking a loaf of bread)

61 κρῑβανίτᾱς, *baked* (in a κρίβανος)

τῶν ἀλαζονευμάτων, *what  humbug!* (for the genitive, see line 47 above; for
the word, see line 43)

62 τριπλάσιον Κλεωνύμου, *three times as big as Cleonymus.* Aristophanes frequently poked fun at Cleonymus for having thrown away his shield to escape
from battle, for being a glutton and a perjurer, and, as here, for the huge bulk of
his body.

63 φένᾱξ, *cheat,* with a pun on the word φοῖνιξ, the fabled Oriental phoenix; translate *cheatiebird*

64 ταῦτ' . . . ἐφενάκιζες, *this is how you were cheating* (us)

ἄρ(α), *as it seems* (distinguish this from ἆρα, which introduces a question)

65 Ψευδαρτάβᾱν, *Falseartabas.* The second half of the name rings true. Xerxes
had an uncle named Artabanes (see Herodotus 7.10).

66 τὸν βασιλέως Ὀφθαλμόν, *the King's Eye* is the actual title of the Persian
king's intelligence official (see Herodotus 1.114).

ἐκκόψειέ γε / κόραξ πατάξᾱς, *may a raven* (κόραξ), *having struck* (πατάξᾱς)
*it, knock it out* (ἐκκόψειέ)

67 τόν γε σὸν τοῦ πρέσβεως, *and yours too, the ambassador's*

68 ὦναξ Ἡράκλεις = ὦ ἄναξ Ἡράκλεις, crasis, see line 8, *O lord Heracles!*–an
exclamation expressing disgust

69 σὺ βασιλεὺς . . . Ἀθηναίοισιν (70): = σὺ φράσον ἅττα (= ἅτινα) βασιλεὺς
ἀπέπεμψέ σε λέξοντα Ἀθηναίοισιν

| | | |
|---|---|---|
| 46 | | μισθὸν φέροντας δύο δραχμὰς τῆς ἡμέρας |
| 47 | | ἐπ' Εὐθυμένους ἄρχοντος. **ΔΙΚ.** οἴμοι τῶν δραχμῶν. . . . |
| 48 | **ΠΡΕ.** | (*ignoring Dicaeopolis and continuing his speech*) |
| | | ξενιζόμενοι δὲ πρὸς βίαν ἐπίνομεν |
| 49 | | ἐξ ὑαλίνων ἐκπωμάτων καὶ χρῡσίδων |
| 50 | | ἄκρᾱτον οἶνον ἡδύν. **ΔΙΚ.** ὦ Κραναὰ πόλις, |
| 51 | | ἆρ' αἰσθάνει τὸν κατάγελων τῶν πρέσβεων; |
| 52 | **ΠΡΕ.** | (*continuing to ignore Dicaeopolis*) οἱ βάρβαροι γὰρ |
| | | ἄνδρας ἡγοῦνται μόνους |
| 53 | | τοὺς πλεῖστα δυναμένους καταφαγεῖν καὶ πιεῖν. . . . |
| 54 | | ἔτει τετάρτῳ δ' εἰς τὰ βασίλει' ἤλθομεν· |
| 55 | | ἀλλ' εἰς ἀπόπατον ᾤχετο στρατιὰν λαβών, |
| 56 | | κἄχεζεν ὀκτὼ μῆνας ἐπὶ χρῡσῶν ὀρῶν. |
| 57 | **ΔΙΚ.** | πόσου δὲ τὸν πρωκτὸν χρόνου ξυνήγαγεν; |
| 58 | | τῇ πανσελήνῳ; |
| | **ΠΡΕ.** | (*continuing his speech*) κᾆτ' ἀπῆλθεν οἴκαδε. |
| 59 | | εἶτ' ἐξένιζε παρετίθει θ' ἡμῖν ὅλους |
| 60 | | ἐκ κρῑβάνου βοῦς. **ΔΙΚ.** καὶ τίς εἶδε πώποτε |
| 61 | | βοῦς κρῑβανίτᾱς; τῶν ἀλαζονευμάτων. |
| 62 | **ΠΡΕ.** | (*ignoring Dicaeopolis*) καὶ ναὶ μὰ Δί' ὄρνῑν τριπλάσιον |
| | | Κλεωνύμου |
| 63 | | παρέθηκεν ἡμῖν· ὄνομα δ' ἦν αὐτῷ φένᾱξ. |
| 64 | **ΔΙΚ.** | ταῦτ' ἄρ' ἐφενάκιζες σὺ δύο δραχμὰς φέρων. |
| 65 | **ΠΡΕ.** | (*ignoring Dicaeopolis*) καὶ νῦν ἄγοντες ἥκομεν |
| | | Ψευδαρτάβᾱν, |
| 66 | | τὸν βασιλέως 'Οφθαλμόν. **ΔΙΚ.** ἐκκόψειέ γε |
| 67 | | κόραξ πατάξᾱς, τόν γε σὸν τοῦ πρέσβεως. |
| 68 | **ΚΗΡ.** | (*formally presenting Pseudartabas to the Assembly*) |
| | | ὁ βασιλέως 'Οφθαλμός. **ΔΙΚ.** ὦναξ 'Ηράκλεις. . . . |
| 69 | **ΠΡΕ.** | (*to Pseudartabas*) ἄγε δὴ σὺ βασιλεὺς ἄττα σ' ἀπέπεμψεν |
| | | φράσον |

71    "Comic Persian, suggesting King (Arta)xerxes and Pissuthnes, satrap of Sardis"
         (Henderson, page 69).

72    ξυνήκαθ' = ξυνήκατε = συνεῖτε (aorist of συνίημι), *Did you understand?*
       'γὼ = ἐγὼ, prodelision, see line 25

74    μεῖζον, *louder*

75    This time Pseudartabas speaks a sort of pidgin Greek, of which sense of a sort can
         be made: *No getty goldy, wide-assed Ioni.*

76    δαὶ: colloquial for δή

77    λέγει, *he calls* + two accusatives

79    ἀχάνᾱς, *bushels;* ἡ ἀχάνη can mean either a basket for provisions or the Greek
         name for a Persian measure.
       ὅδε γε: the words suggest that the ambassador has hold of the King's Eye and is
         trying to make him say his piece again.

83    εἰς τὸ πρυτανεῖον, *to the Prytaneum* (for a public banquet)
       ταῦτα δῆτ' οὐκ ἀγχόνη; *well, isn't this a hanging (matter)?* i.e., enough to
         make you hang yourself

85    'στιν = ἐστιν, prodelision, see line 25
       πάρα = πάρειμι

87    ποιῆσαι: singular aorist middle imperative
       μόνῳ: take with ἐμοὶ (86)

88    τοῖσι παιδίοισι, *for my young children*        τῇ πλάτιδι, *for my wife*

89    πρεσβεύεσθε, *be ambassadors!*
       κεχήνατε: perfect (with present meaning) imperative of χάσκω, *I gape;* the use
         of the perfect may suggest that their mouths are always hanging open, either
         because they are naive fools or because they are always half asleep (yawning).

The theater of Dionysus in the second half of the fifth century

70          λέξοντ' 'Αθηναίοισιν, ὦ Ψευδαρτάβᾱ.

71   **ΨΕΥΔΑΡΤΑΒΑΣ** (*making his announcement to the Assembly*)
         ιαρτα ναμε ξαρξανα πισονα σατρα.

72   **ΠΡΕ.** (*to the Assembly*) ξυνήκαθ' ὃ λέγει;   **ΔΙΚ.** μὰ τὸν
         'Απόλλω 'γὼ μὲν οὔ.

73   **ΠΡΕ.** (*to the Assembly*) πέμψειν βασιλέᾱ φησὶν ὑμῖν χρῡσίον.

74          (*to Pseudartabas*) λέγε δὴ σὺ μεῖζον καὶ σαφῶς τὸ
         χρῡσίον.

75   **ΨΕΥ.** οὐ λῆψι χρῡσό, χαυνόπρωκτ' 'Ιᾱοναῦ.

76   **ΔΙΚ.** οἴμοι κακοδαίμων ὡς σαφῶς.   **ΠΡΕ.** τί δαὶ λέγει;

    **ΔΙΚ.** (*standing up and shouting to the ambassador*)
77          ὅ τι; χαυνοπρώκτους τοὺς 'Ιᾱονας λέγει,
78          εἰ προσδοκῶσι χρῡσίον ἐκ τῶν βαρβάρων.

79   **ΠΡΕ.** (*answering Dicaeopolis*) οὔκ, ἀλλ' ἀχᾱνᾱς ὅδε γε χρῡσίου
         λέγει.

80   **ΔΙΚ.** (*to the ambassador*) ποίᾱς ἀχᾱνᾱς; σὺ μὲν ἀλαζὼν εἶ
         μέγας. . . .

81   **ΚΗΡ.** (*to Dicaeopolis*) σῖγᾱ, κάθιζε.

82          (*to the Assembly*) τὸν βασιλέως 'Οφθαλμὸν ἡ βουλὴ
         καλεῖ

83          εἰς τὸ πρυτανεῖον.   **ΔΙΚ.** (*refusing to sit down and*
         *thoroughly disgusted with the ambassador's announcement*)
         ταῦτα δῆτ' οὐκ ἀγχόνη; . . .

84          (*aside*) ἀλλ' ἐργάσομαί τι δεινὸν ἔργον καὶ μέγα.
85          (*calling out*) ἀλλ' 'Αμφίθεός μοι ποῦ 'στιν;   **ΑΜΦ.**
         οὑτοσὶ πάρα.

86   **ΔΙΚ.** (*to Amphitheus*) ἐμοὶ σὺ ταυτᾱσὶ λαβὼν ὀκτὼ δραχμᾱς
87          σπονδᾱς ποιῆσαι πρὸς Λακεδαιμονίους μόνῳ
88          καὶ τοῖσι παιδίοισι καὶ τῇ πλᾱτιδι.
89          (*to the ambassadors*) ὑμεῖς δὲ πρεσβεύεσθε καὶ κεχήνατε. . . .
         (*Amphitheus rushes off to begin his trip to Sparta.*)

# ΑΧΑΡΝΗΣ (γ)

## VOCABULARY

*Verbs*

ἀνακράζω, ἀνέκραγον, *I shout*

σπένδω, σπείσω, ἔσπεισα,
ἔσπεισμαι, *I pour a libation;*
middle, *I make a treaty; I
make peace* (by pouring a libation with the other party)

*Nouns*

ἡ ἄμπελος, τῆς ἀμπέλου,
*grapevine*

τὸ στόμα, τοῦ στόματος, *mouth*

*Adjective*

μιαρός, -ά, -όν, *defiled; foul;
villainous*

90  ἀλλ' . . . γάρ, *but (look), for* . . .
    ὁδί, *this here*, i.e., *here he is*
91  μήπω γε, *don't (greet me) yet.* . . .
93  σπονδάς: the word can mean truces or the wine poured in libations to sanctify a
    truce or the libations themselves. Aristophanes cleverly plays on these mean-
    ings in this passage.
94  ὦσφροντο (from ὀσφραίνομαι), *smelled* (the wine)     πρεσβῦταί, *old men*
95  στιπτοί, *trodden down;* of old men, *tough, sturdy*
    πρίνινοι, *oaken*
96  ἀτεράμονες, *unsoftened, hard, tough*
    Μαραθωνομάχαι, *fighters at the Battle of Marathon*
    σφενδάμνινοι, *made of maple wood*
97  ἀνέκραγον: ingressive aorist, *they began to shout*
99  κᾆς = καὶ εἰς, crasis, see line 8
    τρίβωνας, *cloaks* (usually old and threadbare)
    ξυνελέγοντο + partitive gen. here, *they began gathering (some of the) stones*
100 ἔφυγον . . . ἐδίωκον κᾀβόων: ingressive aorist and inchoative imperfects
    κᾀβόων = καὶ ἐβόων, crasis, see line 8
101 βοώντων: 3rd person plural imperative, *let them shout*
102 γεύματα, *tastes;* here, *vintages*
103 αὗται: the antecedent is τὰς σπονδάς (101).
    πεντέτεις, *five-years old; for five years*
    γεῦσαι (aorist imperative of γεύομαι), *taste*
104 αἰβοῖ, *ugh* (an expression of disgust)     ὅτι, *because*
105 ὄζουσι + gen., *they smell of*
    πίττης, *pitch;* pitch or resin was used both to caulk ships and to line wine jars (it
    is still used in making some Greek wine today, called retsina). There is a
    double-entendre here; both meanings are intended.
106 δεκέτεις, *ten years old; for ten years*
107 χαὗται = καὶ αὗται, crasis, see line 8, *this too;* if a truce were made for only ten
    years, both sides would be sending ambassadors to other cities to gain allies,
    preparing for the next war.
108 ὀξύτατον, *very sharply*

*The Assembly continues, with more interruptions from Dicaeopolis. Just as proceedings are coming to an end, Dicaeopolis sees Amphitheus rushing in breathless, having returned from Sparta. He brings with him three specimen truces, which are in the form of wine for libations contained in wine skins.*

90 **ΔΙΚ.** ἀλλ' ἐκ Λακεδαίμονος γὰρ Ἀμφίθεος ὁδί.

91 χαῖρ' Ἀμφίθεε. **ΑΜΦ.** (*still running*) μήπω γε πρίν γ' ἂν στῶ τρέχων.

(*looking behind himself with trepidation*)

92 δεῖ γάρ με φεύγοντ' ἐκφυγεῖν Ἀχαρνέας.

93 **ΔΙΚ.** τί δ' ἔστ'; **ΑΜΦ.** ἐγὼ μὲν δεῦρό σοι σπονδὰς φέρων

94 ἔσπευδον· οἱ δ' ὤσφροντο πρεσβῦταί τινες

95 Ἀχαρνικοί, στιπτοὶ γέροντες, πρίνινοι,

96 ἀτεράμονες, Μαραθωνομάχαι, σφενδάμνινοι.

97 ἔπειτ' ἀνέκραγον πάντες· "ὦ μιαρώτατε,

98 σπονδὰς φέρεις τῶν ἀμπέλων τετμημένων;"

99 κᾆς τοὺς τρίβωνας ξυνελέγοντο τῶν λίθων·

100 ἐγὼ δ' ἔφευγον· οἱ δ' ἐδίωκον κᾆβόων.

101 **ΔΙΚ.** (*reassuring Amphitheus*) οἱ δ' οὖν βοώντων. ἀλλὰ τὰς σπονδὰς φέρεις;

102 **ΑΜΦ.** (*holding up the wine skins for Dicaeopolis to see*) ἔγωγέ, φημι, τρία γε ταυτὶ γεύματα.

103 (*holding out one of the wine skins*) αὗται μέν εἰσι πεντέτεις. γεῦσαι λαβών.

104 **ΔΙΚ.** (*taking the skin and smelling the wine*) αἰβοῖ. **ΑΜΦ.** τί ἐστιν; **ΔΙΚ.** οὐκ ἀρέσκουσίν μ' ὅτι

105 ὄζουσι πίττης καὶ παρασκευῆς νεῶν.

106 **ΑΜΦ.** (*offering another wine skin*) σὺ δ' ἀλλὰ τᾶσδὶ τὰς δεκέτεις γεῦσαι λαβών.

**ΔΙΚ.** (*taking the second wine skin and smelling the wine*)

107 ὄζουσι χαῦται πρέσβεων εἰς τὰς πόλεις

108 ὀξύτατον. . . .

109    τριᾱκοντούτιδες, *thirty years old; for thirty years*
110    ὦ Διονΰσια, *O festival of Dionysus!*
111    ἀμβροσίᾱς καὶ νέκταρος: ambrosia was the food of the gods, and nectar was
        their drink.
112    κᾆν = καὶ ἐν, crasis, see line 8
        ὅπῃ, *where*
113    κᾆκπίομαι = καὶ ἐκπίομαι, crasis, see line 8, *and I will drink it off*
114    χαίρειν κελεύων πολλά, *bidding a long farewell to*, i.e., wishing to have
        nothing to do with
116    ἀπαλλαγεὶς (aorist passive participle of ἀπαλλάττω) + gen., *rid of*
117    τὰ κατ᾽ ἀγροὺς . . . Διονΰσια, *the Rural Dionysia*
        εἰσιών, *going into* (my house); we are no longer on the Pnyx but outside Di-
        caeopolis's house in the country. Such changes of scene, indicated only by the
        actors' words, are common in comedy.

A       The great altar
        of Dionysus
D–D     Drainage
        channel
M       Choregic
        monuments
O       Odeon of
        Pericles
S       Long stoa
T1      Early
        temple
T2      Later
        temple

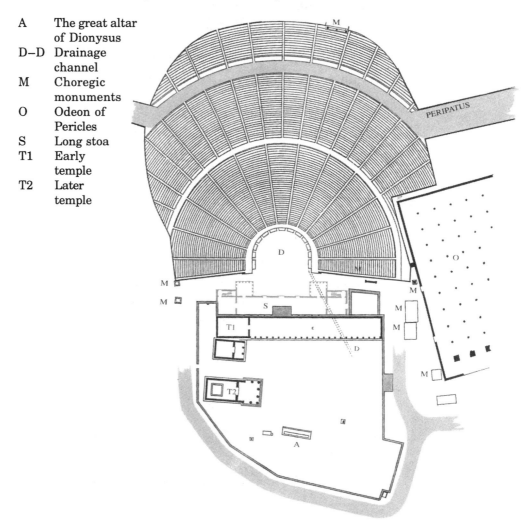

Plan of the theater of Dionysus in the mid fourth century

109 **ΑΜΦ.** (*offering the third wine skin*) ἀλλ' αὑταιὶ σπονδαὶ
τριᾱκοντούτιδες

110 κατὰ γῆν τε καὶ θάλατταν. **ΔΙΚ.** (*taking the third wine
skin and smelling the wine*) ὦ Διονύσια,

111 αὗται μὲν ὄζουσ' ἀμβροσίᾱς καὶ νέκταρος . . .

112 (*tasting the wine*) κἀν τῷ στόματι λέγουσι· "βαῖν' ὅπη
θέλεις."

(*clutching the wine skin, pouring a libation, and drinking
deeply of the wine*)

113 ταύτᾱς δέχομαι καὶ σπένδομαι κἀκπίομαι,

114 χαίρειν κελεύων πολλὰ τοὺς Ἀχαρνέᾱς.

(*running off stage*)

115 **ΑΜΦ.** ἐγὼ δὲ φευξοῦμαί γε τοὺς Ἀχαρνέᾱς.

116 **ΔΙΚ.** ἐγὼ δὲ πολέμου καὶ κακῶν ἀπαλλαγεὶς

117 ἄξω τὰ κατ' ἀγροὺς εἰσιὼν Διονύσια.

(*exiting into the house*)

Statuette of a comic Heracles

# ΑΧΑΡΝΗΣ (δ)

## VOCABULARY

*Verbs*

ᾄδω, ᾄσομαι, ᾖσα, ᾖσμαι,
ᾔσθην, *I sing*

ἀκολουθέω + dat., *I follow*

ἀπάρχομαι, *I begin*

εὐφημέω, *I keep holy silence*

καταχέω, καταχέω, κατ-
έχεα, κατακέχυκα, κατα-
κέχυμαι, κατεχύθην, *I pour*
X (acc.) *over* Y (gen.)

μηνύω, μηνύσω, ἐμήνῡσα, μεμήνῡκα, μεμήνῡμαι, ἐμηνύ-
θην, *I inform*

*Nouns*

ἡ εὐφημίᾱ, τῆς εὐφημίᾱς, *call
for holy silence*

οἱ οἰκέται, τῶν οἰκετῶν,
*household*

*Adjective*

μακάριος, -ᾱ, -ον, *blessed;
happy*

*Adverb or Preposition*

ἐξόπισθε(ν) + gen., *behind*

*Adverbs*

μήν or καὶ μήν, *truly, indeed*

σφόδρα, *very much*

119  ὁδοιπόρων, *wayfarers, passers-by*
ἄξιόν (ἐστι) + dat. and infin., *it is fit,* i.e., *it is worth while for* X *to do* Y

121  ὅποι . . . γῆς, *where in the world*
τέτραπται (perfect of τρέπω), *has turned, has gone*

120  ξυλλαβεῖν (from συλλαμβάνω), here + acc., *to seize, apprehend, arrest*
(compare the use of this verb + dat. = *I help*)

122  φροῦδος, *gone, fled, vanished*

123  Βαλλήναδε: a comic coinage punning on the verb βάλλω, *I pelt,* and the name
of an Attic deme, Παλλήνη, + suffix -δε = *toward;* translate *toward Pelting,
Peltingward.*

124  γῆν πρὸ γῆς, *through land* (acc. of extent of space) *after land* (πρό + gen. usually means *before,* but in a few idioms it has the sense of *further, forward, on-
ward*)

125  ἐμπλήμην (2nd aorist passive optative of ἐμπίμπλημι, *I fill full;* passive, *I sate
myself*), potential optative, *I could never have my fill of*
λίθοις: take with βάλλων

128  δεῦρο πᾶς/ ἐκποδών, *everyone (come) here, out of the way*

129  ἀνήρ = ὁ ἀνήρ, crasis, see line 8

131  πρόιθ(ι), *come forward*
ἡ κανηφόρος, *the basket-bearer;* the daughter carries the basket on her head.

132  τὸν φαλλόν, *phallus-pole,* an image carried in Dionysiac processions
στησάτω: 3rd person singular imperative, *let him* (i.e., Xanthias) *stand* X *up*

*The chorus of old Acharnian men rush in, armed with stones, in pursuit of Amphitheus.*

118 **ΧΟΡΟΣ**  τῇδε πᾶς ἕπου, δίωκε καὶ τὸν ἄνδρα πυνθάνου

119         τῶν ὁδοιπόρων ἁπάντων· τῇ πόλει γὰρ ἄξιον

120         ξυλλαβεῖν τὸν ἄνδρα τοῦτον. *(to the audience)* ἀλλά μοι
               μηνύσατε,

121         εἴ τις οἶδ' ὅποι τέτραπται γῆς ὁ τὰς σπονδὰς φέρων.

122         ἐκπέφευγ', οἴχεται φροῦδος. . . .

123         ἀλλὰ δεῖ ζητεῖν τὸν ἄνδρα καὶ βλέπειν Βαλλήναδε

124         καὶ διώκειν γῆν πρὸ γῆς, ἕως ἂν εὑρεθῇ ποτέ·

125         ὡς ἐγὼ βάλλων ἐκεῖνον οὐκ ἂν ἐμπλήμην λίθοις.


*As the chorus search fruitlessly for Amphitheus, Dicaeopolis is heard from within the house calling for holy silence.*

126 **ΔΙΚ.**  εὐφημεῖτε, εὐφημεῖτε.

127 **ΧΟΡ.**  *(addressing its own members)* σῖγα πᾶς. ἠκούσατ',
               ἄνδρες, ἆρα τῆς εὐφημίας;

128         οὗτος αὐτός ἐστιν ὃν ζητοῦμεν. *(retiring to one side of the
               stage)* ἀλλὰ δεῦρο πᾶς

129         ἐκποδών· θύσων γὰρ ἀνήρ, ὡς ἔοικ', ἐξέρχεται.


*As the members of the chorus withdraw, Dicaeopolis, carrying a pot, leads his family out of his house—his wife, his daughter, who carries a sacred basket, and Xanthias and a second slave, who carry a phallus-pole.*

130 **ΔΙΚ.**  εὐφημεῖτε, εὐφημεῖτε.

131         *(to his daughter)* πρόιθ' εἰς τὸ πρόσθεν ὀλίγον, ἡ
               κανηφόρος.

132         *(referring to his slave Xanthias)* ὁ Ξανθίας τὸν φαλλὸν
               ὀρθὸν στησάτω.

133  τὸ κανοῦν, *basket;*  the daughter sets the basket down near the altar.

134  τὴν ἐτνήρυσιν, *soup-ladle*

135  ἔτνος, *soup,* made of peas or beans and contained in the pot that Dicaeopolis
     carries

     τοὐλατῆρος = τοῦ ἐλατῆρος, crasis, see line 8, *broad, flat cake;* the daughter
     takes one of these cakes from the basket, places it on the altar, and pours the
     soup over it.

136  καὶ μὴν . . . γ(ε), *and indeed. . . .*

137  κεχαρισμένως (adverb formed from the perfect participle of χαρίζομαι) + dat.,
     *acceptably, in a manner pleasing to*

     ἐμὲ . . . ἀγαγεῖν (139) . . . τὰς σπονδὰς (140) . . . ξυνενεγκεῖν (141; see
     note below): the infinitives express prayers, *(grant) that I may conduct the Ru-
     ral Dionysia . . . and (grant) that this truce may turn out well. . . .*

139  τυχηρῶς, *with good fortune, with good luck*

140  ἀπαλλαχθέντα + gen. (see line 115 above), *rid of*

141  ξυνενεγκεῖν (aorist infinitive of συμφέρει, *it is useful, it is profitable*), with
     καλῶς, *may turn out well*

     τριᾱκοντούτιδας, *of / lasting thirty years*

142  ὅπως, *(see to it) that. . . .*

143  βλέπουσα θυμβροφάγον, *looking as if you have eaten savory* (the eating of
     the bitter herb, savory, would pucker the lips up, and give a prim, demure look
     to the girl's face –W. W. Merry)

144  ὀπύσει, *will marry* (the Greek verb is from a root meaning *nourish, maintain* )

145  κἂν = καὶ ἐν, crasis, see line 8

     τὤχλῳ = τῷ ὄχλῳ, crasis, see line 8, *the crowd*

     φυλάττεσθαι (infinitive for imperative), *watch out!*

146  περιτράγῃ (from περιτρώγω, aorist, περιέτραγον), *nibble at,* i.e., *steal*

     τὰ χρῡσία, *your golden jewelry*

147  σφῷν, dual, *by the two of you*          ἐστὶν . . . ἑκτέος / ὁ φαλλός (verbal ad-
     jective from ἔχω, see Chapter 26, Grammar 4, page 173), *the phallus-pole must
     be held*

150  θεῶ: singular imperative of θεάομαι

     τοῦ τέγους, *the roof*

     πρόβᾱ = πρόβηθι

151  Βακχίου, *of Bacchus*

152  ἕκτῳ, *sixth*

     σ' = σε

Dionysus with a panther at his altar

133    (*to his daughter*) κατάθου τὸ κανοῦν, ὦ θύγατερ, ἵν'
       ἀπαρξώμεθα.

134  **ΘΥΓΑΤΗΡ** ὦ μῆτερ, ἀνάδος δεῦρο τὴν ἐτνήρυσιν,
135       ἵν' ἔτνος καταχέω τοὐλατῆρος τουτουί.

   **ΔΙΚ.** (*addressing Dionysus, at his altar on the stage*)
136       καὶ μὴν καλόν γ' ἔστ'. ὦ Διόνυσε δέσποτα,
137       κεχαρισμένως σοι τήνδε τὴν πομπὴν ἐμὲ
138       πέμψαντα καὶ θύσαντα μετὰ τῶν οἰκετῶν
139       ἀγαγεῖν τυχηρῶς τὰ κατ' ἀγροὺς Διονύσια,
140       στρατιᾶς ἀπαλλαχθέντα, τὰς σπονδὰς δέ μοι
141       καλῶς ξυνενεγκεῖν τὰς τριακοντούτιδας.
142    (*addressing his daughter and arranging the procession*)
       ἄγ', ὦ θύγατερ, ὅπως τὸ κανοῦν καλὴ καλῶς
143       οἴσεις βλέπουσα θυμβροφάγον. ὡς μακάριος
144       ὅστις σ' ὀπύσει. . . .
   (*urging his daughter to lead the procession forward, into the*
145    *audience*) πρόβαινε, κἂν τὤχλῳ φυλάττεσθαι σφόδρα
146       μή τις λαθών σου περιτράγῃ τὰ χρυσία.
   (*urging Xanthias and the second slave to perform their duty*
       *properly*) ὦ Ξανθία, σφῷν δ' ἐστὶν ὀρθὸς ἑκτέος
148       ὁ φαλλὸς ἐξόπισθε τῆς κανηφόρου·
149       ἐγὼ δ' ἀκολουθῶν ᾄσομαι τὸ φαλλικόν·
150    (*sending his wife to watch from the roof*) σὺ δ', ὦ γύναι, θεῶ
       μ' ἀπὸ τοῦ τέγους. (*urging on his daughter*) πρόβᾱ.

*Dicaeopolis celebrates his own Rural Dionysia by singing the following joyous song to Phales, Dionysiac god of the phallus, in honor of the peace he has made:*

151    Φαλῆς, ἑταῖρε Βακχίου, . . .
152    ἕκτῳ σ' ἔτει προσεῖπον εἰς
153    τὸν δῆμον ἐλθὼν ἄσμενος,
154    σπονδὰς ποιησάμενος ἐμαυ-

156   ἀπαλλαγείς: see lines 115 and 140.
158   ξυμπίης, *drink with*
      ἐκ κραιπάλης, *in* (lit., *from*) *a drinking-bout*
159   ἕωθεν, *from earliest dawn*
      ῥοφήσει (from ῥοφέω, fut., ῥοφήσομαι), *you will gulp down; you will drain dry,*
        *will empty*
      τρύβλιον, *cup*
160   φεψάλῳ, *chimney*
      κρεμήσεται, *will be hung* (cf. line 38)

εἰρήνης ῥοφήσῃ τρύβλιον

155   τῷ, πρᾱγμάτων τε καὶ μαχῶν

156   . . . ἀπαλλαγείς. . . .

157   Φαλῆς Φαλῆς,

158   ἐὰν μεθ᾽ ἡμῶν ξυμπίῃς, ἐκ κραιπάλης

159   ἕωθεν εἰρήνης ῥοφήσει τρύβλιον·

160   ἡ δ᾽ ἀσπὶς ἐν τῷ φεψάλῳ κρεμήσεται.

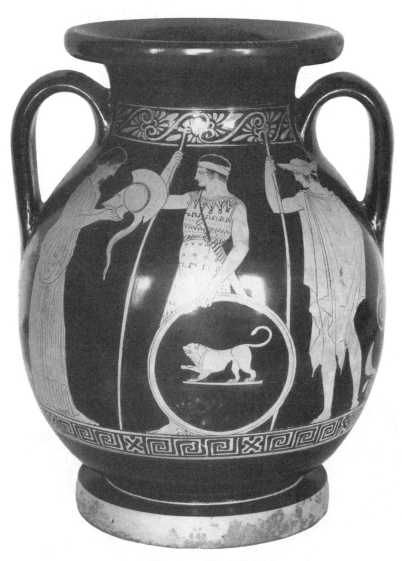

Warrior with shield

## PRINCIPAL PARTS: Verbs in -μι

δείκ-νῡ-μι, δείξω, ἔδειξα, δέδειχα, δέδειγμαι, ἐδείχθην, *I show*

ζεύγ-νῡ-μι, ζεύξω, ἔζευξα, ἔζευγμαι, ἐζεύχθην or ἐζύγην, *I yoke*

ἀνοίγ-νῡ-μι [= ἀνα- + οἴγ-νῡ-μι], imperfect, ἀνέῳγον (double augment), ἀνοίξω, ἀνέῳξα, ἀνέῳχα, ἀνέῳγμαι (*I stand open*), ἀνεῴχθην, *I open*

ῥήγ-νῡ-μι, ῥήξω, ἔρρηξα, ἔρρωγα (*I am broken*), ἐρράγην, aorist passive participle, ῥαγείς, *I break*

σβέν-νῡ-μι, [σβε-] σβέσω, ἔσβεσα, ἔσβηκα (*I have gone out*), ἐσβέσθην, *I put out, extinguish*

δί-δω-μι [δω-/δο-], imperfect, ἐδίδουν, δώσω, ἔδωκα, infinitive, δοῦναι, participle, δούς, imperative, δός, δέδωκα, δέδομαι, ἐδόθην, *I give*

εἰμί [ἐσ-], imperfect, ἦ or ἦν, ἔσομαι, *I am*

εἶμι [εἰ-/ἰ-], imperfect, ᾖα or ᾔειν, *I will go*

ἵημι, imperative, ἵει, infinitive, ἱέναι, participle, ἱείς, imperfect, ἵην, [ἡ-] ἥσω, ἧκα, imperative, [ἑ-] ἕς, infinitive, εἶναι, participle, εἵς, εἷκα, εἷμαι, εἵθην, *I let go, release; I send; I throw;* middle, ἵεμαι, imperfect, ἱέμην, *I hasten*

ἵστημι, imperfect, ἵστην, [στη-] στήσω, ἔστησα, *I make* X *stand; I stop* X; *I am setting* X *(up)*

    athematic 2nd aorist, ἔστην, intransitive, *I stood*

    -κα- 1st perfect, ἕστηκα, intransitive, *I stand*

    -θη- 1st aorist passive, [στα-] ἐστάθην, *I was set (up)*

τί-θη-μι [θη-/θε-], imperfect, ἐτίθην, θήσω, ἔθηκα, infinitive, θεῖναι, participle, θείς, imperative, θές, τέθηκα, (τέθειμαι; κεῖμαι usually used instead), ἐτέθην, *I put, place*

The fertile valley of the river Eurotas, in which Sparta lay,
with the Taygetus range of mountains behind

# GRAMMAR

## 1. Complex Sentences in Indirect Statement: Secondary Sequence

If the introductory verb is in a past tense (imperfect, aorist, or pluperfect), the following rules for secondary sequence apply:

a. An indicative verb in the <u>main clause</u> of the direct statement may be retained or may be changed to the corresponding tense of the optative when the indirect statement is introduced by ὅτι or ὡς in secondary sequence (see Chapter 25, Grammar 6, pages 155–156), e.g.:

Direct Statement:

εἰ ὁ Φίλιππος τοῦτο εἶπεν, **ἐψεύσατο**.     (past particular condition)
*If Philip said this, **he lied**.*

Indirect Statement:

εἶπεν ὅτι/ὡς εἰ ὁ Φίλιππος τοῦτο εἶπεν, **ἐψεύσατο/ψεύσαιτο**.
*He/She said that if Philip said this, **he lied**.*

Note, however, that an indicative with ἄν in the main clause of *contrary to fact conditions* is retained after ὅτι or ὡς, e.g.:

Direct Statement:

εἰ ὁ Φίλιππος τοῦτο εἶπεν, **ἐψεύσατο** <u>ἄν</u>.     (past contrary to fact condition)
*If Philip had said this, **he would have lied**.*

Indirect Statement:

εἶπεν ὅτι/ὡς εἰ ὁ Φίλιππος τοῦτο εἶπεν, **ἐψεύσατο** <u>ἄν</u>.
*He/She said that if Philip had said this, **he would have lied**.*

With ἔφη and ἤδει this sentence would be as follows:

ἔφη τὸν Φίλιππον **ψεύσασθαι** ἄν, εἰ τοῦτο εἶπεν.
*He/She said that Philip **would have lied**, if he had said this.*
ἤδει τὸν Φίλιππον **ψευσάμενον** ἄν, εἰ τοῦτο εἶπεν.
*He/She knew that Philip **would have lied**, if he had said this.*

b. *Secondary tenses of the indicative* in the <u>subordinate clause</u> of the direct statement remain unchanged in mood and tense when put into indirect statements. See the examples above, in which the verbs in the subordinate clauses remain unchanged.

c. *Primary tenses of the indicative* in the <u>subordinate clause</u> of the direct statement may be retained or may be changed to the optative, e.g.:

Direct Statement:

εἰ ὁ Φίλιππος τοῦτο **λέγει**, ψεύδεται.     (present particular condition)
*If Philip **says** this, he is lying.*

Indirect Statement:

εἶπεν ὅτι/ὡς εἰ ὁ Φίλιππος τοῦτο **λέγει/λέγοι**, ψεύδεται.

*He/She said that if Philip **was saying this**, he was lying.*

(Note that we switch to the past tense in English, where Greek keeps the present tense; and note that ψεύδεται could have been changed to ψεύδοιτο according to rule a above.)

d.  All *subjunctives* (with or without ἄν) in the <u>subordinate clause</u> of the direct statement may be retained or may be changed to the corresponding tenses of the optative (ἐάν becomes εἰ, ὅταν becomes ὅτε, πρὶν ἄν becomes πρίν, etc., i.e., the ἄν drops out when the subjunctive is changed to optative).  Greek writers often chose *not* to make the optional changes to the optative but to retain the original indicatives or subjunctives for the sake of vividness.

Direct Statement:

**ἐὰν στρατεύηται** Κροῖσος ἐπὶ Πέρσᾱς, μεγάλην ἀρχὴν καταλύσει.

*If Croesus **wages war** against the Persians, he will destroy a great empire.*                                    (future more vivid condition)

Indirect Statement without Changes:

ἡ δὲ Πῡθίη τάδε ἀπεκρίνατο, ὅτι **ἐὰν στρατεύηται** Κροῖσος ἐπὶ Πέρσᾱς, μεγάλην ἀρχὴν **καταλύσει**.                                    (27α:32–33)

*And the Pythia answered these things, that **if** Croesus **waged war** against the Persians, **he would destroy** a great empire.*

(The ἐάν + subjunctive in the original subordinate clause and the future indicative in the original main clause are here retained in the indirect statement.  See rules a and d above.)

Indirect Statement with Changes:

ἡ δὲ Πῡθίη τάδε ἀπεκρίνατο, ὅτι **εἰ στρατεύοιτο** Κροῖσος ἐπὶ Πέρσᾱς, μεγάλην ἀρχὴν **καταλύσοι**.

*And the Pythia answered these things, that **if** Croesus **waged war** against the Persians, **he would destroy** a great empire.*

(Optatives are here substituted in both clauses, with ἐάν changing to εἰ.  Again, see rules a and d above.)

e.  All optatives in the direct statement remain unchanged in mood and tense after ὅτι or ὡς.

Direct Statement:

εἰ ὁ Φίλιππος τοῦτο **εἴποι**, **ψεύδοιτο ἄν**. (future less vivid condition)

*If Philip **should say** this, **he would be lying**.*

Indirect Statement:

εἶπεν ὅτι/ὡς εἰ ὁ Φίλιππος τοῦτο **εἴποι**, **ψεύδοιτο ἄν**.

*He/She said that if Philip **should say** this, **he would be lying**.*

(Both optatives are retained, along with ἄν.)

With ἔφη and ᾔδει this sentence would be as follows:

ἔφη τὸν Φίλιππόν **ψεύδεσθαι** ἄν, εἰ τοῦτο **εἴποι**.

ᾔδει τὸν Φίλιππον **ψευδόμενον** ἄν, εἰ τοῦτο **εἴποι**.

*He / She said / knew that Philip **would be lying**, if he should say this.*
(The optative of the main clause changes to the same tense of the infinitive after ἔφη and to the same tense of the participle after ᾔδει, with ἄν retained. The optative of the original subordinate clause remains unchanged.)

Note that ἄν with an infinitive or participle in indirect statement may also represent a direct statement with a potential optative, e.g.:

Direct Statement:

**βουλοίμην ἂν** τὸν ἰᾱτρὸν ἰδεῖν.                (potential optative)

*I **would like** to see the doctor.*

Indirect Statements:

οἴομαι τὸν Φίλιππον **ἂν βούλεσθαι** τὸν ἰᾱτρὸν ἰδεῖν.

*I think that Philip **would like** to see the doctor.*

οἶδα τὸν Φίλιππον **ἂν βουλόμενον** τὸν ἰᾱτρὸν ἰδεῖν.

*I know that Philip **would like** to see the doctor.*

## Exercise 30 α

*Translate the following pairs of sentences and explain each change that has been made in the versions in indirect statement, with reference to the rules above.*

1. ἐὰν στρατεύηται ὁ Κροῖσος ἐπὶ Πέρσᾱς, μεγάλην ἀρχὴν καταλύσει.
   ἡ Πυθίᾱ ἔφη τὸν Κροῖσον μεγάλην ἀρχὴν καταλύσειν, εἰ στρατεύοιτο ἐπὶ Πέρσᾱς.

2. οἱ παῖδες πάντα ἐποίησαν ὅσα ἐκέλευσεν ὁ πατήρ.
   οἱ παῖδες εἶπον ὅτι πάντα ποιήσειαν ὅσα ἐκέλευσεν ὁ πατήρ.

3. ὁ ποιμὴν τὰ πρόβατα φυλάξει ἕως ἂν νὺξ γένηται.
   ᾖσμεν τὸν ποιμένα τὰ πρόβατα φυλάξοντα ἕως νύξ γένοιτο.

4. ὅστις ἂν ἔξω τῶν τειχῶν μένῃ, ὑπὸ τῶν πολεμίων ἀποθανεῖται.
   ὁ Δικαιόπολις εἶπεν ὅτι ὅστις ἔξω τῶν τειχῶν μένοι, ὑπὸ τῶν πολεμίων ἀποθανεῖται.

5. οἱ παῖδες, εἰ ταῦτα ἐποίησαν, οὐκ ἂν εἰς κίνδῡνον κατέστησαν.
   ὁ πατὴρ ἔφη τοὺς παῖδας, εἰ ταῦτα ἐποίησαν, οὐκ ἂν εἰς κίνδῡνον καταστῆναι.

# VERB CHART: PRESENT AND IMPERFECT

Principal Parts of Verb: _____

Exercise Number: _____      Voice: _____

## Present

| Indicative | Subjunctive | Optative | Imperative | Infinitive | Participle |
|---|---|---|---|---|---|
| _____ | _____ | _____ | | _____ | _____ |
| _____ | _____ | _____ | _____ | | _____ |
| _____ | _____ | _____ | | | _____ |
| _____ | _____ | _____ | _____ | | _____ |
| _____ | _____ | _____ | | | |
| _____ | _____ | _____ | _____ | | |

## Imperfect

| | | | | | |
|---|---|---|---|---|---|
| _____ | | | | | |
| _____ | | | | | |
| _____ | | | | | |
| _____ | | | | | |
| _____ | | | | | |
| _____ | | | | | |

For participles, fill in the nominative singular, masculine, feminine, and neuter and the genitive singular masculine of participles having 3rd and 1st declension forms.

For middle voice participles, give the masculine nominative singular and the feminine and neuter endings.

# VERB CHART: FUTURE AND AORIST

First Principal Part of Verb: _____

Exercise Number: _____          Voice: _____

## Future

| Indicative | Subjunctive | Optative | Imperative | Infinitive | Participle |
|------------|-------------|----------|------------|------------|------------|

## Aorist

# VERB CHART: PERFECT AND PLUPERFECT

First Principal Part of Verb: _____

Exercise Number: _____          Voice: _____

## Perfect

| Indicative | Subjunctive | Optative | Imperative* | Infinitive | Participle |
|---|---|---|---|---|---|
| _____ | _____ | _____ | | _____ | _____ |
| _____ | _____ | _____ | | | _____ |
| _____ | _____ | _____ | | | _____ |
| _____ | _____ | _____ | | | |
| _____ | _____ | _____ | | | |
| _____ | _____ | _____ | | | |

## Pluperfect

| Indicative |
|---|
| _____ |
| _____ |
| _____ |
| _____ |
| _____ |
| _____ |

*Very rare and not given in charts

# FORMS

## 1.  THE DEFINITE ARTICLE (see Book I, page 50)

|      | Singular |      |      | Plural |      |      |
|------|------|------|------|------|------|------|
|      | **M.** | **F.** | **N.** | **M.** | **F.** | **N.** |
| **N.** | ὁ | ἡ | τό | οἱ | αἱ | τά |
| **G.** | τοῦ | τῆς | τοῦ | τῶν | τῶν | τῶν |
| **D.** | τῷ | τῇ | τῷ | τοῖς | ταῖς | τοῖς |
| **A.** | τόν | τήν | τό | τούς | τάς | τά |

## 2.  NOUNS OF THE 1ST DECLENSION

### Feminine  (see Book I, pages 40–42)

|      | Singular |      | Plural |      |      | Singular |      | Plural |      |
|------|------|------|------|------|--|------|------|------|------|
| **N.** | ἡ | κρήνη | αἱ | κρῆναι | | ἡ | ὑδρίᾱ | αἱ | ὑδρίαι |
| **G.** | τῆς | κρήνης | τῶν | κρηνῶν | | τῆς | ὑδρίας | τῶν | ὑδριῶν |
| **D.** | τῇ | κρήνῃ | ταῖς | κρήναις | | τῇ | ὑδρίᾳ | ταῖς | ὑδρίαις |
| **A.** | τὴν | κρήνην | τᾱς | κρήνᾱς | | τὴν | ὑδρίαν | τᾱς | ὑδρίᾱς |
| **V.** | ὦ | κρήνη | ὦ | κρῆναι | | ὦ | ὑδρίᾱ | ὦ | ὑδρίαι |

|      | Singular |      | Plural |      |  | Singular |      | Plural |      |
|------|------|------|------|------|--|------|------|------|------|
| **N.** | ἡ | μέλιττᾰ | αἱ | μέλιτται | | ἡ | μάχαιρᾰ | αἱ | μάχαιραι |
| **G.** | τῆς | μελίττης | τῶν | μελιττῶν | | τῆς | μαχαίρᾱς | τῶν | μαχαιρῶν |
| **D.** | τῇ | μελίττῃ | ταῖς | μελίτταις | | τῇ | μαχαίρᾳ | ταῖς | μαχαίραις |
| **A.** | τὴν | μέλιττᾰν | τᾱς | μελίττᾱς | | τὴν | μάχαιρᾰν | τᾱς | μαχαίρᾱς |
| **V.** | ὦ | μέλιττᾰ | ὦ | μέλιτται | | ὦ | μάχαιρᾰ | ὦ | μάχαιραι |

### Masculine  (see Book I, pages 47–48)

|      | Singular |      | Plural |      |  | Singular |      | Plural |      |
|------|------|------|------|------|--|------|------|------|------|
| **N.** | ὁ | δεσπότης | οἱ | δεσπόται | | ὁ | νεᾱνίᾱς | οἱ | νεᾱνίαι |
| **G.** | τοῦ | δεσπότου | τῶν | δεσποτῶν | | τοῦ | νεᾱνίου | τῶν | νεᾱνιῶν |
| **D.** | τῷ | δεσπότῃ | τοῖς | δεσπόταις | | τῷ | νεᾱνίᾳ | τοῖς | νεᾱνίαις |
| **A.** | τὸν | δεσπότην | τοὺς | δεσπότᾱς | | τὸν | νεᾱνίαν | τοὺς | νεᾱνίᾱς |
| **V.** | ὦ | δέσποτα* | ὦ | δεσπόται | | ὦ | νεᾱνίᾱ | ὦ | νεᾱνίαι |

*Irregular accent.  Normally the accent is persistent as with the noun ὁ πολίτης, vocative, ὦ πολῖτα.

## 3.  NOUNS OF THE 2ND DECLENSION

**Masculine** (see Book I, page 31)          **Neuter** (see Book I, page 31)

|     | Singular |         | Plural |         |     | Singular |          | Plural |           |
|-----|----------|---------|--------|---------|-----|----------|----------|--------|-----------|
| N.  | ὁ        | ἀγρός   | οἱ     | ἀγροί   | τὸ  | δένδρον  | τὰ       | δένδρα |           |
| G   | τοῦ      | ἀγροῦ   | τῶν    | ἀγρῶν   | τοῦ | δένδρου  | τῶν      | δένδρων |          |
| D.  | τῷ       | ἀγρῷ    | τοῖς   | ἀγροῖς  | τῷ  | δένδρῳ   | τοῖς     | δένδροις |         |
| A.  | τὸν      | ἀγρόν   | τοὺς   | ἀγρούς  | τὸ  | δένδρον  | τὰ       | δένδρα |           |
| V.  | ὦ        | ἀγρέ    | ὦ      | ἀγροί   | ὦ   | δένδρον  | ὦ        | δένδρα |           |

**Feminine:** e.g., ἡ ὁδός (see Book I, page 48)

**Contract:** Masculine              **Attic Declension**
(see Book I, page 263):

|     | Singular |       | Plural |      |     | Singular |           | Plural |         |
|-----|----------|-------|--------|------|-----|----------|-----------|--------|---------|
| N.  | ὁ        | νοῦς  | οἱ     | νοῖ  | ὁ   | λαγώς    | οἱ        | λαγῴ   |         |
| G.  | τοῦ      | νοῦ   | τῶν    | νῶν  | τοῦ | λαγώ     | τῶν       | λαγών  |         |
| D.  | τῷ       | νῷ    | τοῖς   | νοῖς | τῷ  | λαγῴ     | τοῖς      | λαγῴς  |         |
| A.  | τὸν      | νοῦν  | τοὺς   | νοῦς | τὸν | λαγών/ώ  | τοὺς      | λαγώς  |         |
| V.  | ὦ        | νοῦ   | ὦ      | νοῖ  | ὦ   | λαγώς    | ὦ         | λαγῴ   |         |

**Contract Neuter:** τὸ κανοῦν (rare; not formally
presented in this course; for an example, see κανᾶ, 9β:6)

## 4.  NOUNS OF THE 3RD DECLENSION

**Labial Stems** (β, π, φ; see Book I, page 107)

|     | Singular |         | Plural |           |
|-----|----------|---------|--------|-----------|
| N.  | ὁ        | κλώψ    | οἱ     | κλῶπες    |
| G.  | τοῦ      | κλωπός  | τῶν    | κλωπῶν    |
| D.  | τῷ       | κλωπί   | τοῖς   | κλωψί(ν)  |
| A.  | τὸν      | κλῶπα   | τοὺς   | κλῶπας    |
| V.  | ὦ        | κλώψ    | ὦ      | κλῶπες    |

**Velar Stems** (γ, κ, χ; see Book I, page 98)

|     | Singular |          | Plural |           |     | Singular |        | Plural |          |
|-----|----------|----------|--------|-----------|-----|----------|--------|--------|----------|
| N.  | ὁ        | φύλαξ    | οἱ     | φύλακες   | ὁ   | αἴξ      | οἱ     | αἶγες  |          |
| G.  | τοῦ      | φύλακος  | τῶν    | φυλάκων   | τοῦ | αἰγός    | τῶν    | αἰγῶν  |          |
| D.  | τῷ       | φύλακι   | τοῖς   | φύλαξι(ν) | τῷ  | αἰγί     | τοῖς   | αἰξί(ν) |         |
| A.  | τὸν      | φύλακα   | τοὺς   | φύλακας   | τὸν | αἶγα     | τοὺς   | αἶγας  |          |
| V.  | ὦ        | φύλαξ    | ὦ      | φύλακες   | ὦ   | αἴξ      | ὦ      | αἶγες  |          |

## Dental Stems (δ, θ, τ; see Book I, page 99)

| | Singular | | Plural | | | Singular | | Plural | |
|---|---|---|---|---|---|---|---|---|---|
| **N.** | ὁ | παῖς | οἱ | παῖδες | | τό | ὄνομα | τά | ὀνόματα |
| **G.** | τοῦ | παιδός | τῶν | παίδων | | τοῦ | ὀνόματος | τῶν | ὀνομάτων |
| **D.** | τῷ | παιδί | τοῖς | παισί(ν) | | τῷ | ὀνόματι | τοῖς | ὀνόμασι(ν) |
| **A.** | τόν | παῖδα | τούς | παῖδας | | τό | ὄνομα | τά | ὀνόματα |
| **V.** | ὦ | παῖ | ὦ | παῖδες | | ὦ | ὄνομα | ὦ | ὀνόματα |

## Stems in -ντ- (see Book I, page 145)

| | Singular | | Plural | |
|---|---|---|---|---|
| **N.** | ὁ | γέρων | οἱ | γέροντες |
| **G.** | τοῦ | γέροντος | τῶν | γερόντων |
| **D.** | τῷ | γέροντι | τοῖς | γέρουσι(ν) |
| **A.** | τόν | γέροντα | τούς | γέροντας |
| **V.** | ὦ | γέρον | ὦ | γέροντες |

## Liquid Stems (λ, ρ; see Book I, page 107)  Nasal Stems (ν; see Book I, pages 106–107)

| | Singular | | Plural | | | Singular | | Plural | |
|---|---|---|---|---|---|---|---|---|---|
| **N.** | ὁ | ῥήτωρ | οἱ | ῥήτορες | | ὁ | χειμών | οἱ | χειμῶνες |
| **G.** | τοῦ | ῥήτορος | τῶν | ῥητόρων | | τοῦ | χειμῶνος | τῶν | χειμώνων |
| **D.** | τῷ | ῥήτορι | τοῖς | ῥήτορσι(ν) | | τῷ | χειμῶνι | τοῖς | χειμῶσι(ν) |
| **A.** | τόν | ῥήτορα | τούς | ῥήτορας | | τόν | χειμῶνα | τούς | χειμῶνας |
| **V.** | ὦ | ῥήτωρ | ὦ | ῥήτορες | | ὦ | χειμών | ὦ | χειμῶνες |

## Stems in -ρ- (see Book I, pages 124–125)

### Singular

| | | | | | | | | | |
|---|---|---|---|---|---|---|---|---|---|
| **N.** | ὁ | ἀνήρ | ὁ | πατήρ | ἡ | μήτηρ | ἡ | θυγάτηρ |
| **G.** | τοῦ | ἀνδρός | τοῦ | πατρός | τῆς | μητρός | τῆς | θυγατρός |
| **D.** | τῷ | ἀνδρί | τῷ | πατρί | τῇ | μητρί | τῇ | θυγατρί |
| **A.** | τόν | ἄνδρα | τόν | πατέρα | τήν | μητέρα | τήν | θυγατέρα |
| **V.** | ὦ | ἄνερ | ὦ | πάτερ | ὦ | μῆτερ | ὦ | θύγατερ |

### Plural

| | | | | | | | | | |
|---|---|---|---|---|---|---|---|---|---|
| **N.** | οἱ | ἄνδρες | οἱ | πατέρες | αἱ | μητέρες | αἱ | θυγατέρες |
| **G.** | τῶν | ἀνδρῶν | τῶν | πατέρων | τῶν | μητέρων | τῶν | θυγατέρων |
| **D.** | τοῖς | ἀνδράσι(ν) | τοῖς | πατράσι(ν) | ταῖς | μητράσι(ν) | ταῖς | θυγατράσι(ν) |
| **A.** | τούς | ἄνδρας | τούς | πατέρας | τάς | μητέρας | τάς | θυγατέρας |
| **V.** | ὦ | ἄνδρες | ὦ | πατέρες | ὦ | μητέρες | ὦ | θυγατέρες |

### Stems in -εσ- (see Book I, pages 226–227)

|     | Singular |        | Plural |          | Singular |          | Plural |           |
|-----|----------|--------|--------|----------|----------|----------|--------|-----------|
| N.  | τὸ       | τεῖχος | τὰ     | τείχη    | ἡ        | τριήρης  | αἱ     | τριήρεις  |
| G.  | τοῦ      | τείχους| τῶν    | τειχῶν   | τῆς      | τριήρους | τῶν    | τριήρων   |
| D.  | τῷ       | τείχει | τοῖς   | τείχεσι(ν)| τῇ      | τριήρει  | ταῖς   | τριήρεσι(ν|
| A.  | τὸ       | τεῖχος | τὰ     | τείχη    | τὴν      | τριήρη   | τὰς    | τριήρεις  |
| V.  | ὦ        | τεῖχος | ὦ      | τείχη    | ὦ        | τριῆρες  | ὦ      | τριήρεις  |

### Also ὁ Θεμιστοκλῆς (see Book I, page 254)

|     |     |              |
|-----|-----|--------------|
| N.  | ὁ   | Θεμιστοκλῆς   |
| G.  | τοῦ | Θεμιστοκλέους |
| D.  | τῷ  | Θεμιστοκλεῖ   |
| A.  | τὸν | Θεμιστοκλέᾱ   |
| V.  | ὦ   | Θεμιστόκλεις  |

### Stems Ending in a Vowel (see Book I, page 145)

|     | Singular |        | Plural |          | Singular |        | Plural |          |
|-----|----------|--------|--------|----------|----------|--------|--------|----------|
| N.  | ἡ        | πόλις  | αἱ     | πόλεις   | τὸ       | ἄστυ   | τὰ     | ἄστη     |
| G.  | τῆς      | πόλεως | τῶν    | πόλεων   | τοῦ      | ἄστεως | τῶν    | ἄστεων   |
| D.  | τῇ       | πόλει  | ταῖς   | πόλεσι(ν)| τῷ       | ἄστει  | τοῖς   | ἄστεσι(ν)|
| A.  | τὴν      | πόλιν  | τὰς    | πόλεις   | τὸ       | ἄστυ   | τὰ     | ἄστη     |
| V.  | ὦ        | πόλι   | ὦ      | πόλεις   | ὦ        | ἄστυ   | ὦ      | ἄστη     |

### Stems in Diphthongs or Vowels (see Book I, page 146)

|     | Singular |          | Plural |             |
|-----|----------|----------|--------|-------------|
| N.  | ὁ        | βασιλεύς | οἱ     | βασιλῆς     |
| G.  | τοῦ      | βασιλέως | τῶν    | βασιλέων    |
| D.  | τῷ       | βασιλεῖ  | τοῖς   | βασιλεῦσι(ν)|
| A.  | τὸν      | βασιλέᾱ  | τοὺς   | βασιλέᾱς    |
| V.  | ὦ        | βασιλεῦ  | ὦ      | βασιλῆς     |

Irregular

|     | Singular |       | Plural |          | Singular |      | Plural |         |
|-----|----------|-------|--------|----------|----------|------|--------|---------|
| N.  | ἡ        | ναῦς  | αἱ     | νῆες     | ὁ        | βοῦς | οἱ     | βόες    |
| G.  | τῆς      | νεώς  | τῶν    | νεῶν     | τοῦ      | βοός | τῶν    | βοῶν    |
| D.  | τῇ       | νηΐ   | ταῖς   | ναυσί(ν) | τῷ       | βοΐ  | τοῖς   | βουσί(ν)|
| A.  | τὴν      | ναῦν  | τὰς    | ναῦς     | τὸν      | βοῦν | τοὺς   | βοῦς    |
| V.  | ὦ        | ναῦ   | ὦ      | νῆες     | ὦ        | βοῦ  | ὦ      | βόες    |

**Irregular** (see Book I, page 125)

| | Singular | Plural | | Singular | Plural |
|---|---|---|---|---|---|
| **N.** | ἡ γυνή | αἱ γυναῖκες | ἡ χείρ | αἱ χεῖρες |
| **G.** | τῆς γυναικός | τῶν γυναικῶν | τῆς χειρός | τῶν χειρῶν |
| **D.** | τῇ γυναικί | ταῖς γυναιξί(ν) | τῇ χειρί | ταῖς χερσί(ν) |
| **A.** | τὴν γυναῖκα | τὰς γυναῖκας | τὴν χεῖρα | τὰς χεῖρας |
| **V.** | ὦ γύναι | ὦ γυναῖκες | ὦ χείρ | ὦ χεῖρες |

5. ADJECTIVES AND PARTICIPLES OF THE 1ST AND 2ND DECLENSIONS

**Adjectives** (see Book I, pages 48–49)

| | Singular | | | Plural | | |
|---|---|---|---|---|---|---|
| | **M.** | **F.** | **N.** | **M.** | **F.** | **N.** |
| **N.** | καλός | καλή | καλόν | καλοί | καλαί | καλά |
| **G.** | καλοῦ | καλῆς | καλοῦ | καλῶν | καλῶν | καλῶν |
| **D.** | καλῷ | καλῇ | καλῷ | καλοῖς | καλαῖς | καλοῖς |
| **A.** | καλόν | καλήν | καλόν | καλούς | καλάς | καλά |
| **V.** | καλέ | καλή | κᾰλόν | καλοί | καλαί | καλά |

| | Singular | | | Plural | | |
|---|---|---|---|---|---|---|
| | **M.** | **F.** | **N.** | **M.** | **F.** | **N.** |
| **N.** | ῥᾴδιος | ῥᾳδίᾱ | ῥᾴδιον | ῥᾴδιοι | ῥᾴδιαι | ῥᾴδια |
| **G.** | ῥᾳδίου | ῥᾳδίᾱς | ῥᾳδίου | ῥᾳδίων | ῥᾳδίων | ῥᾳδίων |
| **D.** | ῥᾳδίῳ | ῥᾳδίᾳ | ῥᾳδίῳ | ῥᾳδίοις | ῥᾳδίαις | ῥᾳδίοις |
| **A.** | ῥᾴδιον | ῥᾳδίᾱν | ῥᾴδιον | ῥᾳδίους | ῥᾳδίᾱς | ῥᾴδια |
| **V.** | ῥᾴδιε | ῥᾳδίᾱ | ῥᾴδιον | ῥᾴδιοι | ῥᾴδιαι | ῥᾴδια |

**Present or Progressive Middle Participles** (see Book I, pages 115–116, and 262)

| | Singular | | |
|---|---|---|---|
| | **M.** | **F.** | **N.** |
| **N.** | λῡόμενος | λῡομένη | λῡόμενον |
| **G.** | λῡομένου | λῡομένης | λῡομένου |
| **D.** | λῡομένῳ | λῡομένῃ | λῡομένῳ |
| **A.** | λῡόμενον | λῡομένην | λῡόμενον |
| **V.** | λῡόμενε | λῡομένη | λῡόμενον |
| | **Plural** | | |
| **N., V.** | λῡόμενοι | λῡόμεναι | λῡόμενα |
| **G.** | λῡομένων | λῡομένων | λῡομένων |
| **D.** | λῡομένοις | λῡομέναις | λῡομένοις |
| **A.** | λῡομένους | λῡομένᾱς | λῡόμενα |

**Singular**

|      | M.          | F.          | N.          |
|------|-------------|-------------|-------------|
| N.   | φιλούμενος  | φιλουμένη   | φιλούμενον  |
| G.   | φιλουμένου  | φιλουμένης  | φιλουμένου  |
| D.   | φιλουμένῳ   | φιλουμένῃ   | φιλουμένῳ   |
| A.   | φιλούμενον  | φιλουμένην  | φιλούμενον  |
| V    | φιλούμενε   | φιλουμένη   | φιλούμενον  |

**Plural**

|        | M.          | F.          | N.          |
|--------|-------------|-------------|-------------|
| N., V. | φιλούμενοι  | φιλούμεναι  | φιλούμενα   |
| G.     | φιλουμένων  | φιλουμένων  | φιλουμένων  |
| D.     | φιλουμένοις | φιλουμέναις | φιλουμένοις |
| A.     | φιλουμένους | φιλουμένᾱς  | φιλούμενα   |

Exempli gratia:

| N. | τῑμώμενος | τῑμωμένη | τῑμώμενον |

Exempli gratia:

| N. | δηλούμενος | δηλουμένη | δηλούμενον |

### Sigmatic 1st Aorist and Thematic 2nd Aorist Middle Participles (see Book I, pages 199 and 180)

Exempli gratia:

| N. | λῡσάμενος | λῡσαμένη | λῡσάμενον |

| N. | γενόμενος | γενομένη | γενόμενον |

6. ADJECTIVES OF IRREGULAR DECLENSION (see Book I, page 49)

**Singular**                                        **Plural**

|      | M.       | F.       | N.       | M.        | F.        | N.        |
|------|----------|----------|----------|-----------|-----------|-----------|
| N.   | μέγας    | μεγάλη   | μέγα     | μεγάλοι   | μεγάλαι   | μεγάλα    |
| G.   | μεγάλου  | μεγάλης  | μεγάλου  | μεγάλων   | μεγάλων   | μεγάλων   |
| D.   | μεγάλῳ   | μεγάλῃ   | μεγάλῳ   | μεγάλοις  | μεγάλαις  | μεγάλοις  |
| A.   | μέγαν    | μεγάλην  | μέγα     | μεγάλους  | μεγάλᾱς   | μεγάλα    |
| V.   | μεγάλε   | μεγάλη   | μέγα     | μεγάλοι   | μεγάλαι   | μεγάλα    |
| N.   | πολύς    | πολλή    | πολύ     | πολλοί    | πολλαί    | πολλά     |
| G.   | πολλοῦ   | πολλῆς   | πολλοῦ   | πολλῶν    | πολλῶν    | πολλῶν    |
| D.   | πολλῷ    | πολλῇ    | πολλῷ    | πολλοῖς   | πολλαῖς   | πολλοῖς   |
| A.   | πολύν    | πολλήν   | πολύ     | πολλούς   | πολλᾱς    | πολλά     |
| V.   | none     |          |          |           |           |           |

7. ADJECTIVES OF THE 3RD DECLENSION

### Adjectives with Stems in -ον- (see Book I, pages 107–108)

|  | **Singular** |  | **Plural** |  |
|---|---|---|---|---|
|  | **M. & F.** | **N.** | **M. & F.** | **N.** |
| **N.** | σώφρων | σῶφρον | σώφρονες | σώφρονα |
| **G.** | σώφρονος | σώφρονος | σωφρόνων | σωφρόνων |
| **D.** | σώφρονι | σώφρονι | σώφροσι(ν) | σώφροσι(ν) |
| **A.** | σώφρονα | σῶφρον | σώφρονας | σώφρονα |
| **V.** | σῶφρον | σῶφρον | σώφρονες | σώφρονα |

### Comparative Adjectives with Stems in -ον- (see Book II, page 135)

|  | **Singular** |  | **Plural** |  |
|---|---|---|---|---|
|  | **M. & F.** | **N.** | **M. & F.** | **N.** |
| **N.** | βελτίων | βέλτιον | βελτίονες (βελτίους) | βελτίονα (βελτίω) |
| **G.** | βελτίονος | βελτίονος | βελτιόνων | βελτιόνων |
| **D.** | βελτίονι | βελτίονι | βελτίοσι(ν) | βελτίοσι(ν) |
| **A.** | βελτίονα (βελτίω) | βέλτιον | βελτίονας (βελτίους) | βελτίονα (βελτίω) |
| **V** | βέλτιον | βέλτιον | βελτίονες | βελτίονα |

### Adjectives with Stems in -εσ- (see Book I, page 227):

|  | **Singular** |  |
|---|---|---|
|  | **M. & F.** | **N.** |
| **N.** | ἀληθής | ἀληθές |
| **G.** | ἀληθοῦς | ἀληθοῦς |
| **D.** | ἀληθεῖ | ἀληθεῖ |
| **A.** | ἀληθῆ | ἀληθές |
| **V.** | ἀληθές | ἀληθές |
|  | **Plural** |  |
| **N.** | ἀληθεῖς | ἀληθῆ |
| **G.** | ἀληθῶν | ἀληθῶν |
| **D.** | ἀληθέσι(ν) | ἀληθέσι(ν) |
| **A.** | ἀληθεῖς | ἀληθῆ |
| **V.** | ἀληθεῖς | ἀληθῆ |

8.   ADJECTIVES AND PARTICIPLES OF THE 1ST AND 3RD DECLENSIONS

### Adjectives

πᾶς, πᾶσα, πᾶν, *all; every; whole* (see Book I, page 126).

**Singular**

|        | M.      | F.      | N.      |
|--------|---------|---------|---------|
| N., V. | πᾶς     | πᾶσα    | πᾶν     |
| G.     | παντός  | πάσης   | παντός  |
| D.     | παντί   | πάσῃ    | παντί   |
| A.     | πάντα   | πᾶσαν   | πᾶν     |

**Plural**

|        | M.         | F.       | N.       |
|--------|------------|----------|----------|
| N., V. | πάντες     | πᾶσαι    | πάντα    |
| G.     | πάντων     | πᾱσῶν    | πάντων   |
| D.     | πᾶσι(ν)    | πάσαις   | πᾶσι(ν)  |
| A.     | πάντας     | πάσᾱς    | πάντα    |

ταχύς, ταχεῖα, ταχύ, *quick, swift* (see Book I, pages 227–228)

**Singular**

|     | M.      | F.       | N.      |
|-----|---------|----------|---------|
| N.  | ταχύς   | ταχεῖα   | ταχύ    |
| G.  | ταχέος  | ταχείᾱς  | ταχέος  |
| D.  | ταχεῖ   | ταχείᾳ   | ταχεῖ   |
| A.  | ταχύν   | ταχεῖαν  | ταχύ    |
| V.  | ταχύ    | ταχεῖα   | ταχύ    |

**Plural**

|     | M.        | F.        | N.        |
|-----|-----------|-----------|-----------|
| N.  | ταχεῖς    | ταχεῖαι   | ταχέα     |
| G.  | ταχέων    | ταχειῶν   | ταχέων    |
| D.  | ταχέσι(ν) | ταχείαις  | ταχέσι(ν) |
| A.  | ταχεῖς    | ταχείᾱς   | ταχέα     |
| V.  | ταχεῖς    | ταχεῖαι   | ταχέα     |

### Present or Progressive Active Participles

εἰμί (see Book I, page 136):

**Singular**

|        | M.     | F.     | N.     |
|--------|--------|--------|--------|
| N., V. | ὤν     | οὖσα   | ὄν     |
| G.     | ὄντος  | οὔσης  | ὄντος  |
| D.     | ὄντι   | οὔσῃ   | ὄντι   |
| A.     | ὄντα   | οὖσαν  | ὄν     |

**Plural**

|  | M. | F. | N. |
|---|---|---|---|
| **N., V.** | ὄντες | οὖσαι | ὄντα |
| **G.** | ὄντων | οὐσῶν | ὄντων |
| **D.** | οὖσι(ν) | οὔσαις | οὖσι(ν) |
| **A.** | ὄντας | οὔσᾱς | ὄντα |

## λύω (see Book I, page 136):

**Singular**

| **N., V.** | λύων | λύουσα | λῦον |
|---|---|---|---|
| **G.** | λύοντος | λῡούσης | λύοντος |
| **D.** | λύοντι | λῡούσῃ | λύοντι |
| **A.** | λύοντα | λύουσαν | λῦον |

**Plural**

| **N., V.** | λύοντες | λύουσαι | λύοντα |
|---|---|---|---|
| **G.** | λῡόντων | λῡουσῶν | λῡόντων |
| **D.** | λύουσι(ν) | λῡούσαις | λύουσι(ν) |
| **A.** | λύοντας | λῡούσᾱς | λύοντα |

## φιλέω (see Book I, page 136):

**Singular**

| **N., V.** | φιλῶν | φιλοῦσα | φιλοῦν |
|---|---|---|---|
| **G.** | φιλοῦντος | φιλούσης | φιλοῦντος |
| **D.** | φιλοῦντι | φιλούσῃ | φιλοῦντι |
| **A.** | φιλοῦντα | φιλοῦσαν | φιλοῦν |

**Plural**

| **N., V.** | φιλοῦντες | φιλοῦσαι | φιλοῦντα |
|---|---|---|---|
| **G.** | φιλούντων | φιλουσῶν | φιλούντων |
| **D.** | φιλοῦσι | φιλούσαις | φιλοῦσι |
| **A.** | φιλοῦντας | φιλούσᾱς | φιλοῦντα |

## τῑμάω (see Book I, pages 136–137):

**Singular**

| **N., V.** | τῑμῶν | τῑμῶσα | τῑμῶν |
|---|---|---|---|
| **G.** | τῑμῶντος | τῑμώσης | τῑμῶντος |
| **D.** | τῑμῶντι | τῑμώσῃ | τῑμῶντι |
| **A.** | τῑμῶντα | τῑμῶσαν | τῑμῶν |

**Plural**

| | M. | F. | N. |
|---|---|---|---|
| N., V. | τῑμῶντες | τῑμῶσαι | τῑμῶντα |
| G. | τῑμώντων | τῑμωσῶν | τῑμώντων |
| D. | τῑμῶσι | τῑμώσαις | τῑμῶσι |
| A. | τῑμῶντας | τῑμώσᾱς | τῑμῶντα |

δηλόω (see Book I, page 262; declined like φιλῶν above; we give only the nominative):

| | | |
|---|---|---|
| δηλῶν | δηλοῦσα | δηλοῦν |

### Sigmatic 1st Aorist Active Participles (see Book I, page 199)

**Singular**

| | | | |
|---|---|---|---|
| N., V. | λύσᾱς | λύσᾱσα | λῦσαν |
| G. | λύσαντος | λῡσάσης | λύσαντος |
| D. | λύσαντι | λῡσάσῃ | λύσαντι |
| A. | λύσαντα | λύσᾱσαν | λῦσαν |

**Plural**

| | | | |
|---|---|---|---|
| N., V. | λύσαντες | λύσᾱσαι | λύσαντα |
| G. | λῡσάντων | λῡσᾱσῶν | λῡσάντων |
| D. | λύσᾱσι(ν) | λῡσάσαις | λύσᾱσι(ν) |
| A. | λύσαντας | λῡσάσᾱς | λύσαντα |

### Thematic 2nd Aorist Active Participles (see Book I, page 180)

**Singular**

| | | | |
|---|---|---|---|
| N., V. | λιπών | λιποῦσα | λιπόν |
| G. | λιπόντος | λιπούσης | λιπόντος |
| D. | λιπόντι | λιπούσῃ | λιπόντι |
| A. | λιπόντα | λιποῦσαν | λιπόν |

**Plural**

| | | | |
|---|---|---|---|
| N., V. | λιπόντες | λιποῦσαι | λιπόντα |
| G. | λιπόντων | λιπουσῶν | λιπόντων |
| D. | λιποῦσι(ν) | λιπούσαις | λιποῦσι(ν) |
| A. | λιπόντας | λιπούσᾱς | λιπόντα |

### -θη- 1st Aorist Passive Participles (see Book II, page 5)

**Singular**

| | | | |
|---|---|---|---|
| N., V. | λυθείς | λυθεῖσα | λυθέν |
| G. | λυθέντος | λυθείσης | λυθέντος |
| D. | λυθέντι | λυθείσῃ | λυθέντι |
| A. | λυθέντα | λυθεῖσαν | λυθέν |

**Plural**

|        | M. | F. | N. |
|--------|----|----|----|
| **N., V.** | λυθέντες | λυθεῖσαι | λυθέντα |
| **G.** | λυθέντων | λυθεισῶν | λυθέντων |
| **D.** | λυθεῖσι(ν) | λυθείσαις | λυθεῖσι(ν) |
| **A.** | λυθέντας | λυθείσᾱς | λυθέντα |

**-η- 2nd Aorist Passive Participles** (see Book II, page 13)

Exempli gratia:

|        |    |    |    |
|--------|----|----|----|
| **N., V.** | γραφείς | γραφεῖσα | γραφέν |

**-κα 1st Perfect Active Participles** (see Book II, page 208)

**Singular**

|        |    |    |    |
|--------|----|----|----|
| **N., V.** | λελυκώς | λελυκυῖα | λελυκός |
| **G.** | λελυκότος | λελυκυίᾱς | λελυκότος |
| **D.** | λελυκότι | λελυκυίᾳ | λελυκότι |
| **A.** | λελυκότα | λελυκυῖαν | λελυκός |

**Plural**

|        |    |    |    |
|--------|----|----|----|
| **N., V.** | λελυκότες | λελυκυῖαι | λελυκότα |
| **G.** | λελυκότων | λελυκυιῶν | λελυκότων |
| **D.** | λελυκόσι(ν) | λελυκυίαις | λελυκόσι(ν) |
| **A.** | λελυκότας | λελυκυίᾱς | λελυκότα |

**-α 2nd Perfect Active Participles** (see Book II, pages 210–211)

Exempli gratia:

|        |    |    |    |
|--------|----|----|----|
| **N., V.** | γεγονώς | γεγονυῖα | γεγονός |

9. **COMPARISON OF ADJECTIVES** (see Book II, pages 126–128 and 134–135)

| Positive | Comparative | Superlative |
|----------|-------------|-------------|

**Regular** (see Book II, pages 126–127)

1st and 2nd Declension

| | | |
|---|---|---|
| ἀνδρεῖος, -ᾱ, -ον | ἀνδρειότερος, -ᾱ, -ον | ἀνδρειότατος, -η, -ον |
| χαλεπός, -ή, -όν | χαλεπώτερος, -ᾱ, -ον | χαλεπώτατος, -η, -ον |

3rd Declension

| | | |
|---|---|---|
| ἀληθής, ἀληθές | ἀληθέστερος, -ᾱ, -ον | ἀληθέστατος, -η, -ον |
| σώφρων, σῶφρον | σωφρονέστερος, -ᾱ, -ον | σωφρονέστατος, -η, -ον |

**Irregular** (see Book II, pages 127–128 and 134–135)

| | | |
|---|---|---|
| ἀγαθός, -ή, -όν | ἀμείνων, ἄμεινον | ἄριστος, -η, -ον |
| | βελτίων, βέλτῑον | βέλτιστος, -η, -ον |
| | κρείττων, κρεῖττον | κράτιστος, -η, -ον |

| | | |
|---|---|---|
| αἰσχρός, -ά, -όν | αἰσχίων, αἴσχῑον | αἴσχιστος, -η, -ον |
| ἐχθρός, -ά, -όν | ἐχθίων, ἔχθῑον | ἔχθιστος, -η, -ον |
| ἡδύς, ἡδεῖα, ἡδύ | ἡδίων, ἥδῑον | ἥδιστος, -η, -ον |
| κακός, -ή, -όν | κακίων, κάκῑον | κάκιστος, -η, -ον |
| | χείρων, χεῖρον | χείριστος, -η, -ον |
| | ἥττων, ἧττον | |
| καλός, -ή, -όν | καλλίων, κάλλῑον | κάλλιστος, -η, -ον |
| μέγας, μεγάλη, μέγα | μείζων, μεῖζον | μέγιστος, -η, -ον |
| ὀλίγος, -η, -ον | ἐλάττων, ἔλαττον | ὀλίγιστος, -η, -ον |
| | | ἐλάχιστος, -η, -ον |
| πολύς, πολλή, πολύ | πλείων/πλέων, πλεῖον/πλέον | πλεῖστος, -η, -ον |
| ῥᾴδιος, -ᾱ, -ον | ῥᾴων, ῥᾷον | ῥᾷστος, -η, -ον |
| ταχύς, ταχεῖα, ταχύ | θάττων, θᾶττον | τάχιστος, -η, -ον |
| φίλος, -η, -ον | φιλαίτερος, -ᾱ, -ον | φιλαίτατος, -η, -ον or φίλτατος -η, -ον |

For the declension of irregular comparative adjectives, see No. 7 above.

10.  **DEMONSTRATIVE ADJECTIVES**

οὗτος, αὕτη, τοῦτο, *this* (see Book I, pages 244–245)

| | **Singular** | | | **Plural** | | |
|---|---|---|---|---|---|---|
| | **M.** | **F.** | **N.** | **M.** | **F.** | **N.** |
| **N.** | οὗτος | αὕτη | τοῦτο | οὗτοι | αὗται | ταῦτα |
| **G.** | τούτου | ταύτης | τούτου | τούτων | τούτων | τούτων |
| **D.** | τούτῳ | ταύτῃ | τούτῳ | τούτοις | ταύταις | τούτοις |
| **A.** | τοῦτον | ταύτην | τοῦτο | τούτους | ταύτᾱς | ταῦτα |

ἐκεῖνος, ἐκείνη, ἐκεῖνο, *that* (see Book I, page 245):

| | **Singular** | | | **Plural** | | |
|---|---|---|---|---|---|---|
| | **M.** | **F.** | **N.** | **M.** | **F.** | **N.** |
| **N.** | ἐκεῖνος | ἐκείνη | ἐκεῖνο | ἐκεῖνοι | ἐκεῖναι | ἐκεῖνα |
| **G.** | ἐκείνου | ἐκείνης | ἐκείνου | ἐκείνων | ἐκείνων | ἐκείνων |
| **D.** | ἐκείνῳ | ἐκείνῃ | ἐκείνῳ | ἐκείνοις | ἐκείναις | ἐκείνοις |
| **A.** | ἐκεῖνον | ἐκείνην | ἐκεῖνο | ἐκείνους | ἐκείνᾱς | ἐκεῖνα |

ὅδε, ἥδε, τόδε, *this here* (see Book I, page 245):

| | **Singular** | | | **Plural** | | |
|---|---|---|---|---|---|---|
| | **M.** | **F.** | **N.** | **M.** | **F.** | **N.** |
| **N.** | ὅδε | ἥδε | τόδε | οἵδε | αἵδε | τάδε |
| **G.** | τοῦδε | τῆσδε | τοῦδε | τῶνδε | τῶνδε | τῶνδε |
| **D.** | τῷδε | τῇδε | τῷδε | τοῖσδε | ταῖσδε | τοῖσδε |
| **A.** | τόνδε | τήνδε | τόδε | τούσδε | τάσδε | τάδε |

11.  THE ADJECTIVE αὐτός, -ή, -ό, *-self, -selves; same* (see Book I, pages 68–69)

**Singular**

| | M. | F. | N. |
|---|---|---|---|
| N. | αὐτός | αὐτή | αὐτό |
| G. | αὐτοῦ | αὐτῆς | αὐτοῦ |
| D. | αὐτῷ | αὐτῇ | αὐτῷ |
| A. | αὐτόν | αὐτήν | αὐτό |

**Plural**

| | N. | | |
|---|---|---|---|
| N. | αὐτοί | αὐταί | αὐτά |
| G. | αὐτῶν | αὐτῶν | αὐτῶν |
| D. | αὐτοῖς | αὐταῖς | αὐτοῖς |
| A. | αὐτούς | αὐτάς | αὐτά |

12.  THE INTERROGATIVE ADJECTIVE (see Book I, page 108)

| | **Singular** | | **Plural** | |
|---|---|---|---|---|
| | **M. & F.** | **N.** | **M. & F.** | **N.** |
| N. | τίς | τί | τίνες | τίνα |
| G. | τίνος | τίνος | τίνων | τίνων |
| D. | τίνι | τίνι | τίσι(ν) | τίσι(ν) |
| A. | τίνα | τί | τίνας | τίνα |

13.  THE INDEFINITE ADJECTIVE (see Book I, page 109)

| | **Singular** | | **Plural** | |
|---|---|---|---|---|
| | **M. & F.** | **N.** | **M. & F.** | **N.** |
| N. | τις | τι | τινές | τινά |
| G. | τινός | τινός | τινῶν | τινῶν |
| D. | τινί | τινί | τισί(ν) | τισί(ν) |
| A. | τινά | τι | τινάς | τινά |

14   NUMERICAL ADJECTIVES (see Book I, pages 128 and 263–264)

**Cardinals**

| | | | |
|---|---|---|---|
| 1 | εἷς, μία, ἕν | 11 | ἕνδεκα |
| 2 | δύο | 12 | δώδεκα |
| 3 | τρεῖς, τρία | 13 | τρεῖς (τρία) καὶ δέκα or τρεισκαίδεκα |
| 4 | τέτταρες, τέτταρα | 14 | τέτταρες (τέτταρα) καὶ δέκα |
| 5 | πέντε | 15 | πεντεκαίδεκα |
| 6 | ἕξ | 16 | ἐκκαίδεκα |
| 7 | ἑπτά | 17 | ἑπτακαίδεκα |
| 8 | ὀκτώ | 18 | ὀκτωκαίδεκα |
| 9 | ἐννέα | 19 | ἐννεακαίδεκα |
| 10 | δέκα | 20 | εἴκοσι(ν) |

|  | 21 | εἷς καὶ εἴκοσι(ν) |
|--|----|-----------------|
|  | 100 | ἑκατόν |
|  | 1,000 | χίλιοι, -αι, -α |
|  | 10,000 | μύριοι, -αι, -α |

|  | **M.** | **F.** | **N.** |
|--|--------|--------|--------|
| **N.** | εἷς | μία | ἕν |
| **G.** | ἑνός | μιᾶς | ἑνός |
| **D.** | ἑνί | μιᾷ | ἑνί |
| **A.** | ἕνα | μίαν | ἕν |

|  | **M. F. N.** | **M. F.** | **N.** | **M. F.** | **N.** |
|--|--------------|-----------|--------|-----------|--------|
| **N.** | δύο | τρεῖς | τρία | τέτταρες | τέτταρα |
| **G.** | δυοῖν | τριῶν | τριῶν | τεττάρων | τεττάρων |
| **D.** | δυοῖν | τρισί(ν) | τρισί(ν) | τέτταρσι(ν) | τέτταρσι(ν) |
| **A.** | δύο | τρεῖς | τρία | τέτταρας | τέτταρα |

### Ordinals

| 1st | πρῶτος, -η, -ον | 6th | ἕκτος, -η, -ον |
|-----|-----------------|-----|-----------------|
| 2nd | δεύτερος, -ᾱ, -ον | 7th | ἕβδομος, -η, -ον |
| 3rd | τρίτος, -η, -ον | 8th | ὄγδοος, -η, -ον |
| 4th | τέταρτος, -η, -ον | 9th | ἔνατος, -η, -ον |
| 5th | πέμπτος, -η, -ον | 10th | δέκατος, -η, -ον |
|  |  | 11th | ἑνδέκατος, -η, -ον |
|  |  | 12th | δωδέκατος, -η, -ον |
|  |  | 20th | εἰκοστός, -ή, -όν |
|  |  | 100th | ἑκατοστός, -ή, -όν |
|  |  | 1,000th | χῑλιοστός, -ή, -όν |
|  |  | 10,000th | μῡριοστός, -ή, -όν |

15.　PERSONAL PRONOUNS (see Book I, pages 64–65)

|  | **1st Person Singular** | | | **1st Person Plural** | |
|--|-------------------------|--|--|------------------------|--|
| **N.** | ἐγώ | | *I* | ἡμεῖς | *we* |
| **G.** | ἐμοῦ | μου | *of me* | ἡμῶν | *of us* |
| **D.** | ἐμοί | μοι | *to or for me* | ἡμῖν | *to or for us* |
| **A.** | ἐμέ | με | *me* | ἡμᾶς | *us* |

|  | **2nd Person Singular** | | | **2nd Person Plural** | |
|--|-------------------------|--|--|------------------------|--|
| **N.** | σύ | | *you* | ὑμεῖς | *you* |
| **G.** | σοῦ | σου | *of you* | ὑμῶν | *of you* |
| **D.** | σοί | σοι | *to or for you* | ὑμῖν | *to or for you* |
| **A.** | σέ | σε | *you* | ὑμᾶς | *you* |

## 3rd Person

**Singular**

| **M.** | | **F.** | | **N.** | |
|---|---|---|---|---|---|
| **G.** | αὐτοῦ | *of him* or *it* | αὐτῆς | *of her* or *it* | αὐτοῦ | *of it* |
| **D.** | αὐτῷ | *to* or *for him* or *it* | αὐτῇ | *to* or *for her* or *it* | αὐτῷ | *to it* |
| **A.** | αὐτόν | *him* or *it* | αὐτήν | *her* or *it* | αὐτό | *it* |

**Plural**

| **G.** | αὐτῶν | *of them* | αὐτῶν | *of them* | αὐτῶν | *of them* |
|---|---|---|---|---|---|---|
| **D.** | αὐτοῖς | *to* or *for them* | αὐταῖς | *to* or *for them* | αὐτοῖς | *to* or *for them* |
| **A.** | αὐτούς | *them* | αὐτάς | *them* | αὐτά | *them* |

16.   REFLEXIVE PRONOUNS (see Book I, pages 100–101)

**1st Person**                         **2nd Person**

**Singular**

| **M.** | **F.** | **M.** | **F.** |
|---|---|---|---|
| **G.** ἐμαυτοῦ | ἐμαυτῆς | σεαυτοῦ | σεαυτῆς |
| **D.** ἐμαυτῷ | ἐμαυτῇ | σεαυτῷ | σεαυτῇ |
| **A.** ἐμαυτόν | ἐμαυτήν | σεαυτόν | σεαυτήν |

**Plural**

| **G.** ἡμῶν αὐτῶν | ἡμῶν αὐτῶν | ὑμῶν αὐτῶν | ὑμῶν αὐτῶν |
|---|---|---|---|
| **D.** ἡμῖν αὐτοῖς | ἡμῖν αὐταῖς | ὑμῖν αὐτοῖς | ὑμῖν αὐταῖς |
| **A.** ἡμᾶς αὐτούς | ἡμᾶς αὐτάς | ὑμᾶς αὐτούς | ὑμᾶς αὐτάς |

**3rd Person**

**Singular**

| **M.** | **F.** | **N.** |
|---|---|---|
| **G.** ἑαυτοῦ | ἑαυτῆς | ἑαυτοῦ |
| **D.** ἑαυτῷ | ἑαυτῇ | ἑαυτῷ |
| **A.** ἑαυτόν | ἑαυτήν | ἑαυτό |

**Plural**

| **G.** ἑαυτῶν | ἑαυτῶν | ἑαυτῶν |
|---|---|---|
| **D.** ἑαυτοῖς | ἑαυταῖς | ἑαυτοῖς |
| **A.** ἑαυτούς | ἑαυτάς | ἑαυτά |

17.   THE RECIPROCAL PRONOUN

| **M.** | **F.** | **N.** |
|---|---|---|
| **G.** ἀλλήλων | ἀλλήλων | ἀλλήλων |
| **D.** ἀλλήλοις | ἀλλήλαις | ἀλλήλοις |
| **A.** ἀλλήλους | ἀλλήλᾱς | ἄλληλα |

18.  POSSESSIVES (see Book I, pages 66–67)

**Possessive Adjectives**

|              | Singular                       | Plural                                |
|--------------|--------------------------------|---------------------------------------|
| **1st Person** | ἐμός, -ή, -όν, *my, mine*       | ἡμέτερος, -ᾱ, -ον, *our, ours*          |
| **2nd Person** | σός, -ή, -όν, *your, yours*     | ῡμέτερος, -ᾱ, -ον, *your, yours*        |

**Possessive Pronouns** (used for 3rd person possessives)

**Singular**

| **M.** | αὐτοῦ, *of him, his; of it, its* |
|--------|----------------------------------|
| **F.** | αὐτῆς, *of her, her; of it, its* |
| **N.** | αὐτοῦ, *of it, its*              |

**Plural**

| **M., F., N.** | αὐτῶν, *of them, their* |
|----------------|-------------------------|

19.  THE INTERROGATIVE PRONOUN

For the interrogative pronoun τίς, τί, *who? what?* see Book I, page 108.  Its forms are the same as those of the interrogative adjective (see above) and are not repeated here; it always has an acute accent on the first syllable.

20.  THE INDEFINITE PRONOUN

For the indefinite pronoun τις, τι, *someone; something; anyone; anything*, see Book I, page 109.  This pronoun is enclitic, and it has the same forms as the indefinite adjective (see above).

21.  THE RELATIVE PRONOUN (see Book I, pages 224–225)

|        | **Singular** |       |       | **Plural** |       |       |
|--------|--------------|-------|-------|------------|-------|-------|
|        | **M.**       | **F.** | **N.** | **M.**     | **F.** | **N.** |
| **N.** | ὅς           | ἥ      | ὅ      | οἵ         | αἵ     | ἅ      |
| **G.** | οὗ           | ἧς     | οὗ     | ὧν         | ὧν     | ὧν     |
| **D.** | ᾧ            | ᾗ      | ᾧ      | οἷς        | αἷς    | οἷς    |
| **A.** | ὅν           | ἥν     | ὅ      | οὕς        | ἅς     | ἅ      |

22  FORMATION OF ADVERBS (see Book I, page 50):

Adverbs regularly have the same spelling and accent as the genitive plural of the corresponding adjective, but with the final ν changed to ς:

Adjective καλός (genitive plural, καλῶν) > adverb καλῶς

Adjective σώφρων (genitive plural, σωφρόνων) > adverb σωφρόνως

Adjective ἀληθής (genitive plural, ἀληθῶν) > adverb ἀληθῶς

Adjective ταχύς (genitive plural, ταχέων) > adverb ταχέως

23. COMPARISON OF ADVERBS (see Book I, page 236)

For the comparative adverb the neuter singular of the comparative adjective is used, and for the superlative, the neuter plural of the superlative adjective:

**Regular**

| | | |
|---|---|---|
| ἀνδρείως | ἀνδρειότερον | ἀνδρειότατα |
| χαλεπῶς | χαλεπώτερον | χαλεπώτατα |
| ἀληθῶς | ἀληθέστερον | ἀληθέστατα |
| σωφρόνως | σωφρονέστερον | σωφρονέστατα |

**Irregular**

| | | |
|---|---|---|
| εὖ | ἄμεινον | ἄριστα |
| κακῶς | κάκῑον | κάκιστα |
| πόλυ | πλέον | πλεῖστα |
| μάλα | μᾶλλον | μάλιστα |

# Verbs

24. VERBS WITH THEMATIC PRESENTS, SIGMATIC FUTURES, SIGMATIC 1ST
AORISTS, -κα 1ST PERFECTS, -κη 1ST PLUPERFECTS, -θη- 1ST AORIST
PASSIVES, AND -θη- 1ST FUTURE PASSIVES

λύω, λύσω, ἔλῡσα, λέλυκα, λέλυμαι, ἐλύθην, *I loosen, loose;* middle, *I
ransom*

PRESENT ACTIVE (THEMATIC) (see Book I, pages 38 and 136, and Book II, pages
75 and 145)

| Indic. | Subjn. | Opt. | Imper. | Infin. | Part. |
|--------|--------|------|--------|--------|-------|
| λύω | λύω | λύοιμι | | λύειν | λύων, |
| λύεις | λύῃς | λύοις | λῦε | | λύουσα, |
| λύει | λύῃ | λύοι | | | λῦον, |
| λύομεν | λύωμεν | λύοιμεν | | | gen., λύοντος, etc. |
| λύετε | λύητε | λύοιτε | λύετε | | |
| λύουσι(ν) | λύωσι(ν) | λύοιεν | | | |

PRESENT MIDDLE/PASSIVE (THEMATIC) (see Book I, pages 77 and 115, and
Book II, pages 76 and 145)

| | | | | | |
|--------|--------|------|--------|--------|-------|
| λύομαι | λύωμαι | λυοίμην | | λύεσθαι | λυόμενος, |
| λύει/ῃ | λύῃ | λύοιο | λύου | | -η, |
| λύεται | λύηται | λύοιτο | | | - ον |
| λῡόμεθα | λῡώμεθα | λῡοίμεθα | | | |
| λύεσθε | λύησθε | λύοισθε | λύεσθε | | |
| λύονται | λύωνται | λύοιντο | | | |

IMPERFECT ACTIVE (THEMATIC) (see Book I, page 214)

ἔλῡον
ἔλῡες
ἔλῡε(ν)
ἐλύομεν
ἐλύετε
ἔλῡον

IMPERFECT MIDDLE/PASSIVE (THEMATIC) (see Book I, page 214)

ἐλῡόμην
ἐλύου
ἐλύετο
ἐλῡόμεθα
ἐλύεσθε
ἐλύοντο

SIGMATIC FUTURE ACTIVE (THEMATIC) (see Book I, page 158, and Book II, page 146; for consonant-stem verbs, see Book I, pages 158–159)

| Indic. | Opt. | Infin. | Part. |
|---|---|---|---|
| λύσω | λύσοιμι | λύσειν | λύσων, |
| λύσεις | λύσοις | | λύσουσα, |
| λύσει | λύσοι | | λῦσον, |
| λύσομεν | λύσοιμεν | | gen., λύσοντος, etc. |
| λύσετε | λύσοιτε | | |
| λύσουσι(ν) | λύσοιεν | | |

SIGMATIC FUTURE MIDDLE (THEMATIC) (see Book I, page 158, and Book II, page 146; for consonant-stem verbs, see Book I, pages 158–159)

| | | | |
|---|---|---|---|
| λύσομαι | λῡσοίμην | λύσεσθαι | λῡσόμενος, |
| λύσει/ῃ | λύσοιο | | -η, |
| λύσεται | λύσοιτο | | - ον |
| λῡσόμεθα | λῡσοίμεθα | | |
| λύσεσθε | λύσοισθε | | |
| λύσονται | λύσοιντο | | |

-θη- 1ST FUTURE PASSIVE (THEMATIC) (see Book II, pages 5 and 146)

| | | | |
|---|---|---|---|
| λυθήσομαι | λυθησοίμην | λυθήσεσθαι | λυθησόμενος |
| λυθήσει/ῃ | λυθήσοιο | | -η, |
| λυθήσεται | λυθήσοιτο | | - ον |
| λυθησόμεθα | λυθησοίμεθα | | |
| λυθήσεσθε | λυθήσοισθε | | |
| λυθήσονται | λυθήσοιντο | | |

SIGMATIC 1ST AORIST ACTIVE (see Book I, page 196, and Book II, pages 76 and 145; for consonant-stem verbs, see Book I, pages 197–198; for alternative forms of the optative, see Book II, page 145)

| Indic. | Subjn. | Opt. | Imper. | Infin. | Part. |
|---|---|---|---|---|---|
| ἔλῡσα | λύσω | λύσαιμι | | λῦσαι | λύσᾱς, |
| ἔλῡσας | λύῃς | λύσειας | λῦσον | | λύσᾱσα, |
| ἔλῡσε(ν) | λύσῃ | λύσειε | | | λῦσαν, |
| ἐλύσαμεν | λύσωμεν | λύσαιμεν | | | gen., λύσαντος, etc. |
| ἐλύσατε | λύσητε | λύσαιτε | λύσατε | | |
| ἔλῡσαν | λύσωσι(ν) | λύσειαν | | | |

SIGMATIC 1ST AORIST MIDDLE (see Book I, page 197, and Book II, pages 77 and 145; for consonant-stem verbs, see Book I, pages 197–198)

| | | | | | |
|---|---|---|---|---|---|
| ἐλῡσάμην | λύσωμαι | λῡσαίμην | | λύσασθαι | λῡσάμενος, |
| ἐλύσω | λύσῃ | λύσαιο | λῦσαι, | | -η, |
| ἐλύσατο | λύσηται | λύσαιτο | | | - ον |
| ἐλῡσάμεθα | λῡσώμεθα | λῡσαίμεθα | | | |
| ἐλύσασθε | λύσησθε | λύσαισθε | λύσασθε | | |
| ἐλύσαντο | λύσωνται | λύσαιντο | | | |

### -θη- 1ST AORIST PASSIVE (see Book II, pages 5, 77, and 145)

| Indic. | Subjn. | Opt. | Imper. | Infin. | Part. |
|---|---|---|---|---|---|
| ἐλύθην | λυθῶ | λυθείην | | λυθῆναι | λυθείς, |
| ἐλύθης | λυθῇς | λυθείης | λύθητι | | λυθεῖσα, |
| ἐλύθη | λυθῇ | λυθείη | | | λυθέν, |
| ἐλύθημεν | λυθῶμεν | λυθεῖμεν | | | gen., λυθέντος |
| ἐλύθητε | λυθῆτε | λυθεῖτε | λύθητε | | |
| ἐλύθησαν | λυθῶσι(ν) | λυθεῖεν | | | |

### -κα 1ST PERFECT ACTIVE (see Book II page 207; for alternative forms of the subjunctive and optative, see Book II, page 207)

| | | | | | |
|---|---|---|---|---|---|
| λέλυκα | λελυκὼς ὦ | λελυκὼς εἴην | | λελυκέναι | λελυκώς, λελυκυῖα, |
| λέλυκας | λελυκὼς ᾖς | λελυκὼς εἴης | | | λελυκός, gen., λελυκότος |
| λέλυκε(ν) | λελυκὼς ᾖ | λελυκὼς εἴη | | | |
| λελύκαμεν | λελυκότες ὦμεν | λελυκότες εἶμεν or εἴημεν | | | |
| λελύκατε | λελυκότες ἦτε | λελυκότες εἶτε or εἴητε | | | |
| λελύκᾱσι(ν) | λελυκότες ὦσι(ν) | λελυκότες εἶεν or εἴησαν | | | |

### PERFECT MIDDLE/PASSIVE (ATHEMATIC) (see Book II, page 186)

| | | | | | |
|---|---|---|---|---|---|
| λέλυμαι | λελυμένος ὦ | λελυμένος εἴην | | λελύσθαι | λελυμένος, -η, |
| λέλυσαι | λελυμένος ᾖς | λελυμένος εἴης | | | - ον |
| λέλυται | λελυμένος ᾖ | λελυμένος εἴη | | | |
| λελύμεθα | λελυμένοι ὦμεν | λελυμένοι εἶμεν or εἴημεν | | | |
| λέλυσθε | λελυμένοι ἦτε | λελυμένοι εἶτε or εἴητε | | | |
| λέλυνται | λελυμένοι ὦσι(ν) | λελυμένοι εἶεν or εἴησαν | | | |

### -κη 1ST PLUPERFECT ACTIVE (see Book II, page 210)

ἐλελύκη
ἐλελύκης
ἐλελύκει
ἐλελύκεμεν
ἐλελύκετε
ἐλελύκεσαν

PLUPERFECT MIDDLE/PASSIVE (ATHEMATIC) (see Book II, page 187)

**Indic.**

ἐλελύμην
ἐλέλυσο
ἐλέλυτο
ἐλελύμεθα
ἐλέλυσθε
ἐλέλυντο

> For the perfect and pluperfect middle/passive of verbs with stems ending in consonants, see Book II, pages 197–199.

25. VERBS WITH -η- 2ND FUTURE PASSIVES AND -η- 2ND AORIST PASSIVES

**γράφω, γράψω, ἔγραψα, γέγραφα, γέγραμμαι, ἐγράφην,** *I write*

-η- 2ND FUTURE PASSIVE (see Book II, pages 13 and 146)

| Indic. | Opt. | Infin. | Part. |
|---|---|---|---|
| γραφήσομαι | γραφησοίμην | γραφήσεσθαι | γραφησόμενος, |
| γραφήσει/ῃ | γραφήσοιο | | -η |
| γραφήσεται | γραφήσοιτο | | - ον |
| γραφησόμεθα | γραφησοίμεθα | | |
| γραφήσεσθε | γραφήσοισθε | | |
| γραφήσονται | γραφήσοιντο | | |

-η- 2ND AORIST PASSIVE (see Book II, pages 13, 77, and 145)

| Indic. | Subjn. | Opt. | Imper. | Infin. | Part. |
|---|---|---|---|---|---|
| ἐγράφην | γραφῶ | γραφείην | | γραφῆναι | γραφείς, |
| ἐγράφης | γραφῇς | γραφείης | γράφητι | | γραφεῖσα, |
| ἐγράφη | γραφῇ | γραφείη | | | γραφέν, |
| ἐγράφημεν | γραφῶμεν | γραφεῖμεν | | | gen., γραφέντος, etc. |
| ἐγράφητε | γραφῆτε | γραφεῖτε | γράφητε | | |
| ἐγράφησαν | γραφῶσι(ν) | γραφεῖεν | | | |

26. VERBS WITH ATHEMATIC PRESENTS AND IMPERFECTS (see Book I, pages 276–277)

**δύναμαι, δυνήσομαι, ἐδυνήθην,** *I am able; I can*

PRESENT

| Indic. | Subjn. | Opt. | Imper. | Infin. | Part. |
|---|---|---|---|---|---|
| δύναμαι | δύνωμαι | δυναίμην | | δύνασθαι | δυνάμενος, |
| δύνασαι | δύνῃ | δύναιο | δύνασο | | -η, |
| δύναται | δύνηται | δύναιτο | | | - ον |
| δυνάμεθα | δυνώμεθα | δυναίμεθα | | | |
| δύνασθε | δύνησθε | δύναισθε | δύνασθε | | |
| δύνανται | δύνωνται | δύναιντο | | | |

**IMPERFECT**

**Indic.**

ἐδυνάμην
ἐδύνασο or ἐδύνω
ἐδύνατο
ἐδυνάμεθα
ἐδύνασθε
ἐδύναντο

### κεῖμαι, κείσομαι, *I lie*

**PRESENT**

| Indic. | Subjn. | Opt. | Imper. | Infin. | Part. |
|--------|--------|------|--------|--------|-------|
| κεῖμαι | κέωμαι | κεοίμην | | κεῖσθαι | κείμενος, |
| κεῖσαι | κέῃ | κέοιο | κεῖσο | | -η, |
| κεῖται | κέηται | κέοιτο | | | - ον |
| κείμεθα | κεώμεθα | κεοίμεθα | | | |
| κεῖσθε | κέησθε | κέοισθε | κεῖσθε | | |
| κεῖνται | κέωνται | κέοιντο | | | |

**IMPERFECT**

ἐκείμην
ἔκεισο
ἔκειτο
ἐκείμεθα
ἔκεισθε
ἔκειντο

### ἐπίσταμαι, ἐπιστήσομαι, ἠπιστήθην, *I understand; I know*

**PRESENT**

| ἐπίσταμαι | ἐπίστωμαι | ἐπισταίμην | | ἐπίστασθαι | ἐπιστάμενος, |
|-----------|-----------|------------|----------|------------|---------------|
| ἐπίστασαι | ἐπίστῃ | ἐπίσταιο | ἐπίστασο | | -η, |
| ἐπίσταται | ἐπίστηται | ἐπίσταιτο | | | - ον |
| ἐπιστάμεθα | ἐπιστώμεθα | ἐπισταίμεθα | | | |
| ἐπίστασθε | ἐπίστησθε | ἐπίσταισθε | ἐπίστασθε | | |
| ἐπίστανται | ἐπίστωνται | ἐπίσταιντο | | | |

**IMPERFECT**

ἠπιστάμην
ἠπίστασο or ἠπίστω
ἠπίστατο
ἠπιστάμεθα
ἠπίστασθε
ἠπίσταντο

## 27. CONTRACT VERBS

**φιλέω, φιλήσω, ἐφίλησα, πεφίληκα, πεφίλημαι, ἐφιλήθην,** *I love*

### PRESENT ACTIVE (see Book I, pages 39 and 136, and Book II, pages 75 and 145)

| Indic. | Subjn. | Opt. | Imper. | Infin. | Part. |
|---|---|---|---|---|---|
| φιλῶ | φιλῶ | φιλοίην | | φιλεῖν | φιλῶν, |
| φιλεῖς | φιλῇς | φιλοίης | φίλει | | φιλοῦσα, |
| φιλεῖ | φιλῇ | φιλοίη | | | φιλοῦν |
| φιλοῦμεν | φιλῶμεν | φιλοῖμεν | | | gen., φιλοῦντος, etc. |
| φιλεῖτε | φιλῆτε | φιλοῖτε | φιλεῖτε | | |
| φιλοῦσι(ν) | φιλῶσι(ν) | φιλοῖεν | | | |

### PRESENT MIDDLE/PASSIVE (see Book I, pages 77 and 115–116, and Book II, pages 76 and 145)

| | | | | | |
|---|---|---|---|---|---|
| φιλοῦμαι | φιλῶμαι | φιλοίμην | | φιλεῖσθαι | φιλούμενος, |
| φιλεῖ or φιλῇ | φιλῇ | φιλοῖο | φιλοῦ | | -η, |
| φιλεῖται | φιλῆται | φιλοῖτο | | | - ον |
| φιλούμεθα | φιλώμεθα | φιλοίμεθα | | | |
| φιλεῖσθε | φιλῆσθε | φιλοῖσθε | φιλεῖσθε | | |
| φιλοῦνται | φιλῶνται | φιλοῖντο | | | |

### IMPERFECT ACTIVE (see Book I, page 214)

ἐφίλουν
ἐφίλεις
ἐφίλει
ἐφιλοῦμεν
ἐφιλεῖτε
ἐφίλουν

### IMPERFECT MIDDLE/PASSIVE (see Book I, page 214)

ἐφιλούμην
ἐφιλοῦ
ἐφιλεῖτο
ἐφιλούμεθα
ἐφιλεῖσθε
ἐφιλοῦντο

### FUTURE ACTIVE (see Book I, page 159)

φιλήσω, etc., like λύσω above

### FUTURE MIDDLE (see Book I, page 159)

φιλήσομαι, etc., like λύσομαι above

**FUTURE PASSIVE** (see Book II, page 6)

φιληθήσομαι, etc., like λυθήσομαι above

**AORIST ACTIVE** (see Book I, page 198)

ἐφίλησα, etc., like ἔλῡσα above

**AORIST MIDDLE** (see Book I, page 198)

ἐφιλησάμην, etc., like ἐλῡσάμην above

**AORIST PASSIVE** (see Book II, page 6)

ἐφιλήθην, etc., like ἐλύθην above

**PERFECT ACTIVE** (see Book II, page 208)

πεφίληκα etc., like λέλυκα above

**PERFECT MIDDLE/PASSIVE** (see Book II, page 187)

πεφίλημαι etc., like λέλυμαι above

**PLUPERFECT ACTIVE** (see Book II, page 210)

ἐπεφιλήκη, etc., like ἐλελύκη above

**PLUPERFECT MIDDLE/PASSIVE** (see Book II, page 188)

ἐπεφιλήμην, etc., like ἐλελύμην above

**τῑμάω, τῑμήσω, ἐτίμησα, τετίμηκα, τετίμημαι, ἐτῑμήθην**, *I honor*

**PRESENT ACTIVE** (see Book I, pages 56 and 136–137, and Book II, pages 76 and 146)

| Indic. | Subjn. | Opt. | Imper. | Infin. | Part. |
|--------|--------|------|--------|--------|-------|
| τῑμῶ | τῑμῶ | τῑμῴην | | τῑμᾶν | τῑμῶν, |
| τῑμᾷς | τῑμᾷς | τῑμῴης | τίμα | | τῑμῶσα, |
| τῑμᾷ | τῑμᾷ | τῑμῴη | | | τῑμῶν, |
| τῑμῶμεν | τῑμῶμεν | τῑμῷμεν | | | gen., τῑμῶντος, etc. |
| τῑμᾶτε | τῑμᾶτε | τῑμῷτε | τῑμᾶτε | | |
| τῑμῶσι(ν) | τῑμῶσι(ν) | τῑμῷεν | | | |

**PRESENT MIDDLE/PASSIVE** (see Book I, pages 77–78 and 116, and Book II, pages 76 and 146)

| | | | | | |
|--------|--------|------|--------|--------|-------|
| τῑμῶμαι | τῑμῶμαι | τῑμῴμην | | τῑμᾶσθαι | τῑμώμενος, |
| τῑμᾷ | τῑμᾷ | τῑμῷο | τῑμῶ | | -η, |
| τῑμᾶται | τῑμᾶται | τῑμῷτο | | | - ον |

| | | | |
|---|---|---|---|
| τῑμώμεθα | τῑμώμεθα | τῑμώμεθα | |
| τῑμᾶσθε | τῑμᾶσθε | τῑμῷσθε | τῑμᾶσθε |
| τῑμῶνται | τῑμῶνται | τῑμῶντο | |

## IMPERFECT ACTIVE (see Book I, page 214)

**Indic.**

ἐτίμων
ἐτίμᾱς
ἐτίμᾱ
ἐτῑμῶμεν
ἐτῑμᾶτε
ἐτίμων

## IMPERFECT MIDDLE/PASSIVE (see Book I, page 214)

ἐτῑμώμην
ἐτῑμῶ
ἐτῑμᾶτο
ἐτῑμώμεθα
ἐτῑμᾶσθε
ἐτῑμῶντο

## FUTURE ACTIVE (see Book I, page 159)

τῑμήσω, etc., like λῡσω above

## FUTURE MIDDLE (see Book I, page 159)

τῑμήσομαι, etc., like λῡσομαι above

## FUTURE PASSIVE (see Book II, page 6)

τῑμηθήσομαι, etc., like λυθήσομαι above

## AORIST ACTIVE (see Book I, page 198)

ἐτίμησα etc., like ἔλῡσα above

## AORIST MIDDLE (see Book I, page 198)

ἐτῑμησάμην, etc., like ἐλῡσάμην above

## AORIST PASSIVE (see Book II, page 6)

ἐτῑμήθην, etc., like ἐλύθην  above

## PERFECT ACTIVE (see Book II, page 208)

τετίμηκα, etc., like λέλυκα above

PERFECT MIDDLE/PASSIVE (see Book II, page 187)

τετίμημαι etc., like λέλυμαι above

PLUPERFECT ACTIVE (see Book II, page 210)

ἐτετῑμήκη, etc., like ἐλελύκη above

PLUPERFECT MIDDLE/PASSIVE (see Book II, page 188)

ἐτετῑμήμην, etc., like ἐλελύμην above

**δηλόω, δηλώσω, ἐδήλωσα, δεδήλωκα, δεδήλωμαι, ἐδηλώθην,** *I show*

PRESENT ACTIVE (see Book I, page 262, and Book II, pages 76 and 146)

| Indic. | Subjn. | Opt. | Imper. | Infin. | Part. |
|---|---|---|---|---|---|
| δηλῶ | δηλῶ | δηλοίην | | δηλοῦν | δηλῶν, |
| δηλοῖς | δηλοῖς | δηλοίης | δήλου | | δηλοῦσα, |
| δηλοῖ | δηλοῖ | δηλοίη | | | δηλοῦν, |
| δηλοῦμεν | δηλῶμεν | δηλοῖμεν | | | gen., δηλοῦντος, etc. |
| δηλοῦτε | δηλῶτε | δηλοῖτε | δηλοῦτε | | |
| δηλοῦσι(ν) | δηλῶσι(ν) | δηλοῖεν | | | |

PRESENT MIDDLE/PASSIVE (see Book I, page 262, and Book II, pages 76 and 146)

| | | | | | |
|---|---|---|---|---|---|
| δηλοῦμαι | δηλῶμαι | δηλοίμην | | δηλοῦσθαι | δηλούμενος, |
| δηλοῖ | δηλοῖ | δηλοῖο | δηλοῦ | | -η, |
| δηλοῦται | δηλῶται | δηλοῖτο | | | -ον |
| δηλούμεθα | δηλώμεθα | δηλοίμεθα | | | |
| δηλοῦσθε | δηλῶσθε | δηλοῖσθε | δηλοῦσθε | | |
| δηλοῦνται | δηλῶνται | δηλοῖντο | | | |

IMPERFECT ACTIVE (see Book I, page 262)

ἐδήλουν
ἐδήλους
ἐδήλου
ἐδηλοῦμεν
ἐδηλοῦτε
ἐδήλουν

IMPERFECT MIDDLE/PASSIVE (see Book I, page 262)

ἐδηλούμην
ἐδηλοῦ
ἐδηλοῦτο
ἐδηλούμεθα
ἐδηλοῦσθε
ἐδηλοῦντο

FUTURE ACTIVE (see Book I, page 262)

δηλώσω, etc., like λύσω above

FUTURE MIDDLE (see Book I, page 262)

δηλώσυμαι, etc., like λύσομαι above

FUTURE PASSIVE (see Book II, page 6)

δηλωθήσομαι, etc., like λυθήσομαι above

AORIST ACTIVE (see Book I, page 262)

ἐδήλωσα, etc., like ἔλῡσα above

AORIST MIDDLE (see Book I, page 262)

ἐδηλωσάμην, etc., like ἐλῡσάμην above

AORIST PASSIVE (see Book II, page 6)

ἐδηλώθην, etc., like ἐλύθην above

PERFECT ACTIVE (see Book II, page 208)

δεδήλωκα, etc., like λέλυκα above

PERFECT MIDDLE/PASSIVE (see Book II, page 187)

δεδήλωμαι, etc., like λέλυμαι above

PLUPERFECT ACTIVE (see Book II, page 210)

ἐδεδηλώκη, etc., like ἐλελύκη above

PLUPERFECT MIDDLE/PASSIVE (see Book II, page 188)

ἐδεδηλώμην, etc., like ἐλελύμην above

28. ASIGMATIC CONTRACT FUTURE OF VERBS IN -ίζω (see Book I, page 159)

**κομίζω, κομιῶ, ἐκόμισα, κεκόμικα, κεκόμισμαι, ἐκομίσθην,** *I bring; I take;* middle, *I get for myself, acquire*

FUTURE ACTIVE

| **Indic.** | **Opt.** | **Infin.** | **Part.** |
|---|---|---|---|
| κομιῶ | κομιοίην | κομιεῖν | κομιῶν, |
| κομιεῖς | κομιοίης | | κομιοῦσα, |
| κομιεῖ | κομιοίη | | κομιοῦν, |
| κομιοῦμεν | κομιοῖμεν | | gen., κομιοῦντος, etc. |
| κομιεῖτε | κομιοῖτε | | |
| κομιοῦσι(ν) | κομιοῖεν | | |

FUTURE MIDDLE

| Indic. | Opt. | Infin. | Part. |
|--------|------|--------|-------|
| κομιοῦμαι | κομιοίμην | κομιεῖσθαι | κομιούμενος, |
| κομιεῖ/ῇ | κομιοῖο | | -η, |
| κομιεῖται | κομιοῖτο | | -ον |
| κομιούμεθα | κομιοίμεθα | | |
| κομιεῖσθε | κομιοῖσθε | | |
| κομιοῦνται | κομιοῖντο | | |

29. ASIGMATIC CONTRACT FUTURE OF VERBS WITH LIQUID AND NASAL STEMS (see Book I, pages 166–167, and Book II, page 146)

**μένω, μενῶ, ἔμεινα, μεμένηκα,** intransitive, *I stay* (in one place); *I wait;* transitive, *I wait for*

FUTURE ACTIVE

| | | | |
|--------|--------|--------|--------|
| μενῶ | μενοίην | μενεῖν | μενῶν, |
| μενεῖς | μενοίης | | μενοῦσα, |
| μενεῖ | μενοίη | | μενοῦν, |
| μενοῦμεν | μενοῖμεν | | gen., μενοῦντος, etc. |
| μενεῖτε | μενοῖτε | | |
| μενοῦσι(ν) | μενοῖεν | | |

**κάμνω, καμοῦμαι, ἔκαμον, κέκμηκα,** *I am sick; I am tired*

FUTURE MIDDLE

| | | | |
|--------|--------|--------|--------|
| καμοῦμαι | καμοίμην | καμεῖσθαι | καμούμενος, |
| καμεῖ/ῇ | καμοῖο | | -η, |
| καμεῖται | καμοῖτο | | -ον |
| καμούμεθα | καμοίμεθα | | |
| καμεῖσθε | καμοῖσθε | | |
| καμοῦνται | καμοῖντο | | |

30. ASIGMATIC 1ST AORIST OF VERBS WITH LIQUID AND NASAL STEMS (see Book I, page 207, and Book II, pages 77 and 145)

**αἴρω, ἀρῶ, ἦρα, ἦρκα, ἦρμαι, ἤρθην,** *I lift, raise up;* with reflexive pronoun, *I get up;* intransitive, *I get under way, set out*

AORIST ACTIVE

| Indic. | Subjn. | Opt. | Imper. | Infin. | Part. |
|--------|--------|------|--------|--------|-------|
| ἦρα | ἄρω | ἄραιμι | | ἆραι | ἄρᾱς, |
| ἦρας | ἄρῃς | ἄρειας/αις | ἆρον | | ἄρᾱσα, |
| ἦρε(ν) | ἄρῃ | ἄρειε/αι | | | ἆραν, |
| ἤραμεν | ἄρωμεν | ἄραιμεν | | | gen., ἄραντος, etc. |
| ἤρατε | ἄρητε | ἄραιτε | ἄρατε | | |
| ἦραν | ἄρωσι(ν) | ἄρειαν/αιεν | | | |

AORIST MIDDLE

| Indic. | Subjn. | Opt. | Imper. | Infin. | Part. |
|--------|--------|------|--------|--------|-------|
| ἠράμην | ἄρωμαι | ἀραίμην | | ἄρασθαι | ἀράμενος, |
| ἤρω | ἄρῃ | ἄραιο | ἆραι | | -η, |
| ἤρατο | ἄρηται | ἄραιτο | | | - ον |
| ἠράμεθα | ἀρώμεθα | ἀραίμεθα | | | |
| ἤρασθε | ἄρησθε | ἄραισθε | ἄρασθε | | |
| ἤραντο | ἄρωνται | ἄραιντο | | | |

31. THEMATIC 2ND AORISTS (see Book I, pages 177–178, and Book II, pages 77 and 146)

**λείπω, λείψω, ἔλιπον, λέλοιπα, λέλειμμαι** (*I am left behind; I am inferior*), **ἐλείφθην,** *I leave*

AORIST ACTIVE

| | | | | | |
|--------|--------|------|------|------|------|
| ἔλιπον | λίπω | λίποιμι | | λιπεῖν | λιπών, |
| ἔλιπες | λίπῃς | λίποις | λίπε | | λιποῦσα, |
| ἔλιπε(ν) | λίπῃ | λίποι | | | λιπόν, |
| ἐλίπομεν | λίπωμεν | λίποιμεν | | | gen., λιπόντος, etc. |
| ἐλίπετε | λίπητε | λίποιτε | λίπετε | | |
| ἔλιπον | λίπωσι(ν) | λίποιεν | | | |

**γίγνομαι, γενήσομαι, ἐγενόμην, γέγονα, γεγένημαι,** *I become*

AORIST MIDDLE

| | | | | | |
|--------|--------|------|------|------|------|
| ἐγενόμην | γένωμαι | γενοίμην | | γενέσθαι | γενόμενος, |
| ἐγένου | γένῃ | γένοιο | γενοῦ | | -η, |
| ἐγένετο | γένηται | γένοιτο | | | - ον |
| ἐγενόμεθα | γενώμεθα | γενοίμεθα | | | |
| ἐγένεσθε | γένησθε | γένοισθε | γένεσθε | | |
| ἐγένοντο | γένωνται | γένοιντο | | | |

32. ATHEMATIC 2ND AORISTS (see Book I, pages 252–253, and Book II, pages 77 and 146)

**βαίνω, βήσομαι, ἔβην, βέβηκα,** *I step; I walk; I go*

AORIST ACTIVE

| | | | | | |
|--------|--------|------|------|------|------|
| ἔβην | βῶ | βαίην | | βῆναι | βάς, |
| ἔβης | βῇς | βαίης | βῆθι | | βᾶσα, |
| ἔβη | βῇ | βαίη | | | βάν |
| ἔβημεν | βῶμεν | βαῖμεν | | | gen., βάντος, etc. |
| ἔβητε | βῆτε | βαῖτε | βῆτε | | |
| ἔβησαν | βῶσι(ν) | βαῖεν | | | |

**γιγνώσκω, γνώσομαι, ἔγνων, ἔγνωκα, ἔγνωσμαι, ἐγνώσθην**, *I come to know; I perceive; I learn*

AORIST ACTIVE

| Indic. | Subjn. | Opt. | Imper. | Infin. | Part. |
|--------|--------|------|--------|--------|-------|
| ἔγνων | γνῶ | γνοίην | | γνῶναι | γνούς, |
| ἔγνως | γνῷς | γνοίης | γνῶθι | | γνοῦσα, |
| ἔγνω | γνῷ | γνοίη | | | γνόν, |
| ἔγνωμεν | γνῶμεν | γνοῖμεν | | | gen., γνόντος, etc. |
| ἔγνωτε | γνῶτε | γνοῖτε | γνῶτε | | |
| ἔγνωσαν | γνῶσι(ν) | γνοῖεν | | | |

**ἵστημι, στήσω, ἔστησα**, *I make X stand; I stop X; I am setting X (up)*;  athematic 2nd aorist, **ἔστην**, intransitive, *I stood;* -κα 1st perfect, **ἕστηκα**, intransitive, *I stand;* -θη- 1st aorist passive, **ἐστάθην**, *I was set (up)*

AORIST ACTIVE

| | | | | | |
|--------|--------|------|--------|--------|-------|
| ἔστην | στῶ | σταίην | | στῆναι | στάς, |
| ἔστης | στῇς | σταίης | στῆθι | | στᾶσα, |
| ἔστη | στῇ | σταίη | | | στάν, |
| ἔστημεν | στῶμεν | σταῖμεν | | | gen., στάντος, etc. |
| ἔστητε | στῆτε | σταῖτε | στῆτε | | |
| ἔστησαν | στῶσι(ν) | σταῖεν | | | |

## 33. THE IRREGULAR VERB εἰμί, *I am*

**εἰμί, ἔσομαι**, *I am*

PRESENT (see Book I, pages 39 and 136, and Book II, pages 75 and 153)

| | | | | | |
|--------|--------|------|--------|--------|-------|
| εἰμί | ὦ | εἴην | | εἶναι | ὤν, |
| εἶ | ᾖς | εἴης | ἴσθι | | οὖσα, |
| ἐστί(ν) | ᾖ | εἴη | | | ὄν, |
| ἐσμέν | ὦμεν | εἶμεν/εἴημεν | | | gen., ὄντος, etc. |
| ἐστέ | ἦτε | εἶτε/εἴητε | ἔστε | | |
| εἰσί(ν) | ὦσι(ν) | εἶεν/εἴησαν | | | |

IMPERFECT (see Book I, page 215)

ἦ or ἦν
ἦσθα
ἦν
ἦμεν
ἦτε
ἦσαν

FUTURE (see Book I, page 160, and Book II, page 154)

| Indic. | Opt. | Infin. | Part. |
|---|---|---|---|
| ἔσομαι | ἐσοίμην | ἔσεσθαι ἐσόμενος, -η, -ον | |
| ἔσει or ἔσῃ | ἔσοιο | | |
| ἔσται | ἔσοιτο | | |
| ἐσόμεθα | ἐσοίμεθα | | |
| ἔσεσθε | ἔσοισθε | | |
| ἔσονται | ἔσοιντο | | |

## 34. THE IRREGULAR VERB εἶμι, *I will go*

FUTURE/PRESENT (see Book I, pages 168–169, and Book II, pages 85 and 153)

| Future | Present | Usually Present | Present | Usually Present | Usually Present |
|---|---|---|---|---|---|
| **Indic.** | **Subjn.** | **Opt.** | **Imper.** | **Infin.** | **Part.** |
| εἶμι | ἴω | ἴοιμι/ἰοίην | | ἰέναι | ἰών, |
| εἶ | ἴῃς | ἴοις | ἴθι | | ἰοῦσα, |
| εἶσι(ν) | ἴῃ | ἴοι | | | ἰόν, |
| ἴμεν | ἴωμεν | ἴοιμεν | | | gen., ἰόντος, etc. |
| ἴτε | ἴητε | ἴοιτε | ἴτε | | |
| ἴᾱσι(ν) | ἴωσι(ν) | ἴοιεν | | | |

IMPERFECT (see Book I, page 215)

| | | |
|---|---|---|
| ᾖα | or | ᾔειν |
| ᾔεισθα | or | ᾔεις |
| ᾔειν | or | ᾔει |
| ᾖμεν | | |
| ᾖτε | | |
| ᾖσαν | or | ᾔεσαν |

## 35. -μι VERBS IN BOOK II

**δίδωμι:** for charts, see Chapter 18, Grammar 1, pages 21–22.
  For the subjunctive, see Chapter 21, Grammar 4, page 85.
  For the optative, see Chapter 25, Grammar 5, page 153.

**τίθημι:** for charts, see Chapter 18, Grammar 2, pages 29–31.
  For the subjunctive, see Chapter 21, Grammar 4, page 85.
  For the optative, see Chapter 25, Grammar 5, page 153.

**ἵστημι:** for charts, see Chapter 19, Grammar 3, pages 49–51.
  For the subjunctive, see Chapter 21, Grammar 4, pages 85–86.
  For the optative, see Chapter 25, Grammar 5, pages 153–154.

**δείκνῡμι:** for charts, see Chapter 20, Grammar 1, page 59.
  For the subjunctive, see Chapter 21, Grammar 4, page 86.
  For the optative, see Chapter 25, Grammar 5, page 154.

ἵημι: for charts, see Chapter 20, Grammar 2, pages 64–66.
For the subjunctive, see Chapter 21, Grammar 4, page 86.
For the optative, see Chapter 25, Grammar 5, page 154.

### 36. THE VERB φημί, φήσω, ἔφησα, *I say*

PRESENT

| Indic. | Subjn. | Opt. | Imper. | Infin. | Part. |
|--------|--------|------|--------|--------|-------|
| φημί | φῶ | φαίην | | φάναι | φάς, |
| φής | φῇς | φαίης | φαθί | | φᾶσα, |
| φησί(ν) | φῇ | φαίη | or φάθι | | φάν, |
| φαμέν | φῶμεν | φαῖμεν | | | gen., φάντος, etc. |
| φατέ | φῆτε | φαῖτε | φάτε | | |
| φᾱσί(ν) | φῶσι(ν) | φαῖεν | | | |

IMPERFECT

ἔφην
ἔφησθα or ἔφης
ἔφη
ἔφαμεν
ἔφατε
ἔφασαν

### 37. NEW VERB FORMS IN BOOK II

Aorist and Future Passive: see Chapter 17, Grammar 1, pages 4–6 and Grammar 2, page 13.

Subjunctive: see Chapter 21, Grammar 2, pages 75–77 and for -μι verbs, see Grammar 4, pages 85–86.

Optative: see Chapter 25, Grammar 4, pages 145–146 and for -μι verbs, see Grammar 5, pages 153–154.

Perfect Active: see Chapter 28, Grammar 2, pages 207–208 and Grammar 7, pages 210–211.

Perfect Middle/Passive: see Chapter 27, Grammar 4, pages 186–187 and Grammar 9, pages 197–199.

Pluperfect Active: see Chapter 28, Grammar 6, page 210 and Grammar 7, pages 210–211.

Pluperfect Middle/Passive: see Chapter 27, Grammar 6, pages 187–188 and Grammar 9, pages 197–199.

The verb οἶδα: see Chapter 28, Grammar 9, pages 219–220.

# INDEX OF LANGUAGE
AND GRAMMAR

This listing of topics will help you find information on language and grammar in this book.

# GREEK TO ENGLISH VOCABULARY

We do not give principal parts of contract verbs except when they are irregular.

We do not give principal parts of compound verbs except when the uncompounded verb is not used in Attic Greek, e.g., ἀφικνέομαι. For the principal parts of most compound verbs, see the corresponding simple verb.

We give the principal parts of all other regular and irregular verbs, with their stems when their stems are different from what is seen in the present indicative form.

For compound verbs we give in brackets the prefix and the simple verb when elision or elision and assimilation take place, e.g. ἀφικνέομαι [= ἀπο- + ἰκνέομαι].

Note: 5β means that the vocabulary item appears in the vocabulary list in the second half of Chapter 5, i.e., in 5β. A notation such as 14 Gr 2 refers to Chapter 14, Grammar 2. A notation such as 22α PP means that the verb appears in the list of Principal Parts after the reading in Chapter 22α. H or S accompanied by a page number means that the word or the meaning is needed only for a Greek Wisdom reading on that page (H = Heraclitus; S = Socrates).

Principal parts of model contract verbs:

φιλέω, φιλήσω, ἐφίλησα, πεφίληκα, πεφίλημαι, ἐφιλήθην
τῑμάω, τῑμήσω, ἐτίμησα, τετίμηκα, τετίμημαι, ἐτῑμήθην
δηλόω, δηλώσω, ἐδήλωσα, δεδήλωκα, δεδήλωμαι, ἐδηλώθην

## A

ἀγαθός, -ή, -όν, good (5β and 14 Gr 2)

  ἀμείνων, ἄμεινον, better (14 Gr 2 and 24 Gr 2)

  ἄριστος, -η, -ον, best; very good; noble (9β, 14 Gr 2, and 24 Gr 2)

  See 24 Gr 2 for other comparatives and superlatives of ἀγαθός.

ἄγαλμα, ἀγάλματος, τό, statue (of a god) (H., p. 156)

Ἀγαμέμνων, Ἀγαμέμνονος, ὁ, Agamemnon (7α)

ἀγγέλλω, [ἀγγελε-] ἀγγελῶ, [ἀγγειλ-] ἤγγειλα, [ἀγγελ-] ἤγγελκα, ἤγγελμαι, ἠγγέλθην, I announce; I tell (14β, 22α PP, and 27 Gr 9)

ἄγγελος, ἀγγέλου, ὁ, messenger (4α)

ἄγε; pl., ἄγετε, come on! (9α)

ἀγείρω, [ἀγερε-] ἀγερῶ, [ἀγειρ-] ἤγειρα, I gather (27α)

ἀγνοέω, I do not know (19β)

ἄγομαι γυναῖκα + dat., I bring home a wife (for someone)

ἀγορά, ἀγορᾶς, ἡ, agora, city center, market place (8β)

ἀγορεύω, I speak in the Assembly; more generally, I speak; I say (21α)

ἄγρᾱ, ἄγρᾱς, ἡ, hunt; hunting (26β)

ἄγριος, -ᾱ, -ον, savage; wild; fierce (5β)

  ἀγρίως, adv., savagely; wildly; fiercely

ἀγρός, ἀγροῦ, ὁ, field (1α and 3 Gr 2)
ἐν τοῖς ἀγροῖς, in the country

ἄγω, ἄξω, [ἄγαγ-] ἤγαγον, [ἀγ-] ἦχα, ἦγμαι, ἤχθην, I lead; I take (2β, 20γ PP)

  ἄγε; pl., ἄγετε, come on! (9α)

ἀγών, ἀγῶνος, ὁ, struggle; contest (15β)

ἀγωνίζομαι, [ἀγωνιε-] ἀγωνιοῦμαι, [ἀγωνι-] ἠγωνισάμην, ἠγώνισμαι, I contend (27α)

ἀδελφός, ἀδελφοῦ, ὁ, ὦ ἄδελφε,
brother (11α)

ἀδικέω, intransitive, I do wrong; transitive, I wrong; I injure (30β)

ἄδικος, -ον, unjust (24α)

Ἄδρηστος, Ionic, (Ἄδραστος, Attic),
Ἀδρήστου, ὁ, Adrastus (26α)

ἀδύνατος, -ον, impossible; incapable
(21β)

ᾄδω, ᾄσομαι, ᾖσα, ᾖσμαι, ᾔσθην, I
sing (30δ)

ἀεί, adv., always (4β)

ἀέναος, -ον, ever-flowing; everlasting
(H., p. 30)

ἀθάνατος, -ον, immortal (30β)
ἀθάνατοι, ἀθανάτων, οἱ, the Immortals

Ἀθήνᾱζε, adv., to Athens (12β)

Ἀθῆναι, Ἀθηνῶν, αἱ, Athens (6α)
Ἀθήνησι, at Athens
ἐν ταῖς Ἀθήναις, in Athens (1α)

Ἀθηνᾶ, Ἀθηνᾶς, ἡ, τῇ Ἀθηνᾷ, τὴν
Ἀθηνᾶν, ὦ Ἀθηνᾶ, Athena (daughter
of Zeus) (9α)

Ἀθηναῖος, -ᾱ, -ον, Athenian (1α)
Ἀθηναῖοι, Ἀθηναίων, οἱ, the
Athenians
Ἀθήνησι, at Athens

ἀθῡμίᾱ, ἀθῡμίᾱς, ἡ, lack of spirit; despair (26β)

Αἰγαῖος πόντος, Αἰγαίου πόντου,
ὁ, Aegean Sea

Αἰγεύς, Αἰγέως, ὁ, Aegeus (king of
Athens) (6α)

Αἰγύπτιοι, Αἰγυπτίων, οἱ, Egyptians

Αἴγυπτος, Αἰγύπτου, ἡ, Egypt (16α)

αἰεί = ἀεί

αἷμα, αἵματος, τό, blood (20γ)

αἴξ, αἰγός, ὁ or ἡ, goat (7α and 7 Gr
3a)

Αἴολος, Αἰόλου, ὁ, Aeolus

αἰρέω, αἱρήσω, [ἑλ-] εἷλον (irregular
augment), [αἱρε-] ᾕρηκα, ᾕρημαι,
ᾑρέθην, I take (7α, 11β, and 27α PP);
middle, I choose (28β)

αἴρω, [ἀρε-] ἀρῶ, [ἀρ-] ἦρα, ἦρκα,

ἦρμαι, ἤρθην, I lift, raise up; with
reflexive pronoun, I get (myself) up; intransitive, I get under way, set out (1β,
10β, 12 Gr 3, 17α, and 23α PP)

αἰσθάνομαι, [αἰσθε-] αἰσθήσομαι,
[αἰσθ-] ᾐσθόμην, [αἰσθε-] ᾔσθημαι
+ gen. or acc., I perceive; I learn; I apprehend (30β)

αἰσχρός, -ά, -όν, shameful (24α and
24 Gr 4)
αἰσχίων, αἴσχῑον, more shameful
(24 Gr 4)
αἴσχιστος, -η, -ον, most
shameful (24 Gr 4)

Αἰσχύλος, Αἰσχύλου ὁ, Aeschylus
(15β)

αἰτέω, I ask; I ask for (11α)

αἰτίᾱ, αἰτίᾱς, ἡ, blame; responsibility;
cause (23α)

αἴτιος, -ᾱ, -ον, responsible (for); to
blame (3α)

Αἰτναῖον ὄρος, Αἰτναίου ὄρους,
τό, Mount Etna (16β)

αἰχμή, αἰχμῆς, ἡ, spear point

Ἀκαρνᾱνίᾱ Ἀκαρνᾱνίᾱς, ἡ, Acarnania (29α)

ἀκέομαι, ἀκοῦμαι, ἠκεσάμην (note
ε instead of η), I heal (17β)

ἀκίνητος, -ον, motionless, unmoved

ἀκολουθέω + dat., I follow (30δ)

ἀκοντίζω, [ἀκοντιε-] ἀκοντιῶ,
[ἀκοντι-] ἠκόντισα + gen., I throw a
javelin at

ἀκούω, ἀκούσομαι, ἤκουσα, [ἀκο-]
ἀκήκοα, [ἀκου-] ἠκούσθην, intransitive, I listen; transitive + gen. of
person, acc. of thing, I listen to; I hear
(4α and 29β PP)

ἀκρόπολις, ἀκροπόλεως, ἡ, citadel
(28α)
Ἀκρόπολις, Ἀκροπόλεως, ἡ,
the Acropolis (the citadel of
Athens) (8β)

ἄκρος, -ᾱ, -ον, top (of) (5α)
ἄκρον τὸ ὄρος, the top of the moun-
tain/hill (5α)

ἄκων, ἄκουσα, ἄκον, *unwilling(ly); in-*
*voluntary(-ily)* (26α)

ἀλαζών, ἀλαζόνος, ὁ or ἡ, *imposter,*
*charlatan, quack* (30β)

ἀλήθεια, ἀληθείᾱς, ἡ, *truth* (26α)

ἀληθής, ἀληθές, *true* (13β, 13 Gr 4,
and 14 Gr 1)

ἀληθέστερος, -ᾱ, -ον, *truer* (24
Gr 1)

ἀληθέστατος, -η, -ον, *truest* (24
Gr 1)

ἀληθῶς, adv., *truly* (14 Gr 3)

ἀληθέστερον, adv., *more truly* (14
Gr 3)

ἀληθέστατα, adv., *most truly* (14
Gr 3)

ἀληθές, ἀληθοῦς, τό, *the truth*

ἀληθῆ, ἀληθῶν, τά, *the truth* (13β)

ἀλίσκομαι, [ἀλο-] ἀλώσομαι,
ἑάλων or ἥλων, ἑάλωκα or
ἥλωκα, *I am caught; I am taken* (28α)

ἀλλά, conj., *but* (1α)

ἀλλᾱντοπώλης, ἀλλᾱντοπώλου, ὁ,
*sausage-seller*

ἀλλήλων, *of one another* (13α)

ἄλλος, -η, -ο, *other, another* (4β)

ἄλλοι . . . ἄλλοι, *some . . . others*

ἄλλοι ἄλλοσε, *some to some places*
*. . . others to other places* (27α)

ἄλλοσε, adv., *to another place; to other*
*places* (27α)

Ἀλυάττης, τοῦ Ἀλυάττου, (Ionic,
Ἀλυάττεω), ὁ, *Alyattes* (25α)

Ἅλυς, Ἅλυος, ὁ, *Halys  River* (27α)

ἀλῶναι: aorist infinitive of ἀλίσκομαι

ἅμα, adv., *together, at the same time*
(13β)

ἅμα, prep. + dat., *together with*

ἅμα ἔῳ, *at dawn* (29δ)

ἀμαθής, ἀμαθές, *stupid*

ἀμαθίᾱ, ἀμαθίᾱς, ἡ, *ignorance* (H.,
p. 243)

ἅμαξα, ἀμάξης, ἡ, *wagon* (22β)

ἁμαρτάνω, [ἁμαρτε-] ἁμαρτήσομαι,
[ἁμαρτ-] ἥμαρτον, [ἁμαρτε-]
ἡμάρτηκα, ἡμάρτημαι,

ἡμαρτήθην + gen., *I miss; I make a*
*mistake, am mistaken* (18β)

ἁμαρτίᾱ, ἁμαρτίᾱς, ἡ, *mistake*

Ἄμασις, Ἀμάσεως, ὁ, *Amasis* (25α)

ἀμείνων, ἄμεινον, *better* (14 Gr 2, 24
Gr 2)

ἄμεινον, adv., *better* (14 Gr 3)

ἀμέλγω, ἀμέλξω, ἤμελξα, *I milk*

ἄμπελος, ἀμπέλου, ἡ, *grapevine* (30γ)

ἀμῡνω, [ἀμυνε-] ἀμυνῶ, [ἀμῡν-]
ἤμῡνα, active, transitive, *I ward off* X
(acc.) *from* Y (dat.); middle, transitive, *I*
*ward off* X (acc.); *I defend myself*
*against* X (acc.) (13β)

ἀμφότερος, -ᾱ, -ον, *both* (25β)

ἄν: used with subjunctive (22 Gr 2); potential particle (25 Gr 2)

ἀνά, prep. + acc., *up* (5α)

ἀναβαίνω, *I go up, get up;* + ἐπί + acc., *I*
*climb, go up onto* (8β)

ἀναβλέπω, *I look up*

ἀναγιγνώσκω, *I read* (21α)

ἀναγκάζω, ἀναγκάσω, ἠνάγκασα,
ἠνάγκακα, ἠνάγκασμαι,
ἠναγκάσθην, *I compel* (15α)

ἀνάγκη, ἀνάγκης, ἡ, *necessity* (21β)

ἀνάγκη ἐστί(ν), *it is necessary*
(21β)

ἀνάγομαι [= ἀνα- + ἄγομαι], *I put out*
*to sea* (29δ)

ἀνάθημα, ἀναθήματος, τό, *temple*
*offering* (27α)

ἀναιρέομαι [= ἀνα- + αἱρέομαι], *I take*
*up; I pick up* (28α)

ἀνακράζω, [κραγ-] ἀνέκραγον, *I*
*shout* (30γ)

ἀναμιμνῄσκω, [μνη-] ἀναμνήσω,
ἀνέμνησα, *I remind* someone (acc.) *of*
something (acc. or gen.)

μέμνημαι (perfect middle = present), *I have reminded myself = I*
*remember*

μνησθήσομαι (future passive in
middle sense), *I will remember*

ἐμνήσθην (aorist passive in middle

sense), *I remembered* (28β and 29δ
PP)

ἀναπαύομαι, ἀναπαύσομαι, ἀνεπαυσάμην, ἀναπέπαυμαι, *I rest*
(19β)

ἄναξ, ἄνακτος, ὁ, *lord; master* (H., p.
158)

ἀνάστασις, ἀναστάσεως, ἡ, *forced
move; move; evacuation* (22α)

ἀναστενάζω, *I groan aloud* (28β)

ἀναστρέφω, *I turn around* (27β)

ἀνατίθημι, *I set up; I dedicate* (18β)

ἀναχωρέω, *I retreat, withdraw* (14β)

ἀνδρεῖος, -ᾱ, -ον, *brave* (3β, 14 Gr 1,
and 24 Gr 1)

ἀνδρείως, adv., *bravely* (14 Gr 3)

ἄνεμος, ἀνέμου, ὁ, *wind* (13α)

ἀνεξέταστος, -ον, *not searched out,
not inquired into, unexamined* (S., p.
246)

ἀνέρχομαι, *I go up*

ἀνέχομαι [= ἀνα- + ἔχομαι], imperfect,
ἠνειχόμην (double augment), ἀνέξομαι (irregular), [σχ-] ἠνεσχόμην, *I endure; I am patient* (27β)

ἀνήρ, ἀνδρός, ὁ, *man; husband* (4α
and 8 Gr 2)

ἀνθίσταμαι [= ἀντι- + ἵσταμαι], [στη-]
ἀντιστήσομαι, ἀντέστην, ἀνθέστηκα + dat., *I stand up against,
withstand* (22α)

ἄνθρωπος, ἀνθρώπου, ὁ, *man; human being; person* (1α and 3 Gr 3)

ἀνίστημι [= ἀνα- + ἵστημι], ἀνα-
στήσω, ἀνέστησα, transitive, *I make
X stand up; I raise X* (19α)

ἀνίσταμαι [= ἀνα- + ἵσταμαι],
[στη-] ἀναστήσομαι, ἀν-
έστην, ἀνέστηκα, *I stand up; I
am forced to move; I move; I
evacuate* (22α)

ἀνόητος, -ον, *foolish* (28β)

ἀνοίγνῡμι [= ἀνα- + οἴγνῡμι], imperfect, [οἰγ-] ἀνέῳγον (double augment),
ἀνοίξω, ἀνέῳξα, ἀνέῳχα, ἀν-

ἐῷγμαι (*I stand open*), ἀνεῴχθην,
*I open* (20 Gr 1 and 30δ PP)

ἀντέχω [= ἀντι- + ἔχω], imperfect,
ἀντεῖχον (irregular augment), ἀνθ-
έξω (irregular), [σχ-] ἀντέσχον +
dat., *I resist* (14β)

ἀντί, prep. + gen., *instead of; against*
(28β); *in preference to, above* (H., p. 32)

ἀντιόομαι, ἀντιώσομαι, ἠντιώθην
+ dat., *I oppose* (27α)

ἄντρον, ἄντρου, τό, *cave*

ἄνω, adv., *up; above* (20γ)

ἄξιος, -ᾱ, -ον, *worthy;* + gen., *worthy
of* (16β)

ἀοιδός, ἀοιδοῦ, ὁ, *singer; bard* (H., p.
211)

ἀπάγω, *I lead away*

ἀπάρχομαι, *I begin* (30δ)

ἅπᾱς, ἅπᾱσα, ἅπαν, *all; every; whole*
(14β)

ἄπειμι [= ἀπο- + εἰμί], *I am away (from)*
(5α)

ἀπελαύνω [= ἀπο- + ἐλαύνω], transitive, *I drive away;* intransitive, *I march
away*

ἀπέρχομαι [= ἀπο- + ἔρχομαι], *I go
away* (6α)

ἀπέχω [= ἀπο- + ἔχω], imperfect, ἀπεῖχον (irregular augment), ἀφέξω
(irregular), [σχ-] ἀπέσχον, *I am distant;* + gen., *I am distant from;* middle, +
gen., *I abstain from* (17α)

ἀπό, prep. + gen., *from* (4α)

ἀπο-, as a prefix in compound verbs,
*away* (4α)

ἀποβαίνω, *I go away*

ἀποβλέπω, *I look away*

ἀποδημέω, *I am abroad; I go abroad*
(25α)

ἀποδίδωμι, *I give back, return; I pay;*
middle, *I sell* (18α)

χάριν ἀποδίδωμι + dat., *I give
thanks to; I thank* (18α)

ἀποθνῄσκω, [θανε-] ἀποθανοῦμαι,
[θαν-] ἀπέθανον, [θνη-] τέθνηκα, *I*

*die;* perfect, *I am dead* (11α and 24β PP)

     Sometimes ἀποθνῄσκω supplies the passive of ἀποκτείνω and means *I am killed.*

ἀποκρῑ́νομαι, [κρινε-] ἀπο- κρινοῦμαι, [κρῑν] ἀπεκρῑνάμην, [κριν-]ἀποκέκριμαι, [κρι-] ἀπ- εκρίθην (New Testament Greek regularly uses the aorist passive and not the aorist middle), *I answer* (7β and 22β PP)

ἀποκτείνω, [κτενε-] ἀποκτενῶ, [κτειν-] ἀπέκτεινα, [κτον-] ἀπ- έκτονα, *I kill* (6α, 10β, and 22β PP)

     The passive of ἀποκτείνω is supplied by ἀποθνῄσκω, *I die; I am killed.*

ἀπολαμβάνω, *I cut off, intercept* (29δ)

ἀπόλλῡμι [= ἀπο- + ὄλλῡμι], [ολε-] ἀπολῶ, ἀπώλεσα, *I destroy; I ruin; I lose*

     Middle: ἀπόλλυμαι, [ολε-] ἀπ- ολοῦμαι, [ολ-] ἀπωλόμην, *I perish*

Perfect: [ολε-] ἀπολώλεκα, *I have ruined*, [ολ-] ἀπόλωλα, *I am ruined* (26α)

Ἀπόλλων, Ἀπόλλωνος, ὁ, *Apollo*

ἀποπέμπω, *I send away*

ἀποπλέω, *I sail away*

ἀπορέω, *I am at a loss* (12α)

ἀπορίᾱ, ἀπορίᾱς, ἡ, *perplexity; diffi- culty; the state of being at a loss* (15α)

ἀποστέλλω, *I send off* (29β)

ἀποφαίνω, *I show; I reveal; I prove* (26β)

ἀποφεύγω, *I flee away, escape* (5β and 10β)

ἀποχωρέω, *I go away*

ἆρα, particle; introduces a question (4α and 10 Gr 9)

Ἀργεῖος, -ᾱ, -ον, *Argive* (25β)

Ἄργη, Ἄργης, ἡ, *Arge* (name of a dog) (19β)

Ἄργος, Ἄργου, ὁ, *Argus* (name of a

dog; cf. ἀργός, -ή, -όν, *shining; swift*) (5α)

ἀργός [= ἀεργός = ἀ-, *not* + ἐργ-, *work*], -όν, *not working, idle, lazy* (2α and 4α)

ἀργύριον, ἀργυρίου, τό, *silver; money* (11β)

ἀρέσκει, [ἀρε-] ἀρέσει, ἤρεσε, im- personal + dat., *it is pleasing* (20γ)

ἀρετή, ἀρετῆς, ἡ, *excellence; virtue; courage* (15β)

ἀριθμός, ἀριθμοῦ, ὁ, *number* (27α)

ἀριστερά, ἀριστερᾶς, ἡ, *left hand* (9α)

ἄριστος, -η, -ον, *best; very good; no- ble* (9β)

     ἄριστα, adv., *best* (14 Gr 3)

ἁρμονίᾱ, ἁρμονίᾱς, ἡ, *harmony* (24β)

ἄροτρον, ἀρότρου, τό, *plow* (2α)

ἀρόω, *I plow*

Ἀρτεμίσιον, Ἀρτεμισίου, τό, *Artemisium* (14β)

ἀρτύ́ω, ἀρτύ́σω, ἤρτῡσα, ἤρτῡκα, ἤρτῡμαι, ἠρτύθην, *I arrange, make ready*

ἀρχή, ἀρχῆς, ἡ, *beginning* (13β); *rule; empire* (21α)

Ἀρχίδᾱμος, Ἀρχιδᾱ́μου, ὁ, *Archi- damus* (22β)

Ἀρχιμήδης, Ἀρχιμήδου, ὁ, *Archi- medes* (28ε)

ἄρχω, ἄρξω, ἦρξα, ἦργμαι, ἤρ- χθην + gen., active or middle, *I begin;* + gen., active, *I rule* (21β)

Ἀσίᾱ, Ἀσίᾱς, ἡ, *Asia* (i.e., Asia Minor) (15β)

Ἀσκληπιεῖον, Ἀσκληπιείου, τό, *the sanctuary of Asclepius* (17β)

Ἀσκληπιός, Ἀσκληπιοῦ, ὁ, *Ascle- pius* (the god of healing) (11β)

ἀσκός, ἀσκοῦ, ὁ, *bag*

ἄσμενος, -η, -ον, *glad(ly)* (24α)

ἀσπίς, ἀσπίδος, ἡ, *shield* (30β)

ἀστράγαλος, ἀστραγάλου, ὁ, *knuck- lebone* (used as dice in gaming)

ἄστυ, ἄστεως, τό, *city* (8α and 9 Gr 3)

ἀσφαλής, -ές, *safe* (20γ)

ἄτακτος, -ον, *disordered* (29ε)
ἀτάκτως, *in disorder* (29ε)
ἀταξίᾱ, ἀταξίᾱς, ἡ, *disorder* (29ε)
ἀτεχνῶς, adv., *simply; really* (30α)
ἀτραπός, ἀτραποῦ, ἡ, *path*
'Αττική, 'Αττικῆς, ἡ, *Attica* (14β)
'Αττικός, -ή, -όν, *Attic* (29ε)
"Ατῡς, "Ατῠος, ὁ, *Atys* (26α)
αὖ, adv., *again* (24β)
αὖθις, adv., *again* (3α); *in turn* (H., p. 176)
αὔλιον, αὐλίου, τό, *sheepfold*
αὐξάνω, [αὐξε-] αὐξήσω, ηὔξησα, ηὔξηκα, ηὔξημαι, ηὐξήθην, *I increase* (9β and 23β PP)
αὔριον, adv., *tomorrow* (11α)
αὐτίκα, adv., *straightway, at once* (27α)
αὐτός, -ή, -ό, intensive adjective, *-self, -selves;* adjective, *same;* pronoun in gen., dat., and acc. cases, *him, her, it, them* (5β, 5 Gr 6, and 5 Gr 9)
αὐτουργός, αὐτουργοῦ, ὁ, *farmer* (1α)
ἀφαιρέομαι [= ἀπο- + αἱρέομαι], *I take away for myself; I save* (29δ)
ἀφίημι [= ἀπο- + ἵημι], *I let go, release; I send; I throw* (20δ)
ἀφικνέομαι [= ἀπο- + ἱκνέομαι], [ἱκ-] ἀφίξομαι, ἀφῑκόμην, ἀφῑγμαι, *I arrive;* + εἰς + acc., *I arrive at* (6α, 10α, 17α, and 24α PP)
ἀφίσταμαι [= ἀπο- + ἵσταμαι], [στη-] ἀποστήσομαι, ἀπέστην, *I stand away from; I revolt from* (19β and 19 Gr 4)
'Αχαίᾱ, 'Αχαίᾱς, ἡ, *Achaea* (29α)
'Αχαϊκός, -ή, -όν, *Achaean* (29γ)
'Αχαιοί 'Αχαιῶν, οἱ, *Achaeans; Greeks* (7α)
'Αχαρναί, 'Αχαρνῶν, αἱ, *Acharnae* (23α)
'Αχαρνῆς, 'Αχαρνέων, οἱ, *inhabitants of Acharnae, the Acharnians* (23α)
'Αχαρνικός, -ή, -όν, *Acharnian*
ἄχθομαι, [ἀχθε-] ἀχθέσομαι,

ἠχθέσθην + dat., *I am vexed* (at); *I am grieved* (by) (30β)
ἄχρηστος, -ον, *useless* (27β)

**B**

Βαβυλώνιοι, Βαβυλωνίων, οἱ, *Babylonians* (27α)
βαδίζω, [βαδιε-] βαδιοῦμαι, [βαδι-] ἐβάδισα, βεβάδικα, *I walk; I go* (1β)
βαθύς, -εῖα, -ύ, *deep* (19β)
βαίνω, [βη-] βήσομαι, ἔβην, βέβηκα, *I step; I walk; I go* (2β and 15 Gr 1)
βάλλω, [βαλε-] βαλῶ, [βαλ-] ἔβαλον, [βλη-] βέβληκα, βέβλημαι, ἐβλήθην, *I throw; I put; I pelt; I hit, strike* (7β and 22α PP)
βάρβαρος, βαρβάρου, ὁ, *barbarian* (13β)
βασιλείᾱ, βασιλείᾱς, ἡ, *kingdom* (25α)
βασίλεια, βασιλείων, τά, *palace* (25α)
βασιλεύς, βασιλέως, ὁ, *king* (6α and 9 Gr 4)
βασιλεύω, βασιλεύσω, ἐβασίλευσα, *I rule* (6α)
βέβαιος, -ᾱ, -ον, *firm* (13α)
βέλτιστος, -η, -ον, *best* (24 Gr 2)
βελτῑ́ων, βέλτῑον, *better* (24 Gr 2 and 24 Gr 5)
βίᾱ, βίᾱς, ἡ, *force; violence* (30β)
βιβλίον, βιβλίου, τό, *book* (24β)
βίος, βίου, ὁ, *life* (16β)
Βίτων, Βίτωνος, ὁ, *Biton* (25β)
βιωτός, -όν, *to be lived; worth living* (S., p. 246)
βλάπτω, [βλαβ-] βλάψω, ἔβλαψα, βέβλαφα, βέβλαμμαι, ἐβλάφθην or ἐβλάβην, *I harm, hurt* (15β and 19α PP)
βλέπω, βλέψομαι, ἔβλεψα, usually intransitive, *I look; I see* (2β)
βοάω, βοήσομαι, ἐβόησα, *I shout* (5α)
βοή, βοῆς, ἡ, *shout* (10β)

βοήθεια, βοηθείᾱς, ἡ, *help; aid*(29ε)

βοηθέω, *I come to the rescue;* + dat., *I come to X's aid; I come to rescue/aid X* (6α)

Βοιωτίᾱ, Βοιωτίᾱς, ἡ, *Boeotia* (14β)

Βοιωτοί, Βοιωτῶν, οἱ, *Boeotians* (23β)

βότρυες, βοτρύων, οἱ, *grapes*

βουλεύω, βουλεύσω, ἐβούλευσα, βεβούλευκα, βεβούλευμαι, ἐβουλεύθην, active or middle, *I deliberate; I plan* (21α)

βουλή, βουλῆς, ἡ, *plan; advice; Council* (22β)

βούλομαι, [βουλε-] βουλήσομαι, βεβούλημαι, ἐβουλήθην + infin., *I want; I wish* (6α and 28β PP)

βοῦς, βοός, ὁ, *ox* (2β and 9 Gr 4)

βραδύς, βραδεῖα, βραδύ, *slow* (13 Gr 5)

   βραδέως, adv., *slowly* (2β)

Βρόμιος, Βρομίου, ὁ, *the Thunderer* (a name of Dionysus) (9β)

βωμός, βωμοῦ, ὁ, *altar* (8β)

# Γ

γάμος, γάμου, ὁ, *marriage* (26α)

γάρ, postpositive conj., *for* (1α)

γε, postpositive enclitic; restrictive, *at least;* intensive, *indeed* (6β)

γέγονε (perfect of γίγνομαι), *he/she/it has become; he/she/it is*

γελάω, γελάσομαι (note α instead of η), ἐγέλασα, γεγέλασμαι, ἐγελάσθην, *I laugh* (18α and 18β PP)

γένος, γένους, τό, *race*

γεραιός, -ά, -όν, *old* (12α)

γέρων, γέροντος, *old* (9β and 9 Gr 2)

γέρων, γέροντος, ὁ, *old man* (9β and 9 Gr 2)

γεύομαι, γεύσομαι, ἐγευσάμην, γέγευμαι, *I taste*

γέφῡρα, γεφύρᾱς, ἡ, *bridge*

γεωμετρίᾱ, γεωμετρίᾱς, ἡ, *geometry*

γεωργέω, *I farm*

γῆ, γῆς, ἡ, *land; earth; ground* (4β)

κατὰ γῆν, *by land* (14α)

ποῦ γῆς; *where* (in the world)? (16α)

γίγᾱς, γίγαντος, ὁ, *giant*

γίγνομαι, [γενε-] γενήσομαι, [γεν-] ἐγενόμην, [γον-] γέγονα, [γενε-] γεγένημαι, *I become* (6α, 10α, 11 Gr 2, 11 Gr 4, 26αPP, and 26β PP)

   γίγνεται, *he/she/it becomes; it happens* (6α)

γιγνώσκω, [γνω-] γνώσομαι, ἔγνων, ἔγνωκα, ἔγνωσμαι, ἐγνώσθην, *I come to know; I perceive; I learn* (5β, 15 Gr 1, 17α, 24β PP, and 26α PP)

   ὀρθῶς γιγνώσκω, *I am right* (18β)

γνώμη, γνώμης, ἡ, *opinion; judgment; intention* (18β); *purpose* (H., p. 41)

   τίνα γνώμην ἔχεις; *What do you think?* (18β)

Γορδίης, Ionic (Γορδίᾱς, Attic), Γορδίου, ὁ, *Gordias* (26α)

γράμμα, γράμματος, τό, *letter* (of the alphabet); pl., *writing* (24α)

γραμματιστής, γραμματιστοῦ, ὁ, *schoolmaster* (24α)

γράφω, γράψω, ἔγραψα, γέγραφα, γέγραμμαι, ἐγράφην, *I write* (14β and 19β PP)

γυμναστική, γυμναστικῆς, ἡ, *gymnastics* (24α)

γυνή, γυναικός, ἡ, *woman; wife* (4α and 8 Gr 3)

# Δ

δαίμων, δαίμονος, ὁ, *spirit; god; the power controlling one's destiny, fate, lot* (28α)

δάκνω, [δηκ-] δήξομαι, [δακ-] ἔδακον, [δηκ-] δέδηγμαι, ἐδήχθην, *I bite; I sting* (30α)

δακρύω, δακρύσω, ἐδάκρῡσα, δεδάκρῡκα, δεδάκρῡμαι (*I am in tears*), *I cry, weep* (11α and 17α PP)

δέ, postpositive particle, *and, but* (1α)

δέδοικα, perfect with present meaning, *I am afraid* (28 Gr 8)

δεῖ, impersonal + acc. and infin., *it is nec-*

*essary* (10β and 10 Gr 8)

δεῖ ἡμᾶς παρεῖναι, *we must be there* (10β and 10 Gr 8)

δείκνῡμι, imperfect, ἐδείκνῡν, [δεικ-] δείξω, ἔδειξα, δέδειχα, δέδειγμαι, ἐδείχθην, *I show* (20γ, 20 Gr 1, 21 Gr 4, 24α PP, 25 Gr 5, and 30δ PP)

δειλίᾱ, δειλίᾱς, ἡ, *cowardice* (26β)

δειλός, -ή, -όν, *cowardly* (27β)

δεινός, -ή, -όν, *terrible; clever, skilled;* + infin., *clever at, skilled at* (6α and 19β)

δεινά, *terrible things*

δεινῶς, adv., *terribly, frightfully*

δειπνέω, *I eat dinner* (20δ)

δεῖπνον, δείπνου, τό, *dinner* (3β); *meal*

δέκα, indeclinable, *ten* (8 Gr 5)

δέκατος, -η, -ον, *tenth* (8 Gr 5)

Δελφοί, Δελφῶν, οἱ, *Delphi* (25β)

δένδρον, δένδρου, τό, *tree* (2β and 3 Gr 2)

δεξιός, -ά, -όν, *right* (i.e., on the right hand) (15β)

δεξιά, δεξιᾶς, ἡ, *right hand* (9α)

δέομαι, [δεε-] δεήσομαι, ἐδεήθην, *I ask for* X (acc.) *from* Y (gen.); + infin., *I beg;* + gen., *I want* (26α)

δέος, δέους, τό, *fear* (28α)

δεσμωτήριον, δεσμωτηρίου, τό, *prison*

δεσπότης, δεσπότου, ὁ, ὦ δέσποτα, *master* (2β and 4 Gr 4)

δεῦρο, adv., *here*, i.e., *hither* (3α)

δευτερεῖα, δευτερείων, τά, *second prize*

δεύτερος, -ᾱ, -ον, *second* (8 Gr 5)

δεύτερον or τὸ δεύτερον, adv., *a second time*

δέχομαι, δέξομαι, ἐδεξάμην, δέδεγμαι, *I receive* (6α and 27 Gr 9)

δέω, δήσω, ἔδησα, δέδεκα, δέδεμαι, ἐδέθην, *I tie, bind* (17α)

δή, postpositive particle; emphasizes that what is said is obvious or true, *indeed, in fact* (6β)

δῆλος, -η, -ον, *clear* (18α)

δῆλόν ἐστι(ν), *it is clear* (18α)

δηλόω, *I show* (15β, 15 Gr 3, 17 Gr 1, 18β PP, 21 Gr 2, 25 Gr 4, 27 Gr 4 and 6, and 28 Gr 3 and 6)

δημοκρατίᾱ, δημοκρατίᾱς, ἡ, *democracy*

δῆμος, δήμου, ὁ, *the people* (9β); *township; deme* (23α)

δήπου, particle, *doubtless, surely* (20γ)

διά, prep. + gen., *through* (9α); + acc., *because of* (18β)

δι' ὀλίγου, *soon* (5α)

διαβαίνω, *I cross* (27α)

διαβάλλω, *I pass over, cross*

διαβιβάσαι (aorist infin. of διαβιβάζω), *to take across, transport*

διακομίζω, *I bring over; I take across*

διᾱκόσιοι, -αι, -α, *200* (15 Gr 5 and 16α)

διαλέγομαι, διαλέξομαι or διαλεχθήσομαι, διελεξάμην, διείλεγμαι, διελέχθην + dat., *I talk to, converse with* (8α)

διαλύω, *I disband* (an army); *I disperse* (a fleet) (23β)

διάνοια, διανοίᾱς, ἡ, *intention; intellect* (24β)

διαπέμπω, *I send* X (acc.) *through* Y (dat.)

διὰ πολλοῦ, *after a long time*

διαφέρει, impersonal + dat., (it) *makes a difference to* (28α)

διαφέροντα, διαφερόντων, τά, *things carrying in different directions; opposites* (H., p. 111)

διαφεύγω, *I escape* (29δ)

διαφθείρω, [φθερε-] διαφθερῶ, [φθειρ-] διέφθειρα, [φθαρ-] διέφθαρκα or [φθορ-] διέφθορα, [φθαρ-] διέφθαρμαι, διεφθάρην, *I destroy* (15α, 23α PP, and 26β PP)

διδάσκαλος, διδασκάλου, ὁ, *teacher* (24α)

διδάσκω, [διδαχ-] διδάξω, ἐδίδαξα, δεδίδαχα, δεδίδαγμαι, ἐδιδάχθην, *I teach* someone (acc.)

something (acc.); passive, *I am taught
something* (acc.) (24α and 26α PP)

**δίδωμι** [δω-/δο-], imperfect, ἐδίδουν,
**δώσω, ἔδωκα,** infinitive, **δοῦναι,** participle, **δούς,** imperative, **δός, δέδωκα,
δέδομαι, ἐδόθην,** *I give* (18α, 18 Gr
1, 21 Gr 4, 25 Gr 5, and 30δ PP)

**διέρχομαι** [= δια- + ἔρχομαι], *I come
through; I go through* (14β)

**διίσταμαι,** [στη-] **διαστήσομαι,
διέστην, διέστηκα,** intransitive, *I
separate, part*

**Δικαιόπολις, Δικαιοπόλιδος,** ὁ, τῷ
Δικαιοπόλιδι, τὸν Δικαιόπολιν, ὦ
Δικαιόπολι, *Dicaeopolis* (1α)

**δίκαιος, -ᾱ, -ον,** *just* (24α)

**δίκη, δίκης,** ἡ, *custom; justice; right;
lawsuit; penalty* (21β)

**δι᾽ ὀλίγου,** *soon* (5α)

**Διονύσια, Διονυσίων, τά,** *the festival
of Dionysus* (4α)

     τὰ Διονύσια ποιῶ/ποιοῦμαι, *I
     celebrate the festival of Dionysus*
     (4α)

**Διόνῡσος, Διονύσου,** ὁ, *Dionysus*
(8α)

**διότι,** conj., *because* (18β)

**διώκω, διώξω** or **διώξομαι, ἐδίωξα,
δεδίωχα, ἐδιώχθην,** *I pursue, chase*
(5α and 20δ PP)

**δοκέω,** [δοκ-] **δόξω, ἔδοξα, δέδογμαι, ἐδόχθην,** *I seem; I think*
(18α PP and 20δ PP); *I expect; I imagine* (H., p. 50)

     **δοκεῖ,** [δοκ-] **δόξει, ἔδοξε(ν),
     δέδοκται,** impersonal, *it seems
     (good);* + dat., e.g., **δοκεῖ μοι,** *it
     seems good to me; I think it best*
     (11α); + dat. and infin., e.g., **δοκεῖ
     αὐτοῖς σπεύδειν,** *it seems good
     to them to hurry, they decide to
     hurry* (11β)

     **ὡς δοκεῖ,** *as it seems* (13β)

**δόρυ, δόρατος, τό,** *spear* (26α)

**δοῦλος, δούλου,** ὁ, *slave* (2α)

**δουλόω,** *I enslave*

**δραμεῖν** (aorist infin. of τρέχω), *to run*

**δραχμή, δραχμῆς,** ἡ, *drachma* (a silver coin worth six obols) (11β)

**Δύμη, Δύμης,** ἡ, *Dyme* (29β)

**δύναμαι,** [δυνη-] **δυνήσομαι,
ἐδυνήθην,** *I am able; I can* (16α, 16 Gr
2, and 25α PP)

**δύναμις, δυνάμεως,** ἡ, *power;
strength; forces* (military) (21β)

**δυνατός, -ή, -όν,** *possible* (3α); *capable* (21β); *powerful*

**δύο,** *two* (7β and 8 Gr 5)

**δώδεκα,** indeclinable, *twelve* (15 Gr 5)

     **δωδέκατος, -η, -ον,** *twelfth* (15 Gr
     5)

**Δωδώνη,** Ionic, (Δωδώνᾱ, Attic),
**Δωδώνης,** ἡ, *Dodona* (27α)

**δώματα, δωμάτων, τά,** Homeric
word, *palace*

**δῶρον, δώρου, τό,** *gift* (27α)

**E**

**ἐάν,** conj. + subjunctive, *if* (21α)

**ἔαρ, ἦρος, τό,** *spring* (22β)

**ἑαυτοῦ:** see ἐμαυτοῦ

**ἐάω,** imperfect, εἴων (irregular augment), **ἐάσω** (note that because of the ε
the α lengthens to ᾱ rather than η),
**εἴᾱσα** (irregular augment), **εἴᾱκα,
εἴᾱμαι, εἰᾱθην,** *I allow, let be* (23β
and 25β PP)

**ἑβδομήκοντα,** indeclinable, *seventy* (15
Gr 5)

**ἕβδομος, -η, -ον,** *seventh* (8 Gr 5)

**ἐγγύς,** adv., *nearly; nearby*

**ἐγγύς,** prep. + gen., *near* (13β)

**ἐγείρω,** [ἐγερε-] **ἐγερῶ,** [ἐγειρ-]
**ἤγειρα,** [thematic 2nd aorist middle;
ἐγρ-] **ἠγρόμην** (*I awoke*), [ἐγορ-]
**ἐγρήγορα** (*I am awake*), [ἐγερ-]
**ἐγήγερμαι, ἠγέρθην,** active, transitive, *I wake X up;* middle and passive,
intransitive, *I wake up* (8β, 23α PP, and
26β PP)

**ἐγώ, ἐμοῦ** or **μου,** *I* (2α and 5 Gr 6)

ἔγωγε, strengthened form of ἐγώ, *I indeed*

ἔδραμον: *see* τρέχω

ἐθέλω or θέλω, imperfect, ἤθελον, [ἐθελε-] ἐθελήσω, ἠθέλησα, ἠθέληκα + infin., *I am willing; I wish* (4α and 28β PP)

ἔθνος, ἔθνους, τό, *tribe; people* (27β)

εἰ, conj., *if;* in indirect questions, *whether* (11α)

  εἰ γάρ, *if only; oh, that* (25α)

  εἰ μή, *unless; except*

  εἴ πως, *if somehow, if perhaps*

εἰδότες: participle of οἶδα

εἴθε, note accent, *if only; oh, that* (25α)

εἴκοσι(ν), indeclinable, *twenty* (15 Gr 5)

  εἰκοστός, -ή, -όν, *twentieth* (15 Gr 5)

εἴκω, εἴξω, εἶξα (no augment) + dat., *I yield* (15α)

εἰκών, εἰκόνος, ἡ, *statue*

εἷλον: *see* αἱρέω

εἰμί [ἐσ-], imperfect, ἦ or ἦν, ἔσομαι, *I am* (1α, 4 Gr 1, 10 Gr 1, 13 Gr 1, 21 Gr 4, 25 Gr 5, and 30δ PP)

  οἷός τ᾽ εἰμί, *I am able* (25α)

εἶμι [εἰ-/ἰ-], imperfect, ᾖα or ᾔειν, *I will go* (10 Gr 6, 13 Gr 1, 21 Gr 4, 25 Gr 5, and 30δ PP)

εἵνεκα: Ionic for ἕνεκα

εἶπον (aorist of λέγω), *I / they said; I / they told; I / they spoke*

εἰρήνη, εἰρήνης, ἡ, *peace* (16β)

εἰς, prep. + acc., *into; to; at* (2β); of time, *for; onto; against;* of purpose, *for*

  εἰς ἀπορίᾱν κατέστη, *he fell into perplexity, became perplexed* (19β)

  εἰς καιρόν, *at just the right time*

  εἰς τὸ πρόσθεν, *forward* (30β)

εἷς, μία, ἕν, *one* (7β and 8 Gr 5)

  εἷς καὶ εἴκοσι(ν), *twenty-one* (15 Gr 5)

εἰσάγω, *I lead in; I take in* (2β and 11α)

εἰσβαίνω, *I go in; I come in*

  εἰσβάντες, *having embarked*

εἰς ναῦν εἰσβαίνω, *I go on board ship, embark*

εἰσβάλλω + εἰς + acc., *I invade* (22α)

εἰσβολή, τῆς εἰσβολῆς, ἡ, *invasion* (23α)

εἰσελαύνω, *I drive in*

εἰσέρχομαι, *I come in(to); I go in(to)*

εἰσηγέομαι + dat., *I lead in*

εἰσηκοντίζω, *I throw a javelin at*

εἰσκαλέω, *I call in(to)*

εἰσκομίζω, *I bring in; I take in*

εἴσοδος, εἰσόδου, ἡ, *entrance*

εἰσπίπτω, *I fall (up)on*

εἰσπλέω, *I sail in(to)*

εἰστίθημι, *I put in*

εἰσφέρω, *I bring in(to)*

εἴσω, adv., *inward* (29α)

εἶτα, adv., *then, next* (30α)

εἴτε . . . εἴτε, note the accent, *either . . . or* (28α)

εἴωθα, perfect with present meaning, *I am accustomed to* (28β, 28 Gr 8)

ἐκ, ἐξ, before words beginning with vowels, prep. + gen., *out of* (3α)

  ἐκ τοῦ ὄπισθε(ν), *from the rear*

ἕκαστος, -η, -ον, *each* (23β)

ἑκάτερος, -ᾱ, -ον, *each* (of two) (21β)

ἑκατόν, indeclinable, *100* (15 Gr 5 and 16α)

  ἑκατοστός, -ή, -όν, *hundredth* (15 Gr 5)

ἐκβαίνω, *I step out; I come out* (2α)

  ἐκβαίνω ἐκ τῆς νεώς, *I disembark*

ἐκβάλλω, *I throw out*

ἐκδίδωμι, *I give* (in marriage)

ἐκεῖ, adv., *there* (6α)

ἐκεῖθεν, adv., *from that place, thence*

ἐκεῖνος, ἐκείνη, ἐκεῖνο, *that;* pl., *those* (13β and 14 Gr 6)

ἐκεῖσε, adv., *to that place, thither* (8α)

ἐκκαλέω, *I call out*

ἐκκλησίᾱ, ἐκκλησίᾱς, ἡ, *assembly* (21α)

ἐκκομίζω, *I bring, carry out*

ἐκπέμπω, *I send out*

ἐκπίπτω, *I fall out*

ἐκπλέω, *I sail out*

ἔκπλους, ἔκπλου, ὁ, *escape route*

ἐκπνέω, *I blow out; I blow from* (29α)

ἔκτοπος, -ον, *out of the way, unusual*

ἐκτός, prep. + gen., *outside* (22β)

ἕκτος, -η, -ον, *sixth* (8 Gr 5)

ἐκ τοῦ ὄπισθε(ν), *from the rear*

ἐκφέρω, *I carry out*

ἐκφεύγω, *I flee (out), escape*

ἐλᾶ, ἐλᾶς, ἡ, *olive; olive tree* (19α)

ἐλάττων, ἔλαττον, *smaller*, pl., *fewer* (14 Gr 2 and 24 Gr 4)

ἐλαύνω, [ἐλα-] ἐλῶ, ἐλᾷς, ἐλᾷ, etc., ἤλασα, ἐλήλακα, ἐλήλαμαι, ἠλάθην, transitive, *I drive* (2α); *I march* (an army); intransitive, *I march* (29β PP)

ἐλάχιστος, -η, -ον *smallest; least;* pl., *fewest* (24 Gr 4)

ἐλευθερίᾱ, ἐλευθερίᾱς, ἡ, *freedom* (13β)

ἐλεύθερος, -ᾱ, -ον, *free*

ἐλευθερόω, *I free, set free* (15β)

Ἐλευσίς, Ἐλευσῖνος, ἡ, *Eleusis* (20δ)

ἕλκω, imperfect, εἷλκον (irregular augment), ἕλξω, [ἑλκυ-] εἵλκυσα (irregular augment), εἵλκυκα, εἵλκυσμαι, εἱλκύσθην, *I drag* (25β and 25β PP)

Ἑλλάς, Ἑλλάδος, ἡ, *Hellas, Greece* (13β)

Ἕλλην, Ἕλληνος, ὁ, *Greek;* pl., *the Greeks* (14α)

Ἑλλήσποντος, Ἑλλησπόντου, ὁ, *Hellespont*

ἐλπίζω, [ἐλπιε-] ἐλπιῶ, [ἐλπι-] ἤλπισα, *I hope; I expect; I suppose* (14α)

ἐλπίς, ἐλπίδος, ἡ, *hope; expectation* (23β)

ἔλπομαι, *I hope; I expect; I suppose* (H., p. 50)

ἐμαυτοῦ, σεαυτοῦ, ἑαυτοῦ, *of myself, of yourself, of him-, her-, itself*, etc. (7α and 7 Gr 4)

ἐμβάλλω + dat., *I strike with a ram* (ἔμβολος)

ἐμμένω [= ἐν- + μένω], *I remain in* (23β)

ἐμός, -ή, -όν, *my, mine* (5 Gr 8)

ἔμπειρος, -ον + gen., *skilled in* or *at*

ἐμπίπτω [= ἐν- + πίπτω] + dat., *I fall into; I fall upon; I attack* (15β)

ἐμποδίζω [ἐν- + ποῦς, ποδός, ὁ, *foot*), [ἐμποδιε-] ἐμποδιῶ, no aorist, *I obstruct*

ἔμπορος, ἐμπόρου, ὁ, *merchant* (12β)

ἐν, prep. + dat., *in; on* (3β); *among*

ἐν διδασκάλων, *at school*

ἐν μέσῳ + gen., *between* (14α)

ἐν νῷ ἔχω + infin., *I have in mind; I intend* (4α)

ἐν ταῖς Ἀθήναις, *in Athens* (1α)

ἐν ... τούτῳ, *meanwhile* (8β)

ἐν ᾧ, *while* (8α)

ἐνακόσιοι, -αι, -α, *900* (15 Gr 5)

ἐναντίος, -ᾱ, -ον, *opposed; opposite; hostile;* as noun, *the enemy* (29ε)

ἔνατος, -η, -ον, *ninth* (8 Gr 5)

ἕνδεκα, indeclinable, *eleven* (15 Gr 5)

ἑνδέκατος, -η, -ον, *eleventh* (15 Gr 5)

ἐνδίδωμι, *I give in, yield* (22β)

ἔνδον, adv., *inside*

ἔνειμι, *I am in*

ἕνεκα, prep. + preceding gen., *for the sake of; because of* (21α)

ἐνενήκοντα, indeclinable, *ninety* (15 Gr 5)

ἐνθάδε, adv., *here; hither; there; thither* (7β)

ἐνθῡμέομαι, ἐνθῡμήσομαι, ἐντεθῡμημαι, ἐνεθῡμήθην, *I take to heart; I ponder* (28β)

ἔνιοι, -αι, -α, *some* (20δ)

ἐννέα, indeclinable, *nine* (8 Gr 5)

ἔνοικος, ἐνοίκου, ὁ, *inhabitant* (16α)

ἐνόπλιος, -ον, *in armor, fully armed*

ἐνταῦθα, adv., *then; here; hither; there; thither* (5β)

ἐνταῦθα δή, *at that very moment, then* (5β)

ἐντεῦθεν, adv., *from this place*

ἐντός, adv., *within, inside* (20γ)

ἐντός, prep. + gen., *within, inside* (20γ)

ἐντυγχάνω + dat., *I meet* (19β)

ἐξ: *see* ἐκ

ἕξ, indeclinable, *six* (8 Gr 5)

ἐξάγω, *I lead out*

ἐξαιρέω [= ἐκ + αἱρέω], *I take out, remove*

ἐξαίφνης, adv., *suddenly* (20γ)

ἐξακόσιοι, -αι, -α, *600* (15 Gr 5)

ἐξαμαρτάνω [= ἐκ- + ἁμαρτάνω], *I miss; I fail; I make a mistake* (23β)

ἐξαρτύω [= ἐκ + ἀρτύω], *I equip* (29β)

ἐξεγείρω [= ἐκ + ἐγείρω], *I wake X up*

ἐξελαύνω, *I drive out*

ἐξέρχομαι + ἐκ + gen., *I come out of; I go out of* (6β)

ἔξεστι(ν), impersonal + dat. and infin., *it is allowed/possible* (10β and 10 Gr 8)

ἔξεστιν ἡμῖν μένειν, *we are allowed to stay, we may stay; we can stay* (10β and 10 Gr 8)

ἐξετάζω, *I examine; I question closely* (S., p. 246)

ἐξευρίσκω, *I find out*

ἐξηγέομαι [ἐκ- + ἡγέομαι], *I relate* (12β)

ἐξήκοντα, indeclinable, *sixty* (15 Gr 5)

ἔξοδος, ἐξόδου, ἡ, *going out; marching forth; military expedition* (23β)

ἐξόπισθε(ν), adv., *behind* (30δ)

ἐξόπισθε(ν), prep. + gen., *behind* (30δ)

ἔξω, adv., *outside* (20δ)

ἔξω, prep. + gen., *outside* (20δ)

ἔοικα, perfect with present meaning, *I am like; I am likely to* (28β and 28 Gr 2)

ὡς ἔοικε(ν), *as it seems* (28 Gr 8)

ἑορτή, ἑορτῆς, ἡ, *festival* (4α)

ἑορτὴν ποιῶ/ποιοῦμαι, *I celebrate a festival* (4β)

ἔπαινος, ἐπαίνου, ὁ, *praise* (24β)

ἐπαίρω [ἐπι- + αἴρω], *I lift, raise* (7α); *I induce*

ἐπαίρω ἐμαυτόν, *I get (myself) up* (7α)

ἐπανέρχομαι [= ἐπι- + ἀνα- + ἔρχομαι], *I come back, return;* + εἰς or πρός + acc., *I return to* (9α)

ἐπεί, conj., *when* (3β), *since* (26β)

ἐπειδή, conj., *when; since* (22α)

ἐπειδάν [= ἐπειδή + ἄν], conj., *in indefinite or general clauses with subjunctive, when(ever)* (22α)

ἐπεισβαίνω [= ἐπι- + εἰσ- + βαίνω], *I go into* (29δ)

ἔπειτα, adv., *then; thereafter* (2β)

ἐπεξέρχομαι [= ἐπι- + ἐκ- + ἔρχομαι] + dat., *I march out against, attack* (23α)

ἐπέρχομαι [= ἐπι- + ἔρχομαι], *I approach;* + dat., *I attack* (27α)

ἐπί, prep. + gen., *toward, in the direction of* (20δ); *on* (24β); + dat., *upon, on* (5β); *of price, for* (18β); *of purpose, for;* + acc., *at* (5β, 29α); *against* (5β); *onto, upon* (9α); *of direction or purpose, to, for* (26α); *of time, for* (27α)

ἐπὶ τὴν ἕω, *at dawn* (29α)

ἐπιβαίνω + gen., *I get up on, mount;* + dat., *I board* (28α)

ἐπιβοηθέω + dat., *I come to aid* (29δ)

ἐπιβουλεύω + dat., *I plot against*

ἐπιγίγνομαι, *I come after* (29α)

Ἐπίδαυρος, Ἐπιδαύρου, ἡ, *Epidaurus* (11β)

ἐπιδιώκω, *I pursue* (29ε)

ἐπικαλέω, *I call upon;* middle, *I call upon X to help* (28β)

ἐπίκειμαι + dat., *I lie near, lie off* (of islands with respect to the mainland)

ἐπιλανθάνομαι, [λη-] ἐπιλήσομαι, [λαθ-] ἐπελαθόμην, [λη-] ἐπιλέλησμαι + gen., *I forget*

ἐπιμελέομαι, ἐπιμελήσομαι, ἐπιμεμέλημαι, ἐπεμελήθην + gen., *I take care for;* + ὅπως + future indicative, *I take care (to see to it that)* (24β)

ἐπιπέμπω, *I send against; I send in* (14α)

ἐπιπλέω + dat. or + εἰς + acc., *I sail against* (15β)

ἐπίσταμαι, [ἐπιστη-] ἐπιστήσομαι, ἠπιστήθην, *I understand; I know*

(16α, 16 Gr 2, and 25α PP)

ἐπιστήμη, ἐπιστήμης, ἡ, knowledge (S., p. 242)

ἐπιστρατεύω + dat. or ἐπί + acc., I march against, attack (18β)

ἐπιστρέφω, I turn around (29δ)

ἐπιτήδειος, -ᾱ, -ον, friendly; + infin., suitable for (23α)

ἐπιτίθημι, I put X (acc.) on Y (dat.) (18α)

ἐπιτίθεμαι, [θη-] ἐπιθήσομαι, [θε-] ἐπεθέμην + dat., I attack (29α)

ἐπιτρέπω, I entrust X (acc.) to Y (dat.) (17β)

ἐπιχειρέω + dat., I attempt; I attack (29α)

ἕπομαι, imperfect, εἱπόμην (irregular augment), ἕψομαι, [σπ-] ἑσπόμην + dat., I follow (8α, 17α, and 25β PP)

ἑπτά, indeclinable, seven (8 Gr 5)

ἑπτακόσιοι, -αι, -α, 700 (15 Gr 5)

ἐράω, imperfect, ἤρων, ἐρασθήσομαι, ἠράσθην + gen., I love (30α)

ἐργάζομαι, imperfect, ἠργαζόμην or εἰργαζόμην, ἐργάσομαι, ἠργασάμην or εἰργασάμην, εἴργασμαι, εἰργάσθην, I work; I accomplish (8α and 25β PP)

ἔργον, ἔργου, τό, work; deed (8α)
ἔργα, τά, tilled fields
ἔργῳ, in fact

ἐρέσσω, no future, [ἐρετ-] ἤρεσα, I row (13α)

ἐρέτης, ἐρέτου, ὁ, rower

ἔρημος, -ον, deserted (19β)

Ἐρῑνύες, Ἐρῑνῶν, αἱ, the Furies (avenging spirits) (20γ)

ἑρμηνεύς, ἑρμηνέως, ὁ, interpreter

ἔρχομαι, [εἰ-/ἰ-] εἶμι (irregular), [ἐλθ-] ἦλθον, [ἐλυθ-] ἐλήλυθα, I come; I go (6α, 11β, and 27α PP)

ἐρῶ: see λέγω

ἐρωτάω, ἐρωτήσω, ἠρώτησα or [ἐρ-] ἠρόμην, ἠρώτηκα, I ask (12β)

ἐς = εἰς

ἐσβάλλω = εἰσβάλλω

ἐσθίω, [ἐδ-] ἔδομαι, [φαγ-] ἔφαγον, [ἐδ-] ἐδήδοκα, I eat (9α, 19α, and 29β PP)

ἑσπέρᾱ, ἑσπέρᾱς, ἡ, evening (8a); the west

ἔστω, let it be so! all right!

ἔσχατος, -η, -ον, furthest; extreme (28β)

ἔσω: see εἴσω

ἑταῖρος, ἑταίρου, ὁ, comrade, companion (6α)

ἕτερος, -ᾱ, -ον, one or the other (of two) (26α)
ὁ μὲν ἕτερος ... ὁ δὲ ἕτερος, the one ... the other (26α)

ἔτι, adv., still (3α)

ἕτοιμος, -η, -ον, ready (9β)

ἔτος, ἔτους, τό, year (16β)

εὖ, adv., well (8α and 14 Gr 3)
ἄμεινον, adv., better (14 Gr 3)
ἄριστα, adv., best (14 Gr 3)
εὖ γε, good! well done! (8α)

Εὔβοια, Εὐβοίᾱς, ἡ, Euboea (14α)

εὐγένεια, εὐγενείᾱς, ἡ, nobility of birth (S., p. 242)

εὐδοξίᾱ, εὐδοξίᾱς, ἡ, good reputation, fame (H., p. 118)

εὐδαιμονίᾱ, εὐδαιμονίᾱς, ἡ, happiness; prosperity; good luck (25β)

εὐθύς, εὐθεῖα, εὐθύ, straight
εὐθύς, adv., straightway, immediately, at once (10β); straight

εὐμενής, -ές, kindly (18α)
εὐμενῶς, adv., kindly

εὑρίσκω, [εὑρε-] εὑρήσω, [εὑρ-] ηὗρον or εὗρον, [εὑρε-] ηὕρηκα or εὕρηκα, ηὕρημαι or εὕρημαι, ηὑρέθην or εὑρέθην, I find (7α, 10α, and 24β PP)

Εὐρυμέδων ποταμός, Εὐρυμέδοντος ποταμοῦ, ὁ, the Eurymedon River

εὐρυχωρίᾱ, εὐρυχωρίᾱς, ἡ, broad waters (29γ)

εὐφημέω, I keep holy silence (30δ)

εὐφημίᾱ, εὐφημίᾱς, ἡ, call for holy silence (30δ)

εὐχή, εὐχῆς, ἡ, prayer (25β)

εὔχομαι, εὔξομαι, ηὐξάμην, ηὖγμαι, I pray; + dat., I pray to; + acc. and infin., I pray (that) (8β and 20δ PP)

ἔφαγον: see ἐσθίω

ἔφη, he/she said (11α)

ἔφασαν, they said

'Εφιάλτης, 'Εφιάλτου, ὁ, Ephialtes (14β)

ἐφίημι [= ἐπι- + ἵημι], I throw; + ἐπί + acc., I throw at (20δ)

ἐφίσταμαι [= ἐπι- + ἵσταμαι], [στη-] ἐπέστην + dat., I stand near; of dreams, I appear to (26α)

ἐχθρός, -ά, -όν, hateful; hostile (18β and 24 Gr 4)

ἐχθρός, ἐχθροῦ, ὁ, enemy (18β and 24 Gr 4)

ἐχθίων, ἔχθιον, more hateful, hostile (24 Gr 4)

ἔχθιστος, -η, -ον, most hateful, hostile (24 Gr 4)

ἔχω, imperfect, εἶχον (irregular augment), ἕξω (irregular) (I will have) and [σχε-] σχήσω, (I will get), [σχ-] ἔσχον, [σχε-] ἔσχηκα, ἔσχημαι, I have; I hold; middle + gen., I hold onto (4α, 25β PP)

κᾰλῶς ἔχω, I am well (11α)

πῶς ἔχει τὰ πράγματα; How are things? (18β)

πῶς ἔχεις; How are you? (11α)

ἕως, ἕω, ἡ, dawn (29α)

ἅμα ἕῳ, at dawn (29δ)

ἐπὶ τὴν ἕω, at dawn (29α)

ἕως, conj. + indicative (14β), + subjunctive (22α and 22 Gr 2), until

**Z**

*ζάω (unattested, hypothetical form) (ζῶ, ζῇς, ζῇ, etc.), infinitive, ζῆν, imperfect, ἔζων, ἔζης, ἔζη, etc., ζήσω or ζήσομαι, I live (24α)

ζεύγνῡμι, ζεύξω, ἔζευξα, ἔζευγ-μαι, ἐζεύχθην or ἐζύγην, I yoke (20 Gr 1, 22β, and 30δ PP)

Ζεύς, ὁ, τοῦ Διός, τῷ Διί, τὸν Δία, ὦ Ζεῦ, Zeus (king of the gods) (3α and 8β)

μὰ Δία, by Zeus

ναὶ μὰ Δία, yes, by Zeus! (30β)

ζητέω, I seek, I look for (5α)

ζωή, ζωῆς, ἡ, life (28α)

ζῷον, ζῴου, τό, animal

**H**

ἤ, conj., or (12α)

ἤ . . . ἤ, conj., either . . . or (12α)

ἤ, conj., with comparatives, than (14α)

ἡγέομαι + dat., I lead (6β); I think, consider (30β)

ἤδη, adv., already; now (2β)

ἥδομαι, [ἡσθε-] ἡσθήσομαι, [ἡσθ-] ἥσθην, I am glad, delighted; + participle or dat., I enjoy (24β)

ἡδύς, ἡδεῖα, ἡδύ, sweet; pleasant (24 Gr 4)

ἡδίων, ἥδιον, sweeter; more pleasant (24 Gr 4)

ἥδιστος, -η, -ον, sweetest; most pleasant (24 Gr 4)

ἡδέως, adv., sweetly; pleasantly; gladly (18β)

ἥδιον, adv., more sweetly; more pleasantly; more gladly

ἥδιστα, adv., most sweetly; most pleasantly; most gladly (19β)

ἦθος, ἤθους, τό, character, disposition; moral character (H., p. 113)

ἥκιστα, adv., least

ἥκιστά γε (the opposite of μάλιστά γε), least of all, not at all (16β)

ἥκω, I have come; imperfect, ἧκον, I had come; future, ἥξω, I will have come (5β)

ἥλιος, ἡλίου, ὁ, sun (1β)

ἡμεῖς, ἡμῶν, we (5β and 5 Gr 6)

ἡμέρᾱ, ἡμέρᾱς, ἡ, day (6α)

καθ' ἡμέρᾱν, every day (24α)

ἡμέτερος, -ᾱ, -ον, our (5 Gr 8)

ἡμίονος, ἡμιόνου, ὁ, mule (12α)

ἤπειρος, ἠπείρου, ἡ, *land; mainland* (29α)

ᾗπερ, adv., *where* (23α); *how, just as*

Ἥρᾱ, Ἥρᾱς, ἡ, *Hera* (wife of Zeus and principal deity of Argos) (25β)

Ἡρόδοτος, Ἡροδότου, ὁ, *Herodotus* (24β)

ἠρόμην: *see* ἐρωτάω

ἡσυχάζω, ἡσυχάσω, ἡσύχασα, *I keep quiet; I rest* (13α)

ἡσυχίᾱ, ἡσυχίᾱς, ἡ, *quietness* (28β)

ἥσυχος, -ον, *quiet*

ἧττα, ἥττης, ἡ, *defeat* (29γ)

ἥττων, ἧττον, *inferior; weaker; less* (24 Gr 2)

Ἥφαιστος, Ἡφαίστου, ὁ, *Hephaestus*

## Θ

θάλαττα, θαλάττης, ἡ, *sea* (7α)
κατὰ θάλατταν, *by sea* (11β)

θάνατος, θανάτου, ὁ, *death* (16β)

θάπτω, [θαφ-] θάψω, ἔθαψα, τέθαμμαι, [ταφ-] ἐτάφην, *I bury* (25α)

θαρρέω, *I am confident* (17β)
θάρρει, *Cheer up! Don't be afraid!* (17β)

θάττων, θᾶττον, *quicker, swifter* (24 Gr 4)

θαυμάζω, θαυμάσομαι, ἐθαύμασα, τεθαύμακα, τεθαύμασμαι, ἐθαυμάσθην, intransitive, *I am amazed;* transitive, *I wonder at; I admire* (5β and 21β PP)

θεάομαι, θεάσομαι (note that because of the ε the α lengthens to ᾱ rather than η), ἐθεᾱσάμην, τεθέαμαι, *I see, watch, look at* (8α, 10α, and 18β PP)

θέᾱτρον, θεᾱτρου, τό, *theater*

θέλω = ἐθέλω

Θεμιστοκλῆς, Θεμιστοκλέους, ὁ, *Themistocles* (15α and 15 Gr 2)

θεός, θεοῦ, ἡ, *goddess* (9α)

θεός, θεοῦ, ὁ, *god* (8α)

σὺν θεοῖς, *God willing, with luck* (17α)

θεράπων, θεράποντος, ὁ, *attendant; servant* (25α)

Θερμοπύλαι, Θερμοπυλῶν, αἱ, *Thermopylae* (14α)

θεσπίζω, *I prophesy*

θεωρέω, *I watch; I see* (4α)

θεωρίᾱ, θεωρίᾱς, ἡ, *viewing; sightseeing* (25α)

θηρίον, θηρίου, τό, *beast, wild beast* (26β)

θησαυρός, θησαυροῦ, ὁ, *treasure; treasury* (25α)

Θησεύς, Θησέως, ὁ, *Theseus* (son of King Aegeus) (6α)

θνῄσκω, [θανε-] θανοῦμαι, [θαν-] ἔθανον, [θνη-] τέθνηκα (*I am dead*), *I die*

θνητός, -ή, -όν, *mortal* (H., p. 30)

θόρυβος, θορύβου, ὁ, *uproar, commotion* (15β)

Θριάσιος, -ᾱ, -ον, *Thriasian* (23α)

θυγάτηρ, θυγατρός, ἡ, *daughter* (4α and 8 Gr 2)

θῡμός, θῡμοῦ, ὁ, *spirit* (16β)

θύρᾱ, θύρᾱς, ἡ, *door* (8α)

θυσίᾱ, θυσίᾱς, ἡ, *sacrifice* (18β)

θύω, θύσω, ἔθῡσα, [θυ-] τέθυκα, τέθυμαι, ἐτύθην, *I sacrifice* (21α)

## Ι

ἰᾱτρεύω, ἰᾱτρεύσω, ἰᾱτρευσα, *I heal*

ἰᾱτρός, ἰᾱτροῦ, ὁ, *doctor* (11α)

ἰδίᾳ, adv., *privately* (21β)

ὁ ἰδιώτης, τοῦ ἰδιώτου, *private person* (21β)

ἰδού, adv., *look!* (4α)

ἱερεῖον, ἱερείου, τό, *sacrificial victim* (9β)

ἱερεύς, ἱερέως, ὁ, *priest* (9β)

ἱερόν, ἱεροῦ, τό, *temple* (9α)

ἱερός, -ά, -όν, *holy, sacred* (17β)

ἵημι, imperative, ἵει, infinitive, ἱέναι, participle, ἱείς, imperfect, ἵην, [ἡ-] ἥσω, ἧκα, imperative, [ἑ-] ἕς, infini-

tive, εἶναι, participle, εἴς, εἶκα, εἶμαι,
εἵθην, *I let go, release; I send; I throw;*
middle, ἵεμαι, imperfect, ἱέμην, *I hasten*
(20δ, 20 Gr 2, 21 Gr 4, 25 Gr 5, and 30δ
PP)

ἱκανός, -ή, -όν, *sufficient; capable*
(25β)

ἱκέτης, ἱκέτου, ὁ, *suppliant* (17β)

ἵλεως, acc., ἵλεων, *propitious* (9β)

ἵνα, conj. + subjunctive, *so that, in order
to* (expressing purpose) (21α)

ἱππεύς, ἱππέως, ὁ, *horseman; cavalryman* (28α)

ἱππεύω, ἱππεύσω, ἵππευσα, active or
middle, *I am a horseman; I ride a horse*
(27β)

ἱππικόν, ἱππικοῦ, τό, *cavalry* (27β)

ἵππος, ἵππου, ὁ, *horse* (27β)

ἵππος, ἵππου, ἡ, *cavalry* (27β)

Ἰσθμός, Ἰσθμοῦ, ὁ, *the Isthmus of
Corinth* (22β)

ἵστημι, imperfect, ἵστην, [στη-] στήσω,
ἔστησα, *I make* X *stand; I stop* X; *I am
setting* X *(up)*

    athematic 2nd aorist, ἔστην, intran-
     sitive, *I stood*

    -κα 1st perfect, ἕστηκα, intran-
     sitive, *I stand*

    -θη- 1st aorist passive, [στα-]
     ἐστάθην, *I was set (up)*

    (15 Gr 1, 19α, 19 Gr 2 and 3, 21 Gr 4,
    25 Gr 5, and 30δ PP)

ἱστία, ἱστίων, τά, *sails* (13α)

ἰσχῡρός, -ά, -όν, *strong* (1β)

ἴσως, adv., *perhaps* (17α)

Ἴωνες, Ἰώνων, οἱ, *Ionians*

Ἰωνίᾱ, Ἰωνίᾱς, ἡ, *Ionia*

## K

καθαίρω, [καθαρε-] καθαρῶ,
    [καθηρ-] ἐκάθηρα, [καθαρ-] κεκά-
    θαρμαι, ἐκαθάρθην, *I purify* (26α)

καθαρός, -ά, -όν, *clean, pure* (17β)

κάθαρσις, καθάρσεως, ἡ, *purification*

καθέζομαι [= κατα- + ἕζομαι], [ἑδε-]

καθεδοῦμαι, *I sit down; I encamp*
(23α)

καθέλκω, *I drag down, launch* (a ship)

καθεύδω [= κατα- + εὕδω], imperfect,
καθεῦδον or καθηῦδον, [εὑδε-]
καθευδήσω, no aorist in Attic Greek, *I
sleep* (2α)

κάθημαι [= κατα- + ἧμαι], present and
imperfect only, *I sit* (17α)

καθ' ἡμέρᾱν, *every day* (24α)

καθίζω [= κατα- + ἵζω], [καθιε-] καθ-
ιῶ, [καθι-] ἐκάθισα, active, transitive, *I make* X *sit down; I set; I place;*
active, intransitive, *I sit* (1β); middle, intransitive, *I seat myself, sit down* (8β)

καθίστημι [= κατα- + ἵστημι], when
transitive, *I set* X *up; I appoint* X; *+ εἰς +
acc., I put* X *(acc.) into a certain state* ;
when intransitive, *I am appointed; I am
established; + εἰς + acc., I get / fall into a
certain state; I become* (19β and 19 Gr
4)

καθοράω [= κατα- + ὁράω], [ὀπ-]
κατόψομαι, [ἰδ-] κατεῖδον, *I look
down on* (20γ)

καί, adv., *even; also, too* (4α)

καὶ μήν, *truly, indeed* (30δ)

καί, conj., *and* (1α)

καὶ δὴ καί, *and in particular; and
what is more* (16α)

καί . . . καί, conj., *both . . . and* (5β)

καίπερ + participle, *although* (12α)

καιρός, καιροῦ, ὁ, *time; right time*
(4α)

εἰς καιρόν, *just at the right time*

καίω or κάω, κάεις, κάει, κάομεν, κάετε,
κάουσι(ν), [καυ-] καύσω, ἕκαυσα,
κέκαυκα, κέκαυμαι, ἐκαύθην,
active, transitive, *I kindle, burn;* middle,
intransitive, *I burn, am on fire* (9β)

κακοδαίμων, κακοδαίμονος, *having
an evil spirit, having bad luck* (30β)

οἴμοι κακοδαίμων, *poor devil! oh
misery!* (30β)

κακός, -ή, -όν, *bad; evil* (12α, 14 Gr 2,
and 24 Gr 2)

κακῑ́ων, κάκῑον, *worse* (14 Gr 2 and 24 Gr 2)

κάκιστος, -η, -ον, *worst* (14 Gr 2 and 24 Gr 2)

See 24 Gr 2 for other comparatives and superlatives of κακός.

κακῶς, adv., *badly* (14 Gr 3)

κάκῑον, adv., *worse* (14 Gr 3)

κάκιστα, adv., *worst* (14 Gr 3)

κακά, τά, *evils*

κακόν τι, *something bad*

καλέω, καλῶ, ἐκάλεσα, [κλη-] κέκληκα, κέκλημαι (*I am called*), ἐκλήθην, *I call* (2α and 18α PP)

κάλλος, κάλλους, τό, *beauty* (H., p. 74)

καλός, -ή, -όν, *beautiful* (1α, 3 Gr 2, 4 Gr 3, 4 Gr 6, 14 Gr 2, and 24 Gr 4)

    καλλῑ́ων, κάλλῑον, *more beautiful* (14 Gr 2 and 24 Gr 4)

    κάλλιστος, -η, -ον, *most beautiful* (9α, 14 Gr 2, and 24 Gr 4)

καλῶς, adv., *well* (10α)

    κάλλῑον, adv., *better*

    κάλλιστα, adv., *best*

καλῶς ἔχω, *I am well* (11α)

κάμηλος, καμήλου, ἡ, *camel* (27β)

κάμνω, [καμε-] καμοῦμαι, [καμ-] ἔκαμον, [κμη-] κέκμηκα, *I am sick; I am tired* (9α and 24α PP)

καρδίᾱ, καρδίᾱς, ἡ, *heart* (30α)

καρτερός, -ά, -όν, *strong; fierce* (27α)

κατά, prep. + acc., *down* (5α); distributive, *each, every* (24α); *by* (11β); *on; according to* (17β); of time, *at* (21β); *through* (25α); *along; with regard to* (26α); *after* (28α)

    καθ' ἡμέρᾱν, *every day* (24α)

    κατὰ γῆν, *by land* (14α)

    κατὰ θάλατταν, *by sea* (11β)

    κατὰ μέσον . . . , *in the middle of* . . . (29α)

    κατὰ τάχος, *quickly* (27β)

    κατ' εἰκός, *probably*

καταβαίνω, *I come down; I go down*

καταβάλλω, *I throw down; I drop*

καταγώγιον, καταγωγίου, τό, *inn*

καταδύω, καταδύσω, κατέδῡσα, [δυ-] καταδέδυκα, καταδέδυμαι, κατεδύθην, transitive, *I sink;* athematic 2nd aorist, κατέδῡν, intransitive, *I sank;* of the sun, *set* (29β)

κατακαίω or κατακάω, *I burn completely* (28α)

κατάκειμαι, *I lie down* (16α)

καταλαμβάνω, *I overtake, catch* (16α)

καταλείπω, *I leave behind, desert* (10β)

καταλύω, *I dissolve; I break up; I destroy* (27α)

καταπαύω, *I put an end to* (28α)

καταπῑ́πτω, *I fall down*

κατάρᾱτος, -ον, *cursed*

καταστρέφω, *I overturn;* middle, *I subdue* (25α)

κατατίθημι, *I set down*

καταφεύγω, *I flee for refuge* (29ε)

καταφρονέω + gen., *I despise* (25β)

καταχέω, *I pour X* (acc.) *over Y* (gen.) (30δ)

κατ' εἰκός, *probably*

κατέρχομαι, *I come down*

κατέχω, *I hold back* (29γ)

καττίτερος, καττιτέρου, ὁ, *tin*

κάτω, adv., *down; below* (20γ)

κεῖμαι, κείσομαι, *I lie;* also used in the present and imperfect instead of the perfect and pluperfect passive of τίθημι, with the meanings *I am laid; I am placed* (16α, 16 Gr 2, and 25α PP)

κελεύω, κελεύσω, ἐκέλευσα, κεκέλευκα, κεκέλευσμαι, ἐκελεύσθην + acc. and infin., *I order, tell* (someone to do something) (7α and 17β PP)

κενός, -ή, -όν, *empty* (29δ)

κέρας, κέρως, τό, *wing* (of a fleet or army) (29δ)

κεφαλή, κεφαλῆς, ἡ, *head* (10β)

κῆπος, κήπου, ὁ, *garden*

κῆρυξ, κήρῡκος, ὁ, *herald* (9β)

κιθαρίζω, [κιθαριε-] κιθαριῶ, [κιθαρι-] ἐκιθάρισα, *I play the lyre* (24β) κιθαριστής, κιθαριστοῦ, ὁ, *lyre player* (24α)

Κίμων, Κίμωνος, ὁ, *Cimon*

κινδῡνεύω, κινδῡνεύσω, ἐκινδύνευσα, κεκινδύνευκα, *I run / take a risk*

κίνδῡνος, κινδύνου, ὁ, *danger* (9α)

κῑνέω, *I move* (18α)

Κλέοβις, Κλεόβεως, ὁ, *Cleobis* (25β)

κλέος, κλέους, τό, *fame* (H., p. 30)

κλῆρος, κλήρου, ὁ, *farm*

Κνῆμος, Κνήμου, ὁ, *Cnemus* (29β)

Κνωσός, Κνωσοῦ, ὁ, *Knossos* (6α)

κοινός, -ή, -όν, *common*

κολάζω, κολάσω, ἐκόλασα, κεκόλασμαι, ἐκολάσθην, *I punish*

κόλπος, κόλπου, ὁ, *lap; gulf* (29α)

κομίζω, [κομιε-] κομιῶ, [κομι-] ἐκόμισα, κεκόμικα, κεκόμισμαι, ἐκομίσθην, *I bring; I take* (11α and 21β PP); middle, *I get for myself, acquire*

κόπτω, [κοπ-] κόψω, ἔκοψα, κέκοφα, κέκομμαι, ἐκόπην, *I strike; I knock on* (a door) (11α and 19β PP)

κόρη, κόρης, ἡ, *girl*

Κορίνθιοι, Κορινθίων, οἱ, *Corinthians* (18β)

Κόρινθος, Κορίνθου, ἡ, *Corinth* (14α)

κόσμος, κόσμου, ὁ, *good order* (15β); *world* (H., p. 69)

  κόσμῳ, *in order* (15β)

κρατέω + gen., *I rule, have power over, control; I prevail* (18β)

κράτιστος, -η, -ον, *best; strongest* (24 Gr 2)

κράτος, κράτους, τό, *power* (18β)

κρείττων, κρεῖττον, *better; stronger* (24 Gr 2)

κρήνη, κρήνης, ἡ, *spring* (4α and 4 Gr 3)

Κρήτη, Κρήτης, ἡ, *Crete* (6α)

κρίνω, [κρινε-] κρινῶ, [κρῑν-] ἔκρῑνα, [κρι-] κέκρικα, κέκριμαι, ἐκρίθην, *I judge* (22β PP, 25α, and 27 Gr 9)

Κρῑσαῖος, -ᾱ, -ον, *Crisean* (Crisa was a city in Phocis near Delphi) (29α)

Κροῖσος, Κροίσου, ὁ, *Croesus* (24β)

κρύπτω, [κρυφ-] κρύψω, ἔκρυψα, κέκρυμμαι, ἐκρύφθην, *I hide* (20δ)

κτείνω, usually compounded with ἀπο- in Attic prose, [κτενε-] κτενῶ, [κτειν-] ἔκτεινα, [κτον-] ἔκτονα, *I kill* (27β)

κυβερνέω, *I steer* (H., p. 41)

κυβερνήτης, κυβερνήτου, ὁ, *steersman*

κύκλος, κύκλου, ὁ, *circle* (26β)

Κύκλωψ, Κύκλωπος, ὁ, *Cyclops* (one-eyed monster) (7β)

Κυλλήνη, Κυλλήνης, ἡ, *Cyllene* (29β)

κῦμα, κύματος, τό, *wave* (13β)

κῡμαίνω, [κῡμανε-] κῡμανῶ, [κῡμην-] ἐκύμηνα, *I am rough* (of the sea)

κυνηγέτης, κυνηγέτου, ὁ, *hunter*

Κύπρος, Κύπρου, ἡ, *Cyprus*

Κυρήνη, Κυρήνης, ἡ, *Cyrene*

κύριος, -ᾱ, -ον, *having authority; legitimate; regular* (30α)

Κῦρος, Κύρου, ὁ, *Cyrus* (24β)

κύων, κυνός, ὁ or ἡ, *dog* (5α)

κωμάζω, κωμάσω, ἐκώμασα, *I revel*

κώπη, κώπης, ἡ, *oar* (29ε)


Λ

λαβύρινθος, λαβυρίνθου, ὁ, *labyrinth*

λαγώς, ὁ, acc., τὸν λαγών, *hare* (5α)

Λακεδαιμόνιοι, Λακεδαιμονίων, οἱ, *the Lacedaemonians, Spartans* (14α)

Λακεδαιμόνιος, -ᾱ, -ον, *Lacedaemonian, Spartan*

λαλέω, *I talk; I chatter* (30α)

λαμβάνω, [ληβ-] λήψομαι, [λαβ-] ἔλαβον, [ληβ-] εἴληφα, εἴλημμαι, ἐλήφθην, *I take* (2β); middle + gen., *I seize, take hold of* (11α and 23β PP)

λαμπρός, -ά, -όν, *bright; brilliant* (13α)

  λαμπρῶς, adv., *brightly; brilliantly*

λανθάνω, [ληθ-] λήσω, [λαθ-]
ἔλαθον, [ληθ-] λέληθα + acc. and/or
participle, *I escape someone's notice do-*
*ing something* = I do something without someone's noticing; *I escape the*
*notice of* someone (20δ and 29ε PP)

λέγω, λέξω or [ἐρε-] ἐρῶ, ἔλεξα or
[ἐπ-] εἶπον (irregular augment), [ῥη-]
εἴρηκα, [λεγ-] λέλεγμαι or [ῥη-]
εἴρημαι, [λεγ-] ἐλέχθην or [ῥη-]
ἐρρήθην, *I say; I tell; I speak* (1a, 11β,
and 27β PP)

λείπω, λείψω, [λιπ-] ἔλιπον, [λοιπ-]
λέλοιπα, [λειπ-] λέλειμμαι (*I am*
*left behind; I am inferior*), ἐλείφθην, *I*
*leave* (3β, 11α, 11 Gr 2, 11 Gr 4, 19α PP,
26β PP, and 27 Gr 9)

Λευκάδιος, -ᾱ, -ον, *Leucadian* (29ε)

Λευκάς, Λευκάδος, ἡ, *Leucas* (29β)

λέων, λέοντος, ὁ, *lion* (20γ)

Λεωνίδης, Λεωνίδου, ὁ, *Leonidas*
(14α)

λίθινος, -η, -ον, *of stone, made of*
*stone* (20γ)

λίθος, λίθου, ὁ, *stone* (3α)

λιμήν, λιμένος, ὁ, *harbor* (12α)

λῑμός, λῑμοῦ, ὁ, *hunger*

λίνον, λίνου, τό, *thread*

λογάδες, λογάδων, οἱ, *picked, se-*
*lected men*

λόγος, λόγου, ὁ, *word; story* (11α);
*reason*
     λόγῳ, *in word, ostensibly*

λοιδορέω, *I abuse* (30α)

λούω, λούεις, λούει, λοῦμεν, λοῦτε,
λοῦσι(ν), imperfect, ἔλουν, λούσομαι, ἔλουσα, λέλουμαι, *I wash;*
middle, *I wash myself, bathe* (22α)

Λῡδίᾱ, Λῡδίᾱς, ἡ, *Lydia* (27β)

Λῡδοί, Λῡδῶν, οἱ, *Lydians* (24β)

Λύδιος, -ᾱ, -ον, *Lydian* (27β)

λύκος, λύκου, ὁ, *wolf* (5α)

λῡπέω, *I grieve, vex, cause pain to* X;
passive, *I am grieved, distressed* (16β)

λύω, λύσω, ἔλῡσα, [λυ-] λέλυκα,
λέλυμαι, ἐλύθην, *I loosen, loose* (3β,

4 Gr 1, 6 Gr 3, 9 Gr 1, 10 Gr 1, 12 Gr 1,
12 Gr 2, 13 Gr 1, 17α PP, 17 Gr 1, 21 Gr
2, 25 Gr 4, 27 Gr 4 and 6, and 28 Gr 2
and 6)
     λύομαι, *I ransom* (6 Gr 2c, 6 Gr 3, 8
     Gr 1, 10 Gr 1, 12 Gr 1, 12 Gr 2, 13
     Gr 1, 21 Gr 2, 25 Gr 4, and 27 Gr 4
     and 6)

## M

μὰ Δία, *by Zeus*

μαθηματικά, μαθηματικῶν, τά,
*mathematics*

μαθητής, μαθητοῦ, ὁ, *pupil* (24β)

μακάριος, -ᾱ, -ον, *blessed; happy*
(30δ)

μακρός, -ά, -όν, *long; large* (1α)

μάλα, adv., *very* (4α and 14 Gr 3)
     μᾶλλον, adv., *more; rather* (14 Gr 3
     and 18β)
         μᾶλλον ἤ, *rather than* (14 Gr 3
         and 18β)
     μάλιστα, adv., *most, most of all; very*
     *much; especially* (4β and 14 Gr 3)
         μάλιστά γε, *certainly, indeed*
         (12β)

μανθάνω, [μαθε-] μαθήσομαι, [μαθ-]
ἔμαθον, [μαθε-] μεμάθηκα, *I learn; I*
*understand* (11α and 23β PP)

μαντεῖον, μαντείου, τό, *oracle* (27α)

μάχαιρα, μαχαίρᾱς, ἡ, *knife* (4 Gr 3)

μάχη, μάχης, ἡ, *fight, battle* (13β)

μάχομαι, [μαχε-] μαχοῦμαι,
ἐμαχεσάμην, μεμάχημαι, *I fight;* +
dat., *I fight against* (6β and 28β PP)

Μέγαρα, Μεγάρων, τά, *Megara* (20δ)

μέγας, μεγάλη, μέγα, *big, large; great*
(3α, 4 Gr 6, 14 Gr 2, and 24 Gr 4)
     μείζων, μεῖζον, *bigger, larger;*
     *greater* (14 Gr 2 and 24 Gr 4)
     μέγιστος, -η, -ον, *biggest, largest;*
     *greatest* (7α, 14 Gr 2, and 24 Gr 4)

μέγα, adv., *greatly; loudly* (12β)

μεγάλως, adv., *greatly*

μέγεθος, μεγέθους, τό, *size* (20γ)

μεθίημι [= μετα- + ἵημι], *I set loose; I let go* (26β)

μεθύω, only present and imperfect, *I am drunk*

μείζων, μεῖζον, *bigger, larger; greater* (14 Gr 2 and 24 Gr 4)

μέλᾱς, μέλαινα, μέλαν, *black*

μέλει, [μελε-] μελήσει, ἐμέλησε, μεμέληκε, impersonal + dat., X *is a care to; there is a care to* X (dat.) *for* Y (gen.) (26β)

μελετάω, *I study; I practice* (24α)

μέλιττα, μελίττης, ἡ, *bee* (4 Gr 3)

Μέλιττα, Μελίττης, ἡ, *Melissa* (daughter of Dicaeopolis and Myrrhine) (4α)

μέλλω, [μελλε-] μελλήσω, ἐμέλλησα + present or future infin., *I am about* (to); *I am destined* (to); *I intend* (to) (7β); without infinitive or with present infinitive, *I delay*

μέμνημαι, perfect middle = present, *I have reminded myself; I remember* (28β and 29δ PP)

Μέμφις, Μέμφεως or Μέμφιδος or Μέμφιος, ἡ, *Memphis* (16α)

μέμφομαι, μέμψομαι, ἐμεμψάμην or ἐμέμφθην + dat. or acc., *I blame, find fault with* (27α)

μέν ... δέ ..., postpositive particles, *on the one hand ... and on the other hand ...* or *on the one hand ... but on the other hand ...* (2α)

μέντοι, particle, *certainly; however* (18β)

μένω, [μενε-] μενῶ, [μειν-] ἔμεινα, [μενε-] μεμένηκα, intransitive, *I stay* (in one place); *I wait*; transitive, *I wait for* (3α, 10β, 10 Gr 5, and 22β PP)

μέρος, μέρους, τό, *part* (15β)

μέσος, -η, -ον, *middle (of)* (9β)
  ἐν μέσῳ + gen., *between* (14α)
  κατὰ μέσον ..., *in the middle of ...* (29α)

Μεσσήνιοι, Μεσσηνίων, οἱ, *Messenians* (29δ)

μετά, prep. + gen., *with* (6α); + acc., of time or place, *after* (6α)

μετά, adv., *afterward; later* (25α)

μεταγιγνώσκω, *I change my mind; I repent* (28β)

μεταπέμπομαι, *I send for* (26β)

μέτεστι(ν), impersonal + dat. and infin. as subject, *for* X *there is a share in, a claim to;* X *has the capacity to do* Y (H., p. 21)

μέτρον, μέτρου, τό, *measure* (27α)

μέχρι οὗ, *as long as*

μή, adv., *not;* + imperative, *don't ... !* (2α); + infin., *not* (20δ)
  εἰ μή, *unless*

μηδείς, μηδεμία, μηδέν, used instead of οὐδείς with imperatives and infinitives, *no one, nothing; no* (13β)

Μηδικός, -ή, -όν, *Median* (24β)

Μῆδοι, Μήδων, οἱ, *Medes* (Persians) (24β)

μηκέτι, adv., + imperative, *don't ... any longer!* (3β); + infinitive, *no longer* (15α)

μήν, adv., *truly, indeed* (30δ)

μήν, μηνός, ὁ, *month* (30β)

μηνύω, μηνύσω, ἐμήνῡσα, μεμήνῡκα, μεμήνῡμαι, ἐμηνύθην, *I inform* (30δ)

μήτε, conj., *and not* (29α)
  μήτε ... μήτε, conj., *neither ... nor* (29α)

μήτηρ, μητρός, ἡ, *mother* (4α and 8 Gr 2)

μιαρός, -ά, -όν, *defiled; foul; villainous* (30γ)

μῑκρός, -ά, -όν, *small* (1α)

Μίνως, Μίνω, ὁ, *Minos* (king of Crete) (6α)

Μῑνώταυρος, Μῑνωταύρου, ὁ, *Minotaur* (6α)

μισθός, μισθοῦ, ὁ, *reward; pay* (11β)

μνημεῖον, μνημείου, τό, *monument*

μνησθήσομαι, future passive in middle sense, *I will remember* (28β and 29δ PP) μόλις, adv., *with difficulty; scarcely; reluctantly* (4α)

Μολύκρειον, Μολυκρείου, τό, *Molycreon* (29β)

μόνος, -η, -ον, *alone; only* (15α)
μόνον, adv., *only* (15α)
οὐ μόνον ... ἀλλὰ καί, *not only ... but also* (15α)

μόσχος, μόσχου, ὁ, *calf*

μουσική, μουσικῆς, ἡ, *music* (24α)

μοχλός, μοχλοῦ, ὁ, *stake*

μῦθος, μύθου, ὁ, *story* (5β)

Μυκαλή, Μυκαλῆς, ἡ, *Mycale*

Μυκῆναι, Μυκηνῶν, αἱ, *Mycenae* (20γ)

μύριοι, -αι, -α, *10,000* (15 Gr 5 and 21α)
μῡρίοι -αι, -α, *numberless, countless* (15 Gr 5 and 21α)
μῡριοστός, -ή, -όν, *ten thousandth* (15 Gr 5)

Μυρρίνη, Μυρρίνης, ἡ [= *myrtle*], *Myrrhine* (wife of Dicaeopolis) (4α)

Μῡσοί, Μῡσῶν, οἱ, *Mysians* (26β)

μυχός, μυχοῦ, ὁ, *far corner*

μῶρος, -ᾱ, -ον, *foolish*

## N

ναὶ μὰ Δία, *yes, by Zeus!* (30β)

ναυάγιον, ναυᾱγίου, τό, *wrecked ship* (29ε)

ναύαρχος, ναυάρχου, ὁ, *admiral* (15α)

ναύκληρος, ναυκλήρου, ὁ, *ship's captain* (12β)

ναυμαχέω, *I fight by sea* (15β)

ναυμαχίᾱ, ναυμαχίᾱς, ἡ, *naval battle* (29α)

Ναυπάκτιοι, Ναυπᾱκτίων, οἱ, *inhabitants of Naupactus* (29ε)

Ναύπᾱκτος, Ναυπάκτου, ὁ, *Nuupactus* (29α)

ναῦς, νεώς, ἡ, *ship* (6α and 9 Gr 4)

ναύτης, ναύτου, ὁ, *sailor* (12β)

ναυτικόν, ναυτικοῦ, τό, *fleet* (13β)

νεᾱνίᾱς, νεᾱνίου, ὁ, *young man* (4 Gr 4 and 8β)

Νεῖλος, Νείλου, ὁ, *Nile*

νεκρός, νεκροῦ, ὁ, *corpse* (15β)

νέμεσις, νεμέσεως, ἡ, *retribution* (26α)

νέμω, [νεμε-] νεμῶ, [νειμ-] ἔνειμα, [νεμε-] νενέμηκα, νενέμημαι, ἐνεμήθην, *I distribute*

νέος, -ᾱ, -ον, *young; new* (21α)

νεφέλη, νεφέλης, ἡ, *cloud* (28β)

νῆσος, νήσου, ἡ, *island* (4 Gr 5 and 6α)

νῑκάω, *I defeat; I win* (10α)

νίκη, νίκης, ἡ, *victory* (15β)
Νίκη, Νίκης, ἡ, *Nike* (the goddess of victory) (9α)

νομίζω, [νομιε-] νομιῶ, [νομι-] ἐνόμισα, νενόμικα, νενόμισμαι, ἐνομίσθην, *I think* (21β)

νόμος, νόμου, ὁ, *law; custom* (17β)

νοσέω, *I am sick, ill* (11β)

νόσος, νόσου, ἡ, *sickness, disease; plague*

νοστέω, *I return home* (19α)

νόστος, νόστου, ὁ, *return* (home) (19α)

νοῦς, νοῦ, ὁ, *mind* (15α and 15 Gr 4)
ἐν νῷ ἔχω + infin., *I have in mind; I intend* (4α)

νυκτερεύω, νυκτερεύσω, ἐνυκτέρευσα, *I spend the night*

νύμφη, νύμφης, ἡ, *nymph; bride*

νῦν, adv., *now* (5β)

νύξ, νυκτός, ἡ, *night* (6α)

## Ξ

Ξανθίᾱς, Ξανθίου, ὁ, *Xanthias* (2α and 4 Gr 4)

Ξάνθιππος, Ξανθίππου, ὁ, *Xanthippus* (21β)

ξενίζω, [ξενιε-] ξενιῶ, [ξενι-] ἐξένισα, ἐξενίσθην, *I entertain* (25α)

ξένος, ξένου, ὁ, *foreigner; stranger* (7β)
ξεῖνος = ξένος

Ξενοφάνης, Ξενοφάνους, ὁ, *Zeno-*

*phanes* (early Greek poet and philosopher)

Ξέρξης, Ξέρξου, ὁ, *Xerxes* (14α)

ξίφος, ξίφους, τό, *sword*

## O

ὁ, ἡ, τό, *the* (4 Gr 8)
   ὁ δέ, *and he*

ὀβολός, ὀβολοῦ, ὁ, *obol* (a coin of slight worth) (11β)

ὀγδοήκοντα, indeclinable, *eighty* (15 Gr 5)

ὄγδοος, -η, -ον, *eighth* (8 Gr 5)

ὅδε, ἥδε (note the accent), τόδε, *this here*; pl., *these here* (14β and 14 Gr 5)

ὁδός, ὁδοῦ, ἡ, *road; way; journey* (4β and 4 Gr 5)

ὀδυνάω, ὀδυνηθήσομαι, ὠδυνήθην, *I cause pain;* passive, *I suffer pain* (30α)

ὀδύρομαι, rare in tenses other than present, *I grieve* (22β)

'Οδυσσεύς, 'Οδυσσέως, ὁ, *Odysseus* (7α)

ὄζω, [ὀζε-] ὀζήσω, ὤζησα + gen., *I smell of*

ὅθεν, adv., *from where, whence* (29ε)
   ὅθενπερ: -περ added for emphasis (29ε)

οἶδα, perfect with present meaning, *I know* (17α, 28 Gr 8 and 9, and 29α PP)

οἴκαδε, adv., *homeward, to home* (4β)

οἰκεῖοι, οἰκείων, οἱ, *the members of the household; family; relations* (22β)

οἰκεῖος, -ᾱ, -ον, *of one's own*

οἰκέται, οἰκετῶν, οἱ, *household* (30δ)

οἰκέω, *I live; I dwell* (1α)

οἴκησις, οἰκήσεως, ἡ, *dwelling* (22α)

οἰκίᾱ, οἰκίᾱς, ἡ, *house; home; dwelling* (5α)

οἰκίον, οἰκίου, τό, *house; palace* (often in plural for a single house or palace) (26α)

οἶκος, οἴκου, ὁ, *house; home; dwelling* (1α and 3 Gr 3)
   κατ' οἶκον, *at home* (16α)

οἴκοι (note the accent), adv., *at home* (8α)

οἰκτίρω, [οἰκτιρε-] οἰκτιρῶ, [οἰκτῑρ-] ᾤκτῑρα, *I pity* (20δ)

οἴμοι, note the accent, interjection, *alas!* (11β)
   οἴμοι κακοδαίμων, *poor devil! oh misery!* (30β)

Οἰνόη, Οἰνόης, ἡ, *Oinoe* (23α)

οἰνοπώλιον, οἰνοπωλίου, τό, *wineshop, inn*

οἶνος, οἴνου, ὁ, *wine* (7β)

οἴομαι or οἶμαι, imperfect, ᾠόμην or ᾤμην, [οἰε-] οἰήσομαι, ᾠήθην, *I think* (23β)

οἷός τ' εἰμί, *I am able* (25α)

οἴχομαι, present in perfect sense, *I have gone, have departed;* imperfect in pluperfect sense, *I had gone, had departed* (30β)

ὀκνέω, *I shirk*

ὀκτακόσιοι, -αι, -α, *800* (15 Gr 5)

ὀκτώ, indeclinable, *eight* (8 Gr 5)

ὄλβιος, -ᾱ, -ον, *happy; blessed; prosperous* (24β)

ὄλβος, ὄλβου, ὁ, *happiness, bliss; prosperity* (28β)

ὀλίγος, -η, -ον, *small;* pl., *few* (14α, 14 Gr 2, and 24 Gr 4)
   ἐλάττων, ἔλαττον, *smaller,* pl., *fewer* (14 Gr 2 and 24 Gr 4)
   ὀλίγιστος, -η, -ον, *smallest,* pl., *fewest* (14 Gr 2 and 24 Gr 4)
   ἐλάχιστος, -η, -ον *smallest; least;* pl., *fewest* (24 Gr 4)

ὁλκάς, ὁλκάδος, ἡ, *merchant ship* (29ε)

ὅλος, -η, -ον, *whole, entire* (30β)

'Ολύμπιοι, 'Ολυμπίων, οἱ, *the Olympian gods*

῎Ολυμπος, 'Ολύμπου, ὁ, *Mount Olympus* (a mountain in Mysia) (26β)

ὅμῑλος, ὁμῑλου, ὁ, *crowd* (12α)

ὅμοιος, -ᾱ, -ον + dat., *like* (21β)

ὅμως, conj., *nevertheless* (8α)

ὄνειρος, ὀνείρου, ὁ, *dream* (26α)

ὄνομα, ὀνόματος, τό, *name* (7α and 7
   Gr 3)
   ὀνόματι, dative, *by name, called*
   (7α)
ὀνομάζω, ὀνομάσω, ὠνόμασα,
   ὠνόμακα, ὠνόμασμαι, ὠνο-
   μάσθην, *I name; I call* (26α)
ὄπισθε(ν), adv., *behind* (27β)
ὄπισθε(ν), prep. + gen., *behind* (27β)
   ἐκ τοῦ ὄπισθε(ν), *from the rear*
ὀπίσω, adv., *backward* (27β)
ὅπλα, ὅπλων, τά, *weapons* (29δ)
ὁπλίτης, ὁπλίτου, ὁ, *hoplite* (heavily-
   armed foot soldier) (14α)
ὁπόθεν, indirect interrogative adv.,
   *whence, from where* (26α)
ὁπότε, conj., *when* (23α)
   ὁπόταν [= ὁπότε + ἄν], conj. + subjunctive, *when(ever)* (23α)
ὅπου, adv., *where* (14β and 22 Gr 3)
ὅπως, conj. + subjunctive, *so that, in order to* (22β); + future indicative, *(to see
   to it) that* (24α)
ὁράω, imperfect, ἑώρων (note the double
   augment in this and some of the following forms), [ὀπ-] ὄψομαι, [ἰδ-]
   εἶδον (irregular augment), [ὀρᾱ-]
   ἑόρᾱκα or ἑώρᾱκα, ἑώρᾱμαι or
   [ὀπ-] ὦμμαι, ὤφθην, *I see* (5α, 11β,
   and 29α PP)
ὀργή, ὀργῆς, ἡ, *anger* (20δ)
ὀργίζω, ὤργισα, *I make* X *angry*
   ὀργίζομαι, [ὀργιε-] ὀργιοῦμαι or
   [ὀργισ-] ὀργισθήσομαι, ὤργισμαι, ὠργίσθην, *I grow angry; I
   am angry;* + dat., *I grow angry at; I
   am angry at* (21β PP)
ὀρθός, -ή, -όν, *straight; right, correct*
   (12α)
   ὀρθῶς γιγνώσκω, *I am right* (18β)
ὅρια, ὁρίων, τά, *boundaries*
ὅρκιον, ὁρκίου, τό, *oath;* pl., *treaty*
   (27α)
ὅρκος, ὅρκου, ὁ, *oath*
ὁρμάω, active, transitive, *I set* X *in motion;* active, intransitive, *I start; I rush;*

middle, intransitive, *I set myself in motion; I start; I rush; I hasten* (7β)
ὁρμέω, *I lie at anchor* (29δ)
ὁρμίζω, *I bring* (a ship) *into harbor;*
   middle, *I come to anchor* (29γ)
ὄρνῑς, ὄρνῑθος, ὁ or ἡ, *bird* (30β)
ὄρος, ὄρους, τό, *mountain; hill* (5α)
ὅς, ἥ, ὅ, relative pronoun, *who, whose,
   whom, which, that* (13β and 13 Gr 3)
   ὅσπερ, ἥπερ, ὅπερ, relative pronoun, emphatic forms, *who,
   whose, whom, which, that* (13β)
ὅσιος, -ᾱ, -ον, *holy, pious* (17β)
ὅσος, -η, -ον, *as great as; as much as;*
   pl., *as many as* (22α)
   πάντα ὅσα, *all that, whatever* (22α)
   πάντες ὅσοι, *all that, whoever;*
   (22α)
ὅστις, ἥτις, note the accent, ὅ τι, often
   in indefinite or general clauses with ἄν
   and subjunctive, *anyone who, whoever;
   anything that, whatever;* pl., *all that;
   whoever; whatever* (22α)
ὅταν + subjunctive, *when(ever)* (22 Gr
   2)
ὅτε, adv., *when* (13β)
ὅτι, conj., *that* (5β); *because*
οὐ, οὐκ, οὐχ, οὐχί, adv., *not* (1α)
   οὐ διὰ πολλοῦ, *not much later, soon*
   (17β)
   οὐ μόνον . . . ἀλλὰ καί, *not
   only . . . but also* (15α)
οὐδαμοῦ, adv., *nowhere* (16α)
οὐδαμῶς, adv., *in no way, no* (6β)
οὐδέ, conj., *and . . . not; nor; not even* (5α)
οὐδείς, οὐδεμία, οὐδέν, pronoun, *no
   one; nothing;* adjective, *no* (7α and 8 Gr
   5)
   οὐδέν, adv., *nothing, no*
οὐδέποτε, adv., *never* (22β)
   οὐδεπώποτε, adv., *never yet* (30α)
οὐδέτερος, -ᾱ, -ον, *neither* (27α)
οὐκέτι, adv., *no longer* (3α)
οὔκουν, adv., *certainly not* (18β)
οὖν, a connecting adverb, postpositive, *so*

(i.e., because of this); *then* (i.e., after this) (1α)

οὖπερ, adv., *where* (29γ)

οὐρανός, οὐρανοῦ, ὁ, *sky, heaven* (9β)

οὔτε... οὔτε, note the accent, conj., *neither... nor* (5α)

οὗτος, αὕτη, τοῦτο, *this;* pl., *these* (14α and 14 Gr 5)

οὕτως, adv., before consonants, οὕτω, *so, thus* (2α)

ὀφθαλμός, ὀφθαλμοῦ, ὁ, *eye* (7β)

ὀψέ, adv., *late; too late* (17β)

## Π

πάθος, πάθους, τό, *experience; misfortune* (29γ)

παίδευσις, παιδεύσεως, ἡ, *education* (24α)

παιδεύω, παιδεύσω, ἐπαίδευσα, πεπαίδευκα, πεπαίδευμαι, ἐπαιδεύθην, *I educate* (24α)

παῖς, παιδός, ὁ or ἡ, *boy; girl; son; daughter; child* (3β and 7 Gr 3b)

πάλαι, adv., *long ago* (18β)

πάλαι εἰσί(ν), *they have been for a long time now* (18β)

παλαιός, -ά, -όν, *old; of old* (24β)

πανήγυρις, πανηγύρεως, ἡ, *festival*

Πάνορμος, Πανόρμου, ὁ, *Panormus* (29γ)

πάντα, *everything*

πανταχόσε, adv., *in all directions*

πανταχοῦ, adv., *everywhere* (15β)

πάντες ὅσοι, *all that, whoever;* πάντα ὅσα, *all that, whatever* (22α)

πάνυ, adv., *altogether; very; exceedingly* (27α)

πάππας, πάππου, ὁ, ὦ πάππα, *papa* (6α)

πάππος, πάππου, ὁ, *grandfather* (5α)

παρά + gen., *from* (30β); + dat., *at the house of* (24α); + acc., of persons only, *to* (11α); *along, past* (29δ); *in respect of* (24α)

παραβοηθέω + dat., *I come to X's aid* (29δ)

παραγίγνομαι, *I arrive* (14β)

παραδίδωμι, *I hand over; I give* (18β)

παραινέω [= παρα- + αἰνέω], παραινέσω or παραινέσομαι, παρήνεσα, παρήνεκα, παρήνημαι, παρηνέθην + dat. and infin., *I advise* (someone to do something) (19β)

παρακαλέω, *I summon* (27α)

παρακελεύομαι, *I encourage, exhort* (29γ)

παραπλέω, *I sail by; I sail past; I sail along* (29α)

παρασκευάζω, *I prepare* (7α)

παρασκευή, παρασκευῆς, ἡ, *preparation* (29β)

παρατίθημι, *I put beside, serve*

πάρειμι [παρα- + εἰμί], *I am present; I am here; I am there* (2α); + dat., *I am present at*

παρέρχομαι, *I go past; I pass in, enter; I come forward* (to speak) (20δ)

παρέχω [= παρα- + ἔχω], [σχε-] παρασχήσω, παρέσχον, imperative, παράσχες, [σχε-] παρέσχηκα, παρέσχημαι, *I hand over; I supply; I provide* (6β)

παρθένος, -ον, *virgin, chaste*

παρθένος, παρθένου, ἡ, *maiden, girl* (6α)

Παρθένος, Παρθένου, ἡ, *the Maiden* (= the goddess Athena) (9α)

Παρθενών, Παρθενῶνος, ὁ, *the Parthenon* (the temple of Athena on the Acropolis in Athens) (8β)

παρίσταμαι [= παρα- + ἵσταμαι], παρέστην, παρέστηκα + dat., *I stand near, stand by; I help* (28β)

πᾶς, πᾶσα, πᾶν, *all; every; whole* (7β and 8 Gr 4)

πάντα ὅσα ἄν, *all that, whatever* (22α)

πάντες ὅσοι ἄν, *all that, whoever* (22α)

πάσχω, [πενθ-] πείσομαι, [παθ-]
ἔπαθον, [πονθ-] πέπονθα, *I suffer; I
experience* (5β and 11α)

πατήρ, πατρός, ὁ, *father* (3β and 8 Gr
2)

Πάτραι, Πατρῶν, αἱ, *Patrae* (29α)

πατρίς, πατρίδος, ἡ, *fatherland* (15β)

Παυσανίᾱς, Παυσανίου, ὁ, *Pausanias*

παύω, παύσω, ἔπαυσα, πέπαυκα,
πέπαυμαι, ἐπαύθην, active, transitive, *I stop* X; middle, intransitive +
participle, *I stop doing* X; + gen., *I cease
from* (7β and 17α PP)
    παῦε, *stop!* (7β)

πεδίον, πεδίου, τό, *plain* (19α)

πεζός, -ή, -όν, *on foot* (15β)
    πεζῇ, adv., *on foot* (21β)
    πεζός, πεζοῦ, ὁ, *infantry* (27β)

πείθω, πείσω, ἔπεισα, πέπεικα (*I
have persuaded*) or [ποιθ-] πέποιθα
(+ dat., *I trust*), [πειθ-] πέπεισμαι,
ἐπείσθην, *I persuade;* middle, present,
imperfect, and future + dat., *I obey* (4β,
6α, 21β PP, and 27 Gr 9)

πεῖρα, πείρᾱς, ἡ, *trial; attempt; test*
(23α)

Πειραιεύς, Πειραιῶς, ὁ, τῷ Πειραιεῖ,
τὸν Πειραιᾶ, *the Piraeus* (the port of
Athens) (11β)

πειράω, πειράσω (note that because of
the ρ the α lengthens to ᾱ rather than
η), ἐπείρᾱσα, πεπείρᾱκα, πεπείρᾱμαι, ἐπειράθην, active or middle,
*I try, attempt* (15β and 18β PP)

Πελοποννήσιοι, Πελοποννησίων,
οἱ, *Peloponnesians* (21α)

Πελοπόννησος, Πελοποννήσου, ἡ,
*the Peloponnesus* (14β)

πέμπτος, -η, -ον, *fifth* (8 Gr 5)

πέμπω, πέμψω, ἔπεμψα, [πομπ-]
πέπομφα, [πεμπ-] πέπεμμαι,
ἐπέμφθην, *I send* (6α and 19α PP)

πεντακόσιοι, -αι, -α, *500* (15 Gr 5)

πέντε, indeclinable, *five* (8 Gr 5)

πεντήκοντα, indeclinable, *fifty* (15 Gr
5)

πέπλος, πέπλου, ὁ, *robe; cloth* (15β)

περί, prep. + gen., *about, concerning* (7α);
*around* (18α); + dat., *concerning* (29δ);
+ acc., *around* (7α)
    περὶ οὐδενὸς ποιοῦμαι, *I con-
sider of no importance* (28β)
    περὶ πολλοῦ ποιοῦμαι, *I consider
of great importance* (24α)
    περὶ πλείστου ποιοῦμαι, *I con-
sider of greatest importance* (24α)

περιάγω, *I lead around* (25α)

περιίσταμαι, περιστήσομαι, περι-
έστην, *I stand around*

Περικλῆς, Περικλέους, ὁ, *Pericles*
(21β)

περιμένω, *I wait for* (29ε)

περιοράω, *I overlook, disregard* (23α)

περιπέμπω, *I send around*

περιπλέω, *I sail around*

Πέρσαι, Περσῶν, οἱ, *the Persians*
(14α)

Πέρσης, Πέρσου, ὁ, *Persian* (28α)

Περσικός, -ή, -όν, *Persian* (15β)

πεσεῖν (aorist infin. of πίπτω), *to fall*

πέφῡκα, perfect with present meaning, *I
am by nature* (28 Gr 8)

πίθηκος, πιθήκου, ὁ, *ape; monkey*
(H., p. 74)

πίνω, [πῑ-] πίομαι, [πι-] ἔπιον, [πω-]
πέπωκα, [πο-] πέπομαι, ἐπόθην, *I
drink* (9α)

πίπτω, πεσοῦμαι (irregular), ἔπεσον
(irregular), [πτω-] πέπτωκα, *I fall* (3α
and 26α PP)

πιστεύω, πιστεύσω, ἐπίστευσα,
πεπίστευκα, πεπίστευμαι, ἐπιστεύθην + dat., *I trust, am confident
(in); I believe;* + ὡς or infin., *I believe
(that)* (15β and 17β PP)

Πλάτων, Πλάτωνος, ὁ, *Plato* (24α)

πλεῖστος, -η, -ον, *most; very great;*
pl., *very many* (12β, 14 Gr 2, and 24 Gr
4)
    πλεῖστα, adv., *most* (14 Gr 3)

πλείων/πλέων, alternative forms for either masculine or feminine, πλέον, neuter, *more* (12 β and 24 Gr 4)

πλέον, adv., *more* (14 Gr 3)

πλέω, [πλευ-] πλεύσομαι or [πλευσε-] πλευσοῦμαι, [πλευ-] ἔπλευσα, πέπλευκα, *I sail* (6α, 6 Gr 1, and 18 α PP)

πλῆθος, πλήθους, τό, *number, multitude* (14α); *size*

πλήν, prep. + gen., *except, except for* (29 ε)

πληρόω, *I fill* (21β)

πλοῖον, πλοίου, τό, *boat* (29α)

πλούσιος, -ᾱ, -ον, *rich*

πλοῦτος, πλούτου, ὁ, *wealth* (25β)

πνεῦμα, πνεύματος, τό, *breeze* (29α)

πνέω, [πνευσε-] πνευσοῦμαι or [πνευ-] πνεύσομαι, ἔπνευσα, πέπνευκα, *I blow*

Πνύξ, Πυκνός, ἡ, *the Pnyx* (the hill in Athens on which the Assemblies were held) (21α)

πόθεν; adv., *from where? whence?* (7β, 10 Gr 9, and 14 Gr 6)

ποθέν, enclitic, *from somewhere* (14 Gr 6)

ποθέω, *I long for* (30α)

ποῖ; *to where? whither?* (10 Gr 9, 14 Gr 6, and 17α)

ποι, enclitic, *to somewhere* (14 Gr 6)

ποιέω, *I make; I do* (4α)

περὶ οὐδενὸς ποιοῦμαι, *I consider of no importance* (28β)

περὶ πολλοῦ ποιοῦμαι, *I consider of great importance* (24α)

περὶ πλείστου ποιοῦμαι, *I consider of greatest importance* (24α)

ποίημα, ποιήματος, τό, *poem*

ποιητής, ποιητοῦ, ὁ, *poet* (8α)

ποιμήν, ποιμένος, ὁ, *shepherd* (19β)

ποῖος; ποία; ποῖον; *what kind of?* (26β)

ποιός, -ά, -όν, enclitic, *of some kind*

πολεμέω, *I make war; I go to war* (21α)

πολέμιος, -ᾱ, -ον, *hostile; enemy* (14β)

πολέμιοι, πολεμίων, οἱ, *the enemy* (14β)

πόλεμος, πολέμου, ὁ, *war* (14β)

πολιορκέω [= πόλις, *city* + ἕρκος, *wall*], *I besiege* (16β)

πόλις, πόλεως, ἡ, *city* (7α and 9 Gr 3)

πολίτης, πολίτου, ὁ, *citizen* (8β)

πολλάκις, adv., *many times, often* (6β)

πολλαχόσε, adv., *to many parts* (16α)

πολυμαθίᾱ, πολυμαθίᾱς, ἡ, *much learning* (H., p. 176)

πολύς, πολλή, πολύ, *much* (1α, 4 Gr 6, and 14 Gr 2); pl., *many* (3β)

διὰ πολλοῦ, *after a long time*

περὶ πολλοῦ ποιοῦμαι, *I consider of great importance* (24α)

πλείων/πλέων, alternative forms for either masculine or feminine, πλέον, neuter, *more* (12β, 14 Gr 2, and 24 Gr 4)

πλεῖστος, -η, -ον, *most; very great;* pl., *very many* (12β, 14 Gr 2, and 24 Gr 4)

περὶ πλείστου ποιοῦμαι, *I consider of greatest importance* (24α)

πολύ, adv., *much* (14 Gr 3), *far, by far* (20δ)

πλέον, adv., *more* (14 Gr 3)

πλεῖστα, adv., *most* (14 Gr 3)

πομπή, πομπῆς, ἡ, *procession* (9β)

πονέω, *I work* (1α)

πονηρίᾱ, πονηρίᾱς, ἡ, *fault; wickedness* (24β)

πόνος, πόνου, ὁ, *toil, work* (1α)

Πόντος, Πόντου, ὁ, *Pontus, the Black Sea*

πορεύομαι, πορεύσομαι, ἐπορευσάμην (only in compounds), πεπόρευμαι, ἐπορεύθην (active in meaning), *I go; I walk; I march; I journey* (6β and 17β PP)

πορθέω, *I sack* (28α)

Ποσειδῶν, Ποσειδῶνος, ὁ, *Poseidon* (13 β)

πόσος; πόση; πόσον; *how much?* pl., *how many?* (16 α)

   ποσός, ποσή, ποσόν, enclitic, *of some size*

ποταμός, ποταμοῦ, ὁ, *river* (16 β)

πότε; adv., *when?* (10 Gr 9 and 14 Gr 6)

   ποτέ, enclitic, *at some time, at one time, once, ever* (10 β and 14 Gr 6)

πότερος, -ᾱ, -ον, *which* (of two)?

   πότερον . . . ἤ, *(whether . . .) or* (17 α)

ποῦ; adv., *where?* (5 α and 14 Gr 6)

   που, enclitic, *somewhere, anywhere* (10 Gr 9 and 14 Gr 6); *perhaps, I suppose*

ποῦ γῆς; *where (in the world)?* (16 α)

πούς, ποδός, ὁ, *foot*

πότερον . . . ἤ, conj., *(whether . . .) or* (17 α)

πρᾶγμα, πράγματος, τό, *matter; trouble* (18 β)

   πῶς ἔχει τὰ πράγματα; *How are things?* (18 β)

πρᾶξις, πράξεως, ἡ, *deed* (24 β)

πράττω [πρᾱκ-], πράξω, ἔπρᾱξα, πέπρᾱγα, πέπρᾱγμαι, ἐπρᾱχθην, intransitive, *I fare;* transitive, *I do* (14 α and 20 γ PP)

πρέσβυς, πρέσβεως, ὁ, *old man; ambassador* (21 α)

   οἱ πρέσβεις, τῶν πρέσβεων, *ambassadors* (21 α)

πρίν, conj., + indicative or + ἄν and subjunctive, *until;* + infinitive, *before* (22 α)

πρό, prep. + gen., of time or place, *before* (10 β); *in preference to*

προάγω, *I lead forward* (21 β)

προβαίνω, imperfect, προῦβαινον, προβήσομαι, προῦβην, *I go forward*

πρόβατα, προβάτων, τά, *sheep* (5 α)

πρόγονος, προγόνου, ὁ, *ancestor* (15 β)

προέρχομαι, *I go forward, advance* (20 δ)

προθῡμίᾱ, προθῡμίᾱς, ἡ, *eagerness, spirit*

πρόθῡμος, -ον, *eager* (29 γ)

πρόκειμαι, προκείσομαι + dat., *I lie before* (21 α)

προλέγω, *I proclaim* (28 α)

πρός, prep. + gen., *from* (i.e., *at the hand of*) (26 β); + dat., *at, near, by* (4 α); *in addition to* (24 β); + acc., *to, toward* (1 β); *upon, onto; against* (11 β); *with* (i.e., *in relation to*) (27 α); *in comparison with* (H., p. 74)

προσβαίνω, *I approach*

προσβάλλω + dat., *I attack* (14 α)

προσβολή, προσβολῆς, ἡ, *attack* (23 α)

προσδέχομαι, *I receive, admit; I await, expect* (22 β)

προσδοκάω, *I expect* (30 β)

προσέρχομαι + dat. or πρός + acc., *I approach* (11 β)

πρόσθε(ν), adv., *before* (of time or place) (30 β)

   εἰς τὸ πρόσθε(ν), *forward* (30 β)

προσπίπτω + dat., *I fall against; I fall on* (29 β)

προσπλέω, *I sail toward*

προστάττω, *I command* (27 β)

προστρέχω, *I run toward* (18 β)

προσχωρέω + dat., *I go toward, approach* (3 α)

πρότερος, -ᾱ, -ον, *former*

   προτεραίᾳ, τῇ, *on the day before* (14 β)

   πρότερον, adv., *formerly, before, earlier; first* (17 α)

προχωρέω, *I go forward; I come forward, advance* (6 β); + ἐπί + acc., *I advance against*

πρύμνη, πρύμνης, ἡ, *stern* (of a ship) (29 α)

πρυτάνεις, πρυτάνεων, οἱ, *prytaneis = presidents* (see essay in Chapter 22) (30 α)

πρῷρα, πρῴρᾱς, ἡ, *bow* (of a ship)
(29 α)

Πρωταγόρᾱς, Πρωταγόρου, ὁ, *Protagoras* (24α)

πρῶτος, -η, -ον, *first* (5 β and 8 Gr 5)
πρῶτοι, πρώτων, οἱ, *the leaders*
πρῶτον, adv., *first* (4 α)
τὸ πρῶτον, *at first*

Πτερίᾱ, Πτερίᾱς, ἡ, *Pteria* (27 β)

Πτέριοι, Πτερίων, οἱ, *Pterians* (27α)

Πῡθίᾱ, Πῡθίᾱς, ἡ, *Pythia* (the Delphic priestess of Apollo) (27 α)

Πῡθαγόρᾱς, Πῡθαγόρου, ὁ, *Pythagoras* (early Greek philosopher) (H., p. 176)

πύλη, πύλης, ἡ, *gate*
πύλαι, πυλῶν, αἱ, pl., *double gates* (6 β); *pass* (through the mountains) (14 β)

πυνθάνομαι, [πευθ-] πεύσομαι, [πυθ-] ἐπυθόμην, πέπυσμαι, *I inquire; I learn by inquiry; I hear; I find out about* X (acc.) *from* Y (gen.) (26α)

πῦρ, πυρός, τό, *fire* (7β)

πυρά, πυρᾶς, ἡ, *funeral pyre* (28 α)

πυραμίς, πυραμίδος, ἡ, *pyramid*

πύργος, πύργου, ὁ, *tower* (22β)

πυρκαϊά, πυρκαϊᾶς, ἡ, *conflagration* (H., p. 58)

πώποτε, adv., *ever* (30β)

πῶς; adv., *how?* (7β, 10 Gr 9, and 14 Gr 6)
πῶς ἔχει τὰ πράγματα; *How are things?* (18β)
πῶς ἔχεις; *How are you?* (11α)

πως, enclitic adv., *somehow; in any way* (14 Gr 6 and 17β)

**Ρ**

ῥάβδος, ῥάβδου, ἡ, *wand*

ῥᾴδιος, -ᾱ, -ον, *easy* (4β, 4 Gr 6, and 24 Gr 4)
ῥᾴων, ῥᾷον, *easier* (24 Gr 4)
ῥᾷστος, -η, -ον, *easiest* (24 GR 4)

ῥᾴθῡμος [= ῥᾷ, *easily* + θῡμός, *spirit*], -ον, *careless* (5α)

ῥήγνῡμι, [ῥηγ-] ῥήξω, ἔρρηξα, [ῥωγ-] ἔρρωγα (intransitive, *I have broken out*), [ῥαγ-] ἐρράγην, *I break* (20 Gr 1 and 30δ PP)

ῥῆμα, ῥήματος, τό, *word*

ῥήτωρ, ῥήτορος, ὁ, *speaker; politician* (21α)

Ῥίον, Ῥίου, τό, *Headland* (29β)

ῥυθμός, ῥυθμοῦ, ὁ, *rhythm* (24β)

ῥώμη, ῥώμης, ἡ, *strength* (25β)

**Σ**

Σαλαμίς, Σαλαμῖνος, ἡ, *Salamis* (13α)

Σάμος, Σάμου, ἡ, *Samos*

αἱ Σάρδεις, τῶν Σάρδεων; Ionic, αἱ Σάρδιες, τῶν Σαρδίων, τὰς Σάρδῑς, *Sardis* (25α)

σαφῶς, adv., *clearly* (30β)

σβέννῡμι, [σβε-] σβέσω, ἔσβεσα, ἔσβηκα (intransitive, *I have gone out*), ἐσβέσθην, *I put out, extinguish* (20 Gr 1 and 30δ PP)

σεαυτοῦ: see ἐμαυτοῦ

σεμνός, -ή, -όν, *holy; august* (18α); *worthy of respect; honorable* (H., p. 243)

σημαίνω, [σημανε-] σημανῶ, [σημην-] ἐσήμηνα, [σημαν-] σεσήμασμαι, ἐσημάνθην, *I signal; I sign; I show* (19β)

σημεῖον, σημείου, τό, *sign* (29δ)

σῑγάω, *I am silent* (9β)

σῑγή, σῑγῆς, ἡ, *silence* (28β)

Σικελίᾱ, Σικελίᾱς, ἡ, *Sicily*

Σιμωνίδης, Σιμωνίδου, ὁ, *Simonides* (15β)

σῖτος, σίτου, ὁ, pl., τὰ σῖτα, *grain; food* (1α)

σκοπέω, [σκεπ-] σκέψομαι, ἐσκεψάμην, ἔσκεμμαι, *I look at, examine; I consider* (11α and 18α PP)

σκότος, σκότου, ὁ, *darkness*

Σκυθίᾱ, Σκυθίᾱς, ἡ, *Scythia*

σμῑκρός, -ά, -όν, *small* (24α)

Σόλων, Σόλωνος, ὁ, *Solon* (25α)

σός, -ή, -όν, *your*, sing. (5 Gr 8)

σοφίᾱ, σοφίᾱς, ἡ, *wisdom* (25α)

σοφιστής, σοφιστοῦ, ὁ, *wise man; sophist* (24α)

σοφός, -ή, -όν, *skilled; wise; clever* (11α)

Σπαρτιᾱ́της, Σπαρτιᾱ́του, ὁ, *a Spartan* (14β)

σπείρω, [σπερε-] σπερῶ, [σπειρ-] ἔσπειρα, [σπαρ-] ἔσπαρμαι, ἐσπάρην, *I sow*

σπένδω, [σπει-] σπείσω, ἔσπεισα, ἔσπεισμαι, *I pour a libation;* middle, *I make a treaty; I make peace* (by pouring a libation with the other party) (30γ)

σπέρμα, σπέρματος, τό, *seed*

σπεύδω, σπεύσω, ἔσπευσα, ἔσπευκα, ἔσπευσμαι, *I hurry* (2α and 21α PP)

σπονδή, σπονδῆς, ἡ, *libation* (drink offering) (16β)

   σπονδαί, σπονδῶν, αἱ, *peace treaty* (16β)

      σπονδὰς ποιοῦμαι, *I make a peace treaty*

      σπονδὴν ποιοῦμαι, *I make a libation*

σπουδή, σπουδῆς, ἡ, *haste; eagerness* (15β)

τὸ στάδιον, τοῦ σταδίου, pl., τὰ στάδια or οἱ στάδιοι, *stade* (1 stade = 607 feet or 185 meters; 8.7 stades = 1 mile; 5.4 stades = 1 kilometer) (23β)

στέλλω, [στελε-] στελῶ, [στειλ-] ἔστειλα, [σταλ-] ἔσταλκα, ἔσταλμαι, ἐστάλην, *I send; I equip; I take down* (sails) (29α)

στενάζω, [υτεναγ-] στενάξω, ἐστέναξα, *I groan* (4β)

στενός, -ή, -όν, *narrow* (14α)

   στενά, στενῶν, τά, *narrows, straits; mountain pass* (13β)

στοά, στοᾶς, ἡ, *colonnade*

στόλος, στόλου, ὁ, *expedition; army; fleet* (14α)

στόμα, στόματος, τό, *mouth* (30γ)

στράτευμα, στρατεύματος, τό, *army* (27α)

στρατεύω, στρατεύσω, ἐστράτευσα, ἐστράτευκα, ἐστράτευμαι, active or middle, *I wage war, campaign;* + ἐπί + acc., *I campaign* (against) (16α)

στρατηγός, στρατηγοῦ, ὁ, *general* (15α)

στρατιᾱ́, στρατιᾶς, ἡ, *army* (21β)

στρατιώτης, στρατιώτου, ὁ, *soldier* (14α)

στρατόπεδον, στρατοπέδου, τό, *camp; army* (22β)

στρατός, στρατοῦ, ὁ, *army* (14α)

στρέφω, στρέψω, ἔστρεψα, [στραφ-] ἔστραμμαι, ἐστράφην, *I turn*

στρογγύλος, -η, -ον, *round*

στυγέω, *I hate* (30α)

σύ, σοῦ or σου, *you*, sing. (3β and 5 Gr 6)

συγκαλέω, *I call together*

συλλαμβάνω [= συν- + λαμβάνω], *I help* (2β); + dat., *I help* X (6 Gr 6g)

συλλέγω [= συν- + λέγω, *I pick up, gather; I say, tell, speak*], συλλέξω, συνέλεξα, [λογ-] συνείλοχα, [λεγ-] συνείλεγμαι, συνελέγην, *I collect, gather* (19α)

συμβάλλω [= συν- + βάλλω], *I join battle;* + dat., *I join battle with* (14α)

σύμβουλος, συμβούλου, ὁ, *adviser*

συμμαχίᾱ, συμμαχίᾱς, ἡ, *alliance* (27α)

σύμμαχος, συμμάχου, ὁ, *ally* (16α)

συμπέμπω, *I send with*

συμπίπτω [= συν- + πίπτω], *I clash;* + dat., *I clash with* (15β)

συμπλέω, *I sail with*

συμφορά, συμφορᾶς, ἡ, *misfortune; disaster* (16α)

σύν, prep. + dat., *with* (17α)

   σὺν θεοῖς, *God willing; with luck* (17α)

συναγείρω, active, transitive, *I gather* X;

middle, intransitive, *I gather together*
(16α)

συνάγω, *I bring together; I compress*
(29α)

συνέρχομαι, *I come together* (14α)

συνθήκη, συνθήκης, ἡ, *compact*

συνίημι + gen. of person, acc. of thing, *I understand* (20δ)

σύντομος, -ον, *cut short; short* (H., p. 118)

συντρέχω, *I run together*

σφάζω or σφάττω, [σφαγ-] σφάξω, ἔσφαξα, ἔσφαγμαι, ἐσφάγην, *I slay* (29ε)

Σφίγξ, Σφιγγός, ἡ, *Sphinx*

σφόδρα, adv., *very much* (30δ)

σῴζω, σώσω, ἔσωσα, σέσωκα, σέσωσμαι, ἐσώθην, *I save* (6α)

σῶμα, σώματος, τό, *body* (24β)

σωφρονέω, *I am of sound mind, prudent, moderate, self-controlled* (H., pp. 20 and 21)

σωφροσύνη, σωφροσύνης, ἡ, *soundness of mind, prudence; moderation, self-control* (24β)

σώφρων, σῶφρον, *of sound mind; prudent; self-controlled* (7β, 7 Gr 7, 14 Gr 1, and 24 Gr 1)

**Τ**

τάξις, τάξεως, ἡ, *rank; position* (29α)

ταράττω (ταράσσω), [ταραχ-] ταράξω, ἐτάραξα, τετάραγμαι, ἐταράχθην, *I confuse* (29β)

ταραχή, ταραχῆς, ἡ, *confusion* (29α)

ταύτῃ, adv., *in this way; here* (14 Gr 5)

τάττω, [τακ-] τάξω, ἔταξα, τέταχα, τέταγμαι, ἐτάχθην, *I marshal, draw up in battle array; I station, post* (23α)

τάφρος, τάφρου, ἡ, *ditch*

τάχος, τάχους, τό, *speed*
  κατὰ τάχος, *quickly* (27β)

ταχύς, ταχεῖα, ταχύ, *quick, swift* (13α, 13 Gr 5, and 24 Gr 4)
  θάττων, θᾶττον, *quicker, swifter* (24 Gr 4)

τάχιστος, -η, -ον, *quickest, swiftest* (24 Gr 4)

ταχέως, adv., *quickly, swiftly* (4α)
  θᾶττον, adv., *more quickly, more swiftly*
  τάχιστα, adv., *most quickly, most swiftly* (12α)
  ὡς τάχιστα, *as quickly as possible* (12α)

τε . . . καί or τε καί, the τε is postpositive and enclitic, particle and conjunction, *both . . . and* (3α)

τείχισμα, τειχίσματος, τό, *wall; fort*

τεῖχος, τείχους, τό, *wall* (12α and 13 Gr 4)

τέκνον, τέκνου, τό, *child* (20γ)

τεκών, τεκόντος, ὁ, *parent* (24α)

τελευταῖος, -ᾱ, -ον, *last*

τελευτάω, *I end; I die* (16α)

τελευτή, τελευτῆς, ἡ, *end* (25α)

Τέλλος, Τέλλου, ὁ, *Tellus* (25α)

τέλος, adv., *in the end, finally* (8β)

τέμενος, τεμένους, τό, *sacred precinct* (17β)

τέμνω, [τεμε-] τεμῶ, [τεμ-] ἔτεμον, [τμε-] τέτμηκα, τέτμημαι, ἐτμήθην, *I cut; I ravage* (23α)

τέρπομαι, τέρψομαι, ἐτερψάμην, τερψάμενος, *I enjoy myself;* + dat., *I enjoy* X; + participle, *I enjoy doing* X (9β)

τέταρτος, -η, -ον, *fourth* (8 Gr 5)

τετρακόσιοι, -αι, -α, *400* (15 Gr 5)

τετταράκοντα, indeclinable, *forty* (15 Gr 5)

τέτταρες, τέτταρα, *four* (8 Gr 5)

τῇδε, adv., *in this way; here* (14 Gr 5)

τήμερον, adv., *today* (20δ)

τῇ προτεραίᾳ, *on the day before* (14β)

τῇ ὑστεραίᾳ, *on the next day* (8β)

τί; adv., *why?* (2α and 10 Gr 9)

τί; pronoun, *what?* (4β and 10 Gr 9)

τίθημι [θη-/θε-], imperfect, ἐτίθην, θήσω, ἔθηκα, infinitive, θεῖναι, participle, θείς, imperative, θές, τέθηκα, (τέθειμαι; κεῖμαι usually used instead),

ἐτέθην, *I put, place* (18α, 18 Gr 2, 21
Gr 4, 25 Gr 5, and 30δ PP); *I make*
τῑμάω, *I honor* (5α, 5 Gr 1, 6 Gr 3, 8 Gr 1,
9 Gr 1, 13 Gr 1, 17 Gr 1, 18β PP, 21 Gr 2,
25 Gr 4, 27 Gr 4 and 6, 28 Gr 3 and 6)
τῑμή, τῑμῆς, ἡ, *honor* (21β)
Τῑμοκράτης, Τῑμοκράτου, ὁ, *Timocrates* (29ε)
τίς; τί; gen., τίνος; interrogative adjective, *which . . . ? what . . . ?* (7α and 7 Gr
8)
τίς; τί; gen., τίνος; interrogative pronoun, *who? what?* (7α, 7 Gr 8, and 10
Gr 9)
τις, τι, gen., τινός, enclitic indefinite
adjective, *a certain; some; a, an* (7α and
7 Gr 9)
τις, τι, gen., τινός, enclitic indefinite
pronoun, *someone; something; anyone;
anything* (7α and 7 Gr 9)
    τίνα γνώμην ἔχεις; *What do you
think?* (18β)
τλήμων, τλήμονος, *poor; wretched*
τοιόσδε, τοιάδε, note the accent,
    τοιόνδε, *such* (as the following) (21β)
τοιοῦτος, τοιαύτη, τοιοῦτο, *such*
(21β)
τολμάω, *I dare* (18β)
τοξότης, τοξότου, ὁ, *archer*
τόπος, τόπου, ὁ, *place* (20γ)
τοσόσδε, τοσήδε, note the accent,
    τοσόνδε, *so great;* pl., *so many* (22β)
τοσοῦτος, τοσαύτη, τοσοῦτο, *so
great;* pl., *so great; so many* (3β)
τοὐναντίον = τὸ ἐναντίον (S., p. 242)
τούτῳ, ἐν, *meanwhile* (8β)
τότε, adv., *then* (12β)
τραγῳδίᾱ, τραγῳδίᾱς, ἡ, *tragedy*
τρᾱχύς, -εῖα, -ύ, *rough* (19β)
τρεῖς, τρία, *three* (8 Gr 5)
    τρεῖς καὶ δέκα, *thirteen* (15 Gr 5)
τρέπω, τρέψω, ἔτρεψα, [τροπ-]
τέτροφα, [τραπ-] τέτραμμαι,
ἐτράπην, active, transitive, *I turn* X;
middle, intransitive, *I turn myself, turn*
(10β)

τρέφω, [θρεφ-] θρέψω, ἔθρεψα,
[τροφ-] τέτροφα, [τραφ] τέθραμμαι,
ἐτράφην, *I support; I nourish*
τρέχω, [δραμε-] δραμοῦμαι, [δραμ-]
ἔδραμον, [δραμε-] δεδράμηκα,
δεδράμημαι, *I run; I sail* (5α, 18β, and
27α PP)
τριάκοντα, indeclinable, *thirty* (15 Gr 5)
τριᾱκόσιοι, -αι, -α, *300* (15 Gr 5)
τριήρης, τριήρους, ἡ, *trireme* (a
warship) (13β and 13 Gr 4)
τρίτος, -η, -ον, *third* (8 Gr 5)
Τροίᾱ, Τροίᾱς, ἡ, *Troy* (7α)
τρόπαιον, τροπαίου, τό, *trophy* (29β)
τροπή, τροπῆς, ἡ, *turn; turning; rout*
(of the enemy) (29ε)
τρόπος, τρόπου, ὁ, *manner; way* (21β)
τυγχάνω, [τευχ-] τεύξομαι, [τυχ-]
ἔτυχον, [τυχε-] τετύχηκα + gen., *I
hit; I hit upon; I get;* + participle, *I happen* to be doing X (17α, 20 Gr 3, and 29ε
PP)
τύπτω, [τυπτε-] τυπτήσω, no other
principal parts of this verb in Attic, *I
strike, hit* (19β PP)
τυφλός, -ή, -όν, *blind* (11α)
τύχη, τύχης, ἡ, *chance; luck; fortune*
(15β)
τῷ ὄντι, *in truth* (13β)

**Υ**

ὕβρις, ὕβρεως, ἡ, *wanton violence; in-
solence; arrogance; pride* (H., p. 58)
ὑγιής, -ές, *healthy* (18β)
ὑδρίᾱ, ὑδρίᾱς, ἡ, *water jar* (4α and 4
Gr 3)
ὕδωρ, ὕδατος, τό, *water* (10β)
υἱός, υἱοῦ, ὁ, *son* (24α)
ὑλακτέω, *I bark*
ὕλη, ὕλης, ἡ, *woods, forest* (19β)
ὑμεῖς, ὑμῶν, *you*, pl. (5β and 5 Gr 6)
ὑμέτερος, -ᾱ, -ον, *your*, pl. (5 Gr 8)
ὑμνέω, *I hymn, praise*
ὑπάρχω [= ὑπο- + ἄρχω], *I am; I exist; I
am ready* (22α)
ὑπειλήφᾱσιν (perfect indicative, 3rd

person pl. of ὑπολαμβάνω), *have sup-
posed, suppose* (H. p. 218)

ὑπεκφεύγω [= ὑπο- + ἐκ- + φεύγω], *I escape* (29δ)

ὑπέρ, prep. + gen., *on behalf of, for* (8β);
*over, above;* + acc., *over, above* (18α)

ὑπηρέτης, ὑπηρέτου, ὁ, *servant; attendant* (17β)

ὕπνος, ὕπνου, ὁ, *sleep* (18α)

ὑπό, prep. + gen., *under;* of agent, *by*
(16α); *because of;* + dat., *under* (5β); +
acc., of motion, *under;* of time, *at* (29ε)

ὑποκρούω, *I interrupt*

ὑπομένω, *I await* (an attack); *I stand
firm* (29ε)

ὑποχωρέω, *I retire*

Ὑροιάδης, Ὑροιάδου, ὁ, *Hyroeades* (28α)

ὗς, ὑός, ὁ, *wild boar*

ὑστεραίᾳ, τῇ, *on the next day* (8β)

ὕστερον, adv., *later* (16α)

ὑφαίνω, *I weave*

## Φ

φαγεῖν: aorist infinitive of ἐσθίω

φαίνω, [φανε-] φανῶ or φανοῦμαι,
[φην-] ἔφηνα, [φαν-] πέφασμαι, *I
show* (22α PP and 26α)

   φαίνομαι, [φανε-] φανήσομαι
   (2nd future passive) or [φανε-]
   φανοῦμαι, [φην-] πέφηνα,
   [φαν-] ἐφάνην + infinitive, *I appear; I seem;* + participle, *I am
   shown to be; I am proved to be; I
   am clearly* (12β, 20 Gr 3, 22α PP,
   and 27 Gr 9)

Φάληρον, Φαλήρου, τό, *Phalerum*
(the old harbor of Athens) (14β)

φᾱσί(ν), postpositive enclitic, *they say*
(6β)

Φειδίᾱς, Φειδίου, ὁ, *Pheidias* (the
great Athenian sculptor) (9α)

φείδομαι, φεισόμαι, ἐφεισάμην
+ gen., *I spare* (27β)

φέρω, [οἰ-] οἴσω, [ἐνεγκ-] ἤνεγκα or
ἤνεγκον, [ἐνεκ-] ἐνήνοχα, ἐνή-

νεγμαι, ἠνέχθην, *I carry* (1β); of
roads, *lead* (28α PP)

φεῦ, interjection, often used with gen. of
cause, *alas!* (10α)

φεύγω, φεύξομαι, [φυγ-] ἔφυγον,
[φευγ-] πέφευγα, *I flee; I escape* (5α
and 20γ PP)

φήμη, φήμης, ἡ, *saying; report; voice;
message* (26β)

φημί, postpositive enclitic, imperfect,
ἔφην, φήσω, ἔφησα, *I say* (3α and 23
Gr 4)

φθάνω, [φθη-] φθήσομαι, [φθα-]
ἔφθασα or [φθη-] ἔφθην + acc.
and/or participle, *I anticipate; I do
something* before *someone else* (20 Gr
3, 29ε, and 29ε PP)

φιλέω, *I love* (1α, 4 Gr 1, 6 Gr 3, 8 Gr 1, 9
Gr 1, 13 Gr 1, 17 Gr 1, 18α PP, 21 Gr 2,
25 Gr 4, 27 Gr 4 and 6, 28 Gr 3 and 6)

Φίλιππος, Φιλίππου, ὁ, *Philip* (3β)

φίλος, -η, -ον, *dear* (4α and 24 Gr 4)

   φιλαίτερος, -ᾱ, -ον, *dearer* (18β and
   24 Gr 4)

   φιλαίτατος, -η, -ον or φίλτατος,
   -η, -ον, *dearest* (18β and 24 Gr 4)

   φίλος, φίλου, ὁ or φίλη, φίλης, ἡ,
   *friend* (4α)

φλᾱρέω, *I talk nonsense*

φοβέομαι, imperfect, usually used for
fearing in past time, ἐφοβούμην,
φοβήσομαι, πεφόβημαι, ἐφοβή-
θην, intransitive, *I am frightened, am
afraid;* transitive, *I fear, am afraid of*
(something or someone) (6α)

φοβερός, -ά, -όν, *terrifying, frightening*

φόβος, φόβου, ὁ, *fear; panic* (19β)

φοιτάω, *I go; I visit* (24α)

φονεύς, φονέως, ὁ, *murderer*

φονεύω, φονεύσω, ἐφόνευσα, πεφόνευκα, πεφόνευμαι, ἐφονεύθην, *I slay* (26α)

φόνος, φόνου, ὁ, *murder* (26β)

Φορμίων, Φορμίονος, ὁ, *Phormio*
(29α)

φράζω, φράσω, ἔφρασα, πέφρακα,
πέφρασμαι, ἐφράσθην, *I show; I tell
(of); I explain;* middle and aorist passive in middle sense, *I think about; I
consider* (14β and 21β PP)

φρονέω, *I think; I am minded* (17β)

φροντίζω, [φρομτιε-] φροντιοῦμαι,
[φροντι-] ἐφρόντισα, πεφρόντικα, *I
worry; I care* (12α)

φρουρέω, transitive, *I guard;* intransitive, *I am on guard* (29α)

φρούριον, φρουρίου, τό, *garrison*
(23α)

Φρύγιος, -ᾱ, -ον, *Phrygian*

φυγή, φυγῆς, ἡ, *flight* (15α)

φυλακή, φυλακῆς, ἡ, *guard; garrison*
(22α)

φύλαξ, φύλακος, ὁ, *guard* (7 Gr 3 and
26β)

φυλάττω, [φυλακ-] φυλάξω, ἐφύλαξα, πεφύλαχα, πεφύλαγμαι (*I
am on my guard*), ἐφυλάχθην, *I
guard* (5α and 20δ PP)

φύσις, φύσεως, ἡ, *nature*

φύω, φύσω, ἔφῡσα, ἔφῡν (*I grew*),
πέφῡκα (*I am by nature, am*), *I produce* (28 Gr 8)

φωνέω, *I speak* (27α)

φωνή, φωνῆς, ἡ, *voice; speech* (24β)


**Χ**

χαίρω, [χαιρε-] χαιρήσω, [χαρε-]
κεχάρηκα, [χαρ-] ἐχάρην (*I re-
joiced*), *I rejoice;* + participle, *I am glad
to* (1α, 4α, and 28β PP)

χαῖρε; pl., χαίρετε, *greetings!* (4α)

χαίρειν κελεύω + acc., *I bid X farewell,
I bid farewell to X* (12α)

χαλεπός, -ή, -όν, *difficult* (1β, 14 Gr
1, and 24 Gr 1)

Χαλκίς, Χαλκίδος, ἡ, *Chalcis* (29α)

χαρίζομαι, [χαριε-] χαριοῦμαι,
[χαρι-] ἐχαρισάμην, κεχάρισμαι
+ dat., *I show favor to; I oblige* (26β)

χάρις, χάριτος, ἡ, *thanks; gratitude*
(18α)

χάριν ἀποδίδωμι + dat., *I give
thanks to; I thank* (18α)

χειμών, χειμῶνος, ὁ, *storm; winter*
(7β and 7 Gr 5)

χείρ, χειρός, ἡ, *hand* (8β)

χείριστος, -η, -ον, *worst* (24 Gr 2)

χείρων, χεῖρον, *worse* (24 Gr 2)

χέω, χέω, ἔχεα, [χυ-] κέχυκα,
κέχυμαι, ἐχύθην, *I pour*

χίλιοι, -αι, -α, *1,000* (15 Gr 5)

χῑλιοστός, -ή, -όν, *thousandth* (15
Gr 5)

χορός, χοροῦ, ὁ, *dance; chorus* (4α)

χράομαι (present and imperfect have η
where α would be expected: χρῶμαι,
χρῇ, χρῆται, etc.), χρήσομαι (note
that here the α changes to η even after
the ρ), ἐχρησάμην, κέχρημαι,
ἐχρήσθην + dat., *I use; I enjoy; I consult* (an oracle) (14α and 18β PP)

χρή, impersonal, imperfect, ἐχρῆν +
infin. or acc. and infin., *it is necessary;
ought, must* (17β)

χρήματα, χρημάτων, τά, *things;
goods; money* (18β)

χρήσιμος, -η, -ον, *useful* (24β)

χρησμός, χρησμοῦ, ὁ, *oracular response* (27α)

χρηστήριον, χρηστηρίου, τό (often
pl. with sing. meaning), *oracle* (either
the seat of the oracle or the oracular response) (27α)

χρηστός, -ή, -όν, *useful; good* (24β)

χρόνιος, -ᾱ, -ον, *lengthy* (21β)

χρόνος, χρόνου, ὁ, *time* (1β)

χρῡσίον, χρῡσίου, τό, *gold coin;
money; jewelry* (30β)

χρῡσοῦς, -ῆ, -οῦν, *golden* (30β)

χώρᾱ, χώρᾱς, ἡ, *land* (21β)

χωρέω, *I go; I come* (29β)

χωρίον, χωρίου, τό, *place; district*
(23α)

χῶρος, χώρου, ὁ, *place* (23α)


**Ψ**

ψευδής, -ές, *false* (13β)

ψευδῆ, ψευδῶν, τά, *lies* (13β)

ψεύδομαι, ψεύσομαι, ἐψευσάμην, ἔψευσμαι, *I lie*

ψηφίζομαι, [ψηφιε-] ψηφιοῦμαι, [ψηφι-] ἐψηφισάμην, ἐψήφισμαι, *I vote* (21α)

ψόφος, ψόφου, ὁ, *noise*

ψῡχή, ψῡχῆς, ἡ, *soul* (17β)

Ω

ὦ, interjection, introducing a vocative
ὦ Ζεῦ, *O Zeus* (3α)

ὧδε, adv., *thus*

ᾧ, ἐν, *while* (8α)

ὠθίζομαι, no future or aorist, *I push*

ὦμος, ὤμου, ὁ, *shoulder* (19β)

ὤν, οὖσα, ὄν, participle of εἰμί, *being* (9 Gr 1)

ὤνια, ὠνίων, τά, *wares*

ὡς, adv., in exclamations, *how!* (6β and 15 Gr 6a)

ὡς, adv. + future participle to express purpose, *to* (10 Gr 7 and 15 Gr 6a)

ὡς, adv. + superlative adjective or adverb, e.g., ὡς τάχιστα, *as quickly as possible* (12α, 14 Gr 4d, and 15 Gr 6a)

ὡς, adv., *as* (13β and 15 Gr 6a)
ὡς δοκεῖ, *as it seems* (13β and 15 Gr 6a)

ὡς, conj., temporal, *when* (14β and 15 Gr 6b)

ὡς, conj., *that* (15β and 15 Gr 6b)

ὥσπερ, note the accent, adv., *just as* (8α and 15 Gr 6a)

ὥστε, note the accent, conj. + indicative or infinitive, introducing a clause that expresses result, *so that, that, so as to* (5α and 15 Gr 6b)

ὠφελέω, *I help; I benefit* (11β)

# ENGLISH TO GREEK VOCABULARY

This English to Greek vocabulary is provided merely as a reminder of approximate Greek equivalents of English words. For further information about the Greek words, you must consult the Greek to English vocabulary and the readings and grammar sections in the various chapters of this book.

## A

a (certain), τις
able, I am, δύναμαι, οἷός τ' εἰμί
about, περί
about (to), I am, μέλλω
above, ἄνω, ὑπέρ
abroad, I am/go, ἀποδημέω
abstain from, I, ἀπέχομαι
abuse, I, λοιδορέω
Acarnania, Ἀκαρνᾱνίᾱ
accomplish, I, ἐργάζομαι
according to, κατά
accustomed to, I am, εἴωθα
Achaea, Ἀχαΐᾱ
Achaeans, Ἀχαιοί
Acharnae, Ἀχαρναί
Acharnian, Ἀχαρνικός
Acharnians, Ἀχαρνῆς
Acropolis, Ἀκρόπολις
admiral, ναύαρχος
admire, I, θαυμάζω
admit, I, προσδέχομαι
Adrastus, Ἄδρηστος
advance, I, προέρχομαι
advance (against), I, προχωρέω
advice, βουλή
advise (someone to do something), I, παραινέω
Aegean Sea, Αἰγαῖος πόντος
Aegeus, Αἰγεύς
Aeolus, Αἴολος
Aeschylus, Αἰσχύλος

afraid, don't be, θάρρει
afraid, I am, δέδοικα
afraid (of), I am, φοβέομαι
after, κατά, μετά
after a long time, διὰ πολλοῦ
afterward, μετά
again, αὖ, αὖθις
against, ἀντί, εἰς, ἐπί, πρός
Agamemnon, Ἀγαμέμνων
agora, ἀγορά
aid, βοήθεια
alas! οἴμοι, φεῦ
all, ἅπᾱς, πᾶς
all right! ἔστω
all that, πάντα ὅσα ἄν, πάντες ὅσοι ἄν
alliance, συμμαχίᾱ
allow, I, ἐάω
allowed, being, ἐξόν
allowed, I am, ἔξεστί μοι
allowed, it is, ἔξεστι(ν)
ally, σύμμαχος
alone, μόνος
along, κατά, παρά
already, ἤδη
also, καί
altar, βωμός
although, καίπερ
altogether, πάνυ
always, ἀεί
Alyattes, Ἀλυάττης
am, I, εἰμί, ὑπάρχω
amazed, I am, θαυμάζω
Amasis, Ἄμασις
ambassador, πρέσβυς
among, ἐν

an, τις
ancestor, πρόγονος
and, δέ, καί
and in particular, καὶ δὴ καί
and ... not, μηδέ, μήτε, οὐδέ
and so ... not, οὔκουν
and what is more, καὶ δὴ καί
anger, ὀργή
angry (at), I grow/am, ὀργίζομαι
animal, ζῷον
announce, I, ἀγγέλλω
another, ἄλλος
another, of one, ἀλλήλων
answer, I, ἀποκρίνομαι
anticipate, I, φθάνω
anyone, anything, τις, τι
anyone who, ὅστις ἄν
anything that, ὅ τι ἄν
anywhere, που
Apollo, Ἀπόλλων
appear, I, φαίνομαι
appoint, I, καθίστημι
apprehend, I, αἰσθάνομαι
approach, I, ἐπέρχομαι, προσβαίνω, προσέρχομαι, προσχωρέω
Archidamus, Ἀρχίδᾱμος
Archimedes, Ἀρχιμήδης
Arge (name of a dog), Ἀργή
Argive, Ἀργεῖος

Argus (name of a dog),
  Ἄργος
army, στόλος, στρά-
  τευμα, στρατός,
  στρατιά, στρατόπε-
  δον
around, περί
arrange, I, ἀρτύω
arrive (at), I, ἀφικνέ-
  ομαι, παραγίγνομαι
Artemisium, Ἀρτεμί-
  σιον
as, ὡς
as great as, ὅσος
as it seems, ὡς δοκεῖ, ὡς
  ἔοικε(ν)
as many as, ὅσοι
as much as, ὅσος
as quickly as possible, ὡς
  τάχιστα
Asclepius, Ἀσκληπιός
Asia (Minor), Ἀσία
ask, I, αἰτέω, ἐρωτάω
ask for, I, αἰτέω
ask for X from Y, I, δέ-
  ομαι
assembly, ἐκκλησία
at, εἰς, ἐπί, κατά,
  πρός, ὑπό
at a loss, I am, ἀπορέω
at dawn, ἅμα ἕω, ἐπὶ
  τὴν ἕω
at first, τὸ πρῶτον
at home, κατ' οἶκον,
  οἴκοι
at just the right time, εἰς
  καιρόν
at least, γε
at once, αὐτίκα, εὐθύς
at one time, ποτέ
at school, ἐν διδασκά-
  λων
at some time, ποτέ
at that very moment, ἐν-
  ταῦθα δή
at the house of, παρά
at the same time, ἅμα
Athena, Ἀθηνᾶ, Παρ-
  θένος
Athenian, Ἀθηναῖος

Athenians, Ἀθηναῖοι
Athens, Ἀθῆναι
Athens, at, Ἀθήνησι
Athens, in, ἐν ταῖς
  Ἀθήναις
Athens, to, Ἀθήναζε
attack, προσβολή
attack, I, ἐμπίπτω, ἐπ-
  εξέρχομαι, ἐπ-
  έρχομαι, ἐπιστρα-
  τεύω, ἐπιτίθεμαι,
  ἐπιχειρέω, προσ-
  βάλλω
attempt, πεῖρα
attempt, I, ἐπιχειρέω,
  πειράω, πειράομαι
attendant, θεράπων,
  ὑπηρέτης
at the hand of, πρός
at the same time, ἅμα
Attic, Ἀττικός
Attica, Ἀττική
Atys, Ἄτυς
august, σεμνός
await, I, προσδέχομαι
await (an attack), I, ὑπομένω
away, I am, ἄπειμι

**B**

Babylonians, Βαβυ-
  λώνιοι
backward, ὀπίσω
bad, κακός
badly, κακῶς
bag, ἀσκός
barbarian, βάρβαρος
bark, I, ὑλακτέω
bathe, I, λούομαι
battle, μάχη, ναυμαχία
be so!, let it, ἔστω
beast, θηρίον
beautiful, καλός
beautiful, more, καλλίων
beautiful, most, κάλλι-
  στος
because, διότι, ὅτι
because of, διά, ἕνεκα
become, I, γίγνομαι,
  καθίσταμαι

bee, μέλιττα
before, πρίν, πρό,
  πρόσθεν, πρότερον
begin, I, ἀπάρχομαι,
  ἄρχομαι, ἄρχω
beginning, ἀρχή
behind, ὄπισθε(ν)
believe (that), I, πιστεύω
below, κάτω
benefit, I, ὠφελέω
besiege, I, πολιορκέω
best, ἄριστα, ἄριστος,
  βέλτιστος, κάλ-
  λιστα, κράτιστος
better, ἄμεινον, ἀμεί-
  νων, βελτίων, κάλ-
  λῑον, κρείττων
between, ἐν μέσῳ
bid farewell to X, bid X
  farewell, I, χαίρειν
  κελεύω
big, μέγας
bigger, μείζων
biggest, μέγιστος
bind, I, δέω
bird, ὄρνῑς
bite, I, δάκνω
Biton, Βίτων
black, μέλᾱς
Black Sea, the, Πόντος
blame, αἰτίᾱ
blame, I, μέμφομαι
blame, to (adj.), αἴτιος
blessed, μακάριος, ὄλ-
  βιος
blind, τυφλός
bliss, ὄλβος
blood, αἷμα
blow, I, πνέω
blow from, I, ἐκπνέω
blow out, I, ἐκπνέω
boar, ὗς
board, I, εἰσβαίνω,
  ἐπεισβαίνω, ἐπι-
  βαίνω
boat, πλοῖον
body, σῶμα
Boeotia, Βοιωτία
Boeotians, Βοιωτοί
book, βιβλίον

both... and, καί ...
καί, τε ... καί
both, ἀμφότερος
bow (of a ship), πρῷρα
boy, παῖς
brave, ἀνδρεῖος
bravely, ἀνδρείως
bread, σῖτος
break, I, ῥήγνῡμι
break up, I, καταλύω
breeze, πνεῦμα
bride, νύμφη
bridge, γέφῡρα
bright, λαμπρός
brilliant, λαμπρός
bring, I, διακομίζω,
κομίζω
bring (a ship) into harbor,
I, ὁρμίζω
bring in(to), I, εἰσφέρω,
εἰσκομίζω
bring out, I, ἐκκομίζω
bring over, I, διακομίζω
bring to an end, I, τελευτάω
bring together, I, συνάγω
broad waters, εὐρυ-
χωρίᾱ
brother, ἀδελφός
burn, I, καίω, κάω
burn completely, I, κατα-
καίω, κατακάω
bury, I, θάπτω
but, ἀλλά, δέ
by, κατά, πρός, ὑπό
by far, πολύ
by land, κατὰ γῆν
by nature, I am, πέφῡκα
by night, νυκτός
by sea, κατὰ θάλατταν

C
calf, μόσχος
call, I, καλέω, ὀνομάζω
call for holy silence, εὐφημίᾱ
call for holy silence, I, εὐφημέω
call in(to), I, εἰσκαλέω
call out, I, ἐκκαλέω

call together, I, συγ-
καλέω
call upon, I, ἐπικαλέω
call upon X to help, I,
ἐπικαλέομαι
called, ὀνόματι
camel, κάμηλος
camp, στρατόπεδον
campaign, I, στρατεύο-
μαι
campaign (against), I,
στρατεύω
can, I, δύναμαι, ἔξεστί
μοι
capable, δυνατός, ἱκα-
νός
captain: see ship's captain
care, I, φροντίζω
care to, X is a, μέλει
care to X for Y, there is a,
μέλει
careless, ῥᾴθυμος
carry, I, φέρω
carry out, I, ἐκφέρω, ἐκ-
κομίζω
catch, I, καταλαμβάνω
caught, I am, ἁλίσκομαι
cause, αἰτίᾱ
cause pain, I, ὀδυνάω
cause pain to, I, λῡπέω
cavalry, ἱππικόν, ἵππος
cavalryman, ἱππεύς
cave, ἄντρον
cease from, I, παύομαι
celebrate a festival, I,
ἑορτὴν ποιῶ/ ποι-
οῦμαι
celebrate the festival of
Dionysus, I, τὰ Διο-
νύσια ποιῶ/ποιοῦ-
μαι
certain, a, τις
certainly, μάλιστά γε,
μέντοι
certainly not, οὔκουν
Chalcis, Χαλκίς
chance, τύχη
change my mind, I,
μεταγιγνώσκω
charlatan, ἀλαζών

chase, I, διώκω
chatter, I, λαλέω
cheer up! θάρρει
child, παῖς, τέκνον
choose, I, αἱρέομαι
chorus, χορός
Cimon, Κίμων
circle, κύκλος
citadel, ἀκρόπολις
citizen, πολίτης
city, ἄστυ, πόλις
city center, ἀγορά
clash (with), I, συμπίπτω
clean, καθαρός
clear, δῆλος
clear, it is, δῆλόν ἐστι(ν)
clearly, σαφῶς
clearly, I am, φαίνομαι
Cleobis, Κλέοβις
clever, σοφός
clever at, δεινός
climb, I, ἀναβαίνω
cloth, πέπλος
cloud, νεφέλη
Cnemus, Κνῆμος
collect, I, συλλέγω
colonnade, στοά
come!, ἐλθέ
come, I, ἔρχομαι, χω-
ρέω
come, I have, ἥκω
come after, I, ἐπι-
γίγνομαι
come back, I, ἐπαν-
έρχομαι
come down, I, κατα-
βαίνω, κατέρχομαι
come forward, I, προ-
χωρέω
come forward (to speak),
I, παρέρχομαι
come in(to), I, εἰσβαίνω,
εἰσέρχομαι
come on! ἄγε
come out (of), I, ἐκ-
βαίνω, ἐξέρχομαι
come through, I δι-
έρχομαι
come to aid X, I ,

βοηθέω, παρα-
βοηθέω
come to an end, I, τελευ-
τάω
come to anchor, I, ὁρμί-
ζομαι
come to know, I, γιγνώ-
σκω
come to rescue/aid X, I,
βοηθέω, ἐπιβοηθέω,
παραβοηθέω
come to the rescue, I, βοηθέω
come together, I, συνέρ-
χομαι
come upon, I, ἐπέρχομαι
command, I, προστάττω
commotion, θόρυβος
companion, ἑταῖρος
compel, I, ἀναγκάζω
compress, I, συνάγω
comrade, ἑταῖρος
concerning, περί
confident, I am, θαρρέω
confident (in), I am, πιστεύω
confuse, I, ταράττω
confusion, ταραχή
consider, I, ἡγέομαι,
σκοπέω, φράζομαι
consider of great impor-
tance, I, περὶ πολλοῦ
ποιοῦμαι
consider of greatest im-
portance, I, περὶ πλεί-
στου ποιοῦμαι
consider of no importance,
I, περὶ οὐδενὸς ποι-
οῦμαι
consult (an oracle), I,
χράομαι
contend, I, ἀγωνίζομαι
contest, ἀγών
control, I, κρατέω
converse with, I, δια-
λέγομαι
Corinth, Κόρινθος
Corinthians, Κορίνθιοι
corpse, νεκρός
correct, ὀρθός

Council, βουλή
countless, μῦριοι
country, in the, ἐν τοῖς
ἀγροῖς
country, to the, εἰς τοὺς
ἀγρούς
courage, ἀρετή
cowardice, δειλίᾱ
cowardly, δειλός
Crete, Κρήτη
Crisean, Κρῖσαῖος
Croesus, Κροῖσος
cross, I, διαβαίνω, δια-
βάλλω
crowd, ὅμῑλος
cry, I, δακρύω
cursed, κατάρᾱτος
custom, δίκη, νόμος
cut off, I, ἀπολαμβάνω
cut, I, τέμνω
Cyclopes, the, Κύκλωπες
Cyclops, Κύκλωψ
Cyllene, Κυλλήνη
Cyprus, Κύπρος
Cyrus, Κῦρος
Cyrene, Κυρήνη

**D**

dance, χορός
danger, κίνδῡνος
dare, I, τολμάω
darkness, σκότος
daughter, θυγάτηρ,
παῖς
dawn, ἕως
dawn, at, ἅμα ἔῳ, ἐπὶ
τὴν ἕω
day, ἡμέρᾱ
day before, on the, τῇ
προτεραίᾳ
day, on the next, τῇ
ὑστεραίᾳ
dead, I am: perfect of
ἀποθνῄσκω
dear, φίλος
death, θάνατος
decide, I, δοκεῖ μοι
decided, he, ἔδοξεν
αὐτῷ
dedicate, I, ἀνατίθημι

deed, ἔργον, πρᾶξις
deep, βαθύς
defeat, ἧττα
defeat, I, νῑκάω
defend myself (against X),
I, ἀμύνομαι
defiled, μιαρός
deliberate, I, βουλεύο-
μαι, βουλεύω
delighted, I am, ἥδομαι
Delphi, Δελφοί
deme, δῆμος
democracy, δημοκρατίᾱ
deny, I, οὐ φημί
departed, I have, οἴχομαι
desert, I, καταλείπω
deserted, ἔρημος
despair, ἀθῡμίᾱ
despise, I, καταφρονέω
destined (to), I am, μέλλω
destroy, I, ἀπόλλῡμι,
διαφθείρω, καταλύω
Dicaeopolis,
Δικαιόπολις
die, I, ἀποθνῄσκω, τε-
λευτάω
difference to, it makes a,
διαφέρει
difficult, χαλεπός
difficulty, ἀπορίᾱ
difficulty, with, μόλις
dinner, δεῖπνον
Dionysus, Διόνῡσος
direction of, in the, ἐπί
directions, in all, πανταχόσε
disaster, συμφορά
disband (an army), I,
διαλύω
disembark, I, ἐκβαίνω ἐκ
τῆς νεώς
disorder, ἀταξίᾱ
disorder, in, ἀτάκτως,
οὐδενὶ κόσμῳ
disordered, ἄτακτος
disperse, I, διαλύω
disregard, I, περιοράω
dissolve, I, καταλύω
distant (from), I am, ἀπ-
έχω

distressed, I am, βαρΰ-
νομαι, λῡπέομαι
distribute, I, νέμω
district, χωρίον
do, I, ἐργάζομαι,
ποιέω, πρᾱττω
do (something) before
(someone else), I,
φθάνω
do wrong, I, ἀδικέω
doctor, ῑᾱτρός
Dodona, Δωδώνη
dog, κύων
don't, μή
don't . . . any longer, μηκέτι
don't be afraid! θάρρει
door, θύρᾱ
double gates, πύλαι
doubtless, δήπου
down, κατά, κάτω
drachma, δραχμή
drag, I, ἕλκω
draw up in battle array, I,
τάττω
dream, ὄνειρος
drink, I, πῑνω
drive, I, ἐλαύνω
drive away, I, ἀπελαύνω
drive in, I, εἰσελαύνω
drive out, I, ἐξελαύνω
drop, I, καταβάλλω
drunk, I am, μεθύω
dwell, I, οἰκέω
dwelling, οἴκησις, οἰ-
κίᾱ, οἶκος
Dyme, Δύμη

**E**

each, ἕκαστος, κατά
each (of two), ἑκάτερος
each other, ἀλλήλων
eager, πρόθῡμος
eagerness, προθῡμίᾱ,
σπουδή
earlier, πρότερον
earth, γῆ
easier, ῥᾱων
easist, ῥᾷστος
easily, ῥᾳδίως

easy, ῥᾴδιος
eat, I, δειπνέω, ἐσθίω
educate, I, παιδεύω
education, παίδευσις
Egypt, Αἴγυπτος
Egyptians, Αἰγύπτιοι
eight, ὀκτώ
eight hundred, ὀκτα-
κόσιοι
eighth, ὄγδοος
eighty, ὀγδοήκοντα
either . . . or, εἴτε . . .
εἴτε . . . , ἤ . . . ἤ
Eleusis, Ἐλευσίς
eleven, ἕνδεκα
eleventh, ἑνδέκατος
embark, I, εἰς ναῦν
εἰσβαίνω
empire, ἀρχή
empty, κενός
encamp, I, καθέζομαι,
στρατοπεδεύω
encourage, I, παρα-
κελεύομαι
end, τελευτή
end, I, τελευτάω
end, in the, τέλος
end to, I put an, κατα-
παύω
endure, I, ἀνέχομαι
enemy, ἐχθρός, πολέ-
μιος
enemy, the, ἐναντίοι,
πολέμιοι
enjoy, I, ἥδομαι, χρά-
ομαι
enjoy (myself), I, τέρπο-
μαι
enslave, I, δουλόω
enter, I, παρέρχομαι
entertain, I, ξενίζω
entire, ὅλος
entrance, εἴσοδος
entrust X to Y, I, ἐπι-
τρέπω
Ephialtes, Ἐφιάλτης
Epidaurus, Ἐπίδαυρος
equip, I, ἐξαρτύω,
στέλλω

err, I, ἁμαρτάνω, ἐξ-
αμαρτάνω
escape (from), I, ἀπο-
φεύγω, διαφεύγω,
ἐκφεύγω, ὑπεκ-
φεύγω, φεύγω
escape the notice of, I,
λανθάνω
especially, μάλιστα
Euboea, Εὔβοια
Eurymedon River, the,
Εὐρυμέδων ποταμός
evacuate, I ἀνίσταμαι
evacuation, ἀνάστασις
even, καί
evening, ἑσπέρᾱ
ever, ποτέ, πώποτε
every, ἅπᾱς, πᾶς, κατά
every day, καθ' ἡμέρᾱν
everything, πάντα
everywhere, πανταχοῦ
evil, κακός
examine, I, σκοπέω
exceedingly, πάνυ
excellence, ἀρετή
except, εἰ μή
except (for), πλήν
exhort, I, παρα-
κελεύομαι
exist, I, ὑπάρχω
expect, I, δοκέω, ἐλπί-
ζω, προσδέχομαι,
προσδοκάω
expectation, ἐλπίς
expedition, στόλος
experience, πάθος
experience, I, πάσχω
explain, I, φράζω
extinguish, I, σβέννῡμι
extreme, ἔσχατος
eye, ὀφθαλμός

**F**

fail, I, ἐξαμαρτάνω
fall, I, πῑπτω
fall against, I, προσπῑπτω
fall down, I, καταπῑπτω
fall into, I, ἐμπῑπτω
fall into a certain state, I,
καθίσταμαι

fall (of evening, etc.), γίγνεται

fall out, I, ἐκπίπτω

fall (up)on, I, εἰσπίπτω, ἐμπίπτω, προσπίπτω

false, ψευδής

family, οἰκεῖοι

family, of the, οἰκεῖος

far, πολύ

fare, I, πράττω

farm, κλῆρος

farm, I, γεωργέω

farmer, αὐτουργός

fate, δαίμων

father, πάππας, πατήρ

fatherland, πατρίς

fault, πονηρίᾱ

fear, δέος, φόβος

fear, I, φοβέομαι

festival, ἑορτή, πανήγυρις

festival of Dionysus, Διονύσια

few, pl. of ὀλίγος

fewer, pl. of ἐλάττων

fewest, pl. of ἐλάχιστος, ὀλίγιστος

field, ἀγρός

fierce, ἄγριος, καρτερός

fiercely, ἀγρίως

fifth, πέμπτος

fifty, πεντήκοντα

fight, μάχη

fight (against), I, μάχομαι

fight by sea, I, ναυμαχέω

fill, I, πληρόω

finally, τέλος

find, I, εὑρίσκω

find fault with, I, μέμφομαι

find out, I, ἐξευρίσκω

find out about X from Y, I, πυνθάνομαι

fire, πῦρ

fire, I am on, καίομαι, κάομαι

firm, βέβαιος

first, πρότερον, πρῶτον, πρῶτος

first, at, τὸ πρῶτον

five, πέντε

five hundred, πεντακόσιοι

flee, I, φεύγω

flee (away), I, ἀποφεύγω

flee for refuge, I, καταφεύγω

flee (out), I, ἐκφεύγω

fleet, ναυτικόν, στόλος

flight, φυγή

flow in, I, εἰσρέω

follow, I, ἀκολουθέω, ἕπομαι

food, σῖτος

foolish, ἀνόητος, μῶρος

foot, πούς

foot, on, πεζῇ, πεζός

for, γάρ, εἰς, ἐπί, ὑπέρ

for the sake of, ἕνεκα

force, βίᾱ

forced move, ἀνάστασις

forced to move, I am, ἀνίσταμαι

forces (military), δύναμις

foreigner, ξένος

forest, ὕλη

forget, I, ἐπιλανθάνομαι

former, πρότερος

formerly, πρότερον

fortune, τύχη

forty, τετταράκοντα

forward, εἰς τὸ πρόσθε(ν)

foul, μιαρός

four, τέτταρες

four hundred, τετρακόσιοι

fourth, τέταρτος

free, ἐλεύθερος

free, I, ἐλευθερόω

freedom, ἐλευθερίᾱ

friend, φίλη, φίλος

friendly, ἐπιτήδειος

frightened, I am, φοβέομαι

frightening, φοβερός

frightfully, δεινῶς

from, ἀπό, παρά, πρός

from somewhere, ποθέν

from that place, ἐκεῖθε(ν)

from the rear, ἐκ τοῦ ὄπισθε(ν)

from this place, ἐντεῦθεν

from where, ὅθεν, ὁπόθεν

from where? πόθεν;

fully armed, ἐνόπλιος

funeral pyre, πυρά

Furies, the, Ἐρῑνύες

furthest, ἔσχατος

## G

garden, κῆπος

garrison, φρούριον, φυλακή

gates, double, πύλαι

gather, I, ἀγείρω, συλλέγω, συναγείρω

gather together, I, συναγείρομαι

general, στρατηγός

geometry, γεωμετρίᾱ

get, I, τυγχάνω

get (into a certain state), I, καθίσταμαι

get (myself) up, I, see αἴρω, ἐπαίρω

get under way, I, αἴρω

get up, I, ἀναβαίνω

get up on, I, ἐπιβαίνω

giant, γίγᾱς

gift, δῶρον

girl, κόρη, παῖς, παρθένος

give, I, δίδωμι, παραδίδωμι

give back, I, ἀποδίδωμι

give in, I, ἐνδίδωμι

give (in marriage), I, ἐκδίδωμι

give thanks to, I, χάριν ἀποδίδωμι

glad, ἄσμενος
glad, I am, ἥδομαι
glad to, I am, χαίρω
gladly, ἀσμενῶς, ἡδέως
go! ἴθι
go, I, βαδίζω, βαίνω,
    ἔρχομαι, πορεύο-
    μαι, φοιτάω, χωρέω
go, I will, εἶμι
go, to, ἰέναι
go away, I, ἀπέρχομαι,
    ἀποβαίνω, ἀπο-
    χωρέω
go down, I, καταβαίνω
go forward, I, προ-
    έρχομαι, προβαίνω,
    προχωρέω
go in(to), I, εἰσβαίνω,
    εἰσέρχομαι, ἐπεισ-
    βαίνω
go on! ἴθι δή
go on board ship, I, εἰς
    ναῦν εἰσβαίνω
go out against, I, ἐπεξ-
    έρχομαι
go out (of), I, ἐκβαίνω,
    ἐξέρχομαι
go over, I, ἐπέρχομαι
go past, I, παρέρχομαι
go through, I, διέρχομαι
go to war, I, πολεμέω
go toward, I, προσχωρέω
go up, I, ἀνέρχομαι
go up (onto), I, ἀνα-
    βαίνω
goat, αἴξ
God willing, σὺν θεοῖς
god, δαίμων, θεός
goddess, θεός
going out, ἔξοδος
gold coin, χρῡσίον
golden, χρῡσοῦς
gone, I have, οἴχομαι
good, ἀγαθός, χρηστός
good! εὖ γε
good luck, εὐδαιμονίᾱ
good order, κόσμος
goods χρήματα
Gordias, Γορδίης
grain, σῖτος

grandfather, πάππος
grapes, βότρυες
grapevine, ἄμπελος
gratitude, χάρις
great, μέγας
greater, μείζων
greatest, μέγιστος
greatly, μέγα, μεγάλως
Greece, Ἑλλάς
Greek(s), Ἕλλην(ες)
Greeks, Ἀχαιοί
greetings! χαῖρε
grieve, I, λῡπέω, ὀδύ-
    ρομαι
grieved (by), I am, ἄχθο-
    μαι, λῡπέομαι
groan, I, στενάζω
groan aloud, I, ἀνα-
    στενάζω
ground, γῆ
grow angry (at), I, ὀργί-
    ζομαι
guard, φυλακή, φύλαξ
guard, I, φρουρέω, φυ-
    λάττω
gulf, κόλπος
gymnastics, γυμναστική

**H**
Halys River, Ἅλυς
hand, χείρ
hand over, I, παρα-
    δίδωμι, παρέχω
happen (to be doing X), I,
    τυγχάνω
happens, it, γίγνεται
happiness, εὐδαιμονίᾱ,
    ὄλβος
happy, μακάριος, ὄλ-
    βιος
harbor, λιμήν
hare, λαγώς
harm, I, βλάπτω
harmony, ἁρμονίᾱ
haste, σπουδή
hasten, I, ὁρμάομαι,
    ἵεμαι
hate, I, στυγέω
hateful, ἐχθρός
have, I, ἔχω

have come, I, ἥκω
have departed/gone, I,
    οἴχομαι
have in mind, I, ἐν νῷ
    ἔχω
have power over, I, κρα-
    τέω
having authority, κύριος
he, and, ὁ δέ
head, κεφαλή
headland, ῥίον
heal, I, ἀκέομαι, ἰᾱ-
    τρεύω
healthy, ὑγιής
hear, I, ἀκούω, πυνθά-
    νομαι
heart, καρδίᾱ
heaven, οὐρανός
Hellas, Ἑλλάς
Hellespont, Ἑλλήσπον-
    τος
help, βοήθεια
help, I, παρίσταμαι,
    συλλαμβάνω, ὠφε-
    λέω
her, αὐτήν
Hera, Ἥρᾱ
herald, κῆρυξ
here, δεῦρο, ἐνθάδε,
    ἐνταῦθα, ταύτῃ,
    τῇδε
here, I am, πάρειμι
Herodotus, Ἡρόδοτος
herself, of: see ἐμαυτοῦ
hide, I, κρύπτω
hill, ὄρος
him, αὐτόν
himself, of: see ἐμαυτοῦ
hit, I, βάλλω, τυγχάνω,
    τύπτω
hit (upon), I τυγχάνω
hither, δεῦρο, ἐνθάδε,
    ἐνταῦθα
hold out against, I, ἀντ-
    έχω
hold, I, ἔχω
hold back, I, κατέχω
hold onto, I, ἔχομαι
holy, ἱερός, ὅσιος, σε-
    μνός

home, οἰκίᾱ, οἶκος
home, at, κατ' οἶκον, οἴκοι
home, to, οἴκαδε
homeward, οἴκαδε
honor, I, τῑμάω
honor, τῑμή
hope, ἐλπίς
hope, I, ἐλπίζω
hoplite, ὁπλίτης
horse, ἵππος
horseman, ἱππεύς
horseman, I am a, ἱππεύω
hostile, ἐναντίος, ἐχθρός, πολέμιος
house, οἰκίᾱ, οἶκος, οἰκίον
house, of the, οἰκεῖος
how, ὡς
how? πῶς;
How are things? πῶς ἔχει τὰ πράγματα;
How are you? πῶς ἔχεις;
How are you off for food? πῶς ἔχετε τοῦ σίτου;
how many? pl. of πόσος;
how much? πόσος;
however, μέντοι
human being, ἄνθρωπος
hundred, a, ἑκατόν
hundredth, ἑκατοστός
hunger, λῑμός
hunt(ing), ἄγρᾱ
hurry, I, σπεύδω
hurt, βλάπτω
husband, ἀνήρ
Hyroeades, Ὑροιάδης
hymn, I, ὑμνέω

I

I, ἐγώ; emphatic, ἔγωγε
I am, εἰμί
idle, ἀργός
if, εἰ, ἐάν
if only, εἰ γάρ, εἴθε
if perhaps, εἴ πως
if somehow, εἴ πως
ill, I am, νοσέω
immediately, εὐθύς
immortal, ἀθάνατος

impossible, ἀδύνατος
imposter, ἀλαζών
in, ἐν
in, I am, ἔνειμι
in addition to, πρός
in all directions, παντα- χόσε
in any way, πως
in armor, ἐνόπλιος
in fact, δή, ἔργῳ
in no way, οὐδαμῶς
in order, κόσμῳ
in order to, ἵνα, ὅπως, ὡς
in respect of, παρά
in the end, τέλος
in the middle of, κατὰ μέσον
in this way, ταύτῃ, τῇδε
in time, ἐν καιρῷ
in truth, τῷ ὄντι
in turn, αὖ
incapable, ἀδύνατος
increase, I, αὐξάνω
indeed, γε, δή, καὶ μήν, μάλιστά γε, μήν
infantry, πεζός
inferior, ἥττων
inform, I, μηνύω
inhabit, I, οἰκέω
inhabitant, ἔνοικος
injure, I, ἀδικέω
inn, οἰνοπώλιον
inquire, I, πυνθάνομαι
inside, ἔνδον, ἐντός
instead of, ἀντί
intellect, διάνοια
intend (to), I, ἐν νῷ ἔχω, μέλλω
intention, γνώμη, διά- νοια
intercept, I, ἀπολαμ- βάνω
interpreter, ἑρμηνεύς
into, εἰς
invade, I, εἰσβάλλω
invasion, εἰσβολή
involuntary(-ily), ἄκων
inward, εἴσω

Ionia, Ἰωνίᾱ
Ionians, Ἴωνες
is, he/she/it, ἐστί(ν)
island, νῆσος
Isthmus of Corinth, Ἰσθμός
it, αὐτόν, αὐτήν, αὐτό
it is necessary, δεῖ
itself, of: see ἐμαυτοῦ

J

jar, water, ὑδρίᾱ
jewelry, χρῡσίον
join battle (with), I, συμ- βάλλω
journey, ὁδός
journey, I, πορεύομαι
judge, I, κρίνω
judgment, γνώμη
just, δίκαιος
just as, ὥσπερ
justice, δίκη

K

heep holy silence, I, εὐ- φημέω
keep quiet, I, ἡσυχάζω
kill, I, ἀποκτείνω, κτείνω,
kindle, I, καίω or κάω
kindly, εὐμενής, εὐ- μενῶς
king, βασιλεύς
kingdom, βασιλείᾱ
knife, μάχαιρα
knock on (a door), I, κόπτω
Knossos, Κνωσός
know, I, ἐπίσταμαι, οἶδα
know, I do not, ἀγνοέω
know, come to, I, γιγνώ- σκω
knucklebone, ἀστράγα- λος

L

labyrinth, λαβύρινθος
Lacedaemonians, the, Λακεδαιμόνιοι

lack of spirit, ἀθῡμίᾱ
Laconian, Λάκαινος
land, γῆ, ἤπειρος,
   χώρᾱ
land, on *or* by, κατὰ γῆν
lap, κόλπος
large, μακρός, μέγας
larger, μείζων
largest, μέγιστος
last, τελευταῖος
late, ὀψέ
later, μετά, ὕστερον
later, not much, οὐ διὰ
   πολλοῦ
laugh I, γελάω
law, νόμος
lawsuit, δίκη
lazy, ἀργός
lead, I, ἄγω, ἡγέομαι;
   (of roads) φέρω
lead around, I, περιάγω
lead away, I, ἀπάγω
lead forward, I, προάγω
lead in, I, εἰσάγω, εἰσ-
   ηγέομαι
lead out, I, ἐξάγω
leaders, πρῶτοι
learn, I, αἰσθάνομαι,
   γιγνώσκω, μανθάνω
learn by inquiry, I, πυν-
   θάνομαι
least, ἐλάχιστος, ἥκι-
   στα
least of all, ἥκιστά γε
leave, I, λείπω
leave behind, I, κατα-
   λείπω
left hand, ἀριστερά
legitimate, κύριος
lengthy, χρόνιος
Leonidas, Λεωνίδης
less, ἥττων
let be, I, ἐάω
let go, I, ἀφίημι, ἵημι,
   μεθίημι
let it be so! ἔστω
letter (of the alphabet),
   γράμμα
Leucadian, Λευκάδιος
Leucas, Λευκάς

libation, σπονδή
lie, I, κεῖμαι, ψεύδομαι
lie at anchor, I, ὁρμέω
lie before, I, πρόκειμαι
lie down, I, κατάκειμαι
lie near, I, ἐπίκειμαι
lie off, I, ἐπίκειμαι
lies, ψευδῆ
life, βίος, ζωή
lift, I, αἴρω, ἐπαίρω
light, I, καίω, κάω
like, ὅμοιος
like, I am, ἔοικα
likely to, I am, ἔοικα
lion, λέων
listen (to), I, ἀκούω
live, I, *ζάω, οἰκέω
long, μακρός
long ago, πάλαι
long (of time), πολύς
long time, after a, διὰ
   πολλοῦ
look! ἰδού
look, I, βλέπω
look at, I, θεάομαι, σκο-
   πέω
look away, I, ἀποβλέπω
look down on, I, καθ-
   οράω
look for, I, ζητέω
look up, I, ἀναβλέπω
loose/loosen, I, λύω
lose, I, ἀπόλλῡμι
loss, I am at a, ἀπορέω
loss, state of being at a,
   ἀπορίᾱ
lot, δαίμων
loudly, μέγα
love, I, ἐράω, φιλέω
luck, τύχη
luck, with, σὺν θεοῖς
Lydia, Λῡδίᾱ
Lydian, Λύδιος
Lydians, Λῡδοί
lyre player, κιθαριστής

**M**

made of stone, λίθινος
maiden, παρθένος
Maiden, the, Παρθένος

mainland, ἤπειρος
make, I, ποιέω
make a libation, I, σπον-
   δὴν ποιοῦμαι
make a mistake, I, ἁμαρ-
   τάνω, ἐξαμαρτάνω
make a (peace) treaty, I,
   σπένδομαι, σπονδὰς
   ποιοῦμαι
make peace, I, σπένδο-
   μαι
make ready, I, ἀρτύω
make war, I, πολεμέω,
   πόλεμον ποιοῦμαι
make X angry, I, ὀργίζω
make X sit down, I, καθ-
   ίζω
make X stand up, I, ἀν-
   ίστημι, ἵστημι
makes a difference to, it,
   διαφέρει
man, ἀνήρ, ἄνθρωπος
man, young, νεᾱνίᾱς
manner, τρόπος
many, pl. of πολύς
many times, πολλάκις
march, I, ἐλαύνω, πο-
   ρεύομαι
march against, I, ἐπι-
   στρατεύω
march away, I, ἀπ-
   ελαύνω
march out against, I, ἐπ-
   εξέρχομαι
marching forth, ἔξοδος
market place, ἀγορά
marriage, γάμος
marshal, I, τάττω
master, δεσπότης
mathematics, μαθημα-
   τικά
matter, πρᾶγμα
may, ἔξεστι(ν)
me, με
meal, δεῖπνον
meanwhile, ἐν . . .
   τούτῳ
measure, μέτρον
Medes, Μῆδοι
Median, Μηδικός

meet, I, ἐντυγχάνω
Megara, Μέγαρα
Melissa, Μέλιττα
members of the house-
hold, οἰκεῖοι
Memphis, Μέμφις
merchant, ἔμπορος
merchant ship, ὁλκάς
message, φήμη
messenger, ἄγγελος
Messenians, Μεσσήνιοι
middle (of), μέσος
middle of, in the, κατὰ
μέσον
military expedition, ἔξ-
οδος
mind, νοῦς
mind, have in, I, ἐν νῷ
ἔχω
minded, I am, φρονέω
mine, ἐμός
Minos, Μίνως
Minotaur, Μῑνώταυρος
misfortune, πάθος,
συμφορά
miss, I, ἁμαρτάνω, ἐξ-
αμαρτάνω
mistake, I make a, ἁμαρ-
τάνω
mistaken, I am, ἁμαρ-
τάνω
moderation, σωφροσύνη
Molycreon, Μολύκρειον
money, ἀργύριον,
χρήματα, χρῡσίον
month, μήν
monument, μνημεῖον
more, μᾶλλον, πλεί-
ων/πλέων, πλέον
more, and what is, καὶ
δὴ καί
most, μάλιστα, πλεῖ-
στα, πλεῖστος
most of all, μάλιστα
most swiftly/quickly, τά-
χιστα
mother, μήτηρ
motion, set in, I, ὁρμάω
motionless, ἀκίνητος
mount, I, ἐπιβαίνω

Mount Olympus, Ὄ-
λυμπος
mountain, ὄρος
mountain pass, στενά
mouth, στόμα
move, ἀνάστασις
move, I, ἀνίσταμαι,
κῑνέω
much, πολύ, πολύς
mule, ἡμίονος
multitude, πλῆθος
murder, φόνος
music, μουσική
must, δεῖ, χρή
my, ἐμός
Mycale, Μυκαλή
Mycenae, Μυκῆναι
Myrrhine, Μυρρίνη
Mysians, Μῡσοί
myself, of, ἐμαυτοῦ

**N**

name, ὄνομα
name, by, ὀνόματι
name, I, ὀνομάζω
narrow, στενός
narrows, στενά
nature, φύσις
nature, I am by, πέφῡκα
Naupactus, Ναύπᾱκτος
naval battle, ναυμαχίᾱ
near, ἐγγύς, πρός
nearby, ἐγγύς
nearly, ἐγγύς
necessary, it is, ἀνάγκη
ἐστί(ν), δεῖ, χρή
necessity ἀνάγκη
neither ... nor, μήτε ...
μήτε, οὔτε ... οὔτε
neither, οὐδέτερος
never, οὐδέποτε
never yet, οὐδεπώποτε
nevertheless, ὅμως
new, νέος
next, εἶτα
next day, on the, τῇ
ὑστεραίᾳ
night, νύξ
Nike, Νίκη
Nile, Νεῖλος

nine, ἐννέα
nine hundred, ἐνακόσιοι
ninety, ἐνενήκοντα
ninth, ἔνατος
no, μηδείς, οὐδαμῶς,
οὐδείς, οὐδέν, οὐχί
no longer, μηκέτι, οὐκ-
έτι
no one, μηδείς, οὐδείς
noble, ἄριστος
nor, μηδέ, μήτε, οὐδέ
not, μή, οὐ, οὐκ, οὐχ,
οὐχί
not, and, μηδέ, οὐδέ
not at all, ἥκιστά γε
not even, οὐδέ
not much later, οὐ διὰ
πολλοῦ
not only ... but also, οὐ
μόνον ... ἀλλὰ καί
not working, ἀργός
nothing, μηδέν, οὐδέν
now, ἤδη, νῦν
nowhere, οὐδαμοῦ
number, ἀριθμός, πλῆ-
θος
numberless, μῡρίοι
nymph, νύμφη

**O**

O, ὦ
oar, κώπη
oath, ὅρκιον, ὅρκος
obey, πείθομαι
oblige, I, χαρίζομαι
obol, ὀβολός
obstruct, I, ἐμποδίζω
Odysseus, Ὀδυσσεύς
of one another, ἀλλήλων
of some kind, ποιός
of some size, ποσός
of sound mind, σώφρων
of stone, λίθινος
offering, temple, ἀνά-
θημα
often, πολλάκις
oh, that, εἰ γάρ, εἴθε
oh misery! οἴμοι κακο-
δαίμων
Oinoe, Οἰνόη

old, γεραιός, γέρων
old, (of), παλαιός
old man, γέρων
olive, ἐλάā
olive tree, ἐλάā
on, ἐν, ἐπί, κατά, πρός
on behalf of, ὑπέρ
on fire, I am, καίομαι,
　κάομαι
on foot, πεζῇ, πεζός
on guard, I am, φρουρέω
on the day before, τῇ
　προτεραίᾳ
on the next day, τῇ ὑστε-
　ραίᾳ
on the one hand . . . and on
　the other hand . . .; on
　the one hand . . . but on
　the other hand . . . , μέν
　. . . δέ . . .
once, ποτέ
one, εἷς
one another, of, ἀλλή-
　λων
one or the other (of two),
　ἕτερος
one . . . the other, the, ὁ
　μὲν ἕτερος . . . ὁ δὲ
　ἕτερος
only, μόνον, μόνος
onto, εἰς, ἐπί, πρός
open, I, ἀνοίγνῡμι
opinion, γνώμη
oppose, I, ἀντιόομαι
opposed, ἐναντίος
opposite, ἐναντίος
or, ἤ
oracle, μαντεῖον, χρη-
　στήριον
oracular response,
　χρησμός
order, I, κελεύω
other, ἄλλος
ought, χρή
our, ἡμέτερος
out of, ἐκ, ἐξ
out of the way, ἔκτοπος
outside of, ἐκτός, ἔξω
over, ὑπέρ
overlook, I, περιοράω

overtake, I, κατα-
　λαμβάνω
overturn, I, καταστρέφω
ox, βοῦς

**P**

pain to X, cause, I, λῡπέω
palace, βασίλεια, οἰ-
　κίον
panic, φόβος
Panormus, Πάνορμος
papa, πάππας
parent, τεκών
part, μέρος
part, I, διίσταμαι
Parthenon, Παρθενών
particular, and in, καὶ δὴ
　καί
parts, to many, πολλα-
　χόσε
pass in, I, παρέρχομαι
pass over, I, διαβάλλω
pass (through the moun-
　tains), πύλαι
past, παρά
path, ἀτραπός
patient, I am, ἀνέχομαι
Patrae, Πάτραι
Pausanias, Παυσανίᾱς
pay, ἀποδίδωμι, μισ-
　θός
peace, εἰρήνη
peace treaty, σπονδαί
Peloponnesians, Πελο-
　ποννήσιοι
Peloponnesus, the, Πε-
　λοπόννησος
pelt, I, βάλλω
penalty, δίκη
people, ἔθνος
people, the, δῆμος
perceive, I, αἰσθάνομαι,
　γιγνώσκω
perhaps, ἴσως, πού
Pericles, Περικλῆς
perish, I, ἀπόλλυμαι
perplexity, ἀπορίᾱ
Persian, Περσικός
Persians, the, Πέρσαι
person, ἄνθρωπος

persuade, I, πείθω
Phalerum, Φάληρον
Pheidias, Φειδίᾱς
Philip, Φίλιππος
Phormio, Φορμίων
Phrygian, Φρύγιος
pick up, I, ἀναιρέομαι
pious, ὅσιος
Piraeus, Πειραιεύς
pity, I, οἰκτίρω
place, τόπος, χωρίον,
　χῶρος
place, I, καθίζω, τίθημι
place, to another, ἄλλοσε
place, to this, ἐνθάδε
plague, νόσος
plain, πεδίον
plan, βουλή
plan, I, βουλεύομαι,
　βουλεύω
Plato, Πλάτων
play the lyre, I, κιθαρίζω
pleasant, ἡδύς
pleasantly, ἡδέως
pleasing, it is, ἀρέσκει
plot against, I, ἐπι-
　βουλεύω
plow, I, ἀρόω
plow, ἄροτρον
Pnyx, the, Πνύξ
poet, ποιητής
politician, ῥήτωρ
ponder, I, ἐνθῡμέομαι
Pontus, Πόντος
poor, τλήμων
poor devil! οἴμοι κακο-
　δαίμων
Poseidon, Ποσειδῶν
position, τάξις
possible, δυνατός
possible, it is, ἔξεστι(ν)
post, I, τάττω
pour, I, χέω
pour a libation, I, σπένδω
pour X over Y, I, κατα-
　χέω
power, δύναμις, κρά-
　τος
power controlling one's
　destiny, δαίμων

power over, I have, κρα-
τέω
powerful, δυνατός
practice, I, μελετάω
praise, ἔπαινος
praise, I, ὑμνέω
prayer, εὐχή
pray that, I, εὔχομαι
pray (to), I, εὔχομαι
precinct, sacred, τέμενος
preparation, παρασκευή
prepare, I, παρασκευά-
ζομαι, παρασκευ-
άζω
present (at), I am, πάρ-
ειμι
presidents, πρυτάνεις
prevail, I, κρατέω
priest, ἱερεύς
prison, δεσμωτήριον
private person, ἰδιώτης
privately, ἰδίᾳ
probably, κατ' εἰκός
procession, πομπή
proclaim, I, προλέγω
produce, I, φύω
propitious, ἵλεως
prosperity, εὐδαιμονίᾱ,
ὄλβος
prosperous, ὄλβιος
Protagoras, Πρωταγό-
ρᾱς
prove, I, ἀποφαίνω
proved to be, I am, φαί-
νομαι
provide, I, παρέχω
prudence, σωφροσύνη
prudent, σώφρων
Pteria, Πτερίᾱ
Pterians, Πτέριοι
punish, I, κολάζω
pupil, μαθητής
pure, καθαρός
purify, I, καθαίρω
pursue, I, διώκω, ἐπι-
διώκω
push, I, ὠθίζομαι
put, I, βάλλω, τίθημι
put an end to, I, κατα-
παύω

put in, I, εἰστίθημι
put out, I, σβέννῡμι
put out to sea, I, ἀν-
άγομαι
put X into a certain state, I,
καθίστημι
put X on Y, I, ἐπιτίθημι
pyramid, πυραμίς
Pythia, the, Πῡθίᾱ

**Q**

quack, ἀλάζων
quick, ταχύς
quickly, κατὰ τάχος,
ταχέως
quickly, most, τάχιστα
quiet, ἥσυχος
quiet, keep, I, ἡσυχάζω
quietness, ἡσυχίᾱ

**R**

race, γένος
raise (up), I, αἴρω, ἀν-
ίστημι, ἐπαίρω
rank, τάξις
ransom, I, λῡομαι
rather, μᾶλλον
rather than, μᾶλλον ἤ
ravage, I, τέμνω
read, I, ἀναγιγνώσκω
ready, ἕτοιμος
ready, I am, ὑπάρχω
really, ἀτεχνῶς
rear, from the, ἐκ τοῦ
ὄπισθε(ν)
reason, λόγος
receive, I, δέχομαι
regard to, with, κατά
regular, κύριος
rejoice, I, τέρπομαι,
χαίρω
relate, I, ἐξηγέομαι
relations, οἰκεῖοι
release, I, ἀφίημι, ἵημι
reluctantly, μόλις
remain, I, παραμένω
remain in, I, ἐμμένω
remember, I, μέμνημαι
remind, I, ἀναμιμνήσκω
removal, ἀνάστασις

remove, I, ἐξαιρέω
repent, I, μεταγιγνώσκω
report, φήμη
resist, I, ἀντέχω
responsibility, αἰτίᾱ
responsible (for), αἴτιος
rest, I, ἀναπαύομαι,
ἡσυχάζω
rest (of), ἄλλος
retire, I, ὑποχωρέω
retreat, I, ἀναχωρέω
retribution, νέμεσις
return, I, ἀναχωρέω,
ἀποδίδωμι, ἐπαν-
έρχομαι
return (home), νόστος
return home, I, νοστέω
revel, I, κωμάζω
reveal, ἀποφαίνω
revolt from, I, ἀφ-
ίσταμαι
reward, μισθός
Rhion, Ῥίον
rhythm, ῥυθμός
ride a horse, I, ἱππεύω
right, δεξιός, δίκη,
ὀρθός
right, I am, ὀρθῶς
γιγνώσκω
right hand, δεξιά
right time, καιρός
right time, just at the, εἰς
καιρόν
river, ποταμός
road, ὁδός
robe, πέπλος
rough, τρᾱχύς
rough, I am, κῡμαίνω
round, στρογγύλος
rout, τροπή
row, I, ἐρέσσω
rower, ἐρέτης
ruin, I, ἀπόλλῡμι
rule, ἀρχή
rule, I, ἄρχω, βασι-
λεύω, κρατέω
rule (over), I, βασιλεύω
run, I, τρέχω
run together, I, συντρέχω

run toward, I, προσ-
τρέχω
rush, I, ὁρμάομαι, ὁρ-
μάω

S

sack, I, πορθέω
sacred, ἱερός
sacred precinct, τέμενος
sacrificial victim, ἱερεῖον
sacrifice, θυσίᾱ
sacrifice, I, θῡω
sad, I am, λῡπέομαι
safe, ἀσφαλής
said, he/she, ἔφη
said, I/they, εἶπον
said, they, ἔφασαν
sail, I, πλέω
sail against, I, ἐπιπλέω
sail along, I, παραπλέω
sail around, I, περιπλέω
sail away, I, ἀποπλέω,
ἐκπλέω
sail by, I, παραπλέω
sail in(to), I, εἰσπλέω
sail out, I, ἐκπλέω
sail past, I, παραπλέω
sail toward, I, προσπλέω
sail with, I, συμπλέω
sailor, ναύτης
sails, ἱστία
Salamis, Σαλαμίς
same, αὐτός
same time, at the, ἅμα
Samos, Σάμος
sanctuary of Asclepius,
Ἀσκληπιεῖον
Sardis, Σάρδεις
sausage-seller, ἀλλᾱντο-
πώλης
savage, ἄγριος
savagely, ἀγρίως
save, I, ἀφαιρέομαι,
σῴζω
say, I, ἀγορεύω, λέγω,
φημί
say, they, φᾱσί(ν)
saying, φήμη
says, he/she, φησί(ν)
scarcely, μόλις

schoolmaster, γραμμα-
τιστής
Scythia, Σκυθίᾱ
sea, θάλαττα
sea, by, κατὰ θάλατταν
sea battle, ναυμαχίᾱ
seat myself, I, καθίζομαι
second, δεύτερος
second prize, δευτερεῖα
second time, a, (τὸ) δεύ-
τερον
see, I, βλέπω, θεάομαι,
θεωρέω, ὁράω
seed, σπέρμα
seek, I, ζητέω
seem, I, δοκέω,
φαίνομαι
seems, as it, ὡς δοκεῖ
seems (good), it, δοκεῖ
seems good to me, it,
δοκεῖ μοι
seize, I, λαμβάνομαι
-self, -selves, αὐτός
self-controlled, σώφρων
self-control, σωφροσύνη
sell, I, ἀποδίδομαι
send, I, ἀφῑημι, ῑημι,
πέμπω, στέλλω
send against, I, ἐπιπέμπω
send around, I, περι-
πέμπω
send away, I, ἀποπέμπω,
ἀφῑημι
send for, I, μετα-
πέμπομαι
send in, I, ἐπιπέμπω
send off, I, ἀποστέλλω
send out, I, ἐκπέμπω
send with, I, συμπέμπω
send X through Y, I, δια-
πέμπω
separate, I, διίσταμαι
servant, θεράπων, ὑπη-
ρέτης
set, I, καθίζω
set down, I, κατατίθημι
set free, I, ἐλευθερόω
set loose, I, μεθῑημι
set myself in motion, I,
ὁρμάομαι

set out, I, αἴρω, ὁρμάο-
μαι, ὁρμάω
set up house, I, κατα-
σκευάζομαι
set X down, I, κατα-
τίθημι
set X in motion, I, ὁρμάω
set X up, I, ἀνατίθημι,
ἀνίστημι, ἵστημι,
καθίστημι
seven, ἑπτά
seven hundred, ἑπτα-
κόσιοι
seventh, ἕβδομος
seventy, ἑβδομήκοντα
shameful, αἰσχρός
sheep, πρόβατα
sheepfold, αὔλιον
shepherd, ποιμήν
shield, ἀσπίς
ship, ναῦς
ship, merchant, ὁλκάς
ship's captain, ναύ-
κληρος
shirk, I, ὀκνέω
shoulder, ὦμος
shout, βοή
shout, I, ἀνακράζω,
βοάω
show, I, ἀποφαίνω,
δείκνῡμι, δηλόω,
σημαίνω, φαίνω,
φράζω
show favor to, I,
χαρίζομαι
shown to be, I am, φαί-
νομαι
Sicily, Σικελίᾱ
sick, I am, κάμνω,
νοσέω
sight-seeing, θεωρίᾱ
sign, σημεῖον
sign, I, σημαίνω
signal, I, σημαίνω
silence, σῑγή
silent, I am, σῑγάω
silver, ἀργύριον
Simonides, Σιμωνίδης
simply, ἀτεχνῶς
since, ἐπεί, ἐπειδή

sing, I, ᾄδω
sink, I, καταδύω
sit (down), I, καθ-
  έζομαι, κάθημαι,
  καθίζομαι, καθίζω
sit down, I make X, καθ-
  ίζω
six, ἕξ
six hundred, ἑξακόσιοι
sixth, ἕκτος
sixty, ἑξήκοντα
size, μέγεθος, πλῆθος
skilled, σοφός
skilled (at), δεινός
skilled in or at, ἔμπειρος
sky, οὐρανός
slave, δοῦλος
slay, I, σφάζω, φονεύω
sleep, ὕπνος
sleep, I, καθεύδω
slow, βραδύς
slowly, βραδέως
small, μῑκρός, ὀλίγος,
  σμῑκρός
smaller, ἐλάττων, μῑ-
  κρότερος
smallest, ἐλάχιστος, μῑ-
  κρότατος, ὀλίγιστος
so, οὖν, οὕτω(ς)
so as to, ὥστε
so great, τοσόσδε, το-
  σοῦτος
so many, pl. of τοσόσδε,
  τοσοῦτος
so that, ἵνα, ὅπως, ὥστε
so that . . . not, ἵνα μή
soldier, στρατιώτης
Solon, Σόλων
some, ἔνιοι, τις
some . . . others, ἄλλοι
  . . . ἄλλοι
some to some places . . .
  others to other places,
  ἄλλοι ἄλλοσε
somehow, πως
someone, something, τις,
  τι
sometime, ποτέ
somewhere, που
somewhere, from, ποθέν

somewhere, to, ποι
son, παῖς, υἱός
soon, δι' ὀλίγου, οὐ
  διὰ πολλοῦ
sophist, σοφιστής
sorrowful, I am, λῡπέ-
  ομαι
soul, ψῡχή
soundness of mind, σω-
  φροσύνη
sow, I, σπείρω
spare, I, φείδομαι
Spartan, Σπαρτιάτης
Spartans, the, Λακεδαι-
  μόνιοι
speak, I, ἀγορεύω,
  λέγω, φωνέω
speaker, ῥήτωρ
spear, δόρυ
speech, φωνή
Sphinx, Σφίγξ
spirit, δαίμων, θῡμός,
  προθῡμίᾱ
spoke, I/they, εἶπον
spring, ἔαρ, κρήνη
stade, στάδιον
stake, μοχλός
stand around, I, περι-
  ίσταμαι
stand away from, I, ἀφ-
  ίσταμαι
stand by, I, παρίσταμαι
stand firm, I, ὑπομένω
stand near, I, ἐφίσταμαι,
  παρίσταμαι
stand up! ἀνάστηθι
stand up, I, ἀνίσταμαι
stand up against, I, ἀνθ-
  ίσταμαι
stand X up, I, ἀνίστημι
start, I, ὁρμάομαι, ὁρ-
  μάω
state of being at a loss, the,
  ἀπορίᾱ
station, I, τάττω
statue, εἰκών
stay, I, μένω
steady, βέβαιος
steersman, κυβερνήτης
step, I, βαίνω

step out, I, ἐκβαίνω
stern (of a ship), πρύμνη
still, ἔτι
sting, I, δάκνω
stone, λίθος
stone, of, λίθινος
stop X, I, ἵστημι, παύω
stop (doing X), I, παύο-
  μαι
storm, χειμών
story, λόγος, μῦθος
straight, εὐθύς, ὀρθός
straightway, αὐτίκα,
  εὐθύς
straits, στενά
stranger, ξένος
strength, δύναμις,
  ῥώμη
strike, I, βάλλω, κόπτω,
  τύπτω
strike with a ram, I, ἐμ-
  βάλλω
strong, καρτερός, ἰσχῡ-
  ρός
stronger, κρείττων
strongest, κράτιστος
struggle, ἀγών
study, I, μελετάω
stupid, ἀμαθής
subdue, I, καταστρέ-
  φομαι
such as the following,
  τοιόσδε
such, τοιοῦτος, τοι-
  όσδε
suddenly, ἐξαίφνης
suffer, I, πάσχω
suffer pain, I, ὀδυνῶμαι
sufficient, ἱκανός
suitable for, ἐπιτήδειος
summon, I, παρακαλέω
sun, ἥλιος
suppliant, ἱκέτης
supply, I, παρέχω
suppose, I, δήπου, ἐλπί-
  ζω, που
surely, δήπου
survive, I, παραμένω
sweet, ἡδύς
sweetly, ἡδέως

swift, ταχύς
swiftly, ταχέως
sword, ξίφος

**T**

take, I, ἄγω, αἱρέω, κο-
μίζω, λαμβάνω
take across, I, διακομίζω
take away for myself, I,
ἀφαιρέομαι
take care (for), I, ἐπι-
μελέομαι
take down (sails), I,
στέλλω
take hold of, I, λαμβάνο-
μαι
take in, I, εἰσάγω,
εἰσκομίζω
take out, I, ἐξαιρέω
take to heart, I, ἐνθῡμέ-
ομαι
take to the field, I, στρατεύω
take up, I, ἀναιρέομαι
taken, I am, ἁλίσκομαι
talk, I, λαλέω
talk nonsense, I, φλυᾱρέω
talk to, I, διαλέγομαι
taste, I, γεύομαι
teach, I, διδάσκω
teacher, διδάσκαλος
tell! εἰπέ
tell, I, ἀγγέλλω, λέγω
tell (of), I, φράζω
tell (someone to do some-
thing), I, κελεύω
Tellus, Τέλλος
temple, ἱερόν
temple offering, ἀνάθημα
ten, δέκα
tenth, δέκατος
ten thousand, μύριοι
ten thousandth, μῡρι-
οστός
terrible, δεινός
terrible things, δεινά
terribly, δεινῶς
terrifying, φοβερός
test, πεῖρα
than, ἤ

thank, I, χάριν ἀπο-
δίδωμι
thanks, χάρις
that, ἐκεῖνος, ὅπως, ὅς,
ὅσπερ, ὅτι, ὡς, ὥστε
the, ὁ, ἡ, τό
theater, θέᾱτρον
them, αὐτούς, αὐτάς,
αὐτά
Themistocles, Θεμισ-
τοκλῆς
then, εἶτα, ἐνταῦθα
(δή), ἔπειτα, οὖν,
τότε
thence, ἐκεῖθεν
there, ἐκεῖ, ἐνθάδε,
ἐνταῦθα
there, I am, πάρειμι
there, to, ἐκεῖσε
thereafter, ἔπειτα
Thermopylae, Θερ-
μοπύλαι
Theseus, Θησεύς
things: use neuter plural of
adjective
things, χρήματα
think, I, γιγνώσκω, δο-
κέω, ἡγέομαι, νο-
μίζω, οἴομαι, φρο-
νέω
think?, What do you, τίνα
γνώμην ἔχεις;
think about, I, φράζομαι
think it best, I, δοκεῖ μοι
third, τρίτος
thirteen, τρεῖς καὶ δέκα
thirty, τριάκοντα
this, pl., these, οὗτος
this here, pl., these here,
ὅδε
thither, ἐκεῖσε, ἐνθάδε,
ἐνταῦθα
those, pl., of ἐκεῖνος
thousand, a, χίλιοι
thousandth, χῑλιοστός
thread, λίνον
three, τρεῖς
three hundred, τριᾱ-
κόσιοι
Thriasian, Θριᾱσιος

through, διά, κατά
throw, I, ἀφίημι, ἵημι,
βάλλω
throw a javelin at, I, εἰσηκοντίζω
throw (at), I, ἐφίημι
throw down, I, κατα-
βάλλω
throw out, I, ἐκβάλλω
Thunderer, Βρόμιος
thus, οὕτω(ς)
tie, I, δέω
tilled fields, τὰ ἔργα
time, χρόνος
time, (right), καιρός
Timocrates, Τῑμοκράτης
tin, κασσίτερος
tired, I am, κάμνω
to, εἰς, ἐπί, παρά,
πρός, ὡς
to another place, ἄλλοσε
to Athens, Ἀθήνᾱζε
to blame (adj.), αἴτιος
to home, οἴκαδε
to many parts, πολλα-
χόσε
to other places, ἄλλοσε
to school, εἰς διδασκά-
λων
(to see to it) that, ὅπως
to somewhere, ποι
to that place, ἐκεῖσε
to where? ποῖ;
today, τήμερον
together (with), ἅμα
toil, πόνος
told, I/they, εἶπον
tomorrow, αὔριον
too, καί
too late, ὀψέ
top (of), ἄκρος
toward, ἐπί, πρός
tower, πύργος
township, δῆμος
tragedy, τραγῳδίᾱ
treasure, θησαυρός
treasury, θησαυρός
treaty, ὅρκια
tree, δένδρον
trial, πεῖρα

tribe, ἔθνος
trireme, τριήρης
trophy, τροπαῖον
trouble, πρᾶγμα
Troy, Τροία
true, ἀληθής
truely, ἀληθῶς, καὶ
  μήν, μήν
trust, I, πιστεύω
truth, ἀλήθεια, ἀλη-
  θές, ἀληθῆ
truth, in, τῷ ὄντι
try, I, πειράομαι, πει-
  ράω
turn, I, στρέφω, τρέπω
turn around, I, ἀνα-
  στρέφω, ἐπιστρέφω
turn(ing), τροπή
turn (myself), I, τρέ-
  πομαι
twelfth, δωδέκατος
twelve, δώδεκα
twentieth, εἰκοστός
twenty, εἴκοσι(ν)
twenty-one, εἷς καὶ
  εἴκοσι(ν)
two, δύο
two hundred, διᾱκόσιοι

U

under, ὑπό
understand, I, συνίημι,
  ἐπίσταμαι, μαν-
  θάνω
unjust, ἄδικος
unless, εἰ μή
unmoved, ἀκίνητος
until, ἔως, ἔως ἄν,
  πρίν, πρὶν ἄν
unusual, ἔκτοπος
unwilling(ly), ἄκων
up, ἀνά, ἄνω
upon, ἐπί, πρός
uproar, θόρυβος
us, ἡμῶν, ἡμῖν, ἡμᾶς
use, I, χράομαι
useful, χρήσιμος,
  χρηστός
useless, ἄχρηστος

V

very, μάλα, πάνυ
very big, μέγιστος
very good, ἄριστος
very great, πλεῖστος
very many, pl. of πλεῖ-
  στος
very much, μάλιστα,
  σφόδρα
vex, I, λῦπέω
vexed (at), I am, ἄχθο-
  μαι
victim, sacrificial,
  ἱερεῖον
victory, νίκη
viewing, θεωρίᾱ
villainous, μιαρός
violence, βίᾱ
virtue, ἀρετή
visit, I, φοιτάω
voice, φήμη, φωνή
vote, I, ψηφίζομαι

W

wage war, I, στρατεύ-
  ομαι, στρατεύω
wagon, ἄμαξα
wait (for), I, μένω, περιμένω, ὑπομένω
wake up, I, ἐγείρομαι
wake X up, I, ἐγείρω,
  ἐξεγείρω
walk, I, βαδίζω, βαίνω,
  πορεύομαι
wall, τεῖχος
wand, ῥάβδος
want, I, βούλομαι, δέ-
  ομαι
war, πόλεμος
war, I go to, πολεμέω
war, I make, πολεμέω
ward off, I, ἀμύνω
ward off X from myself, I,
  ἀμύνομαι
wares, ὤνια
wash X, I, λούω
watch, I, θεάομαι, θε-
  ωρέω
water, ὕδωρ
water jar, ὑδρίᾱ

wave, κῦμα
way, ὁδός, τρόπος
way, in any, πως
way, in this, ταύτῃ
we, ἡμεῖς
weaker, ἥττων
wealth, πλοῦτος
weapons, ὅπλα
weep, I, δακρύω
well, εὖ, καλῶς
well, I am, καλῶς ἔχω
well done! εὖ γε
what? τί; τίς;
What do you think? τίνα
  γνώμην ἔχεις;
whatever, ὅ τι ἄν,
  (πάντα) ὅσα ἄν
when, ἐπεί, ἐπειδή,
  ὁπότε, ὅτε, ὡς
when? πότε;
whence, ὅθεν, ὁπόθεν
whence? πόθεν;
whenever, ἐπειδάν,
  ὅταν, ὁπόταν
where, ᾗπερ, ὅπου,
  οὗπερ
where? ποῦ;
where?, from, πόθεν;
where (in the world)? ποῦ
  γῆς;
where to? ποῖ;
whether, εἰ
(whether) . . . or,
  πότερον . . . ἤ
which, ὅς, ὅσπερ
which? τί; τίς;
which (of two)? πότερος
while, ἐν ᾧ, ἔως
whither? ποι;
who? τίς;
who, whose, whom,
  which, that, ὅς, ὅσπερ
whoever, ὅστις ἄν,
  ὅσοι ἄν, πάντες
  ὅσοι ἄν
whole, ἅπᾱς, ὅλος, πᾶς
why? τί;
wickedness, πονηρίᾱ
wife, γυνή
wild, ἄγριος

wildly, ἀγρίως
wild beast, θηρίον
will go, I, εἶμι
willing, I am, ἐθέλω
win, I, νῑκάω
wind, ἄνεμος, πνεῦμα
wine, οἶνος
wine-shop, οἰνοπώλιον
wing, κέρας
winter, χειμών
wisdom, σοφίᾱ, σωφρο-
     σύνη
wise, σοφός
wise man, σοφιστής
wish, I, βούλομαι,
     ἐθέλω
with, μετά, σύν
with difficulty, μόλις
with luck, σὺν θεοῖς
with regard to, κατά
withdraw, I, ἀναχωρέω

within, ἐντός
withstand, I, ἀνθίσταμαι
wolf, λύκος
woman, γυνή
wonder at, I, θαυμάζω
woods, ὕλη
word, λόγος
work, ἔργον, πόνος
work, I, ἐργάζομαι,
     πονέω
worry, I, φροντίζω
worse, κάκῑον, κακίων,
     χείρων
worst, κάκιστα, κάκι-
     στος, χείριστος
worthy (of), ἄξιος
wrecked ship, ναυάγιον
wretched, τλήμων
write, I, γράφω
writing, γράμματα
wrong X, I, ἀδικέω

**X**

Xanthias, Ξανθίᾱς
Xanthippus, Ξανθίππος
Xerxes, Ξέρξης

**Y**

year, ἔτος
yield, I, εἴκω, ἐνδίδωμι
yoke, I, ζεύγνῡμι
you, pl., ὑμεῖς
you, sing., σύ
young man, νεᾱνίᾱς
young, νέος
your, pl., ὑμέτερος
your, sing., σός,
yourself, of, σεαυτοῦ

**Z**

Zeus, Ζεύς
Zeus, by, μὰ Δία
Zeus, O, ὦ Ζεῦ
Zeus, yes by, ναὶ μὰ Δία

# GENERAL INDEX

This index is selective. It does not include the names of the family members when they appear in the stories, but it does include them when they appear in essays. Numbers in boldface refer to illustrations or maps.

# LIST OF MAPS

# ACKNOWLEDGMENTS

Most of the passages in the Classical Greek readings and some of the quotations from Greek authors in the stories are taken from Loeb Classical Library editions (Cambridge, Mass.: Harvard University Press) with permission of the publishers and the Trustees of the Loeb Classical Library.

The selections from the Gospel of John in Book II are taken from *The Greek New Testament*, Fourth Revised Edition, edited by Barbara Aland, Kurt Aland, Johannes Karavidopoulos, Carlo M. Martini, and Bruce M. Metzger, © 1993 Deutsche Bibelgesellschaft, Stuttgart (available in the U.S.A. from the American Bible Society, 1865 Broadway, New York, NY 10023).

# LIST OF ILLUSTRATIONS

Page

189 Detail of an Attic red figure cup. Berlin, Antikenmuseum F 2538. (Photo: Museum).

190 Detail of bronze statue of charioteer. Delphi, Archaeological Museum. (Photo: Nimatallah/Art Resource, NY).

193 The stadium at Delphi. (Photo: Marburg/Art Resource, NY).

203 Detail of an Attic red figure neck amphora. Vase E270. Reproduced by courtesy of the Trustees of the British Museum, London. (Photo: Museum).

214 Detail of Attic red figure hydria. Ht. 14 1/16 in. All rights reserved, New York, The Metropolitan Museum of Art 56.171.53, Fletcher Fund, 1956. (Photo: Museum).

215 Detail of an Attic red figure stamnos. Vase E440. Reproduced by courtesy of the Trustees of the British Museum, London. (Photo: Museum).

222 Drawing: from vase painting. From Peter Connolly and Hazel Dodge, *The Ancient City: Life in Classical Athens & Rome*, Oxford University Press, 1998, p. 61. (Drawing: Peter Connolly).

223 Attic red figure hydria. Ht. 58.5 cm. All rights reserved, New York, The Metropolitan Museum of Art SL 1990.1.109, The Shelby White and Leon Levy Collection. (Photo: Sheldan Collins).

225 Detail of belly amphora. Paris, Musée du Louvre. (Photo: M. and P. Chuzeville).

237 Trireme. From *The Athenian Trireme* by J. S. Morrison, J. F. Coates, and N. B. Rankov © 2nd ed., 2000 by Cambridge University Press, page 232.

240 Plan of the reconstructed trireme *Olympias*. From *The Athenian Trireme* by J. S. Morrison, J. F. Coates, and N. B. Rankov © 2nd ed., 2000 by Cambridge University Press, page 208.

243 Relief. Athens, Acropolis Museum. (Photo: Museum).

248 Detail of an Attic red figure pelike. Ht. 31 cm. (12 3/16 in). © 2002 Museum of Fine Arts, Boston 20.187, Francis Bartlett Donation of 1912. (Photo: Museum).

253 (Photo: Alison Frantz).

254 Attic red figure plate. Vase E135. Reproduced by courtesy of the Trustees of the British Museum, London. (Photo: Museum).

258 Theater of Dionysus. From Peter Connolly and Hazel Dodge, *The Ancient City: Life in Classical Athens & Rome*, Oxford University Press, 1998, p. 94. (Drawing: Peter Connolly).

262 Plan of the theater of Dionysus. From Peter Connolly and Hazel Dodge, *The Ancient City: Life in Classical Athens & Rome*, Oxford University Press, 1998, p. 99. (Drawing: Peter Connolly).

263 Terracotta statuette. Ht. 7 cm (2 3/4 in.). © 2002 Museum of Fine Arts, Boston 01.8014, Gift by contribution. (Photo: Museum).

266 Detail of an Attic red figure cup. Ht. 9.5 cm. (3 3/4 in.); di. 22.7 cm (8 15/16 in.). © 2002 Museum of Fine Arts, Boston 95.30, Catharine Page Perkins Fund. (Photo: Museum).

268 Detail of an Attic red figure cup. Vase E49. Reproduced by courtesy of the Trustees of the British Museum, London. (Photo: Museum).

269 Attic red figure pelike. Ht. 36.1 cm. (14 3/16 in.); di. 44.8 cm (17 5/8 in.). © 2002 Museum of Fine Arts, Boston 03.793, Francis Bartlett Donation. (Photo: Museum).

270 The valley of the river Eurotas. (Photo: Alison Frantz).